Happy Birthday 1987



RCH.

# COMPREHENSIVE

# GUIDE

TO THE

# COUNTY OF NORTHUMBERLAND

BY

W. W. TOMLINSON

DAVIS BOOKS LTD
NEWCASTLE-UPON-TYNE

*Republished 1985*
*by*
DAVIS BOOKS LTD
140, Westgate Road
Newcastle-Upon-Tyne

ISBN 0 946865 03 5

*Printed and Bound*
*by*
SMITH SETTLE
Otley, West Yorkshire

# INTRODUCTION

1985 REPRINT

To anyone interested in the history and topography of Northumberland, the name *'Tomlinson'* is sufficient to identify, what over the years has become 'the' guide to the County.

**'The Comprehensive Guide to the County of Northumberland'** was first published in 1888 and has been reprinted many times. William Weaver Tomlinson died on the 26th November 1916 at which time nearly thirty years after its first publication, the Guide was described as 'one of the best of its kind'.

This description still applies, and, as the last reprint issued in 1968 is long out of print and the book still in great demand it has been decided to reprint the Guide.

The print size has been slightly increased for ease of reading, as the original was quite small by modern standards.

The three section maps have been included, but not the full map which in earlier editions was in a pocket in the binding.

CW

# TABLE OF CONTENTS.


| | PAGES |
|---|---|
| INTRODUCTION | v—xi |
| NEWCASTLE SECTION— | |
| Newcastle-upon-Tyne | 1—37 |
| Newcastle to Tynemouth | 38—54 |
| Tynemouth to Blyth and Bedlington | 55—69 |
| Newcastle to Killingworth and Stannington | 70—75 |
| Newcastle to Belsay and Stamfordham | 76—84 |
| Newcastle to Harlow Hill and Horsley | 85—91 |
| Newcastle to Ovingham | 92—101 |
| HEXHAM SECTION— | |
| Hexham | 102—113 |
| Hexham to Hexham Levels and Blanchland | 114—118 |
| Hexham to Dilston and Stocksfield | 119—133 |
| Hexham to Bywell and Matfen | 134—149 |
| Hexham to Haydon Bridge | 150—153 |
| Haydon Bridge to Allendale | 154—161 |
| Haydon Bridge to Haltwhistle and Gilsland | 162—174 |
| Haltwhistle to Alston | 175—180 |
| Hexham to St. Oswald's and Chollerford | 181—186 |
| Chollerford to Haltwhistle | 187—197 |
| Hexham to Haughton Castle and Wark | 198—208 |
| Hexham to Hallington and Wark | 209—213 |
| BELLINGHAM SECTION— | |
| Bellingham | 214—216 |
| Bellingham to Lee Hall and Shitlington | 217—218 |
| Bellingham to Hesleyside and Falstone | 219—221 |
| Bellingham to Falstone and Kielder | 222—229 |
| Bellingham to Birtley | 230—231 |
| Bellingham to Sweethope Loughs | 232—233 |
| Bellingham to Kirkwhelpington and Capheaton | 234—241 |
| MORPETH SECTION— | |
| Morpeth | 242—247 |
| Morpeth to Mitford and Wallington | 248—266 |
| Morpeth to Bolam and Shafthoe Crags | 267—272 |
| Morpeth to Nunnykirk | 273—276 |
| Morpeth to Longhorsley and Weldon Bridge | 277 |
| Morpeth to Cockle Park Tower and Felton | 278, 279 |
| Morpeth to Widdrington and Low Chibburn | 280—284 |
| Morpeth to Newbiggin and Cresswell | 285—295 |

| | PAGES |
|---|---|
| ELSDON SECTION— | |
| Redesdale | 296—301 |
| Elsdon and Neighbourhood | 301—310 |
| Elsdon to Otterburn and Carter Fell | 311—326 |
| ROTHBURY SECTION— | |
| Rothbury | 327—334 |
| Rothbury to Simonside and Fallowlees | 335—337 |
| Rothbury to Tosson Hill | 338, 339 |
| Rothbury to Alwinton and Coquethead | 340—351 |
| Rothbury to Biddlestone and Alnham | 352, 353 |
| Rothbury to Whittingham and Linhope | 354—366 |
| Rothbury to Brinkburn and Felton | 367—371 |
| ALNWICK SECTION— | |
| Alnwick | 372—393 |
| Alnwick to Ratcheugh Crag and Cawledge Dene | 394 |
| Alnwick to Edlingham | 395—397 |
| Alnwick to Bolton and Eglingham | 398—401 |
| Alnwick to Shilbottle and Newton-on-the-Moor | 402, 403 |
| Alnwick to Alnmouth and Warkworth | 404—417 |
| Alnwick to Longhoughton and Craster | 418—423 |
| Alnwick to Rock | 424, 425 |
| BAMBURGH SECTION— | |
| Bamburgh | 426—437 |
| Bamburgh to Budle and Spindlestone | 438—441 |
| Bamburgh to Lucker and Ellingham | 442, 443 |
| Bamburgh to Belford and Beal | 444—447 |
| Bamburgh to Dunstanburgh | 448—454 |
| Bamburgh to Holy Island | 455—464 |
| Bamburgh to the Farnes | 465—473 |
| WOOLER SECTION— | |
| Wooler | 474—476 |
| Wooler to Langleeford and Cheviot | 477—483 |
| Wooler to Hedgehope | 484, 485 |
| Wooler to Hedgeley Moor | 486—489 |
| Wooler to Chillingham and Old Bewick | 490—501 |
| Wooler to Humbleton and the Valley of the Glen | 502—510 |
| Wooler to Flodden Field | 511—518 |
| Wooler to Ford and Etal | 519—524 |
| Wooler to Doddington and Lowick | 525—529 |
| BERWICK SECTION— | |
| Berwick | 530—537 |
| Berwick to Beal | 538—542 |
| Berwick to Etal and Cornhill | 543—545 |
| Berwick to Norham and Carham | 546—557 |
| LISTS— | |
| Hills, Loughs, Crags, etc. | 558 |
| Pre-Reformation Churches | 559, 560 |
| Principal Camps of the Ancient Britons | 561 |
| Castles and Pele-Towers; Roman Stations and Camps | 561 |
| Ruined Churches and Chapels; Remains of Monastic Houses | 562 |
| PRINCIPAL HOTELS AND INNS IN THE COUNTY | 563—565 |
| INDEX— | 567—574 |

# INTRODUCTION.

THE County of Northumberland is roughly triangular in shape, embracing an area of 2016 square miles. Its greatest length is seventy miles, and its greatest breadth forty-seven miles. It is bounded on the north by the Tweed, on the south by the Tyne and the Derwent, on the west by Cumberland and the Cheviot Hills, and on the east by the German Ocean. The physical aspect of the county is varied, being low and flat near the coast, hilly in the centre, and mountainous towards the west. The geological strata, as a whole, slope to the sea, the direction of this general dip lying between south-east and east, so that, as Professor Lebour says, "anyone travelling from the coast to the Scottish Border across the country would be always encountering older and older formations. As he trudged along he might gradually pass over Permian, Coal-measure, Mill-stone Grit, Carboniferous Limestone; Bernician, Tuedian, and Silurian rocks." Volcanic agency has, however, interfered with this simplicity of arrangement, breaking and dislocating the strata. The porphyry rocks of the Cheviots, the great Whin Sill, stretching across the county from Kyloe to Hartington and Thirlwall into Cumberland, together with the various basaltic dykes, afford abundant evidence of the subterranean disturbances which took place shortly after the deposition of the carboniferous limestone. This last-named series of rocks are found chiefly in the upper part of the county; the mill-stone grit forms a high ridge down the centre, and the coal-measures occupy the lower portion. The immense northern coal-field, which comprises a part of Durham, and extends for some distance under the sea, has an area of eight hundred square miles, the total thickness of the seams being about thirty-six feet. These underground treasures of Northumberland, with the great engineering and chemical works and shipbuilding yards for which it is famous, lie chiefly in the south-east and south-west corners of the county, and here it is that the greater part of the population is massed. The rest of the county is pastoral and agricultural in its character, and hence preserves much of that primitive charm and natural beauty which make it so eminently a touring-district for the dwellers in our large towns. Gently-moulded hills, all green to the summit, wild whinstone or sandstone crags, bosky denes, romantic trout streams, richly-cultivated plains, over which are scattered arcadian villages, and a finely-indented coast, presenting to the sea a line of tall wave-worn cliffs, or low monotonous sand-hills—these are some of the attractive features of Northumberland from the tourist's point of view. But these are not all. Northumberland, in the words of Mr. Freeman, is the "land of castles," and not merely, as is popularly imagined, the land of collieries. In no other part of England is there such a remarkable and interesting collection of military antiquities as in this. "One cannot," says Fuller, "rationally expect fair fabrics here, where the vicinity of the Scots made men to build, not for state, but for strength. Here it was the rule with the ancient inhabitants, 'what was firm, that was fair;' so it may be said of the houses of the gentry herein, *quot mansiones, tot munitiones*, as being either all castles or castle-like, able to resist (though no solemn siege) a tumultuary invasion." Of these military antiquities there are—firstly, the rude camps of the old Celtic population, in which the principle of the Norman castle may be traced—a series of fortifications round a central stronghold; secondly, the Roman stations and camps; thirdly, the great castles of feudal times; and, finally, the pele-towers and bastle-houses, which "show the type of the Norman keep continued on a small scale to a very late period." Their picturesque outlines add a characteristic feature to every Northumbrian landscape. So many remarkable relics of the past being still extant, it is not to be wondered at that archæology is a favourite study in the North, and that travellers find the Northumbrians "great antiquaries within their own bounds," from Roger North, who wrote in 1676, to the tourist who described for the readers of *All the Year Round* a "Northumbrian Fortress" in February 1888. Many scraps of folk-lore, and many old customs and superstitions, still linger in remote villages among the hills and in out-of-the-way places. "The Northumbrians between the Tyne and Tweed," says Mr. Ralph Carr, "are nearly of pure Anglican breed, with very little intermixture, save on Tyneside, where the people are more mercurial, more excitable, more restless, showing signs of Cymric interblending." Hence the Northumbrian dialect, strange and uncouth as it may sound in a stranger's ears, is a peculiarly interesting study to philologists.

Northumberland is rich in its historical associations. Of the early Celtic tribes who formerly occupied the hills and valleys of the county in great numbers but little is known, and that chiefly obtained from a careful examination of the camps and burial-mounds of this ancient people. The forts of Agricola, and the gigantic military works of Hadrian, are not only monuments of the indomitable perseverance and engineering skill of the Romans, but also of the courage and warlike character of the Britons. The Romans left Britain in the fifth century; and then the Saxons swooped down on the defenceless coasts, but, unlike the Romans, they colonised, as well as governed, the conquered states. Ida, significantly styled the flame-bearer, overran Northumberland with his hordes of Saxon freebooters about the middle of the sixth century, and made Bamburgh (at that time known as Dynguayrdi) the capital of his new kingdom of Bernicia. He fell in battle after a reign of twelve years. Adda, Hussa, Theodoric, and Æthelfrith successively occupied the Bernician throne, and on the death of the latter at Retford, Eadwine became king of the united realms of Bernicia and Deira in 617. Nine years after he married Ædelberga, an adherent of the new faith. Through the preaching of Paulinus, a Roman missionary who accompanied the new queen, the king and his subjects were converted to Christianity. For some years Bernicia was scourged by the pagan Cadwallon, who slew Eadwine and his successor Eanfrid in battle, and seemed to be invincible till Oswald put an end to his victorious career at the battle of Hefenfeldt. The history of Northumberland, from the time of Oswald to that of Eanrid, with whom the line of Bernician kinglets came to an end, may be inferred from the fact that most of these Saxon rulers died by a violent death. The great feature of this period is the development of the monastic system in Northumberland. Tynemouth, Hexham, and Lindisfarne became centres of light, secular as well as spiritual, to the surrounding districts. Under the direction of the monks, churches were built, forests cleared, marshes drained, and a rude form of art developed. "Northumbria had done its work," says Mr. Green in his *Short History of the English People.* "By its missionaries, and by its sword, it had won England from heathendom to the Christian church. It had given her a new poetic literature. Its monasteries were already the seat of whatever intellectual life the country possessed, and above all, it had been the first to gather together into a loose political unity the various tribes of the English people, and by standing at their head for nearly a century to accustom them to a national life, out of which England, as we have it now, was to spring." Towards the close of the eighth century, the Danes appeared off the coasts of Northumberland, and soon the smouldering ruins of monasteries, towns, and villages told the awful tale of their ravages. In 876, under Halfdene, they laid the country waste once more, and for many years continued to make piratical descents on the coast. Northumberland, for a time, was under Danish dominion, but it does not appear as if the Danes settled in any numbers there. Mr. J. V. Gregory has shown that they have left hardly a trace of their presence in the place-names of the county, which are almost entirely Saxon. With Osulph, in the reign of Edred, began the line of Northumbrian earls, who were to exercise almost as much power as the old Bernician kings. His successors were men of great force of character, but unfortunate. Uchtred, defeated by the Danes, was assassinated by them at the court of Canute, at Wiheal. Siward assisted Malcolm to wrest the Scottish crown from the hands of the usurper, Macbeth. Tostig, the fiery and haughty son of Godwin, fell in battle at Stamford Bridge. Earl Copsi, the favourite of the Conqueror, was slain in the porch of Newburn Church by his rival, Osulph. Gospatric, to whom William afterwards sold the earldom, was banished on suspicion of intriguing against the Norman rule. His successor, Waltheof, was beheaded for treason. William the Conqueror visited Northumberland, and left a scene of desolation behind him. Then Malcolm of Scotland made a destructive inroad, but fell by the spear of Moræl, near Alnwick, in 1093. Robert de Mowbray, the powerful Earl of Northumberland, rebelled against the Red King, and brought down the Norman vengeance on the county as well as on himself. Great fortresses, grimly frowning, rose on every hand, as if in preparation for the terrible conflict which was to rage between the English and the Scots for so many centuries.

David I., in 1138, and William the Lion, in 1174, overran Northumberland, inflicting horrible barbarities on the inhabitants. In cruelty, however, they were outdone by King John, in an expedition that he undertook to punish the disaffected barons who had sworn allegiance to Alexander at Felton. He burnt castles, towns, and villages, killing and plundering without regard to age or sex. Wallace, striking for freedom, led his wild Scots into Northumberland, and laid waste the country. From the south came Edward I., through the desolated districts, to wreak his anger on the hapless Scots. Robert Bruce next appears on the scene, and bitterly had the Northumbrians cause to lament the weakness and incompetency of Edward II. After Bannockburn they were subjected to all the calamities which the victorious Scots could inflict upon them. Edward III., however, retrieved the honour of England at Halidon Hill in 1333, and at Neville's Cross in 1346. A more terrible foe than Wallace or Bruce ravaged the northern counties in 1348-9, and this was the Black Death, which destroyed about one-third of the inhabitants. In 1388 a party of Scots made an incursion into Northumberland, which resulted in the battle of Otterburn, when Earl Douglas was slain and Sir Henry and Sir Ralph Percy were made prisoners. But backward swung the pendulum of fortune again in 1402, when Hotspur defeated the Scots under Earl Douglas at Homildon Hill. The fourth Earl of Northumberland having rebelled against Henry IV., this king marched an army of 3000 men against him, and reduced the castles of Prudhoe, Warkworth, and Alnwick, driving the earl across the Borders. A marauding party of Scots were defeated in 1414 at Yeavering by Sir Robert de Umfraville. After this the Northumbrians shared with the rest of England in the troubles of the fifteenth century, known as "The Wars of the Roses." The Percies espoused the Lancastrian interest, and the castles of Alnwick, Bamburgh, and Dunstanburgh were the last retreats of the intrepid but unfortunate Queen Margaret. A battle took place at Hedgeley Moor, near Wooler, in 1463, when the Lancastrians were defeated by Lord Montagu, and the following year they suffered another reverse at a place called the Linnels, near Hexham, and Queen Margaret had to seek safety in flight among the bosky recesses of Deepden. In the reign of Henry VIII. Lord Home, with a few thousand Borderers, ravaged Northumberland, but was intercepted by Sir William Bulmer on Millfield Plain, near Wooler, and defeated with a loss of a third of his men. This engagement preceded by a few months the terrible battle of Flodden Field (September 1513), so disastrous to Scotland. The last Border fight took place two years later (July 5th, 1513), and is known as the Raid of the Redeswire. The dissolution of monasteries and religious houses by Henry VIII. aroused the indignation of the northern gentry, and a rising was organised, called the "Pilgrimage of Grace," the object of which was to reinstate the ejected monks in their monasteries. John Heron, of Chipchase, and Sir Thomas Percy, brother to the Earl of Northumberland, took an active part in it. An ill-starred attempt to re-establish the ancient faith by an appeal to arms, called the "Rising of the North," was made in 1569, at the instigation of the Earls of Northumberland and Westmoreland, one of whom died on the scaffold, the other in exile. In 1588, and again ten years later, the Plague visited the northern counties. With the accession of James VI. of Scotland to the throne of England, the national feuds and rivalries ceased, though the lawless spirit of the Borders still found a congenial outlet in cattle-lifting. In the struggle between Charles I. and his Parliament, Northumberland played a comparatively unimportant part. The Scots, who had declared for the Parliament, despatched a body of 26,000 men, under Lesley, across the Borders. They marched without opposition to Newburn, where they found a body of 6000 English, under Lord Conway, entrenched on Stella Haugh. Under cover of their cannon, posted on the tower of Newburn Church, the Scots crossed the river by the ford, and drove their opponents up the opposite slopes. They entered Newcastle, and billeted themselves on the inhabitants for some time. Charles I. passed through Northumberland the following year, 1641. In 1644 the Scots once more crossed the Tweed, and appeared before the walls of Newcastle. The good old town, however, was not in such a hurry to admit the hungry Covenanters, and, after beleaguering the walls from the 3rd of February to the 22nd, the Scots retreated, and, crossing the Tyne at the fords of Ovingham, Bywell, and Eltringham, marched by way of Ebchester to Sunderland. The next event of importance in Northumbrian history is the Jacobite rising of 1715, which brought irretrievable ruin on so many famous families. The so-called rebels—The Earl of Derwentwater, Thomas Forster, Esq., and about sixty of the local gentry—met at a hill called the Waterfalls, near Tone, on October 6th. After proclaiming the Pretender at Rothbury, Warkworth, Morpeth, and Hexham, they proceeded northward to Kelso, to meet the Scottish Jacobites, under the Earl of Kenmure and Brigadier Mackintosh. At Preston their ill-timed rebellion came to a disastrous end. The rebellion of 1745 did not affect Northumberland, beyond reviving for a time the hopes of the faithful adherents of the House of Stuart still remaining in the county. The events which have stirred the public life of Northumberland since this period have chiefly been industrial or political, notably the adaptation of the steam-engine to the practical uses of mankind by George Stephenson, and the passing of the Reform Bill, with which the name of Earl Grey of Howick is so indissolubly connected. The uncertain tenure by which life and property were held till the

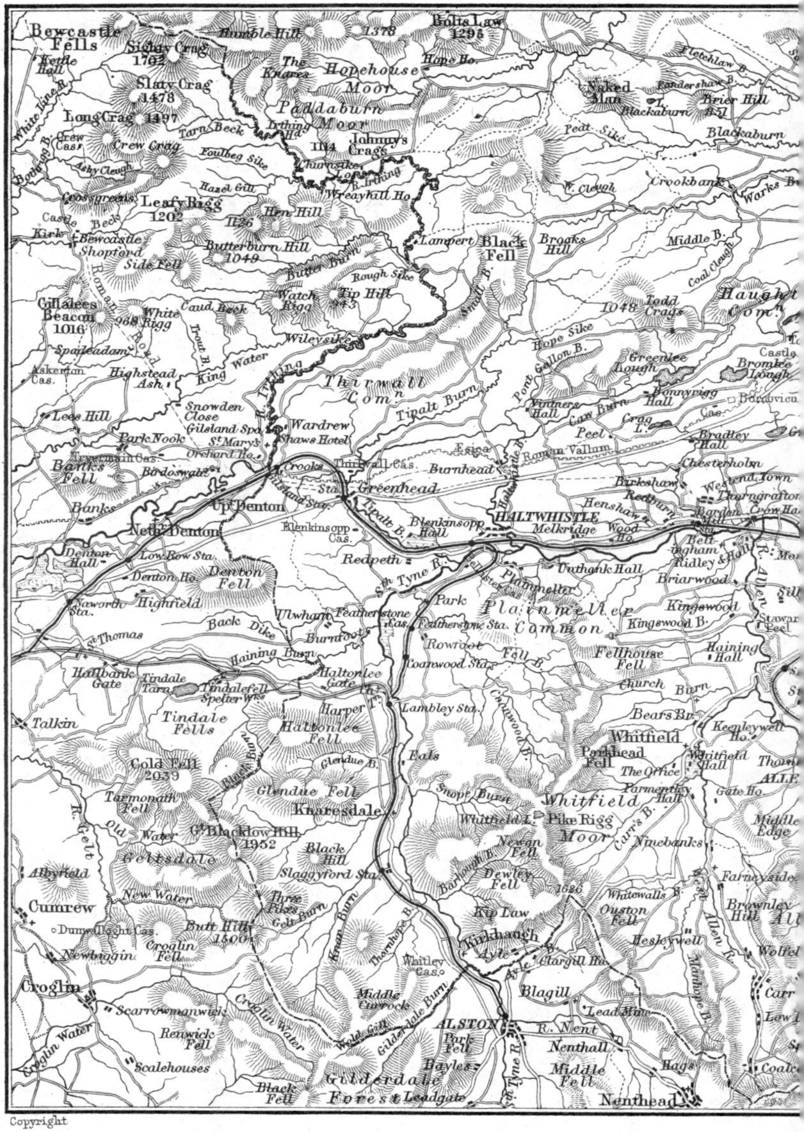

Bewcastle Fells
Sighty Crag 1702
Humble Hill
1378
Bolts Law 1295
Kettle Hall
The Knares
Hopehouse Moor
Hope Ho.
Slaty Crag 1478
Naked Man
Kandershaw B.
Brier Hill 1351
Blackaburn
Long Crag 1497
Paddaburn Moor
Irthing Ho.
Tarn Beck
Johnny's Crags
1114
Peat Sike
Crew Cas.
Crew Crag
Foulbeg Sike
Churnsike Lodge
R. Irthing
Askey Cleugh
Hazel Gill
Wreayhill Ho.
W. Cleugh
Crookbank
Warks B.
Crossgreens
Leafy Rigg 1202
Hen Hill
1126
Castle Kirk
Bewcastle
Shopford
Lampert
Black Fell
Brooks Hill
Middle B.
Butterburn Hill 1049
Side Fell
Butter Burn
Rough Sike
Coal Cleugh
Gillalees Beacon 1016
968
White Rigg
Caud Beck
Watch Rigg
Tip Hill 943
1048
Todd Crags
Roman Road
Trout B.
Spadeadam
Wileysike
Hope Sike
Pont Gallon B.
Greenlee Lough
Castle
Bromlee Lough
Askerton Cas.
Highstead Ash
King Water
R. Irthing
Thirwall Com.n
Tipalt Burn
Bonnyrigg Hall
Lees Hill
Snowden Close
Gilsland Spa
Wardrew
Shaws Hotel
Vinners Hall
Caw Burn
Crag L.
Park Nook
St. Mary's
Orchard Ho.
Peel
Esica
Roman Vallum
Bradley Hall
Banks Fell
Triermain Cas.
Birdoswald
Crooks
Thirwall Cas.
Burnhead
Chesterholm
Birkshaw
West end Town
Thorngrafton
Greenhead
Redburn
Banks
Up.r Denton
Tipalt B.
Henshaw
Crow Hall
Bardon Mill
Neth.r Denton
Blenkinsopp Cas.
Blenkinsopp Hall
HALTWHISTLE
Melkridge
Wood Ho.
Beltingham
Denton Hall
Low Row Sta.
Redpeth
Unthank Hall
Ridley Hall
R. Allen
Denton Ho.
Denton Fell
S.th Tyne R.
Plainmeller
Briarwood
Naworth Sta.
Highfield
Park
Plainmeller Common
Kingswood
Ulwham
Featherstone Cas.
Featherstone Sta.
Kingswood B.
Staward Peel
Back Dike
St. Thomas
Burnfoot
Rowfoot
Haining Hall
Haining Burn
Coanwood Sta.
Fell B.
Fellhouse Fell
Hallbank Gate
Tindale Tarn
Tindalefell Spelter Wks.
Haltonlee Gate
Church Burn
Talkin
Tindale Fells
Harper T.
Lambley Sta.
Bears Br.
Keenleywell Ho.
Haltonlee Fell
Whitfield
Cold Fell 2039
Black Burn
Glendue B.
Eals
Parkhead Fell
Whitfield Hall
The Office
ALLEN
Tarmonath Fell
Glendue Fell
Snope Burn
Whitfield Moor
Farmentley Hall
Gate Ho.
R. Gelt
Knaresdale
Whitfield L.
Pike Rigg
Carr's B.
Middle Edge
Old Water
Gt. Blacklow Hill 1952
Moor
Ninebanks
Geltsdale
Black Hill
Newan Fell
Albyfield
Slaggyford Sta.
Barhaugh B.
Dewley Fell
Farneyside
New Water
1626
Whitewalls B.
Three Pikes
Gelt Burn
Ouston Fell
Cumrew
Kip Law
Brownley Hill
Dumwallaght Cas.
Butt Hill 1500
Knar Burn
Thornhope B.
Kirkhaugh
Hesleywell
Allen R.
Croglin Fell
Ayle
Clargill Ho.
Newbiggin
Whitley Cas.
Mohope B.
Croglin
Middle Carrock
Blagill
Scarrowmanwick
Croglin Water
Gilderdale Burn
Lead Mine
Weld Gill
ALSTON
R. Nent
Renwick Fell
Park Fell
Nenthall
Croglin Water
Scalehouses
Hayles
Middle Fell
Hags
S.th Tyne R.
Gilderdale Forest
Leadgate
Black Fell
Nenthead


Copyright

# Comprehensive Guide to Northumberland.

## NEWCASTLE-UPON-TYNE.

Here, stately, on Northumbrian soil, she stands,
With brow imperial, pondering vast designs,
While rumours of her greatness and the Tyne's
Are wafted to her ears from distant lands—
Queen in the realm of Force, whose loyal bands
Quit the fair sunlight for the deadly mines
To conquer from the gnomes their guarded shrines
That she may reign queen of the mighty hands.
Her robes are wrought with quaint embroiderings:
The fashion of them is both new and old:
Her crown of beauty is beyond all praise:
Her dusky hair in many a tangle clings
About her, and her looks, though stern and cold,
Grow tender with the dreams of by-gone days.

BEAUTIFUL for situation! will be the mental comment of the spectator who gazes on Newcastle for the first time from a "coigne of vantage" like the Windmill Hills at Gateshead. From the side of the river, where the quaintly-built mansions of other days, with their overhanging stories and picturesque lattices, are yet standing, degraded into warehouses and offices—to the crown of the hill, where the degenerate structures of modern times huddle together for mutual support, the eye may travel in wonder over miles of smoke-blackened stone and brickwork, from which rise tower and spire and monument. Very different now is the view from what it was a century and a-half ago, when John Wesley wrote that he knew no place in Great Britain comparable to Newcastle for pleasantness. Then the inhabitants of the far-famed town were content to abide within the shadow of the grey old walls, amongst gardens and meadows. At the present time those walls exist only in fragments; and the town, now raised to the rank of a city, has spread far beyond the bowshot of the lustiest archers who used to man its turrets. Though many of the details of the picture will offend a fastidious taste, the spectator will find the general effect imposing; and his first view of a town which is associated in his mind with the greatest engineering triumphs of the century will not, on the whole, prove disappointing. If he be a follower of Mr. Whistler or Mr. Oscar Wilde, he will find that, even when mantled in its proverbial smoke, Newcastle has much to commend it to an artistic eye for a certain sombre, Dantesque kind of picturesqueness. It is perhaps, however, at night-time that the presence of a great city like Newcastle will appeal with most power to the imagination of a visitor; when the vast outlines of its stately streets and more conspicuous buildings are weirdly defined as silhouettes on the darkness—when multitudinous rows of lamps stretch along and across the steep hill-side, forming a wonderful network of illumination, mysteriously and grandly suggestive. Before we proceed to view Newcastle at closer quarters, it may be advisable to say a little about the vicissitudes of the town before it attained its present importance and magnitude.

## HISTORY OF THE TOWN.

NEWCASTLE owes its origin to Hadrian, who, when constructing his wonderful rampart through the dangerous territory of the Ottadini, recognised the strategical importance of the present position of Newcastle, and built there in A.D. 120 one of his great military stations, which he called after the neighbouring bridge across the Tyne—Pons Ælii. As to the position of this station, says Dr. Bruce —"We shall not greatly err if we suppose Pons Ælii to have lain between St. Nicholas' Church on the one side and the Literary and Philosophical Society on the other; and having the north side of Collingwood Street for the site of its north rampart, to have extended as far south as Bailiffgate, where the ground begins to dip rapidly down towards the river." After the departure of the Roman legions Pons Ælii sank into a heap of ruins. Some monks having settled there in Saxon times, it became known as Monkchester. Whether this colony of monks suffered from the ravages of the Danes, at the time when all the neighbouring monasteries and religious houses were burnt, historians are unable to say. The probability is, that Monkchester would possess at this period few attractions for the northern freebooters in the shape of gold or grain. When the Conqueror, after desolating Northumberland with fire and sword, found the turbulent inhabitants still unsubdued, he saw the necessity of having a stronghold in their midst; and in A.D. 1080 his eldest son, Robert Curthose, when returning from an expedition against the Scots, erected, on the site of the old Roman Station, a fortress, which was called the New Castle. This was evidently but a temporary erection, for a few years later a second and much stronger castle was built by William Rufus. This new castle was the nucleus of a young town, and the Red King endeavoured to promote its growth and develop its resources by granting several privileges and immunities to the infant community. In the reign of Stephen, Northumberland was under the rule of David, King of Scotland, who is supposed to have built the Church of St. Andrew, and to have made considerable grants of land to the Hospital of St. Mary the Virgin and the

Nunnery of St. Bartholomew, at this period outside the town. In the reign of Henry II. the possession of Northumberland reverted to the crown of England. Newcastle was of great importance to the English kings as the basis of their military operations against the Scots, for it was to Newcastle that the loyal burghers of the different towns were requested to send their contingent of archers or hobelers.

As the feud between the two nations continued, it soon became apparent that the existing walls were inadequate to protect the inhabitants of the town from the sudden inroads of the Scots, and so, in the reign of Edward I., new walls were commenced, on a scale of unusual strength and magnitude, to enclose not only the whole of the houses of the town, but also the more outlying parts, where lay the monasteries with their grounds and gardens, and, in addition, the ancient villa of Pandon. These extensive fortifications, above two miles in extent, from twelve to twenty feet high, according to the nature of the ground, and eight feet thick, were completed in the reign of Edward III. Leland, in his *Itinerary*, says—"The strength and magnificence of the walling of this town surpasseth all the walls of the cities of England, and most of the towns of Europe."

In the "new hall of the king," which formerly stood on the ground now occupied by the Moot Hall, John Baliol did homage to Edward I. for the crown of Scotland, December 12, 1292.

In the chapel of the Blackfriars Edward Baliol did homage to Edward III. for the crown of Scotland in 1333.

Important as the town had now become from a military point of view, it was far more so from a commercial one; for the coal-trade and the woollen manufacture had begun to give Newcastle a prominence in the markets of England, which her geographical advantages enabled her to sustain. In the reign of Richard II. the Scots, under Douglas, penetrated as far as Newcastle, and it was the incident of the encounter between that great Scotch leader and Sir Henry Percy which led to the battle of Otterburn, so famous in the history of song. In 1400 Newcastle, by royal charter, was created a county of itself, and from that period to the time of the Stuarts there are but few events of much moment to record. In 1635-6 the plague devastated the town, carrying off 5000 of the inhabitants. A few years later the town was thrown into a state of consternation by the tidings that Lesley and his Scots had defeated Lord Conway and his forces on Stella Haughs. Being unprepared to resist the victorious army, the town was compelled to open the gates after "great assurance was given of sincerity and peacefulness of their intentions." In the struggle between Charles I. and his Parliament, Newcastle espoused the Royalist side, and in 1644 had to show its devotion to the King's cause by sustaining a siege of ten weeks' duration. The mayor at this time was a man of singular courage and ability, Sir John Marley, who, with an effective fighting force of only 1500 men, opposed a force of about 30,000. The stubborn resistance offered by the town so irritated the Earl of Leven, that he threatened to destroy the spire of St. Nicholas' Church if the town were not immediately surrendered; but Sir John Marley placed the Scotch prisoners in the lantern of the tower, and his answer is thus given by Bourne—"that they would upon no terms deliver up the town, but would to the last moment defend it. That the steeple of St. Nicholas was indeed a beautiful and magnificent piece of architecture, and one of the great ornaments of their town, but yet should it be blown into atoms before ransomed at such a rate. That, however, if it was to fall, it should not fall alone: that the same moment he destroyed the beautiful structure, he should bathe his hands in the blood of his countrymen, who were placed there on purpose either to preserve it from ruin or to die along with it." The Earl did not execute his threat, however, but on the 20th of October 1644 commenced an assault of the town, which, after an obstinate struggle, was taken, though the brave Sir John Marley and his officers held out in the keep of the Castle for four days longer. It was on account of this celebrated resistance to the troops of the Parliament that Newcastle had conferred upon her by the King the motto which she still bears on her arms, "Fortiter defendit triumphans." In 1646 Charles I. was for ten months a captive in Newcastle, occupying the stately mansion of Anderson Place, which stood on the site of Lambton's Bank. It was here that there passed those papers "betwixt his sacred Majestie and Mr. Al. Henderson concerning the change of church government" which appear at the end of "Eikon Basilike." An attempt to escape along the side of the Lort Burn was frustrated, and the King was strictly guarded during the rest of the time he remained in Newcastle. He was finally delivered up by the Scots to the Parliament. The terrible Cromwell visited the town more than once in his journeys to Scotland, and to the governor of the town, Sir Arthur Haselrigg, he despatched a characteristic letter just before the battle of Dunbar. In 1715 considerable excitement was caused in the town by the news of the Jacobite rising in Northumberland; but the mayor and corporation took prompt steps to stamp out any signs of disaffection by imprisoning all Papists and suspected persons, and by putting the town in a proper state of defence. They walled up the gates and armed the inhabitants, so that General Forster, instead of surprising the town as he expected to do, found the gates shut and a determined body of Hanoverian supporters ready to oppose him. He therefore turned aside to Hexham, and the town was soon relieved of any further anxiety on his account. The rebellion of 1745 stirred up the town once more to look after its defences. The walls were repaired and mounted with cannon, and the gates walled up. Fires were lit and kept burning outside the town to prevent surprise, and volunteers were enrolled and exercised in the various military manœuvres. The movement of troops to and from Newcastle kept the sense of danger alive in the hearts of the inhabitants; but the storm broke in the distance, and Newcastle only heard the far-off rumbling of the rebellion. From that time to the present the history of Newcastle is chiefly concerned with the improvement of her streets and the development of her industries. The most eventful dates in the present century as regards Newcastle are, perhaps, 1831 and 1853, when the Asiatic cholera devastated the town; 1838, when the Newcastle and Carlisle Railway was opened; 1850, when the High Level and Central Station were opened for traffic by Her Majesty; 1854, when the great fire and explosion took place, which quite destroyed a large portion of old Newcastle, situated by the river-side; and 1881, when the centenary of the birth of George Stephenson was celebrated. Necessarily, much that would have been of the greatest interest to the antiquary and the lover of the picturesque has had to be sacrificed in the name of Progress; but still there is—what is lacking in many modern towns—a sufficient blending of the old with the new to suggest the idea of continuity, and tinge the hard features of the present with the hues of the past. It is to those famous structures, consecrated by the touch of Time, that the modern pilgrim will first direct his footsteps.

## THE NORMAN KEEP.

[*Open in summer from* 10 A.M. *to* 5 P.M., *and in winter from* 10 A.M. *to* 4 P.M. *Admission* 6*d. each, or* 1*s. for a party of three.*]

FIRST and foremost is the NORMAN KEEP, the grim old ancestor of Newcastle-upon-Tyne, which, in an architectural sense, still dominates the town with its mediæval grandeur, while its walls re-echo to a note more imperious than ever trumpet blew, as the steam-engines thunder past to the north or the south. The old Keep, with the grime of centuries upon it, still overlooks the world-famed river, unchanged amidst change — a glorious anachronism. It is a rectangular structure, with a forebuilding on its east side, measuring at its base (not including the plinth) from east to west, 73 feet, and from north to south, 62 feet. To the top of the parapet it is 85 feet high, and to the top of the turret, on the south-west corner, 107 feet. The walls are of colossal strength, being in the lower part from 15 to 18 feet in thickness, and in the upper, from 12 to 17 feet. The north-west corner has been rounded so as to lead the enemy to suppose that it contained the stairway, and was therefore a vulnerable point to attack, whereas it is the most solid corner of the building. Proceeding to the east side of the Keep, and ascending the stairs, on each side of which is a lamp-niche, the visitor enters a chamber, which some have supposed to have been a priest's chamber, and others the governor's room, where he received strangers. Around three of its sides is a rich Norman arcade. It contains some finely-carved oak furniture, some ancient weapons, and one of the old watchman's rattles, which will be of interest to the visitor. Passing through a beautiful Norman doorway, an exact reproduction of the original, we enter the GREAT HALL of the Keep on the second floor. This room is about 40 feet in height. The arched vault is of comparatively recent date. Beneath the openings of a gallery which runs round the whole building there was once another floor, the joist-holes of which may still be seen in the walls. The fire-place is modern. The carved chimney-piece above it was taken from the Mansion House. The centre panel of the over-mantel represents King James I. being carried up to heaven by angels. To the right of the fire-place will be seen some old guns from China, and opposite, a rack of pikes and halberts. On the walls are various specimens of old armour, and some pieces of tapestry taken from an old house at Wallsend. Two old wheels recovered from the Tyne at Stella will be observed, one on the right of the entrance-door, and the other in a recess of the window close by. Ascending a few steps, we enter the WELL-CHAMBER. The well-shaft goes down through the solid masonry into the rock beneath, and is 94 feet deep. The depth of the water therein in 46 feet. On each side of the well-chamber we notice a basin in the wall. These were for the reception of water, which was conveyed from them through pipes in the solid wall to cisterns in distant parts of the Keep. One of these cisterns still exists over the external door of the chapel, and the communication from the well-chamber is still perfect. On the south of the hall, opposite the recess just referred to, is the KING'S CHAMBER, in the thickness of the walls. It contains a fire-place which will repay examination, as it is one of the only two original fire-places in the castle. Here will be observed the top of a wine-cask with the head of Charles I. carved upon it, a chest with the original padlock and keys formerly belonging to the Maison Dieu of Newcastle, and a portion of a Roman water-wheel from Tartessus, in Spain. Ascending one of the staircases leading to the top of the building, we pass through a low door on to the stone-flagged ROOF, occupied only by a few old guns that are silent now in their small wooden carriages.

The roof of the castle, its battlements and flag-tower, are all modern, and, as Dr. Bruce adds, are not in character with a Norman building. The view from the top embraces most of the old and much of the new town, with the river and Gateshead. We descend by the other staircase to the apartment used as the LIBRARY of the Society of Antiquaries of Newcastle-upon-Tyne. Here it is that they hold their meetings. The fire-place in this chamber is original. The pillar in the centre and the arches springing from it are modern, as is also the fire-place. Round this pillar is a curiously-shaped table, made from the oak dredged out of the bed of the river Tyne. The President's chair at the head is of oak dug up from below the foundation of the Roman Wall, close to its western terminus. A number of helmets, breastplates, cross-bows, battle-axes, swords, halberts, morning-stars, and other weapons and armour, will be observed on the walls and round the pillar of this room. The visitor will also notice with interest a view of the Sandhill, in oils, by Ralph Waters, painted about the middle of the last century, and a water-colour of the interior of St. Nicholas' Church, by Ralph Waters, Jun., together with various old engravings and prints ; a model of the guillotine, made by French prisoners in England out of the bones of their food ; a copy of the

Roman silver lanx found near Corbridge in 1735; casts from the concentric circles in the rocks of Argyleshire; a cast of the catstane,—an ancient Pictish inscription; a model of the old Exchange, and a case of ancient chirurgery.

Descending to the floor below, which is the basement, we enter a large apartment, called THE GUARD-ROOM, or DUNGEON. The shaft in the centre, which supports the six arched ribs of the roof, is original. Near the base of it is the opening of a pipe which conveyed water from the well to a cistern here. The iron ring on the other side of the pillar was one to which prisoners were formerly chained. In the chamber may be seen some old guns, some stone figures from the town walls, and a large defaced stone figure of James I., which stood above the north entrance to Newgate. John Howard, the philanthropist, visited this dungeon, and thus describes the state of the prisoners:—"During the assizes at Newcastle the county prisoners are, men and women, confined together seven or eight nights in a dirty, damp dungeon, six steps down in the old castle, which having no roof, in wet seasons the water is some inches deep. The felons are chained to rings in the wall." The memory of such sufferings will no doubt cause a shudder to pass through the visitor as he stands in this dark, cold chamber, gazing at the rings so gruesomely suggestive.

"Ascending the stairs which lead to the south window, we enter a small chamber which takes to the sally-port. The whole of the arrangements in this part of the castle are exceedingly curious. Immediately opposite the window, in the chamber just referred to, and solidly lodged in the joint of the masonry, is the head of an arrow shot from a crossbow—an interesting relic of ancient warfare. In this chamber the sallying party was no doubt marshalled." Leaving the dungeon, we pass through a gloomy chamber, where, on the ground floor, we notice an ancient British grave found near Lesbury, and enter the CHAPEL. This occupies the basement of the small wing on the east side of the castle. Here a vision of architectural beauty greets us that we were scarcely prepared to expect after the rugged severity of the chambers just visited. The beautiful round arches, the ribs of the groining decorated so exquisitely with the chevron or zigzag ornament, seem fresh and clean-cut as from the sculptor's chisel. On the walls will be observed a cast of a hunting-piece from Glasgow Cathedral, and a cast of the dedication-stone of Bede's old church at Jarrow. The visitor will examine with interest some ancient stone coffins, some carved fonts from the Blackfriars, Newcastle, and Easby Abbey; an effigy, a fragment of a Saxon cross from Rothbury, and various fragments of ancient ecclesiastical sculpture. Over a doorway leading to this chapel from the outside is a small gallery, where we have the cistern into which water can still be poured from one of the basins in the well-room. The last time this mighty keep was used for military purposes was in 1644, when Sir John Marley put it into temporary repair, and for a few days longer defied the Scotish army after they had secured the town.

## THE BLACK GATE.

[*Open in summer from* 10 A.M. *to* 5 P.M., *and in winter from* 10 A.M. *to* 4 P.M. *Admission* 3*d*.]

THE BLACK GATE, supposed to be named after one Patrick Black, a local magnate, who lived about the year 1617, was formerly the main entrance to the castle. It is believed to have been built by Henry III. in the year 1247. Its original aspect has been very much altered by the building operations of Alexander Stevenson—a Scotchman who, in the reign of James I., obtained a lease of the castle—and also of one John Pickle. It has also suffered from decay, for in the middle of the eighteenth century part of it fell, and was patched up again with brickwork. It is the lower part which is old, and the visitor will naturally examine with most interest the arched passage and the finely vaulted chambers on each side of it. No trace remains of its double portcullis and drawbridge. Ascending a few stairs to a balcony, at the end of which is the custodian's lodge, we pay a small fee, and enter the room in which are contained the invaluable collection of inscribed and sculptured stones of the Roman period, belonging to the Society of Antiquaries of Newcastle-upon-Tyne. Here around us are the defaced and broken altars of unremembered gods—relics of faiths outworn, which once, no doubt, were potent in the lives of those strong-armed rulers of the world. The visitor who is not a professed antiquary will have no difficulty in deciphering the inscriptions or interpreting the symbols, for all this has been carefully done for him on illustrated labels attached to each stone. A most interesting and carefully prepared catalogue (price 2s. 6d.) may also be obtained from the attendant. The antiquities which will, perhaps, be regarded with most interest are:—No. 2, where the mother goddesses are represented in triplets and seated; No. 13, an altar with a trident and dolphin carved upon it, dedicated to Neptune by the Sixth Legion; No. 70, a sculpture from the Mithraic cave at Housesteads, representing the god Mithras coming out of an egg with the signs of the zodiac around him; Nos. 71 and 72, fragments of a large tablet found in the same cave, representing Mithras with an uplifted torch; No. 80, a Roman in his civic dress; No. 83, a monumental stone erected by Aurelius Marcus to his most holy wife, who lived thirty-three years without any stain; No. 86, large figure of Hercules; No. 88, fine figure of a Roman soldier; No. 93, a figure of Victory careering with outstretched wings over the round earth; No. 101, a Roman tombstone, a lady—Aurelia Aureliana—holding a bunch of flowers in her left hand; No. 138, portion of fine slab found at Habitancum, with the name of Geta erased (by command of his brother, who had murdered him); No. 150, funereal monument representing two invalids upon a bed; No. 157, a mutilated figure of Neptune; No. 158, three female figures, partially clothed, and standing; No. 160, fragment of a sculptured lion; No. 172, the upper portion of a human figure set in a niche; Nos. 175-179, headless figures of the Deæ Matres; No. 200, a funereal monument of a Roman lady; No. 205, heads of male and female figures. These are ranged on a shelf over the fire-place at the south end of the room. No. 206, flue tiles for conveying the hot air from the hypocausts up into the walls of the building; stone mortar, etc. These may be found on a shelf over the fire-place at the north end of the room. Ascending to the room above, the visitor will see around the walls fac-similes of the Bayeux tapestry. By examining a model of the castle he will obtain a better idea of the original appearance of this massive stronghold than he would from the most careful description. In this room there are a great many British and Roman antiquities, chiefly lent, however, to the Society of Antiquaries, among which may be mentioned: Implements of bronze and stone, earthenware vases and bronze amphoræ, pieces of tesselated pavement, rings, brooches, necklaces, hair-pins, combs, keys, seals, etc. There are also various prints and drawings illustrative of the topography of the district, some interesting cases of coins and mediæval antiquities, old family and ecclesiastical plate, with autograph letters from George and Robert Stephenson, William Blake, Queen Elizabeth, Sir William Herschell, Charles I., Judge Jeffreys, Linnæus, Melancthon, Sir Isaac Newton, Bishop Percy, Archdeacon Paley, William Martin, Rev. John Brand, Charles Hutton, John Locke, the Earl of Derwentwater, and others. In the room above will be found some ancient clocks, spinning wheels, mediæval shoes, old armour, rare books, and illuminated missals, with many other objects of antiquarian interest. The Black Gate till recently consisted of about eleven rooms, and was let off in tenements by the Corporation, but the Society of Antiquaries, on obtaining a lease of the building, completely gutted the inside, and altered it to its present condition.

The visitor should not omit to see another remnant of the old castle—the SOUTH POSTERN—of special interest, because it is said to be the only remaining Norman postern in England. Let him cross the Castle Garth, pass the Moot Hall—or County Court of Northumberland, which, with its yard, occupies the sites of the ancient Moot Hall, the King's Chamber, and the Half Moon Battery—and go a short way down the Castle Stairs, and he will observe the arched passage with a portion of its massive tower before him. The oblique direction of the passage is noteworthy. This postern is the oldest remaining fragment of the castle, and may possibly be a part of the works of Robert Curthose. Many portions of the castle wall may be observed between the Postern and the High Level Bridge.

## ANCIENT CHURCHES OF NEWCASTLE.

NEWCASTLE is more celebrated for its military and domestic, than for its ecclesiastical architecture. The old churches are commodious and well proportioned, but they do not effloresce with those rich groinings, traceries, and mouldings, that in more southern towns illustrate so wonderfully the luxuriant imagination of the Middle Ages. We look in vain for those elegant buttresses, with their panelling and crocketed pinnacles, that seem rather to adorn than support the hallowed walls. There is not that marvellous union of grace and strength which make St. Mary's, Beverley, so precious an heirloom of the past. We must ascribe this deficiency to the benumbing sense of insecurity, and not to the lack of devotion or imaginative vigour in the ancient inhabitants of Newcastle. One architectural possession of incomparable beauty the town has, and that is the beautiful steeple of St. Nicholas' Church. ST. NICHOLAS' CHURCH, raised in 1881 to the dignity of a Cathedral, dates back to the middle of the fourteenth century. It rose on the site of a previous church, which is said to have been consecrated by Osmond, Bishop of Salisbury and nephew of the Conqueror, in 1091, and was destroyed by fire in 1216. The first important event connected with the church was the ratification of the truce between England and Scotland, which took place in the vestry on the 13th of August 1451. The Princess Margaret, daughter of Henry VII., on her way north to espouse King James IV. of Scotland, attended "the church masse" with her retinue of noblemen and churchmen. John Knox held the appointment of preacher in the church for two years, in the reign of Edward VI., and here made his defence before the Council of the North for teaching that the mass was idolatrous. James I., when on his way from Scotland to England to assume the crown of England, stayed a short time in Newcastle, and attended service in St. Nicholas' Church. Toby Mathew, Lord Bishop of Durham, preached before him, welcoming him to his new kingdom. Charles I., when a prisoner in Newcastle, attended this church, and no doubt received many a rude admonishment from the fanatical preachers of the Covenant, who would be more likely to preach at the unfortunate king than to him. One of these gentlemen, at the conclusion of his discourse, gave out the opening lines of the Fifty-second Psalm :—

"Why dost thou, tyrant, boast abroad,
Thy wicked works to praise?"

The allusion was obvious, and the king, with ready wit, stood up and called for the Fifty-sixth Psalm instead—

"Have mercy, Lord, on me, I pray,
For man would me devour."

The sympathies of the congregation were with the king, and the latter psalm was sung. I have already referred to the famous threat of the Scottish general to blow down the spire of St. Nicholas' Church if the town did not surrender, and the stratagem of the brave Sir John Marley to prevent such a calamity. On entering the town, General Lesley and his victorious army attended service in the church, when Alexander Henderson preached to them. After the battle of Dunbar, a large number of the Scotch prisoners whom Cromwell had sent south were quartered for a night in St. Nicholas' Church. From 1784 to 1787 the church was subjected to a restoration, which left it bare of nearly all its monuments and brasses. In 1867 the steeple, which had long shown signs of decay, was entirely repaired, under the direction of Sir Gilbert Scott, at a cost of £8,368 ; and in 1873 the restoration of the body of the church was commenced, and on May 31st, 1877, the church was re-opened. The sum of £21,400 has been required for this work. The visitor will naturally direct his attention to that which has given St. Nicholas' Church its special value in the eyes of all lovers of architectural beauty—namely,

THE TOWER AND STEEPLE, built about the middle of the fifteenth century by Robert Rhodes, a lawyer of Newcastle, who was one of its members in Parliament for five years. The tower measures at the base 36 feet 9 inches by 35 feet, and the whole structure is 193 feet 6 inches high from the pavement to the top of the lantern. It is divided into three storeys, the lowest of which forms the western vestibule or entrance to the church, and is covered with a very rich and beautiful vault, bearing in the centre the inscription, "Orate pro anima Roberti Rodes." In the second storey is the clock, which has two dials, one on the north and one on the south side. In the third storey are the bells, nine in number, the largest of which is called the "Major," in commemoration of the donor, Major George Anderson, and is used for striking the hours. One of the bells is called the "Pancake Bell," and is still rung on Shrove Tuesday, at night. The common "Thief and Reiver" bell, re-cast in 1755, is used for calling the burgesses together ; it was always rung before the annual fairs, to let all thieves and doubtful characters know that they might come into the town during the fair without fear of being molested or examined. "With this storey commence the decorations which have excited the admiration of many generations. Each face of it is divided by a delicate buttress, rising up square as far as the battlements, and then is ingeniously continued as an octagonal turret crowned by a pinnacle. On each side of the central buttress are elegant windows, divided by a transom across the centre, and perpendicularly by a mullion ; through these, being unglazed, passes the sound of the bells. The tower terminates with perforated battlements, and from thence rise eight turrets and pinnacles of matchless elegance. The pinnacles are crocketted, and each finishes with a lofty vane, ornamented with the fleur-de-lis at the angles and sides. From the base of the four angular turrets spring four segments of arches, elegantly curved and cut into mouldings. At their intersection, twenty feet above the battlements, they support a very elegant and lofty square lantern, which has an open window on each side, divided by a mullion and cross-bar. There are small buttresses at the angles, surmounted by ornamented pinnacles, each of which supports a vane ; and from the top of the lantern rises a lofty pinnacle, which crowns the work. This pinnacle is hollow within, and is composed of stones only four inches in breadth." "This steeple," says Rickman, "is the type of which there are various imitations : the best known are St. Giles's, Edinburgh ; the Church at Linlithgow ; the College Tower at Aberdeen ; and its modern imitation by Sir C. Wren at St. Dunstan'sin-the-East, London ; but all those fall far short of the original." The following enigma, having the steeple for its subject, is attributed by Gray in his *Chorographia* to Ben Jonson :

"My Altitude high, my Body foure square,
My Foot in the Grave, my Head in the Ayre,
My Eyes in my Sides, five Tongues in my Wombe,
Thirteen Heads upon my Body, foure Images alone.
I can direct you where the Winde doth stay,
And I turn God's Precepts thrice a day.
I am seen where I am not, I am heard where I is not,
Tell me now what I am, and see that you misse not."

Entering by the West Porch we observe under the tower the ancient font of St. Nicholas, a plain octagonal marble vase supported on a plain octagonal pillar, the base of which rests on a stone pedestal. The eight faces of the vase are sculptured with shields of arms, six of them being the arms of Robert Rhodes. Over the font, and partly supported by two iron bars in the rim, is a lofty and elegant canopy, exhibiting most curious and elegant workmanship.

THE NAVE.--The view of the inside of the church is imposing ; the architecture, though plain, being very effective. The total length of the interior is 245 feet. The only stained glass window on the north side is in memory of the officers and privates of the fifth battalion of the Northumberland Fusiliers who were killed in the Indian mutiny ; and the two banners which hang above were used in the action. On the south side is the Bewicke Porch, anciently called Saint Margaret's Chantry. The beautiful Gothic monument on the east side, in memory of Colonel Bewicke, is by Bailey, from a design by Theed ; part of it was exhibited at the Royal Academy in 1819. Opposite to it is an effigy, which lay formerly under a recess in the south transept. The figure is habited in a hauberk of chain mail and surcoat, with a sword and shield of arms. The animal at the feet is described by Bourne as a dog, but is thought by others to be a lion. It is not known exactly whom the figure represents. Brand suggests Peter de Mauley, and Bourne one of the family of the Scroopes ; and Mr. Thompson, in his little guide to the Cathedral, thinks that it is most likely meant for Peter-le-Marechal, the shield-bearer of King Edward I., as the costume of the figure agrees with that period, and it is known that Edward II. paid for the funeral services at his burial in Saint Nicholas. In one of the windows of this south aisle is the only fragment in the church of the original coloured glass, representing the Virgin and Child, very delicately treated. At the east end of the nave, against the pillar of the north aisle, is a fine monument, by Flaxman, of Sir Matthew White Ridley, who was three times mayor of Newcastle, and represented the town in Parliament for thirty-two years. Against the opposite pillar in the south aisle is a cenotaph, by Rossi, of Lord Collingwood, the hero of Trafalgar, who was a native of Newcastle. Embedded in the masonry of the north-east pier of the nave may be seen an early English pillar and capital, a fragment of the earlier church.

THE SOUTH TRANSEPT was formerly called St. Mary's Chapel. Underneath the large south window is the mutilated niche of the Peter-le-Marechal effigy, and on the left of it there are the remains of a piscina. On the west side of this transept is the famous Maddison monument, which appears to have been erected some time between the years 1635 and 1640. It is a very beautiful and elaborate sculpture. At the top are statues of Faith, Hope, and Charity. In the body of the monument are six kneeling figures—three men and three women. The central effigies are those of Henry Maddison—sheriff of Newcastle in 1605, and mayor in 1623—in his robes as an alderman, and Elizabeth his wife; behind Henry is the figure of his father, Lionel Maddison, who was mayor of Newcastle in 1693, 1705, and 1617, and his mother Jane Maddison, of the family of Seymour. On the other side of the monument are Sir Lionel Maddison, eldest son of Henry, with his wife Anne, daughter of William Hall. Below the central effigies are sixteen smaller ones, representing the sixteen children of Henry and Elizabeth Maddison, and a series of small shields of arms, indicating their respective marriages. Opposite to this fine work of art is a beautiful monument, erected to the memory of the Rev. Hugh Moises, M.A., who was for many years head-master of Newcastle Grammar School, by his pupils. It is of marble, by Flaxman, and represents Religion in the form of a woman, with her eyes fixed on heaven, leaning on a cippus, which bears a medallion portrait of the deceased, and is surmounted by an urn. The inscription is by one of his pupils, William Scott, Lord Stowell. All the windows are filled with stained glass. The large one was erected to the memory of the Rev. Clement Moody, M.A., vicar of St. Nicholas, from 1853 to 1871, and the subjects illustrated are the Sermon on the Mount and Christ weeping over Jerusalem. The two windows on the east side are to the memory of Margaret Coates Gibbs and Eliza Harper, the subject of the former being Christ meeting Mary Magdalene and Mary the mother of James after his resurrection.

THE NORTH TRANSEPT.—In this part of the church now stands the organ—a magnificent instrument, built by Messrs. T. C. Lewis & Co., of Brixton, London, and considered to be one of the finest in the north. Beneath the north end of this transept is a crypt, which is generally known as Saint Catherine's Chantry, and is believed to have formed a part of the church that preceded the present edifice; its length is 23 feet 6 inches, and its width 11 feet 1 inch, inside measurement. The roof is semi-circular, and strengthened by five bold longitudinal ribs. In the south wall is a piscina, and there is a window looking into St. George's Porch, resembling a St. Catharine's wheel. A beautiful oak screen separates this porch from the church.

THE CHOIR OR CHANCEL.—Across the body of the chancel has been erected a beautiful reredos of very fine Uttoxeter alabaster, the design of which is based on the great mediæval altar-pieces of Winchester and St. Alban's. It is 20 feet high and 16 feet wide, with splayed wings of Caen stone, richly panelled, connecting it with the side walls of the choir. Immediately above the altar ledge, which is of red Italian marble, nine canopied niches contain as many angels of white alabaster bearing shields with the emblems of the Passion. In the upper part, ranged round the central figure of Christ, are various statues of Northumbrian saints and the four Evangelists. The saints in the top row are St. Oswald, Ven. Bede, St. Cuthbert, St. Benedict Biscop, St. Aidan, and St. Edwin ; below are St. Gabriel, St. Matthew, St. Mark, St. Luke, St. John, St. Mary, and lower still, St. Wilfrid and St. Paulinus. On each side of the central figures are the Virtues in a vertical series of niches. All the figures have been specially modelled and sculptured by Mr. J. Sherwood Westmacott, of London. The Bishop's Throne is raised on three steps of black marble, and is crowned with lofty tabernacle-work of oak, ending in a crocketted spire 36 feet high from the pavement. Eastward of the choir the church has been excavated so as to disclose the original bases of the pillars about 2½ feet below the level of the other part of the church. A broad flight of steps across each aisle leads down to this excavated area, which is formed into a chapel for smaller services. The great east window was erected in 1859 from a design by Mr. A. Dunn, in memory of Dr. Ions, for more than twenty years organist of the church. The principal subject is the Crucifixion. Beneath it is a second altar with an oak reredos richly carved and coloured. This is divided into three compartments, having pictures representing the Nativity, the Annunciation, and the Visitation. Hung up at the back of the principal reredos is a painting 17 feet by 7 feet, by Tintoretto, the subject of which is "Christ washing the feet of the Disciples." It was presented in 1818 by Sir Matthew White Ridley, Bart. Here is preserved a finely-carved Communion chest, with this inscription upon it, "This Communion chest, which had disappeared about one hundred years before from the church of St. Nicholas, Newcastle-upon-Tyne, was bought by Edwin Fenwick Boyd, of Moor House, in the county of Durham, Esquire, for the purpose of restoring it to the vicar and churchwardens, to be held by them in trust for ever." On the wall above are two small paintings, "The Flight into Egypt" and "The Adoration of the Magi," presented by Hugh Taylor, Esq., of Chipchase Castle, in 1879. Passing down the south aisle of the chancel we come to the Hall monument, somewhat similar in design to the Maddison monument. In arched recesses are the effigies of William Hall and his wife, kneeling at a desk with books upon it. Below are the effigies of their children in the same posture, one of whom, their son, is represented kneeling at one side of a desk with an open book upon it ; and five daughters on the other side of it, kneeling one after the other. Two other monuments demand special notice—first, the Askew monument, by Henry Webber. It was erected to the memory of Henry Askew, of Redheugh, by one of his nephews. In the centre of the monument is an urn, raised on a pedestal. On the face of the urn are profile portraits of the deceased, whose ashes are supposed to be deposited within. A figure representing Gratitude is directing two children, a boy and a girl, to present wreaths of flowers to Benevolence, who stands on the other side of the urn, which she embraces with one arm, while with the other she enwreaths it with the children's offering. At the children's feet a dove nestles; behind Benevolence is a pelican feeding her young, and beside Gratitude a stork, emblem also of parental care and affection. The other monument is that of Matthew Ridley, Esquire, of Blagdon and Heaton, who was for four years mayor of Newcastle, and represented the town in five successive parliaments. During his mayoralty in 1745 he particularly distinguished himself in preparing the town to resist the Pretender. The stained glass windows on the south side of the chancel are as follow :—In memory of James Dale, representing the Ascension; in memory of the children of James Dale, representing Christ blessing little children; in memory of Joseph Garnett, representing the six corporal acts of Mercy (the principal figure in each of the six groups is the donor, Mr. Joseph Garnett, chemist, by whose executors the window was erected); in memory of the Rev. James Snape, master of the Grammar School, representing Christ sowing the seed, and St. Paul preaching at Athens.

THE VESTRY, attached to the south side of the church, was built by Sir Walter Blackett in 1736. In the room above, called the chapter room or upper vestry, is the old or parish library, containing a famous MS. Bible illuminated by the monks of Hexham about seven hundred years ago, and many other rare MSS., some of them said to date back as far as the Conquest. The chains by which the bibles were fastened to the desks are still kept here. Permission to see these literary treasures must be obtained of the churchwardens. The churchyard contains the tombs of many who once were of note in the town. One gravestone bears the name of Joseph Barber, the famous bookseller of Amen Corner, who died July 4th, 1781. His great grandson and namesake is Joseph Barber Lightfoot, the present Lord Bishop of Durham.

ALL SAINTS' CHURCH stands at the foot of Pilgrim Street. It was built in the year 1789 on the site of an older building called "All Hallows," which in its turn is supposed to have risen from the ruins of a Roman Pantheon, the temple to all the gods. The position of the church is very commanding, and the churchyard, planted with trees and flowers, is like a green oasis in the midst of the wretched tenements around. The steeple consists of a square tower, from which rises a succession of stages, terminating in a light and elegant spire. It has an elevation from the ground of 202 feet. "A singular incident with regard to the round top-stone in which the vase is fixed is recorded. This stone is thirty inches in circumference, and when it was placed in position, one John Burdikin, a militiaman, and afterwards a barber in Gateshead, ascended the scaffolding, and stood on his head on the extreme summit—a feat, strange to say, repeated by his son during some repairs in 1816." Ascending a broad flight of steps, we stand beneath a handsome Doric portico, consisting of four stately columns supporting a pediment, the apex of which is ornamented by a beautifully sculptured vase. We now enter a lofty vestibule of circular form, having a nobly-vaulted roof, supported by eight coupled Ionic pilasters. On our left is a small chapel for morning prayer and the services of baptism and burial, and on the right is a vestry. On the walls of the vestibule are a few mural tablets. The watch which hangs here belonged to a son of the Rev. Hugh Moises, master of the Grammar School. He was unfortunately drowned, and the watch, having stopped when he sank, marks the correct time of the sad occurrence. The main body of the church is elliptical in form, the diameter 86 by 72 feet, exclusive of a semi-circular recess in the east wall, which contains the pulpit, and another in the east wall, which contains the gallery stairs and the organ. The pews are made of solid mahogany. The beautiful curvature and decoration of the roof, which is without any supporting pillars, produce a very fine effect. A spacious gallery, resting on twelve fluted columns of the Doric order, extends in a semi-circle round the church. Behind the pulpit are three painted windows to the memory of Joseph Garnett, who died 14th December 1861, aged ninety years. There are two other painted windows, representing the apostles Peter and Paul. In the vestry, in a wooden frame, is the splendid monumental brass which covered the altar tomb of Roger Thornton and his wife. Besides the chief figures are numerous small images of the apostles and saints in beautifully carved niches or canopies. Round the rim of the plate runs the inscription, "Hic jacet Domicella Agnes quondam uxor Rogeri Thornton que obiit in vigilia Sancte Katerine anno Domini MCCCCXI., Propitietur Deus amen. Hic jacet Rogerus Thornton mercator Novi Castri super Tinam qui obiit anno Domini MCCCCXXIX. et III die Januarii." This Roger Thornton, a munificent merchant of Newcastle, like so many other Tyneside celebrities, commenced his career with very little stock-in-trade beside his own energy, if we may credit local tradition, which tells us that—

> "At the Westgate came Thornton in,
> With a hap, and a halfpenny, and a lamb's skin."

In the Parish Register are some curious entries—

| | | | | |
|---|---|---|---|---|
| 1725.—Paid for two Otters' heads . . . | £0 | 0 | 8 |
| 1727.—Paid for a Badger's head . . . | 0 | 1 | 0 |
| 1730.—Paid for a Foumart's head . . . | 0 | 0 | 4 |

According to an old custom, whoever brought the heads of foxes and other vermin, and nailed them to the church door of the parish in which they were killed, was entitled to be rewarded by the churchwardens according to a fixed scale.

ST. ANDREW'S CHURCH, in all probability the oldest church of the town, stands at the top of Newgate Street, and was formerly just within the town walls, near the site of the old gate. Tradition ascribes its erection to King David, and the fashion of the architecture and the fact of the church being dedicated to St. Andrew, the patron Saint of Scotland, give colour to this belief. During the siege of Newcastle in 1644 a breach was battered in the walls close by, and the Scottish cannon on the Leazes almost ruined the church, so that no service was performed in it for a year afterwards. It has been subject to so many repairs and alterations since its erection, that few traces of the original are left which have not undergone some innovation, and it exhibits so many styles of architecture that Mr. Charleton is justified in calling it a "much be-patched edifice." The tower is low and square, strengthened by exceedingly large buttresses. On the west side are marks of a doorway and three windows which have been built up, and on the east side is the mark of the original high-pitched roof of the nave. Entering through the chancel, the antiquity of the church is evidenced by the round Norman arch of the chancel, with its zigzag ornamentation, and by the low cylindrical columns of the nave, on whose octagon capitals rest the heavy semicircular arches. Above the pillars of the north side a dead wall extends to the roof, and on the left side it is broken by a number of not very elegant windows, one of which, near the chancel arch, is filled with stained glass. The font is plain, but has a very richly-carved canopy. The chancel is 58 feet in length, and 18 feet in breadth, and contains some very finely-carved black oak stalls. The east window is to the memory of the Rev. William Dodd, M.A., and represents the Ascension. On the north wall of the chancel, above the altar, is a fine old painting, representing the Last Supper, by the celebrated Luca Giordano. It was presented by Major George Anderson to St. Andrew's Parish in 1804. The obtuse-pointed arch in the nave leads to a chantry, which was founded by the person who is supposed to have given the Town Moor to Newcastle—Sir Adam de Athol, Knight, Lord of Jesmond and Sheriff of Northumberland under Richard II. In it he was buried, together with his wife, Lady Mary. Along the north side of the churchyard may be seen some remnants of the town wall, surmounted by a ruined turret. Opposite the south entrance is the grave of the musical composer, Avison, author of "An Essay on Musical Expression."

ST. JOHN'S CHURCH stands at the corner of Grainger Street and Westgate Road, and its blackened, weather-beaten walls contrast strangely with the more modern buildings whose splendid façades we regard with so much admiration. The date when this church was founded is not definitely known. Bourne mentions, on the authority of a charter of the date 15 Edward I., the existence of the church at that time. The greater part of the church belongs to the Decorated and Perpendicular periods, though there are fragments of Norman masonry in the building. The large projecting buttresses at the corners of the tower terminate in gracefully crocketed pinnacles. A difference will be observed between the north and south walls of the church, one being finished with a plain parapet, the other, evidently later in date, being ornamented with battlements. The pointed arches which separate the nave from the aisles are plain and simple in character. On the altar-piece, painted by Henry Mort, are represented cherubs ascending and descending in the clouds. A funnel or spout is said to have hung from the choir of this church, through which a dove was conveyed on the day of Pentecost, in imitation of the descent of the Holy Ghost. The cover of the font is richly decorated. In the south transept is a window to the memory of John Cunningham, a pastoral poet, who died in Newcastle, September 18th, 1773, aged forty-four years. It is a beautiful design—representing Faith, Hope, and Charity—and was presented by Joseph Cowen, Esq. In the churchyard, not far from the east window, is his gravestone—a stone slab raised on four pillars, recently restored by public subscription. As his name is likely to prove unfamiliar to the visitor, a few words about this "pastoral poet" will not be out of place. He was a native of Dublin, and like another unfortunate poet of later days—Albert Glatigny—led a Bohemian life as a strolling player. Necessarily he was often in want, and there is a world of pathos underlying the quaint humour of a reply he made to a clergyman who once rebuked him for fishing on the Sunday in the Wear, near Durham. He hoped God and his reverence would forgive his seeming profanity of that sacred day, as he had no dinner to eat but what lay at the bottom of that pool. Cunningham had a delicate appreciation of the minuter charms of nature, and a subtle grace of diction, which in a less artificial age would have given birth to poems of exquisite beauty; but he succumbed to the fashion of the time, and the majority of his poems, conventional alike in subject and style, are no longer read, and the world has agreed to forget him. But even as it is, we find in his poems delicate touches of colour such as are never met with in Akenside's "verses of rhetorical exposition." I select at random a few charming little vignettes from the writings of the "poor inhabitant below":—

"From the low-roof'd cottage ridge,
See the chatt'ring swallow spring;
Darting through the one-arch'd bridge;
Quick she dips her dappled wing."

(From "Morning.")

. . . . . . .

"O'er the heath the heifer strays
Free—(the furrow'd task is done),
*Now the village windows blaze,*
*Burnished by the setting sun.*"

. . . . . .

"Tripping through the silken grass,
O'er the path-divided dale,
Mark the rose-complexion'd lass,
With her well-pois'd milking-pail."

(From "Evening.")

. . . . . .

"Upon the green the virgins wait
In rosy chaplets gay,
*Till morn unbar her golden gate*
*And give the promis'd May.*"
(From "May Eve; or, Kate of Aberdeen.")

. . . . . .

"High upon the daisied hill
Rising from the slope of trees,
*How the wings of yonder mill*
*Labour* in the busy breeze!"
(From "A Landscape.")

Edward Chicken, the author of the "Collier's Wedding," is also buried here. This interesting and once famous local poem, which may perhaps offend some tastes by its rough Doric realism, is valuable for the sprightly and humorous description it contains of the manner in which an important event in the collier's life was celebrated half a century ago.

THE TOWN WALLS.—The principal portions of the ancient walls of Newcastle which still remain are to be found between Hanover Square and the railway, and between Westgate Road and St. Andrew's Church. Hanover Square is not far from the old Keep. Proceeding down Bailiffgate, under the railway, and past Clavering Street Mission, and turning to the right, the visitor will come to a handsome square brick house adjoining Fletcher's Brewery. Passing round to the front, he will see a long stretch of the wall in fair condition; along the top of it, outside, runs an embrasured parapet intact, coping stones and all, probably built in 1715 or 1745. The point where the wall leaves Westgate Road is in Cross Street, opposite the new Police Station. Proceeding up a narrow lane, still called "The West Walls," the visitor will see the largest remaining portion of the town wall. It is only broken in one place, where a breach was made a few years ago to allow Stowell Street to join Bath Lane. He will soon reach the Durham Tower, and then, shortly afterwards, near the gateway of the Fever Hospital, the Heber Tower. Continuing, he will notice, a little way along, a small pointed doorway in the wall, now built up, which was constructed by permission of Edward II., to afford the Dominican, or Black Friars, convenient access to their garden outside the wall. Further on, past the remains of a turret, he will come to the Morden or Mordaunt's Tower, and then, past another turret, the end of the walls is reached at a large warehouse which stands on the site of the Ever Tower. Behind a picturesque old windmill, a well-known feature of this part of the town, a fragment of the wall runs along the north end of St. Andrew's Church. At the foot of Croft Street, which branches off from New Bridge Street, opposite to the Free Library, is the Plummer Tower, at present used as a school. An important remnant of the ancient fortifications is the Sally-port or Carpenters' or Wall Knoll Tower, the only gate now standing. It is a picturesque object, banked up from the New

Road, which runs from Pilgrim Street past the Manors Station to Sandgate. At the west side of the massive archway is a vaulted chamber, at present inhabited. Here several loop-holes may be seen. There is also a small mural-staircase leading to the postern, whence a sortie used to be made. The wall from this point is supposed to have been built on the site of the Roman Wall.

ANCIENT STREETS.—Proceeding from Westgate Road across Charlotte Square we come to LOW FRIAR STREET. A little way along, on the right side, the visitor will notice a curious old house with sporting dolphins and winged heads carved upon it. It is traditionally said to be the oldest house in Newcastle. Turning to the left, down Monk Street to the Friars, he will come upon one of the most interesting parts of old Newcastle, the Blackfriars' Monastery, which, in spite of considerable alterations, still retains its old-world aspect. The buildings are arranged in the form of a square, some being used as poor dwelling-houses, and others being the meeting-halls of the various trades' companies. Over one door we see the inscription—

"By hammer and hand
All artes do stand."

This is the Smiths' Hall, and was formerly the chapel of the monastery. Here it was that, on the 19th June 1334, Edward Baliol, King of Scotland, did homage to Edward I. for the kingdom of Scotland. Passing through a pointed archway, along a short passage roofed with massive beams of wood, we enter the quadrangle, or old cloister garth, called "Friars Green." Around us we see in the walls the mouldings of the Gothic windows and doorways of the monastic buildings, built up in the walls of the houses and trades' meeting-halls. On the east side we see the back door of the Smiths' Hall, with three hammers, the emblems of their ancient craft, and the motto already given carved on a shield above it.

HIGH FRIAR STREET, which runs from Newgate Street to Grey Street, contains the birthplace, now considerably altered, of Richard Grainger, the great builder, who has effected such a transformation in the appearance of Newcastle. The CASTLE GARTH, extending from the Black Gate to the Moot Hall, contains a number of tumble-down tenements, which are gradually being "improved" out of the way. Already several of them are in process of demolition. They are chiefly occupied by the vendors of old clothes and boots. The CASTLE STAIRS, which descend from the Castle Garth to the Sandhill, are lined on both sides with an infinite number of clogs and second-hand boots, which, in spite of the brilliancy of their polish, cannot conceal the wrinkles of age. It is curious how the humbler votaries of St. Crispin have monopolised the wretched buildings that are reared on the steep banks of the Castle Hill.

THE SIDE.—Between St. Nicholas' Church and the Black Gate a curved and narrow street, called the Side, runs down to the bottom of Dean Street. It still preserves many of those curious, yet picturesque, old houses with overhanging storeys, which date back to the time of Elizabeth. In a brick house at the head of this street, on the left-hand side, Lord Collingwood was born, on the 26th of September 1750. It is now a public-house, having the sign of "The Meters' Arms." Further down on the right are the "Dog Leap Stairs," at the top of which stood one of the posterns of the castle. The Side, which in Bourne's day was filled with shops of merchants, goldsmiths, milliners, and upholsterers, is now occupied by shoemakers and the dealers in old clothes. At the foot of the Side a lofty railway arch, spanning Dean Street with a magnificent curve, will excite the admiration of the ordinary sight-seer as well as the practical engineer.

THE BUTCHER BANK, or AKENSIDE HILL, is on the left of the Side. It contains several old houses, and derives its chief interest from the fact that the didactic poet, Mark Akenside, the son of a butcher, was born here on the 9th of November 1721. The house where he first saw the light has been removed, and its site is occupied by a tall, plain, modern building, No. 33.

SANDHILL.—On the south side of the Sandhill is the Guild Hall and Exchange. The Exchange is on the ground floor, and contains a large statue of Charles II., in a Roman toga. The Guildhall is a spacious apartment, with the usual fittings of a court of justice at its west end. The grotesque masks carved in wood, and attached to the beams overhead, are curious. The Merchants' Court adjoins the Guildhall. It is a large square room, with panelled oak wainscoting reaching almost to the ceiling, and terminating in a very finely-carved cornice. Among the arms and names emblazoned on the sides of the room are those of the leading Northumbrian families —the Bewicks, Claverings, Ellisons, Fenwicks, and Ridleys. The large oak chimney-piece is elaborately carved. Two of its panels above the mantel-shelf will especially attract attention—one representing the Judgment of Solomon, and the other the Miraculous Draught of Fishes. The Mayor's Chamber is also wainscoted, and contains several paintings in the panels of the old buildings and streets of Newcastle. From the old stone steps that led to the upper storey of the Guildhall John Wesley was accustomed to preach ; and here it was that on one occasion, when his words had aroused the enmity of several roughs in the crowd, he owed his safety to a sturdy fisherwoman of the name of Bailes, who, putting her arms round his waist, and shaking her clenched fist at the rioters, exclaimed, "If ony yen o' ye lift up another hand to touch ma canny man, ayl floor ye direckly." The desired effect was produced. Opposite to the Guildhall will be seen a picturesque old house with innumerable windows. It bears the name of James D. Hedley over the doorway. This was formerly the residence of Aubone Surtees, Esq., the banker, and from a small casement, marked by a blue pane, Miss Bessy Surtees eloped on the 18th of November 1772, with Mr. Jack Scott, who afterwards became Lord Eldon. The ladder by which the fair damsel descended into the arms of her lover was concealed during the evening in the shop underneath by a clothier's apprentice, one John Wilkinson, a friend of young Scott's. A few doors to the east is another old mansion, No. 33 Sandhill, at present unoccupied, which contains an elaborately carved chimney-piece, and is said to have been the town residence of Lord Derwentwater.

THE CLOSE is a continuation of Sandhill, and was formerly the quarter where the principal inhabitants of the town lived. About the middle of the street, on the south or river-side, stands the Old Mansion House, now let to a timber merchant. It bears few traces of its pristine magnificence. Opposite the Mansion House are the Tuthill Stairs, leading to Clavering Place. Half-way up is a curious and interesting old house, built in the reign of Queen Elizabeth. It was bought by the Baptists in 1720 for a chapel. The first Sunday school in Newcastle is said to have been held here, and one of the ministers who officiated for a short time in the quaintly-carved little room was John Foster, the essayist. A stone tablet on the north wall of the Close, near Messrs. John Davidson & Sons' mills, indicates the site of the Close Gate. The street is spanned at its east end by one of the magnificent arches of the High Level Bridge.

Proceeding along THE QUAYSIDE, where the Custom House and steamboat landings are situated, the visitor will notice a number of narrow streets called "chares," known in Scotland as "wynds,' and in the south of England as "alleys." Into one of them, called "Trinity Chare," let him enter, and visit the hospitals, chapel, and hall of the Trinity House, which he will find at the upper end. In the entrance-hall are various curiosities. Here in a glass-case may be seen models of a full-rigged line-of-battle ship, the *Ville de Paris* (on board of which Lord Collingwood died), made by French prisoners at Portsmouth out of their beef bones; some charges of grapeshot; a Turkish caique and Indian surf-boat; also the knight-head of the *Betsy Cains*, the vessel which brought William III. over to England. In the corner opposite is a model of the Groyne Lighthouse at South Shields. On the walls are some old pictures, "The Journey to Emaus" and "Shields in the Olden Time," an ancient harpoon, and other relics. Hung from the roof are specimens of the hammer-head and shovel-nose sharks, and of the dolphin and tortoise; a Russian musket picked up in the bay of Sebastopol; an Esquimaux canoe; and a relic of the great fire of 1854—viz., a half-burnt rafter, projected by the force of the explosion across the river from Gateshead, and hence metaphorically called "a flying-fish." The visitor is next conducted by the attendant into the chapel, which dates from the year 1491. It is a curious and interesting apartment, with a roof shaped like the under part of a ship's deck, and with ancient pews and pulpit of black oak, finely carved. Over the door are the escutcheons of several of the old benefactors of Trinity House. Passing from the chapel into the library, which contains several old and valuable works, the visitor will notice a framed list of the former masters, bearing their signatures, and a portrait of Mr. Hutton, the mathematician. The next room to be seen is "The Board Room," the walls of which are literally covered with interesting paintings and engravings. Over the fire-place is a magnificent allegorical picture, the subject of which is "The Four Quarters of the Globe." It is said to be by Rubens, and certainly exhibits the salient characteristics of that great master. On the wall opposite is a fine painting (by Backhuysen) of Admiral Van Tromp's *Undracht*, in which he boasted that he had scoured the seas. Nearer the window is an exquisite example of Carmichael's work. It represents North Shields and the mouth of the Tyne, as seen under the transfiguring glow of a great artist's imagination. Over the door is a small portrait of "Blind Willie"—a Newcastle eccentric. The engravings have chiefly for their subjects famous naval engagements. The visitor now proceeds to the hall or dining-room, built 1721, a large and richly-decorated chamber, panelled with oak, and containing some very valuable pictures:—"The Battle of Trafalgar," painted by Carmichael and Balmer, showing the *Royal Sovereign*, flagship of Admiral Lord Collingwood, passing between and firing into two Spanish line-of-battle ships; "The Defeat of the French Squadron," commanded by Monsieur de la Clue, off Cape Lagos, on the 18th August 1759, by the squadron of His Majesty's ships under the command of the Right Hon. Edward Boscawen, Admiral of the Blue; "Conclusion of the Bombardment of Algiers by Admiral Lord Exmouth," on the night of the 27th August 1816, partly painted by Carmichael, but finished by Swift. Above this magnificent picture is a turtle-shell, with the arms and motto of the Trinity House upon it. Portraits of Queen Anne and King James II., and busts of Pitt and Fox, are also to be seen. Above the fire-place are some elaborate carvings in black oak, and on the mantel-piece are little models of ships used in the examination of pilots. Passing down a small passage, containing an old painting of an embarkation scene, the visitor enters once more the vestibule, and is then conducted to the secretary's room, where there is preserved a model of Nelson's ship, the *Victory*, made by English prisoners in France out of their beef bones. Over the main entrance in Broad Chare hangs a rust-eaten old anchor, said to have belonged to one of the vessels of the Spanish Armada. The hours of admission are 10 A.M. to 4 P.M. Monday to Friday, and 10 A.M. to 1 P.M. on Saturdays.

The last "chare" on the left is "Love Lane," in which stood the house where Lord Eldon was born.

SANDGATE is one of the localities immortalised by song; but Sandgate as it is, and Sandgate as it is imagined to be by the many thousands who delight in the "Keel Row," are two different places indeed. At one time, when it stood amid green fields, with a fine sandy beach in front of it, Sandgate was a pleasant locality enough; but now not even a De Quincey, through the mist of an opium dream, could find a picturesque feature about it. Formerly it was the quarter of the once famous Tyne keelmen. As to the sturdy qualities possessed by this now nearly extinct race, the visitor may judge by a visit to the Keelmen's Hospital, which stands on the New Road above Sandgate. It is a fine old square brick building, with an open space in the middle, and was built at the charge of the Newcastle keelmen in 1701, for the benefit of the aged and infirm among them, It cost £2000, to raise which fourpence per tide was levied. It was in Sandgate that, on the 30th May 1742, John Wesley commenced his ministrations among the "poorest and most contemptible part of the town," whose character may be inferred from a passage in his journal:—"So much drunkenness, cursing, and swearing, even from the mouths of little children, do I never remember to have seen or heard before in so short a compass of time." On the occasion of his second visit, in the latter part of the same year, he is found preaching, one bleak November afternoon, in the large square of the Keelmen's Hospital, which gives standing room to several thousands of persons. Passing through the ancient and royal village of Pandon, the visitor, will notice another benevolent institution, the Jesus' Hospital, or Freeman's Hospital, a brick building with a piazza in front, founded in 1681. Adjoining it, at the east end, is an ancient tower about 20 ft. square, the only remnant of the monastery of the Austin Friars, founded about A.D. 1290 by William Ros, Baron of Wark-upon-Tweed. The entrance doorway is a pointed arch of rugged stonework. A well-built newel-staircase leads up to the four apartments of the tower, the middle one of which is known as the "Queen's Room," from a tradition that it was occupied by the Princess Margaret, daughter of Henry VII., when staying at the monastery on her way north in 1503 to espouse James IV. of Scotland. There is a curious stone safe in the wall of this apartment. The dark vaulted room in the basement, once, perhaps, a cellar or store-room, of the monastery was used within comparatively recent times as a temporary cell for the confinement of drunk and disorderly persons, and was called the "Kitty." The iron rings to which the prisoners were fastened may still be seen in the walls. The Manors Brass Works occupy the site of the Friars' burial-ground.

PILGRIM STREET.—This street took its name from the circumstance that pilgrims, on their way to the little chapel at Jesmond, usually passed along it. In the lower part it presents many features of antiquarian interest. Near the Old Fox and Lamb inn is a little barber's shop, the oldest in the town. Tobias Smollett is said to have frequented it, and here it was that Roderick Random, in September 1736, was recognised by his old school-fellow, Strap, who was acting as assistant to the then proprietor. The Liberal Club, a little above Mosley Street, stands near the site of an old building which tradition says was the "pilgrims'" inn. Facing Mosley Street is the Royal Arcade, the entrance to which is adorned with two massive pillars of Doric architecture. At the eastern extremity is a lofty archway, from which a flight of steps leads down to the Manors. The length of the building is 250 feet, its width 20 feet, and the height of the roof, which is richly groined, 35 feet. This was one of the first great works of Grainger, built after a design by Dobson. The stately rows of shops are at present occupied by furniture brokers and second-hand dealers of various kinds.

NEVILLE STREET is the first street with which the visitor to Newcastle is made acquainted, for in it stands the Central Station. This imposing structure took the place of a small building which was the terminus of the Shields and also the Berwick railway, and is now used as a dwelling-house. It stands behind the Gaol, in a corner not far from the subway leading to the Manors Station. The Central Station was designed by Dobson, and was opened by Her Majesty, August 29th, 1850. It cost £120,000, and covers 19,300 square yards. Over its site a large portion of the town walls used to run. The curved roof, divided into three compartments and supported by metal columns, is at once substantial and elegant, and the grandeur and simplicity of the portico in front have been much admired. From the memoir of John Dobson, by his daughter, it is interesting to learn that the great architect, before designing the Central Station, spent three days in a railway station watching the issue of tickets, the passengers getting in and out of the trains, the departure and arrival of trains, in order that he might obtain a thorough knowledge of the sort of work to be performed there, and so harmonise the character of the architecture with the purpose of the building. The result of this careful study is evident in the arrangement of the platforms and the various offices attached. The original plans of Dobson were altered as regards the exterior of the building when the walls were half up, as the company decided to bring the chief offices from York to Newcastle. Consequently Dobson was compelled to rearrange the entire design, making the building two storeys instead of one ; and abandoning the noble classic colonnade which was to have stretched the whole length of the building, with a portico in the centre double the width of the colonnade. In making his design, says Miss Dobson, after studying the various obstacles, he came to the conclusion that a curve not only met and overcame the difficulties of site, but that it was also the most artistic way of treatment. Having determined the general idea of a curved platform he caused everything to fall into harmony with that, carrying out the curve not only in the roof, but in all minor details of the work. The doors and windows opening on the platforms have circular heads, and being placed at equal distances, give the effect of an arcade in harmony with the curved platform. In order to make the roof answer to the rest of the design, Mr. Dobson introduced curved ribs crossing the whole width of the station in three spans of 60 feet. The facility of obtaining malleable iron led Mr. Dobson to originate this new and graceful style of roof effected by curved principals, and, on account of the novelty of this design, he obtained the medal at the Exhibition of Paris 1858.

Near the Station stands STEPHENSON'S MONUMENT. It was fitly designed by a north-country sculptor, J. G, Lough, and was erected at a cost of £5000. It was unveiled October 1862. George Stephenson stands on a pedestal, at the base of which are figures of the miner, the engineer, the navvy, and the smith—intended to represent the handicraftsmen of the district. On the left of this monument are the *Newcastle Chronicle* offices, and a little to the right the Wood Memorial Hall and the Library of the Literary and Philosophical Society. Passing down Collingwood Street, the visitor will come to St. Nicholas' Square. On the left are THE TOWN HALL BUILDINGS, which cost about £50,000, and contain the Corporation Offices, Council Chamber, a large Public Hall, the Corn Market, and many shops and offices. In the Council Chamber are the paintings of Charles II. and James II., of the date 1686, which were formerly hung on the walls of the Guildhall. Portraits of Lords Eldon and Stowell, Alderman Headlam, Alderman Hodgson, Alderman Angus, and Lord Armstrong also adorn this chamber consecrated to municipal wisdom and eloquence. In the Borough Treasurer's office is preserved an ancient treasure-box, called a hutch, in which the town dues were put as they were received. It bears upon it the date 1716. There is also preserved here a half-length portrait, in oils, by H. P. Parker, of Judith Dowlings, or "Old Judy" as she was called, the messenger to the hutch. On Saturday afternoons Dr. Rea, the town organist, gives recitals in the large hall, and visitors with musical tastes will no doubt avail themselves of this opportunity of hearing one whose reputation may, without exaggeration, be said to be European. A narrow lane, passing between St. Nicholas' Church and the back of Mosley Street, leads to the workshop of Thomas Bewick, indicated by a tablet. Here it was that the busy hand traced out on the smooth hard blocks those beautiful representations of birds and quadrupeds that have made his name so famous. Continuing along Mosley Street, the visitor will reach GREY STREET. This magnificent street, which is the pride of Newcastle and the admiration of all visitors, is the crowning work of Grainger, who transformed the narrow irregular streets of old Newcastle into broad and stately thoroughfares, unsurpassed by any in the kingdom. While according every praise to the energetic builder and speculator, we must not forget the great architect who designed the new buildings—Dobson, equal to Grainger in energy, superior in genius. Grey Street stands on the levelled-up valley of the Lort Burn, and the difficulties surmounted by Grainger were very great. From Mosley Street the eye follows the stately curve of the street, with its rich Corinthian architecture, to the lofty monument of Earl Grey at the top. The whole length is 480 yards, and the width averages 80 yards. "In Grey Street," says Miss Dobson, "may be observed the skilful manner in which, by means of throwing up the lifted parts of the sky-line, the descent of the ground has been concealed, so that the eye, satisfied by the artistic grouping of the various masses of the buildings, scarce recognises the difference of level between the top and the bottom of the street. This is in marked contrast to the ordinary treatment of such a slope." Proceeding up the street, the visitor will notice on the west side a majestic pile occupied by the Bank of England. The lower storey consists of rustic masonry, on which stand nine Corinthian columns and two pilasters ; these again support an entablature finished with a double row of balustrades. In the suite of buildings included between High Bridge and Market Street, of which the Turk's Head forms the centre, the order adopted is that of the Temple of Illysus at Athens. The chief ornament of the east side is the Theatre Royal, designed by Benjamin Green. Its noble portico, after the design of the Pantheon at Rome, consists of six Corinthian columns surmounted by an enriched pediment. Between Grey Street and Pilgrim Street are several handsome cross-streets built by Mr. Grainger in the Ionic and Latin styles of architecture—Shakespeare Street, Market Street, and Hood Street. In the upper part of Grey Street is the Central Exchange ; it has three fronts, which are uniform in design, and after the model of the Corinthian Temple of Vesta at Tivoli. The three domes which spring from ranges of Corinthian columns at the angles of the structure are very elegant, and add further variety to the perspective of Grey Street. The interior is a noble semicircular area of 11,835 feet. It was intended by Mr. Grainger for a Corn Market, but is at present used as an Art Gallery and Reading Room. Opposite to the Exchange is an ornate building occupied by Messrs. Lambton and Co., bankers. At the junction of Grey Street and Grainger Street stands a lofty Ionic column, 135 feet high, surmounted by a statue, by Bailey, of Earl Grey of Howick, who was Prime Minister at the time of the passing of the Reform Bill. Crossing the top of Grey Street, to the east and west is BLACKETT STREET, another of Mr. Grainger's streets. On the north side of it is Eldon Square, almost wholly built by him. The open space in front, laid out in walks and planted with trees, relieves somewhat the dark and heavy aspect of the stately stone façades. On the south side of the street, near the buildings of the Young Men's Christian Association, is the Northern Academy of Arts, built after designs by Dobson, in 1827, for Messrs. T. M. Richardson and H. P. Parker, artists, for the exhibition of pictures. It is now the sale-room of Messrs. Davison and Son. The house next to this building, on the east, was occupied by the eminent artist, T. M. Richardson ; that on the west by H. P. Parker. New Bridge Street forms a continuation of Blackett Street on the east, and therein are situated the Public Library and News Room, and the New Bridge Street Station, the terminus of the Blyth and Tyne Railway. We now come to GRAINGER STREET. This fine street has not the beautiful curve nor architectural magnificence of Grey Street, but it has abundant claims to rank second amongst the streets of Newcastle. It is called after one of Newcastle's greatest sons, who began life as a charity-boy, and ended it as the great reconstructor of his native town. He owed little to the advantages of his birth, for his father was a porter on the quay, and his mother was a stocking-engrafter. Parallel with Grainger Street runs CLAYTON STREET, another great thoroughfare, connecting the town with the Railway Station. Between these two streets are Nun Street and Nelson Street. These four streets enclose the Butcher Market, built by Grainger to replace that which was removed from the old theatre when Grey Street was built. It occupies an area of two acres, and is one of the largest and finest covered markets in the country. At the junction of Clayton Street with Neville Street stands St. Mary's Cathedral, the largest and most beautiful of the Roman Catholic churches in the town, built in 1844, after Pugin's designs, in the decorated style of Gothic. Its lofty and delicate spire, 260 feet in height, is one of the architectural ornaments of this part of the town. From a point near this church half-a-dozen streets radiate in different directions. One is Westmoreland Street, which leads to Westmoreland Road, where is situated the Royal Free Grammar School, founded by Alderman Thomas Horsley about the year 1525, and reconstituted by Queen Elizabeth. Another street runs past the Cattle Market, the Infirmary, and the Forth Goods Station to the river. Westward runs a long thoroughfare, SCOTSWOOD ROAD, following the course of the river, past the extensive engineering works of Sir W. G. Armstrong, Mitchell, and Co., Limited, to the oddly-named village of Paradise, and Scotswood.

The lower part of Grainger Street is crossed by WESTGATE ROAD, one of the longest and steepest thoroughfares of Newcastle. From the site of the old West Gate, near the Tyne Theatre, it has a continuous ascent as far as the Workhouse, following almost exactly the course of the Roman Wall. At its lower end, close by the County Court, stand the Assembly Rooms, a stately structure, with a portico consisting of six Ionic columns, built 1774–6. Balls and assemblies are still held here, and it is also used for exhibitions of pictures and chamber concerts. NORTHUMBERLAND STREET is a continuation of Pilgrim Street. On the left, going towards Barras Bridge, are the Orphan House Schools, built on the site of the original Orphan House Chapel and Schools which were founded by John Wesley in 1742. Here it was he lived during the rebellion of 1745, and there are in his journal many references to the state of the town at this critical period. On the right of Northumberland Street —a continuation of Saville Place—is Ellison Place, where at No. 1 are the Judges' Lodgings. The porch is surmounted by the arms of the town. Here may be seen some very fine and locally interesting pictures, belonging to the Corporation, viz.:—T. M. Richardson's famous "View of the Side, with the High Sheriff of Northumberland going out to meet the Judges of Assize;" H. P. Parker's "Sandhill Wine Pant—Coronation of George IV.;" and "Fancy Dress Ball in the Mansion House—Coronation of William IV.;" together with H. Brandling's "Town Hall of Oudenarde," all in the dining-room. Portraits of George III. and Lord Collingwood, formerly hung on the walls of the Guildhall, adorn the vestibule. Leading from Barras Bridge is a small street called Eldon Place, where, in No. 17, the visitor is informed by a tablet in the wall, George and Robert Stephenson resided in 1824-5. Iu another street leading from Barras Bridge—St. Thomas' Crescent—at No. 4 lived William Bell Scott, the eminent poet and artist, whilst he was in Newcastle as the head-master of the School of Art. At his house the late D. G. Rossetti frequently stayed, and here, on one of his visits to the north, he painted the portrait of Mrs. Leathart. By way of New Bridge Street an interesting district called Shieldfield is reached. Here stood the great fort which played an important part during the siege of 1644. In the Shieldfield King Charles I. was allowed, during his captivity in Newcastle, to go and play golf; and tradition says that the quaint old house standing on one side of it is the same in which King Charles rested when he visited the Shieldfield. Pleasant Row, between Shieldfield Green and New Bridge, contains the house—No. 9—where Lord Armstrong was born. In Sandyford Lane, leading from the Shieldfield to Jesmond, is "Lambert's Leap," as the visitor will see from the coping-stone of the parapet. On the 20th of September 1759 the mare of Mr. Cuthbert Lambert, of Newcastle Custom House, took flight, and leapt over the bridge, a distance of 45 feet, falling 36 feet. The intervening branch of an old ash tree broke their fall, and the rider, strange to say, was uninjured. Two other similar accidents have taken place at the same spot—one on the 18th August 1771, and another on 5th December 1827. In the latter case the rider died from injuries he received.

THE HIGH LEVEL BRIDGE.—This massive structure over the deep river-gorge between Newcastle and Gateshead is one of the wonders of Newcastle. It was proposed by Mr. Hudson, the Railway-King, and designed by Robert Stephenson. The difficulties of securing a good foundation for the piers were very great. Huge piles were driven into the bed of the river by Nasmyth's Titanic steam-hammer, the rapid strokes of which evolved so much heat, that on many occasions the pile-head burst into flame. The first pile was driven to a depth of 32 feet in four minutes, and as soon as one was placed, the traveller, moving overhead, presented another, and down it went like a pin into a pincushion.

Great difficulty was experienced in emptying the coffer-dams of water, which forced its way through the bed of quicksand almost as fast as it was pumped out. After some months of unsuccessful effort cement concrete was put in, which set, a foundation was made, and the piers were securely built. The bridge consists of six cast-iron arches springing from piers of solid masonry, 50 feet by 16 feet in thickness, and 125 feet distant from each other. Above these arches is the railway, and beneath them the roadway. The first is 112 feet above the water, the second 85 feet; the whole length of the bridge is 1337½ feet, and its weight 5050 tons. The total cost of the bridge and approaches, etc., was £491,153. The first pile for forming the foundation of the bridge was driven into the river on October 1st, 1846, and the last key closing the arches was driven into its place on January 7th, 1849. It was opened for traffic on the 4th of February 1850. On the Newcastle end of the bridge is the old, primitive locomotive of George Stephenson, known as the "Billy."

THE REDHEUGH BRIDGE.—This elegant structure, designed

and built by Sir Thomas Bouch, the engineer of the unfortunate Tay Bridge, affords a high level communication between the western portions of the boroughs of Newcastle and Gateshead. It was commenced in 1868, and completed and opened for traffic in June 1871. The height of the under side of the bridge is 87 feet above high water line, or about four feet higher than the High Level Bridge. The river spans are formed of two longitudinal wrought-iron lattice girders, each 838 feet long and 22½ feet high, supported on three river piers, each of which is formed of four cast-iron columns. The total length of the bridge and viaducts between the high line on each side of the river is 1453 feet, and the whole cost of the structure was £35,000. A main water-pipe and a gas main are carried across this bridge.

THE SWING BRIDGE.—This, the latest of the bridges over the Tyne, is erected on the site of several old bridges. 1st. There was the bridge of wood and stone built by the Roman Emperor Hadrian in the second century—the bridge that gave the name of Pons Ælii to Newcastle. 2nd. There was the mediæval bridge, erected about 1250, after the fire of 1248, which destroyed the older one. This famous old bridge was washed away by the memorable flood of 1771. And 3rd. There was the stone bridge of modern days, which was built on the ruins of the mediæval one between the years 1773 and 1781. The dredging of the river by the Tyne Commissioners had deepened the channel so that it was navigable much higher than formerly, and as the low arches of the bridge prevented masted vessels from passing, the Commissioners determined to remove it and replace it by the present Swing Bridge. The work was commenced 23rd of September 1868, and opened for traffic 25th June 1876. The piers and abutments are of stone and concrete on foundations of cast-iron cylinders filled with cement, sunk down to the rock about 45 feet below low water. The superstructure, made by Sir W. G. Armstrong & Co., is of wrought iron, supporting a carriage road of 24 feet wide, and footways on each side 8 feet wide. The swinging portion of the bridge, which weighs 1450 tons, and spans the two middle openings, is turned with wonderful ease and smoothness by the hydraulic machinery of Lord Armstrong. The total cost of the bridge was £233,000.

The LIBRARY of the LITERARY AND PHILOSOPHICAL SOCIETY.—Standing a little back from Westgate Road, not far from Stephenson's Monument, is a large, sombre, and impressive building belonging to the Literary and Philosophical Society. This society was founded in 1793 by a few townspeople who were interested in literary and scientific matters, the foremost of them being the Rev. William Turner and the Rev. Edward Moises. It developed, and after several changes of quarters, it built in 1825, at a cost of £16,000, the building referred to, which stands on the site of the town house of the Earls of Westmoreland. In the erection of the building the great sculptor Lough was engaged as a stonemason. Robert Stephenson left the institution £10,000, and Lord

Armstrong built at his own cost the lecture theatre. As a specimen of architecture the building will not rank so high as some large and ornate structures of more recent date, like that, for example, which contains the Free Library. The façade is heavy and unornamented, and draped in the "sable stole" of accumulated coal-dust. The doorway, which is raised three or four steps above the street level, is adorned with two fluted columns. Entering the vestibule, the visitor will notice, on ascending the grand staircase, a full-length marble statue of Mr. Losh, formerly Recorder of Newcastle. Around the walls are some four beautifully sculptured slabs from Nineveh, the gift of W. K. Loftus, Esq., a native of Newcastle, who assisted Sir H. Rawlinson in the East, and some casts of the Elgin marbles, representing the battles of the Centaurs and the Lapithæ. On the top of the staircase may be seen William Bell Scott's historical picture of the building of the Castle by Robert Curthose. This great artist, who is also a poet, in a striking poem, where he restores Saint Bede to life again, and brings him to the Library of the Literary and Philosophical Society, describes the wonder of the saint at the sight of so many goodly volumes; and even to our modern eyes the first glimpse of the large and handsome and commodious room, crowded with books from floor to ceiling, is impressive. It is estimated that the library contains now about 50,000 volumes. Near the entrance is a model by Lough of "Milo." Arranged on pedestals around the room are marble busts of distinguished men, among which may be specially mentioned George and Robert Stephenson, Thomas Bewick, Lord Armstrong, and Lord Brougham. There is a comfortable reading-room adjoining the library, hung with oil paintings of George and Robert Stephenson, Lord Brougham, the Rev. Edward Moises, Rev. Robert Morrison, Sir J. E. Swinburne, Bart., F.R.S., Thomas Bewick, and Charles Hutton. Several alterations and additions are proposed to be shortly made to the building of this valuable institution, which has far outgrown the expectations of its original promoters.

THE PUBLIC LIBRARY.—This library, which was opened on the 7th of December 1881, with a stock of 20,069 books, is situated in New Bridge Street. The foundation of the present stately building was laid on the 13th of September 1880, and it was found necessary, much to the regret of antiquaries, to remove the Carliol or Weavers' Tower. The structure is in the Corinthian and Doric orders of architecture. The principal entrance is in the centre, and is approached by seven steps through a portico with Doric columns supporting an entablature surmounted by a balustrade. The floor is semi-circular in shape; it is approached from the principal hall or vestibule, 43 feet long by 20 feet wide. On each side of the entrance are statues of Lords Eldon and Stowell. On the left is the lending library, in which the library indicator is in use, and facilitates very considerably the issuing of books. On the right is the reading-room, containing all the principal newpapers and periodicals of the day. Ascending the broad flight of stairs, at the foot of which is a fine marble statue of the Archangel Michael subduing Satan, by Lough, we reach the next storey, that contains the reference library, opened by the Prince of Wales, August 20th, 1884. Some more beautiful marble statues by Lough will be noticed, representing Hamlet, Macbeth, Lady Macbeth, Iago, and Edgar. These, together with the one downstairs, were presented to the library by Sir M. W. Ridley. At present both the lending and reference library contain nearly 29,000 volumes. In addition to these there are the books of the Thomlinson Library, 4365 in number, which were transferred to the Public Library from the room over the vestry of St. Nicholas' Cathedral. Alderman Cowen was the first to be enrolled as a borrower, and to his reader's-ticket, was entered at his request, John Stuart Mill's *Essay on Liberty*. There are in connection with the central building branch news-rooms situated in Byker, Elswick, and Westgate.

THE MUSEUM.—The Museum of the Natural History Society stands at the top of Barras Bridge, on the North Road. It is a plain and substantial building, commodious and well-lighted, in every way adapted for the arrangement of such a collection as that possessed by the society. In the entrance-hall is the original design of Dobson for the Central Station. Passing into the first room we notice the magnificent Hancock collection of birds. The specimens illustrating "Falconry" are especially interesting—The 'hooded falcon,' 'struggle with the quarry,' and 'gorged falcon.' The "Eagle attacking Swans," and "Falcon and Raven," and "The Falcon's fate in the nineteenth century," are wonderfully lifelike. The museum contains two specimens of the Great Auk, a bird now extinct; one is in the case along the wall, the other stands on a long table opposite. This and another specimen with two eggs were brought from Iceland, and, as far as is known, are the last captures of this rare bird. An egg of the Great Auk, kept in one of the drawers by the Curator, is considered of great value. The visitor will examine with some degree of curiosity specimens of several New Zealand birds, the Kiwis (Apteryx Oweni) in particular. The collection of natural history also includes fine specimens of the Grey Seal (Halichœrus Gryphus) taken at Warkworth, 1858, and of the Sunfish (Orthagoriscus Mola) taken at Whitby, 1855. In the adjoining apartment, on the east side of the building, is a large skeleton of Rudolphi's Rorqual, washed into the bay of Newbiggin, 1869. A fine collection of corals, a considerable proportion of which were contributed by the Earl of Tankerville, will be noticed in the first room. In the next room is one of the finest collections of fossils from the coal measures to be found in the United Kingdom. They include specimens of fossil trees (Sigillaria). In the upstairs rooms are cases of curiosities from the South Sea Islands, India, China, Persia, Assyria, and Egypt, and other countries of the world. Some Egyptian mummies, Roman urns, and New Zealand paddles (richly carved) will scarcely escape the eye of the curious visitor. Round the galleries are hung a unique and invaluable collection of Bewick's original drawings.

The Museum is open from 10 to 4. Admission—Adults, 3d.; Children, 1d.

The TOWN MOOR AND LEAZES.—This fine expanse of green pasture-land rises gradually from the north and north-west of the town towards its most elevated point, the Cow-hill, where the cattle fairs are held. The area of the Town Moor, Castle Leazes, and Nun's Moor is about twelve hundred acres. This great tract of herbage was once, it is said, a forest of trees, and tradition adds that all the houses of mediæval Newcastle, as well as hundreds of ships, were built of wood grown here. The Newcastle races used to be run over the Moor, but they have now been transferred to Gosforth Park. In place of this popular sport, a Temperance Festival is now held during the summer. At holiday times the Town Moor presents a very gay appearance, with the bowling, cricket, football, and other sports practised upon its velvety surface. The Leazes is divided from the Moor by a long row of houses, extending from Eldon Street to Spital Tongues.

THE LEAZES PARK occupies the centre of the Leazes. It may be approached from Percy Street *via* St. Thomas' Crescent, or from the North Road running from Gallowgate. This beautiful Park has been laid out with much taste and care, and with its shrubberies and flower-beds, its lake and quiet alleys, its bowling-greens, its tennis-courts, its rustic summer-houses, its aviaries and conservatories, is one of the most attractive pleasure-resorts of the people of Newcastle.

THE ELSWICK PARK.—This Park lies between Westmoreland Road and Elswick Road, on the west part of the town, and is situated on a slope. It is much smaller than the Leazes Park, but it has much larger and older trees, and commands a magnificent view of the Team Valley and the heights of Whickham. It also has a lake, bowling-green, rockery, etc. On a terrace in front of the aviaries is a fine granite drinking-fountain, erected by public subscription in 1881, in recognition of the public spirit of six gentlemen—Joseph Cowen, Thomas Forster, Thomas Gray, T. Hodgkin, William Smith, William H. Stephenson—who had been instrumental in procuring the park for the people of Newcastle. Elswick Hall, a large impressive-looking stone building, with a front composed of four Ionic columns, stands in the centre of the park. It was built about the beginning of the present century, probably on the site of an old house once the seat of the Jenisons, who obtained possession of the estate on the dissolution of the monasteries, for of old this place belonged to the Priors of Tynemouth. It is the repository of the Lough and Noble Models, presented to the town by the widows of the deceased sculptors. The town is indeed to be congratulated on the possession of such a noble collection of beautiful works. Speaking of Lough, Mr. Joseph Cowen, M.P., in his inaugural address, said, "He was recognised as the worthy successor of Banks and Flaxman, of Chantrey and Westmacott. His works might be divided into four classes—the Poetic, Classic, Religious, and Historical: there are illustrations of the first two orders of his models, which the works of no modern sculptor surpass in purity, in elegance, in simplicity, and in taste.

His groups exhibit that high sense of the beautiful and harmonious in composition which was equally conspicuous in the martial 'Knight Banneret,' in the homely heroine of the 'Heart of Midlothian,' and the plaintive 'Mourners,'—as fine an example of motionless poetry as was to be found in England. His statuary combined in happy proportions the heroic and the familiar, the poetic and the real." Besides the models mentioned by Mr. Cowen, there are others equally great in imagination, conception, and realistic embodiment. "Group of Horses and Tigers" (No. 74); "Samson slaying the Philistines" (No. 100); "Michael" (No. 106); "Satan" (No. 112); "Milo" (No. 113); and the splendid bas-relief, "The Siege of Troy," where the sculptor's power of combining his creations is marvellously exemplified. The statues of "Warren Hastings," "The Prince Consort," "Lord Lawrence," "Southey," and "Her Majesty," should not be passed unnoticed by all who would understand the many-sided genius of Lough. In the rooms above are the models of Matthew Noble, the great bust-sculptor. In this collection the visitor will recognise most of the prominent men of the century—"John Bright," "Richard Cobden," "The Prince Consort," "The Prince of Wales," "Palmerston," "Sir Robert Peel," "Earl Derby," "W. E. Gladstone," "Wellington," "General Havelock, K.C.B.," "Sir John Franklin," "Nelson," "Lord Mayo," and others. His more ideal work is seen in the Models (No. 24), "Alto-Relief of Religion;" (No. 25), Monument to commemorate the son and daughter of Robert Heath, Esq.; and (No. 68) "Purity."

THE BRANDLING PARK.—This is a pretty enclosure near the Museum, opposite to Brandling Place. It contains a small sheet of water, and a number of shrubs and young trees. The beds are tastefully laid out, and set with a great variety of flowers.

THE HEATON PARK.—This is one of the latest acquisitions to the town, and lies at the extreme east of Jesmond. It was formerly part of the Heaton estate. Perhaps this is the best wooded of the Newcastle parks. A fine terrace, backed by extensive hot-houses, aviaries, and monkey-houses, overlooks the bowling-greens. Near the lake is a bear-pit, where Bruin shambles sullenly around his pole. A large eagle, a racoon, and several monkeys are kept here for the delectation of juvenile students of natural history. Near the new bowling-green, close to the north-east boundary of the park, are the ruins of a mediæval building, popularly known as

KING JOHN'S PALACE. Three sides of a square tower covered with ivy are all that remains of it. In the north wall are the joist-holes of an upper floor, and at the north-west corner of the tower a sort of turret. On the west side there is a round arched doorway in the upper storey; on the north side a pointed window; on the east side a similar but smaller one, and beneath it an arrow-slit. These ruins in Heaton Park, according to Mr. Cadwallader I. Bates, are those of the Camera, or principal seat of Adam de Gesemuth (Jesmond)—a baron of considerable wealth and influence in the thirteenth century. He was high sheriff of Northumberland in 1267, as he had been for three former years—viz., 1262-1264; and having acquired the same odious character for peculation and extortion that was common to nearly all the sheriffs of that time, he found it necessary to obtain a license from King Henry III. to enclose, fortify, and crenellate his house. He apparently left no family, as Ralph de Stikelowe, chaplain, and Marjory de Trewick appear as his heirs in 1275. The circular, temple-like building on the hill in this park was presented to Sir Matthew White Ridley, the former proprietor of the Heaton estate, by his tenants and friends. This beautiful park, which possesses so many natural advantages, and will always repay a visit, is only about five minutes' walk from the Heaton Station. Passing from the Heaton Park, the visitor will enter THE ARMSTRONG PARK. Both this possession and Jesmond Dene the town owes to the munificence of Sir William G. Armstrong. The Park is well-wooded, and extends along the valley-side to the Benton Road. The remains of an old windmill stand picturesquely on the hill. There is a good carriage drive all the way. By the side of it is an old memorial stone, recording the death of Abigail Tisack, who "departed this life the 7th weack of her life, anno 1679." Further on is "Ye well of King John." A fine iron bridge, built by Sir William Armstrong, and known as "Sir William's Bridge," crosses the valley.

JESMOND DENE is continuous with the Armstrong Park, separated from it merely by the Benton Road. Here art and nature have combined to form one of the most beautiful spots in the "north countreè." The glowing rhododendron is in close proximity to the heather, and the tulip is only separated from the cowslip by a foot-path. The transition from the grimy streets of Newcastle to the winding paths of this charming vale of Tempe is magical indeed. The Ouseburn, that lower down is a little Erebus, is here an Arethusa. But how describe all the loveliness of this happy valley—from the cool little dell of moss and fern to the bracken and heather-crowned height above? Such a scene of beauty requires a Keats, with his lines of linkèd sweetness long drawn out, to bring it adequately before the mental vision of those who have not seen it. The picturesque water-mill near the head of the dene, with the shadowy pools and glancing cascades, have been frequently painted by local artists, chief among whom must be mentioned T. M. Richardson. On the west side of the dene is the Banqueting Hall, in the midst of verdure. The interior is superbly decorated. Around the walls of the Reception Room are several fine pictures—"The Wreck" and "Fisher Life at Cullercoats," by R. Jobling; "The Lost Child" and "A Foreign Invasion," by H. H. Emmerson; "St. Abb's Head," by R. Watson; "De Vrow Jacobi off to Sea," by R. Watson; a large picture at the end of the room, "Prince Henry trying on his father's (Henry the Fourth) Crown," by John Calcott Horsley, R.A., and a few others. The Banqueting Hall, which is separated from the Reception Room by a small organ, commands, from its long windows, a series of lovely glimpses into the dene. Stationed around the walls, in niches or on pedestals, are statues in a variety of positions.

THE CHAPEL OF OUR LADY OF JESMOND.—The ruins of this picturesque little chapel stand amidst a clump of trees in a field behind the lodge of the Banqueting Hall. They may be reached by following a passage leading under the road from the dene. Not much is known concerning this little chapel, or the date when it was founded. In 1351 Sir Alexander de Hilton and Matilda his wife presented the chaplainship to Sir William de Heighington. It then seems to have fallen into the possession of the Priors of Tynemouth. Edward VI. granted the chapel and hospital of the Virgin Mary to the Corporation of Newcastle, which in turn sold them to Sir Robert Brandling. For long the chapel was used as a barn and stable, and the hospital was re-built and converted into a dwelling-house.

ST. MARY'S WELL.—This famous well, which attracted pilgrims from all parts of England, is situated in a little wooded dell that lies between the chapel and Captain Coulson's house. It is not very easy to discover. Let the modern pilgrim proceed a short distance along a cross-road that runs by the side of this dell from the edge of Jesmond Dene, and when opposite the yard-doors of Captain Coulson's house, let him look over the railings on his right, and he will observe a few steps—a remnant, no doubt, of the steps that were formerly as numerous as the articles in the Apostles' Creed—amongst the shrubs. Descending, under a moss-grown arch with the word "Gratia" inscribed upon it, will be found the object of his search.

STOTE'S HALL is an old Elizabethan house overlooking the dene, not far from the end of "Sir William's" Bridge. It belonged to the Stotes, an ancient family of yeomen, originally of Hedworth, county of Durham. Dr. Charles Hutton, the great mathematician, kept a school here for a time.

HEATON HALL is delightfully situated on the steep and wooded banks of the Ouseburn. From the grounds which were formerly attached to it the Armstrong Park, as has already been stated, was formed. On the site of it there was a mediæval building, traces of which are still to be seen in parts of the present building. Here are the remains of the chapel at which, in 1299, King Edward I. attended, to hear a boy-bishop (in connection with one of the church spectacles or plays) perform the vespers of St. Nicholas, on the 6th of December, on which occasion, as the wardrobe accounts of that year testify, he gave the juvenile prelate and his companions the sum of forty shillings.

The manor of Heaton was anciently part of the extensive barony of Robert de Gaugy, who was one of the principal and most trusty adherents of King John, and on more than one occasion had the questionable honour of entertaining that monarch when in the North. It belonged for many years to the Babbingtons of Harnham; and one member of this family, Henry Babbington, Esq., received the honour of knighthood from King James I. for the loyal entertainment he had provided for that monarch at his hall on the 1st of May 1617. The estate passed into the hands of the Ridleys, and in 1713 Richard Ridley, Esq., who was an alderman and mayor of Newcastle, re-built Heaton Hall. The present elegant appearance of the Hall is due to the first Sir Matthew White Ridley, who added the two towers and faced the front with stone from designs by Mr. Newton, architect. In or about the year 1840, the chief of the Ridleys having removed to Blagdon, the estate was disposed of to Mr. Addison Langhorne Potter, and the hall is now occupied by his son, Addison Potter, Esq., C.B.

Just within the walls of Heaton plantations is Robin Sheep's Cave, a cold and solitary excavation, in which, tradition says, Robin, a poor mendicant, lived for some years.

HEATON MAIN COLLIERY was the scene of a terrible accident, April 30th, 1850, caused by the inundation of the workings at the lowest extremity of the mine. At the time there were ninty-five persons in the pit; thirty escaped on the first alarm, but seventy-five persons—viz., forty-one men, including the under-viewer, and thirty-four boys—perished.

RUINED CHAPEL OF ST. LAWRENCE.—About half-a-mile eastward from the end of the New Road, not far from the Mushroom landing, is the ruined chapel of St. Lawrence. It stands a little way behind the houses which form the north side of the street, in a wilderness of a yard, amongst ruins of glass-houses, stables, and other buildings. In the certificate of colleges and chantries of Northumberland and Durham (37, Henry VIII.) remaining in the Augmentation Office, is the following account:—"No. 14. The free chapel of Saynt Lawrence, in the Lordshippe of Bycar, within the parish of Saint Nicholas', in the town of Newcastle-upon-Tyne. The said free chapel was founded by the ancesters of the late Erle of Northumberland toward the fynding of a priest to pray for their sowles, and also to herbour sicke persons and wayfayring men in time of need, as it is reported." Of this ancient chapel not much remains. The pointed east window may still be seen, built up solid with brickwork, amidst which are fragments of the original stone mullions. There are other windows and doorways, some round-arched, and one of the latter still retaining the iron crooks on which the door hung. Behind it was an ancient burial-ground.

---

PRINCIPAL HOTELS.—*Alexandra*, 22 Clayton Street West; *Central Exchange Hotel*, 95 Grey Street; *County Hotel*, Neville Street and Grainger Street West; *Crown Hotel*, 12 Clayton Street West; *Crown and Mitre Hotel*, 13 Grey Street; *Crown and Thistle*, Groat Market; *Douglas Hotel*, Grainger Street West; *Midland Hotel*, 17 Westgate Road; *Nag's Head*, 34 Cloth Market; *Norfolk Hotel*, 90 Grey Street; *Old George*, 46 Cloth Market; *Royal Exchange Hotel*, 106 Grey Street and Hood Street; *Royal Scotch Arms*, Newgate Street; *Royal Turf Hotel*, Collingwood Street; *Station Hotel*, Neville Street; *Three Indian Kings*, Three Indian Kings' Court; *Turk's Head Hotel*, 73 Grey Street; *Waverley Hotel*, 92 Pilgrim Street; *White Hart Hotel*, 12 Cloth Market. TEMPERANCE HOTELS.—MRS. E. AVERY, 18 Grey Street and 2 Higham Place; R. N. ELLIS, Neville Street; R. FOSTER, 1 Charlotte Square; *The Excelsior Temperance Hotel*, 6 Clayton Street West.

# NEWCASTLE TO TYNEMOUTH.

**Walker, 3 miles ; Wallsend, 4½ miles ; Willington Quay, 5 miles ; Howdon, 5 miles ; Chirton, 7 miles ; North Shields, 8 miles ; Tynemouth, 9 miles.**

EXCEPT to those who are interested in the industrial development of the North, a walk along the north bank of the Tyne from Newcastle to Tynemouth will scarcely be productive of pleasure. Vanished are the idyllic scenes once sketched by Carmichael ! and the tourist may look in vain for the charming "St. Anthony's" of the painter. Unsightly bastilles of labour, with barrack-like rows of dingy houses, have taken the place of green fields and hedgerows. Shipyards, foundries, glass and chemical works, colour factories, cinder ovens, etc.—these, however, and not hedgerows, are what make the Tyne so famous. The lover of nature must console himself with the fact that the genii of steam which desecrate these lovely scenes will convey him to others still undefiled and equally fair not a dozen miles away. Under certain conditions there is a sombre grandeur about these fire-wasted landscapes that appeals with irresistible power to a truly poetic nature. Yet around those chimneys and furnaces that darken the skies with their billowing fumes, there toils a hardy population, manifesting in social and political life the vigour and independence of character which was so conspicuous in George Stephenson. A trip down the river should not be omitted by any visitor who wishes to know something more than by hearsay of those industries which have made the Tyne one of the most famous of rivers. The principal sights to be seen may be gathered from the following descriptive catalogue of Mr. Walter White :—" River and shore show more and more signs of trade and labour as we descend : half a dozen steamers on the stocks —rows of coke-ovens all a-glow—troops of boiler-makers raising a deafening clatter—heaps, nay, mountains of slag and refuse ballast—more steamers on the stocks—cranes, sheds, chimneys staithes—the big beam of a steam-engine rising and falling in the distance—piles of timber-inclines that resemble railway cuttings sloping down to the water's edge—while here and there a green field and hedgerow amid the havoc and encroachment plead with silent eloquence for Nature."

WALKER.—"There's no place like Walker," says the proverb, "for general ugliness, at any rate," ejaculates the visitor as he contemplates the unpicturesque conglomeration of iron foundries, alkali and copperas works, and dingy rows of workmen's dwellings. Yet even a village so unpromising as this has found someone to sing its praises—

"When aw cam to Walker wark,
Aw had ne coat nor ne pit sark;
But noo aw've getten twe or three—
Walker pit's deun weel for me.
    Byker Hill and Walker shore,
    Collery lads for evermore;
    Byker Hill and Walker shore,
    Collery lads for evermore!"

In the farm-house of Old Walker are many Roman stones, and the fosse is used as a duck-pond. Between this place and Stote's Houses was the first mile-castle on the Roman Wall.

WALLSEND.—The village of Wallsend, once so famous for its coal, takes its name from the Roman Wall. Here was the eastern extremity of the great structure which extended into the river as far as low-water mark. Well-situated upon an angle of the river, formed by two of the longest reaches which the stream makes in the whole of its course, stood the station of Segedunum, the first of those given in the Notitia as being *per lineam valli*. Its site covered an area of three acres and a half. It is supposed to have been garrisoned by the 4th cohort of the Lingones. Recent building operations have removed nearly all the traces of this extensive military station. Roman pottery and coins and a few inscribed stones have frequently been found, and bones of all kinds have been dug up in considerable quantities. A little to the west of the western rampart of the station is the shaft of the famous Wallsend Colliery. The first operations at this colliery were unsuccessful, and the place was sold, in consequence, to the Messrs. Russell, who deepened the shaft and won the world-famed Wallsend coal, which long brought in its owners a profit of £1000 a-week. All that was got by the original owners was a piece of Samian ware, now in the possession of the Society of Antiquaries at Newcastle. In this colliery a dreadful explosion took place, October 23rd, 1821, by which fifty-two men were killed.

There is a good anecdote recorded in *Chambers's Journal* of a visit paid to this pit by a distinguished foreigner when the allied sovereigns of Russia and Prussia were in England after the overthrow of Napoleon. Having donned the picturesque garb usually worn by pitmen—viz., thick flannel trousers, called "duds," and a jacket—he was escorted to the mouth of the pit. When Mr. Buddle, the viewer, conducted him up the ladder leading to the platform of the pit mouth and introduced him to the scene of operations, he suddenly stopped short and asked with alarm whether that was really the place which he had been recommended to visit. Upon being assured that such was actually the case, he went forward to the very edge of the pit, at sight of which, however, he stepped precipitately back, and holding up his hands, exclaimed in French,

"Ah! my God, it is the mouth of hell; none but a madman would venture into it!" Upon uttering these words he hastily retreated, and, slippping off his flannels as quickly as he could, again assumed his splendid uniform of a Russian general, and soon left the Wallsend colliery far behind him. The person who thus displayed so infirm a purpose was——Nicholas the First, Autocrat of all the Russias.

The view of the river, both down the Long Reach to South Shields and up the Bill Reach to Walker, from the rounded hill on which the Roman station stood, is very extensive, when the weather is at all fine and comparatively clear. A realistic sonnet, entitled, "Wallsend-on-Tyne," by a local writer, Mr. Will H. Dircks, may not inappropriately be introduced at this point:—

"Look, painter, look. What Acheron is there,
That floats, a deathly olive hue, along
The blackened shores, where, iron-girded, throng
Gaunt chimney-shafts, that columned high in air,
Half shrouded in the mist, their offering bear
To dun low-sagging clouds! Dog-daisies strong
And rank, here at our feet, seek root among
Scant patches of stained grass, that everywhere—
Round broken walls, in furtive spots—begs life
For memory of green fields! Mark all the mud,
O Zola, all the grime—those furnace cones
Grotesque, this framework of dank staithes, the strife
Of staggering piles that half invade the flood—
And make a picture Labour loves and owns!"

The village of Wallsend is situated on the north side of the railway. The church of St. Peter was built in 1807-9, superseding the old parish church of Holy Cross, which was erected between the middle and the close of the twelfth century in the Norman style of English architecture. Little remains but the round-headed doorway on the south side, and the foundations of the walls a few feet high, together with a porch of later date. The church and churchyard occupy a plateau surrounded on three sides by deep ravines, and approached by a flight of steps, so arranged as to afford resting-places for the bearers of a corpse. On the north side the ravine seems to have been made steeper by art. Mr. Septimus Oswald suggests that the site was formerly an outpost of Segedunum. Many of the stones of which the church is built have been obtained from the Roman wall or station. The disused graveyard still retains the crumbling memorials of those who died two centuries ago. Many of these stones commemorate members of the Henzell family—emigrants from Alsace and Lorraine—who were so closely identified with the glass manufactures on the Tyne. The dates range from 1686 to 1734-5. It is said that many of the tombstones were used by the people of the neighbouring villages in the construction of ovens, and that ancient Wallsend loaves have borne such inscriptions as "Sacred to," and "In memory of." The old church was, according to a tradition narrated by Mr. Robert White in Richardson's *Table Book*, the scene of a Tam O'Shanterlike adventure, of which one of the lords of Delaval was the hero. Returning home late one night he was surprised to see the church lit up, and looking through one of the windows he beheld a number of withered hags engaged in their unholy rites. They had a cauldron filled with abominable ingredients suspended over a fire which was fed with broken pieces of coffins. He burst open the door and succeeded in capturing an old beldam, who was afterwards burnt on the sea-shore near Seaton Delaval. In the present churchyard are the old parish stocks, where many a scold and brawler has sat exposed to public ridicule.

WILLINGTON QUAY.—This village is of interest to all admirers of George Stephenson as the place where, in a little cottage of two rooms, the great engineer set up housekeeping, and where, on the 16th October 1803, Robert Stephenson was born. The cottage has been pulled down, but the exact spot where it stood is now the boys' playground in the rear of the "Stephenson Memorial Schools." "George Stephenson did not remain long at Willington, but his brief residence on the quayside was marked by other incidents besides the birth of his child. It was there that his intercourse with Robert Hawthorn first took the form of personal intimacy. It was at Willington, too, that he first took to clock-mending and clock-cleaning as an additional field of industry."—*J. C. Jeaffreson.* Near the railway viaduct on the Newcastle and Tynemouth line stands the Willington Mill, a huge and empty building fast falling into ruin. Separated from it by a cart-way is "the haunted house of Willington," which has gained a more than local notoriety by reason of the strange noises and apparitions associated with it during the last fifty years. No satisfactory explanation has been given of these extraordinary occurrences. The popular mind accounts for them thus:—About two hundred years ago, in a cottage which stood on the site now occupied by the mill-house, there lived a fortune-telling old woman who was suspected of having dealings with a certain mythical gentleman in black, and now, instead of being at rest, revisits the glimpses of the moon, making the blood of poor mortals run cold in their veins. There are also vague reports of some deed of darkness having been done when the premises were building in the year 1800 or 1801. A brief account of the visitations may be of interest to the reader. The mill belonged to Messrs. Unthank and Proctor, corn-millers, and the house at the time was occupied by Mr. Proctor and his family, who were members of the Quaker body. About fifty years ago the most unaccountable noises were heard in the house, and these appeared to get more alarming as the time wore on, so that Mr. Proctor entered into an arrangement with Mr. Unthank to reside four years alternately in the house. Sounds as of a mangle going all night disturbed Mr. Unthank, but the visitations seem to have increased when Mr. Proctor came back again to take up his abode in the house. Then a lady in a lavender-coloured dress was seen by one of the family servants, and a whitish cat, a rabbit, a large and luminous sheep, all equally impalpable, were seen by the girl's sweetheart. The noises increased so that not one of the family or servants could get any sleep. Mr. Proctor tried every means to discover the cause of the noises and apparitions. The floors were taken up, they were covered with feeding stuff to detect feet marks, but all in vain. A gentleman named Mr. Edward Drury received the sanction of Mr. Proctor to sit up all night, and endeavour to lay the ghost and account for any noises he might hear in a philosophical manner. He was accompanied by a friend, Mr. Thomas Hudson, and armed with a brace of pistols, they sat down on the third storey landing about eleven o'clock at night. About ten minutes to twelve they both heard a noise as if a number of people were pattering with their bare feet upon the floor. A few minutes afterwards they heard a noise, as if someone was knocking with his knuckles amongst their feet, and this was followed by a hollow cough. About ten minutes to one Drury saw the closet door open and the form of a female attired in greyish garments, with head declining downwards and one hand pressed upon the chest as if in pain, and the other—viz., the right hand—extending towards the floor with the index finger pointing downward. It approached Hudson, who was slumbering, when Drury rushed at it, giving, as Mr. Proctor states, a most awful yell, but instead of grasping the figure he fell upon his friend, and recollected nothing distinctly for nearly three hours afterwards. He was known to declare that for £10,000 he would not put his foot across the door-step of that house again. The noises were not restricted to the ears of one person, but were heard by all in the house. The sounds have been likened to the thumping of a pavior's rammer, the galloping of a donkey in the room overhead, the falling of scrap iron over the fire-place and fender, the clattering of peas or pebbles upon the floor, the crackling of sticks when burning, the crumpling of newspapers, and the tapping of a pencil. The bed on which the Misses Carr—two of Mrs. Proctor's sisters—slept was shaken, the curtains suddenly held up all round to the very tester, as if pulled up and as rapidly let down again several times in succession. The young ladies saw a female figure, of a misty substance and bluish-grey hue, go out of the wall at the head of the bed and through the head-boards in a horizontal position, and lean over them. Their terror, as may be imagined, was intense, and one of the young ladies would not sleep in the house again, but during her stay, and on the occasion of subsequent visits, slept at the house of one of the millers. Mrs. Mann, the wife of the foreman at the mill, saw an apparition in the large window that reaches from the top of the house down to the first landing, and being struck with the peculiarity, went and brought out her husband, her daughter, and Miss Carr, and all four saw the figure of a bald-headed old man, in a flowing robe like a surplice, gliding backwards and forwards about three feet from the floor, or nearly level with the bottom of the second storey window. He seemed to enter the wall on either side, and thus presented side views in passing. Mr. Thomas Davidson and Mr. John Ridley sat up all night, and after midnight heard sounds like those made by a rivetter riveting a boiler. Mr. J. D. Carr and Mr. Proctor on one occasion, and the Rev. Mr. Caldwell, Congregational minister of Howdon, and the Rev. Mr. Robertson, the Presbyterian minister of Wallsend, on another, kept up their vigils through the night, and all heard the mysterious sounds. One of the children saw a lady with eye-holes, but no eyes, in Mrs. Proctor's room, and this apparition was beheld on another occasion by the engineman. Numerous other sights and sounds disturbed the family, all of which have been recorded by Mr. Robert Davidson of Rosehill in his "True story of the Willington ghost." As regards the number and character of the witnesses, it would be difficult to find a story of the supernatural so well substantiated, and among the various haunted houses of Great Britain the Willington Mill-house must always occupy a unique position. Since the Proctor family left these visitations seem to have ceased, and the house is now let off in tenements.

HOWDON.—This place is generally called Howdon-Pans, from the numerous salt-pans which once existed here. It has also been celebrated for its glass-works, established here during the reign of Elizabeth by a colony of German emigrants, under the direction of a family named Henzel. Here is the Northumberland Dock, which was the first public dock in the Tyne. It was opened for traffic in June 1857, and the last stone of the masonry was laid on by His Grace the Duke of Northumberland on the 22nd October 1857. A very popular local song has been founded on the fact of Howdon being the place where the river is crossed to Jarrow. The Martin family resided for some time at Howdon, and John, William, and Jonathan were employed as boys at the rope-works of Mr Hurry, there.

CHIRTON is a small village to the west of North Shields. Ralph Gardiner, the patriot of the Tyne during the Commonwealth, author of *England's Grievance discovered in relation to the Coal Trade*, was born here. His cottage was removed in 1856 to make way for the house now occupied by Mr. Alderman J. F. Spence. A monument, designed by C. T. Gomosznski, was erected to his memory on Chirton Green in 1882. Ralph Gardiner's claim to remembrance is that he disputed very vigorously the right of the brewers, shipwrights, and other "free-traders" of Newcastle to monopolise the markets of the Tyne. Like many other reformers, he was slandered, persecuted, and imprisoned. His monument bears a very appropriate motto from Tennyson :—

> "Who suffered countless ills
> And battled for the true and just."

A profligate Duke of Argyle resided here for several years in the reign of William the III. Ralph Waters, whose painting of the Sandhill in the middle of the last century (at present in the Old Keep at Newcastle) has a considerable local value, belonged to Chirton. John

Dobson, the celebrated local architect, was born at the Pine Apple Inn, a little to the west of Chirton, in 1787. "At a very early age," says Miss Dobson, "he showed a remarkable talent for drawing; and amusing stories are told of the wrath of the villagers, which was often roused on finding their gates and shutters decorated with sketches in chalk by his furtive hand. Mr. Lawson, the village schoolmaster, perceiving his bent, gave him a set of drawing materials, whereupon he ceased his *al fresco* efforts." Another distinguished person was associated with Chirton—Admiral Lord Collingwood, who had an estate here. Lady Collingwood and her two daughters resided in Chirton House for a short time, but the Admiral was not on shore when it became his property. His mansion bears upon it the date 1693. Of Chirton Hall only the piers of the gateway and portions of the outbuildings remain. It was built in 1672 by one Joseph Clarke, who obtained his materials from the ruins of Warkworth Castle, by permission of the Countess of Northumberland. The manor of Chirton was for many generations the seat and the property of a branch of the Lawson family, from whom it passed in a curious manner to a Mr. Cardonnel. "Being acquainted with old Lawson, he called on him one day, when Mr. Lawson informed him that he had just been making his will, and, to prevent any future litigation, he had entailed his estate on every relative he had to his knowledge; and that in fourteen families, on whom he had entailed it, there would always be some one to heir it. Cardonnel, after some conversation, laughingly told him that he might put him in at the end of the entail, which Mr. Lawson, seeing very little chance of his getting anything by it, did." Strange to relate, in less than a dozen years the whole of the fourteen families became extinct, and Mr. Cardonnel succeeded to the estate, assuming the name of Lawson in addition to his own.

NORTH SHIELDS.—North Shields, which derives its name from the shiels or sheds which formerly occupied its site, is a large and important seaport town at the mouth of the Tyne, with a large and commodious harbour. Its growth is of comparatively recent date, ever since those unjust privileges and chartered rights of Newcastle, which interfered so much with the development of other towns on the river, were abolished, chiefly through the efforts made by Ralph Gardiner, of Chirton, for the liberation of the Tyne. How unjust these privileges were we may gather from the plea of the Corporation of Newcastle in their action of the year 1290 against the Priors of Tynemouth and Durham for building towns "where no towns ought to be." The Corporation declare, "that at the visit of John de Vallibus and his colleagues to the County of Northumberland in the seventh year of the reign of our now King Edward, it was presented on oath that the Prior of Tynemouth had raised a town on the bank of the water of Tyne at Sheles on the one side of the water, and that the Prior of Durham had raised another on the other side of the water, where no town ought to be, but only huts for sheltering fishermen ; and that fishermen sold fish there which ought to be sold at Newcastle, to the great injury of the whole borough, and in detriment of the tolls of Our Lord the King at the Castle, because the fish and other merchandise on which Our Lord the King is wont to take toll, which are now sold in the above manner, ought to be sold at the borough of Newcastle, where Our Lord the King takes his tolls ; and that the said Prior had also made a brewery at Sheles, and had large fishing craft where there ought to be only boats, whereby Our Lord the King lost his tolls, and the borough of Newcastle its customs, to the great loss of Our Lord the King and of the borough aforesaid." For ages Shields is described in old references as consisting of only a few huts or shielings for fishermen. The Priors of Tynemouth seem to have had a small harbour there, for, in digging to make gas tanks at the Low Lights, in a place called the Salt Marsh in Pow Dean, at the depth of twelve feet six inches from the surface, the workmen came to a framing of large oak beams, black as ebony, pinned together with wooden pins or tree-nails, the whole resembling a wharf or pier whither ships drawing nine or ten feet of water had come. This had probably been part of the erection by the Prior of Tynemouth, who, at his own cost, was obliged to remove, destroy, or abolish the use of such wharfs, markets, buildings, etc., as he had formed at North Shields. The mouth of this burn must have been a secure estuary, guarded from the sea by a peninsula of clay and sandy land now called Prior's Point, whereon Clifford's Fort was erected in 1672. A prior fort first occupied the same, or nearly the same, site. On the side of the peninsula above referred to, next to the estuary, salt-pans were working in the time of the Priory at Tynemouth—probably as early as the year 800, and so to the dissolution in 1539—and according to local history and other records, the Pow Pans were making salt in the reign of Queen Elizabeth. These antiquarian facts take us back to Saxon times ; but it is almost possible to go back further still, for at the western extremity of North Shields, at a place called Blake Chesters, about midway between Wallsend and Tynemouth Priory, were to be seen till lately the remains of a fortlet which is believed to have been Roman. The modern town has not inappropriately been compared to Wapping. The narrow, dirty, irregular streets near the river exhibit some of the most unsavoury aspects of a seaport town. The following lines, from a poetical squib by Mr. William Brockie, have, as he admits, a "spice of exaggeration" in them, but do not unfairly hit off the more conspicuous characteristics of North Shields :—

> "Farewell to Shields, the filthiest place
> On old Northumbria's dirty face,
> The coal-hole of the British nation,
> The fag-end of the whole creation.
>
> . . . . . .
>
> A mass of houses—not a town—
> On heaps of cinders squatted down,
> Close to the river's oozy edge."

The motley groups of sailors, watermen, teemers, and trimmers are not altogether unpicturesque, and, taken in conjunction with their surroundings, have much to recommend them to the artistic eye. And so, as Wapping has its Turner, North Shields has its George Balmer, who has represented the quaint features of his native town and river in many of his pictures. Unprepossessing as the town may appear to the stranger, it has charms which endear it to the local bard—to him it is "Canny Shields."

> "What darkly-distant see I yonder
> O'er the hedges, ditches, fields?
> Whence the busy hum, I wonder?
> Wonder not—'tis Canny Shields.
>
> Giddy topmasts, thick as rushes,
> Crowds of boats, and dirty keels;
> Ballast-hills, like gooseb'ry bushes,
> Altogether—Canny Shields."

The river at this point has a very busy aspect, being crowded with shipping of every description. The Fish-quay, near the Low Lights, presents a scene of considerable interest when the cobles and other boats come in with their freight of fish. Not far away from the Low Lights may be seen the old hulks of the "Castor" and the Wellesley Training Ship. The parish church of North Shields, on the Preston Road, was built in 1659, and restored in 1792. In the churchyard are preserved the parish stocks. North Shields possesses a good-sized Free Library, and has recently acquired a public park, a part of Spital Dene having been laid out very prettily for that purpose. When this park was being formed, the site of "St. Leonard's Hospital," a record of which appears as early as 1320, was discovered in 1885. During the progress of the excavations the workmen exhumed two stone coffins, one or two mediæval grave-covers, and a number of skeletons; they also came upon a tiled floor about two feet below the surface. In Dotwick Street is the site of an old house with which there is connected one of the most blood-curdling of Northumbrian ghost-stories. Many years ago it was occupied by an aged couple named Fafty, who were exceedingly poor. Their married daughter, one evening, brought them a young sailor, apparently in search of lodgings. They received him kindly, and the rough seaman, in the fulness of his heart, showed them the gold and jewels he had amassed in foreign lands. The cupidity of the old couple was aroused, and in the middle of the night they murdered their guest in his bed. The next morning their daughter came to inquire about the lodger, and struck terror to their hearts by informing them that he was their long-lost son Jim, who had run away to sea when a boy, and had now returned to comfort and lighten the lot of his aged parents. He had wished to give them a surprise before making himself known. The spirit of the murdered man is long said to have haunted the house as a black Newfoundland dog. On the Tynemouth road is the Master Mariners' Asylum, a large stone building in the Tudor style of architecture, erected in 1837-8. A full-length statue of the late Duke of Northumberland stands on a pedestal in front of the building. North Shields has its fair proportion of celebrities. In an old house in Liddell Street was born William Wouldhave, a rather eccentric character, upon whom public opinion bestows, what official authority denies him, the honour of having originated the life-boat. George Balmer (b. 1805, d. 1846) and Birket Foster (born 1812), water-colour painters, were both natives of North Shields. In the grounds of Cleveland House may be seen John Wesley's Newcastle study, which was purchased by the late Mr. Solomon Mease when the old Orphan House was taken down in 1857, and erected here, as far as possible, in its original form.

TYNEMOUTH.—This popular watering-place, so much resorted to by the inhabitants of Newcastle, is situated, as its name implies, at the mouth of the Tyne, on a commanding promontory, which is said to have been called "Pen-Bal Crag, or the head of the rampier on the rock." On the point which is now occupied by the ruins of the priory, the lighthouse, and the barracks, it is believed that the Romans had a camp dependent on the station of Wallsend. All remains of its ramparts have long since disappeared, but occasional relics have been disinterred which proves the fact. The position is exceedingly strong. Three of its sides are guarded by the ocean, and the fourth, partaking of the nature of an isthmus, admits of easy defence. From an inscription on a Roman altar which was found here in 1783, it is probable the camp was garrisoned by the 4th cohort of the Lingones.

*Tynemouth Castle.*—The remains of this ancient fortification are very inconsiderable. They have been incorporated into the present barracks. The massive old gateway is suggestive of the original strength of the place. It was formerly defended by a portcullis and drawbridge. Beneath are two dungeons, at present closed. This fortress seems to have been erected for the protection of the monastery, which had suffered much from the attacks of the Danes. It was in the possession of the Earls of Northumberland, and was held by Earl Tosti just after the Conquest. William I. afterwards conferred it, with considerable lands, upon Robert de Mowbray. This powerful earl rebelled against William Rufus, and sustained a siege of two months in the castle, escaping therefrom to Bamburgh Castle. The fortress then became vested in the Prior and Convent, and in the fourteenth century, during the Scottish invasions, Prior Richard de Tewing maintained eighty armed men there for the defence of his monastery of Tynemouth. Just previous to the wars between Charles I. and his Parliament the fortifications were strengthened, and in 1633 the king paid a visit to Tynemouth Castle. In 1644 it was besieged by General Leven and the Scottish army, and the garrison, having suffered as much from the plague as from the Scots, was obliged to surrender. Then it was repaired and garrisoned by the Parliament, and Colonel Lilburn appointed governor. He, however, declared shortly afterwards for the king, and Sir Arthur Haslerigg marched against him from Newcastle and took the castle by storm. Lilburn was slain and his head stuck on a pole. In September 1681 the castle was in a ruinous state and only maintained by a slender garrison. It was replaced by Clifford's Fort at North Shields, newly built. In the castle-yard are rows of guns and pyramids of shot, with powder magazines that are said to contain a sufficient quantity of the dangerous material to blow up the whole of Tynemouth.

*The Ruins of the Priory of St. Mary and St. Oswyn.*—To the mariner as well as to the lover of the picturesque these ruins will ever be of interest, for they crown the high sandstone crags that guard the mouth of the Tyne. They are associated with many important events in history, and carry the mind back for twelve hundred years. Edwin, the first Christian King of Northumberland, we are told, built here, probably not long after the year 627, a chapel of wood, wherein his daughter Rosella took the veil. This edifice was rebuilt of stone by St. Oswald about A.D. 640. The body of St. Oswyn, King of Deira, who had nobly sacrificed his crown and life at Wilfaresdune, near Gilling in Yorkshire, was brought hither for burial, and interred in the Oratory, A.D. 651. The church was destroyed by the Danes in the reign of Ecgfrid and restored by his pious care. In 792 Osric, King of Northumberland, was interred at Tynemouth. The Priory was burnt and plundered by the Danes in 865, when the nuns of St. Hilda, who had fled from Hartlepool to Tynemouth for refuge, were "translated by martyrdom to Heaven." In 870 it was again the scene of devastation. Deserted and roofless, it was given by Waltheof, Earl of Northumberland, to the monks of Jarrow about the year 1075. A miraculous event, if we may believe the old legend, restored the church to its pristine glory. The spirit of St. Oswyn, in a radiant human form, appeared to Edmund, the sacrist of the church, and revealed to him his burial-place, then long-lost and forgotten. The Lady Judith, wife of Tosti, at that time Earl of Northumberland, came with the Bishop of Durham to search for St. Oswyn's place of sepulture. The relics were discovered and the foundations of a new monastery commenced. In 1090 Mowbray, Earl of Northumberland, re-founded Tynemouth monastery, and filled it with black canons, and, out of enmity to the Bishop of Durham, made it a cell to the monastery of St. Albans. Here, in 1095, he took sanctuary, after he had escaped from the guards of William II., and was dragged out by violence and made a prisoner. In 1094 Malcolm Canmore, king of Scotland, and his son Edward (both slain at Alnwick), were buried here. In 1110 the new church was completed, and the sanctuary of St. Oswyn's Peace drawn for a mile round his shrine. On the invasion of Northumberland in 1138 by David, King of Scotland, the monks of Tynemouth had to pay a heavy ransom in silver to save their possessions from being ravaged by the Scottish army, and thereupon the king granted to them a charter of peace and protection. Many wealthy endowments were made to the Priory. The queen of Edward I. resided here for some time in 1303, and the queen of Edward II. in 1312. Edward II. was here in 1312, and with Piers Gaveston fled hence to Scarborough. He also visited the Priory in 1322. In the reign of Edward III. John of Tynemouth, a learned monk, who was a great collector of English annals, a biographer of saints, and author of the work celebrated as *The Golden History*, was vicar of the parochial church here. Thomas de la Mare, another illustrious monk, succeeded to the office of Prior of Tynemouth about 1341. While he was prior, David, King of Scots, captured after the battle of Neville's Cross, was brought to Tynemouth as a prisoner on his way to Bamburgh Castle before his removal to the Tower. In 1523 the right of sanctuary was claimed by Robert Lambert, who with others had murdered Christopher Radcliff at Shereston, in the diocese of Durham. Cardinal Wolsey, roused by the evasion of justice in the case of a crime so heinous, wrote to Lord Dacre, warden of the North Marches, to use every means to get the "grithsman out." On the 12th January 1539 the monastery was surrendered to the crown by Robert Blakeney, last prior of Tynemouth, and eighteen monks. The monastic buildings were dismantled; the church and the prior's house only were preserved—the former as a parochial church, and the latter as a residence for the farmer or purchaser of the demesne. In November 1659 the soldiers of the garrison of Tynemouth Castle having been drawn into the church for the purpose of signing an engagement to stand by General Lambert, who had just arrived at Newcastle, the roof fell in and killed five or six of them. The old church was used for divine service till the year 1668, when a new church (Christ's Church), then just completed, was consecrated by the Bishop of Durham. The principal ruins are those of the church. They probably date from the eleventh to the fourteenth centuries. A circular-headed doorway on the south side (which was an entrance from the cloister) and a cylindrical pillar remaining in the nave are fragments of the earlier Norman building, which, being limited in extent, was enlarged during the thirteenth century in such a manner as to lose most of its original character. The Norman chancel was destroyed, and eastward of the central tower a choir was added, terminated by a noble chancel or presbytery. The eastern and southern walls of this chancel are still standing, and constitute the finest portions of the existing ruins, the architecture being singularly light and beautiful. The eastern wall contains three tall lancet windows; the centre one is nearly 20 feet high, and is richly ornamented with rose-work and zigzag mouldings. Above these are three smaller lights, the centre one in the eastern gable being oval in form, and the series is crowned by a third tall narrow window. On each side are the openings of a gallery. The southern wall is illuminated by four windows, in form like those of the eastern wall, and equally ornamented, though not of the same height. Above these are four smaller windows, in the divisions of which spring the groins of the arches forming the roof. These tall and graceful arches are of red freestone, and are in a wonderful state of preservation considering their exposed situation. Beneath the centre window at the east end is a doorway of excellent workmanship, leading to the Oratory of St. Mary, which was probably a mortuary chapel of some noble Percy. Its dimensions are small, being only 18 feet by 12 feet within the walls. It has a vaulted roof, with curiously intersecting ribs terminating in three bosses adorned with figures of "The Saviour," "The Virgin Mary," and "The Twelve Apostles," which are surrounded by legends now nearly effaced. Several heraldic bearings of the Percy family are sculptured in this chapel, and the arms of the Delaval family also can still be seen on the inside of the door. Light was admitted by a circular or wheel window in the eastern wall, and by broad windows divided by plain mullions on the northern and southern sides. There are two canopied recesses in the eastern wall for statues. The shrine of St. Oswyn is supposed by Hutchinson to have been kept in this chapel, but Sidney Gibson says it was more probably exalted in the middle of the choir. This little chapel was for some time used by the Board of Ordnance as a powder magazine, but attention having been directed to the condition of such an interesting remnant of the famous Priory, it was carefully restored. One of the stained-glass windows represents St. Mary, and another St. Cuthbert holding the head of St. Oswald, King of Bernicia (Northumbria), in his hands. Beneath the figures of the saints is the following inscription :—

"Erected by Subscription to the Memory of
William Sidney Gibson, M.A., F.S.A.,
Historian of Tynemouth Priory,
who died 3rd January 1871,
and was buried here."

The interior of this chapel may be seen by applying to the Vicar. Tynemouth Priory forms the subject of pictures by Turner, Richardson, and Carmichael. The graveyard, which is no longer used for interments, contains many curious epitaphs and inscriptions. The half-moon battery on the east was erected during the great rebellion, and commands a fine view of the coast and harbour. The visitor should, if possible, ascend to the Lighthouse, which is 62 feet high and 128 feet above the level of the sea. It throws a light visible at about 20 miles distance. From the top may be seen, on a clear day, the massive form of Huntcliff Nab on the south and Newbiggin Point and Coquet Island on the north. The promontory contains two caves—the Paddies' Cave on the north side of the pier, and the Cats' Cave a little further on, but higher up the cliff. The most famous cave disappeared through the subsidence of the cliff on the 24th December 1886. This was *Jingling Geordie's Hole*, just above the Short Sands, on the north side of the castle. The entrance was partly formed by the solid rocks and partly by masonry said to be Roman. When explored, about forty years ago, it was found to lead to two arched apartments excavated in the rock. Many theories have been broached to account for this singular structure and its name.

According to one story, the inhabitant of the cave was a mysterious stranger, who prowled about, frightening the children by making a clanking noise as if with fetters. According to another, he was a wrecker, with a jingling iron leg, who lured ships to their destruction on the rocks below by exhibiting lights at the entrance of the cave. It is also said that the famous "hole" admitted to a subterranean passage under the Tyne to Jarrow, by which the monks from the Priory visited their distant brethren. The chambers may possibly have formed part of an outlying tower to the Priory. This was also known as "The Wizards' Cave," and has an interesting legend connected with it:—A mother excited the imagination of her first-born, young Walter, by telling him how

. . . "by Tinmouth's towers grey,
Where chant the cowl'd monks all by night and by day,
In a cavern of rock scoop'd under the sea
Lye treasures in keeping of Sorcerie.
It avails not the cross were sainted and true,
It avails not the prayers of the Prior Sir Hugh,
It avails not, O dread, Holy Virgin's fond care,
Great treasure long held by dark Sathan is there."

When he grew up and "became a goodly knight, he determined to go in search of the treasures, and, armed with basnet and brand, set out one stormy eve of St. John on his adventurous quest. Entering the cave, he descended towards the treasure-chamber, and, though fiends and dragons and eyeless spectres stood in his way, reached a grim portal, where, suspended by a golden cord, hung a bugle. Seizing it he blew three blasts." The doors flew open, and, behold! twelve jasper pillars in a double row support the roof, beneath which he now enters. Twelve pillars of fine crystal rear themselves beyond; the floor sparkles with amethyst, topaz, and flashing beryls, glittering in the light of refulgent lamps; twelve golden lamps shed a soft and serene light from the magic dome; whilst on twelve altars of onyx-stone incense burned.

"It may not be sung what treasures were seen,
Gold heaped upon gold and emeralds green,
And diamonds, and rubies, and sapphires untold,
Rewarded the courage of Walter the Bold."

Below the barracks is a wide moat, which was formed by the contractor of the pier in the expectation of finding stone for his works, but he met with disappointment. He had been misled by boring immediately upon the remains of an old long-buried wall. Looking at the cliff on which the lighthouse stands, from near Sharpness Point on the north, the visitor may, perhaps, be able to detect, in the conformation of the cliff, a resemblance to the Duke of Wellington's nose, and also to a lion. The pier, which forms one of the most pleasant promenades in the North of England, is about half-a-mile in length, and is built of concrete blocks. The foundation-stone was laid in 1854. Over a million and a-half has been already expended on the work. To the south of the pier is the Prior's Haven, the banks of which, according to tradition, formed the scene of a sanguinary encounter between a Lord of Delaval and a Danish chief, Red Eric, who had plundered his domain :—

"Their bucklers were splintered, their helmets were riven,
In their flesh the sharp edge of the fragments were driven,
Till a heart-splitting stab caused Red Eric to fall
With a howl of despair before brave Delaval.
He has hacked off the head ere the blood ceased to flow,
He has hied to the horde who were feasting below,
He flung it among them, his war-cry he raised ;
The Norsemen all rushed to their galleys amazed.

. . . . . . .

Nor yet they escaped, for a tempest arose,
And wrecked on the beach fair Northumbria's foes.
Some perished, engulphed in the depths of the waves,
And some to the serfs they had mocked became slaves."

The Tynemouth Life Brigade was the first Volunteer Life Brigade in the kingdom. It was formed on the 5th December 1869, and has been of invaluable service in rescuing the crews of the numerous vessels that have gone ashore since that period. Crossing an old moat, which formerly extended from Tynemouth Castle to the Spanish Battery (now removed), the visitor will reach Galley Hill, where stands Lord Collingwood's Monument, erected in 1845, from a design by Lough. The statue is 23 feet high, and the pedestal 50 feet. The four guns on the pedestal are from Lord Collingwood's ship, the *Royal Sovereign*. The hollow to the north is called the Howland, and contained in ancient times the Priory fish-pond.

Below the Spanish Battery lies that dangerous reef of rocks known as the Black Middens, which has been fatal to many a goodly vessel. The most appalling disaster that has occurred on these rocks was the wreck, on the 24th November 1864, of the passenger steamer *Stanley*, which was bound from Aberdeen to London. She had at the time a crew of twenty-nine hands all told, and thirty passengers, about half of whom were women. On the deck were about forty-eight cattle and thirty sheep. In spite of the efforts of the coastguardmen, who did what they could to rescue the crew and passengers with the rocket apparatus, twenty-six lives were lost during this terrible November night. On these rocks was wrecked, on February 17th 1827, the *Betsy Cains*, formerly the *Princess Mary*, which is said to have brought King William III. to England in 1688. The Herd Sand beyond, on the Durham side, has also a tragical record. On the south side of Front Street is a plain, two-storied brick house, No. 57, which will always be of interest to the lovers of literature, for on the first floor of this unpretentious little house Harriet Martineau occupied two rooms from March 1840 to January 1845. Here she wrote many of her most interesting works, and was visited by eminent men and women like Richard Cobden, Miss Brontë, Henry Hallam, Robert Chambers,

Lord Houghton (then R. Monckton Milnes), William Howitt, Macready, Kemble and his accomplished daughters, and others. From the crescent-shaped bow-window at the back of the house there was a very pleasant view, which the celebrated invalid describes very charmingly :—" Between my window and the sea is a green down, as green as any field in Ireland, and on the nearer half of this down haymaking goes forward in its season. It slopes down to a hollow, where the Prior of old preserved his fish, there being sluices formerly at either end, the one opening upon the river and the other upon the little haven below the Priory, whose ruins still crown the rock. From the Prior's fish-pond the green down slopes upward again to a ridge ; and on the slope are cows grazing all the summer and half-way into the winter. Over the ridge I survey the harbour and all its traffic, the view extending from the lighthouses far to the right to a horizon of sea to the left."

Above the Long Sands, on the Tynemouth Links, is a magnificent place of amusement, which, unfortunately, has not realised the expectations of its projectors—viz., the Aquarium and Winter Garden. This sea-side Crystal Palace was erected in 1877 and 1878 at a total cost of upwards of £82,500. It was opened by T. E. Smith, Esq., M.P. for the borough, on the 28th of August 1878, and though its collection of birds, beasts, fishes, and particularly sea-anemones, was very good, and the entertainments of an excellent character, the attendances were not such as to bring a satisfactory return to the shareholders for their outlay. The building has been twice sold, and at present is only opened at holiday seasons. There is a Skating Rink detached from the main building, measuring 200 feet by 125 feet. On the sands, just below the end of Percy Park Terrace, is a Chalybeate Well. C. N. Hemy, the artist, is a native of Tynemouth, having been born at Mariner's Cottages.

*The Monk's Stone.*—In front of "The Monk's House," a farm-stead not far from the road leading northward from Holy Saviour's Church, stands a mutilated whinstone pillar, surrounded with wooden rails, called "The Monk's Stone." Traces of ornamentation of a rich and intricate design may still be seen upon its worn surface. It was most probably erected to denote the limit of sanctuary assigned to the monastery of Tynemouth, and originally stood in a field to the east of its present site. A similar fragment of a sanctuary-cross exists near Beverley, the minster-church of which had the right of sanctuary. On the pedestal of the Monk's Stone is said to have been inscribed the following couplet :—

" O horrid dede,
To kill a man for a pigges hede."

This has reference to a legend which has been cast into ballad form by Mr. Robert Owen, of North Shields. "A monk of Tynemouth Monastery strolling abroad came to the hall of Lord Delaval, who was absent on a hunting expedition, and bore off from the kitchen a pig's head. Lord Delaval, on his return, was wroth at this, and set off in pursuit of the holy epicure. He overtook him about a mile east of Preston."

"'But stay! but stay! thou friar knave,
But stay and show to me
What thou hast in that leathern poke
Which thou mayest carry so hie!'—
'Now Christ ye save!' said the friar knave,
'Firewood for the Priorie.'

'Thou liest! thou liest! thou knavish priest,
Thou liest unto me!'—
The knight he took the leathern poke
And his boar's hede did espie,
And still the reek from the scorched cheek
Did seem right savourie.

God's wot! but had ye seen the friar
With his skin of livid hue,
When the knight drew out the reeking snout,
And flourished his hunting thew;
'Grammercie, grammercie! Sir Knight on me,
As the Virgin will mercy shew.'

But the knight he banged the friar about,
And beat his hide full sore;
And he beat him as he rolled on the sward,
Till the friar did loudly roar;
No mote he spare the friar mare
Than Mahound on eastern shore.

'Now take ye that, ye dog of a monk,
Now take ye that from me!'—
And away rode the knight in great delight
At his feat of flagellrie,
And the sands did resound to his war-steed's bound
As he rode near the margined sea."

The friar died in a year and a day, and the knight was obliged to do penance and make over three of his estates to the monastery.

"Now at this day, while years roll on,
And the knight doth coldly lie,
The stone doth stand on the silent land,
To tellen the strangers nigh,
That a horrid dede for a pig his hede
Did thence to heavenward cry."

The principal hotels at Tynemouth are the Bath, the Grand, the Royal, the Salutation, the Turk's Head, and the Union.

# TYNEMOUTH TO BLYTH AND BEDLINGTON.

**Cullercoats, 1½ miles ; Whitley, 2¼ miles ; St. Mary's Island, 4 miles ; Monkseaton, 2½ miles ; Earsdon, 4 miles ; Hartley, 5 miles ; Seaton Sluice, 5½ miles, Seaton Delaval, 7 miles ; Blyth, 9 miles ; Bedlington, 13 miles.**

A FINE promenade extends along the sea banks from Tynemouth to CULLERCOATS.—(Hotel, Hudleston Arms.) This little fishing village, which is said to derive its name from the Anglo-Saxon Culfre Cotes—*i.e.*, dovecotes—and to have been connected with the Tynemouth Monastery, stands on the edge of the cliff above a picturesque little bay, a mile from Tynemouth. Like Runswick, on the Yorkshire coast, it has been a great favourite with artists, among whom may be mentioned the names of Birket Foster, J. D. Watson, F. Holl, Winslow Homer, Mole, H. H. Emmerson, and R. Jobling. It was once more than a mere fishing village, for salt, grindstones, coals, etc., were exported from the haven. A waggon-way ran from the Whitley collieries to the harbour, and the coals were shipped from a wooden jetty or pier. The owners of a colliery at North Shields, we are told, not being permitted to load their coals there, sent them in carts to Cullercoats, where they were shipped. On the site where the corner houses of Beverley Terrace and Mast Lane now stand was a large ballast hill, proving the number of vessels that loaded here, few of which exceeded 100 tons burden. Amongst the ballast old pipes of the Stuart period were frequently found, identifying the date of the deposits with the introduction of tobacco into England. The last clearance from the port of Cullercoats was the *Fortune* of Whitby, on the 18th July 1726, with a cargo of 21 tons of salt. The remains of some old salt-pans may still be seen above the end of the South Pier ; and the round hole in the Smuggler's Cave is the opening through which the pump pipes were run. From the records of the Blyth Custom House, it appears that, in the Michaelmas quarter of 1723, 1962 tons of salt were exported from the small harbour and port of Cullercoats. The oldest house in Cullercoats is called "Sparrow Hall." It is a weather-stained, grim-looking mansion, built by one of the Doves—a Quaker family who formerly had much property here—probably in 1682, as that date is cut on the lintel of one of the windows. The initials, J. D. E. D., appear on an ornament surmounting one of the gables. A dove is also carved upon it, but the village people, not being ornithologists, imagined it was a sparrow, and hence always referred to the house as "Sparrow Hall." The yards recently built in front of it, and the additions made on one side, do not render the old house more picturesque. Above the north pier is the Life-Brigade Look-out, with its quaint little steeple; and on the foreshore below are the Life-Boat House and the Salt-Water Baths. At the end of Beverley Terrace is a large and beautiful church in the early English style of architecture, built 1882-4 by the Duke of Northumberland, and dedicated to St. George. Its tall and delicate spire, so graceful in its symmetry, is one of the principal features of the coast. The Crab Hill and Bear's Back Rocks are happy hunting grounds for the naturalist, and the cliffs present a feature of considerable interest to the geologist, for at the north end of the Long Sands the coal measures, which are seen side by side with the sandstone of which the Smugglers' Cave is composed, suddenly sink to a depth of eighty or ninety fathoms. This is the Ninety Fathom Dyke or Fault, which appears to continue seaward to the north of the Bear's Back, and can be seen cutting across Cullercoats Haven from a few yards inside the concrete pier to the Beacon Point. At the present time there are about forty fishing-boats in use at Cullercoats. They are termed "cobles," and with their brown-red sail swelling in the breeze, have a very graceful appearance as they glide through the water. The names they bear will be regarded with considerable interest by the curious visitor. A good deal of ingenuity was no doubt expended before the right name was fixed upon, and many a strange motive, in all probability, determined the final choice. A large number are called after the mothers, wives, sisters, or sweethearts of their owners. Others bear the designations of many of the virtues, such as *Moderation*, *Gratitude*, *Amity*, etc. Some are exceedingly picturesque and quaint, as will be seen by the following selection :—*Sea-Flower*, *Star of Peace*, *Pilgrim*, *Pride of the Cliff*, *Lily of the Valley*, *Swiftsure*, *Quickstep*, *Cock Robin*, *Robin Hood*, *Good Samaritan*, *Good Design*, *Ancient Promise*, *Welcome Home*, *Village Belle*. To each boat there are three men and a boy. The success of their toil is due very much to the women, who are helpmates indeed. They prepare the bait, carry down the fishing-gear and ballast to the boats, and above all, sell the fish in the towns on Tyneside. Very familiar indeed is the figure of the Cullercoats fish-wife, as, clad in blue serge jacket, short petticoats with ample skirts, large apron and black straw bonnet she trudges along with a heavy creel of fish on her shoulders, calling, in shrill and not unmusical tones of voice, "Buy fee-s-ch."

WHITLEY.—(Hotels: Victoria, Fat Ox.) This very popular sea-side resort, that has grown during the last few years from a small village to a place of considerable importance, is pleasantly situated amongst fields, about a mile and a-half from Tynemouth. In Speede's map of Northumberland (1610) it is spelt Whitlathe. There used to be collieries and ironstone-mines here, on the links, but they are no longer worked. The collieries belonged to Mr. Taylor, father of the owner of Chipchase Castle, and it was through the successful working of these collieries that he laid the foundation of his vast wealth. Whitley was formerly in the possession of the Priors of Tynemouth; and during the Christmas festival there was an entertainment given to the servants of the monastery, the homagers, the farm labourers, and the men called "kelers," who served in their barges. The lands at Whitley appear to have been held by the service of holding this entertainment. The quaint little church of St. Paul, in the early English style, was erected in 1864. Near it are the Northumberland Village-Homes, consisting of four blocks of two houses each, with a large and convenient school-room. The first of these was opened on the 11th May 1880, and the last completed in March 1884. They will accommodate 125 children. Homes in every sense of the word they are to the red-cloaked and red-cheeked little maidens who may be seen playing on the sands or walking demurely along the sea-banks. Standing a little way back from the Whitley links is another valuable charitable institution—the Prudhoe Memorial Convalescent Home, which was opened on the 14th September 1869 by her Grace the Dowager-Duchess of Northumberland. It is a stone building arranged on the pavilion plan, consisting of a central block with a corridor running at right angles, out of which the various day and sleeping rooms project, with open spaces between for ventilation and light. The whole of the apartments have a sea view. The building is raised several feet above the level of the surrounding ground, and is approached by means of an elevated terrace, with steps at the centre and an inclined roadway at each side. It will hold 140 patients—100 males and 40 females. The building has been so arranged as to be capable of extension at any future time. It is surrounded by beautiful gardens and grounds. The tall and picturesque sandstone cliffs between Whitley and Cullercoats are much admired on account of their rugged grandeur and rich neutral tints. The headland known as "Brown's Point," a little to the north of Cullercoats Haven, is a striking object in the scenery of this coast. There is no road along the top, but the visitor who does not mind scrambling about boulders tressed with slippery sea-wrack will be rewarded for his trouble by the view he will get of the bold sandstone bluffs with their irregular outlines and vast proportions. At the base of them huge masses of rock which have fallen bear witness to the violence of past storms, and others, dislodged and loosened from the cliff-side, seem destined to follow before long. Here and there little hollows, which have been scooped out of the rock by the waves, and are always filled with the clear sea-water, form natural aquaria. A long and deep cleft just round the Point is called "Askett's Hole" by the fishermen, and bids fair, as it grows larger and larger every year, to become as interesting a haunt to juveniles as the Smuggler's Cave behind the south breakwater. A wreck was curiously driven into it a few years ago. What are called the North or Table Rocks by the visitors, and the Crawley Rocks by the fishermen, are very picturesque, especially when, during rough weather, fountains of delicate foam are playing above them. Good swimmers will find these rocks the best bathing-place on the coast. The ridge of rocks northwards is called Whitley Skeers. Opposite to the road leading down to the sands are the Half-Moon Rocks. A strong current sweeps round them during certain states of the tide, and is very dangerous to inexperienced bathers. Many fatalities have occurred here. From Whitley northward there is a magnificent stretch of sands, smooth and firm as could be desired, giving to Whitley a decided advantage over Tynemouth in this respect. On the banks may be found a dwarf variety of the Burnet Rose—Rosa pimpinellifolia [Spinosissima.] A little past the Convalescent Home to the left is Briar Dene. "Singing sands," says Dr. J. Carrick Murray, "are to be found at Whitley, on the way to St. Mary's Island. The sound is not musical, but rather a harsh whirring, or as Miller, in his *Cruise of the Betsy*, calls it, a 'woo, woo, woo.' It is most marked when walking over, or rather through, the high dry oolitic sand beyond the slipping stones at the Briar Dene, just below where the volunteers encamp."

ST. MARY'S ISLAND.—(Inn, John Ewen s.) Opposite to Curry's Point, where the body of Michael Curry (executed at Newcastle for murder, 4th September 1739) was hung in chains, is St. Mary's Island, looking very picturesque as it rises from the edge of a black reef of fucus-covered rocks. Above a banked-up slope, whereon some painted cobles lie, are a few cottages and a small inn with green railings in front. A little chantry, an offshoot of the old monastery of Tynemouth, once stood here, but no vestige of it now remains. The only guide to the sacred spot where the ancient chantry stood is a little inlet in the rocks, where the fishermen still run for shelter when caught by a storm, known by the name of St. Mary's Bay. Tradition tells that in the sanctuary a lamp always burned to warn the passing mariners. In the tower hung a bell, which was rung to summon aid in cases of shipwreck upon the coast; and a cemetery was attached wherein the bodies of the victims of the storm were buried, and in which interments took place until about a century ago. In December 1765 a woodcock was shot here, in the stomach of which was found a diamond of considerable value.

MONKSEATON.—(Inns: Black Horse, Ship). Monkseaton is a pretty little village about half-a-mile from Whitley, and was the sea town belonging to the monks of Tynemouth. When its garden trees are in full leaf the village has a very picturesque appearance, situated as it is on a very slight eminence, and many visitors who wish to combine some of the charms of the country with those of the sea-side patronise it during the summer months. The old Whitley railway station is now called after the village, and is a few hundred yards distant.

EARSDON.—This pleasant rustic village of one street, with a little grove of white poplars in the middle of it, is situated on the highest point of ground in the district, two and a-half miles from the sea. The square, dark, pinnacled tower of its church is conspicuous for a considerable distance by land and sea. The church of St. Albans is situated on the east end of the site of a former church, and was consecrated by the Bishop of Durham on the 12th of October 1837. It is in the early English character, from plans by Messrs. John and Benjamin Green, of Newcastle, and is 79 feet long by 30 feet broad. In the churchyard is a granite obelisk, erected by public subscription, to the memory of victims of the Hartley accident. Their names and ages are inscribed on the sides of the monument, which has a pathetic interest to the visitor.

HARTLEY, just above St. Mary's Island, occupies another hill, and is a long and tame-looking village, which has lost much of its importance since the Bottle Works were closed. From a distance it looks well, for the red tiles of its houses give a glow to the landscape. In the reign of King John it was in possession of Adam de Jesmont. The cliffs are very lofty and fine between Hartley and Seaton Sluice. They have witnessed some terrible scenes. On October 28th, 1880, the Dutch galliot *Trebroders*, driven on to the rocks at Crag Point, near Seaton Sluice, was dashing to pieces, and all on board seemed doomed, when Thomas Langley, known afterwards as the "Hartley Hero," allowed himself to be lowered over the cliffs at the risk of his life, and succeeded in saving the lives of the master's wife and child and two seamen, after the captain and his little son had been washed overboard. Shortly afterwards another ship came on shore, and Langley again rushed to the rescue, waded through the heavy surf, established communication with the ship, and saved the crew. These acts of bravery were at once recognised, and Langley was presented with the bronze medal of the Royal Humane Society, and with a purse of gold by the merchants on 'Change at Newcastle. He also received medals from the Board of Trade and the King of the Netherlands—the latter accompanied by an address. Descending past the Wesleyan Chapel (built in 1840) towards Seaton Sluice, the visitor will notice a huge mass of rock standing isolated on the beach. This is called "Charlie's Garden," after an old man named "Charlie Dockwray," who, many years ago, cultivated the top of the rock, producing the earliest cabbages, peas, etc., in the neighbourhood. A cave between this point and Hartley is the habitat of the "Sea-Spleenwort."

To the west of Hartley is *Holywell Dene*, a charming place for a pic-nic, as the visitors to the sea-side have long since discovered. It may be reached by pleasant paths through the fields from Whitley and Monkseaton; the one is entered just opposite Whitley Park, the other behind the Monkseaton Brewery. The Seaton Burn flows through the dene, and in the upper part, especially near the mill-dam, where the branches of lofty trees over-arch it, forms some exquisite little pictures of sylvan loveliness. Gowden's Hole could at one time be seen, but the railway embankment closed it to the public. An excellent tea is supplied to the visitor at the Crow Hall Farm, which stands about the left bank of the dene, and is reached by a broad and shady path leading from the wooden bridge over the stream.

SEATON SLUICE. (Inn, Waterford Arms.) Seaton Sluice, about half-a-mile north from Hartley, was in the possession of the Prior of Tynemouth in 1097, but in 1121 this manor comprised a part of the barony of Delaval, and has continued in that family to the present time. Since the works of the Hartley Bottle Company were closed the village has suffered a deal of depression. The great feature of the place is the passage cut fifty feet down through the solid sandstone cliff to the now disused harbour, which was once of so much importance as to be defended by a battery on the ballast-mount close by, and a party of soldiers. It was originally of small extent, dry at low water and difficult at the entrance. A new haven was therefore constructed, with some difficulty, by Sir Ralph Delaval, Bart. The stone pier which covered it from the north-east wind was carried away by the sea more than once; and when he had overcome this difficulty a new inconvenience arose. His port filled with mud and sand, though a pretty sharp streamlet ran through it. In order to remove this nuisance he placed a strong sluice with floodgates upon this burn, and these being shut by the coming in of the tide, the backwater collected into a body, and, forcing a passage at the ebb, carried all before it, and twice in twenty-four hours scoured the bed of the haven clean. This haven was afterwards improved by Sir John Hussey Delaval, who cut through a solid freestone rock from the point where the river anciently turned to the north, to the sea on the east side of the angle, so that the current now discharges itself into the sea in a straight direction, and forms a harbour accessible with every wind, and a moorage secure against every storm. The entrance into the harbour is fifty-two feet deep, thirty feet broad, and nine hundred feet long. The seaward end of the cut is closed by booms, or balks of timber sliding in a grove, after the manner of a portcullis, and in heavy gales a double set is let down for greater security. A large crane for lowering them stands above. Twelve or fourteen sail of vessels, each of two or three hundred tons burden, could be accommodated in the harbour. This harbour was opened for traffic on the 20th March 1763. The quaint octagonal stone tower in the village by the side of the road was once the coal-office, and is now used as a news-room.

*Seaton Delaval Hall.*—This stately mansion, which is unsurpassed for grandeur and dignity by any other in the north of England, is situated on a gentle slope about one mile west from the sea. It was built in 1707 for Admiral Delaval by Sir John Vanbrugh, the architect of Blenheim, and ranks as the greatest monument of his genius. A flight of sixteen steps ascends to a lofty Doric portico, whose superb columns, with their richly-embellished entablatures, form a most commanding entrance. In the tympanum of the pediment above, the arms of the family and various trophies are carved. The whole of the finely-sculptured façade is crowned with a balustrade, on which are arranged several elegant vases on pedestals. Two immense wings, with beautiful arcades running along the whole length of their fronts, enclose a spacious court. In the east wing are the stables. The largest is 62 feet long and 41 feet wide, the lofty roof being supported by three superb arches 21 feet 4 inches high. The divisions of all the stalls and the niches for the hay are of stone. Over them are plates bearing the names of the valuable race-horses which were kept here previous to the fire. The west wing, which at present contains the principal apartments, was burnt down on May 6th, 1752, but re-built on the original plan. On January 3rd, 1822, the main building was reduced to a splendid ruin by a fire originating in a chimney to which a large beam of wood was affixed. By great exertions the two wings were saved. The heat was so intense that the glass in the windows was reduced to a liquid state, and the lead on the roof poured down like water. From the portico the visitor enters a stately but ruined hall 44 feet long, paved with diamond-shaped black and white marble tiles. In a niche, to the right of the entrance, is a stone slab which was found built up in the wall of a neighbouring farm. It bears upon it the date 1103—the year possibly when the old pele tower of the Delavals was built. Hanging on the wall close by are three ancient man-traps. Opposite to the door is a grand music gallery, faced with elegant iron balustrades. It rests upon a fine entablature, supported by beautiful consoles. In the uppermost niches are six mutilated statues representing Music, Painting, Geography, Sculpture, Architecture, and Astronomy. The massy fire-place has two caryatides as supporters, and a central frieze tablet of figures in Roman togas. Near to it is a large leaden statue removed from the grounds. From the hall we pass into a splendid saloon, 75 feet long and 30 feet wide, fronting the pleasure-grounds. The Corinthian columns and pilasters around it are beautifully carved. On the east side of the entrance-hall is an apartment which is supposed to have been the library. The richly-carved capitals of several broken columns are preserved here. The staircase descends from this floor to a long passage communicating with the stone-arched kitchens, wine-cellars, etc. From a chamber on the left an iron door, with the initials F.B.D. and the date 1753 upon it, admits into a small vault where the plate and other valuables were probably kept. A room on the second floor, looking into the court-yard, is known as the "ghost chamber." Here the "White Lady of Seaton Delaval" is said to keep her melancholy vigils at the window, looking for the return of her absent lord. This apparition can be accounted for on quite natural grounds. When the sun is setting, its last rays strike through one of the windows on to the centre division of a broken mirror not unlike the shape of a female figure, and the reflection as seen on another window may, without any great effort of imagination, take the form of a phantom watcher. The walls were covered with tapestry. The boards to which it was attached still retain some faded fragments of it. The other apartments on this floor still exhibit traces of their former magnificence. From the leads there is a magnificent view in every direction. In the west wing are the apartments occupied by Lord Hastings when he vists Seaton Delaval. A room on the ground floor contains the portraits of Sir John Hussey Delaval (afterwards raised to the peerage as Baron Delaval); Admiral George Delaval, who built the hall; Lady Hussey Delaval and two of her daughters—all painted by William Bell. There are several interesting pictures in the bedrooms. In that of Lord Hastings are portraits of four of the daughters of Lord Delaval, Lady Tyrconnel being one. In another is an old painting representing Christ and the Woman of Samaria, and in a third a Dutch painting—one of the finest in the hall—entitled "The killing of the fatted calf." The gallery facing the court-yard contains several family portraits—Lady Astley, Lady Tyrconnel (Sarah Hussey Delaval) as a child, Lady Stanhope, "The Delaval Family," in which two of the young Delavals are so much alike that it is said there was some difficulty in distinguishing one from the other. A contemporary portrait of Queen Elizabeth, presented by her, it is said, to the Delaval of the time, is a fine piece of work, the lace around the neck and wrists being exquisitely painted. An allegorical picture, representing the struggle between Vice and Virtue, is said, on somewhat doubtful grounds, to be by Rubens.

The south front of the hall is approached through a magnificent portico of the Ionic order. In the garden to the west of it is an old sun-dial inscribed "Ralph Delaval, 1692."

A brief sketch of the history of the famous family who owned this splendid possession will, no doubt, interest the visitor. The Delavals came over with the Conqueror. Guy Delaval married Dionesia, the second daughter of Robert, Earl of Mortagne, and niece of the Conqueror. Gilbert Delaval was one of the twenty-five barons sworn to see the Magna Charta and Charta de Foresta granted by John at Runnymede confirmed by the Pope. From that period to the reign of William III. the Delavals were often to be found serving their country in the field or the senate. The family became extinct in the person of Edward Hussey Delaval, Esq., a gentleman of great culture and scientific attainments, who died August 14th, 1814, aged 85 years, and was buried in Westminster Abbey. The members of the family who, by their wild and reckless mode of life, brought the name of Delaval into somewhat unenviable notoriety, were Sir Francis Blake Delaval and his brother, Lord Delaval. Many were the mad escapades and mischievous pranks perpetrated by "the wicked Delavals" at their magnificent ancestral hall. Beds were suspended by pulleys over trap-doors, and the boon associates of the Lord of Delaval in his midnight revellings had no sooner dropped asleep than they were rapidly let down into darkness and cold water, where their feelings may be better imagined than described. The partitions between the bedrooms were so arranged that they could be suddenly hoisted up into the ceiling by pulleys, so when ladies and gentlemen were retiring to rest, and had doffed all their finery of wigs and hoop-petticoats, they were in a moment astonished to see the walls of their rooms disappear, and to find themselves in a miscellaneous assembly of the oddest and most embarrassing description. In company with Foote, who encouraged him in his excesses, Sir Francis pursued a course of dissipation and frivolity that gave him the reputation of being the gayest and most accomplished Lothario of his age. Cooke, in his *Memoirs of Foote*, says that "in modern honour and modern gallantry he vied with the first fashionables in Europe. He had not a grain of Nero's cruelty, but had he been born in his court would have rode with him as a charioteer, fiddled with him as a musician, fenced with him as a gladiator, and strutted with him as a player. Though indolent in business, he was active in his pleasures; and so strongly did he possess the spirit of emulation that he would be the leading showman of his day, whatever species of frivolity was the fashion." With a host so handsome, gay, and frolicsome, it is not to be wondered at that Seaton Delaval was a centre of attraction to the fashionable world, for there a series of amusements was provided of endless variety, from a grinning match and sack-race to a masquerade and carousal. On one occasion the Delaval family acted in Drury Lane Theatre by permission of Garrick. The play fixed upon was Othello. The part of Othello was taken by Sir Francis; Iago, by his brother, afterwards Lord Delaval; Desdemona, by his sister, Lady Mexborough. Probably one of the most extraordinary schemes that ever entered into a whimsical brain was one that Sir Francis undertook with Foote. Sir Francis set up as a conjuror and fortune-teller, with Foote for his coadjutor, and soon achieved an extraordinary reputation, for by the extensive knowledge that they had of the secret intrigues and gallantries of the city they were able to make some startling disclosures. The upshot of this scheme was that the pretended conjuror came into a fortune of £90,000 by persuading Lady Nassau Paulet, widow of the Earl of Thanet, that fate had determined her marriage with the young and gallant Sir Francis Delaval. They were duly married, but a divorce took place soon after by mutual consent. He closed his eccentric career in August 1771. Many amusing stories are told of the equally gay life led by his brother, Lord Delaval. The daughters of Lord Delaval were celebrated for their beauty, especially Lady Tyrconnel, whose hair was so luxuriant that it floated upon her saddle as she rode. When the Delavals became extinct in the male line their estates descended to Sir Jacob Astley, Bart., grandson of Rhoda, daughter of Sir Francis Delaval. He was, on the 18th May 1841, summoned to the House of Peers as Baron Hastings, he being one of the race of Sir John de Hastings summoned to Parliament by the above title in the eighteenth year of the reign of King Edward I. He died on the 27th December 1859. His son, Jacob Henry Delaval, succeeded him, and died March 9th, 1871. The grandson of Sir Jacob Astley, Lord Hastings, is the present proprietor of Seaton Delaval Hall. In a meadow between the hall and the avenue is a group of leaden statuary representing David slaying Goliath. The giant, with the stone in his forehead, is making a last futile effort to rise from the ground, while the young hero, with uplifted sword, is about to decapitate him. There is a curious feature about the fists of Goliath. They are clenched, but the thumbs are doubled up inside the palms. The reason for this peculiarity may, no doubt, be found in an old Northumbrian superstition. "Children," says Hutchinson, "to avoid approaching danger are taught to double the thumb within the hand. This was much practised while the terrors of witchcraft remained;" and again, "It was the custom to fold the thumbs of dead persons within the hands to prevent the powers of evil spirits over the deceased, the thumb in that position forming the similitude of that character in the Hebrew alphabet which is commonly used to denote the name of God." It was certainly a stroke of imagination on the sculptor's part to represent the blaspheming Philistine making, in his dying moments, the sign of the mystical word. There is another explanation. The thumb, in chiromancy, is the symbol of will power When an effort of will is being exerted, as in fighting, the thumb is closed over the fingers, but when the will is overcome the fingers close over the thumb. In the case of the statue, Goliath symbolically acknowledges himself vanquished, and yields to a stronger power than his own, the peculiarity referred to being the sign of submission. The little *Chapel dedicated to Our Lady*, which belonged to the feudal stronghold of the Delavals, and has stood through all the fortunes of the family since the beginning of the twelfth century, is an interesting specimen of Norman workmanship. There is little to attract the eye on the outside, except, perhaps, a small round-headed window, now built up, in the north wall. Several of the slabs of Scotch slate on the roof are fastened in the ancient manner with sheep-shank bones. The entrance is at the west end. Over the doorway was a sculptured tympanum, now defaced. The round arch is enriched with indented moulding. Over it are three panels with armorial bearings carved upon them—parts of a fourteenth-century altar-tomb. Other panels are inserted in the wall over the door inside the chapel, and also behind one of the hatchments. The effigies which rested on this tomb—a knight with crossed legs and a lady with uplifted hands—recline, one in the south-west and the other in the north-west corner of the church. The most attractive part of this ancient edifice is the chancel, the two arches of which are especially beautiful. They are enriched with the chevron and billet ornaments, and spring from the heavy-cushioned capitals of low massy responds, the abaci of which are continued as string-courses to the east wall. The moulded ceiling of the nave is of the same date as the hall. The chancel is barrel-vaulted. In its south wall is a piscina of fourteenth-century date, with an aumbry above it. There are two aumbries in the north wall. Projecting from the east wall is a bracket for an image, inserted during the restorations of the Decorated period. A small stained-glass window in the south wall, representing a Prince of Wales kneeling under a canopy before a book, while around him are angels with various musical instruments in their hands, is modern, but evidently copied from an old window of sixteenth-century date. Several banner-staffs, from which the silk flags have decayed away, project from the east wall of the church. A few old pennons still remain on the north side of the nave, together with a helmet, surmounted by a crest and a pair of gauntlets. In the vaults below the chapel are six coffins, containing the mortal remains of Francis Blake Delaval, ob. 1752, æt. 59; the Hon. Sir Francis Blake Delaval, K.B., ob. 1771, æt. 44; George Delaval, ob. 1723, æt 55; Sir Alex. Ruthven, ob. 1722, æt. 34; Eliz. Hicks, ob. 1796, æt. 23; Louisa Delaval, ob. 17—.

Not far from the Hall in the park is the Mausoleum, a beautiful edifice raised by Sir John and Lady Hussey Delaval to their only son John, who died 1775, aged 20. It is crowned by a majestic leaden cupola, and approached through a Doric portico, the columns of which are each formed of one single stone, weighing several tons. The inside is in the form of a chapel, having a nave in the middle, with an altar, or communion-table. Above this is a solemn dome, supported by semi-circular arches, and beneath are vaults, strongly arched, and of most durable workmanship. On the way to the Mausoleum the visitor passes a fine leaden statue of Diana. The gardens are let to a market-gardener, and the visitor can buy grapes, flowers, fruit, etc. By the side of the fish-pond, which still contains a good many fine carp, are two or three old statues. The two obelisks that stand on the estate seem to have been erected as pleasant objects in the landscape. The obelisk in the avenue is said to mark the spot where Admiral Delaval was thrown from a restive horse and killed, 1723. The country-people say that they mark the place where certain cannon-balls fell when the French, or Paul Jones, bombarded the Hall—when, or on what occasion, history saith not. As this part of the coast seemed adapted for a new sea-side resort, the land on the north side of the road has been laid out for building sites, but, so far, the new watering-place which is to rival Tynemouth and Whitley exists only on paper. An old thatched house, called Seaton Lodge, was formerly occupied by Sir John Delaval, the third baronet, who is said to have boasted that it was the "finest thatched house in the kingdom."

HARTLEY NEW PIT.—About half-a-mile from the Hall, and close to the railway station of New Hartley, is the old shaft of the Hartley New Pit, made memorable by the terrible catastrophe which occurred there on Thursday, January 16th, 1862. The details of this accident may be briefly given thus:—On the top of the pit-head, or platform, was the engine-house, containing the engine in use for pumping the water out of the pit. One half of the massive beam, weighing altogether about 43 tons, worked over the mouth of the shaft. Suddenly, and without a moment's warning, this ponderous mass of iron snapped at the centre, and the half, weighing twenty-one tons, thundered down the shaft, shivering the strong wooden bratticing which divided the pit into upcast and downcast shafts, and tearing and throwing down the walling, filling the shaft with *debris* as far down as the yard seam. A cage containing eight men was ascending the shaft at the time the beam broke. It was at once smashed, and torn as if it had been manufactured of the weakest tin instead of the strongest wrought iron. Six of the occupants were instantly killed, and three, more or less injured, escaped most miraculously. This shaft—the only approach to the mine—being blocked by the mass of iron and woodwork, the supply of fresh air was cut off from the men imprisoned in the workings, without a hope of escape. By the Friday afternoon it is probable that all of the entombed miners had succumbed to the deadly effects of the "stythe," or choke-damp. In the meantime unremitting efforts were made by devoted friends and relatives to force a passage to the workings. Day after day, and night after night, they toiled heroically, frequently overcome by the deadly "stythe." The whole country was roused by the terrible tidings, and manifested the utmost interest and anxiety in the fate of the imprisoned men. On the Sunday after the accident an immense crowd gathered on the scene, and by the afternoon at least 60,000 persons were swarming round the pit. By trap, by railroad, and on foot, they arrived from all parts. Steadily Mr. Coulson and his brave assistants and volunteers proceeded with the clearing of the shaft, and on Wednesday morning three of the sinkers, headed by Emmerson, Mr. Coulson's chief assistant, were able to advance into the furnace drift, but were unable to proceed far on account of the gas. In the afternoon one of the shift-men, William Adams, managed to penetrate into the yard seam through the furnace drift. He was fearfully excited when he came to bank, and he tore his hair like a maniac while relating his dread news in spasmodic jerks, screaming and leaping at intervals. The bodies of the men and boys were found lying in rows, all quiet and placid, as if sleeping off a heavy day's work. Boys were lying with their hands on the shoulders of their fathers, and one poor fellow had his arms clasped round the neck of his brother. The sleep-like approach of their death has been pathetically described by Mr. Joseph Skipsey, the poet of the Coal-fields, in his ballad on "The Hartley Calamity."

"'Oh, father, till the shaft is rid,
Close, close beside me keep;
My eyelids are together glued,
And I—and I—must sleep.'

'Sleep, darling, sleep, and I will keep
Close by—heigh-ho!'—To keep
Himself awake the father strives;
But he—he too—must sleep.

'O, brother, till the shaft is rid,
Close, close beside me keep;
My eyelids are together glued,
And I—and I—must sleep.'

'Sleep, brother, sleep, and I will keep
Close by—heigh-ho!'—To keep
Himself awake the brother strives;
But he—he too—must sleep.

'O, mother dear! wert, wert thou near
  Whilst—sleep!'——The orphan slept;
And all night long, by the black pit-heap,
  The mother a dumb watch kept.

And fathers and mothers and sisters and brothers,
  The lover and the new-made bride,
A vigil kept for those who slept,
  From eve to morning tide."

The scene at the mouth of the pit, where the friends and relatives of the entombed men are waiting in an agony of suspense, has been graphically represented on canvas by H. H. Emmerson.

On the body of Armour, the back-overman, was found a small memorandum-book, containing the brief but significant entry:—"Friday afternoon, at half-past two, Edward Armstrong, Thomas Gledstone, John Hardy, Thomas Bell, and others took extremely ill. We had a prayer-meeting at a quarter to two, when Tibbs, Henry Sharp, J. Campbell, Henry Gibson, and William Palmer——. Tibbs exhorted us again, and Sharp also." On a shot-box belonging to a hewer named James Bewick the following pathetic words were scratched, evidently with the point of a nail:—"Friday afternoon. My dear Sarah,—I leave you——." No doubt the writer died immediately afterwards. The bodies were interred in Earsdon churchyard on Sunday, the 26th January, in ground set apart for the purpose, in the presence of a vast concourse of spectators. The sad procession was necessarily a long one, and many of the bodies were in the ground before the last had left the desolated village, which was four miles distant. The terrible calamity called forth the sympathy of all classes of society for the widows and children of the Hartley men, and a noble fund for their relief was speedily subscribed.

From Seaton Sluice to Blyth there is a fine stretch of smooth, firm, and elastic sands, about three and a-half miles in length. Meggie's Burn, which spreads itself over the sand, is apt to prove an obstacle to the pedestrian, but by turning up to Meggie's Burn Cottage he will find just behind the links a bridge erected in 1875-6. The coast-line is somewhat tame and desolate, being composed of barren hills and drifts of sand, covered with a sparse, reedy kind of grass.

"Miles and miles and miles of desolation!
  Leagues on leagues without a change!
Sign or token of some eldest nation
  Here would make the strange land not so strange.
Time-forgotten, yea, since Time's creation,
  Seem these borders where the sea-birds range."

BLYTH.—Blyth is a considerable village and seaport, situate at the mouth of the river Blyth, nine miles north from Shields and nine south-east from Morpeth. It has a very safe and commodious harbour, with a south-easterly outlet, and, with the wind in any point north-north-east to west-south-west, can be entered by vessels under canvas. There are two lighthouses, one on the north and one on the south side of the harbour. The pier, built partly of stone and wood, extends into the sea for nearly a mile. Large quantities of coal, brought down from Cowpen, Newsham, North Seaton, and Cambois collieries, are shipped from Blyth Creek, estimated to exceed 200,000 tons yearly. The fishing industry is also carried on very vigorously here during the salmon and herring season. In ancient times several of the monasteries had salt-pans at Blyth. Blyth was the residence, during the latter half of the eighteenth and beginning of the present century, of William Carr, a local Samson, concerning whom many extraordinary stories are told. At thirty years of age he measured 6 feet 4 inches, and weighed twenty-four stones. So great was his strength at this time that it is said he carried an anchor (10 cwt.) from the sands to his father's shop for repairs. His agility was also very remarkable, as was demonstrated on one occasion, when he leaped over a five-barred gate with a young woman, eight stones in weight, under his arm. He is said to have once worked 132 consecutive hours without cessation, and then, after resting himself for twelve hours, to have continued toiling for 120 hours longer. He died at Blyth on the 6th of September 1825, in the sixtieth year of his age.

HORTON is situated four miles south-west of Blyth, on a high ridge. The *Church of St. Mary* was re-built in 1827, on the site of a very ancient chapel. Built into the south wall on the outside is an old grave-cover, bearing, in bas-relief, a pair of shears and the following inscription—"Orate pro anima anne barbowl S.I.O."—that is, "Pray for the soul of Anne Barbowl." The bell in the tower is inscribed, "Thos. Ogle, Esq., 1681." Beneath the tower is preserved an ancient British quern, found in the graveyard. At Low Horton there stood till 1809 the remains of a strong castle, defended by a double fosse and rampart of earth. The deep moat still encircles the farm-buildings. Guiscard de Charron obtained leave in 1293 to fortify his manor-house of Horton. A few years later, in 1317, it gave shelter to Sir Walter de Selby and the lawless band which fled from Mitford Castle after the capture of Sir Gilbert de Middleton, their leader. The castle was subsequently held by the Monbouchers and the Delavals. Two maiden sisters of Admiral Delaval were the last of that family who resided in it.

BEBSIDE, a considerable mining village, three miles north-west from Blyth, anciently belonged to the Prior of Tynemouth. Edward I. pardoned the Prior for acquiring lands in "Hertford, Bebesset-on-Blythe, Cowpen, etc., without license of mortmain." Bebside Grange, with a small tower in the centre of its south front, was the old mansion-house of this estate.

BEDLINGTON (the ton of the Bœdlings, or family of Bœda) stands on an elevated situation, above the river Blyth, which at this point is finely wooded. The parish of Bedlington in ancient times formed part of the patrimony of St. Cuthbert. It was purchased by Bishop Cuthcard about the beginning of the tenth century, and given to the see of Durham, so that in civil and ecclesiastical matters it was totally distinct and unconnected with Northumberland. It anciently had courts of its own, with justices, sheriffs, escheators, coroners, and all other offices of justice, till its privileges were taken away in the twenty-seventh year of Henry VIII. Here the monks of Durham, flying from the Conqueror to Lindisfarne with the body of St. Cuthbert, rested all night. At the south-east end of the village is the *Church of St. Cuthbert*, which is supposed to have been founded shortly after 1089, on the site of a Saxon edifice. The chancel was rebuilt in 1736, and the tower in 1863. The semi-circular part of the nave was also erected in 1863. The south wall of the nave and the chancel arch, with its beautiful Norman ornaments, belong to the eleventh-century building. The south porch, of the pointed style, has been converted into a vestry. During the restorations of 1818 were discovered three grave-covers with incised crosses and swords upon them, and a portionof the shaft of a Saxon cross, which was ornamented with characteristic knot-work, and had carved upon it the figure of a griffin and the words, "Crux or lux udiq (undique) fulget amata." The tombstones stand at the west end of the church, close to the font. In the wall, on each side of the chancel arch, is a trefoil-headed hagioscope; or, as Mr. Raine holds, "a niche intended for a statue." Built up in the south-east wall of the nave is a fragment of old carved work, representing two figures with musical instruments in their hands. On February 14th, 1669, Cuthbert Watson, a noted somnambulist, rose in his sleep, and, wandering to the church, climbed a buttress on the north-east side of the town. A person passing at the time, alarmed for his safety, called out to poor Watson, who, waking suddenly, fell, and was killed on the spot. His name and the date of the occurrence were carved on the old buttress; and though this has been removed, the visitor may still see carved on the new portion of the church—"Watson's Wake, 1669." In the churchyard is a tombstone inscribed :—

> "Poems and epitaphs are but stuff;
> Here lies Robert Barras, that's enough."

At the upper end of the village is the Market-Cross. The old Hall, of which a picturesque tower remains, is let off in tenements. Bedlington gave its name to a well-known breed of terriers. The principal inns here are the King's Arms and the Black Bull.

## NEWCASTLE TO KILLINGWORTH AND STANNINGTON.

**South Gosforth, 2½ miles; North Gosforth, 5 miles; Killingworth, 6½ miles; Blagdon, 8 miles; Hartford Dene, 9 miles; Stannington, 10 miles.**

THE great North Road, crossing the Newcastle Moor and proceeding through Gosforth to Morpeth, has been from time immemorial a portion of the principal highway from the English metropolis to the capital of Scotland. Along this road ran the old mail coaches with wonderful regularity. "The glory of the North Road," writes Mr. John Hodgson Hinde, in the *Archæologia Æliana*, "was no doubt the posting. On other roads the coaches were as well, in some even better appointed, and the speed greater; but nowhere could you drive up to an inn-door with the certainty that, as you drew up, a relay of horses, with mounted post-boys, would issue from the yard, and that one minute's delay was all that was required to replace the steeds that had brought you twelve miles within the hour by a fresh team, to carry you forward at the same rate. This system, however, which was brought to such perfection, was destined to 'flourish and to fade' in a single generation; and some of those who had seen it supplant the jog-trot pace of the last century lived to witness its prostration before the energies of railway enterprise. The road-side inns also, where the wealthiest magnate could be regaled as sumptuously as in his own castle, are many of them altogether desolate—all shorn of their former honours. If a stray pair of horses is required, they have to be taken from the hay-cart or the plough; and if the unfrequent traveller finds a well-aired bed, it is due to the providence of his hostess, and not to the frequency of its occupation."

GOSFORTH.—This village, which lies 2½ miles north-east from Newcastle, possesses many attractions, and is a popular place of residence with men of business in the town, with which it is connected by train and tram. Gosforth, according to the derivation of the name, is the ford over the Gos, Gose, or Ose, a streamlet known now as the Ouseburn. It is divided into South Gosforth and North Gosforth. SOUTH GOSFORTH, 2½ miles from Newcastle, was formerly in the parish of Whalton, held in the 7th Henry II. (1161) by Walter Fitz-William for a service of three knights. In 1616 it came into the possession of the Brandling family. The church of St.

Nicholas, a small plain structure, with an octagonal spire rising from a square tower, was rebuilt and enlarged between the years 1799 and 1820, so that most of its ancient character is lost. The old church was founded at a very remote period. In the reign of Henry II. there is positive evidence of its existence, for it formed part of the dowry of Richard Canville's daughter in 1170. In the church are stained glass windows in memory of the Brandlings and Smiths. The churchyard contains a quaint epitaph on John Ramsay, who died January 13th, 1782. It runs as follows :—

"Ye Politicians, stop and pause—
A Patriot lieth here,
Who lov'd his country and its laws,
And liberty held dear.

To Mathematics he inclin'd ;
His mind was always gay.
A husband good, and parent kind,
Was honest John Ramsay."

Here was buried Thomas Doubleday, historian, dramatist, radical reformer, journalist, and song-writer, who died in Gosforth Villas, December 18th, 1870.

In the sinking of *Gosforth Colliery* great expense was incurred, from the geological phenomenon—the intersection of the great ninety-fathom dyke. To celebrate the winning of the coal, it was arranged to have a grand subterranean ball. The ball-room was situated at a depth of nearly 1100 feet below the surface of the earth, and was brilliantly illuminated with lamps and candles. The company was composed of the men engaged in the work, with their wives and daughters and sweethearts ; several neighbours, with their wives ; the proprietors and agents, with their ladies ; and sundry friends of both sexes, who had courage to avail themselves of the privilege. Between 200 and 300 persons are estimated to have been present.

Near this colliery lived, till within the last six or seven years, Thomas Atthey—a genius in humble life—who was well known as an authority upon the fossil remains of fishes and reptiles of the coal-measures. He discovered several unknown genera, one of which is now connected with his name as the *Attheya decora.* He died in April 1880.

About a quarter of a mile to the east of the railway station, and close to the Ouseburn, is *Haddrick's Mill*, or *Hatherick's Mill*, as it was formerly called. "There is a tradition in the neighbourhood that this place took its name from a notorious Danish freebooter named Hendrik or Hadderick, who made the dene beside the mill his home, and set the authorities at defiance. On what foundation this story rests is not clearly shewn, but it is at least a coincidence that Sir Walter Scott gives nearly the same name—'Dirk Hatterick'—to his smuggler and pirate in *Guy Mannering*. It has been said also, that the old play of 'The Miller and his Men' was taken from incidents which occured at Haddrick's Mill."—*Welford.*

In that part of modern Gosforth known as *Coxlodge*, formerly a township belonging to the Barony of Whalton, stands "The Lunatic Asylum" of the borough of Newcastle, built in 1869, containing about 250 patients.

NORTH GOSFORTH, which for three hundred years was in the possession of the famous local family of the Brandlings, is about five miles north from Newcastle. Gosforth House was erected in 1760 by Mr. Charles Brandling, from a design by Payne. It is a large and elegant structure of white freestone, and being situated on a slightly rising ground, commands a fine and extensive view. Gosforth Park covers 790 acres, and is beautifully wooded. The lake, which is about a mile and a-half from the house, is fifty acres in extent, and during the winter months affords the best and safest skating in the district. Being sheltered in position, the ice forms earlier, and remains firmer for a longer period, than on the other popular sheets of water. During the summer months it is frequented by many varieties of wild fowl, an account of which is given by Mr. John Hancock in the sixth volume of the Tyneside Naturalists' Field Club. Mr. Smiles relates that George Stephenson, when resident at West Moor, "contrived a wonderful lamp which burned under water, with which he was afterwards wont to amuse the Brandling family at Gosforth, going into the fish-pond [lake] at night, lamp in hand, attracting and catching the fish, which rushed wildly towards the flame." In 1852, when the property of the Brandlings came under the hammer, Gosforth House and estate were bought by Thomas Smith, Esq., for £25,100. In 1880 the hall and park were sold by T. E. Smith, Esq., to the High Gosforth Park Company, Limited, who laid out part of the grounds for coursing meetings, transformed the hall into a grand-stand and hotel, with stabling for 115 horses, and transferred the "Pitman's Derby" from Newcastle Moor to Gosforth. The nearest railway station to Gosforth Park is Killingworth, on the north line.

In the grounds at Low Gosforth, about half-a-mile from the hamlet known as the Three Mile Bridge, are the ruins of an ancient chapel, destroyed, probably by fire, during the latter half of the seventeenth century.

KILLINGWORTH, picturesquely seated on a rounded hill, with fine trees around it, is five and a quarter miles north by east from Newcastle, and four from Gosforth, from which it is approached by the Salter's Road. In an old house in the village Admiral Robert Roddam, who distinguished himself in innumerable engagements between the years 1735-80, resided for some time. The neighbourhood is of interest as the scene of the early labours and engineering triumphs of George Stephenson, who came here in 1804 as brakesman to the West Moor Colliery. He occupied a small cottage standing by the side of the road leading from West Moor Pit to Killingworth. A sun-dial over the door, bearing the date "August 11th, MDCCCXVI.," the joint production of George and Robert Stephenson, still indicates the cottage. Here it was that his young wife died of consumption. The many small mechanical improvements that he was continually making at the colliery gained him a local reputation as a man of resource and ingenuity, and he was asked to try to remedy a defect in the pumping-engine, at Killingworth High Pit, which had baffled all the enginemen in the neighbourhood. He set to work, and pulling the engine to pieces, effected several alterations, that made the pumping apparatus work most successfully. In 1812 he was appointed engine-wright of the colliery, at a salary of £100 a-year. Mending the neighbours' clocks and watches, inventing ingenious scare-crows, and connecting the cradles of the women with the smoke-jack, and making them self-acting—his mechanical genius was gradually developed. His cottage was quite a curiosity-shop of models of engines, self-acting planes, and perpetual-motion machines, which last contrivance baffled him as effectually as it had done hundreds of preceding inventors. It was at Killingworth Colliery, in 1813, that, under the patronage of Sir T. H. Liddell, afterwards Lord Ravensworth, he constructed his first locomotive—"Blucher," as it was popularly called. It was tried with success on the Killingworth Railway, July 25th, 1814. This somewhat cumbrous and clumsy engine was succeeded in the following year by a much improved engine, different in construction and mechanical arrangement, that clearly manifested to the far-reaching mind of George Stephenson those wonderful possibilities which he was afterwards to realise. Here it was that he invented, in 1815, the steam-blast, fraught with such important consequences to railway locomotion, and the safety-lamp, so invaluable to the miner in his subterranean toil. At Burradon, or Briardene, three miles to the north, forming part of a farm-house, there is an old pele-tower, of which the vaulted chamber on the ground-floor, and the circular stone staircase leading to the upper apartments, are in a good state of preservation. It was the manor-house of the Andersons, who were resident here in 1552.

*Blagdon Hall*, the seat of Sir Matthew White Ridley, stands on the west side of the North Road, about nine miles from Newcastle, and is a handsome stone building, having east and south fronts, the latter of which is very imposing. It was built by Matthew White, Esq., in the earlier part of the eighteenth century, but additions were made and porticos added from designs of Bonomi in 1826 and 1830. The south portico has its intercolumination closed with a screen of stained glass, beautifully enriched with classical figures, by Mr. John Gibson of Newcastle. It is used as a conservatory. It contains, together with many valuable pictures, a large collection of marble and bronze statues by Lough, purchased by the late Sir Matthew White Ridley who was a generous patron of the sculptor. The statues in bronze of "The Mourners" and "Milo" are undoubtedly amongst the greatest of Lough's works. The pleasure-grounds and gardens are beautiful and extensive, and are ornamented by a fine sheet of water. In the grounds are preserved the ancient Kale Cross, which once stood at the foot of the Side in Newcastle, and the portcullis of the Newgate. The two lodges, each surmounted by a finely-executed white bull, at the chief entrance, have a stately appearance. The Prince of Wales and his two sons were the guests of Sir Matthew during the Royal Agricultural Show which was held at Newcastle in 1887. The manor of Blagdon, formerly Blakedene, was held of the barony of Morpeth by John de Plessis in the time of Henry III. In 1567 it belonged to the Fenwicks, who, after disposing of Little Harle, had their residence here until they sold it to the Whites. On the marriage of Elizabeth, eldest daughter, and at length heiress of Matthew White, Esq., November 18th, 1842, the estate passed into the possession of the renowned family of the Ridleys, whose ancient seat was Hardriding, near Haltwhistle. One celebrated member of this old Border house was Nicholas Ridley, Bishop of London, who was burnt in the reign of Queen Mary. The Ridleys of Blagdon have, for over a century, exercised a very powerful influence on the commercial and political life of the North, and probably in no member of this family have the qualities that, of old, made the name so much respected been more conspicuous than in the present representative, Sir Matthew White Ridley. A little further north, beyond Blagdon, is the picturesque Stannington Bridge, crossing the river Blyth, which takes its course eastward through *Hartford Dene*—one of the prettiest denes in the county, and a favourite haunt of pic-nic parties. A delightful path, over-arched with trees, runs by the side of the stream, passing under the railway viaduct, to Plessey Mill, which is situated in the midst of a sheltered haugh, and in former times had some connection with the Convent of St. Bartholomew in Newcastle. Here the visitor may, if he desires it, obtain tea and refreshments. The pathway, branching off from the river for a time, continues to Hartford Bridge The nearest station to Hartford Dene is Plessey, whence it may be entered at the point just indicated, or by proceeding a little along the road towards Hartford Bridge, and then turning into the fields at Plessey Mill.

STANNINGTON, ten miles north from Newcastle, and four and a-half from Morpeth, is a small, irregular-built village, with a few farm-steads and low-thatched cottages. The church of St. Mary, erected in 1871, stands upon the site of the old structure, which, in consequence of its dilapidated condition, was removed, though the old arcades and piers have been built up again. It is in the early English style, and has a tower 80 feet high, which forms a very conspicuous object to the surrounding country. There is an arcade round the lower part of the chancel, supported on marble shafts, and the chancel arch is also shafted with marble. The fittings of the church are very handsome. The vestry contains some ancient stained glass, presented by Sir M. W. Ridley in 1772. The subjects represented are :—The Virgin, with the infants Jesus and John ; a saint sitting on a chest, his right hand slightly elevated towards the handle of a sword placed horizontally in his mouth, the arms of England and France, and two shields. Near Stannington is the Reformatory School for boys. Of these there are about 200, who farm 500 acres of land, and manufacture agricultural implements, and are taught several useful trades.

# NEWCASTLE TO BELSAY AND STAMFORDHAM.

Kenton, 3 miles; Wolsington, 5 miles; Ponteland, 7 miles; Kirkley, 9½ miles; Ogle, 11½ miles; Milbourne Hall, 11 miles; Belsay, 13 miles; Dalton, 11 miles; Stamfordham, 13 miles; Black Heddon, 15 miles.

THIS is an excellent road, formerly traversed by the famous "Chevy Chase" coach, which ran daily between Newcastle and Edinburgh. It crosses the Town Moor to the Cowgate, whence it diverges to Kenton Bar. This point is an admirable one for obtaining fine panoramic views of the surrounding country.

A little to the east is the ancient village of KENTON, or Kyngton (King's Town), as it was formerly called. Kenton Colliery, a little to the south-east of the village, is of very ancient date. A hundred years ago it was remarkable for its subterranean connection with the Tyne, called "Kitty's Drift." This tunnel was three miles long, six feet high, and about the same breadth. On the tramway leading from Kenton to Coxlodge an interesting experiment was made on the 2nd September 1813 with a steam-engine, patented by Mr. Blenkinsop of Leeds, in 1811. This locomotive was made to work by a cog-wheel upon toothed rails, and drew seventy tons at the rate of nearly three miles an hour. The occasion is memorable from the fact that among the spectators was George Stephenson, the engineer of Killingworth Colliery, who thus had an opportunity of examining the engine and observing its performances. His opinion of the invention may be gathered from a remark he made to his companion, that "he thought he could make a better engine than that to go upon legs." Certain it is, says Mr. Smiles, that shortly after the inspection of the Coxlodge engine he contemplated the construction, of a new locomotive, which was to surpass all that preceded it. Thomas Atthey, naturalist and palæontologist, was born here in 1811.

*Wolsington Hall* (Captain Henry Bell), an old manorial house, with several modern additions, situated in a pleasant and well-wooded park, through which runs the Ouseburn. The manor of Wolsington formed part of the possessions of the Priory of Tynemouth.

PONTELAND (Pont-island) is a pretty rural village on the river Pont, from which it derives its name. Fine trees line both sides of the turnpike road near the village, thus making the entrance to it very picturesque. By the side of the Pont are some charming walks. Ponteland has some claim to antiquity. A peace between England and Scotland was negotiated here in 1244, and both the town and castle (the lord of which at the time was Sir Haymon d'Alphel) were burnt by the Scottish army on its march from Newcastle to Otterburn. Adjoining the Blackbird Inn, a quaint old building, once the villa of the Erringtons, as may be seen from the initials M.E. above the doorway, is a vaulted chamber, now used as a cow-byre, which is all that remains of Ponteland Castle. *The Church of Saint Mary* was founded in Norman times. The lower part of the tower and the west door, with its round-headed arch and characteristic zigzag moulding, are remnants of the early building. Certain features in the tower—the low semi-circular arches over the cusped headings to the windows—correspond with similar work at Embleton, and would seem to imply that the two churches were executed by the same masons from the same design. Built up at the west end, inside the tower is a Saxon cross of plain form. The chancel arch rests on carved corbels. The chancel is a good specimen of decorated work, c. 1330. The nave belongs to the late Decorated period. The transepts are early English work. In each of them is the site of an altar, proving the existence of chantries. A beautiful piscina, with network ornaments, will be noticed with interest. In 1810 the north wall fell, but the whole structure has since that time been repaired. In the chancel are the burial-places and stones inscribed to the memory of the Goftons and Wilkies of Eland Hall, the Horsleys of Milbourne Grange, and the Ogles of Kirkley and the Carrs of Dunston. On the north side of the chancel is a hatchment and a flat sepulchral stone over Cuthbert Ogle, Esq., of Kirkley, who died 14th January 1655. Near the organ is the incised slab of a bishop, in rich robes, found near the door. In the south transept is a handsome stained window, erected by Miss Bates of Milbourne Hall. There is also some fourteenth-century glass in the church. On the north side of the village is the grey tower of the old fortified vicarage—a remnant of moss-trooping days.

A little east of the village, and about seven miles north from Newcastle, is PRESTWICK CAR, which, before it was drained, formed one "of the principal breeding stations of wild birds in the north, and one of the most famous of Nature's nurseries." Speaking of this hunting-ground of the naturalist, Mr. Hancock says—"Rich as it was in botanical and entomological specimens, it was not less remarkable for its ornithological features. I know of no locality of the same limited area where so many species of water-fowl were to be found breeding as bred yearly at Prestwick Car."

KIRKLEY stands two and a-half miles north by west from Ponteland, on the river Blyth. The family of Eure held this manor in the reign of Edward II., by annually presenting a barbed arrow at the manor court. The lands of Sir John de Eure were seized by the

Crown in the reign of Edward III., because his father, John de Eure, had aided the Scots in the preceding reign. They were afterwards restored to the family. Sir Ralph de Eure was Lord Warden of the East Marches in the reign of Henry VIII., and his power and authority were such that during the whole term of his government he was able to maintain peace and order in a district so often exposed to the ravages of the Scots. He burnt the town of Jedworth in 1544, and re-entering Scotland with 4000 men in 1545, was slain at Halidon Hill. His son, Sir William de Eure, was raised to the peerage in the same reign. Kirkley afterwards became the seat of a branch of the noble family of Ogle (*temp.* James I.) Here was born Sir Chaloner Ogle, admiral and commander-in-chief of the fleet, who, when in command of the *Swallow* man-of-war, captured the squadron of Roberts, the famous pirate, on the coast of Africa, 5th February 1722. The mansion-house is a handsome square building, commanding extensive and picturesque views. In the park is an obelisk, put up by Dean Ogle in 1789 *(anno centesimo)*, in memory of the landing of William III. in 1689.

Two miles further north are the remains of *Ogle Castle*, incorporated with the walls of a picturesque manor-house of the time of Charles I. Several early pointed arches remain in the interior of the building. It was formerly a long quadrangular edifice, with towers at the four corners, and surrounded by a double moat, which was crossed by a drawbridge. The Ogle family, which is of very great antiquity, was seated here before the Conquest. Humphrey de Ogle had his manor and seat confirmed to him, with all its ancient privileges, by Walter Fitz-William, baron of Whalton, for the service of one knight's fee and a-half. The manor-house was converted into a castle in 1340 by Robert de Ogle, and here the Ogles flourished till 1809, when the estate was sold to Thomas Brown, Esq., an opulent shipowner in London. Here, according to Froissart, John Copeland, after the battle of Neville's Cross (October 17, 1346), brought his captive, David, King of Scotland, arriving about vespers, after having carried him twenty-five miles. Few families have so long a pedigree as the Ogles, and so proud were they of this fact, that when a Milburn in 1583 protested that the Dacres were of as good blood as the Ogles, "four of the Ogles set upon him and slew him."

Nearly four miles north-west of Ponteland is Milbourne Hall, the seat of the Rev. J. E. Elliott-Bates, and separated from it by a deep narrow glen is Milbourne Grange, which played a considerable part in the early history of Nonconformity in the North. Mr. George Horsley, an ancestor of the present Lord Decies, espoused the cause of the ejected ministers, and is said to have paid as much as £30 for two sermons, preached at his house in one day by Mr. Owen and Mr. Leaver. In August 1684 it is recorded—"Mr. Robert Leaver, ejected from Bolam, was apprehended at his inn in Gateshead for being the preacher at a conventicle at George Horsley's, of Milbourne Grange." Many of the Nonconformists objected to the use of the ritual for the burial of the dead, and chose to be interred in unconsecrated ground. The grave of George Horsley may yet be seen in a plantation, near the site of the old hall, enclosed by a circular wall.

Thirteen miles from Newcastle, and six from Ponteland, is BELSAY, a picturesque little village, consisting of an arcade (a handsome row of stone buildings), with piazza in front, and a few farmsteads and cottages. The nearest railway station is Angerton, four miles distant. In the arcade is a Temperance Hotel, the nearest inn being "The Highlander," two miles to the south. A mile to the west of the village, approached by a long and stately carriage drive, is *Belsay Castle*, the seat of Sir Arthur Edward Middleton, Bart., M.P. It is a large and splendid mansion, situated on gently rising ground, and built according to the purest models of Grecian architecture by Sir C. M. L. Monck. It is a square of about 104 feet, and partly occupies the site of the late chapel of Belsay. Two tiers of lights appear on the east, south, and west fronts, around which a Doric entablature of great beauty is continued. The entrance hall on the east, built wholly of polished stone, is impressive, by reason of its simple grandeur. It opens into a staircase hall, which is also of polished stone, and which is surrounded within by a gallery six feet broad, and supported by twelve Ionic columns and four double pilasters, one at each corner. Adjoining the mansion are some beautiful gardens. Behind are the deep quarries from which the stones were obtained for the new mansion. These have been transformed by the power of art into haunts of the wildest sylvan beauty. Passing under a lofty arch wreathed with ivy—by rugged hollows filled with ferns and ornamental shrubs—along steep and narrow defiles overhung with graceful trees—the visitor strolls in wonder through these picturesque quarries, where, on the jutting ledges, may it be seen the *Allosorus crispus* and *Anchusa sempervirens* growing in friendly proximity to the exotic palm. Near the "great arch" is a handsome specimen of the "Cupressus Macrocarpa." In the park, a little north-west from the new mansion, are the old and picturesque ruins of *Belsay Castle*, surrounded by fine trees. It was erected in the time of Edward III. by John de Middleton, and, as Mr. Hodgson says, is certainly one of the most perfect, and by far the most imposing, specimen of castellated architecture in Northumberland. It consists of a square tower or keep, measuring on the outside, from north to south, 51½ feet, and from east to west, 47 feet 3 inches, and has had four tiers of apartments. Those on the ground floor are covered with a stone arch, and have been used as a kitchen and cellars. On the second floor is a room, 43 feet long by 21½ wide and 17 high. It is lighted on the south by large pointed windows of two lights, the southern one being adorned with trefoil tracery. The walls were formerly ornamented with shields and armorial bearings. At each of the corners of the battlements is a turret projecting considerably over the walls; three of these are round, and the fourth, over the south angle, is square, and contains the staircase. The view from the battlements is exceedingly fine. The numerous additions made to the tower at different times were from the time of James I. the residence of the Middleton family, but most of these were taken down when the modern house was built. The portion which remains is used as the steward's residence, and still bears on a tablet in its south front the inscription, "Thomas Middleton and Dorothy his wife builded this house, anno 1614." On another tablet, immediately below, are the arms of Middleton quartering Strivelyn, and "T. M., 1629." The family of the Middletons, of Belsay, is of very ancient origin, dating, at least, as far back as 1160. In 1278 they were honoured by a royal visit from Edward I. In the reign, however, of his feeble successor, Edward II., Sir Gilbert Middleton, the representative of the family at that time, quarrelled with the Crown, raised a large army of Border riders, ravaged Northumberland and Durham, and seized upon two Romish cardinals and the bishop-elect of Durham, whom they were about to induct into his see, and exacted from them a heavy ransom. He was, after considerable trouble, at last defeated and put to death, and his lands confiscated. They were afterwards, however, recovered by the marriage of one of his descendants with the heiress of the grantee of the Crown, daughter of Sir John de Striveling. Another member of the family married the heiress of the Lamberts of Craven, descendants of William I., and another married the heiress of the Moncks of Caenby, in Lincolnshire, by whom respectively the names of Lambert and Monck came to be adopted by the family. In the grounds, near the mansion and old castle, the botanist will find some very fine and vigorous trees, of which mention may be made of a large oak, 500 yards south-east of the house, with a girth, at a height of four feet, 13 feet 2 inches, and a height of 54 feet; and of a splendid old walnut, thirty yards south of the old castle, with a girth, as it rises from the ground, of 16 feet 1 inch, and a height of 45 feet. To the south of the Hall is Belsay Craig, crossed by many charming paths and planted with stately trees, among which are some very fine birches. An old ash on the top, 45 feet in height, has a girth of 14 feet 7 inches at a height of 8 feet. The bottom of this romantic crag is washed by a picturesque lake or fish-pond. Above a small waterfall at the outlet of this lake is a venerable tree, which is popularly known as "Silky's Seat," for amid its complicated limbs the mischievous ghost of Black Heddon possessed a rude chair, where, in her moody moments, she was wont to sit, wind-rocked, enjoying the rustling of the storm in the dark woods, or the murmur of the cascade below. A mile and a-half south-west of Belsay is West Bitchfield, a farm-house that was formerly a Border pele. It was the seat and property of Roger Fenwick, Esq., second son of Sir John Fenwick of Wallington, in the seventeenth century, and his initials, R. F., with the date 1622, are still to be seen above the door inside the kitchen. This room appears to have been used as an armoury in the olden times, and the racks still remain on its walls.

Three miles north-west from Ponteland, and ten miles north-west from Newcastle, is DALTON, a prettily situated rural village, overlooking the Pont. There is a small chapel here dedicated to the Holy Trinity. At Dalton Hill Head is one of those gradually decreasing houses said to be "haunted." The story in connection with it may be told in the language of the Rev. J. F. Bigge, M.A. :—"This place once belonged to the family of Hedley, of Newcastle, who sold it to Mr. Collingwood, of Dissington. Some years ago a woman, Mary Henderson, had sole charge of the house. Her sister was the wife of George Stephenson, the engineer. A gardener lived close by, and had a mastiff named 'Ball.' In the house there was a closet, which the housekeeper had the most positive orders never to open. Her curiosity, however, got the better of her prudence, and she told the gardener what she intended to do. He strongly advised her against it. She got an axe and broke open the door of the closet, and found a quantity of children's bones—some in hat-boxes, some wrapped up in clothes. She fastened up the door and went to bed. At night she awoke, and heard strange sounds of people dancing and singing upstairs. She thought she would go and see what all the noise was about. She called the dog 'Ball' from under the bed, but he only whined, and was unwilling to follow, and showed symptoms of fear, when in general he was most courageous. So she carried him in her arms upstairs, and proceeded to the room whence the sound came. She entered and found the room empty; an attic window was open. In the morning she told the gardener of these strange doings. He also had heard strange noises, and had been much disturbed during the night."

Adjoining Dalton are the beautiful grounds of North Dissington. *Dissington Hall*, ten miles north-west from Newcastle, the residence of E. M. Bainbridge, Esq., was the birthplace of Sir Ralph Delaval, who served at the battles of Beachy Head and La Hogue, and at his death, in January 1707, was interred in Westminster Abbey.

Half-a-mile to the south of Dissington Hall is EACHWICK—anciently called Achewic—a small village, consisting of a few farmsteads and cottages. It was anciently a place of some consequence. The family of Akenside the Poet had lands here for many generations. In making a road through an old camp near the village, several hand-mill stones, a sacrificial knife, and a flint axe were discovered. The hall is a large old turreted building. Ralph Spearman, the celebrated local antiquary, who is said to have been the Monkbarns of the *Antiquary*, had possession of this estate and lived here. Half-a-mile south-east of Eachwick is *South Dissington*, a manor and seat of the Delavals soon after the Conquest. It was part of the possessions of Tynemouth Priory in the reign of James I., 1613. From the Delavals it passed to the Collingwoods. In the garden here are two figures of Hercules and Flora, which have stood very perfect since 1700, with "Fd. Delavall, Esq.," and "Mad : Mary Delavall," inscribed on the pedestals. About two miles from North Dissington, and one mile east-south-east from Stamfordham, is *Cheeseburn Grange*, the residence of Francis Henry Riddell, Esq., beautifully situated in a well-wooded park, bounded by the river Pont. Adjoining the hall is a Catholic chapel, with a fine painting over the altar representing "The Descent of Our Saviour from the Cross." The manor belonged formerly to the Priory of Hexham, afterwards to the Widdringtons. The Widdringtons of Cheeseburn Grange were deeply engaged in the rebellion of 1715. Ralph Widdrington, Esq., was imprisoned and under sentence of death at Liverpool, but, with his servant, he managed to escape out of the gaol by means of a rope thrown across the ditch or fosse. Mr. Widdrington lost all the nails off one hand by clinging to the rope. They had the gaol-fever when they escaped, but recovered. Mr. Widdrington lived long after 1745, and was never molested. He retired for a few years to the Continent.

There are some charming bits of scenery near the Pont in this part of the country, especially in the vicinity of the Heugh Bridge, which is situated in a very picturesque milieu. On its way to Dissington the streamlet wanders through a lovely little dell, the sides of which are covered with shrubs and trees. A pleasant footpath, called "Captain's Walk," runs eastward along the Pont side towards Eachwick and Dissington.

STAMFORDHAM, 12 miles from Newcastle, Hexham, and Morpeth, is a large rural village, once a market-town, pleasantly situated on rising ground, the river Pont skirting its southern boundary. It is in the township of Heugh, formerly called Hoghe (a village about a mile to the north), and consists principally of one long and broad street, sloping towards the river. The old name of this village is Stannerton—that is, the Ton, the common Anglo-Saxon suffix to so many places, and Stanner, a stony ford. On the green, in the centre of the village, is an ancient covered building, called the Market Cross, resting on four open arches, erected by Sir John Swinburne, Bart., 1735. Not far from this cross, on the north side of the village, there is a high brick house, behind which is a bowling-green, where, it is stated, the ill-fated Lord Derwentwater used to come and play at bowls; but probably, also, for another purpose, which eventually led him to his ruin. There is here a Free Grammar School, founded and endowed in 1663 by Sir Thomas Widdrington.

*The Church of St. Mary*, surrounded on the south and east sides by trees, stands at the west end of the village. The body of the church, with the exception of the chancel arch and the south chancel wall, was entirely rebuilt in 1848-9, under the direction of Mr. Benjamin Ferry, the architect, but the ancient tower being in a good state of preservation, was repaired and left standing. The style of architecture is early English, or first pointed, and the present church was probably built about 1220, though there must have been a more ancient one, for when it was re-built many carved stones of an earlier date were found built up in the walls; among others, part of the shaft of a Saxon Cross, which is now in the Dean and Chapter Library in Durham. Inserted in the walls of the porch are some ancient foliated grave-crosses which were found during the restoration of the church. The two western pillars have ornamented caps. Built into the east end of the south aisle is a very rude piece of sculpture, which was found lying below the old floor, and had, no doubt, been a reredos to an altar in a chantry-chapel. It represents Our Lord on the Cross, with a dove above. On one side are figures of the Virgin Mary and St. Andrew, and on the other St. John and an Archbishop. At the west end of the north aisle is a large stone altar-shaped monument, "To the memory of John Swinburne, of Black Heddon, and Marie, his wife, and son of Thomas Swinburne, of Capheaton, and the sole daughter of Thomas Collingwood, of Eslington; they left four daughters." On the edge of the stone slab is this rhyme:—

> "A loving wife and mother dear, such a one
> She was who now lieth here"—1627.

This monument is about 12 feet high, and is very rudely carved. The chancel, 42 feet long by 18 wide, is of great beauty, and the most striking part of the church. The arch between it and the nave is very peculiar in form, being almost the shape of a horse's shoe. On the south wall of the chancel is the coat-of-arms of the family of Dixon of Inghoe, together with a monument which was painted and emblazoned a few years ago at the cost of the Rev. Dixon Brown, of Unthank Hall. Near the vestry is the mutilated legless figure of a knight in armour. "This is a remarkable effigy; the knight is resting his head on a tilting helmet; the crest on the front had been a lion; the head is gone, but the plume which is on the front of the helmet, was said by the late Rev. Charles H. Hartshorne, Rector of Holdenby, a person most learned on this subject, to be unique, certainly in England, if not in Europe. This is supposed to be the figure of Sir John de Felton, who was lord of the manor of Matfen. He was Sheriff of Northumberland in 1390, in the fourteenth year of the reign of Richard II. He is mentioned by Froissart as being at the battle of Otterburn, which was fought in August 1388, and he says 'he was deputed by the king, August 20th, 1388, to go with Nicholas Dagworth and Gerard Heron to the Exchequer of the King of Scotland, according to articles of a truce concluded between England and France, and forthwith to certify the king what they should in the premises.' He died 1402." Within the altar rail, in a niche in the north wall, is an effigy of a priest in his robes; in a similar niche, within an arch on the south wall, is the figure of a cross-legged knight in armour, and on his shield are six marlets, which prove him to have been a member of the illustrious house of Fenwick. The Vicarage lies to the south side of the church. Over the south entrance to the house is a coat-of-arms; on the dexter side are the arms of Dr. Dochwray (vicar from 1761 to 1783), and on the sinister those of his wife, who was an Ellison, and below:—

> "Œdes hasce labentes refecit, Thomas Dochwray, 1762."

In front of the house is a most remarkable specimen of the Larch

(*Larix Europæa*), resembling a cedar, the circumference of which, on the ground, is 14 feet, and one yard high, 9 feet 10 inches. The gardens are extensive, and there is a fine terrace before the house, below which is a grass lawn bordered with shrubs. Fairs are held at Stamfordham on the Thursday before the 26th of April, for horses, cattle, and sheep; and on the Thursday before the 26th of August, for cattle, sheep, and lambs. The inns are Bay Horse, Masons' Arms, and Swinburne Arms. On the south bank of the Pont, opposite to Stamfordham, to which it is united by a stone bridge of two arches, is the village of Hawkwell.

A mile and a quarter west by north from Stamfordham, built into the walls of a modern farm-house, are the remains of *Fenwick Tower*, which was the original seat of the ancient family of Fenwick, so celebrated in Border warfare. The name is derived from the position of the old villa on the borders of a fen that adjoined the Pont. In pulling down part of the old tower in 1775, 226 gold nobles of Edward III., Richard II., and one of David II., King of Scotland, were found.

BLACK HEDDON, three miles north of Stamfordham, was formerly a possession of the Fenwicks. To the student of popular superstitions it is interesting as the scene of the pranks and frolics of a mischievous spirit, called "Silky," because she usually appeared as a lady dressed in silks. The rustling of this fine-spun raiment of hers struck terror to the hearts of many a bold rustic in the neighbourhood of Black Heddon a hundred years ago. Many are the stories told of this wayward and capricious being, half ghost and half brownie, who was only to be baffled in her midnight pleasures by witch-wood (mountain ash). A bridge a little to the south of Black Heddon, on the road between that place and Stamfordham, is called "Silky's Bridge," in consequence of a scurvy trick she played on a farm servant and his team. She is said to have been the troubled phantom of some person who had died before disclosing where a great treasure, of which she was possessed, lay hid, and on that account she could not lie still in her grave. At last, however, the ceiling of a house in Black Heddon gave way, and something black and uncouth fell from it with a clash upon the floor. This was found to be a great dog or calf's skin filled with gold. After this Silky was never more heard or seen.

# NEWCASTLE TO HARLOW HILL AND HORSLEY.

Benwell, 2½ miles; Denton, 3 miles; Walbottle, 5 miles; Black Callerton, 7 miles; Throckley, 6 miles; Heddon-on-the-Wall, 7 miles; Rutchester, 8½ miles; Harlow Hill, 11 miles; Welton, 11½ miles; Horsley, 10 miles.

THIS road, popularly known as the Military Road, across the high ground from Newcastle to Carlisle, was constructed by General Wade, who, when summoned from Newcastle to defend Carlisle against Prince Charles Edward, found the old road utterly impracticable for the transit of artillery. An old couplet describes its condition—

> "If you'd seen this road before it was made,
> You'd lift up your hands and bless General Wade."

The present road frequently follows the course of the old Roman road, and runs for a great distance near the line of the Wall. Opposite to the Union Workhouse the mounds and fosse of the vallum may be made out on the left of the road.

BENWELL, two and a-half miles west from Newcastle, is a small rural village pleasantly situated on the high ground above the Tyne, sheltered from the winds on the east and north, and with a magnificent open view of the Tyne and Derwent valleys. It was formerly a possession of the Delavals and Shafthoes. The imposing castellated building, still called Benwell Tower, stands on the site of an old tower which belonged to the priors of Tynemouth, and was their summer residence; and it is said that after Prior Blakeney had surrendered the priory of Tynemouth to Henry VIII. he retired hither. Attached to the tower was a small domestic chapel (kept open for the good of the villagers till the beginning of the eighteenth century) and a burying-ground wherein interments took place till 1759. In 1779 Benwell Hall and grounds were purchased by the notorious Andrew Robinson Bowes, an unprincipled adventurer, whose inhuman treatment of his second wife, the Countess of Strathmore, has stamped his name with infamy, To the Benwell estate, says Mackenzie, he clung with peculiar fondness, and could not be prevailed upon to dispose of it. Benwell Tower was purchased by J. W. Pease, Esq., D.C.L., of Pendower, and presented by him in 1881 to the Bishop of Durham, to be used as the palace of the Bishop of Newcastle when the new see was created. Benwell Dene House is the residence of Dr. Hodgkin, B.A., D.C.L., the author of *Italy and her Invaders*, and the editor of *The Letters of Cassiodorus*. On Benwell Hill are the remains of the Roman station of *Condercum*, the third on the line of the wall. It lay partly to the north of the road and partly to the south. The northern portion is now occupied by the high-service reservoir of the Newcastle Water Company. In the grounds of Colonel Dyer and Mr. Mulcaster the eastern, southern, and western ramparts of the station are very distinct. On the lawn in front of Condercum House are the foundations of a small temple which stood a little to the east of the station. It has a round apse at its southern extremity, in which were three skeletons lying side by side, and, beneath them, about twelve Roman coins with the bronze handle of a box. Two altars found in the temple now stand in the place which they originally occupied. That on the right is dedicated to a god unknown to classical mythology, Antenociticus, and to the deities of the emperors, by Ælius Vibius, a centurion of the 20th legion, surnamed the Valerian and Victorious. It is very handsomely sculptured. On one side is the culter or sacrificial knife ; on the other the præfericulum, or jug, with ornaments above each. The other altar is of a ruder kind, and is dedicated to the god Anociticus (probably a contracted form of Antenociticus), by Tineius Longus, a paymaster to the legion. Benwell is surposed to have been the first place in Great Britain where coal was wrought. A coal-mine near Benwell took fire some time in the seventeenth century, and burned for nearly thirty years.

When proceeding down the steep brink between Benwell and Denton on the 20th June 1774, the horses of the Rev. John Wesley took fright, and he, together with his wife's daughter and two grandchildren, who were also in the chaise, had a marvellous escape from danger and death. The episode is best described in his own words :—"About nine I set out for Horsley, with Mr. Hopper and Mr. Smith. I took Mrs. Smith and her two little girls in the chaise with me. About two miles from the town, just on the brow of the hill, on a sudden both the horses set out, without any visible cause, and flew down the hill like an arrow. In a minute John fell off the coach-box. The horses then went on full speed, sometimes to the edge of the ditch on the right, sometimes on the left. A cart came up against them ; they avoided it as exactly as if the man had been on the box. A narrow bridge was at the foot of the hill. They went directly over the middle of it. They ran up the next hill with the same speed ; many persons meeting us, but getting out of the way. Near the top of the hill was a gate, which led into a farmer's yard. It stood open. They turned short and ran through it without touching the gate on one side or the post on the other. I thought, 'The gate which is on the other side of the yard, and is shut, will stop them ;' but they rushed through it as if it had been a cobweb, and galloped on through the corn-field. The little girls cried out, 'Grandpapa, save us !' I told them, 'Nothing will hurt you ; do not be afraid ;' feeling no more fear or care than if I had been sitting in my study. The horses ran on till they came to the edge of a steep precipice. Just then Mr. Smith, who could not overtake us before, galloped in between. They stopped in a moment. Had they gone on ever so little, he and we must have gone down together."

On the left hand side of the road, not far from the bridge referred to in the preceding narrative, is a fragment of the Roman Wall, 9½ feet wide, surrounded by wooden rails. To the south of the road is *Denton Dene*, a picturesque little glen at a convenient distance from the town. Along the well-wooded sides of the ravine are some pleasantly winding paths, but so much damage has been done to the trees and shrubs by mischievous persons, that only those are now admitted who have obtained permission from Messrs. T. & R. Armstrong, 14 Hawthorn Terrace, the agents of the proprietor—Mrs. Blackett Ord. The casual visitor will no doubt obtain permission by applying to the gamekeeper, Mr. George Brooks, Owlet Lane, Denton. On the north side of the road, a little beyond Denton Burn, is *Denton Hall*, a picturesque ivy-clad mansion, approached through a fine avenue of trees. It was built by the monks of Tynemouth in 1503, and used by them as a summer residence. The materials were obtained from the Roman Wall close by. The interior has lost much of its ancient character in the process of renovation, but the original windows, divided into three, four, and five lights by stone mullions, remain. The part of the house which has been least altered is the hall, now used as a museum of antiquities. Here a few sculptured stones from the wall are preserved. Of the manor of Denton there is mention in records as far back as A.D. 1240. In 1380 it was assigned to the prior and convent of Tynemouth, and afterwards passed into the hands of the Widdringtons, the Erringtons, and the Rogers, a family related to the Earl of Sandwich. In 1760, by the death of Miss Rogers, Denton became the property of a relative, the Hon. Edward Montague, a gentleman eminent for his scientific attainments. His wife was the celebrated Lady Mary Wortley Montague, whose conversational and literary talents attracted to the hall many distinguished people of that day. Among her guests were Dr. Johnson, Sir Joshua Reynolds, Beattie, and Garrick. Many of her published letters are dated from Denton Hall, and contain descriptive references to the surrounding scenery. Tradition preserves the memory of the great lexicographer's visits in the names, "Dr. Johnson's Chamber" and "Dr. Johnson's Walk" on the east side of the house. The desk and bookcase which he is said to have used are still shown to the curious. Denton Hall has its mysterious visitant, which is said to take the form of a woman, and is familiarly known as Barbara. Mr. Thomas Doubleday, however, who has recorded a marvellous story related to him by an aged lady of his acquaintance, speaks of her as "Silky." She has been seen flitting along the passages, up the stone staircases, and outside the house in the shady walks. "On one occasion," writes Mr. W. Aubone Hoyle, in Ingram's 'Haunted Homes,' "to the terror of an old nurse, she stood silently in the doorway, barring the entrance; on another she seized the hand of a sleeping inmate of the house, in the middle of the night, and drew it towards her, leaving a touch that was felt with pain for days. A death in the family is frequently marked by her sudden appearance, apparently indiscriminately, to anyone in the house; or the same occasions are marked by unearthly noises. It was but lately (1884) that Silky was heard apparently dragging something through two unoccupied rooms, down a flight of stairs, to a window which was flung open." In an outbuilding is an ancient British canoe which was found in the Tyne, and is undergoing a process of drying. It has been rudely hollowed out of a log of wood. A little to the south-west stood a chapel, of which a baptismal font and a few sculptured stones remain; in the grounds attached was a burial-ground, now a part of the garden. An incised slab with a memorial cross and sword and some large stone coffins were found here several years ago. The chapel was removed shortly after the Reformation. Tradition relates that the monks had an underground passage leading from Denton to their residence at Benwell Tower. To the east of the hall a pear-tree, said to be two hundred years old, still flourishes. The present owner of Denton is Lord Henry Paulet. From the summit of the long ascent above Denton at the Chapel House the view is both beautiful and extensive. In his celebrated picture, "The Plains of Heaven," Martin is said to have represented the glorious valley of the Tyne as seen from this point.

Three quarters of a mile beyond is WALBOTTLE, a village dating back to Saxon times, for its name is Saxon, signifying the "botel" or the "abode" on the wall. Here it was that George Stephenson received his first lessons in reading and spelling from a poor teacher named Robin Cowens. The engineer at Walbottle Colliery at that time was Robert Hawthorn, an ingenious and enterprising man, whose sons founded the celebrated engine factory in Newcastle that bears their name.

At *Walbottle Dean House* the remains of the southern gateway of a mile-castle may be seen by looking over the low garden-wall at its eastern extremity. Close by is *Walbottle Dene*, extending nearly to Newburn, and unfolding here and there several charming bits of sylvan scenery. Through it runs the New burn. On 24th July 1796 the stream being choked up at one point, collected its waters into a huge lake that burst away the embankment, and rushing down to the Tyne, caused a good deal of destruction, three houses at the east end of the village of Newburn being carried away and three lives lost.

Two and a-half miles north of Walbottle is BLACK CALLERTON, a colliery village of no pretensions to picturesqueness, but notable as the place where George Stephenson as a boy drove the "Gin" at eightpence a-day, walking early in the morning from Dewley Burn (a small village west of Throckley Fell, where his parents then lived) two miles across the fields, and returning late in the evening. Here, at the age of twenty, he was appointed to the responsible office of brakesman at the Dolly Pit. In the Dolly Pit Field he had his first and last fight with a roistering bully named Ned Nelson, who was the terror of the village, and was enabled, by his wiry muscles and practised strength, to gain an easy victory. It was at Callerton, his son Robert states, that he began to try his hand at original invention; and for some time he applied his attention to a machine of the nature of an engine-brake, which reversed itself by its own action.

In a field opposite to the Filter Beds at Throckley is the gateway of a mile-castle. *Frenchmen's Row*, a little further up the hill on the north side of the road, was the residence of a number of French refugees who fled to England on the occasion of the first Revolution. The dial was constructed by them. On the left-hand side of the road, before entering the village of Heddon-on-the-Wall, is a small fragment of the wall. Its north face is destroyed, but five courses of its southern face remain. Somewhat nearer the farm-house the remains of a circular chamber, supposed to have been a turret, appear in the substance of the wall, having a diameter of seven feet, with a small aperture leading out of it in a slanting direction. This is the only structure of its kind that remains along the line of the wall, and is deserving, therefore, of special notice.

HEDDON-ON-THE-WALL, seven miles from Newcastle, stands on the summit of a lofty hill, and possesses a fine outlook over the valley below. From its high and open situation it possesses many strategical advantages, and is supposed to have been of importance in the time of the Saxons. When forming the military road through it, in 1752, the workmen discovered in the Roman Wall here a large and very valuable collection of silver and copper Roman coins and medals deposited in wooden boxes which were much decayed. Several of the medals were as fresh as if newly struck. The *Church of St. Philip and St. James* was built about the beginning of the twelfth century, and possesses an interesting Norman chancel. The chancel arch, which has a curious depression in the middle, is enriched with the characteristic zigzag ornament of that period. The north side is transitional work of a very peculiar character. Over the vestry door is an arch of an early date. In the stone stairs, at the west end of the parsonage-house, is a stone with a Roman inscription.

At Heddon the military road takes the higher ground to Harlow Hill. About a mile and a-half beyond Heddon, and just where the second lane crosses the road, is *Rutchester*, the ancient Vindobala. The remains of this station, the fourth on the line of the wall, are very indistinct. The western and southern ramparts remain in a fair state of preservation. The station covered an area of 3½ acres, and was garrisoned by the 1st Cohort, the Frixagi or Frisii. The present farm-house, to the south of the camp, is formed on the nucleus of a mediæval stronghold, some of its ancient features being retained.

Rutchester Tower was inhabited by the family de Rutchester in the reign of King Edward I. It was the chief seat of the Rutherfords, of whom was

"A hot and haughty Rutherford,
Men called him Dickon-draw-the-sword."

*Lay*, canto vi. 7.

Dr. Charlton mentions that there was a "priest's hole or hiding-place" here, and relates the following incident connected with it:—"When Rutchester was searched for priests by Fenwick, the pursuivant in Elizabeth's time, Mrs. Rutherford, who was by birth a Swinburne, hid herself in this concealed chamber while her husband fled to the woods along the banks of the Tyne. But Fenwick was well up to his work. He felt certain from the suddenness of the attack and the surrounding of the house that the inmates had not all had time to escape, so he quietly took up his quarters there, till, on the third day, Rutherford himself returned from the woods and gave himself up, as he knew well that his wife and daughter, having no time to gather provision, would be faint with hunger in their hiding-place." To the west of the farm-house, on the brow of the hill, there is an ancient trough, 12 feet long, 4 feet 6 inches broad, and 2 feet deep, cut in the solid rock, popularly called "The Giants' Grave." Further on is Harlow Hill, a corruption of Hare-law, the hill or station of the army. Here are the Whittle Dene Waterworks. There are eight reservoirs, covering upwards of 150 acres and having an aggregate storage of 525 million gallons of water. The great northern reservoir covers an area of 40 acres, and the great southern one an area of 45 acres. Some barrows, to the north of this place, and graves filled with human bones, confirm the traditionary account of bloody battles having been fought here in the troublous times.

Half-a-mile to the south is the village of Welton, or Wall-town, built upon the line of the vallum. Its most prominent feature is an ancient manor-house called Welton Hall, which is entirely built of Roman stones. The oldest part is a ruined pele at the rear. The more modern building has the initials W. W. and the date 1614 sculptured over the lintel of the back-door. The picturesque front is relieved by a large bay, in which all the mullions remain. The lower apartment at the west end is a kitchen of vast proportions, having a wide chimney and mantel. From the garden there is a fine view of the front of the house, the adjoining pele, and the mantling ivy at the west end. This was the seat of the ancient family of the Weltons, resident here from the time of Henry IV. to that of Charles I. Old Will o' Welton, whose initials appear on the tower, was celebrated for his great strength. One of his feats of prowess is said to have been exhibited when age had deprived him of sight. This blind Samson, sitting outside the tower, called a plough-boy to him, and asked him to let him feel his arm, as he wished to find what sort of bones folk had now-a-days. The lad, apprehensive of his grip, held forth, instead of his arm, the iron plough coulter, which Will, forthwith, snapped in twain, pensively observing, "Men's banes are nought but girsels (gristles) to what they were in my day."

South-east of Welton, and 2½ miles from Heddon-on-the-Wall, is HORSLEY, a long and pretty rural village at a considerable elevation above the Tyne, seated on both sides of the Hexham road. The prospect over the valley is very extensive and beautiful. When, in 1662, the 2000 clergymen left the Church of England rather than submit to the conditions of the Act of Uniformity, Horsley was one of the places on the Tyne where the Nonconformists first assembled, the meeting-place being, as was required by law, more than five miles from a parish church. The meetings were held in the loft of the house adjoining the present chapel. The congregation had first to climb up a step-ladder which, as a precaution against informers, was drawn up afterwards, and then to pass through a small trap-door in order to reach their "conventicle." The present Independent Chapel was built towards the close of the seventeenth or beginning of the eighteenth century, but the exact date cannot be fixed. It was provided with a gallery in 1729. At the west end of the village, slightly raised above the level of the road, is an old house which bears over its doorway the initials of several members of the Richardson family, and the date 1700. Here, in 1742, lived Jonathan Simpson, who was one of Wesley's earliest adherents in the village. The new-formed society held its services in one of his rooms. The present occupant still preserves as a precious heirloom Wesley's plain wooden reading-desk, which only differs from others of its class in having a slight rest for the knees, and a primitive arrangement for holding a candle. One or two specimens of modern carpentry in the shape of slight supports for the base of the stand prove that "decay's effacing fingers" have already been at work on the venerable relic. From the east end of the village there is a pleasant walk through the fields to Wylam by way of Holeyn Hall.

# NEWCASTLE TO OVINGHAM.

Scotswood, $3\frac{1}{2}$ miles ; Newburn, 5 miles ; Wylam, 9 miles ; Prudhoe, $10\frac{1}{2}$ miles ; Cherryburn, $11\frac{1}{2}$ miles ; Ovingham, 11 miles.

THE dredging operations of the River Tyne Commissioners have very considerably deepened the bed of the river above bridge, and, as a consequence, local industries have been "stepping westward" at a rapid pace. The road between Newcastle and Scotswood is quite lined with factories and shipyards. 3½ miles from Newcastle is SCOTSWOOD, a village of considerable industrial importance, which takes its name from the encampment of the Scottish army in the time of Charles the First. The camp was formed above the village in the shape of a crescent. A handsome suspension bridge, erected from the designs of Mr. Green, and opened on the 12th April 1831, here unites the counties of Northumberland and Durham. It forms the goal of the great boat races for which the Tyne is famous.

NEWBURN, 5 miles from Newcastle, is prettily situated on a slight eminence above the Tyne. It is of great antiquity, and is said to have been a place of note before the Conquest, due possibly to the fact of the river being fordable here in two places, and there being no ford nearer to Newcastle. Its knolls, says Dr. Bruce, bear marks of early fortification, and several stones in the present church are undoubtedly Roman. There is reason to believe that the Romans laid a framework of stones across the bed of the river to improve the ford. A quantity of black oak was found at this spot, evidently used to fix the stones in their place. The Romans are thought to have had a fort here commanding the passage of the river. The borough, in the time of the Norman and the Plantagenet monarchs, enjoyed many royal privileges and exemptions ; but from the time when the town of Newcastle became its rival in these, Newburn ceased to be a flourishing place.

*The Church of St. Michael and All Angels*, crowning the hill on which the village stands, is a cruciform building with a square tower, which is supposed to be of early Norman, if not of Saxon, architecture. In 1827 some parts of the church were re-built, and in 1872 it was repaired and reseated. The north aisle was added in the Transitional period, the columns of the arcade being of the ordinary style of Henry II.'s time. The arches are completely without mouldings, having the appearance, says Mr. Longstaffe, of countrified work. The south aisle belongs to the early English period. The church contains some ancient monuments of the Delaval family, and several stained-glass windows. One or two historic events are connected with Newburn and its church. In March 1072, Osulph, who had been deprived of the earldom of Northumberland, besieged Earl Copsi in Newburn. The latter took refuge in the church, but Osulph set fire to it, and his rival, in attempting to escape, was seized and murdered. In 1346 David, King of Scotland, crossed the ford here on his way to Neville's Cross. On the 27th August 1640 two armies faced each other here. The Scots, said to have numbered 20,000, under General Lesley, occupied the high ground above the village; and the English, 3000 foot and 1500 horse, under Lord Conway, were encamped on the haughs opposite, having raised several sconces, or breastworks, against the two fords, to hinder the Scots from passing over. On the 28th August the Scots mounted their cannon (rude engines made of bar iron, and hooped with cord and wet raw hides) on the church-tower, and placed their musketeers in the church, houses, lanes, and hedges in and about Newburn. Having made a breach in the greater sconce and driven out the somewhat faint-hearted defenders, the Scots waded across the river and drove the king's troops up the Ryton and Stella banks, taking many of them prisoners, and completing what Clarendon has described as "that infamous, irreparable rout at Newburn." Thus, through the cowardice or incompetency of the Cavalier general (and Lord Conway has been accused of both), was lost this battle, so fatal to the king's cause. The breastwork thrown up by the English is still to be seen on Stella Haughs. It is a conspicuous object from the Newcastle and Carlisle Railway.

George Stephenson was married in Newburn Church, November 28th, 1802, to his first wife, Fanny Henderson, a servant in the house of the small farmer with whom he lodged. "George's signature," says Mr. Smiles, "as it stands in the books, is that of a person who seems to have just learnt to write. With all his care he had not been able to avoid a blotch: the word Stephenson has been brushed over before the ink was dry." After the wedding the bridal pair rode on a pillion to their home at Willington Quay. Eighteen years afterwards—March 20th, 1820—he married his second wife, Elizabeth Hindmarsh, in the same church, his son Robert being one of the attesting witnesses. George Stephenson spent several years of his boyhood at Newburn, his family residing at "Jolly's Close,' just behind the village (a place now covered with earth, shale, and *débris*), in a poor cottage of only one room, that served for parlour, kitchen, sleeping-room, and all. A pumping-engine having been erected at Water-row Pit, about half-a-mile west of Newburn, old Stephenson went to work it as fireman, his son George acting as the engineman or plugman. It was while working at the Water-row Pit that George Stephenson first learnt the art of braking an engine. It was at Newburn that he acquired a knowledge of arithmetic and writing in a night-school, set up there in the winter of 1799 by a Scotch dominie, named Andrew Robertson. Newburn Hall, at present used as a pattern-shop for the Steel Works, is a fortified manor-house of thirteenth-century architecture, belonging to the Duke of Northumberland. It is, probably, says Mr. C. J. Bates, the oldest non-ecclesiastical building on the north bank of the Tyne between Newcastle and Aydon Castle. Part of it has been demolished. What remains possesses an arched doorway, some corbelling, traces of a small original window, and a curious zigzag chimney. Its walls are in some places six or seven feet in thickness. A little to the west of Newburn are the Hedwin Streams, which form the boundary of the jurisdiction of the Tyne Conservancy. Here it is that an interesting ceremony takes place once in five years, on "Barge Day," when the Corporation of Newcastle and the Commissioners inspect the river throughout the extent of its tidal flow, from a point in the sea called Spar Hawk, ten miles below Newcastle, to Hedwin Streams, anciently called, seven miles above Newcastle.

On the opposite side of the river, crowning a wooded bank, is RYTON, in the county of Durham. The lofty spire of its interesting early English church, rising above the surrounding foliage, is a picturesque object visible from a great distance.

WYLAM, 9 miles west from Newcastle, is a large uninteresting village, chiefly composed of pitmen's dwellings. The manor of Wylam once belonged to the Monastery of Tynemouth, and came into the possession of the Blackett family in the reign of Charles II. Above the village, on a slope looking south-west, is *Holeyn Hall*, the seat of Major Matthew Charles Wood, a fine stone-built mansion, standing in a park of thirty acres. To the south of Wylam, on the opposite side of the river, is Bradley Vale, finely-wooded, and watered by the Stanley Burn. There is a wooden bridge across the Tyne to Wylam Station, on the Newcastle and Carlisle line. Wylam is also the terminus of a small branch line, once "The Scotswood, Newburn, and Wylam Railway." The light and elegant railway bridge that so picturesquely spans the Tyne here was designed by Mr. T. E. Harrison. The chief object at Wylam is the cottage where George Stephenson was born, July 9th, 1781. It may be reached by following for a few hundred yards the waggon-way that runs from Wylam to Lemington. It is a common, two-storeyed, red-tiled, rubble house, and is known by the name of *High Street House*, originally so called because it stands by the side of what used to be the old riding post-road or street between Newcastle and Hexham. The lower room in the west end of this house was the home of the Stephenson family. The apartment is now, what it was then, an ordinary labourer's dwelling—its walls are unplastered, its floor is of clay, and the bare rafters are exposed overhead. The Wylam waggon-way is one of the oldest in the North of England. It was formed of wooden spars or rails, and was worked by horses, and passing, as it did, in front of the cottage, would be one of the earliest sights which met the infant eyes of George Stephenson. It was the first waggon-way in the district on which the experiment of a locomotive engine was tried. Mr Blackett, the owner of Wylam Colliery, was the first colliery-owner in the North who took an active interest in the locomotive. As early as 1804 he had an engine constructed after Trevithick's patent, but owing to the imperfections in its structure it was never put on the Wylam line, but was used as a fixed engine in a Newcastle iron-foundry. In 1812 he tried a second engine on his waggon-way, which was so designed as to work with a toothed driving-wheel upon a rack-rail. In these experiments he was assisted by William Hedley, the viewer of the colliery, an ingenious man, whom many persons consider to have as good claims to the invention of the steam-engine as a practical means of locomotion as George Stephenson. He it was who demonstrated by successive experiments that the weight of the engine would of itself produce sufficient adhesion to enable it to draw upon a smooth railroad a number of wagons, and thus showed that rack-rails and toothed wheels were unnecessary. George Stephenson, when living at Killingworth, frequently came over to Wylam to see Mr. Blackett's engines at work, gathering suggestions which he was to turn to practical account.

*Prudhoe Castle*, 10½ miles west from Newcastle on the south side of the Tyne, is one of the most celebrated and picturesque of Northumbrian fortresses. It derives its name from the proud eminence on which it stands—a steep promontory which communicates with the adjoining grounds by a narrow neck and pass towards the south. The barony of Prudhoe was bestowed by William the Conqueror on one of his followers, "Robert with the Beard," the first of the powerful family of Umfravilles. For nearly three hundred years, with the exception of a short period when the barony was alienated through the disaffection of Richard de Umfraville in the reign of King John, Prudhoe was the capital seat of this powerful family. The castle is thought to have been founded by Odonel de Umfraville between the years 1161-1182, possibly on the foundation of a former stronghold. Almost impregnable must it have been, for William the Lion, who, in the same campaign, had destroyed and sacked the massive fortresses of Harbottle and Wark, besides reducing Carlisle, attacked it in 1174, and after an unsuccessful siege of three days was compelled to retreat towards Alnwick, where he was taken prisoner by Odonel de Umfraville, Barnard de Baliol, and others. The last feudal baron was Gilbert de Umfraville, who died 1381. His widow, the Countess Maud, became the wife of Henry de Percy, fourth lord of Alnwick, and so Prudhoe came into possession of the Percys, and has continued in the family, though not without interruption of attainders during the Wars of the Roses and the eventful contests which followed the Reformation. Algernon Percy, fourth Duke of Northumberland, was created Baron Prudhoe in 1816. The castle, with its moat and garden, occupies three acres of ground. The situation of the castle is exceedingly strong. The steep escarpment of the ridge, which rises to a height of sixty feet on the north, sufficiently protects it on that side. On the south and east is a deep ravine, through which a small burn runs, and towards the west and south-west a broad moat completes the circuit. The castle overlooks, on the north, luxuriant meadows and corn-fields, and on the south, tall and ancient oak, ash, beech, and sycamore trees, and gardens creeping up to its very walls. Fruit-trees seem to have been growing here from a very early period, for the old chroniclers relate how the baffled Scots, on retiring from the walls of the castle, spitefully stripped the bark off all the apple-trees. From the road on the south the visitor crosses the dam which formerly held back the water of the burn in a deep pool, thus forming a head for the castle mill, the ruins of which may be seen on the left bank of the ravine further down. To reach the castle it is necessary, in the first place, to pass through a pointed gateway of Decorated date, ribbed and vaulted within, and flanked by two thick lateral walls projecting about twelve feet. We then proceed along an open passage eighty feet long, between two battlemented walls, in each of which there is a doorway opening right and left upon the scarp of the castle ditch, whereby an enemy undermining the walls might be attacked in front. The main Gatehouse is a rectangular building with a barrel-vaulted passage beneath it. The basement storey is Norman. An outer stone staircase ascends from the court-yard to the first floor, which is of early English date, and contains the chapel of St. Mary, 25 feet long and 15 feet broad. Here is "the earliest known oriel window (1300), one of the simplest and most graceful pieces of work of its kind"—to quote Mr. Freeman. It is projected on corbels, and composed of two lancet lights on the east, and one on the south-east. A drapery of ivy on the outside lends to it additional beauty. In the south-west corner of the chapel is an oblique window—a squint—flanking the barbican. The curtain walls which surround the base-court are from 20 to 30 feet high on the outside, and 10 to 12 feet high within, and are pierced in various places by cruciform loops. At the south-west and north-west angles are the remains of loop-holed bastion towers erected in the Decorated period. That on the north-west contains chambers so low in height that the defendants could not possibly stand upright in them. The Keep stands at the west end of the court, much obscured by the modern residence of the duke's agent, which is attached to it on the east. This, the strongest part of a Norman castle, is rectangular, 42 feet north and east by 60 feet south and west, and about 65 feet high. The walls are about 10 feet thick, and for the most part in ruins. There were probably turrets at the four angles, of which the south-western one remains. In the south wall near the south-east angle are the remains of a bell stair, which seems to have ascended from the base to the roof. In the north-west angle at the first floor level commenced a mural staircase, of which forty-two steps remain. In one of the chambers of the basement storey are the remains of a fire-place. A small bridge, with curiously-shaped arches, over the burn to the south of the castle, is believed to be one of the earliest in the north. In the village of Prudhoe, on the brow of the hill, is a farm-house built from the ruins of an old chapel. A doorway with early English mouldings, walls of great thickness, and the shape of the building testify to its ancient character. It is supposed to owe its origin to Richard de Umfraville, who, on regaining possession of his lands, which he had forfeited by joining the barons against King John, celebrated the event by many gifts to the church.

One mile west from Prudhoe Castle is *Cherryburn House*, the birthplace of the engravers, Thomas and John Bewick. The latter died at the early age of thirty-five, though not before giving abundant instances of great artistic powers. It is with his more celebrated brother that Cherryburn is associated. In his memoir he thus describes it :—"Cherryburn House, the place of my nativity, and which for many years my eyes beheld with cherished delight, is situated on the south side of the Tyne, in the county of Northumberland, a short distance from the river. The house, stables, etc., stand on the west side of a little dean, at the foot of which runs a burn. The dean was embellished with a number of cherry and plum-trees, which were terminated by a garden on the north. Near the house were two large ash-trees growing from one root, and, at a little distance, stood another of the same kind. At the south end of the premises was a spring well, overhung by a large hawthorn bush, behind which was a holly hedge, and further away was a little boggy dean with underwood and trees of different kinds. . . . To the westward, adjoining the house, lay the common or fell, which extended some few miles in length, and was of various breadths." This birthplace of genius was a thatched cottage, containing three apartments and a dairy or milk-house on the ground floor and a chamber above. The east end of this has been pulled down and the rest converted into a byre. Thus the place has lost some of its charm. Below the house lies the old orchard, still answering to Bewick's description of it. Here may be seen the grave-stone of his father and mother, which, having by some accident been broken, was brought here and a larger one erected in Ovingham Churchyard. With such beautiful scenery around him as may be found in the neighbourhood of Cherryburn and Ovingham, it is not surprising that the great wood-engraver became a lover and observer of Nature, reproducing in his wood-cuts the scenes he loved so well.

OVINGHAM stands on the north bank of the Tyne, 11 miles west of Newcastle. It is connected with Prudhoe station by a wooden bridge. This quiet, quaint, old-fashioned village is supposed to be of some antiquity. Its name signifies, we are told by some, "The home of the Offings, or sons and daughters of Offa," some Saxon settler ; just as Eltringham, a little to the west, on the south side of the water, was once the abode of the Eldrings, or offspring of Eldric, or Eldred. Sidney Gibson thinks the name of the village may be derived from Ovatio—a petty triumph upon some victory obtained over the Britons by their conquerors.

*The Church dedicated to St. Mary the Virgin* is an ancient cruciform structure, erected on the site of an early Saxon building about the middle of the eleventh century. The low square tower is part of the original edifice. It bears the strongest resemblance to the early towers of Bywell, St. Andrews, Corbridge, Warden, Bolam, and Billingham, which are of similar date. The characteristics of this tower are well described by Mr. C. C. Hodges—"It rises from the ground without any plinth or base-course, has no buttresses at its angles, and the superficies of the walls is not broken by any set-offs or string-courses until the belfry stage is reached. Here is a plain unmoulded projecting course of thin stones. In the lower portion of the west side 'Roman Wall stones' have clearly been made use of. Many of the quoins have cramp and lewis holes. . . . The disposition of the windows in the lower portion is worthy of remark. These are four in number, and are in no case opposite to one another. Supposing the tower to have been originally divided into five storeys, then each of the four storeys was lighted by a single window. The lowest window is on the south side; the next on the west side; the next, on the east, looks into the nave of the church; the next is on the south again, and is about twice as large each way as the other three. Judging from the disposition of these windows, it is a reasonable inference that this tower was built for purposes of habitation and defence." The four double-lighted windows in the belfry stage, with their rude balusters, their through capitals, rubble borderings, and tympanums pierced with a single circular opening, are eminently characteristic of Saxon work. Beneath the tower, against the west wall, is the vault of several members of the Bewick family, surrounded by iron palisades. Three mural tablets fixed to the wall above are inscribed as follows:—"In memory of John Bewick, engraver, who died December 5th, 1795, aged 35 years. His ingenuity as an artist was excelled only by his conduct as a man." "The burial place of Thomas Bewick, engraver, of Newcastle. Isabella, his wife, died 1st February, 1826, aged 72 years. Thomas Bewick, died 8th of November, 1828, aged 75 years." On the south side of the church is a tablet erected to the memory of another artist, Robert Johnson, a pupil of Bewick's, who, after showing great talent, died in his youth in Perthshire.

The porch is of fourteenth-century date. Above it is a sun-dial, placed there in 1804; and within it are ten early grave-covers, bearing incised crosses, plain and floriated, two of the latter being of elegant design. The church is entered through a richly-moulded early English doorway. The west end of the nave is part of the early church. The rest of the building eastward is early English in character. Aisles were added to the nave about 1378. Against the west wall is placed an original altar slab, marked with five dedication crosses. The transepts are remarkable for their length, similar in their design and details to those of Hexham Abbey, though on a smaller scale. There is an aisle on the west side of them, the arches of which were taken down and rebuilt at the same time as the additions were being made to the nave. The respond corbels against the north and south walls are of considerable beauty, that on the south being ornamented with two vertical strips of dog-tooth moulding. A beautiful bit of carving of this date is built in behind the pulpit. In the south wall of the south transept are two pointed arches near the ground, which appear to belong to a double doorway, now built up, and in the east side is a piscina, indicating the former existence of a chantry altar. Some of the stones used in the construction of this part of the church are Roman. The capital of the column upon which the arcades of the south aisle of the nave and south transept meet is very beautifully carved. "An isolated carved capital," says Mr. C. C. Hodges, "is not uncommonly seen in ancient churches, and is supposed to be the gift to the building of the master mason or chief carver, his 'sign manual,' upon which he displayed his greatest skill." The chancel is a fine specimen of bold, plain, early English work, very early in the style. It is lighted by nine lofty windows, three on each side, and a beautifully-proportioned triplet at the east end. In the angle formed by the walls of the transept and chancel is a 'low-side' or 'leper' window of lancet form. Two early trefoiled sedilia remain in the south wall of the chancel. Some fine slabs lie on the floor. The chancel arch is plain, and of fourteenth century date. There are several stained-glass windows in the church. One of them is to the memory of the Rev. Charles James Fuller, M.A., vicar of the parish, who was struck with paralysis on Easter Sunday, 1873, whilst preaching a sermon in the church on the memorable text, "Why seek ye the living among the dead." The font is ancient, of sixteenth century date. There are three bells in the tower, two of them belonging to pre-Reformation times. Two persons were publicly excommunicated by Archdeacon Sharp as late as 1769. The parsonage house, which has a pretty little fourteenth century window on the east side, occupies the site of a cell of Black Canons, founded here about 1378 by Henry Percy, Earl of Northumberland, subordinate to the Augustinian Priory at Hexham. Two brethren and a superior, styled "The Master of Ovingham," resided here. The last person who held this position of master was evidently a member of the church militant, for, on the suppression of monasteries, the Royal Commissioners, when at Hexham, found "the gates and doors fast shut, and a canon called the master of Ovingham, belonging to the same hous, being in harnes with a bowe bentt with arrowes, accompanyed with diverse other persons, all standing upon the leads and walls of the hous and steple, whiche master of Ovingham answeryd these words hereunder written, 'We be xxii brethren in this hous, and we shall dye all or that shall ye have this hous.'" On the terrace before the vicarage are inscribed stones marking the heights of the great floods of 1771 and 1815. The mother of George Stephenson was a native of Ovingham, being the second daughter of Robert Carr, a dyer in the village. The Carrs were for several generations the owners of a house adjoining the churchyard, and the family tombstone may still be seen standing against the east end of the chancel underneath the centre lancet window. However interesting the village and its old church may be to the antiquary, it is the memory of Thomas Bewick that invests it with its greatest charm to the casual visitor. Here, in the natural environment of beauty, was unfolded the genius of the great wood-engraver. "As soon as I filled all the blank places in my books," he says in his memoirs, "I had recourse at all spare times to the gravestones and the floor of the church porch with a bit of chalk, to give vent to this propensity of mind of figuring whatever I had seen. At that time I had never heard of the word 'drawing,' nor did I know of any other paintings besides the king's arms in the church, and the signs in Ovingham of the Black Bull, the White Horse, the Salmon, and the Hounds and Hare. I always thought I could make a far better hunting scene than the latter; the others were beyond my hand." Inn—The White Swan.

A little north is *Whittle Dene*, a beautifully wooded dell that has the reputation of being haunted by fairies. The burn that flows romantically through it to the Tyne is peculiarly soft and clear, and is celebrated for its power of bleaching linen-cloth. About a quarter of a mile above the water mill, and twenty yards on the east of the burn, is a fine specimen of the larch, whose girth at the height of 5 feet from the ground is 9 feet 3 inches. It is 103 feet in height. On the north side of the road that runs from Heddon-on-the-Wall to Corbridge and crosses the dene is *Nafferton Tower*, an unfinished fortress commenced by Philip de Ulecote, Constable of Chinon, and forester of Northumberland in the reign of King John. This Norman baron, presuming on the influence he possessed with the Crown, had proceeded so far with the erection of a castle on his manor here, when Richard de Umfraville complained of the injury that this rising fortress was to his castle of Prudhoe. The Crown immediately issued a writ to Philip de Ulecote, commanding him to desist from his building operations. Strange to say, the work was never recommenced, and the castle still remains in the same state as it was when abandoned by the workmen of the thirteenth century. There remain the walls of the keep, 20 feet square, and two outer baileys of moderate dimensions, placed on the summit of a gentle slope. In course of time this ruinous hold became known as "Lang Lonkin's Castle," for here a gigantic freebooter of that name is said to have resided, to the terror of the neighbourhood. A fragmentary ballad, taken down from the recitation of an old woman at Ovington some years ago, commemorates one of Lonkin's crimes. Through the treachery of a serving-maid, named Orange, he gained admission to Welton Hall during the absence of the good man, and murdered the lady and child.

"The lord said to his ladie,
As he mounted his horse,
'Beware of Long Lonkin
That lies in the moss.'

The lord said to his ladie,
  As he rode away,
'Beware of Long Lonkin
  That lies in the clay.'

'What care I for Lonkin,
  Or any of his gang;
My doors are all shut,
  And my windows penned in.'

There are six little windows,
  And they were all shut;
But one little window,
  And that was forgot.

. . . .

And at that little window
  Long Lonkin crept in.

'Where's the Lord of the Hall?'
  Says the Lonkin;
'He's gone up to London,'
  Says Orange to him.

'Where's the Ladies of the Hall?'
  Says the Lonkin;
'They're up in their chambers,'
  Says Orange to him.

'How shall we get them down?'
  Says the Lonkin;
'Prick the babe in the cradle,'
  Says Orange to him."

The cry of the child brings the mother down, and she is killed by Lonkin, and then dragged by him into the dene, and thrown into a deep pool in the burn, which may be seen to this day, in confirmation of the story, under the name of "Lang Lonkin's Hole." It is said that the terrible Lonkin hanged himself, or fell from a huge tree overlooking the well, and that his skull lay knocking about the castle for some time. His ghost, however, continued to haunt the district, to keep green the memory of his name, and a mother at the present day has but to shake a bunch of keys and call out, "There's Lang Lonkin!" to recall her wandering offspring at nightfall to the shelter of home. Some relics have been found in the ruins, among which were a brace of silver-mounted pistols. Higher up the burn a small cascade falls into a deep pool, called "The Whirl Dub." The local legend describes the enormous depth of this "dub," and tells circumstantially how, when Lang Lonkin was hard pressed, he sewed his rich booty in a bull's hide, and cast it in here, where it still remains below, awaiting some lucky adventurer to make a fortunate haul. The same story is told at Cyper's Linn, how the treasure was nearly recovered on one occasion, but irrevocably lost through the profanity of the adventurous countryman. "Bogle Burn," which joins the streamlet further up, has no doubt some connection with Lonkin.

Permission to enter Whittle Dene must be obtained from George Hinde, Esq., Ovington.

# HEXHAM SECTION.

## HEXHAM.

THE district of which Hexham is the centre comprises all that the most enthusiastic of antiquaries and the most devoted of nature-worshippers could desire. Roman stations, Saxon churches, mediæval castles, and pele-houses are to be found in the midst of scenery that for beauty and variety is unsurpassed in the north of England. It is a veritable land of Beulah to the modern pilgrim travelling from the great industrial towns of Tyneside. Hexham itself is a picturesque old town, charmingly situated on a terrace or plateau overlooking the wide and rich valley of the Tyne. It is naturally defended on its east and north sides, and partially so on its west, whilst at no great distance it is enclosed by an amphitheatre of hills. A lovely environment of luxuriant nurseries, gardens, shrubberies, plantations, and fields of the richest fertility complete the natural advantages of Hexham. As in all ancient towns, the streets are narrow and irregular, the houses quaint and picturesque, and above these, draped in the neutral greys of the Past, rise the three most prominent buildings—the Church, the Moot Hall, and the Keep. The antiquity of Hexham is very great. In pre-historic times it would be of importance, if the surmise of some geologists be correct, that the valley from above Warden Hill to the sand-banks east of Corbridge was at one time a large lake, for then the site of Hexham would stand out as a promontory, and as such would hardly be disregarded by the primitive inhabitants. Dr. Bruce ascribes a Roman origin to Hexham, and the large number of tooled stones that compose the crypt beneath the Abbey Church, with many others that have been found with inscriptions upon them built into old houses, favour this opinion ; and further confirmation may be found from the fact that on the ground being opened in the vicinity of the manor office, Mr. Fairless discovered a connected chain of earthenware pipes, of manifest Roman workmanship, lying in *situ*, and intended, to all appearance, for the conveyance of water. Other writers, however, consider that there are but slender grounds for believing that Hexham was a Roman station. Perhaps the real explanation of the case may be that two or three prominent Roman officials had large villas here. In Saxon times it was a place of great magnificence and magnitude. The early forms of the name of the town are

Halgutstadt, Hangustald, Hagustald, Hextildesham, Hextoldesham, Hexam, etc., derived from its position at the confluence of small burns, anciently known as the Halgut and the Hextol, now the Cockshaw Burn and the Cowgarth Burn. From the former it was called Halgutstadt, the town on the holy burn; and from the latter Hextoldesham, the homestead on the Hextol. It was from St. Wilfrid, however, that it derived its episcopal dignity, its splendour and celebrity. This eminent ecclesiastic, born about the year 634, and educated in the monastery of Lindisfarne, had visited Lyons and Rome, and seen there the wonders of sacred architecture. The splendour and pomp of the foreign churches powerfully impressed his haughty and ambitious mind, and he returned to England full of great projects for the glory of the Romish Church, and in every way equipped to be the most magnificent church-builder of his time. Appointed to the see of York, he repaired and beautified the Cathedral, and built the church of Ripon. He had the government of nine abbeys, and lived in almost kingly splendour, being served at his table, it is said, out of gold. He was in high favour at the court of Ecgfrid, and Queen Etheldreda gave him for ecclesiastical purposes the land which had formed a portion of her dowry—viz., the district known as Hexhamshire, including the parishes of Hexham, St. John Lee, and Allendale.

He then founded a monastery, in which he most probably placed Benedictine monks, and built the church of St. Andrew, which eclipsed by its magnificence all his other works. This was the fifth church of stone that was reared in Saxon times, its predecessors being Withern, York, Lincoln, and Ripon. What its splendours were may be gathered from the descriptions given by Eddius, who wrote in the same age as that in which the saint lived, and Prior Pichard, who lived in the reign of Henry II. The latter says:—"He began his church by laying foundations and forming crypts and subterranean oratories with winding passages made with great labour. The walls were of immense height and length, divided into three storeys, and supported on polished columns formed of squared stones. Even the capitals and bases of the columns and the arch of the sanctuary were adorned with historical and imaginary and various symbolical figures carved in relief upon the stones, and were decorated with pictures and colours of great and wonderful variety. The body of the church was surrounded with aisles and porches, which, with wonderful and inexplicable artifice, connected both above and below with winding staircases in towers. . . . So the chronicles and ancient histories bear witness that among nine monasteries of which St. Wilfrid was the founder and patron, and of all others throughout England, this church was deemed the first for workmanship, design, and unequalled beauty; and, lastly, that in those days nothing equal to it existed on this side of the Alps." St. Wilfrid obtained for his church the right of sanctuary, which extended for one mile round it. The outer boundaries were marked by four crosses, one to each of the four cardinal points of the compass. He also built a church in honour of St. Mary the Virgin, which stood near to the wall of the mother church. When Queen Etheldreda took the veil and retired into the Abbey of Coldingham, the king married Ermenburga, who hated St. Wilfrid, and persuaded the king to curtail the power of the haughty prelate, the result being that in a Synod under Archbishop Theodore the immense diocese of Wilfrid was divided into the four bishoprics of York, Hexham, Lindisfarne, and Withern, or Candida Casa, in Galloway. Wilfrid travelled to Rome and appealed to the Pope, and, though vigorously opposed by Cœnwald, the envoy and advocate of the Archbishop, obtained a decree of restitution. Armed with the Pope's mandate, he returned to England, but was seized by the king's orders and cast into prison. At the expiration of nine months he was released and banished from Northumbria. He took refuge among the inhabitants of the southern portions of England, and while there founded the monastery of Bosenham. In the meantime a see was created at Hagustald in 681, and Trumbriht was made first bishop. He was succeeded in 684 by Cuthbert, who made an exchange of the diocese of Hagustald for that of Lindisfarne with Eata, who died in 685. The next bishop, St. John of Beverley, held the see but one year, resigning in favour of Wilfrid, who, on the death of Ecgfrid, returned and was reinstated by King Alfrid. For five years this somewhat contentious bishop resided in a state of comparative peace at Hexham, but being called upon to resign possession of Ripon that it might be made the seat of a bishop, he refused to comply, and, in 692 A.D., was driven into exile, and his see of Hexham was conferred once more upon St. John of Beverley. For nine years Wilfrid dwelt in the kingdom of Mercia under the protection of Ethelred, and, finally, after another journey to Rome in his seventieth year, and an endless amount of disputation, he was permitted, on the death of Alfrid, to retain his favourite monasteries of Ripon and Hexham, and four years afterwards, in 709, died in peace at his monastery of Oundle, near Stamford, and was buried in the Church of St. Peter at Ripon.

Wilfrid was succeeded by Acca, who had been a faithful companion in his wanderings and a useful coadjutor in the administration of his see. This worthy prelate enjoyed the friendship of Bede, who dedicated to him his "Hexameron" and his "Commentary on St. Mark's Gospel," which were written at Acca's suggestion, as was also a similar treatise on Luke. He added many costly decorations to the church, procured relics for its shrines, and improved the choral services of the church. After fulfilling the office of a bishop for twenty-four years he was deposed from his see for reasons which have not been stated, and died in 740. His successors were Frithbert, 744; Alchmund, 767; Tilbert, 781; Ethelbert, 789; Eadred, 797; Eanbert, 800; and Tidfirth, 806-21. With the last-named bishop the diocese of Hexham came to an end. The Church of St. Andrew, though it had lost its dignity as a cathedral, continued as a monastic church under Eardulf, Bishop of Lindisfarne, who afterwards set up his see at Chester-le-Street. On the removal of this see to Durham, Hexham was included in that diocese for 106 years. It was then taken away by Henry I. in a dispute he had with Bishop Flambard and given to the see of York, under which it remained till January 1837, when Hexhamshire was restored to the see of Durham.

In 875 the beautiful church and monastery that Wilfrid had built, containing St. Acca's books and vestments, shrines full of relics, and his richly-decorated altars, were destroyed by fire by the Danes under Haldane, and remained in a dilapidated condition for more than two hundred years, when, in 1113, they were restored by Thomas II., Archbishop of York. King John visited Hexham on three occasions—viz., in 1202, in 1208, and in 1212.

In 1296 the Scots made a destructive inroad into England, plundering and burning every town, village, and church on their route. The restored buildings of Hexham were burnt down by the northern barbarians. They also set fire to the grammar school, wherein, at the time, were two hundred scholars, who all perished in the flames. In this conflagration all the charters, monuments, and deeds of the monastery were consumed. In 1297 William Wallace visited Hexham and destroyed all that the men of Galloway had left. Between the years 1312-1318 the town was repeatedly ravaged by the Scottish marauders, and the sufferings of the inhabitants and canons were augmented by a famine which desolated Tynedale. In 1346 the church was plundered by David of Scotland, but the town was spared. The Wars of the Roses affected Hexhamshire, and a battle was fought on the 8th May 1464 between the Lancastrians, under Henry Beaufort, Duke of Somerset, and the Yorkists, under Lord Montacute, resulting in the defeat of the former, and the capture of Somerset, who was afterwards beheaded. The priors at this period did much to restore and embellish the church, and with this work the names of Rowland Leschman and Thomas Smithson especially are associated.

The rising known as the "Pilgrimage of Grace," the object of which was to prevent the dissolution and destruction of monastic houses, may be said to have commenced at Hexham, when the canons of Hexham under the Master of Ovingham resisted by force of arms the Royal Commissioners in 1536. This rebellion was suppressed by the Duke of Norfolk, and many of the monks and canons, according to the instructions of Henry VIII., were "tyed uppe, without further delaye or ceremony, to the terrible example of others." The site and demesnes of the priory were granted to Sir Reginald Carnaby in 1538, and then to Sir Christopher Hatton, from whom they passed successively into the amilies of the Fenwicks, the Blacketts, and the Beaumonts.

"Hexham, writes De Foe, "is famous, or rather infamous, for having the first blood drawn at it in the war against their Prince by the Scots, in King Charles the First's time." On March 9th, 1761, a serious riot, in which forty-five persons were killed and three hundred wounded, took place in Hexham, originating in the great dissatisfaction felt at the mode of electing men for the militia by ballot instead of being hired by the landowners as formerly. The town was connected by rail with Blaydon in 1835. Hexham was formerly celebrated for its gloves, and as many as 23,504 dozen pairs of gloves used to be made and exported sixty years ago. Tanners, glove manufacturers, and hatters were the chief tradesmen of the town; but modern competition has reduced their number very considerably, and the commercial importance of the town is due now more to its extensive market gardens than its manufactories. Though exposed so much to Scottish raids, Hexham does not appear to have been walled. Its streets, both in appearance and name, bear evidences of antiquity. The town is divided, roughly speaking, by a long street stretching, with a gradual ascent, from east to west. It is named in its several parts Priestpopple, supposed to have been the part allotted for the residence of the people or servants and dependants of the priory; Battle Hill, the scene of an encounter between the English and the Scots during the Edwardian wars; and Hencotes, suggestive of the place where the monks kept their poultry. Anent the etymology of this word Mr. A. B. Wright has a rather comic note—"How fond," he says, "must the monks have been of conventual purity and propriety! the hens kept at one end of the town and the cocks at the other! for surely Hencotes and Cockshaw bear some relation to each other." The Market Place, to which most of the streets converge, is an irregular space of some interest both to the lover of the picturesque and the antiquary. Many of the oldest houses, however, have been rebuilt or removed, rendering it more commodious though less picturesque. On the west side is the eastern end of the Abbey Church, and on the south is a covered market with piazzas, erected by Sir Walter Calverley Blackett in 1766. During the hirings in May and November this square presents a very animated appearance, and the spectator will obtain a good deal of amusement from the scene. The old pant that stood here with the inscription, "Ex dono Roberti Allgood Armigeri, anno D.M. 1703," has been swept away. The north-west angle of the Market Place opens from Gilligate, or St. Giles's Street, so-called from St. Giles' Hospital, to which it leads. Together with the Row and Bull Bank, this street forms a steep descent to the north. There is a fine recreation ground or park—the Seal—which once formed part of the abbey grounds.

THE ABBEY CHURCH (once the cathedral) of St. Andrew.—This venerable structure, which is said to form a very text-book of the early English period of pointed church architecture, has suffered much from "destructive restoration." Vandals have impaired its Gothic beauty. The east end was restored in a barbarous manner, and the beautiful fourteenth-century chapels under the great east window demolished. Looked at from the outside, the church has a noble weather-stained appearance that the few modern additions do little to disfigure. It is surmounted by a tower that rises but 35 feet above the ridge of the roof, and seems somewhat low in comparison with the height of the body of the building. Below the plain, embattled parapet, and between the buttresses that enclose the angles, an arcade of five members is carried along each face of the tower, two of the openings being pierced as windows, the other three remaining blank. The church was no doubt originally intended to have been cruciform, but for some cause or other the nave was never completed, and at present we have merely the chancel and transepts.

The entrance to the church is at the south end of the south transept, which is the longest remaining portion, 156 feet in length. The light and elegant arches that sustain the tower, with the tall clustered pillars on which they rest, at once impress the visitor with a sense of height and proportion. In the south transept are some Roman and Mediæval antiquities—viz., two Roman altars of large size, of which one only bears an inscription; a sculptured slab, of Roman workmanship, discovered on the 19th September 1881 by Mr. Charles Clement Hodges, when making an excavation under the floor of the slype, with a view to finding a crypt which was said to exist there. It represents a well-armed cavalry soldier, with a standard in his hand and plumes in his helmet, riding over the crouching nude body of a repulsive-looking barbarian. In a sunken panel below is an inscription, rendered as follows by Dr. Bruce:—"To the gods the shades. Flavinus, a horse-soldier of the cavalry regiment of Petriana, standard-bearer of the troop of Candidus, twenty-five years of age, having served seven years in the army, is laid here." It may have formed, he says, the front of a cippus, in which were deposited the ashes of the young man, and probably belongs to the second century. The eastern aisle of this transept contains a curiously-carved Saxon tombstone and a beautiful oratory, formerly considered to be the Shrine of Prior Richard, but now understood to be that of Prior Rowland Leschman, who died in 1491. His effigy, resting on an altar-tomb, represents him vested as an Austin Canon, with long coat, tunic, and cloak, the hood of which is drawn over his face. The basement of the shrine is of stone, rudely carved on the one side with various heads, and on the other with some grotesque figures representing St. George, the fox in the garb of a monk preaching to the geese, the thumb-screw, the nightmare, etc.

The lattice, divided into seven compartments, exhibits the most delicate flamboyant tracery; and the roof, divided into eight compartments, is ornamented with carved bosses, the centre one representing the figure of an angel holding a shield with Prior Leschman's monogram upon it. Inside the shrine is a stone altar, quite perfect, bearing the five consecration crosses. Behind it is a painted subject in four panels; the upper ones represent St. Peter with the keys, St. Andrew holding the cross, and St. Paul with the sword; the lower one represents the figure of the Saviour crowned with thorns, while around him are the cords and scourges, the ladder, the spear, and the sponge tied to a reed, the dice, etc.

The visitor will observe a peculiarity in this part of the building which does not occur in any other conventual church in England. The slype, or passage from the cloister garth to the conventual cemetery, is within the church instead of immediately to the south of it. The massive stone staircase which formerly led to the dormitory of the canons (now destroyed), and was called the Night-stair, will also be noticed with interest, as it has been considered one of the finest examples of its kind in the country. On the platform at the top are two doorways, one opening on to a spiral flight of steps leading to the roof, the other opening on to a small and ancient room, now used as a vestry for the church, but in former times "most probably used by the man who watched during stated hours for any one fleeing to the church for sanctuary, as its position would command the town and the Market Place, across which anyone must have gone when running to the church from any of the four sanctuary crosses, and seeking to enter the precincts of the Priory by the east gate."

The North Transept, with its vaulted eastern aisle and elaborately-pierced and arcaded western wall, will, to the lover of beautiful architecture, prove one of the most interesting portions of the church. The north wall presents a contrast to the south wall of the transept, the place of the balcony and stone staircase being supplied by a gallery that is carried round in the wall but open to the church. In this transept are many interesting monuments which have been collected from different parts of the church. Where the walls of the transept and choir aisles meet is a beautiful monumental arch flanked by two canopies. A large slab beneath has its upper side entirely covered with a floriated cross of exquisite workmanship, consisting of a vine stem with its leaves and fruit. Tradition ascribes this elaborate altar-tomb to King Elfwold, who was murdered on the 23rd September 788, by one of his nobles, at Sytlechester or Cilchester (probably Cilurnum). As the date of it, however, is not much earlier than 1270, it can only be assumed that the monument was erected to his memory by the canons of the thirteenth century. Adjoining this tomb is a much-defaced effigy of a lady unknown, whose head-dress is a wimple of the fashion worn in the reign of Edward I. Near it are two knightly effigies. The earlier of them, in full armour with a sleeveless surcoat, once covered the tomb of Sir Thomas Devilstone, who died in 1290, and appears to have always lain where it does now—viz., in the north transept aisle, and at the north end, where it is believed the Devilstone family had a chantry. The other bears the Umfreville arms, and represents, no doubt, Sir Gilbert de Umfreville, Earl of Angus, who died in 1307. He is completely attired in mail, and the legs being crossed, indicate that he had been a crusader. A doorway in the north-west angle of this transept leads to the clerestory and tower. Built up in the top of the staircase at the north-west angle of the tower is a Roman altar finely carved in relief. In the belfry, especially on the east wall, are distinct marks of fire, the stones being much calcined and split with the heat.

The vestry contains some interesting specimens of the ancient wood-work of the church. On the partition within it are full-length paintings of the seven bishops of Hexham who were afterwards honoured as saints. Here may also be seen an iron-bound and double-locked alms-box.

Separating the choir from the transept is a richly-carved rood-screen, which was erected, according to an inscription on its cornice, by Prior Thomas Smithson, 1491-1524.—"Orate pro anima domin

Thomae Smithson, prioris hujus ecclesiae qui fecit hoc opus." On the four centre panels at the top are some time-bedimmed paintings from the "Dance of Death" wherein are seen the Cardinal, Monarch, Bishop, and Pope.

The services of the parish are held in the choir, which, in spite of the disfiguring restorations, retains its early English character. It consists of six bays or arches, having a total length of 92 feet 10 inches, and having the three great divisions in height of main arcade, or ground storey, triforium, or blind-storey, and clerestory. The roof is supported by huge blocks of oak, forming plain low sharp-pointed arches. The idea of height is suggested by the triple vaulting shafts that rise from the string-course below the triforium. Traces of the Norman influences may be seen in the mouldings of the columns, which belong to the Transitional period—1145 to 1190. The principal architectural feature of the choir is the clerestory, which is of unusual design, and is said to have but one parallel in England, that of Romsey Abbey in Hampshire. Each opening is composed of three arches, which are stilted. A gallery in the thickness of the wall traverses the clerestory. The arrangement of the arches, with their supporting shafts in the three divisions of the choir, the semi-circular ones in the middle, and pointed ones above and below them, affords a contrast that is decidedly effective. In the south side of the choir are some inscribed grave-covers, commemorating deceased canons of Hexham who died during the twelfth and thirteenth centuries. A monument beside these, bearing the inscription, "Johannes Malerbe jacet hic," is said by Mr. Wright to be the oldest in the church, and to commemorate perhaps an immediate follower of the Norman William. The most ancient and probably the most interesting object to the visitor is the Frithstool, or Sanctuary Chair, which stands to the south of the communion table. It is the centre of the sanctuary, which extended a mile round the church. The outer boundaries were marked by four crosses—one to each of the four cardinal points of the compass. The sites of two are known from the names Maiden Cross to the west and White Cross fields on the east; that to the north was in the river. Heavy fines were imposed by the church on anyone who dared to seize the fugitive within the limits of the sanctuary, being proportioned to the distance of the fugitive from the church; but if anyone seized a malefactor when seated within the stool of peace, the offence was not redeemable with any sum. The privileges of sanctuary were much curtailed in the reign of Henry VIII., and finally abolished in that of James I., 1624. This venerable relic is ornamented on the arms with bands of twisted knot-work, and on the front with incised lines following the outline of the chair. It is believed by some writers to have been the "cathedra" of the see of Hagustald, wherein the bishops were consecrated and perhaps some of the kings of Northumbria crowned.

On the north wall of the choir hangs the helmet of Sir J. Fenwick, killed in the battle of Marston Moor, 1644. His skull, which formerly was preserved in the Manor Office, has been removed to Newcastle. Scott, in his "Rokeby," refers to an old custom of hanging up a glove in this church as a challenge :—

> "Edmund, thy years were scarcely mine,
> When challenging the clans of Tyne,
> To bring their best my brand to prove,
> O'er Hexham's altar hung my glove ;
> But Tynedale nor in tower nor town,
> Held champion meet to take it down."

In the recess, which is the commencement of the nave, stands the baptismal font of a date coeval with the building. Close to the south-west pier of the tower, and entered by means of a trap-door and a ladder, is the Saxon crypt, discovered in 1726, which no visitor should forget to see, as it is the only portion remaining of the church that St. Wilfrid built, and with the exception of a similar subterranean oratory at Ripon, also built by St. Wilfrid, is unique in the country. It consists of two chambers, the central one of which measures 7 feet 9 inches by 13 feet 6 inches and 8 feet 9 inches high, and has a plain arched roof of semi-circular form. Passages lead to these apartments, but the one on the north is now blocked by the north-west pier of the tower. Curious lamp niches, mere hollow cups for holding tallow and a wick, will be noticed in the walls of the crypt. This ancient structure is of special interest, because it is entirely composed of Roman masonry. Many of the walling stones are fine examples of the broached tooling, and several finely-carved fragments of elaborate capitals and cornices are built up into the walls. A roofing slab in the north passage is of considerable historical importance, for the name of the emperor Geta has been erased from the inscription, as in all similar monuments, in accordance with the instructions of Marcus Aurelius after the murder of his brother.

In the old graveyard, called the Campy Hill, on the west side of the north transept, there was found, in 1832, a bronze vessel, shaped like a bucket, containing about 9000 Saxon stycas of bronze, which had been struck during the reigns of the kings of Northumbria—Redulf, Edred, and Ethelred, and Vigmund and Eanbald, Archbishops of York. Nine years later 2000 more were found in the same grave, having fallen from the bucket on the occasion of the first discovery. They are supposed to have been deposited here by the treasurer of the church on the arrival of the Danes in 875. South of the church are the remains of a low vaulted vestibule to the west of the Chapter House, which is now entirely gone. Traces of the lavatory erected about 1280 remain, and some fine ornamented tracery covers the wall behind the trough. The large open space on the west was formerly occupied by the cloisters, in the north wall of which is a wide-arched recess once filled with the carrells or reading-closets of the canons. Of the Prior's House, successively occupied by the Carnabys, Fenwicks, Blacketts, and Beaumonts, and now used as a dwelling-house and police station, very little original work remains, as it has been burnt and rebuilt more than once. In the precinct wall of the Priory on the north is the ancient gateway, not later than 1160 in date. A small bridge of thirteenth-century date spans the Cowgarth burn in the garden of Hexham House.

Portions of the old Church of St. Mary's, built by St. Wilfrid, a little to the south-east of the Abbey Church still remain incorporated in the houses on the south side of the Market Place, behind the shambles. In the house and shop of Mr. Laing, baker, in the meal market, are two of the columns of the nave with their capitals and bases ; more are to be seen, with one arch complete, in the rooms over the archway opening into St. Mary's Chare.

Two ancient buildings on the east side of the Market Place, known as the Moot Hall and the Manor Office, surrounded, in all probability, at one time by a wall, formed portions of the defensive works of the town. THE MOOT HALL, so named because it was used for holding all courts pertaining to the Regality of Hexham, is a strongly-constructed square building, with a passage or covered barbican beneath, defended by two gateway towers. The external stone staircase on the east side was added about the middle of the seventeenth century, probably on the site of a forebuilding similar to that of the Keep at Newcastle. On the upper or third floor was the great hall, a fine apartment, 45 feet 7 inches by 20 feet, and 20 feet in height, open to the roof, which was formerly much higher than at present. The curious range of corbels at the north end of this hall is supposed to have supported a hanging-gallery or platform, which, in conjunction with the gateway towers, would render the defence of the building very complete. Around three sides of the building machicolations are carried, between which are spaces for hurling down missiles and shooting arrows upon the heads of an attacking party below. The town stocks, which formerly stood in the Market Place, are preserved in one of the chambers. Seventy yards to the south-east is the other tower, once the principal stronghold of the place, known by the name of THE MANOR OFFICE, because it was used probably from the time of Elizabeth till the year 1868 for the transaction of all business connected with the manor of Hexham. It is a grim and massive structure, with long ranges of overhanging corbels, and walls in some places as much as eleven feet thick. It was once the prison of the Regality, but its gloomy dungeons underground have been long since disused. From the many stones in its masonry, bearing marks of Roman handling, it is surmised that the tower was built on the site of an earlier fortress, the materials of which had been obtained from some Roman station or villa. The skull of Sir John Fenwick, already referred to, was formerly preserved here, and the popular belief is that whenever it has been taken away it has always returned of its own accord. An object of interest here is an old oak mantel-beam, carved with figures of a man's head and rude coats-of-arms, and bearing inscriptions that have long baffled the antiquary's attempts to decipher them. They are believed to be the work of prisoners confined in the tower, and are clearly not all of one date or by the same hand. Close to the Manor Office is the old Grammar School, erected in 1684, but now used as a private residence. The old houses of Hexham are fast disappearing. A few, however, with initials and dates above the doorways, remain, to give it still an antique air, and may be found in Cockshaw and Fore Street, and on Holy Island, the Tyne Green, and the Battle Hill. Over the door of the Tanners' Arms Inn, at the foot of Gilligate, is an interesting inscription, somewhat defaced, which read, when perfect—

C. D. 1683.—J. D.

"Reason doth wonder, but faith he can tell
That a maid was a mother, and God was a man.
Let reason look down and faith see the wonder,
For faith sees above, and reason sees under.
Reason doth wonder what by Scripture is meant,
Which saith that Christ's body is our Sacrament;
That our bread is his body, and our drink is his blood,
Which cannot by reason be well understood;
For faith sees above and reason below,
For faith can see more than reason doth know."

In St. Mary's Catholic Church, which is situated near the top of Battle Hill, are deposited the remains of several members of the Derwentwater family, removed from Dilston when that estate was sold by the Lords of the Admiralty to W. B. Beaumont, Esq., in 1874. The body of the last Earl, however, is not amongst them, having been taken to Thorndon, in Essex.

Just beyond the outskirts of the town, on the Alston Road, is the Tynedale Hydropathic Mansion, situated on a gentle declivity amid grounds of great beauty. It was erected in 1878-9 at a cost of something over £30,000. The bridge over the Tyne at Hexham was built in 1793, after several previous erections had been washed away by the great floods for which the river is famous. In addition to the eminent natives of Hexham who have already been referred to in connection with the Priory, may be mentioned the names of Joseph Richardson, the author of "The Fugitive," a comedy, "The Rolliad," and other satires, who was born in 1756, and Dr. Parker, the popular preacher of the present day. Hotels: White Hart, Royal, Grey Bull, North-Eastern; Temperance Hotel, Priestpopple.

THE QUEEN'S CAVE.—One of the most delightful excursions from Hexham is that to the Queen's Cave, not only on account of the interesting associations of the place, but also on account of the wild and romantic scenery amidst which it is situated. Let the visitor attend to the following directions:—Proceed westward from the street known as Hencotes for about half-a-mile to Causey Hill, near the foot of which one of the sanctuary crosses used to stand. Ascend the bank to the left, and at the point where the road joins another at right angles, turn to the right past some cottages known as High Yarridge, and then make for the Black Hill farm-house, which occupies a conspicuous position on the left. Pass through the farm-yard to the bottom of the hill, and keep to the right along the edge of the dene for about 150 yards, then follow a path which will be observed running down to the burn, and on the opposite side a few mossy steps lead up to the cave, which is at the base of a tall, picturesque sandstone crag. The entrance is very low, and the height of the cave inside—formerly, it is said, much greater—is not sufficient to admit of a person standing upright. The cave cannot be seen from the burn, and were it not for the pathway to it, half hidden even as it is with briers and brackens, this historical spot would be extremely difficult to find. The dimensions of it are 34 feet by 14 feet, and it is said to have been divided into two distinct apartments. The story connected with the cave is as follows:—After the battle of Hexham Queen Margaret and her young son, Prince Edward, with only one attendant, named De Brezé, fled for safety into the dense woods of Dipton, not far from the Hexham Levels. Here she met a large band of robbers, who stripped her of her jewels and robes of state. Escaping from their hands while they disputed about the division of the spoil, the queen took refuge in a distant thicket, and as soon as the shades of evening closed round, crept fearfully forth and began to thread the tangled mazes of the forest, when, by the light of the moon, she saw another robber advancing towards her with a drawn sword. With great courage and presence of mind she addressed him boldly, "I am the Queen of England, and to you I commit the safety of the king's son." The outlaw accepted the trust reposed in him, and conducted the unhappy fugitives to his lonely retreat. Here the queen lay concealed for two days, until her host encountered Sir Pierre de Brezé and his squire Barville, who had eluded the robbers and were making an anxious search for the queen, and by their aid she contrived to escape into Scotland with the prince.

Deepdene, or Dipton, is one of the most beautiful ravines in Northumberland. Its steep sides are covered with the "squadron'd pines," beneath which grow in great profusion ferns, brackens, and bilberries. On the lower ground, beside the richly-coloured burn that traverses the dene, are sheltered groves of beech, elm, and sycamore, and lovely hazel coppices divided by cool and quiet glades. A mossy pathway leads through these secluded haunts, which are extremely pleasant to the pensive tourist from the "busy haunts of men" who is fond of solitude and botany. The tourist, after visiting the Queen's Cave, should follow the ravine eastward, along a path that crosses the stream a great many more times perhaps than he may care for, as far as Dipton Mill. Here refreshments can be obtained, a fact of some importance in this lovely but lonely district. A straight, though steep, road will take him back to Hexham. About half-a-mile or more to the south of Dipton Bridge is Dotland Park, a farm-house that has incorporated into its structure the remains of an old country-house belonging to the priors of Hexham.

From Dipton Bridge the dene becomes less wild and rugged in character, unfolding new charms and sylvan graces, while the moorland burn, instead of being hemmed in by jagged rocks and heathery slopes, runs through lawns and meadows of the softest green to its meeting-place with a larger and more famous stream.

# HEXHAM TO HEXHAM LEVELS AND BLANCHLAND.

Linnel's Bridge, 2 miles; Slaley, 5½ miles; Blanchland, 11½ miles.

A GOOD road leads from the Cattle Market past the Dukeshouse Woods to the Linnel's Bridge, which lies about two miles south-east of Hexham. It is a hoary, picturesque arch over the Devil's Water, with an inscription on the centre stone, "God preserve Wilfrid Erengton, who builded this bridge," and the date of its erection, 1530, somewhat defaced. Half-a-mile south of the Linnel's Bridge, near the point where a branch road from Corbridge joins the road from Hexham to Slaley, is a group of Hollies, consisting of twelve or fourteen stems, and extending about forty feet from north to south, growing closely together and about twenty feet high. It is known in the neighbourhood as "The Hollin Bush of the Linnels," and is said to be one of the places where, during the rebellions of 1715 and 1745, the rebels and their friends exchanged letters. At that date there was very likely a large hollow tree here, in which the letters of either party might have been deposited. The place is "weel kenned by the drovers," say the people round about, "but it aye had a bad name." A little to the south of the bridge, on the east side of the Devil's Water, are the haughs known as the Hexham Levels, where a decisive battle was fought on the 8th May 1464, between the Lancastrians, under the command of the Duke of Somerset, and the Yorkists, led by Lord Montacute, who had previously gained the Battle of Hedgeley Moor. Henry VI. and his queen, with an army composed of English and Scotch adherents and a contingent of French soldiers, whom the intrepid Margaret of Anjou had enlisted in her cause, were encamped on this lovely spot, which is half girdled by the rapid stream, when Lord Montacute and his army, far outnumbering the king's, appeared on the ridge above. A short and sanguinary engagement took place, which resulted in a disastrous defeat for the Lancastrians, the more so as they had imprudently occupied a position with the stream behind them, thus making an orderly retreat almost impossible. Henry VI., putting spurs to his steed, sought safety in flight, leaving a follower to impersonate him by wearing the high cap of state called "Abacot," adorned with two rich crowns, which was presented to the victorious

Edward at York. Queen Margaret and her son fled into the dark woods of Deepdene, which spread westward from the field of battle, and met with the adventure already alluded to in the account of the Queen's Cave. The Duke of Somerset was captured and beheaded at Hexham, where he was buried, and several other lords and gentlemen shared his fate both at Hexham and on the Sandhill at Newcastle. This was the last struggle made by the Lancastrian party. The globe-flower (*Trollius Europæus*) grows in the meadows here.

The river scenery above the Levels is of the most romantic and beautiful character. The burn tumbles and foams in a succession of miniature cataracts down a rocky incline that is charmingly fringed with birch and rowan-trees, while the banks on each side glow with the masses of purple heather that seem to have crept down from the neighbouring moors. At a place called Nunsbrough the river, swirling round the base of high and densely-wooded cliffs, makes a striking bend in the exact form of a horseshoe, enclosing "a little enchanted vale" of great beauty and interest. "This," says the enthusiastic Mr. Hutchinson, the author of the phrase just quoted, "is the finest natural theatre I ever saw. The circle is geometrically just; the plain would have suited those exhibitions of which we read with an anxious curiosity in the history of the ancients. They would have given it life, taken away the rusticity, and made it noble." This lovely spot has its legend, and a weird one it is. The young Earl of Derwentwater, before rising in the Stuart cause, is said to have roamed one evening, sad and pensive, along the wooded banks of the Devil's Water, past Linnel's Bridge and Dotland Park, until he reached the Maiden's Walk, a terrace on the margin of a cliff overhung with copsewood looking down upon the vale of Nunsbrough. Here, as he was reclining beneath a tree on this cliff, listening to the murmuring of the stream, a figure appeared before him in robe and hood of grey, and having told him in solemn tones that he should be riding for his king, presented him with a crucifix which should act as a talisman to preserve him against sword or bullet. This apparition is said to have been mysteriously connected with the fortunes of the Derwentwater family, and to have appeared at different times to its lords, either to warn them of danger or to announce impending calamity. In a cottage near Newbiggen House, on the other side of the stream, the young earl is said to have been concealed when the Government messengers were expected at his mansion of Dilston with a warrant for his apprehension. Not far from Nunsbrough the Devil's Water is joined by the Rowley Water, a stream that has been identified with the Deniseburn, near which Cadwalla was slain after the battle of Heavenfield. The road, which runs parallel with the stream from the Linnel's Bridge, branches off to the south-east to SLALEY, a long straggling village five and a half miles from Hexham. Its small church, re-built in 1832, contains some fragments of the former early English edifice. Over the door of the "Travellers' Rest" is the amusing address in rhyme to travellers—

"If you go by, and thirsty be,
The fault's on you and not on me;
Fixed I am here, and hinder none
To refresh, pay, and travel on."

A lonely road over the high and bleak moorland leads to BLANCHLAND, a quaint old village beautifully situated on the banks of the Derwent, about two miles below the source. It lies twelve miles south by east of Hexham, and ten miles south-west of Riding Mill station. The stream is luxuriantly fringed with trees and shrubs, and the charming valley through which it runs contrasts strikingly in its fertility with the desolate hills that close it in on every side. The form of the village reminds the visitor of those turbulent times when life and property were held by a very precarious tenure—when the frequent raids of the plundering Scots drove men to unite their homesteads for mutual protection. The ancient grey stone buildings are arranged in the form of a square, which is entered by an old battlemented gateway on the north, corresponding, probably, with a similar one on the other side. In his interesting historical novel of *Dorothy Forster*, which deals very much with Blanchland, Mr. Walter Besant thus describes the village—"Blanchland lies along the valley of the Derwent, in a deep hollow, about the middle of the great moor called Hexhamshire Common, and ten or eleven miles south of Hexham; the stream here is quite little and shallow, babbling over pebbles and under trees; it is crossed by the stout old bridge built by the monks themselves, who once farmed the valley. The fields are now tilled by a few hands, who live about and around the quadrangle of the old monastery, still marked by the ancient walls, behind which the rustics have built their cottages. The place has the aspect of an ancient and decayed college." An abbey in honour of the Blessed Virgin was founded here in 1175 by Walter de Bolbeck, the lord of the manor, for twelve Premonstratensian canons, missionary monks of St. Norbert's severe rule, said to be more rigorous than that of St. Augustine. From the colour of their habit they were called the white canons, and it is probable that the district received from them its name of Blanchland, or White Land, though it may have been called after an abbey of that name in Normandy. The abbey was enriched with several benefactions by the powerful family of Neville, and in the reign of the first Edward had attained a position of some importance, for its abbot was one of the few summoned to Parliament, and therefore privileged to wear the mitre. Though occupying a secluded position, in the midst of a thinly populated district, it did not escape the destructive visitations of marauding Scots. A party of them, so it is related, on their way to pillage the monastery, lost the track to Blanchland over the fells, and, after wandering vainly about in the mist, had come to a spot called the Dead Friars' Hill, to the south of Blanchland, on the Durham side of the river, when they heard the sound of bells, which the monks were ringing for joy at their supposed deliverance, and, guided by the merry peal, they found their way to the convent, broke through the gates, set fire to the buildings, and after slaughtering several of the imprudent brethren, rode off with the unhallowed spoil. The Scots were not alone in their experience of the difficulties to be overcome in traversing the fells and bogs around Blanchland, for in that great but inglorious campaign of 1327 King Edward III. set out from Durham with an army of 60,000 men in search of the devastating Scots. In their eagerness, starting at midnight, they made slow progress at first. "Day began to appear," says Froissart, "as the battalions were assembled at different posts; the banner-bearers then hastened over heaths, mountains, valleys, rocks, and many dangerous places, without meeting with any level country. On the summits of the mountains and in the valleys were large mosses and bogs, and of such extent that it was a miracle many were not lost in them. False alarms were occasionally raised of the enemy being at hand, which were caused by the stags that, startled at the tumult of men on the heath, ran about distractedly in large herds among the troops. The march was continued into Tynedale, the South Tyne being crossed at Haydon, and here the army remained for about a week, but seeing nothing of the foe they re-crossed the river, and on the fourth day afterwards news of the Scots arrived. It was on his way to meet Douglas that, arriving on the north bank of the Derwent, the king turned his horses to feed in the fields near a monastery of white monks, which had been burnt, and which was called in King Arthur's time Blanchland."

Here the king, received by the abbot, proceeded to the church, and there confessed, ordering masses to be said. At the dissolution of monasteries Henry VIII. granted the abbey lands, etc., to John Bellow and John Broxham. They afterwards came into the possession of the Forsters, and were subsequently purchased by Lord Crewe, Bishop of Durham, who left them in trust for charitable purposes. His trustees are now lords of the manor and owners of all the land. A portrait of the bishop adorns the principal room in the well-known Lord Crewe Arms. The monastic buildings have all been destroyed, with the exception of a portion of the refectory, which is appropriately turned into the inn, and the massive gateway already referred to. The cloisters can be traced in the garden of the inn.

The church, dedicated to St. Mary the Virgin, is a portion of the ruins of the ancient Abbey Church, which was repaired and made into a chapel-of-ease in 1752 by Lord Crewe's trustees. It is in the early English style, and consists of chancel, nave, and square tower. North of the altar are some sedilia, partly ancient, wherein sat, during certain portions of the mass, the officiating priest and his attendant deacon and sub-deacon. On the chancel floor opposite is the tombstone of an abbot. Carved upon it is a beautiful cross, with a crosier on one side of it and a chalice on the other. Another tombstone has a pair of shears cut upon it. A baptistery was added on the south-east in 1844. It contains the old font and a slab inscribed with a pastoral staff, which probably covered the remains of another abbot. No stone perpetuates the name of any abbot or monk here, but there is one slab carved with a horn, bow, and arrow, and sword, and inscribed with the name of Robert de Egleston, who had evidently been forester to the abbots of old. In the tower is a painted window of St. John, given as a Christmas offering by Archbishop Thorp in 1850. In the churchyard is an ancient stone cross, without inscription or date.

Where the Knucton and Beldon burns unite to form the Derwent, about a mile from Blanchland, is a romantic cliff, called "Gibraltar Rock," situated in the midst of sylvan loveliness. Blanchland is a good centre for making excursions to several places of interest near the border line between Durham and Northumberland:—to Stanhope, high up among the bleak moors; to Hunstanworth, with the byre of an old pele in its churchyard; to Muggleswick, where is to be seen in the churchyard the earliest attempt of Lough at sculpture; to Shotley Bridge, and other places.

# HEXHAM TO STOCKSFIELD.

**Dilston, $2\frac{1}{2}$ miles; Riding Mill, 5 miles; Minsteracres, 9 miles; Stocksfield, 7 miles.**

A PLEASANT road, well bordered with trees, runs parallel with the railway to *Dilston Castle*, which is situated on a lovely eminence above the Devil's Water, two and a-half miles from Hexham, and about one mile south-west of Corbridge. Probably few places can compare with it for beauty of environment and interest of associations; for this was the home and inheritance of the noble and unfortunate James, last Earl of Derwentwater, whose romantic history and sad fate have inspired alike poets, novelists, and historians.

Dilston is a contraction of Dyvelston, the name of a family which was seated here in the reign of Henry II. This name again appears to have been originally D'Eivill, and as such it occurs in the reign of Henry I. The Dyvelstons possessed the manor for a few generations, and one of them, Sir Thomas, was Sheriff of Northumberland in the ninth year of the reign of Edward III. Issue failing, the estate passed to the Tynedales, lords of the barony of Langley, and from them to the Claxtons, collateral descendants on the female side. The latter family ended in an heiress, who carried the Dilston estates in marriage to John Cartington, Esq., a Northumbrian gentleman. Their daughter and heiress married Sir Edward Radcliffe, younger son of Sir Thomas Radcliffe, whose father had married a descendant of the ancient family of Derwentwater. In the troublous times of Charles I. the estates of the lord of Dilston were sequestrated by the Commonwealth for his attachment to the royal cause. They were restored to him, however, by Charles II. His son and heir, Sir Francis, was created by James II. Baron Dilston, Viscount Radcliffe and Langley, and Earl of Derwentwater. He was succeeded by his eldest son, Edward, who had married Lady Mary Tudor, youngest natural daughter of Charles II., and so established a blood-relationship with the Stuart family, which was afterwards to prove so fatal to his race. This union, however, did not prove a happy one, and they entered into a deed of separation, dated the 6th February 1700, and five years later they were parted by the death of the earl. Four children were the offspring of this marriage—James, the unfortunate third and last earl; Francis, who died unmarried in 1715; Lady Mary Tudor Radcliffe, who married William Petre, of Stamford Rivers; and Charles, who survived his brother for thirty years, and then followed him to the scaffold on a sentence passed in 1716. It is around the last earl that most of the interest connected with this family centres, and few indeed can gaze on the grey old ruins of Dilston Castle, or tread the lovely glades around it, uninfluenced by the tragic story of his short but eventful life. Born in London on the 28th June 1689, he was taken to Paris, where he lived at the Court of the exiled monarch, James II., and was educated with his kinsman, Charles Stuart, afterwards called "The Pretender," who was about his own age. To the Chateau of St. Germains resorted the loyal adherents of the house of Stuart; and so, amid powerful Jacobite influences, the young earl passed his early years, forming an attachment to the exiled family, which would, no doubt, be rendered warmer still when, on the death of James II., his friend and companion, the Prince of Wales was saluted as James III. by the English in Paris. His education completed, he returned to his Northumbrian home in 1710, when he was in his twenty-first year. It was not long before he was actively, though secretly, engaged in the Pretender's cause, for in 1711 he was mayor of a whimsical corporation in Lancashire, known as "The Mayor and Corporation of the ancient Borough of Walton-le-Dale," which concealed a political purpose under the appearance of a convivial association. During his residence at Dilston he rendered himself extremely popular amongst all classes of society by his frank, chivalrous, and hospitable manners. In person he is described as being rather under the middle size, slender and delicate in figure, but of active habits. His hair was light, his eyes grey, his countenance handsome and noble, expressive of openness and benevolence of character. This description is well borne out in the portraits of him at Thorndon and elsewhere, and also in the ballad of "Derwentwater"—

> "O, Derwentwater's a bonnie lord,
> And golden is his hair,
> And glinting is his hawking e'e,
> Wi' kind love dwelling there."

The Rev. Robert Patten, whose *History of the late Rebellion* is a contemptible palinode on his connection with "this mad as well as wicked undertaking," thus describes the character of the earl, whom it was his interest rather to disparage than to praise:—"The sweetness of his temper and disposition, in which he had few equals, had so secured him the affection of all his tenants, neighbours, and dependants, that multitudes would have lived and died for him; he was a man formed by nature to be generally beloved; and he had a beneficence so universal that he seemed to live for others. As he lived among his own people, there he spent his estate; and continually did offices of kindness and good-neighbourhood to everybody as opportunity offered. He kept a house of generous hospitality and noble entertainment, which few in that county do and none come up to. He was very charitable to poor and distressed families on all occasions, whether known to him or not, and whether Papist or Protestant." On the 10th of July 1712, when in his twenty-third year,

Lord Derwentwater married Anna, daughter of Sir John Webb, of Canford, in Dorset, a lady whose acquaintance he had made in Paris, where, in the Convent of Ursuline Nuns, she had been placed for her education. In accordance with a stipulation in the marriage contract that Sir John Webb should provide the residence and table of the noble pair for two years, the young earl and his bride spent that period at Hatherhope, which was a seat of the Webb family. In the meantime considerable improvements and additions were being made to the mansion at Dilston. A west front was begun, but, according to all accounts, was never completed. Early in the autumn of 1714 the earl returned again to his ancestral home, but already secret preparations were being made amongst the Jacobites for a rising in favour of the young Pretender, and his domestic happiness was only to be of a year's duration. When, on August 16th, 1715, James VIII. was proclaimed in Scotland, the well-known sympathies of Lord Derwentwater, and his connection with the house of Stuart, excited the suspicion of the Government, and they issued a warrant for his arrest. Timely notice, however, reached the earl, and he withdrew from Dilston, hiding himself, according to tradition, in the cottage of one of his dependants, not far from the Linnel's Bridge. It is probable, however, that he found a safe retreat in one of the secret chambers in Beaufront Castle, known as "Priests' hiding-holes." The prospects of a successful rising were not very bright, and it was only by the exercise of the utmost caution that the Jacobites were able to communicate with one another. An old Roman altar near Fourstones was the receptacle of their correspondence, and a little boy, clad in fairy livery of green, came in the twilight every evening to receive the letters which had been deposited there, and to leave others, which, in like manner, were spirited away. Messages were also carried by female equestrians—the two Misses Swinburne of Capheaton, and Miss Mary Hodgshon of Tone, doing good service in this way. The ladies were the most enthusiastic adherents of the Pretender, and it is said the Countess reproached her lord, during one of his stealthy visits to her, for continuing to hide his head in hovels from the light of day, when the gentry were in arms for the cause of their rightful sovereign, and then, throwing down her fan, told him to take it and give his sword to her. This action, and the tone of raillery in which she spoke, decided him to throw in his lot with the rebels. That he should have hesitated and hung back a little was natural in one with such princely possessions :—

"I could not lose my bonnie holts,
Or shawes and knowes so green,
Where, poppling by the moss-grown stanes,
The waters flash between.

Were all around me not my ain,
I'd freely gang the gate ;
Wha has nae fortune fights mair bauld
Than one wi' large estate."

On the morning of the 6th of October 1715 the fatal step was taken. The meeting-place was decided upon—Greenrig, a piece of waste land adjoining the Watling Street on the east side, about three miles south from Reedsdale; and the earl, accompanied by his brother and a few friends and servants, all mounted and well armed, set out from Dilston—not without omens of evil, if we may believe the tales yet lingering in the neighbourhood which tell how his favourite dog howled lamentably; how his horse became restive, and could with difficulty be urged forward; and how he soon afterwards found that he had lost from his finger a highly-prized ring, the gift of his revered grandmother, which he constantly wore. In passing through Corbridge they all drew their swords, and proceeding to Beaufront, were reinforced by several other gentlemen. Riding northward, they joined Mr. Forster of Bamborough, with about twenty gentlemen, at the Waterfalls, a small hill near Greenrig, which commands a good view of the Watling Street for miles. The whole party, consisting of about sixty horse, mostly gentlemen and their attendants, forthwith rode on to Plainfield, near the Coquet, where they were joined by others, and then proceeded to Rothbury. After proclaiming James III. at Warkworth and Alnwick, they visited Morpeth, having increased their numbers to about three hundred, all horse, for they would entertain no foot. Mr. Forster was appointed general, not for any special fitness he possessed, but because being a Protestant it was thought his influence would have weight with the High Church party. Finding the gates of Newcastle shut against them, they turned aside to Hexham, where they proclaimed James III. in the Market Place. For some days the army lay encamped on Corbridge Common, near Dilston, waiting for an opportunity of attacking Newcastle. Disappointed in their expectations of securing that important town, they proceeded to Rothbury, to effect a junction with the forces of Lord Kenmure. Thus, augmented in numbers, the little army marched to Kelso, where, on the 22nd October, they were joined by about 1400 foot under Brigadier Mackintosh. At Hawick dissensions arose in the camp, and five or six hundred Highland foot refused to cross the frontier, and returned again to their native hills. An invasion of Lancashire having been decided upon, the united forces entered England, and at Penrith put to flight 12,000 of the *posse comitatus* which had been assembled to oppose them. On the 10th of November they entered Preston, somewhat disheartened by their reception in Lancashire. They numbered about 1600 strong, and were preparing to march to Manchester when news reached them that the king's forces were approaching. They at first took up a position in a narrow and deep lane commanding the bridge over the river, where Oliver Cromwell once met with a stout resistance from the king's forces, and himself narrowly escaped being killed by the huge stones rolled down upon him from above. Then, by a strange infatuation, they abandoned this advantageous post, and retreated to the town. Throwing up barricades across the four principal streets, they prepared to make a vigorous defence. General Willis, with four regiments of dragoons and one of foot, was repulsed on all sides. The earl and his brother displayed great bravery—the former, it is said, having stripped to his waistcoat, that he might be less encumbered in the fight.

> "Now a' is done that men can do,
> And a' is done in vain."

The arrival of General Carpenter with reinforcements quite disheartened the rebels; and General Forster, hoping to get better terms by a timely submission, sent Colonel Oxburgh, without the knowledge of his principal colleagues, to propose a capitulation. He was an utterly incompetent general, but there is no evidence to prove that he was the "traitor" which an old ballad represents him to be:—

> "Lord Derwentwater to Forster said,
> 'Thou hast ruined the cause and all betray'd;
> For thou didst vow to stand our friend,
> But hast prov'd traitor in the end.
> Thou brought us from our own country;
> We left our homes and came with thee;
> But thou art a rogue and a traitor both,
> And has broke thy honour and thy oath.'"

An unconditional surrender being demanded, the rebels, on the 14th November 1715, laid down their arms, and 75 noblemen and gentlemen, chiefly from Northumberland, and 143 from Scotland, with about 1400 of humbler grade, were made prisoners. Terrible was the punishment meted out to these unfortunate adherents of the house of Stuart by the brutal Hanoverian. Many died from the rigour of their treatment; some were executed, and others transported to the American plantations. It was about the beginning of December when the Earl of Derwentwater and the other leaders were conducted to London. His loyalty to the Pretender, in the midst of these adverse circumstances, was still undiminished, as may be gathered from the old ballad already quoted:—

> "Lord Derwentwater to Litchfield did ride,
> With armed men on every side;
> But still he swore, by the point of his sword,
> To drink a health to his rightful lord."

He was committed to the Tower, and having lain there till the 9th of February 1716, was carried to Westminster Hall and impeached of high treason. On the 19th he made a dignified and touching defence, pleading his youth and inexperience; declaring that "he rashly, and without premeditation, engaged in the affair;" and that though his offence was sudden, his submission was early. But all he could say was in vain, and the usual sentence was pronounced. Every effort was made to save the young earl's life; and though the Lords seemed inclined to show clemency, the king remained inexorable, even when the young Countess, attended by a number of noble ladies, implored him with all the eloquence of grief to pardon her unfortunate husband. On the 23rd of February the Countess and Lady Nithsdale, accompanied by a still larger number of ladies of rank, again repaired to the Palace, but they were refused an audience of the king, who on the same day ordered the execution of Lords Derwentwater, Nithsdale, and Kenmure. The last hours of his life he spent in prayer and devout meditation, and in writing letters to the different members of his family. Some of these have been preserved, and are very touching and magnanimous. A beautiful ballad by Surtees expresses the thoughts that would naturally pass through the earl's mind in these last few moments of his life. It is entitled

LORD DERWENTWATER'S FAREWELL.

Farewell to pleasant Dilston Hall,
My father's ancient seat;
A stranger now must call thee his,
Which gars my heart to greet.
Farewell each kindly well-known face
My heart has held so dear;
My tenants now must leave their lord,
Or hold their lives in fear.

No more along the banks of Tyne
I'll rove in autumn grey;
No more I'll hear, at early dawn,
The lav'rocks wake the day;
Then fare thee well, brave Witherington,
And Forster ever true;
Dear Shaftsbury and Errington,
Receive my last adieu.

And fare thee well, George Collingwood,
Since fate has put us down;
If thou and I have lost our lives,
Our king has lost his crown.
Farewell, farewell, my lady dear,
Ill, ill thou counsell'dst me;
I never more may see the babe
That smiles upon thy knee.

And fare thee well, my bonny gray steed,
That carried me aye so free;
I wish I had been asleep in my bed
The last time I mounted thee;
The warning bell now bids me cease,
My trouble's nearly o'er;
Yon sun that rises from the sea
Shall rise on me no more.

Albeit that here in London town
It is my fate to die;
O carry me to Northumberland,
In my father's grave to lie.
There chant my solemn requiem
In Hexham's holy towers;
And let six maids of fair Tynedale
Scatter my grave with flowers.

And when the head that wears the crown
  Shall be laid low like mine,
Some honest hearts may then lament
  For Radcliffe's fallen line.
Farewell to pleasant Dilston Hall,
  My father's ancient seat;
A stranger now must call thee his,
  Which gars my heart to greet.

The Lord Witherington referred to in this ballad had been reprieved, and was with the earl in his last hour, exclaiming, as he took his departure, "My Lord Derwentwater, were I to live a thousand years, I should never forget you: so much courage, and so much resignation, in so much youth!" Lord Derwentwater and Lord Kenmure were conveyed to Tower Hill, where the scaffold, hung with black, was erected. The earl was attired in a complete suit of black velvet, and wore a broad-brimmed beaver hat turned up on one side, and attached with loop and button to the low round crown, adorned with a black drooping plume. As he ascended the steps, he was observed to look pale, but on the scaffold his behaviour was resolute and sedate. Here, it is said, he was offered his life and fortune if he would conform to the Established Church and the house of Hanover, but he answered that "these terms would be too dear a purchase." He died intrepidly, declaring himself a Catholic and a faithful subject of James III. On the night of this fatal 24th of February 1716 an exceptionally brilliant display of the aurora borealis took place in the north, staining the waters of the Devil's Water with its crimson glow, and this phenomenon was naturally associated in the minds of a superstitious peasantry with the death of their beloved earl, and hence the red streamers have ever since been known as "Lord Derwentwater's Lights." The remains of the earl were surreptitiously taken from the Tower and embalmed, and then conveyed to Dagenham Park, near Romford, whither the Countess had retired. Here they rested in the Catholic Chapel for some days, and were afterwards conveyed to Dilston and buried in the family vault. Tradition says that his spirit used to haunt the glades of his ancestral woods, and an old ash near Dilston High Town, called the "Earl's Tree," is still pointed out as the spot where his apparition has been seen of recent years. This fine tree cannot be less than one hundred and fifty years old, and measures twelve feet in girth at a height of five feet from the ground. Lady Derwentwater accompanied the corpse of the earl to Dilston, and after a short sojourn there, she visited the house and estates at Derwentwater; but the peasantry, who attached some blame to her for the tragic fate of their master, rose against her, and she was forced to flee from their vengeance up a wild chasm in Wallow Crag, still known as "The Lady's Rake." She died at Louvain, in Belgium, 30th August 1723. Her immaterial form, like that of her hapless lord, has been said to revisit the glimpses of the moon, and to rekindle the cresset on the top of the ruined tower, as it was wont to shine when in life she was watching there for her lord's return. Charles Radcliffe was condemned to death three months after the execution of his brother, but escaped from Newgate and succeeded ultimately in reaching France, where he married Lady Charlotte Livingstone, Countess of Newburgh. In 1733 and 1735 he returned to England unmolested; and on revisiting Dilston caused no little sensation among the peasantry, who, meeting him wandering in the woods, took him for the ghost of the murdered earl. In 1745, when on his way to join in the rebellion that had broken out in Scotland, he was captured at sea, and after being kept a prisoner in the Tower for a year, was executed on Tower Hill, 8th December 1746. His heart was enclosed in a casket, and conveyed to the vault at Dilston. The only son of Lord Derwentwater *is said* to have died in France from the effects of an accident, at the age of nineteen; but there are conflicting accounts about his death. One is, that he died in France; another, that he died in London; and a third, that he died in Austria at a good old age, leaving two sons behind him to continue the title. The earl's daughter, Anna Maria, married Lord Petre, whose descendants still preserve, at the family seat at Thorndon, several relics of the earl, among which are several portraits and the suit of black velvet that he wore on the scaffold.

The Derwentwater estates were confiscated in 1716, and were held by trustees till 1735, when they were conferred upon the Greenwich Hospital. The management of the Dilston estate seems to have been for many years exceedingly lax, for the furniture, ornaments, and kitchen utensils of the hall gradually found their way—no doubt through the connivance of the servants—into most of the houses in Dilston, Corbridge, and neighbourhood, where they were treasured as relics of the Derwentwater family. A number of families established themselves in the house, which was never repaired, and suffered to go to ruin. It was finally taken down, and the materials sold for building purposes. The Golden Lion public-house in Corbridge, and many of the old houses adjoining, are built with the stones of the Derwentwater mansion.

In 1868 an eccentric lady, of considerable ability, styling herself "The Lady Amelia, Countess of Derwentwater," laid claim to the estates on the ground that she was the grand-daughter, and the heiress by entail, of John, the only son of the unfortunate Earl of Derwentwater. The pedigree which she produced was based on the alleged fact that this John Radcliffe did not die, as was reported in 1731, but that the rumour of his death was a scheme on the part of his friends to protect him from the hostile designs of the Hanoverian government. She had in her possession a number of valuable relics, consisting of jewellery, plate, pictures, furniture, and furnishings, purporting to have been removed from the family mansions on the Lord's Island, Derwentwater, and at Dilston during the time that James, third and last Earl of Derwentwater, lay in the Tower of London. These, she affirmed, had been placed, towards the close of the last century, in a secret vault in Hesse-Darmstadt, from which, in 1866, she caused them to be removed, by permission of the authorities, to Blaydon, where, for some time, she had been residing. After vainly petitioning Parliament, and warning the tenants on the Dilston estate to pay no more rents to the receiver, Mr. Charles Grey, she resorted to a somewhat sensational expedient. Collecting her antique furniture and rare articles of *virtu* together, she set out from Blaydon, accompanied by two faithful followers, and took up her abode in one of the rooms of the old castle at Dilston, which had formed the nursery in the Radcliffe mansion. Then a tarpaulin roof was stretched across by her retainers; two or three windows were stopped with bundles of straw, and others covered up with old canvas, and the walls hung with the Derwentwater family pictures, to some of which, it was remarked, the countess bore a close resemblance; and the old baronial flag of the unfortunate Radcliffe family was hoisted from the summit of the tower, proclaiming that she was now in possession of her ancestral home. Mr. Grey had finally, with as much courtesy as the circumstances would allow, to eject her ladyship. When the men were taking the roof from over her head she seized a sword which she had beside her, and struck lustily at them right and left. She was promptly disarmed, and conveyed in a camp-stool to the highway, and there deposited with her boxes. Here, in a tarpaulin tent, for a time, and then in a wooden pavilion, 7 feet long by 4 feet 8 inches broad, sent to her by some of her Blaydon sympathisers, she dwelt, visited by numerous and distinguished persons, until removed from the carriage-way by the magistrates of Hexham as an obstruction. The novelty and romance of the whole affair created a deal of interest in the neighbourhood, and her uncomfortable situation was quite a theme for the local muse:—

"At Dilston, a countess sits by the roadside,
All through the long night and all day,
And thousands have been from their homes far and wide,
Their tribute of pity to pay;
For so lonely she sits, near her ancestors' home,
'Neath the folds of a tarpaulin shed.
To think that a Stuart so strangely should roam
With a pallet of straw for her bed!
Then stir up the nation its duty to own,
For a Radcliffe we know her to be;
And her claims must be righted, her wrongs be made known,
In England, the land of the free."

For several years afterwards, by the aid of her faithful retainers—hailing from the borders of the Derwent—she continued to annoy the officials of the Greenwich Hospital During the last few years of her life she resided in the neighbourhood of Consett. She died in 1880. The antecedents of this remarkable woman were never satisfactorily known. The Dilston estate was sold on the 13th October 1874 by the Commissioners to Wentworth Blackett Beaumont, Esq., for the sum of £231,000, exclusive of woodlands, which, with other items, raised the purchase-money to £270,000.

The grey old ruins of Dilston Tower, standing so picturesquely in the midst of the most luxuriant foliage, formed part of the ancient baronial castle of the Devylestones, which was probably erected in the early part of the fourteenth century. It was the western front of the mansion built by Sir Francis Radcliffe in 1616. The apartments in it are described in old plans as "the nurserie" and "nurses' rooms," and as such must have a mournful interest for the visitor as he muses here on the vicissitudes of a once illustrious family. Below the entrance floor of the castle is a vault or dungeon. On the west side of the present ruins a range of buildings, comprising several rooms, were added by Lord Derwentwater, but those rooms were never finished in the interior. Dilston Hall at this time occupied three sides of a square, enclosing a handsome court, paved with black limestone, in the middle of which was a fountain supplied with water from a considerable distance. The principal part of the mansion was on the north side. In the centre was a large entrance hall, popularly known as "the marble hall," approached by a flight of stone steps from the courtyard. The servants' apartments were on the east side, and separated from them by a yard, or open space, were all the out-houses of the establishment. The carriage-way from the Fountain Court was through the large gateway, which is still standing, with the initials, F. R. (Francis Radcliffe) and I. R. (Isabel, wife of Sir Francis Radcliffe), and the date 1616 upon it; then north, along the open space just referred to, through an archway and down the bank north of the mansion, over the handsome one-arch bridge, and by a sharp turn northward on to the mill road. The Radcliffe mansion was, as has already been stated, destroyed in 1768.

The little domestic chapel still stands near the old ruins, sheltered by stately trees. It is oblong in form, with a tower at the west end, and is lighted by square-headed windows, divided by two mullions into three lights with pointed heads. It contains at present a reading-desk, a few oaken pews, and a seat secured along the whole length of the south wall, which, judging from the appearance of the timber and the nature of the mouldings and panels, must have been there in the time of the Earls. Under the east window is built into the wall on the outside a Roman monumental stone, bearing an effigy of the deceased clad in the garment of the sick chamber. As in many other instances, food has been placed in the hands of the departing traveller. The individual to whom this stone refers was probably interred by the side of an old Roman road which ran from Corbridge and crossed the Devil's Water, not far from the spot. Above the window are the arms of the Radcliffe family, which had been covered with ivy for generations, finely chiselled, and in a good state of preservation. On another stone, in the north wall, is a cross standing on three Calvary steps, and carrying a circlet of thorns. Beneath the desk and pews, at the east end of the chapel, is the vault, with a flight of stone steps leading down to it, now covered by large stone flags. It was the burial-place of the Radcliffe family, and previous to the sale of the estate contained six leaden coffins, laid upon low brick walls to keep them from the earthy floor, in which bodies at one time must have been deposited, the *débris* bearing clearly the marks of "human mould." These coffins contained the ashes of Francis Radcliffe, the first earl, who died in 1696;

Edward, the second earl, who died in 1705; Mr. Francis Radcliffe, who died in 1704; Ladies Barbara and Mary Radcliffe, whose deaths occurred in 1696 and 1724; and James, the third and last earl. For many years after the last interment had taken place, the vault was so desecrated by curious visitors, that in 1775 the Commissioners of Greenwich Hospital ordered "that the entrance to the vault should be closed, so as to prevent the bodies of the dead from being made a show of." In 1784, however, when Mr. Howard of Corby visited Dilston, the vault was open, and he found the coffin of Lord Derwentwater uninjured by decay or sacrilegious hands.

In 1805, as a doubt had been expressed whether the earl's head was buried with the body, two of the Greenwich Hospital Commissioners, on a tour in the North of England, had the vault opened, and a piece of the coffin lid, extending over the face and neck, cut out, when the body was found embalmed in a state of complete preservation, the head lying by it with the marks of the axe clearly discernible. The hair was quite perfect; the features regular, and wearing the appearance of youth, and the shroud but little decayed. Orders were given to have the coffin repaired and properly soldered, and the vault made secure; but a few days afterwards some curious persons, by means of a forged letter, purporting to have come from the receivers of the Greenwich Hospital at Newcastle, gained admission to the vault and inspected the remains. They left without giving any instructions as to the closing of the vault or coffin, and the consequence was that several persons took advantage of the occasion to visit the vault, and one of them, a blacksmith in the neighbourhood, named Rutter, extracted several of the earl's teeth, which he sold for half-a-crown a-piece. The earl's teeth, like other relics, must have had the power of reproducing themselves, to judge by the quantity disposed of at the price. The vault was again opened in 1838 by Mr. Grey, in consequence of the accidental loosening of some of the stones, but this time the coffin was not interfered with, though a square leaden box, which had lain undiscovered before, was found beneath it, containing a human heart. It is believed that this was the heart of Charles Radcliffe, the earl's brother, which tradition states was brought hither by two servants of the Earl of Newburgh. The earl's heart was placed in a casket and deposited in the care of a body of English nuns at Angers. It was afterwards removed to the chapel of the Augustine nuns at Paris, from which it was taken, by order of Robespierre, and buried in a neighbouring cemetery. The niche in the wall where it rested is still to be seen. The earl's coffin was removed in 1874 to Thorndon, in Essex, and there deposited in the family vault of Lord Petre; the rest of the coffins were taken to Hexham, and re-interred in the cemetery of the Catholic church of that town. The dwelling-house adjoining the chapel is said to have been the residence of the priest. Near to it is a venerable apple-tree, blown down in 1839, a relic of the old orchard. It is called "Lord Derwentwater's tree." The site of the flower-garden, with a fountain in the centre, may be traced on the west side of the old tower. Over the brink of the cliff, a little to the south-east of the old tower, are two subterannean passages, which are said to lead to a vaulted chamber beneath the ruins, where demons guard their hoarded treasure. And it is further affirmed that there was a communication, by a stair of many steps in a vaulted way, cut through the rock, from this chamber to the Devils' Water. One of these passages, close to the carriage-road, is almost stopped up at the entrance, but immediately inside, it is possible to stand upright. A person of an adventurous turn of mind can still penetrate several yards along these mysterious passages.

The foundations of the old village of Dilston may be traced in the field a little east of the ruined tower. It adjoined the outhouses of the mansion, and consisted, in the time of the earl, of two rows of cottages close to the park wall, running east and west, and separated by a village green called the "Town Geaete." A few years ago the large mound on the west of the castle was removed, and a surprising mass of ruins, consisting of walls, six feet thick, chambers, culverts, etc., discovered. These had evidently formed part of the old Devilstone Castle, and the last earl had taken advantage of their solid construction to rear upon them his new range of apartments. Wooden posts were found in the walls, on which it is probable that tapestry was formerly hung. Not far from the old tower stands the residence of W. B. Beaumont, Esq. It was built by John Grey, Esq.—a notable figure in the annals of Dilston, and a leading name in English agriculture, who was appointed in 1833 to take charge of the Greenwich estates. The powerful personality of this high-minded and kind-hearted Northumbrian worthy has been made familiar to north-country readers by his daughter, the justly-celebrated Mrs. Josephine Butler, in her charming biography of her father. The situation of the house is thus described by her :—"Our house at Dilston was a very beautiful one ; its romantic historical associations, the wild informal beauty all round its doors, the bright large family circle, and the kind and hospitable character of its master and mistress, made it a very attractive place to many friends and guests. Among our pleasantest visitors there were Swedes, Russians, and French, who came to England on missions of agricultural or other inquiry, and who sometimes spent weeks with us. It was a house the door of which stood wide open as if to welcome all comers through the livelong summer day (all the days seem like summer days when looking back). It was a place where one could glide out of a lower window and be hidden in a moment, plunging straight among wild-wood paths and beds of fern, or find one's self quickly in some cool concealment beneath slender birch-trees, or by the dry bed of a mountain stream. It was a place where the sweet hushing sound of waterfalls and clear streams murmuring over shallows were heard all day and night, though winter storms turned those sweet sounds into an angry roar." Under the shrubs in front of the house is a fragment of a Saxon cross, and on the west side of the house is a rockery composed of antique stones. Here are fragments of a pier from the Roman bridge near the Cor burn, and stones and tiles from the station of Corstopitum. There are stones and slabs from the old hall, some of them richly moulded. The walks along the side of the ravine above the Devil's Water are extremely beautiful. Under the shade of pine, beech, rowan, and birch trees the visitor saunters along the winding pathway, by banks covered with the trailing flowers of the blue periwinkle or the snowy woodruff. Here, on a rustic bench, he may rest awhile, listening to the dreamy song of the river below, or gazing on the level haughs golden with buttercups. Then, continuing his stroll, he crosses by a small bridge a moist little dell, where the loveliest ferns and the brightest mosses and liver-worts border a modest rill, and wanders to an open space in the woods, where the grass-covered ruins of an old paper-mill and the remains of a garden lend human associations to the scene. Passing down a dusky little glade he comes to the edge of the stream, and has a view of a charming little reach, bordered with alders and willows, where the bright brown waters ripple and swirl over the rocky bed on their way to the Tyne. Crossing a narrow plank, he proceeds to the right, along a rustic pathway, through a tangled copse, perfumed by the honey-suckle and wild rose, until he reaches the haughs already seen from the heights above. Here he seems to stand in the arena of a vast amphitheatre, with tiers on tiers of foliage sloping upward from the river's edge. In the autumn, when the woods are aflame with the gold and coppery hues of a gorgeous pageant, the view is inexpressibly beautiful, as the trees, being sheltered, are able to retain their leaves to the very last A stroll across the meadows and through another copse brings the visitor to the top of a steep scaur, riddled with the holes of the sand-martins. Continuing along the crown of this cliff, he descends to the shady bank of the stream. In the dusk of even he may chance to come upon a heron, standing motionless in some darkling pool. From the picturesque weir, which forms a series of lovely cascades, the path runs between a mill-race on the one hand and the stream on the other, to the ivy-and-moss-covered arch of the old Radcliffe bridge, skirting all the way the ancient "deer park." From this bridge a grass-grown carriage-way winds up the bank to the castle. A little lower down is Dilston Mill, charmingly situated, Close to it, hidden by shrubs and grasses, is the pier of an old bridge. which is thought to have conveyed a Roman road over the Devil's Water. The view of the castle from the modern bridge, a short distance further down, is exceedingly fine, and has frequently been reproduced on canvas. It is necessary to make application to Mr. Balden, the agent of W. B. Beaumont, Esq., at Upper Dilston, to visit the castle and grounds. Pleasant excursions may be made from Dilston to different places—to that elysium of picnic parties, *Swallowship*, further up the river-glen, reached by following the road past Dilston Mill for a mile and a-half. A magnificent view of the Hexham Bridge and valley of the Tyne may be gained from Corbridge Common, which may be reached by following a bridle-road to Dilston High Town, and proceeding through the Snokoe Hill plantation. From Dilston the turnpike-road runs on the south of the Tyne past

Farnley Gate to RIDING MILL, a pretty village, becoming very popular as a country place of residence. It is situated somewhat low, in the midst of luxuriant foliage, and surrounded by charming scenery. Near the village the soft-rippling Dipton burn enters the Tyne, and the last half-mile of its course is through a fairyland of flowers and trees. One of the best roads to Blanchland is from Riding Mill. Four miles to the south along this road is

MINSTERACRES, situated in the midst of an extensive park, near to the bleak moorlands which occupy the southern border of the county. Plantations and pleasure-grounds give variety to the landscape. In the gardens are many rare trees, brought from foreign lands. One is a remarkably fine specimen of the silver fir from California. In the grounds are three Roman altars and other objects of antiquarian interest. The hall is a fine stately building, and was improved and enlarged in 1867 by the addition of a north wing. The drawing-room contains many fine family portraits, and the walls of the dining-room are adorned with tapestry brought from Rome, representing scenes in the lives of Antony and Cleopatra. Against the south wall, and reaching from the ceiling to the floor, is an exquisite piece of carving by the celebrated Italian sculptor, Signor Bulletti. A painting of a nun, in another room, will be viewed with considerable interest, on account of the strange vicissitudes through which it has passed, as evidenced by the four perforations in it—three of which were caused by shot from the guns of Cromwell's soldiers, and the fourth by a cannon-ball during the French siege of Rome in 1849. Among the splendid statuary at Minsteracres is a copy of that masterpiece of Lough's, "The Mourners." George Silvertop was one of the famous sculptor's earliest patrons, and may, in fact, be said to have discovered the young genius; for returning from hunting one day, he saw in a garden attached to the cottage of Lough's parents hundreds of models of legs and arms lying about in all directions. He alighted, walked in, and found the ceiling of the cottage covered with drawings, and models lying about the floor. The future sculptor was sent for, and invited by Mr. Silvertop to his house, where he was shown several works of art by Michael Angelo and Canova. This was the first glimpse Lough had of the beautiful art which he himself lived to enrich so much. Mr. Silvertop, the patron of Lough, visited Napoleon at Elba, and in the course of conversation related that he had dined a few weeks before with the Duke de Fleury, who had laughed at him for supposing that the sum of money granted by the Allied Powers to the exile would be paid, saying they were not such fools. "This," said Napoleon afterwards, "was one of the reasons which induced me to quit Elba."

A handsome Catholic church, in the decorated style of Gothic, dedicated to St. Elizabeth, is connected with the hall by a triforium, or cloister. Built by the owner of the mansion, it was opened by the Bishop of Hexham on the 24th August 1854. In the sanctuary is an exquisitely-carved Madonna, in white marble, executed in Rome at a cost of £200.

BLACK HEDLEY, the birthplace of Lough, is situated about five miles south-east of Minsteracres, near the village of Greenhead. An avenue leads from the house to the high road, and at the end is an embattled archway, above which are some rooms, the janitor's residence. Here the celebrated sculptor was born in January 1798. At Shotley Field, a small village about a mile to the north, he served his apprenticeship to a stonemason.

Two miles eastward from Riding Mill is STOCKSFIELD, a pretty rural village, with a picturesque environment of wood and valley scenery. At Stocksfield station the visitor gets out for Bywell, which lies about half-a-mile distant, on the north side of the river. There is a good inn here, The Bywell. Along the wooded side of the burn are some lovely rambles, which may with advantage be extended from the point where the burn crosses the Riding Mill and Ebchester road to *Whittonstall*, three miles south-west of Stocksfield. Perched on the summit of the ridge which separates the valleys of the Tyne and the Derwent the village has a magnificent outlook in every direction. The church of SS. Philip and James was re-built in 1832. An early English capital and some tomb-slabs are remnants of the former building. The inn here is The Anchor.

# HEXHAM TO BYWELL AND MATFEN.

**Beaufront, 2 miles ; Corbridge, 4 miles ; Aydon Castle, 5½ miles ; Bywell, 8 miles ; Matfen (*via* Aydon), 10½ miles.**

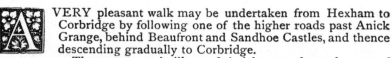

A VERY pleasant walk may be undertaken from Hexham to Corbridge by following one of the higher roads past Anick Grange, behind Beaufront and Sandhoe Castles, and thence descending gradually to Corbridge.

The manor and village of Anick were formerly part of possessions of Hexham Priory, and here was the grange in which the some lay brother dwelt, whose duty it was to superintend the farming operations and look after the interests of the priory.

*Beaufront Castle*, an elegant building of the domestic castellated style, occupies an elevated position, and is surrounded by some magnificent trees. It was built about fifty years ago by W. Cuthbert, Esq., on the site of a more ancient mansion, which was the seat of the Carnabys in the reign of Queen Elizabeth, and subsequently the seat of the Erringtons. The old hall was surmounted by a battlemented parapet, on which were several figures in stone, representing the various heathen deities. Many of these have been preserved, and may be seen on the north wall of the present castle. Beaufront is associated with the fortunes of the Earl of Derwentwater. In a hiding-place under the oak stair-case he is said to have lain concealed from the government messengers, and on the day before he set forth on his fatal expedition, Mr. Errington, the chief of Beaufront, is stated to have taken him to an eminence commanding a view of Dilston Hall and its stately demesne, and to have besought him to pause before he risked so noble an inheritance. When, however, the unfortunate earl and his followers left Dilston Hall on the fatal morning of the 6th October, on their way to the meeting-place at Greenrig, they halted at Beaufront, where they were joined by Thomas Errington Esq., and other adherents of the Pretender. Errington commanded Lord Widdrington's troop in the disastrous expedition. Patten says that he would not have joined the rebellion had not his many obligations to the Earl of Derwentwater prevailed with him. He was, however, pardoned after the surrender at Preston.

The lawns, gardens, and plantations which surround the castle are very extensive, and are said to have cost John Errington, Esq., in improvements alone, upwards of £20,000. In one of the plantations is a seat commanding four striking vistas. Looking through one of these, on the left, the mansion-house opens on the view ; turning the eye towards the next, the church and bridge of Corbridge are discovered ; while the front offers a clear, uninterrupted view of Dilston

Hall; and from the opening on the right, Hexham, with its antique church and towers, is seen. Beaufront is now the residence of Mrs. Kate Abbott, who holds it on lease.

*Sandhoe* adjoins Beaufront on the east, and has a superb situation, above a landscape of unrivalled beauty. The house, a quaint modern mansion, built somewhat in the Elizabethan style of architecture, contains a small theatre. It is the property of Sir John Massey Stanley Errington, but at present occupied by Hugh Fenwick, Esq.

Still further east is *Stagshaw Close House*, four miles north-east of Hexham. It was restored and greatly enlarged by the late Mr. Straker, and is at present the property and residence of his widow, Mrs. Isabella Straker. It is approached from the ancient Watling Street by a beautiful avenue of lime trees, the uniform growth and great height of which have been much admired. The extensive common above is Stagshaw Bank, famous for its fairs, which are held on the 6th May for cattle and sheep; on Whitsun Eve for horses, cattle, etc.; on the 4th of July for horses, cattle, and sheep; and on the 26th of September for cattle and sheep. There are also two "Wiste" fairs, held on the 5th of August and the 24th of October—the former for the sale of lambs and the latter for ewes.

At the east end of the common are the kennels of the famous pack of Tynedale foxhounds.

A little to the north-west of Stagbank Close House is the private chapel of St. Aidan, a handsome edifice in the Decorated Gothic style of the thirteenth century, erected by the late Mr. Straker in 1885.

Four miles east of Hexham, and seventeen miles west of Newcastle, is CORBRIDGE, one of the most picturesque and interesting of Northumbrian villages, as it is one of the most considerable. From its high and dry situation on a gravelly hill, which is sheltered on the north and south by the steep sides of the river gorge, combined with the loveliness of the surrounding country, Corbridge has become one of the most popular health resorts in the county. Few villages, indeed, have so many natural advantages, and these are supplemented by historic associations of exceptional interest. Going back to prehistoric times, it would seem, judging from the cliffs at Thornbrough and on the south side of the river, that the valley of the Tyne, a mile east of Corbridge, had at one time been choked across by an enormous deposit of glacial *débris*, and consequently that the waters of the river accumulating here must have spread themselves into a broad lake, the depth of which is indicated by the height of the cliffs at Thornbrough. Corbridge was at an early period the site of an important Roman station, called in the *Antonine Itinerary* Corstopitum, which has been supposed to be the Latinised form of an earlier name, Caerstobadh—the stockaded fortress or town. That the Britons possessed considerable settlements in this fertile valley is evidenced by the camps, tumuli, and kist-vaens existing in the immediate neighbourhood. The station occupied a gentle knoll near the Cor burn, about 600 yards west of the town, and was approached from the south by a bridge, the foundations of which may still be seen when the water is clear. It is believed to be one of the stations planted by Agricola when he raised a line of forts between the Solway Firth and the mouth of the Tyne. It appears to have covered an area of twenty acres, and to have been, unlike all other Roman stations, in the form of an irregular ellipse. From its well-chosen position to the south of the wall, and on the very line of the Watling Street, the station acquired a considerable importance and magnificence. Roman remains have been found from time to time, consisting of altars, monumental and other inscribed stones, pottery, seals, signet-rings, coins, brooches, etc. Of the altars, which are of great value to antiquaries, two were discovered in the churchyard. They both bear Greek inscriptions, one being dedicated to the Tyrian Hercules, the other to Astarte—the Ashtaroth of the Scriptures. The most curious and valuable relic, however, which Corstopitum has contributed is a large silver plate, or dish, not unlike a tea-tray, measuring 19¾ inches by 15 inches, and weighing nearly 150 ounces. It is adorned by figures in bas-relief, representing Apollo, Vesta, Juno, Minerva, and Diana, each with his or her proper symbols, etc. It is known as the "Corbridge Lanx." It was discovered in 1734, by a little girl whilst gathering sticks on the north side of the river, about two hundred yards below the bridge, and after being sold to a goldsmith in Newcastle, was recovered as treasure-trove, and is now preserved at Alnwick. Almost opposite to the place where the lanx was discovered a silver cup was found two years afterwards. The site of the station is now a ploughed field, the remains of the Pretorium and other buildings, which were visible in Horsley's time, being now quite obliterated. The visitor may take a pleasant walk around three sides of it by following the road past Prior Manor to a bridge (composed of Roman stones) over the Cor burn, following the course of the stream to the Tyne, and returning by the river-side to Corbridge. Several chiselled stones, bearing inscriptions or figures incised or cut in bas-relief, may be seen built up in the old cottage and garden walls. A few of these may be pointed out for the benefit of the curious antiquary.

| | |
|---|---|
| Altar, with inscription much defaced | In the north wall of house, now called Orchard Vale, adjoining the road. |
| Incised stone—strung bow . . | In the west wall of garden of Orchard Vale. |
| Altar . . . . . . . . . . . . | In the wall of a house in the Vicarage yard. |
| Sculptured stone — symbols and figures . . . . . . . . . | Ditto. |
| Sculptured stone—Roman officer | —Ditto. |
| Sculptured stone—owl . . . . . | In the west side of a brick house in Market Place, belonging to Mr. Thos. Harle. |
| " " —coiled snake . . | —Inside of church tower. |

| | |
|---|---|
| Sculptured stone—human figure . | Above doorway of an old house in the Middle Street, opposite the Black Bull public-house. |
| Inscribed stone, dedicated to Marcus Aurelius . . . . . . . . . . | In the forewall of an old house at east end of village. |
| Moulded stone . . . . . . . . | In garden wall in Gos Croft Lane, near its junction with St. Helen's Lane. |

The Roman cemetery appears to have been on the west side of the Cor Burn, for immense quantities of bones have been discovered from time to time, and when, a few years ago, the course of the burn was altered, apparently to its original channel, and the cliff sloped, whole skeletons were unearthed, besides several Roman venel stones. Within the memory of the older inhabitants, portions of the pillars on which the Roman bridge rested, three feet or four feet in height, were standing on the south side of the river, but were, unfortunately, demolished by the orders of Mr. Grey, the agent of the Greenwich Hospital, for the sake of the chiselled stones. One of these covers the mouth of a culvert in the embankment a little further down the river. An interesting fact is mentioned regarding the masonry of the bridge. The surface stones betwixt the base of each pillar were firmly secured together with iron cramps sunk into the stones, and covered with lead, which was found to run from stone to stone at right angles, and when taken out in large squares looked something like window-frames. The southern abutment of this bridge is believed to be in the plantation, covered with sandy soil, which will, no doubt, be some day removed by enterprising antiquaries. But to return to the history of the town. In Saxon times it was a place of importance, and is believed, on good grounds, to have been one of the royal residences. As far back as 771 A.D. there was a monastery here, which was then in a flourishing condition, and must have been founded many years previously, probably by St. Wilfrid whilst he presided over the see of Hexham. In 795 Ethelred, King of Northumbria, was slain at Corbridge, and in 923 the convent and town were probably destroyed when Ragnal, the Dane, defeated Prince Eabald at Corbridge, and took possession of South Northumbria. In 1138, according to John of Hexham, David, King of Scotland, encamped with his army at Corbridge, and during his stay committed the most horrid barbarities throughout the whole neighbourhood. In 1201, when King John was in the north, he caused a diligent search to be made at Corbridge, being impressed with the idea that the town had once been large and populous, and must have been ruined by an earthquake, or some sudden and terrible invasion, and that in either case the inhabitants would have been unable to move their wealth. According to tradition, the search proved fruitless. Within the space of fifty years Corbridge suffered three terrible visitations, being burnt by Wallace in 1296, by Robert Bruce in 1312, and by David II. in 1346. A field, about a quarter of a mile east of the town bears the name of Bloody Acres, where, according to tradition, a sanguinary battle was fought, but at what period is uncertain. Towards the end of the thirteenth century Corbridge was at the height of its prosperity. It had a weekly market, and was one of the three Northumbrian towns which possessed the privilege of sending members to Parliament—a privilege subsequently relinquished to escape the burden of the members' expenses. The plague which devastated so many fair scenes in the Middle Ages is said to have raged here with such violence, that the only inhabitants who survived it were a few who encamped on the north of the town in an open field, called the Leazes, and when they returned the streets were green with grass. In 1644 a skirmish took place here between two regiments of Scots and some Royalist troops, led by Sir Marmaduke Langdale and Colonel Fenwick, in which the former were routed. From this period till the first half of the present century Corbridge seems to have been by no means the pleasant and attractive place that it is at present, for Hutchinson, who visited it in 1765 or 1766, and Hodgson, in 1830, both speak of its appearance in terms of disparagement. Says the latter—"The town (for such its antiquity demands that it be styled) is dirty, and in all the streets except that through which the Newcastle and Carlisle road passes, is filthy with middens and pigsties, with railing before them of split board, etc. The population seem half-fed; the women sallow, thin-armed, and the men flabby, pot-bellied, and tender-footed; but still the place bears the appearance of being ancient." A flattering picture!

There were formerly four churches at Corbridge, dedicated respectively to St. Andrew, St. Mary, St. Helen, and the Holy Trinity. Beyond their names, nothing appears to be known respecting the last three. The ruins of St. Helen's and St. Mary's were only pulled down at the close of the last century. Of Holy Trinity Church, a portion of the wall still stands *in situ*, in a garden to which it has given a name, and where, about fifty years ago, a large quantity of human remains were discovered.

*The Parish Church of St. Andrew.*—This ancient and interesting structure occupies the site of the monastery which existed here in 771, and is mentioned by Prior Richard, of Hexham, as the scene of the consecration of a bishop of Lichfield, in 786. It is dedicated to St. Andrew, like its neighbours at Hexham and Bywell, and doubtless had St. Wilfrid for its founder. As this church is one of the few ecclesiastical buildings in the county which still retains some remnants of the original Saxon work, it is of unusual interest. Though the churches of Bywell, Warden, Ovingham, Whittingham, Newburn, and Heddon-on-the-Wall, in consequence of certain architectural features which they possess in common, lay claim to a similar antiquity, Corbridge is the only place where any portion of the original church, east of the tower, remains. It must not, however, be supposed that Corbridge church received any more favour at the hands of the Scottish Vandals. It was more than once given to the flames, and traces of the fire can be distinctly seen on several stones built into the walls, and on the stones of the principal doorway, and the tower arch. A peculiarity, due, no doubt, to the repeated restorations which have been necessitated, is that no two of the principal walls are at right angles to each other. The earliest remains of the church are the tower at the west end, and the north-west walls of the nave. The tower has been built almost exclusively of Roman stones, evidently procured from the ruins of the neighbouring station. The lower portion belongs to a very early date, and exhibits the same singularly archaic design and venerable appearance as that of Monkwearmouth church. At the ground level is a large doorway, now blocked, and long since disused. The arch is relieved by another of semi-circular form, and greater span. The belfry windows have been much altered in modern times, but have evidently been originally of the same style as those in the towers of Bywell, Ovingham, and Monkwearmouth—viz., a semi-circular arch, containing two sub-arches. A few courses above them is an embattled parapet. An observable feature from the outside of the church is the difference in height between the roofs of the chancel and nave; this is owing to the former having been raised to its original pitch when the chancel was restored some years ago. The interior of the church has many details that repay a careful examination. On the east side of the porch is the great tower-arch which opened to the church in the days of its first erection, as it does now. It is of Roman workmanship, and has been transferred in its entirety from some important building in the neighbouring Roman town. A peculiarity about it is that instead of springing from the impost, it rises from a stone built on the top of the impost, and so has the appearance of being stilted. Inside the space now walled-off at the west end of the north aisle, the north-west angle of the early church is still to be seen, which has large quoins of Roman stones; it stands out three feet five inches from the tower wall, and shows the width of the west front. The nave is separated from the aisles by three arches on each side, resting on octagonal pillars. The south aisle was added to the old nave about the middle of the twelfth century. It is the western part of the wall of the south aisle that remains, containing the beautiful south doorway, with its semi-circular arch of two orders covered with chevron mouldings, and the star ornament on the soffit features, which mark the work of Henry First's reign. The north aisle was added about the year 1200. The chancel is a fine specimen of early English architecture, and opens to the church by an arch of peculiar design, and singularly lofty proportions, which has the appearence of an arch within an arch. There is a piscina in the south wall, near the east end, with a trefoiled arch. A "low-side" window, near the reading-desk, has a stone head made of a flat grave-cover. The priest's door here has a finely-proportioned trefoil head. In the chancel aisle is a fine grave-cover, much shattered, with a beautiful cross, and pair of shears incised, and the words, "✠ Hic. Jacet. Alicia. Vxor. Willehmi. De. Tyndale. Orate. Pro Anima." There is also here the fragment of a Saxon gable cross, probably belonging to the earliest church. In an arched recess at the end of the north transept the visitor will notice another interesting monument of ancient date, inscribed with the following hexameter verse:—"Hic. Jacet. in. Terris. Aslini. Filius. Hugo"—"Here lies underground Hugh Fitz Aseline." This worthy was a small land-holder at Corbridge in the time of Edward I. In the west wall of the south transept is a fine marble slab, with a neatly-carved figure in the lower portion, to the memory of Lionel Winship, of Aydon. In the tower are three bells, one of them inscribed with the name of John Walton, vicar, 1729.

On the south side of the churchyard, not many yards from the south wall of the chancel, is an excellent specimen of those ancient pele towers, which were erected for the protection of adjoining churches, and occupied by their ecclesiastics. It is remarkable for the perfect state of the interior, showing the whole of the domestic arrangements peculiar to the times to which it belongs—viz., about the beginning of the fourteenth century. Nothing has been destroyed except the roof, the upper floor, and the inside doors. The original entrance, door at the north end remains, and is protected by a grille of flat iron bars, fastened to its outer side, and moving with it. The pele is three storeys in height, the chief apartment being on the first floor. A fire-place, now built up, on the north side of the room, was originally the only one in the building. The lower floor is arched with the customary barrel vault. The window-slits are few. On the west front there is only one such small aperture. It is made to let light full upon a stone book-rest, where the early vicars of Corbridge must have meditated over their rare parchments. The tower has been battlemented, having three merlons on the north and south sides, and two on the east and west ends, with corbelled turrets at the corners.

Another pele tower, called "The Low Hall," stands at the east end of the village. It is three storeys in height, and retains its old roof of a high pitch; but the only ancient features remaining internally are the barrel vault to the ground floor, the stone newel stair giving access to the upper floors, the entrance doorway on the ground floor, and the small slits which light the newel stair.

The old Market Cross, which was replaced in 1810 by the present one, had for its base a finely-carved Roman altar, at present in the possession of the Society of Antiquaries at Newcastle. The Golden Lion public-house, and the houses adjoining, were built with the stones taken from that portion of Dilston Hall erected by Sir Francis Radcliffe in 1618. The bridge which crosses the river at the entrance of the village consists of seven very wide arches, and is a structure of remarkable strength. It was erected in 1674, and was the only bridge on the Tyne which survived the tremendous floods of 1771. Such was the height to which the river rose on that occasion, that some of the inhabitants are said to have leaned over the parapet and washed their hands. The Tyne is, as Mrs. Butler says, peculiarly subject to heavy floods, from the sudden pouring in after rain of the waters from its many feeders from the hills; and even yet the strong embankment on the south side of the river is frequently overflowed. Near one of the pillars of the bridge the body of Henry Whitfield, a farmer, who had been drowned in the Tyne, near Featherstone Castle, on the 3rd February 1881, was discovered on the 17th of the following month, by two tramps, under somewhat curious circumstances. One of them, having his imagination excited, no doubt, by a reward of £100, dreamt two or three nights that he saw the body lying against a bridge. After making, one day, a careful search under the railway bridge above Hexham, and also under the Hexham bridge, he went on the next day to Corbridge, and the first sight that met his gaze, as he looked over the parapet of the bridge, was a hand of the missing man, who was lying in a pool about four feet deep. The remains of the mediæval bridge, founded in 1235, may be seen at low water in the same line as the existing structure. These consist of the oak tie-beams by which the pier foundations have been braced together. An accumulation of gravel has covered the line of facing-stones, and the portion of a cutwater of the older bridge, which were visible two years ago in the bed of the river beneath the northernmost arch of the present bridge. The Plantation Walk leading west to Dilston, and the Stanners' Walk leading east to Farnley, start from the south end of the bridge. The former of those would have been lost to the village in 1879, but for the public spirit manifested by one of its inhabitants.

By following the road to the village of Aydon for about two hundred yards, and turning to the left along Deadridge Lane, the visitor will find a delightful pathway through the fields to Aydon Castle, distant from Corbridge about a mile and a-half.

*Aydon Castle*, or "Aydon Halle," as it was called in the thirteenth and fourteenth centuries, occupies a position of great strength and beauty above the well-wooded slope of a charming little dene, through which the Cor wanders musically on its way to the Tyne. It is at present a better-class farm-house, though still retaining many of its ancient features. Belonging, in the first instance, to the Baliols, Aydon passed in the thirteenth century to the family of Aydon. The male line failing in the reign of Edward I., he gave Emma, the heiress of the family who was a royal ward, in marriage to Peter de Vallibus. Aydon subsequently became the property of the Raymeses of Bolam, the Carnabys, the Claverings, the Carrs, and the Collinsons, and it is now the property of Sir Edward Blackett, Bart., of Matfen. It is supposed to have been built about the year 1250, by Peter de Vallibus, and, on account of several architectural features still remaining, is one of the most interesting examples of a fortified house in the county. In Mr. J. Hudson Turner's *Domestic Architecture in England from the Conquest to the end of the Thirteenth Century*, there is a good account of Aydon. Under the head of "Fire-place," Mr. J. H. Parker, in his concise *Glossary of Architecture*, gives an illustration of one in Aydon Castle, the date of which he states to be c. 1270 The Scots, on their way to Durham in 1346, assaulted the castle, and soon compelled the inmates to capitulate on condition of being allowed to depart with their lives. The building stands on the side of a ravine, and is defended by an outer wall, pierced with arrow-slits, and enclosing three court-yards, two of them being large, and one small. At the north-east corner of this wall is a building now appropriated to the storage of agricultural implements, etc., which was formerly the prison. The castle is erected in the form of the letter H, with four towers, one at the end of each wing. The walls are very thick, and one of the towers is upwards of sixty feet high, so that in feudal times it was regarded as a place of great strength.

The outer stone staircase leading to the great hall still remains in the innermost court. Formerly it was, no doubt, covered with a wooden roof. The landing at the top is protected by a stone parapet carried on corbels. The stables, with arched roof and mangers of stone, are interesting memorials of the turbulent times, when the less timber there was about a building the more chance it had of escaping the flames of Scottish marauders. Inside the house there is much to repay a careful examination. The fire-places, of which there are four remaining, will especially be examined with interest. Over the mantel-piece of one of the upper rooms the arms of the Carnabys are carved in stone, and above the fire-place in the kitchen (already referred to) are several curiously carved faces. A window looking on the garden is decorated with a head of our Saviour between its two lights. The outer north wall has been defended by a fosse. At the west angle is the ruin of a turret, the upper storey of which has been supported by corbels and machicolated; below this there is a small postern or sally-port. At the north-west angle is a second turret, with a barrel-vaulted dungeon beneath. Below the castle is a rock called "Jack's Leep," not so formidable now as it used to be, on account of the frequent falls of stone. It acquired its name, according to tradition, from an exploit of a Scottish moss-trooper, who escaped from the hands of Sir Robert Clavering when the rest of his party were precipitated from the cliff. It is also stated, on the same authority, that a Scottish officer in this engagement, being hard set by a sturdy yeoman, of Corbridge, Will Greenwell, took to his heels, throwing money over his shoulder in the hope of stopping his pursuer, but he was caught and killed. Several Roman remains have been found here, among which were two urns, and the effigy of a man. On the walls of the castle, and at their base, overhanging the dene, may be gathered the wallflower (*Cheiranthus Cheiri*), pellitory (*Parietaria Officinalis*), common mallow (*Malva Sylvestris*), giant bell-flower (*Campanula Latifolia*), and in the inner court-yard common celandine (*Chelidonium Majus*), ivy-leaved toad-flax (*Linaria Cymbularia*), plantain-leaved sandwort (*Arenaria Trinervis*), hedge galium (*Galium Mollugo*), black spleenwort (*Asplenium Adiantum-nigrum*), common broom (*Cytisus Scoparius*).

Half-a-mile north of Aydon Castle is *Halton Tower*, a portion of the old castle, which, in its entirety, was an oblong structure, with four towers, built of stones from the Roman Wall and the station of Hunnum. It was the ancient seat of the Haltons, erected, it is supposed, about the same time as Aydon Castle, or a little earlier. In the fourteenth century, however, it passed into the possession of the Carnabys, by the marriage of a member of that family with the daughter of John de Halton. The estate is now the property of Sir Edward Blackett. The existing tower measures 30 feet by 22½ feet, and carries four small look-out turrets at each corner, which are reached by winding staircases in the thickness of the wall. Two Roman funereal tablets are built into the walls. In the Jacobean farm-house attached to it are some massive oak beams, resting on stone corbels, and some fine specimens of oak joisting of that period. Close by is a little chapel-of-ease, rebuilt on the site of an old fourteenth-century church. Of the old edifice nothing remains but the chancel arch and the east window. A portion of the communion service, engraved "Halton Chapel, 1697," was recently discovered by the vicar at a farm-house in Great Whittington, where it was used for feeding fowls. A Roman altar, with the inscription now defaced, stands in the chapel yard. A quarter of a mile to the north, intersected by the turnpike road, are the remains of the Roman station of *Hunnum*, or *Halton Chesters*. This important military camp, which covers about four acres and a-quarter, has not been so carefully excavated as others on the line, and hence the traces of the various streets and buildings are somewhat indistinct. The foundations of several buildings were discovered in 1827, on the north side of the road. One was an elaborate structure, 132 feet in length, which had contained ten or twelve apartments, with arrangements for the transmission of hot air under the floors. Various inscribed and sculptured stones, and also several busts of emperors and empresses, have been found in this station, which was garrisoned by the Ala Sabiniana, probably so named from Sabina, the wife of Hadrian. The route from Corbridge to Bywell is a very pleasant one, and lies along the turnpike road for about two miles, past the grounds of Styford Hall to the river, and then a short distance eastward by its side.

BYWELL seems to be a lovely patch of Arcadia preserved to the modern world amid all the industrial changes that have transformed some of the fairest scenes in Northumberland into black and hideous wastes—the retreat of the old, doomed divinities of wood and fountain, banished from their native haunts. From this "pleasing land of drowsy-head," with its

> "Images of rest
> Sleep-soothing groves and quiet lawns between,"

may the mining engineer, the railway contractor, and the speculative builder long be kept aloof, and

> "Whate'er smacks of noyance and unrest,
> Be far, far off expell'd from this delicious nest!"

May poets and lovers of nature for many years to come meditate and dream in the shadow of this "Castle of Indolence," and painters transfer to canvas the beauty of its ivy-mantled walls!

Bywell is a place of considerable antiquity. A Roman bridge

crossed the Tyne here, and its piers remained standing in the middle of the river till a few years ago, when they were wantonly blown up and destroyed. A silver cup of Roman workmanship, having an inscription around the neck, "Desideri vivas," found in the river here in 1760, had probably been washed down from Corbridge. We may judge of the importance of the place in Saxon times from the fact of a church being erected here by St. Wilfrid. Soon after the subjection of these northern parts by the Normans, the barony of Bywell was transferred from its Saxon owner to Guy de Baliol for "good and faithful services" rendered, but the family forfeited it in the reign of Edward I. by disloyalty to the Crown. In the reign of Richard II. we find it in the possession of the Nevilles, Lords of Raby and Earls of Westmoreland, by whom it was held until the reign of Elizabeth, when Charles, the last Earl of Westmoreland of the Neville family, joined the Duke of Northumberland and other northern lords in an abortive attempt to restore the old religion, and the earl, attainted of high treason in 1571, forfeited all his honours and extensive possessions to the Crown. The estate, after being held for three or four years by the Queen, was sold to a branch of the Fenwick family, of Fenwick Tower, and is now the property of W. B. Beaumont, Esq.

The picturesque, ivy-clad old fortress, sometimes erroneously styled Baliol's Castle, is the gate-tower of an unfinished castle of the Nevilles, and was erected in the fifteenth century. It stands near the brink of the river, surrounded by trees, and is a massive, machicolated structure of three storeys, surmounted by four turrets, one at each corner. Close by is a modern-built house, occupied during the season by John Hall, Esq.

Of the ancient village of Bywell nothing now remains but Bywell House (once the White Horse Inn), St. Peter's Vicarage, and the two churches. What was the size of the village and the character of its inhabitants about the time of "The Rising in the North," may be gathered from a survey of the Royal Commissioners in 1570:—"The town of Bywell is builded in length all of one street upon the river or water of Tyne, on the north and west part of the same; and is divided into two several parishes, and inhabited with handicraftsmen, whose trade is all in iron-work for the horsemen and Borderers of that country, as in making bits, stirrups, buckles, and such others, wherein they are very expert and cunning; and are subject to the incursions of the thieves of Tynedale, and compelled winter and summer to bring all their cattle and sheep into the street in the night season, and watch both ends of the street; and when the enemy approacheth, to raise hue and cry, whereupon all the town prepareth for rescue of their goods; which is very populous, by reason of their trade, and stout and hardy by continual practice against the enemy."

A curious picture is presented of the inhabitants of the village a century later in Roger North's life of his brother, then Lord Chief-Justice of the Common Pleas. In 1676, when the judge was on the Northern Circuit, his progress from Newcastle to Carlisle took him through the barony of Bywell, and such was the state of the country and the roads that a law then in force obliged the tenants of the several manors of the barony to guard the judges through their precincts ; and, says North, "out of it they would not go—no, not an inch, to save the souls of them. They were a comical sort of people, riding upon negs, as they called their small horses, with long beards, cloaks, and long broad swords, with basket-hilts, hanging in broad belts, that their legs and swords almost touched the ground ; and everyone in his turn, with his short cloak and other equipage, came up cheek-by-jowl and talked with my lord judge. His lordship was very well pleased with their discourse, for they were great antiquarians in their own bounds."

The presence of two churches close together in a village, that at no time can have been very large, is sure to set the visitor of an inquiring turn of mind asking for the reason. Tradition will tell him about two sisters, co-heiresses, who quarrelled for precedency, and so each of them founded a church of her own, of which she exercised the patronage to the exclusion of the other. As there are several places in England where a similar occurrence of two churches side by side is met with, and the same story of the two quarrelsome sisters narrated, the explanation is not very satisfactory. Canon Tristram suggests that the ladies, having adjoining manors, built their churches side by side for the sake of society for their exiled chaplains. They are popularly designated the Black and White Churches, from the fact, no doubt, of their being served respectively by the Benedictine or Black Monks, and the Premonstratensian or White Canons. They are picturesquely covered with ivy and surounded by trees.

*St. Andrew's Church* (the "White" Church), restored in 1857, stands on the site of a very early building, erected by St. Wilfrid, and undoubtedly exhibits in its tower the usual characteristics of early Saxon work. It was in the old church (at Biguell) that, according to Symeon, of Durham, Egbert, the twelfth Bishop of Lindisfarne, was consecrated on the 11th June 803, by Archbishop Eanbald, assisted by Eanbert, Badulf, and other bishops. Little original work remains in the body of the church beyond the three-light window of the chancel, the hagioscope, or squint, on the right side of the pointed chancel arch, and a piscina in the south transept. The chancel is two feet longer than the nave—a somewhat unusual feature. There is a holy-water stoup in the porch. No less than twenty-eight early English sepulchral slabs, many of them bearing incised crosses, etc., have been built into the outer wall of the church.

*St. Peter's Church* (the "Black" Church) is an ancient edifice in the early Norman style of architecture, and supposed to have been erected about the middle of the eleventh century. In the low square embattled tower, which is carried no higher than the roof of the nave, are two very old bells, with Latin inscriptions. On one is a monkish hexameter verse in large Gothic capitals, ✠ UTSURGANTGENTESVOCORHORNETCITOJACETES, which has been translated thus—"I proclaim the hour for people rising, and summon those still in bed."

On the other are the words, ✠ TU ES PETRUS ✠ (Thou art Peter), followed by the letters of the alphabet. On the north side of the nave is an interesting series of small round-headed clerestory windows, apparently of early date. In the chantry, or more probably the Lady Chapel, on the north side of the church, is the effigy of a knight in armour, but there is neither inscription nor heraldic emblem to point out his name or his lineage. There is an aisle on the south side of the nave, with plain circular columns, surmounted by octagonal capitals. An interesting relic of mediæval times is the low-side or leper window, on the south side of the chancel, through which the sacrament was administered to lepers, or sick persons, during the time of the plague. During the great flood of 1771 most of the valuable horses belonging to Mr. Fenwick's stud were got into the church. Some of them only saved themselves from being drowned by holding on to the top of the pews, and a mare belonging to Mr. Elliott, the father-in-law of Thomas Bewick, escaped the rising waters by mounting the altar. Both churches suffered much damage from the flood, the churchyards being more or less destroyed. Ten houses in the village were swept away, and six persons perished.

*Bywell Hall*, at present in the occupation of George Anthony Fenwick, Esq., is an elegant stone mansion, with a magnificent lawn in front of it. The trees that grow in the grounds, and in the vicinity, are exceptionally fine. A short list of some of the largest may be found useful to the visitor.

Ash.—50 yards east of St. Peter's Church; girth at the ground, 18 feet, and at a height of 5 feet, 13 feet 9 inches; height, 60 feet.

English Elm.—50 yards west of St. Peter's Church; girth, at a height of 5 feet, 11 feet 1 inch.

Spanish Chestnut.—On lawn, 50 yards north-east of hall door; girth, at a height of 5 feet, 12 feet 2 inches; height, 60 feet. This is as large and finely-shaped a tree of its kind as there is in the county.

Lime.—The most north, and finest of three, 400 yards west-west-north of hall; girth at a height of 5 feet, 11 feet 4 inches.

Mulberry.—About 200 yards east-south-east of hall, very near the Tyne, on the west side of the Black Church, and between the river and the entrance gate. This old decayed tree is a great rarity and curiosity, at least in this part of England. It is about 25 feet high, and its girth at a height of 4 feet, 7 feet 7 inches.

Oak.—Called the King of Bywell, opposite to Bywell Hall, on the south side of the Tyne, and in the north hedge of the road to Riding Mill (760 yards west of Stocksfield Station); girth, at a height of 5 feet, 13 feet 3 inches; height, 86 feet.

Turkish Oak.—On lawn, about 100 yards east of hall; girth, at a height of 5 feet, 9 feet 4 inches; height, about 50 feet.

Some fine walnut, sycamore, and pine trees also are growing in a vigorous state at Bywell.

The river is crossed at Bywell by a handsome and substantial bridge, of five arches, erected in 1838 by the late T. W. Beaumont, Esq., at a cost of nearly £17,000. T. M. Richardson, Carmichael,

Emmerson, and other artists have represented, on canvas, the beauty of Bywell.

Two and a-half miles north of Bywell is *Newton Hall*, rebuilt in 1811 by R. Jobling, Esq., and now the seat of Mrs. Joicey. An observatory, rising above the pine-trees that surround the hall, is a conspicuous object in the landscape. The boat, in which William Darling and his daughter Grace performed their heroic act, was bought, in 1873, by the late Colonel Joicey, and is now in the possession of Mrs. Joicey of Newton Hall.

The *Church of St. James* stands below the village, and looks very picturesque on the hill-side, with its quaint pantiled roof and pinnacled tower. It was built in 1874 by the late John Joicey, Esq., on the site of a former chapel-of-ease to Bywell St. Peter's. In the churchyard is a splendid granite monument to the founder of the church, who died in 1881.

A straight road, commanding very extensive views over the valley of the Tyne, leads up the hill-side to the Newcastle and Carlisle road. Then a pleasant carriage-drive, beautifully bordered with trees, branches off from Matfen Piers, where there stood one of the mile-castles of the Wall to the village of Matfen, two miles distant. About a mile and a quarter along this drive, the tourist will do well to turn aside, a little to the right, where, near an old-fashioned cottage, known as "The Standing Stone Farm," there stands a huge monolith, which is evidently a pre-historic menhir.

From the military road, a gentle descent has been made up to this point, and the sheltered hollow between the ridge traversed by the Roman Wall on the south, and the high ground on the north, is rendered beautiful by the ancestral trees that surround Matfen Hall. Shortly after crossing the Pont, the richly-sculptured park gates are reached, and the road skirting the high park walls makes a sudden bend, and the tourist is fain to admit that few villages have a more picturesque entrance than Matfen.

MATFEN.—This charming little village, from its sheltered position and sweet rural attractions, bids fair to become a favourite resort of the dwellers in our large towns in need of rest and quiet. It is agreeably remote from the sound of the railway whistle, and still retains some of the old Arcadian peace and simplicity. The streamlet belonging to the Whittle Dene Water Company courses merrily through the middle of the village, at the east end of which it enters a tunnel, and is thence conveyed to the reservoirs at Harlow Hill. The village green gains a lovely freshness from its proximity to the running water. The houses are well built, with gardens either before or behind them, and are arranged with none of that barrack-like regularity which makes the colliery villages so monotonous and ugly in their appearance. There is an excellent temperance hotel on the north side of the stream, and on the south is a reading-room, with a picturesque piazza in front; on the slight elevation above the village stands the elegant church, erected in 1842 at the sole cost of Sir

Edward Blackett, and dedicated to the Holy Trinity. The style of architecture is the early English, with single lancet windows. Its graceful spire, rising above the foliage of the Matfen woods, is the only object that betrays to the country round about the existence of the village nestling beneath it. Near the farm-house, called Matfen Low Hall, there formerly stood a tumulus, in which were discovered two cist-vaens, or stone coffins, containing the cremated ashes of some illustrious Briton.

*Matfen Hall* is a large and beautiful mansion on a gentle elevation above the Pont, which flows through the park. A stately doorway, surmounted by the arms of the Blackett family, finely carved, gives admission to a very lofty Gothic hall, rising through the whole length of the building, and surrounded by open arcaded galleries. Here are preserved several relics, among which are the double-headed Spanish shot described by Lord Collingwood in his letter after the battle of Trafalgar as having been fired upon his ship from the *Santissima Trinidada*, weighing 50 lbs., and presented by him to his father-in-law, the owner of Matfen; the celebrated sword of Sir John Conyers, with which he is said to have slain the Sockburne Worm; and the sword of Sir John Carnaby, of Halton Castle. Among the many valuable pictures in the house may be mentioned a half-length portrait of Charles I.—*Vandyke;* Herodias's daughter with the head of St. John Baptist—*Caravaggio;* Holy Family—*Bronzino.*

In the gardens adjoining the hall are preserved several inscribed and sculptured stones and other antiquities obtained from the Wall and the Roman Station at Halton Chesters (Hunnum). To the east of the hall is a vista of considerable extent, opening on to the military road. The trees that form so beautiful a background to the hall are very fine. Regarding the age of several of them, the Rev. J. F. Bigge says:—"I was told by an old man near Matfen, in the parish of Stamfordham, that when his father was engaged in planting the trees on the west side of Matfen Hall, the seat of Sir Edward Blackett, Bart., that he, and the rest of the labourers present, distinctly heard the troops fire on the mob in Hexham, which fixes the age of the trees in a very remarkable manner; that event took place on the 9th day of March 1761." White squirrels are said to have been seen in the Matfen woods.

Pleasant walks abound in the neighbourhood of Matfen. Two and a-half miles, by the road, past the hamlet of Waterloo, or a mile and three quarters through the fields, past the farmstead of Delight, is the small village of *Ryall*, whence many delightful views may be obtained of the low-lying village of Matfen, and the pastoral district around. Near to it passes the old Roman road known as the Devil's Causeway, which is still traceable in many places. The old church of All Saints, after being disused for several years, was restored in 1879, and is now used as a chapel-of-ease to Matfen. Fragments of Transitional work, and twenty-four ancient tomb-slabs are, preserved in the renovated building.

A mile to the south of this village is *Grindstone*, or *Grunstane Law*, a hill which probably takes its name from some large stone or stones fixed in the earth and rising above the surface. On the top of the hill, which slopes rapidly to the north and east, occurs one of those fortified places which are so common in this district, and which were probably the strongholds of the British tribes. This camp is surrounded by a mound and ditch, and is circular in form. On the south side, a few yards distant from the mound, is situated a tumulus which, when opened, yielded some interesting relics. From Grindstone Law the eye has a fine range over the valley of the North Tyne, and the country bordering on the Watling Street. Matfen, which is 2½ miles distant, may be reached by following the road leading from Ryall to Great Whittington for half-a-mile, and then taking another branching off to the east near a farm-stead with the peculiar name of Clickemin. A longer round may be made by continuing a mile further south to Great Whittington, and then turning off to the left to Matfen.

Two miles north-east of Matfen is the village of *Inghoe*, occupying an elevated position, as might be inferred from its name—the *ing*, or meadow, on the *hoe*, or hill. The pedestrian has an uphill walk all the way, direct north to Waterloo, and then north-east through the fields to the conspicuous little village. The Romans are believed by many to have had outposts here, and the commanding position of the place, and the discovery of many ancient coins, go far to confirm such a supposition. No vestiges of such a station remain. Near Inghoe Low Hall Farm are traces of an ancient chapel. The term "Inghoe grits" is well known to geological students as one employed by Professor Lebour to describe the coarse-grained and conglomeritic sandstone rocks of which Inghoe, Shafthoe, and Rothley crags are composed.

A very enjoyable round may be made from Matfen to Ryall through the fields (1¾ miles), thence northward (1½) to the hill called Moot Law, which commands some very delightful views (it lies a little to the left of the road after passing the first gate); then, a mile further, to the quaint little village of *Kirkheaton*, built on a slight eminence around a very large green, with a small church dedicated to St. Bartholomew, and a parsonage, formerly the old Manor House, concerning which there is a tradition that Oliver Cromwell was once a guest within its walls; from Kirkheaton eastwards to Bog Hall Farm (1½ miles), and then south through the fields past the farmsteads of Mount Huley and The Rink to Ingoe (2½ miles), from which a gradual descent is made past the hamlet of Waterloo to Matfen (2 miles)—total distance about 12 miles. Matfen is a good centre for making a visit to the lovely village and park of Capheaton, and the celebrated Shaftoe Crags.

# HEXHAM TO HAYDON BRIDGE.

**Fourstones, 4 miles ; Newbrough, 5 miles ; Haydon Bridge (direct), 6 miles ; Chesterwood, 7 miles.**

A STRAIGHT road leads from Hexham to Haydon Bridge, which is six miles distant, but another route may be indicated. Passing over the Tyne Green, and following for a short distance a path by the side of the railway, the visitor will come to the Suspension Bridge, near the confluence of the North and South Tyne, and, crossing to Warden, will turn to the east, along the side of the river to

FOURSTONES, which is two miles north-west of Warden. This place derives its name from four stones which marked its boundaries, and are said to have been Roman altars. One of these was made the receptacle of the secret correspondence between the Jacobite leaders just before the rising of 1715. The focus was formed into a square recess, with a cover, and a little boy, clad in green, came every evening in the twilight to carry away the letters left in it for the Earl of Derwentwater, and deposited his answers, which were spirited away in a similar manner by the agency of some of his friends. Hence, among the peasantry, this altar came to be known as "The Fairy Stone." The *Limestone Quarries*, near *Fourstones*, on *Frankham Fell*, are very interesting to geologists. The undulation of the strata will attract much notice, and a good supply of fossils may be obtained. The *Prudham Freestone Quarries*, which produce the fine sandstone so much used in these northern parts, will repay a visit. The immense blocks used in the erection of several important buildings in London, Edinburgh, Glasgow, Newcastle, and other large towns, are sawn and dressed on the spot by powerful machinery.

A mile further west is NEWBROUGH, founded and formed into a borough by the Cumin family, at the beginning of the reign of Henry III., when they obtained a charter for a market at Thornton, the name of the estate upon which this *new burgh* was situated. The grant for the market was dated June 20, 1221. Here it was that Edward I. and his court, on their march westward, in 1306, lingered from July to September. The present chapel stands on the site of an ancient building founded in 1242. St. Mary's Well, in a field hard by, close to the path from Newbrough to the chapel, is reputed to have effected, in old times, by the aid of the Virgin Mary, many marvellous cures, and the popular belief is still that no reptile can live in it. Occupying a prominent position in the village is the Town Hall—a handsome building erected in 1876-78—at the sole expense of Miss Jane Todd, of Newbrough Park. An interesting geological feature of the district is the presence of a sheet of hard basaltic rock, known as the Great Whin Sill. Here, contrary to the general rule, it yields a considerable amount of lead ore and carbonate of barytes.

Three miles south-west is HAYDON BRIDGE, which has received its name from the bridge which here crosses the South Tyne. It is a quiet agricultural village, with modern-looking houses, built of the local white stone, and roofed with blue slate. The ancient village of Haydon, whose name is derived from the Saxon words signifying an enclosed place, was located on the hill-side, a short distance north of Haydon Bridge, but of this, the renovated chancel of the old chapel, and a few scattered houses, are all that remain. The church, dedicated to St. Cuthbert, was erected in 1796, and is a plain, but neat, structure, with a small square tower terminating in a quadrangular spire. The remnant of the old church, left standing on the hill-side, north of the railway, is used chiefly as a chapel for funeral services. It consists of the chancel proper, which appears from architectural evidence to have been erected about the year 1190, and a chantry chapel to the south of it, which dates from the fourteenth century. Many of the facing-stones and quoins in the building are Roman, and have been obtained, no doubt, from the ruins of Borcovicus. The principal architectural feature of the interior of the chancel is the triplet of lancets at the east end. The lights are only seven inches wide. The rounded door and lancet, on the south side of the chantry, occupied a similar position in the south wall of the chancel prior to the fourteenth century. At the east end of the chantry is a beautiful window of the later Decorated period (1315-1360). Several grave-covers have been found in connection with the church. One forms the lintel of the south door. Others, sculptured with armorial bearings, are used as the sills of windows in the south wall. One small slab is to the memory of a child. Another has a curious wheel ornament upon it in place of a cross. A fine monumental slab in the chancel is inscribed with leaded letters to the memory of John de Elrington, who was probably the agent of the Boltbyes, of Langley Castle. Fixed in the south-west corner of the church is the fragment of an effigy found in the churchyard. A relic of the old pagan worship, in the form of a Roman altar, has curiously enough been fashioned into the font of this little Christian edifice.

At the south-west side of the churchyard is a gravestone lying flat, upon which is the following curious inscription:—"Here lyeth the body of M. (illegible) Simon, who died on the 18th March 1710, in the 49th year of his age. During the last four years of his life he was tapped four times for dropsy, and three times he had taken away from him about MCCC pints of water. He bore his disease with wonderful resolution, and in the intervals of the tappings pursued his business with cheerfulness, and never dreaded the operations. He was remarkable for his amiability. He was an affectionate husband, sincere friend, and good neighbour. Margaret, his wife, obit., Jan. 23 (illegible), aged 86." Near the church is a small burn called "The Cruel Syke," traditionally the scene of some desperate fray, in which the streamlet is said to have run blood. There is an old couplet referring to it—

> "Till the cruel Syke wi' Scottish blode rins rede,
> Thoo mauna sowe corn by Tyneside."

There is a Grammar School at Haydon Bridge, founded by deed of the Rev. John Shafthoe, in 1685, and reorganised in 1879 in accordance with a scheme issued by the Charity Commissioners. In the old school-house (replaced by new buildings) the celebrated painter, John Martin, received the rudiments of his education. It is said by those who knew him that he rarely left the school at playtime, preferring to remain indoors and sketch upon his slate. By means of a burnt stick he made several drawings on the school wall, representing in one case two of his school-fellows fighting, and in another the master thrashing a boy over his knee. As the features of the worthy dominie and the hapless culprit are said to have been limned with striking accuracy, the sketch must have afforded considerable amusement. The house in which Martin was born (on July 19th, 1789) is called East Land Ends, and is situated about half-a-mile from the railway station, on the south side of the river. His parents removed from Land Ends to a small cottage at Low Hall, where his father, a journeyman tanner by trade, taught the sword-and-stick exercise. Shortly afterwards another change was made to a thatched cottage on the north side of Haydon Bridge. While living there young Martin painted several pictures on coarse calico, and once, upon a festive occasion, when the village was illuminated, adorned the thatched roof of his father's cottage by a display of his own pictures, fastened to the ends of short poles. So great was the lad's *penchant* for drawing, that he has been known at times to go down to the river-side, and there, in the absence of better material, sketch with a stick on the smooth sand. When he was fourteen years of age his connection with this quiet country village was severed by the removal of his parents to Newcastle.

A celebrity of Haydon Bridge, very different from Martin, was Ned Coulson, an eccentric character, remarkable for his swiftness of foot, born April 28th, 1784. Various feats of his are recorded. On one stormy winter's night, when the roads were very bad, he went fifty miles with a message, and returned the next morning. On being asked by his master his reason for not going, he replied, "I have been there and back again, and here's an answer to the message I took." Another time, after walking sixty-five miles and performing a piece of work, he reached home in time to take a successful part in some athletic sports which were held on a green by the side of the river. At Brampton races, Ned having said that he could run as fast as the horses, a wager was made, and he tried his speed against a certain horse, the distance being from Brampton to Glen Whelt. They kept pretty even until reaching Denton toll-bar, and, the gate being closed, the rider was obliged to draw his horse up. Ned, however, never halted, but leapt over the toll-bar, astonishing the rider, who inquired of the toll-keeper who the man was. "Ned Coulson," he was told. "No, no," replied the rider, "it must be the devil, as no man can keep pace with this horse!" The rider went no further, but Ned finished the distance; and as a proof that he had done so, got the landlord of the public-house in Glen Whelt to write a few lines to that effect. Ned returned, and arrived at Brampton before the rider, the latter having been completely pumped out. A curious habit of his was to go to the old church near midnight, clothe himself in the minister's surplice, ascend the pulpit, and quietly read aloud a chapter of the Bible by the light of two candles. Among his many other accomplishments was the power to perform on his violin whilst he ran along the road, with the instrument behind his back. In connection with the old church there is a blood-curdling legend given by Mr. William Lee in his "Historical Notes of Haydon Bridge and District."

A mile to the north of Haydon Bridge is CHESTERWOOD, a small village, chiefly composed of the old-fashioned buildings known as "Peel-houses." Some of the old oaken doors may yet be seen. Here lived in the turbulent times a Border celebrity named Frank Stokoe, a man of gigantic stature, a bold and determined character, of whom many stories are told. One winter night he was awakened by a noise, and found that someone was trying to draw back the bolt of his door with a knife. He instructed his daughter to stand behind the door, and as the knife was withdrawn, to push the bolt quickly back again, but without alarming the party. He then took his musket, and loading it with slugs, descended through the trap-door into the cow-house below, and cautiously unbarred the door. At the top of the heavy flight of stone stairs leading to the dwelling apartment he saw four or five men with a dark lantern. After carefully surveying them for a few minutes in order to satisfy himself as to who they were, he broke silence in a thundering voice—"You d—d treacherous rascals, I'll make the starlight shine through some of you!" and discharged his weapon at the same moment. The holder of the lantern staggered across the stair-head, and fell headlong down the steps, shot through the heart. His terrified companions jumped over the wall and fled in all directions. Stokoe hastily entered the house, closed the door, and retired to his bed, as if nothing particular had happened. He was out with the Earl of Derwentwater in 1715, but escaped from Preston by clearing a high wall with his horse. He was one of those who helped to convey the body of the decapitated earl to Dilston.

# HAYDON BRIDGE TO ALLENDALE.

**Langley** Castle, 1½ miles ; Staward-le-Peel, 5 miles ; Whitfield, 8 miles ; Allendale Town, 8 miles ; Allenheads, 15 miles.

THE road from Haydon Bridge to the south keeps by the side of a small dell, through which runs the bright little Langley Burn, forming in one place a pretty waterfall. The tourist will notice on his way a stone cross, erected by Mr. C. J. Bates in 1883, "To the memory of James and Charles, Viscounts Langley, Earls of Derwentwater, beheaded on Tower Hill, London, 24th February 1716, and 8th December 1746, for loyalty to their lawful sovereign." A mile and a-half distant from Haydon Bridge, and three-quarters of a mile from Langley Station, is *Langley Castle*, built about the year 1350 by Sir Thomas de Lucy, most probably on the site of the older residence of the Tindals, to protect his property from the ravages of the Scots. It passed successively into the hands of the Umfravilles, the Percys, the Nevilles, and the Radcliffes. To Sir Francis Radcliffe, who purchased it in 1632, the barony gave the title of Viscount and Baron Langley. Forfeited to the crown, like the rest of the Derwentwater property, after the ill-starred rising of 1715, Langley was eventually settled, in 1749, on the Governors of Greenwich Hospital. In October 1882 the ruined fortress was purchased from the Lords of the Admiralty by C. J Bates, Esq., of Heddon House, Wylam, and is now undergoing a suitable restoration. The castle is believed to have been destroyed in 1405 by Henry IV. as he advanced into Northumberland against the Earl of Northumberland, who had joined in Archbishop Scrope's rebellion. "Thanks," says Mr. Bates, "to its destruction by fire so soon after its erection, paradoxical though it may sound, the castle of Sir Thomas de Lucy retains in an almost, if not quite unique, manner the essential outlines of a fortified English house in the great days of Cressy and Poictiers. Had it continued to be inhabited, it would be sure to have been subjected to all sorts of Perpendicular, Tudor, Elizabethan, Jacobean, Queen Anne, Georgian, and Strawberry-hill Gothic alterations and accretions at the cost of architectural purity." The site chosen for this feudal fortress is a good one, in the angle formed by the little burn from Deanraw and the Langley Burn. Sheltered somewhat from the northern blasts by a low, fertile ridge—the "Lang-lea"—its towers yet possessed a commanding view of the high ranges north of the Tyne, from St. Oswald's to the Wall-town Crags. Foundations, in the modern sense, were dispensed with ; great boulders were laid down, and the walls, averaging six feet in thickness, built on top of them. The castle is an oblong pile, with a square tower at each corner. On to the south-east one is built the entrance tower, a parallelogram of 96 feet by 84 feet, containing some vaulted rooms and a narrow newel-stair. The sole entrance was provided with a small portcullis, that could be drawn up by means of a rope coming down through the mouth of a man's head carved in the stone vault. An elaborately-carved arch and doorway, their shafts ornamented with floriated capitals, led from the stair to what, on the first floor, was probably the great hall. This arch is a skilful piece of workmanship, deserving careful examination, since it is double-centred to fit in with the curve of the newel. To judge from its small windows and two round-arched openings in its walls, up to which goods could readily be hoisted by small external cranes, the second floor was in part used for a granary or storehouse. The third floor, possessing five large windows, was probably that tenanted by the lord and his family. The upper room of the south-east tower, which at its east end has a little traceried window of two lights—the only one in the towers—may, in spite of its fire-place, have been the chapel. The south-west tower is devoted to sanitary purposes, and the arcades on the west side afford an interesting example of the arrangement of the latrines in these mediæval strongholds. The pointed windows of the castle exhibit a profusion of tracery somewhat rare in domestic architecture, advancing, storey on storey, from pure decorated, through traces of flamboyancy, to forecasts of perpendicular. The interior bears unmistakable signs of fire. The ashlar work of the walls is still remarkably perfect, and the appearance of the castle from the outside is little different from what it must have been when the banner of the Lucys floated from its lofty turrets.

About half-a-mile to the south are the Langley Mills, for the smelting of lead ore, established upwards of a century ago by the Commissioners of Greenwich Hospital. They are now carried on by the executors of the late Joseph Dinning & Co. The noxious fumes are conveyed through a horizontal flue, upwards of a mile in length, to two chambers, where they are submitted to a process of condensation to free them from the minute particles of lead with which they are laden. Afterwards they pass up the tall chimney-stalks, 100 feet high, and so escape without injuring the surrounding vegetation.

A mile and a-half further on to the right is the farm-house of *Low Staward*, once the old manor-house, where the Earl of Derwentwater took temporary refuge previous to joining the adherents of the Stuart cause, and where, there is reason to believe, he slept during the occupation of Hexham by the Jacobite army. Rather more than half a-mile from this place are the ruins of *Staward-le-Peel*, which may be reached by following a pathway into the woods, and then turning to the right. The name has been thus analysed :—Staw or Sta, an Anglo-Saxon word, meaning a fenced or enclosed place ; arth or warth—for this is the ancient orthography—is also Anglo-Saxon, and simply means a yard. Peel is a Celtic word for "stronghold."

A more impregnable position for a fortress could scarcely be found than the small platform on which the ruins stand. It forms the top of a pear-shaped promontory, which is joined to the mainland by a narrow strip of land, and washed at its base by the waters of the Allen and its tributary, the Harsondale Burn. Jutting crags, covered with trees, loose masses of rock, and lofty precipices, constitute the natural defences of the pele on three sides. It was further guarded by a deep fosse and a vallum of earth and stone. The latter has disappeared, but a portion of the former may be seen at the west end. The gateway was defended by a draw-bridge and portcullis. There is very little left of the ancient stronghold, a portion of the west wall, seven feet thick, and a fragment of the gateway being all that remains at present to show its former strength and magnitude. Many of the stones composing this gateway are Roman, as is evident from the "broached tooling" and mouldings upon them. They must have been taken from one of the neighbouring stations. A Roman altar, having a bull's head carved upon it, now does duty as a quoin near the top of this shattered mass of masonry. It is not known when the pele was erected, but in 1386 it was given by Edward, Duke of York, to the Friars Eremite of Hexham, to be held by the annual payment of five marks. At the dissolution of religious houses the grant was resumed by the Crown, but the castle subsequently became the property and residence of the Bacon family, one member of which is said to have been a descendant from the same stock as Lord Chancellor Bacon, by a monk of Wetheral Abbey, who conformed and married. In later times it was the haunt of a freebooter, known as Dicky of Kingswood, who is the hero of a very amusing tale, illustrative of the lawless state of Northumbrian society a century or so ago. Passing a farm-house at Denton Burn, near Newcastle, a pair of fat oxen in an adjoining field so attracted his attention that at night-time he drove them off. At Lanercost he sold them to an old farmer whom he met, and, over a bottle of wine, offered to buy the beautiful mare he rode. "My mare ! No," was the reply, "not for all Cumberland would I sell her; her like is not to be found." "I cannot blame you," rejoined Dicky, "but I would recommend you to keep her close, as unlikelier things have happened than that your stable should be empty some morning." "Stable, sir; God bless you! she sleeps in the same house with myself—close at my own bed-foot. I keep her at her manger, and no music can be sweeter to me than to hear her grinding her corn all night long close by me." After drawing on the simple farmer to show him the lock, which he carefully examined, he departed. The next morning the mare was gone. The robber, losing no time, was on his way home, when, crossing Haltwhistle Fell, he met a farmer, who asked him if he had seen a yoke of oxen in his travels. Dicky, without hesitation, said he had, and directed him to the very place where he had sold them. "You ride a good mare," said the farmer, "and I am completely knocked up with tramping; will you sell her?" After some bartering, a price was agreed upon, and the farmer mounting, made the best of his way to recover his cattle, which he soon recognised, grazing in a field. He at once greeted their apparent owner : "I say, friend, those are my cattle in your field. How did you come by them?" "And I'm d—d," replied the other, "that is my mare! How did you come by her?" The two, in comparing notes of the person from whom they had purchased, found that they had been duped by a rogue of no common order.

From the grassy plateau occupied by the ruined pele there is a magnificent view of Alpine grandeur up the wild and romantic ravine of the Allen, with its dense and dark pinewoods, whose sombre foliage is relieved somewhat by the light green of the ash, the alder, the birch, and other woodland trees, while from below come gently borne on the breezes the chiming notes of the stream as it rambles brightly over its stony bed. A precipice, about 250 yards south-east of the pele, overlooking Cyper's Linn, is called "The Thief's Loup," commemorating the feat of some daring freebooter, who, being surprised in the act of stealing a horse from the pele, sprang over the crag, and escaped without sustaining any more damage than the splitting of his clog-sole.

About the year 1827 a cannon-ball was found embedded in the heart of a tree, near the pele, by Mr. Michael Walton's woodman. The relic is now in the possession of Mr. Walton, Huntershields, Whitfield. A descent should now be made to the banks of the Allen, which is exceedingly picturesque at this point. Some massive rocks form a kind of natural lock here, damming back the waters of the stream into a deep pool, from which they emerge through a narrow chasm overhung with trees. This is Cyper's Linn. Across it there has formerly been a draw-bridge, of which nothing at present remains but a large iron staple firmly fixed in the rock. Near this place, tradition says that the first of the Bacon family who came into this neighbourhood forded the stream with his wife on his back, and in doing so addressed himself thus :—"Hold thou thy foot, Bacon, for all thou hast is on thy back." Cyper's Linn, according to Mr. George Dickinson, has its legend, like nearly every other sombre-looking pool in the country. At a very early period, but the exact date is not stated, an avaricious individual determined to obtain, if possible, a box of gold, which, tradition said, lay at the bottom of the Linn. Accordingly, he took two horses, and also a pair of oxen, and yoked them to the sunken treasure by means of ropes. All being ready, he profanely cried to his team, "Hup, Brock! Hup, Bran! we'll have it out in spite of God or man!" In response to this command, the oxen tugged, the horses strained, and slowly, but surely, the coveted prize moved towards the surface. But just as it was appearing to the light of day, and the attempt was apparently about to be crowned with success, an accident occurred, and the whole rolled back into the pool—box, horses, cattle, and all—and there they remain, it is said, to this day. An old angler, who for many years frequented the place, is reported to have said that in fine weather, when the water was low, the horns of the oxen, standing up in the Linn, were to be seen—a fact of some importance to the imaginative visitor. The railway station of Staward is about a mile from the pele, and occupies an elevated situation above the charming river-glen. Hot water for picnic parties may be obtained at a small cottage, on the way to the station, called "The Gingle Pot." As there are no places of refreshment in the immediate neighbourhood, the station-master is ready to oblige a limited number of excursionists with tea.

Proceeding up stream from Staward-le-Peel, through the most delightful woodland scenery, the tourist may gain the height above by ascending a staircase cut in the rock, as nearly vertical as possible, which is found on the right bank of the river near the cupola bridge. At the foot of Cupola Bank, the East and West Allen unite, and the view from the road, as it winds in a zigzag fashion down to the enchantingly beautiful vale of Whitfield, is one to be remembered. A pleasant two miles walk by the side of the West Allen, under embowering trees, brings the tourist to

WHITFIELD, one of the most picturesque of Northumbrian villages, there miles distant from Staward railway station. There is little historical interest about the place. The manor of Whitfield was granted by William the Lion, King of Scotland, and his mother, to the canons of Hexham, in the latter part of the twelfth century. It passed by purchase into the possession of the Whitfields, at the dissolution of Hexham Abbey, and afterwards became the property of the Ords. The estate at present belongs to Mrs. Blackett-Ord. *Whitfield Hall*, the old seat of the Whitfields, occupies an elevated position overlooking the West Allen and the hills beyond. It was rebuilt, some time after its purchase by the Ords, and the adjoining estate greatly improved by enclosures and plantations. Very considerable additions and improvements were made in 1856 by the present owner. Amongst the natural beauties of the place are the Monk-wood and Monk-wood Crags, the latter standing isolated above the stream, crested with oak trees. From the boundaries of the estate stretch the bleak and desolate moors away to Alston, heightening by contrast the loveliness of the spot, which appears, in the words of Mackenzie, "like the Garden of Eden in the midst of a wilderness." A good Temperance Hotel is the only place of public entertainment in the village. A short distance from the inn is the church, dedicated to the Holy Trinity, and erected in 1860 at the sole cost of Mrs. Blackett-Ord, as a tribute to the memory of her uncle. It is a handsome Gothic structure, built of white freestone, in the early English style of architecture, and possesses a graceful spire, rising to a height of 120 feet. The church is lighted by several very beautiful stained-glass windows, inscribed to the memory of the Ord and Hamilton families. Three bronze camp-kettles, of peculiar make, were found near Whitfield in 1849. Proceeding two and a-half miles eastward from Whitfield to the east side of the East Allen, the tourist will come to

OLD TOWN, where there are the vestiges of several ancient pele-houses. On the western extremity of the hill, overlooking the river Allen, there is supposed to have been a Roman station, square in form, surrounded by entrenchments, and identified by some writers with the Alione of the Notitia, no doubt from the similarity of the name with that of the adjoining river, the Allen, or Al aon of the ancient Britons. As there are no traces of any defensive works, unless a shallow ditch at the south-west corner may have been part of the fosse, the existence of the station has been doubted, and Alione is now generally placed at Whitley Castle, near Alston. A Roman Way, however, is said to have passed from Corbridge through Dilston Park over Hexham Fell to this place, and joined the Maiden Way at Whitley Castle. About a mile to the east is Catton Beacon, a hill so named from the beacons which stood on its highest point to give alarm to the inhabitants on the approach of an enemy.

A mile from Catton Road is ALLENDALE TOWN, or Allenton, as it was formerly written, a straggling, dreary-looking place, situated 1400 feet above the sea-level. It is the capital of the lead-mining district, and disputes with Hexham the distinction of being the central spot in Great Britain. The *Church of St. Cuthbert*, erected in the seventeenth century, was rebuilt in 1807, and restored in 1874. Above the door, inside the building, is a beautiful monument to the memory of Ann Stephenson, executed by the celebrated sculptor, John Lough. Mr. Robert Patten, who was appointed chaplain to Mr. Forster, the general of the Pretender's army in 1715, and afterwards obtained his pardon by writing the History of the Rebellion, was one of the vicars of this parish. The reverend gentleman, with six Jacobites from Allendale, met the small contingent from the Derwent at a place since known by the name of "Rebel Hill," on the moor, about a mile north of the village of Catton, and then marched to join the general body of the rebels at Wooler.

Though the district be bleak and unpicturesque, the flower of poetry is in bloom in it, as may be seen by the pathetic ballad of Mr. Robert Anderson, commemorating the fate of an Allendale maiden, whose betrothed died of grief for her loss.

"Say, have you seen the blushing rose,
  The blooming pink, or lily pale?
Fairer than any flower that blows
  Was Lucy Gray of Allendale.

Pensive at eve, down by the burn,
  Where oft the maid they used to hail,
The shepherds now are heard to mourn
  For Lucy Gray of Allendale.

With her to join the sportive dance
  Far have I strayed o'er hill and vale;
Then, pleased, each rustic stole a glance
  At Lucy Gray of Allendale.

I sighing view the hawthorn shade,
Where first I told a lover's tale;
For now low lies the matchless maid,
Sweet Lucy Gray of Allendale.

I cannot toil, and seldom weep;
My parents wonder what I ail;
While others rest, I wake and weep
For Lucy Gray of Allendale.

A load of grief preys on my heart,
In cottage or in darken'd vale;—
Come, welcome Death! O let me rest
Near Lucy Gray of Allendale."

From the Allen Smelt Mills run long flues away on to the moors three miles west of Allendale Town. The soot from the mill contains a considerable proportion of silver, and the sweeping of the flues formerly brought in annually a rich harvest of from six to ten thousand pounds. Mining operations were commenced at an early date in Allendale, and there are, about a quarter of a mile below the Allen Smelt Mills, on the west side of the river, the remains of some primitive smelting works, which are said, on very dubious grounds, to be Roman. The level, or tunnel, of one of the present mines is seven miles long.

Seven and a-half miles south of Allendale Town is the mining village of ALLENHEADS. The road follows the course of the East Allen river through this wild and lonely region, which yet possesses beneath its surface mineral treasure of inestimable value. "It rises higher and higher, and the dale along which flows the East Allen becomes apparently deeper and deeper. The lower slopes are very green; cots are scattered here and there, on small patches of meadow, or struggling gardens sheltered by a few trees; but as we proceed every mile is barer than the last. We pass *St. Peter's*, the mother church of the dale, then the little village of Dirtpot—what a name!—lying in the hollow; then we come to rows of workshops, long rows of bouse-teams and bing-steads on each side of an acre or more of washing-floors, where men and boys are working with noise and activity; a wooden tower, within which is one of the entrances of the lead mines; a row of buildings containing the offices, the library, and reading-room, and we are in Allenheads, one of the most elevated places in England, situate fourteen hundred feet above the sea. It lies, nevertheless, deep within the hollow of the hills, and has all the appearance of a place which has taken to decent ways." At one time the Allenheads mines yielded one-seventh of the total amount of lead produced in the kingdom. The industry of the district has for some years been in a depressed state. *Allenheads Hall*, near the village, is a shooting-box belonging to Mr. Beaumont. The East Allen rises at Allenheads, and the West Allen on Coalcleugh Moor, three miles to the west. A few clumps of firs patch the hill-sides, and then beyond are the wild bleak fells, with their dismal peat-bogs. Away to the west is Kilhope Law, a hill more than 2000 feet high, from the summit of which the eye may range for miles and miles, catching, it may be, a glimpse of the blue heights of Simonside away to the north.

Five miles south-west of Allendale Town, in the hamlet of NINEBANKS, West Allendale, is *Ninebanks Tower*, an ancient stronghold, probably erected about the fourteenth century, and said to have belonged to a Sir John Eden. A coat of arms above one of the windows, which might have thrown some light on its history, is unfortunately undecipherable. At the top are two curious spout-like projecting stones, which are supposed to have been used for pouring melted lead upon the heads of assailants. The *Church of St. Mark* was re-built in the early English style in 1871. The place is passed by the enterprising pedestrian who takes a stiff and breezy walk from Allendale to Alston, or *vice versâ*.

# HAYDON BRIDGE TO HALTWHISTLE.

Ridley Hall, 3½ miles ; Beltingham Church, 4 miles ; Willimoteswick, 5 miles ; Unthank, 8 miles ; Bardon Mill, 4½ miles ; Chesterholm, 6½ miles ; Melkridge, 7 miles ; Haltwhistle, 9 miles ; Bellister, 9½ miles ; Blenkinsopp Castle, 11½ miles ; Thirlwall Castle, 12½ miles ; Gilsland Station, 14½ miles.

FOLLOWING the road on the north side of the river past the hamlet and hall of Lipwood, let the tourist cross the Tyne by the Ridley Bridge (three miles from Haydon Bridge) to *Ridley Hall*. It is situated on the west bank of the Allen, near its confluence with the South Tyne, and derives its name from its ancient owners, the Ridleys of Willimoteswick, who were in possession in 1567. Lovely gardens and lawns adjoin it, while for two miles along the river stretch the justly-celebrated Ridley woods. Nowhere in the county has Nature arranged more harmoniously her wonderful effects of wood and rock and water than in these beautiful and extensive grounds. At the top of the glen are grassy walks that afford at different points enchanting glimpses up and down the lovely glen. The tourist may probably prefer to stroll along the mossy green-arched glade that forms such a long and lovely vista as it follows the straight course of the stream.

No wonder if the poetry of nature wells up within him as he gazes on the green-robed ranks of birch and larch and rowan scaling the opposite heights, or allows his eye to linger on some weather-stained crag, covered with trailing creepers and overhanging ferns, its base aglow with rhododendron bloom, while through the light fresh leaves the soft glints of sunlight flash on the faceted ripples of the Alaon, or White River, as it hastens to the Tyne. Crossing the stream by a narrow suspension bridge, and ascending the steep bank, he may follow a shady pathway that gradually winds up to the top of the ridge, where, surrounded by young firs and larches, is a small lake. Water-lilies float on its still surface. At one end is a rude hut or wigwam. The pathway descends to the *Swiss Cottage*, perched on a narrow ledge above one of the steepest scaurs in the grounds, and commanding a series of charming views up the glen. By a winding staircase cut in the rock he descends to the bridge again. About a mile from the hall the river, which had kept a straight course, makes a bend underneath the Raven's Crag, a bold cliff of yellow sandstone. Half-a-mile further on, approached by a lightly-built chain bridge, is Plankey Mill, underneath a semi-circular hill, which in summer is one mass of whin and broom. A varied walk through a few meadows and groves, along the side of a steep scar, over a romantic little cleugh, and by the shady margin of the stream, will lead the tourist to Staward-le-Peel. Ridley Hall is one of the places associated with the story of the "Long Pack."

Half-a-mile west is *Beltingham Church*, dedicated to St. Cuthbert, which, according to a local tradition, was originally a domestic chapel of the Ridleys. It is interesting, as being the only church in Northumberland which is entirely of the Perpendicular style of architecture. It overlooks on the north the rich valley of the South Tyne. On the east it is bounded by the little Beltingham Burn as it passes through a deep ravine on its way to the Tyne. The chapel is an oblong square, 67½ feet by 18½. Some of the windows on the south side contain on their inner splays small ornaments in relief, one of them representing a dog or wolf. Between the church and the vestry there is a hagioscope or squint (an opening in the direction of the altar through which the elevation of the host could be seen). It was, prior to the restoration of the building, concealed by the back of one of the family pews, but is now exposed to view on the church side. Around the church is an ancient burial-ground, at the east end of which stands the shaft of an ancient cross, the head having disappeared long ago. There are three venerable yew-trees here, supposed to be upwards of 400 years old. The one that stands on the north side of the church, facing the river

> "In the midst
> Of its own darkness as it stood of yore,"

is indeed a patriarch among Northumbrian trees—17 feet in circumference at 6 feet from the ground,

> "Beneath whose sable roof
> Of boughs, as if for festal purpose, decked
> With unrejoicing berries, ghostly shapes
> May meet at noontide—Fear and trembling Hope,
> Silence and Foresight—Death the skeleton
> And Time the shadow—there to celebrate,
> As in a natural temple scattered o'er
> With altars undisturbed of mossy stone,
> United worship."

The graveyard also contains a tombstone erected to the memory of William Atkinson of Penpeugh, his wife, one son, and two daughters, the united ages of the five being three hundred and ninety-eighty years; the oldest was ninety-eight and the youngest fifty-seven years.

From Beltingham the road leads by the side of the river, and, past the bridge to Bardon Mill, curves round up a gentle declivity to *Willimoteswick Castle*, the chief seat of the ancient family of Ridley, and the reputed birthplace of Bishop Ridley, the martyr. The curious name of the place is said, according to one writer, "to signify the *mote* or *keep* and *villa* of William." According to another, it is derived from the *Guillemont*, a species of marine bird, known in Northumberland as the *Willowmont* or *sea-hen*, and *Wick*, a village or hamlet. The castle has been long in ruins, but one of the towers is incorporated with the farm-house which has been built on the site, and is one of the most quaint and picturesque objects in the landscape when viewed from the railway or the opposite heights. Behind the old pele is the steep slope of the hill-side cleft into a pretty little dene, with a border of trees, forming a pleasing background. The tower forms the entrance of the farm-yard, and though considerably dilapidated inside, has its outer walls still intact, these being in many places upwards of seven feet thick. The capacious fire-place still remains, and measures 10 feet 8 inches in width. The top is reached by winding stone steps, and the labour of ascent is well repaid by the splendid view obtained along and across the valley of the Tyne. Considerable care has to be exercised in climbing up the ruined staircase, and in walking along the wall at the top. This hoary stronghold, that nature now decorates with ivy-leaves, tufts of grass, and waving saplings, is a good specimen of the fortified mansions in which the North-country gentlemen lived, when the "good old rule, the simple plan" was in force,

> "That they should take who have the power
> And they should keep who can."

The construction was pretty much the same all over the county: a square tower with an overhanging battlement; the lower storey occupied by the cattle, the upper by the family. When the raids of the Tynedale and Redesdale freebooters were so frequent, a farmer in the olden times was compelled to look well after his live stock and secure it in the barmkin every night. When there was a feud, as was generally the case with some powerful Border family, the greatest precautions were necessary to protect life and property, which were held by a very precarious tenure. One of the Ridleys of Willimoteswick was, according to the famous ballad of Surtees, concerned in the murder of Sir Albany Featherstonehaugh, on October 24th, 1530. It was only twenty years after this tragic affair, in which so many of the Ridleys took part, that the Venerable Nicholas Ridley, Bishop of London, suffered martyrdom with his friend Latimer, being burnt at the stake before Baliol College, Oxford, on the 16th October 1555. In Bishop Ridley's last letter addressed to his various relatives he writes :—

"Farewell, my well-beloved and worshipful cousins, Master Nicholas Ridley of Willimoteswick, and youre wife ; and I thank you for all your kindness showed both to me and also to all your own kinsfolk and mine. Good cousin, as God hath set you in that our stock and kindred, not for any respect to your person, but of his abundant grace and goodness, to be, as it were, the Bell-wether to order and conduct the rest ; and hath also endued you with his manifold, gifts of grace, both heavenly and worldly, above others ; so I pray you, good cousin, as my trust and hope is in you, continue and increase in the maintenance of truth, honesty, righteousness, and all true godliness ; and to the uttermost of your power to withstand falsehood, untruth, unrighteousness, and all ungodliness, which is forbid and condemned by the law of God."

Thirty years after, on the decease of Nicholas Ridley, of Willimoteswick, at the time sheriff of the county, two men and a woman were committed to prison by Sir John Foster on suspicion of having caused his death by witchcraft. Musgrave Ridley having espoused the Royalist cause, his estates were sold in 1652, and passed into the hands of the ancient family of Lowes, who derived their name from the Forest of Lowes, of which they were the lords. One member of this family is a noted character in Border history. He was at feud with Charlton of Leehall, and many were the fights between them. On one occasion a fierce onslaught was made on Lowes near Bellingham. Charlton attempted to stab Lowes in the thigh, but the thrust missed aim, killing instead the horse on which he was seated. The affair is thus alluded to in an old ditty, long sung on the Borders :—

"O, kensta Will Lowes,
O, kensta Leeha',
O, kensta Will Lowes,
The flower o' them a'.

O, had Leeha' been but a man,
As he was never nean,
He wad have stabbed the rider,
And letten the horse alean."

He escaped on a horse standing near, but after another conflict near Sewingshields, was captured by Charlton, who, it is said, chained his enemy to the huge grate of his kitchen fire at Leehall. From this degrading position he was rescued by Frank Stokoe of Chesterwood, and the feud was terminated. Willimoteswick Castle is at present the property of Sir Edward Blackett.

About three miles west is another place associated with the Ridley family—*Unthank Hall*, a splendid mansion, rebuilt in 1862, and retaining few traces of the ancient pele that disputes with Willimoteswick the honour of being the birthplace of Bishop Ridley. The belief that Unthank was his paternal home is strengthened by the fact that his sister was resident there, as we gather from his last letter :—"Farewell, my beloved sister of Unthanke, wyth all youre children, my nephews and nices. Synce the departure of my brother, Hughe, my mynde was to have been unto them as a father ; but the Lord God must and will be their father if they love him and fear him, and live in the trade of his law." This view receives confirmation from the fact that a chamber in the oldest part of the house was traditionally called "The Bishop's Room." Sir Edward Blackett is now the owner of Unthank Hall. Far away to the south stretches the bleak common of Plainmellor.

Between Ridley Hall and Willimoteswick the South Tyne is crossed by a new, lightly-built bridge to BARDON MILL, a quaint little village, which derives its name from the woollen mill established there many years ago. Many of the cottages still retain their old thatched roofs. There is a small inn here, the Greyhound. The railway station here is the one where tourists generally alight for a visit to the Roman stations of Chesterholm and Housesteads, and to the Northumberland lakes. A road a little to the east of the station leads up the steep bank to the pretty rural village of THORNGRAFTON (the town on Thor's graf or dyke), referred to in one of Surtees's ballads as "Sweet Thorngrafton's bowers." Within this, and the adjoining manor of Ridley, is the Forest of Lowes, from which the local family already alluded to derives its name. Above the village rises the heather-clad hill of Barcombe, on the eastern shelf of which the ancient Britons have evidently had a settlement. The ramparts, the stronghold of the chieftain, the pit-like dwellings of his followers, and the enclosures for the cattle, may still be traced. This ancient camp is a little below the summit, near the Long-stone. Here are the old abandoned quarries from which the Romans obtained some of the freestone blocks for building the Wall and the adjoining stations ; "and," says Dr. Bruce, "the tracks are visible by which the quarrymen—no doubt the oppressed natives—at the bidding of their conquerors, carried the stone from the quarries to the Wall." In one of these old quarries, near the Long-stone, some workmen discovered in 1837 a bronze vessel, with a circular handle, containing sixty-three Roman coins—sixty silver ones and three gold ones—the latter carefully wrapped up in a piece of green-coloured leather. One Thomas Pattison was commissioned by his companions to sell the coins, and he accordingly proceeded to Hexham, where he exhibited the bronze vessel and its contents in the public-houses there. Making light of the discovery at first, he came afterwards to entertain the most exaggerated opinion of the value of the coins, and clung tenaciously to his prize. The news of the find soon spread in the district, and the Duke's agent hearing of it, claimed for His Grace the coins by the law of Treasure-Trove ; but Pattison refused to render up his prize, and legal proceedings were taken, and a verdict of £18 damages returned against him. He, however, defied the law, and was lodged in Denbigh Gaol for a year. On being discharged he returned to the North, residing chiefly with his brother William, who held a small farm in the neighbourhood of Blenkinsop, and who had been entrusted with the keeping of the coins. But he was a lost man. His mind was soured—his habits of industry were broken. He never afterwards did a day's work, but wandered restlessly over the country, and soon sank into the grave. Twenty-one years after the discovery of the coins they were purchased by Mr. Clayton from William Pattison for fifty new bright sovereigns. The story of how a life was blighted by this luckless treasure, as told by Dr. Bruce in his account of the "Thorngrafton Find" reads more like a romance than a sober recital of facts. As there are no coins in the collection later than the early period of Hadrian's reign, antiquaries who advocated the claims of that emperor to the honour of building the Roman Wall received a strong confirmation of their belief. A fine view is obtained from the top of Barcombe Hill of the South Tyne valley on the one side, and the mural ridge from Sewingshields to the Nine Nicks of Thirlwall on the other.

Below the hill, where the stream from Crag Lough unites with another from Winshields to form the Chineley Burn, is *Chesterholm*, the Vindolana of the Romans. The station, supposed to have been planted by Agricola, is situated on an elevated platform naturally protected on every side but the west, and occupies an area of three acres and a quarter. The walls, ditches, and gateways, though in a dilapidated condition, may be easily made out. Here many important antiquities have been found, notably two Roman altars, one of which, with a dedication to Jupiter, bears on its sides representations of the stork, and the other, with a dedication to the genius of the Prætorium, bears figures of the instruments used in sacrifice—an axe, a knife, a jug (for the wine), and a ladle—together with the figure of an ox. Both these altars are now at the Chesters. About fifty yards to the west of the station are the ruins, now nearly obliterated, of an extensive building which has been furnished with hypocausts. The pillars long retained the marks of fire and soot, which gave rise to the popular belief that a colony of fairies had here established themselves, and that this was their kitchen. Close by the site of the camp is a neat villa residence, erected by the late Rev. Anthony Hedley, M.A., a devoted student of antiquity. Nearly all the stones were taken from the ruins, and bear the traces of Roman chiselling. In the front wall of the house is a stone, with sculptures upon it, supposed to have reference to the mysteries of Mithraic worship. Several carved and inscribed stones will be found in the walls of the passage leading from the kitchen of the cottage to the burn-side; one of them bears the representation of a boar. Near the north-eastern angle of the station is a Roman milestone, standing in its original position upon the line of the ancient road called the Stanegate, which ran from Cilurnum to Magna. Close to it is a large barrow, possibly the burial-place of some British chief.

*Vindolana* is about two miles from Bardon Mill, and may be reached by climbing the hill-side by the road that runs first on the west and then on the east side of the Chineley Burn, and when to the north of Barcombe Hill, turning to the left along a pathway through the fields for a short distance. A little clump of trees adjoins the camp. Nearly a mile west of Bardon Mill, a little north of the main road, is HENSHAW, a quaint little rural village with thatched cottages. Three-quarters of a mile beyond, on the left of the road, stands *Hardriding*, an ancient seat of the Ridleys, referred to in Surtees's ballad. A mile further on is *Melkridge*, containing a curiously-decorated stone house, and a pele-tower, which formerly belonged to the Blackett family. Another mile to the west is *Whitchester*, near which, on the north side of the road, are the traces of one of the military posts of the Romans. The site is well chosen, being defended on three sides by steep and rugged glens.

The tourist now approaches HALTWHISTLE, a quiet little

country town of some 1600 inhabitants, pleasantly situated on an eminence on the north bank of the South Tyne, fifteen miles west of Hexham. Though in recent years the town has been undergoing a process of modernisation, it still retains some of its ancient features. The name Haltwhistle, or Hautwyesill, to use the old spelling, signifies either "The holy hill of the high water," or "The high watch hill or beacon," and owes its origin to the oval-shaped mound called the Castle Hill, which at some very remote period has been fortified with earthworks. At the east and west ends there are four distinct terraces raised one above another. The summit of the hill is defended by a breastwork of earth, and on the west by an inaccessible precipice, probably of artificial formation. At the rear of this mound will be observed a plain-looking building, with a loop-holed turret built on corbels. This is all that remains of the old tower of Hautwysill, mentioned in the list of the Northumbrian castles in 1416. The old roof, which was removed some twenty years ago, was formed of flags laid on heavy oaken beams, and fastened thereto with sheep-shank bones. The floors also consisted of flags laid on joists formed of the roughly-squared trunks of oak-trees. A winding stone staircase leads to the upper part of the tower. This pele was probably the official residence of the bailiffs of the town acting under the Warden of the Marches. Another old pele is the turreted building near the Market Place, recently converted into the Red Lion Hotel with a modernised front.

The *Church*, dedicated to the *Holy Cross*, is situated on the south side of the town. The oldest part of the building is the chancel, erected in the twelfth century. A fine triplet is noticeable here. The nave belongs to the thirteenth century. The shafts and piers of the arcade are early English in their character, while the capitals exhibit the incoming of the Decorated style. In the south wall of the chancel is a fifteenth century low-side window. The chancel contains a recumbent effigy of a member of the Blenkinsopp family, probably of the fourteenth century. There is also a tombstone bearing the arms of this family, and ornamented with a beautiful flowered crosier, a broken-hilted sword, and a staff and scrip, indicating that the person buried beneath had visited the Holy Land. Standing against the south wall of the chancel is the tombstone, six feet long, of John Ridley, of Walltown, brother of Dr. Nicholas Ridley, Bishop of London, bearing, beneath two shields, a rhyming inscription, which runs thus—

IHON REDLE | THAT SVM | TIM DID BE | THEN: LARD OF THE WALTON
GON IS HE OVT OF THE VAL OF MESRE | HIS BONS LIES VNDER
THES STON; AL FRENDES MAY BE GLAD TO HAER | WHEN HES
SOVL FROM PAEN DID GO | OVT OF THES WORLD AS DOETH
APPER | IN THE YEER OF OVR LORD | A. 1562.

The church possesses a curious font and a handsome carved marble reredos representing the adoration of the Magi. The east window is by Morris, and the west window by Wailes.

From the churchyard, which forms a fine terrace, there is a splendid prospect over the vale from Bellister Castle on the one hand to Haydon Bridge on the other. The inscriptions on the gravestones bear witness to the remarkable longevity of the inhabitants of Haltwhistle.

Few events occur now to disturb the tranquillity of the little town, but between the date when Edward I. rested here a night (September 11th, 1306), on his last journey into Scotland, to the time of the Union, Haltwhistle was the scene of many a deadly conflict.

In 1598 the Armstrongs of Liddesdale plundered Haltwhistle during the time that Sir Robert Carey (afterwards Earl of Monmouth) was Warden of the Middle Marches on the English side. Satisfaction for this was demanded from the King of Scotland, who replied that the Armstrongs were no subjects of his, and recommended the English Warden to take his own revenge. The English accordingly entered Liddesdale and ravaged the land of the Armstrongs, and in a skirmish Sim of the Cathill, an Armstrong, was slain by one of the Ridleys of Haltwhistle. This led to another visit of the Scottish outlaws to Haltwhistle, when they plundered and burnt the greater part of the town, losing one of their leaders in the fray. The state of terror in the country was such that Sir Robert Carey was compelled to take decided steps to destroy the power of the Liddesdale moss-troopers, and bring them into some degree of subjection. So, with a number of hardy volunteers, he set out for the Wastes of Liddesdale, and laid siege to the Tarras, a large and impenetrable forest, surrounded with bogs and marshy ground, whither the chief outlaws had betaken themselves with their goods. So confident were they in the strength of their stronghold that they sent a party into England and plundered the Warden's lands, and, on its return, sent, by a trusty messenger, one of his own cows to him, with a message that, fearing he might fall short of provisions during his stay in Scotland, they had taken the precaution of sending him some English beef. By the skilful strategy, however, of Sir Robert Carey, the leaders were captured and the gang broken up, so that they never again attained to such power and notoriety. A famous ballad, of contemporary authorship, commemorates

THE FRAY OF HAUTWESSEL.

The limmer thieves o' Liddesdale
Wadna leave a kye in the hail countrie,
But an' we gie them the caud steel
Our gear they'll reive it a' awaye ;
Sae pert they stealis I you say :
O' late they came to Hautwessel,
And thowt they there wad drive a fray,
But Alec Ridley shot too well.

'Twas some time gane, they took our naigs,
And left us eke an empty byre :
I wad the deil had had their craigs,
And a' things in a bleeze o' fire ;

Eh! but it raised the warden's ire,
Sir Robert Carey was his name;
But an John Ridley thrust his spear
Right through Sim o' the Cathill's wame.*

For he cam riding o'er the brae,
As gin he could na steal a cow;
And when we'd got our gear awa'
Says—"Wha this day's work will avow?"
I wot he got reply enow,
As ken the Armstrongs to their grief.
For to tine the gear and Simmy too,
The ane to the tither's nae relief.

Then cam Wat Armstrong to the town,
Wi' some three hundred chiels or mair,
An' swore that they wad burn it down;
A' clad in jack, wi' bow and spear.
Harnessed right weel, I trow they were;
But we were aye prepared at need,
And dropt ere lang upon the rear
Amangst them, like an angry gleed.†

Then Alec Ridley he let flee
A clothyard shaft, ahint the wa';
It struck Wat Armstrong in the ee',
Went through his steel cap, heid and a'.
I wot it made him quickly fa',
He could na rise, though he essayed;
The best at thief-craft or the ba'‡
He ne'er again shall ride a raid.

Gin should the Armstrongs promise keep,
And seek our gear to do us wrang;
Or rob us of our kye or sheep,
I trow but some o' them will hang;
Sharp is the sturdy sleuth dog's fang,
At Crawcragge watchers will be set,
At Linthaugh ford too, a' neet lang,
Wow! but the meeting will be het.

Inns: Black Bull, Blue Bell, Grey Bull, Red Lion, and Railway.

Crossing the South Tyne close to the station, and proceeding seven or eight hundred yards to the right, the tourist will observe a branch road on the left leading to *Bellister Castle*. This border stronghold, which is mentioned as being in the possession of one of the Blenkinsopps as early as 1470, was a small pele-tower of considerable strength, but the only portions now remaining are the fragments of the outer walls. The ruins stand, well relieved by dark woods, on a rocky eminence which has been surrounded with a moat. Growing almost out of the rent wall of the old castle is a huge sycamore-tree, 12 feet 10 inches in girth at a height of 5 feet, and 51 feet high. Adjoining the ruins is a modern farm-house in the castellated style.

Bellister has its legend, which tells how many centuries ago a

* Belly. † Kite. ‡ Football.

wandering minstrel came to the castle seeking protection and a night's rest, which the chivalrous and generous feeling of the day readily accorded ; but the boon had not long been conceded ere dark suspicions began to rankle in the breast of the lord of Bellister. That the minstrel was a spy sent by a neighbouring baron, with whom he had a feud, was a conclusion quickly arrived at ; distrust therefore sat upon his countenance, which the lowly guest failed not to notice ; and when the signal was given for withdrawal, the stranger, auguring treachery, disappeared from the castle. The baron's suspicions seemed to be confirmed, and he ordered out the bloodhounds, which, following up the track, came upon the poor old minstrel hard by the willow-trees near the banks of the Tyne, and before any of the party could reach them, they had finished their dreadful work. Remorse for the outrage seized the baron, whose life was kept in a state of fear by the visits to his home of the ghostly "Grey Man of Bellister." Many are the uncanny doings related of the restless spirit who, till recent times, used to haunt this ruined pele.

By following the course of the Tipalt, which is the same as the high road and rail to Carlisle, for about two miles and a-half, a visit may be paid to *Blenkinsopp Castle*, restored in 1880 by W. L. B. Coulson, Esq., and now the property of the Joiceys. The ancient fortress, seated on the summit of a grassy knoll, dates back to 1339, when "Thomas de Blencansopp obtained the royal license to fortify his manor-house of Blenkinsopp." Hodgson says—"The old family residence stood on the right bank of the hope or valley of Glenwhelt ; prior to the Conquest it had probably belonged to one Blencan, from whom the place and township derived its name, for in the oldest writings it is called Blenkan or Blenkens-hope." In the troublous times it was a place of considerable strength, consisting of a square tower built upon vaults, with walls over seven feet in thickness, defended by a deep ditch on the north and west, on the south by a rivulet, and on the east by a steep bank. Material from the Roman wall has evidently been utilised in its construction, judging by the number of stones bearing Roman inscriptions which were found during the recent restorations. In 1542 it had fallen into decay, and was afterwards deserted for Bellister. The only portions of the original building now remaining are the east wall of the entrance-hall block and the north-west corner of the building, which was incorporated with the new work. Some of the inner walls have also been retained, but their thickness has been reduced. During the restoration there was discovered at the north-west corner of the castle the entrance to a secret passage which, it is supposed, connected this stronghold with that of Thirlwall, a mile and a half distant, thus affording the means of escape should either castle be captured by the enemy. In 1727 the castle came into the possession of the Coulsons of Jesmond, near Newcastle, by the marriage of William Coulson with Jane Blenkinsop, the heiress of the estate, and remained in the family till a very short time ago, when it was sold by Major Coulson.

The legend of the White Ladye of Blenkinsopp lends a weird and strange interest to the castle. According to tradition there was once a certain Bryan de Blenkinsop, who, with many excellent qualities, had an inordinate love of wealth. At a festive gathering, among other health-drinkings was given that of Bryan de Blenkinsopp and his "ladye love." "Never!" said he, "never shall that be until I meet with a lady possessed of a chest of gold heavier than ten of my strongest men can carry into my castle." After the lapse of some years his desire was gratified, and he brought home from some far country a wife and the box of gold, but the lady becoming either jealous or revengeful, caused the treasure to be secreted, and would not give it up, till at length the young lord, aggravated by her conduct, suddenly left the castle, and was never heard of again. The lady was inconsolable, and at last, with her attendants, went forth in search of the baron, but never returned It is said the lady, filled with remorse, cannot rest in her grave, but must needs wander back again to the old castle and mourn over the chest of gold, the cause of all her woe. Here she must continue to wander until some one shall follow her to the vault, and by removing the treasure, allow her spirit to rest.

On the opposite side of the valley is *Blenkinsopp Hall*, finely situated on the crest of the hill called Dryburnhaugh, which slopes down to the Tipalt. It is a stately castellated mansion rising from picturesque woods, and was built by Colonel John Blenkinsopp Coulson. There is a tradition here of a black dog which always appears as a warning before a death, and reappears in the chamber of death at the moment of dissolution.

Half-a-mile from Blenkinsopp Castle is the Greenhead Railway Station, and half-a-mile from the station are the ruins of *Thirlwall Castle*, situated on a rocky boss about thirty feet above the stream, with a few pines around it. This cheerless-looking stronghold of the Thirlwalls, with its walls in some places nine feet thick, was entirely built of stones from the neighbouring barrier and the station of Carvoran. The date of its erection is not known. Mr. C. J. Bates does not think it was built earlier than the first half of the fourteenth century. In 1831 the east wall fell into the Tipalt, so that the merest fragment of the dark and shattered walls remains. The castle consists of a main building and a small tower that joins it on the east. The entrance was at the north-east corner. A stair immediately inside the door led up to a sort of turret, the curiously-vaulted basement of which was probably the dungeon. The interior, with its vaulted chambers, into which light was but sparingly admitted through the narrow loop-holed windows, must have been exceptionally comfortless, even in the rough days of Border warfare. A singular feature in the construction was discovered in 1759, when some rubbish being removed from the interior, the flooring of one of the apartments was found to consist of three courses of flags, one above another, with a stratum of sand lying between each.

Thirwall is generally stated to have derived its name from the fact that here the Caledonians first *thirled* or threw down the *wall*. Thirl-ian is an Anglo-Saxon word, signifying to penetrate, and, adds

Dr. Bruce, whatever truth there may be in this etymology, it is certain that this is the weakest part of the wall. The ancient family of De Thirlwall took their name from that of the manor and castle, and one of the early barons must have had the honour of entertaining Edward I., for it is stated he slept here on September 20th, 1306. John Thirlwall was a witness in a suit tried at Newcastle before Richard II. in 1385, of Scrope *versus* Grosvenor, in which both families claimed the right to bear the shield "azure, a bend or." According to the evidence of the witness, his father died at the age of a hundred and forty-five, and had borne arms in his time sixty-nine years. In 1542 the tower, as it was called, is recorded to have been "in measurable good reparations." Sad complaints in 1550 were made to government of the condition of the estates of the gentlemen who had "their inheritance and dwelling-places" on South Tyne; "and surely the inhabitants thereof be much prone and inclined to theft, especially a lordship next to the west border, at Powltrosse, called Thirlwall." The gathering cry, "A Thirlwall! a Thirlwall! a Thirlwall!" was heard in many a border fray. It is supposed that the proprietors ceased to make the fortress their residence after the rebellion of 1646. The last of the Thirlwalls was Eleanora, who carried the manor and castle by marriage to Matthew Swinburne, of Capheaton, by whom they were sold to an ancestor of the present owner, the Earl of Carlisle. In connection with the castle there is a legend which runs as follows:—A baron of Thirlwall returned from the wars with great spoils, having with him a table of solid gold, the report of which spread far and wide. In course of time the castle was attacked and taken by the Scots; the baron and his retainers were slain, and then came a search for the treasure. This had been known to be, night and day, under the guard of a mysterious dwarf. Dungeon and vault were searched in vain; and no wonder, as tradition says the dwarf, during the heat of the fray, threw the treasure into a deep well, and afterwards jumped in himself; then, by diabolical power, he drew the top down over himself and his charge, and there he still remains under the influence of a spell which can be removed by none save the only son of a widow. So far, however, the "dwarf well" has not been discovered.

Not far from Thirlwall Castle is the village of GLENWHELT, connected with Greenhead by a bridge across the Tipalt rivulet. In the house which bears this name, formerly an inn of considerable importance in the old coaching days, but now a farm-stead, are preserved a magnificent pair of red deer's antlers, found in a well at the Roman station of Carvoran. In a stone fence near the house is a colossal much-weathered bust of Roman workmanship. Other relics of Roman times—a small Roman goddess, now preserved in a glass-covered case; a Roman spear; and several altars and inscribed stones—may be seen at the neighbouring farm-house. On the rising ground, westward of Glenwhelt, and on the other side of the Tipalt, are the remains of a temporary camp, supposed to have been thrown up by the ninth legion, when advancing with Agricola into Scotland.

Close to Greenhead and Thirlwall is the water-parting of the North of England—the Tipalt, which belongs to the eastern water-shed, and the Irthing, which belongs to the western water-shed, approaching within two miles of each other.

On the extreme border-line of Northumberland, near to Gilsland railway station, stood *Mumps Ha'*, or *Beggars' Hall*, the house where Dandy Dinmont is represented (in *Guy Mannering*) as telling the news of Ellangowan's death to Meg Merrilies. This once famous hostelry has recently been enlarged. The ancient portion of the walls is yet traceable, and the work of restoration brought into view the small old windows, with their mullions and iron bars; and a secret passage was discovered leading from the kitchen to the attic. The entrance was in a closet at the right side of the fire-place, and the chimney was so built as to serve the purpose of a staircase. In the loft or attic fragments of what had been the dead bones of a child or children were discovered. The landlady of this notorious "hedge alehouse" was Margaret Carrick—nick-named "Meg of Mumps Hall"—who, after a long career of crime, died in peace on the 4th of December 1717, at the advanced age of one hundred, and sleeps in the churchyard of Upper Denton, where her daughter, Margaret Teasdale, who died 1777, aged ninety-eight, is also interred. She is said to have drugged her guests to death that she might rob them, and "a deep pond on the right of the road is shown as the place where Meg disposed of the bodies of her victims, and a phosphorescent light is still believed to float nightly over its waters." Mumps Ha' had a bad reputation for harbouring the lawless freebooters who infested the district, and Meg used to work into their hands by abstracting the charges from the pistols of unsuspecting travellers. In his notes to *Guy Mannering*, Sir Walter Scott recounts a characteristic anecdote of her treachery, the hero of the story being an old and sturdy yeoman belonging to the Scottish side, known as "Fighting Charlie of Liddesdale." The celebrated Gilsland Spa and Popping Stone are about a mile distant, on the Cumberland side of the Irthing, and from the Shaw's Hotel excursions may be made to the various places of interest that have just been described. On the opposite side of the river, a short distance north of the wall, is Wardrew Spa. Wardrew House was built in 1752 on the site of one much older. The poet Burns visited it in June 1787:—"Left Newcastle early and rode over a fine country to Hexham to breakfast, from Hexham to Wardrew, the celebrated spa where we slept." It was at Wardrew that Sir Walter Scott first met with his future spouse. A pane of glass in one of the windows with Sir Walter's name upon it, said to have been written by himself, was taken out by Mr. Hodgson Hinde, when he rented the house, owing to the annoyance caused by the hundreds of strangers who visited the place to see the writing. Far away to the north extends the bleak and desolate Spadeadam Waste.

## HALTWHISTLE TO ALSTON.

Featherstone Castle, 3 miles ; Lambley, 5 miles ; Knaresdale, 8 miles ; Slaggyford, 9 miles ; Kirkhaugh, 11½ miles ; Whitley Chapel, 11½ miles ; Alston, 14 miles.

FOLLOWING the main road in front of Bellister the tourist will notice on the right *Wydon Scar*, where the river has worn away the hill into an abrupt cliff. As he proceeds he will obtain fine views of the barren hills of Tindale, Blacklaw, Thornhope, and Coanwood in the distance. Passing through the richly-wooded park he will reach, after a delightful walk of three miles, *Featherstone Castle*. It occupies a picturesque situation in a little sequestered vale, opposite to the confluence of the Hartley Burn with the South Tyne, so that the scenery around is charmingly varied and beautiful, especially when contrasted with the heathy moorlands which lie beyond. The castle itself is a handsome castellated mansion, which has for its nucleus an old square pele-tower vaulted underneath. Part of the modern work is a gallery 60 feet long. There is also a Gothic chapel, to which has been added a mausoleum. The stern outlines of turrets, gables, window-arches, and merlons are beautifully softened by a profusion of ivy, which adds very much to the picturesque appearance of the castle. The visitor will hardly disagree with Mr. C. J. Bates that "Featherstone Castle, with its corner bartisans and carved corbels, is perhaps the loveliest tower in the county." It is the subject of a beautiful picture by T. M. Richardson. Old writers say the tower of the ancient family who held the place through many generations stood on high ground where there were two stones, Featherstones or Feuderstones, round which the feudal tenants of the manor were assembled ; the old place falling to decay, a castle was built on the haugh below, hence the name of Featherstonehaugh. The family, which boasts a long antiquity, was seated here in the early years of the thirteenth century, when the manor and castle were held by one Helios de Featherstonehalgh. The name appears frequently during the succeeding centuries in connection with important events. One member of the family in particular is not likely to be forgotten so long as English poetry endures—Sir Albany Featherstonehaugh, High Sheriff of Northumberland in 1530. He was killed in a border feud at Greensilhaugh, near the farmhouse of Wydon Eals (situated on the opposite side of the river, about a mile from his castle), by Nicholas Ridley of Unthank, Hugh Ridley of Harden, and others, on the 24th of October 1530. The event is commemorated in Surtees' famous ballad, which so deceived

Sir Walter Scott by its old-world accent and historical accuracy, that he inserted a stanza of it in his poem of "Marmion," stating in the notes that "this old Northumbrian ballad was taken down from the recitation of a woman, eighty years of age, mother of one of the miners in Alston Moor, by an agent for the lead mines there, who communicates it to my friend and correspondent, R. Surtees, Esq., of Mainsforth. 'She had not,' she said, 'heard it for many years; but when she was a girl it used to be sung at merry-makings till the roof rang again.'"

"Hoot awa', lads, hoot awa',
Ha' ye heard how the Ridleys, and Thirlwalls, and a'
Ha' set upon Albany Featherstonhaugh,
And taken his life at the Deadmanshaw?
There was Willemoteswick,
And Hardriding Dick,
And Hughie of Hawden, and Will of the Wa',
I canno' tell a', I canno' tell a',
And mony a mair that the de'il may knaw.

The auld man went down, but Nicol his son
Ran away afore the fight was begun;
And he run, and he run,
And afore they were done,
There was many a Featherston gat sic a stun,
As never was seen since the world begun.

I canna' tell a', I canna tell a',
Some gat a skelp, and some gat a claw;
But they gar'd the Featherstons haud their jaw—
Nicol and Aleck and a'.
Some gat a hurt, and some gat nane,
Some had harness, and some gat staen,
Ane gat a twist o' the craig;
Ane gat a bunch o' the wame;
Symy Haw gat lamed of a leg,
And syne ran wallowing hame.

Hoot, hoot, the auld man's slain outright!
Lay him now wi' his face down:—he's a sorrowful sight.
Janet, thou donot,
I'll lay my best bonnet,
Thou gets a new gude-man afore it be night.

Hoot away, lads, hoot away,
Wi's a' be hanged if we stay;
Tak' up the dead man, and lay him ahint the bigging;
Here's the Bailey o' Haltwhistle,
Wi' his great bull's pizzle,
That supp'd up the broo' and syne—in the piggin."

During the civil wars in the reign of Charles I. Timothy Featherstonehaugh espoused the Royal cause, and raised a troop of horse at his own expense. For his gallant conduct he was knighted under the king's banner, but was subsequently taken prisoner at the battle of Worcester, and beheaded at Bolton, in Lancashire. The castle is now in the possession of J. Hope Wallace, Esq., who, on coming of age in 1860, made several improvements and additions to it. The house contains some fine pictures by Reynolds and Gainsborough. The railway station and Wallace Arms, which are half-a-mile distant, may be reached by ascending the high ground in the rear of the castle. About half-a-mile to the north of the castle the stream is crossed by a picturesque bridge of one arch. In the Bridge End farm-house, close by, are preserved two old oak coffins of primitive construction which were found, along with some others of a similar nature, in a field on the Wydon Eals farm on the north side of the river. A little to the north of the bridge is a romantic little glen called Pynkinscleugh, which, for its size, has rather more than its share of eerie associations. We have the celebrated Mother Shipton predicting that when three boys with two thumbs on each hand should be born at Pinkie's Cleugh, the third should hold the reins of two kings while they contended together; and, if tradition may be believed, two of the four-thumbed boys have already appeared. Then we have a reputed witch named Janet Pearson, better known as "Beardie Grey," from her long hirsute appendage, who, about a hundred and fifty years ago, secured an unenviable local fame by her oracular utterances, and vanished in a mysterious manner one stormy night. A moss-covered wall and gable of the "Witches' Cot" are yet standing by the side of two venerable thorns. At the west corner of the hut there was once a huge grey stone, which served "Beardie" as a tripod during her prophetic visions. Tradition says that she prophesied that when that stone was covered with moss, a great battle would take place here, which would make the burn run red with blood for three days. The stone was rapidly being overgrown with moss, when it was destroyed some years ago. Then we have an account of a ghostly cavalcade of mail-clad warriors and courtly dames being seen at midnight, moving through the woody defile of Pynkinscleugh. Many hundreds of years ago, the story runs, there lived a bold baron of Featherstonhaugh, who committed the parental indiscretion of choosing a husband for his only daughter, Abigail, the last of the famous line. The lady, however, loved Ridley of Hardriding, whose suit had been rejected by the baron on account of an ancient feud. Neither tears nor entreaties prevailed to alter the baron's purpose, and in the small chapel adjoining the castle she was united to a distant relative, Timothy Featherstonhaugh. A hunting excursion took place in honour of the occasion, and as the party was returning home by the gloomy glen of Pynkinscleugh, it was met at a bridge, close to the road, by the rejected lover at the head of a well-appointed band of vassals, who attempted to carry away the lovely bride. A deadly combat ensued, in which the whole of the bridal party were cut down. The lady was accidentally killed while attempting to stop a desperate encounter between the bridegroom and her lover, and the latter, maddened with grief, put an end to his existence. His heart's blood, says the fragment of a wild ballad which still floats in the district, ran into a hollow stone, and the black ravens drank it out, filling the forest with vile croakings over their infernal banquet. This relic, called the Ravens'-stone, is still shown in a wood near the castle, and it is said that the ghostly bridal party traverse the road as surely as the anniversary of the fatal event year after year returns, disappearing at the scene of their murder.

Proceeding a short distance in the direction of the bridge over the Tyne, let the tourist take the first turn to the right, and continue on to the little ravine called "Glen Cune," nearly opposite to the castle. Quitting the road and following the burn to its confluence with the Tyne, he will pass a pretty miniature waterfall called "Bishop's Linn," from Bishop Percy, who first drew attention to it. The Hartley Burn, a little to the south of Glen Cune, will well repay exploring, especially to the geologist. One of its branches, the Blackburn, "abounds in basaltic precipices; the water, after running through a deep and narrow channel, is thrown over a columnar brae in a succession of falls. The basaltic columns below rise to a great height, and further down, where the stream crosses the dyke, the strata are broken, and dip at every angle, and are also intersected by veins of basalt. The diluvium is a bed of reddish clayey gravel, in which are embedded nodules of new red sandstone, masses of granite, and other products of countries to the west and northwards."

A quarter of a mile south of the point where the Blackburn enters the Tyne is the site of a small convent of Benedictine Nuns, founded by Adam de Tindale and Heloise, his wife, in the latter part of the twelfth century. During an incursion of the Scots in 1296 "the house of the holy nuns of Lambley" was burnt, and the country around devastated, while indignities worse than death were inflicted upon the unfortunate sisters. The convent was restored, and at the time of the suppression of religious houses by Henry VIII. contained six inmates. When Camden wrote, the nunnery was still standing, and the Tyne, he tells us, flowed amongst its dismantled walls, but every vestige of the buildings has now been swept away by the river. A pleasant walk of half-a-mile by the river-side past the hamlet of Harper Town, formerly, according to tradition, a large village which the Scots destroyed during one of their incursions, will bring the tourist to Lambley Viaduct, an elegant structure (within a few feet of the height of the High Level Bridge at Newcastle), which even Mr. Ruskin, with all his horror of railways, could not, we think, but admire as a graceful addition to the landscape.

Attached to the side of the viaduct, at a lower level than the railway, is a wooden bridge, by which the Tyne may be crossed to the railway station. Near the east end of the bridge, at a spot known as Castle Hill, is a small Roman camp, defended on three sides by the natural slope of the river bank, and on the fourth by a dry trench of some depth. This locality also presents several features of interest to the geologist, who will here see, perhaps, the best section of the ninety-fathom dyke, and may study the coal measures, as well as the millstone grit and mountain limestone.

Through the woods that crown the high-scarped cliff that has been worn into its present configuration by the action of the river, there is a pathway running all the way to the small and well-sheltered village of EALS, and commanding fine and extensive views over the surrounding country. Instead of proceeding to the village, however, the tourist will do well to cross the river by the wooden bridge, and proceed up the pretty and romantic ravine of *Glen Dhu*. Through narrow rocky defiles, under projecting masses of rock, around and over huge freestone boulders, gliding, swirling, and tumbling, the little burn pursues its way in a most charmingly wild and capricious fashion. Trees and shrubs and mosses grow in rich profusion. From the cool, moist crevices of the rocks spring all varieties of ferns, among which the oak fern is found in great luxuriance. About three-quarters of a mile up the glen, in a lonely and secluded spot, the streamlet leaps over a ledge of rock into a pool below, forming one of the prettiest waterfalls in the district. After a steep climb the tourist gains the road which crosses the ravine at almost the same point as the old Roman road—the *Maiden Way*. Continuing a mile and a quarter to the south, the hamlet of *Burnstones* is reached, a little north-east of which is *Knaresdale Hall*, a seventeenth-century house of considerable strength. This ancient seat of the lairds of Knaresdale lay for a long time in a ruinous and neglected condition, but some years ago it was made habitable, and is now the homestead of a farmer. Around it are signs of what some think was a moat, whilst others see the remains of ancient fish-ponds. The manor was at an early period in the possession of a family named Pratt, who, by some act of disloyalty, forfeited it to the Crown in the reign of Edward I. An extensive forest, well stocked with the now scarce red deer, was anciently a feature of Knaresdale.

There is a story connected with the hall which may be briefly summarised as follows :—The laird marries a young wife, who falls in love with her husband's nephew, and proves unfaithful to her marriage vows. The young man's sister learns the secret, but keeps silence for her brother's sake. The guilty pair, however, grow suspicious of her, and resolve upon a dark deed. One terribly stormy night the girl is sent to close an outer door in the rear of the house, where she is seized by her brother, who was on the watch, and plunged into an old pond much swollen by the rain. The old man, unsuspicious of foul play, falls asleep, but is awakened by the hideous howling of one of his dogs, and starting up in an agony, beholds his niece standing by the kitchen fire wringing the water from her long hair. At the sound of his voice the apparition vanishes. The guilty brother disappears, and is no more seen, and the lady dies from a brain fever, after having revealed in her unconscious ravings the dreadful secret.

*Knaresdale Church*, a little to the south of the hall, is a very plain structure, built in 1838 on the site of an older one. In the churchyard is the curious epitaph of Robert Baxter, who died October 4th, 1796 :—

"All you that please these lines to read,  
It will cause a tender heart to bleed;  
I murdered was upon the fell,  
And by the man I knew full well;  
By bread and butter which he'd laid,  
I, being harmless, was betray'd.  
*I hope he will rewarded be,*  
That laid that poison there for me."

A malicious person with whom Baxter had not long before had a quarrel is believed to have been guilty of this crime; yet, adds Mackenzie, it seems no inquest was held upon Baxter's body; and it is equally strange that the clergyman should permit a malediction on one of his parishioners to be put up in the churchyard. Rising sheer from the opposite side of the river is Williamston Fell.

A mile from Knaresdale is SLAGGYFORD, which once was a market town, and had its fair, but which began to decline when Alston came to the front. A grocer of Alston, some sixty years ago, having dreamed several times in succession that he would find lead at Slaggyford, sank a shaft at considerable expense, and commenced operations, but failed to discover the ore.

Two and a quarter miles further south, past *Kirkhaugh Church*, which is beautifully placed in the middle of the valley, is *Whitley Castle*, the modern name of a Roman outpost or station, measuring 150 yards by 128 yards, and enclosing an area of nearly nine acres. Unlike most Roman stations, which are quadrangular, its form is that of a trapezoid. On the west side it is overlooked by a ridge of high ground, and here, in addition to its ordinary walls, it is defended by seven earthen ramparts, and on the north side by four. The Maiden Way passes the east side of the station. A fine figure of Hercules, with several altars and inscribed stones, have been found here. In the garden belonging to the farm-house, called the Castle Nook, is preserved an altar which is carved on all four sides. The inscription has been nearly obliterated, but it has, no doubt, been dedicated to Apollo. Some antiquaries have tried to identify this station with the Alione of the Notitia. John Wallis, the historian, was born at the Castle Nook, a house "just at the south entry of the station" of Whitley Castle, and was baptised on December 3rd, 1714, at Kirkhaugh Church. "Northumberland," says he, "being Roman ground, and receiving my first breath in Alione or Whitley Castle, one of their castra, I was led by a sort of enthusiasm to an enquiry and search after their towns, their cities, and temples, their baths, their altars, their tumuli, their military ways, and other remains of splendour and magnificence." A short distance from Whitley Castle is the Gilderdale Burn, which forms the south-west boundary of Northumberland. Alston is two miles beyond.

# HEXHAM TO ST. OSWALD'S AND CHOLLERFORD.

**St. John Lee, 1½ miles; Written Crag, 3 miles; St. Oswald's Chapel, 4 miles; Chollerford, 5 miles.**

CROSSING the bridge over the Tyne, let the tourist keep straight on for a short distance, then, turning to the left, proceed along the road for half-a-mile, and take the first turn on the right to the *Church of St. John Lee*, a small and ancient structure, with an elegant spire, standing, it is believed, on the site of the oratory which St. Wilfrid erected and dedicated to St. Michael the Archangel. This bold and woody headland has been identified as Erneshow, or Eagle's Mount, where St. John of Beverley lived for some time in retirement before his exaltation to the bishopric of Hexham. The memory of his seclusion here is perpetuated in the name *Hermitage*, which the place has long borne. A singular marriage took place in this church in January 1765 between an old man of ninety, named Robert Scott, and one Jean Middlemass, who had seen but twenty-five summers. The bridegroom, who was a noted performer on the Northumbrian bagpipes, had for nearly twenty-six years travelled the country upon a pair of crutches; but on the day of the wedding he threw them away, and walked from his residence at Wall to the church and back without their aid. All who took part in the ceremony were either pipers or immediately connected with them. In the flower garden of the modern mansion, "The Hermitage," situated below the mount, is an old tombstone bearing the following Latin inscription:—"Hic jacet Georgius Heslope, Quondam Dominus De Hermitage, Qui Obiit 15 Jan. Anno Dom. 1655." From the church a lane conducts to the village of WEST ACOMB, chiefly inhabited by miners. Proceeding up the dene by the rocky bed of the stream, which has curiously worn for itself some deep and winding channels, the Fallowfield Lead Mines will be reached. The next object is to find the "Written Crag." This can be done by following the dene a little further, and then striking northward across the fell. A cairn on the top of the crag will serve as a landmark. The inscription, "Petra Flavi Carantini," is just under the heather-crowned brow, and is as legible as if the Roman mason had but chiselled it yesterday. Proceeding northward past the small fir plantation, the great west road is gained at St. Oswald's Hill Head. Into the front of one of the houses here a centurial stone is built, bearing the inscription, Cho. VIII. CAECILI CLIIME, "the century or company of Cecilius Clemens of the 8th cohort." A little to the west, on the rising ground to the north of the road, stands *St. Oswald's Chapel.* This little church was rebuilt in 1737, and contains but a few fragments of the Norman edifice. The site is considered to be the very spot where King Oswald first raised the standard of the cross in the battle of Hefenfelt, or Heaven's Field, A.D. 635. Opposite to it, on the south side of the road, is a field called Mould's Close, which, according to local tradition, witnessed the hottest of the fight. Here skulls and hilts of swords have been ploughed up. A large silver coin of St. Oswald, with a representation of the saint's head, sceptred, on one side, and the cross on the other, was found on repairing the church, and was for a long time used by the convent at Durham as their common seal in honour of him.

The facts of this famous battle, as gathered from Bede and other writers, seem to be these :—Osric, King of Bernicia, and Eanfrith, King of Deira, having been killed, the one in battle, the other during a parley, by Cadwallon, the duty of avenging their deaths fell upon Oswald, the younger brother of Eanfrith. Collecting a small army, he met the victorious Cadwallon near Hexham, and chose a good site for a pitched battle, protected to the north and west by steep rocky banks, and to the south by the great barrier left by the Romans. Cadwallon brought his immense forces from the north and west, and must have been at a great disadvantage so far as the ground was concerned. Before the battle Oswald erected a wooden cross, which he had ordered to be made, in the sight of all his army, and on his knees prayed to God that he would assist his worshippers in their great distress. Advancing towards the enemy with the first dawn of the day, the battle was begun, and seems to have raged as far as Hallington, where it is probable the defeated forces of Cadwallon may have rallied for a final struggle. Fortune, however, went against the British chieftain, and he fled southwards down the Watling Street, over the Tyne, and away to the south past Dilston, pursued by the victorious followers of Oswald, till, at the Deniseburn, which has been identified as the Rowley Burn, the hero of fourteen battles and sixty skirmishes was caught and. slain. At the spot where King Oswald offered up his prayer many miraculous cures are said to have been performed.

Two and a half miles to the north-east of St. Oswald's, a little beyond the Errington Hill Head farm-house, are the *Redhouse Crags*, on which are the remains of some ancient British camps.

Continuing westward from St. Oswald's the tourist will shortly come to *Plane-Trees Field* on the left side of the road, where a considerable portion of the Wall is yet remaining. Another interesting remnant will be found in the grounds of Brunton Hall, nearly a mile further on. It is seven feet high, and presents nine courses of facing-stones entire. On the south side of the Wall at this place there is a turret—a small quadrangular building, enclosing a space of twelve feet nine inches by eleven feet nine inches. The hamlet of Brunton commemorates in its name some act of Scottish incendiarism.

At the foot of the steep bank is CHOLLERFORD. Situated five miles west by north from Hexham, in the midst of romantic scenery, it is one of the best centres to make excursions from, along the most interesting sections of the Roman wall. It is also within easy distance of Haughton and Chipchase Castles.

The George Inn has gained a great reputation amongst tourists for the excellence of its accommodation, and almost justifies Dr. Johnson's dictum that "there is nothing which has yet been contrived by man by which so much happiness is produced as by a good tavern or inn.'

The river is crossed by a substantial stone bridge, erected in 1775. The older structure, destroyed by the disastrous flood of 1771, was probably the one rebuilt by Walter Skirlaw, Bishop of Durham, who, in 1394, granted "thirteen days' release from enjoined penance" to all who assisted in its restoration. Below the bridge is Chollerford Weir. If an old ballad, entitled "Jock o' the Side," had any foundation in fact, it may be inferred that there was no bridge here at the close of the sixteenth century. Jock o' the Side was a notable borderer in the time of Elizabeth, and assisted the Earl of Westmoreland in his escape after his unfortunate insurrection in 1570, with the Earl of Northumberland, who also was compelled to seek safety in flight, the Countess of Northumberland and her retinue in the meantime remaining in Jock's house in Liddesdale. The ballad commences—

"Now Liddesdale has ridden a raid,
  But I wat they had better hae staid at hame;
For Michael o' Winfield he is dead,
  And Jock o' the Side is prisoner ta'en."

Jock's uncle, Lord Mangerton, promises Lady Downie, the moss-trooper's mother, to attempt a rescue, and he sends three men, harnessed with steel, to Newcastle town for that purpose.

"At the Cholerford they a' light down,
  And there, wi' the help of the light o' the moon,
A tree they cut, wi' fifteen nogs on each side,
  To climb up the wa' of Newcastle toun."

Arriving there,

"They fand their stick baith short and sma'."

"Then up and spak the Laird's ain Jock,
  'There's naething for't, the gates we maun force,'
But when they cam the gate until,
  A proud porter withstood baith men and horse.

His neck in twa the Armstrongs wrang;
  Wi' fute or hand he ne'er play'd pa!
His life and his keys at anes they hae ta'en,
  And cast his body ahint the wa.' "

They reach the jail, burst open the doors, set Jock, who is laden with "full fifteen stane o' Spanish iron," on their steeds, and take their departure.

"The night, tho' wat, they didna mind,
But hied them on fu' merrilie,
Until they cam to Cholerford brae,
Where the waters ran like mountains hie.

But when they cam to Cholerford,
There they met with an auld man;
Says, 'Honest man, will the water ride?
Tell us in haste, if that ye can.'—

'I wat weel no,' quo' the gude auld man,
'I hae lived here thretty years and three,
And I ne'er yet saw the Tyne sae big,
Nor running anes sae like a sea.'"

After a slight demur on the part of "the laird's soft Wat," they take the water, and swim across; but hardly have they reached the other bank when their pursuers, twenty in number, ride up to the stream. These are too faint-hearted to follow, and Jock and his deliverers hie them away to Liddesdale.

Chollerford possesses some of the most interesting relics of the Roman occupation in Britain, and their discovery is chiefly due to the antiquarian enthusiasm of John Clayton, Esq. The remains of the Roman bridge that crossed the river here, and the ruins of the military city of Cilurnum, will long continue to excite the wonder of the visitor as he realises something of "the grandeur that was Rome." To reach the old bridge the visitor must cross the stile at the east end of the modern bridge, and follow a footpath through the plantation by the river-side. The river has, during the last seventeen centuries, shifted its course westward, hence the western abutment is now quite submerged. Two of the piers on which the bridge itself rested can be seen whenever the water is low; a third is buried beneath the accumulations of the river's bank, and the eastern land abutment is far back in the plantation. It was discovered through the sagacity of Mr. W. Coulson, of Corbridge, in 1860. It is a solid mass of masonry, measuring on the side directly fronting the river, twenty-two feet. The facing-stones, which are ornamented with the feathered tooling, have been placed in their position by the *luis*, and they have been bound together by rods of iron embedded in lead. The bridge itself was no doubt constructed of timber. Among the *débris* is a stone about four feet in length, resembling an axle-tree. It has orifices as if for receiving handspikes.

A covered way, formed subsequently to the bridge, will be observed crossing the abutment and cutting the castellum, but no satisfactory theory has been put forward by antiquaries to account for its existence. Built into the abutment are the remains of a pier, where the cramping of the stones is entirely different, and it is believed that this is a relic of the bridge built by Agricola, and used by Hadrian as a nucleus around which to form his own construction. The monolithic pillar here and the portion of another, together with the stone shaped like the nave of a wheel or a barrel, are believed by Mr. Sheriton Holmes to have formed part of an ingenious arrangement for breaking the communication along the line of the bridge, by lifting a portion of the wooden platform out of position. The two pillars he imagines to have been set up on the face line of the abutment, and a beam laid across their heads. "Then athwart this," he says, "place a lever beam on a spindle, and sling from one end a portion of the planked roadway of the bridge's eastern bay, and at the other, as a counterpoise, the barrel-shaped stone (for the proximity of the castellum limited the length of the lever in this direction), and we have a lift and swing-bridge fifteen hundred years old." Returning to the inn, and continuing along the road for half-a-mile westward, the student of Roman antiquities will not fail to visit

THE CHESTERS.—The mansion, situated amidst a profusion of stately trees, was built by John Errington in 1771, and is now the property and residence of John Clayton, Esq., a zealous antiquary, whose good hap it has been to have three of the principal stations on his estate, and has thus been enabled to preserve from the hands of the utilitarian destroyer so many wonderful remnants of Roman power and skill. In the park may be seen all that now remains of *Cilurnum*. Excepting Amboglanna, the modern Birdoswald, it is the largest station on the line of the wall. It occupies 5¼ acres, and is, as usual, in the form of a parallelogram, with the corners slightly rounded off. Its ramparts are five feet thick, and traces of the fosse may in several places be made out. The station is entered by six gateways, two on the east and west sides, and one on the north and south respectively. All the main gateways consist of two portals, separated from each other by a wall, having a narrow passage through it. Each portal has been spanned by an arch, and closed by two-leaved gates, which have moved upon pivots. On each side is a guard-chamber. The two main streets, running from north to south, and east to west, and crossing each other at right angles, are about eighteen feet wide. The other streets of the camp are exceedingly narrow—scarcely a yard in width.

Entering the western gateway, from the south jamb of which the wall takes its departure, and proceeding to the centre of the camp, the visitor will notice the ruins of the *Forum*, or Market-Place, with its public buildings. The street which crossed the station from east to west passed along its northern front, and the street which came from the north gate of the station led directly to the north gate of the Forum, which had also gates on its eastern and western sides. The square enclosure, into which goods were brought, was surrounded by a covered colonnade.

The gutter-stones which received the rain falling from the roof still occupy their original position. Grooves formed by the action of wheels will be noticed in the eastern entrance. At the south end of the Forum are three halls, each having a wide portal. "The central chamber is believed to have been the ærarium of the station, the place where the treasure chest of the regiment was kept, and where all pecuniary business connected with it was transacted; the chambers on each side of it are believed to be the curiæ, in which court-martials were held and the justice of the district dispensed." A vault, which was entered from the original ærarium, was constructed, at a later period, for the more effectual preservation of the treasure chest. Some knowledge of this subterranean chamber had been preserved in the folk-lore of the district, but tradition had elaborated it into a stable capable of accommodating five hundred horses. The peculiar construction of the roof should be noticed. Between the Forum and the eastern rampart an interesting series of buildings will be observed, which are believed to have been the *Prætorium*, or general's quarters. The floors of the chambers are supported upon pillars of brick or stone, so as to leave a considerable space beneath for the transmission of heated air, from a furnace in the south-east corner of the building. The hot air was likewise carried up the walls by means of flue tiles. In this manner the apartment was warmed. Near to these interesting ruins is the Eastern Gateway, by which the station was entered from the bridge. The great wall came up to the southern jamb of this gateway. The guard-chambers are unusually complete, their walls being, in one place, twelve courses high. Passing towards the river, the foundations of a large range of buildings, lately excavated, will be seen. These consist of a court-yard, paved with rough flags, and having its western wall pierced on its inner side by seven niches or recessed arches; a foot-worn passage leading to two chambers furnished with hypocausts; a large hall with floor of concrete; a chamber attached to it having a splayed opening or window, beneath which Dr. Bruce found some fragments of Roman glass; another long apartment with a concrete floor, communicating by three apertures in its north wall with a smaller room.

The burial-ground of the station was to the south of it, at a point where the river bends rapidly to the east. Cilurnum was garrisoned, as numerous inscriptions prove, by the second Ala of Astures, a people from the modern Asturia in Spain. The station was evidently destroyed by an irruption of the Caledonians, when all the buildings were thrown down, and even the heavy stone floors smashed.

In Mr. Clayton's mansion, and in the portico before it, as well as in the Antiquity House, are preserved numerous altars, inscribed stones, statuary, vases of Samian ware, earthen vessels of native manufacture, intaglios, gems, coins and rings, etc., from Cilurnum and other stations on the wall. Among the interesting relics found here may be mentioned a headless figure of Cybele, the mother of the gods, standing upon a bull; a half-sitting, half-reclining figure, supposed to represent the genius of the North Tyne; and a diploma conferring the right of citizenship upon those soldiers in certain divisions of the army who had completed twenty-five campaigns and received honourable discharge. This is written on both sides of two tablets of bronze, and is now in the British Museum.

# CHOLLERFORD TO HALTWHISTLE.

**Carrawburgh, $3\frac{1}{2}$ miles ; Carraw, 4 miles ; Sewingshields, $6\frac{1}{2}$ miles ; Housesteads, 8 miles ; Crag Lough, $9\frac{1}{2}$ miles ; Cawfields Mile-castle, $12\frac{1}{2}$ miles ; Æsica, 14 miles ; Haltwhistle, 16 miles ; Magna, $17\frac{1}{2}$ miles.**

FOR two and a half miles the road westward is uphill the whole way, and thus, from several elevated points, exceedingly fine views may be obtained across the surrounding country. At Walwick, by the road-side, is a wide-spreading Scotch elm, called "General Wade's tree," under which the great road-maker took shelter during a thunderstorm. On the hill called Tower Taye is a small tower, built a century and a half ago out of the stones of the wall. A little beyond are the remains of a mile-castle. On the Black Carts farm, still further on, is a piece of the wall, 6 feet high, and the foundations of a turret remain. Near the summit of Limestone Bank the plantation on the left should be entered, for there the ditch of the vallum is in a condition approaching perfection. A remarkable triumph of engineering skill will be observed at the top of the hill, where the fosse of both wall and vallum have been cut through the hard basaltic rock. Huge masses of that substance lie about the brink. One large block lying on the northern margin, and now split into three pieces, probably by the action of frost, must have been, when lifted from its place, not less than thirteen tons in weight.

A short distance beyond, on the left-hand side of the road, is *Procolitia*, now called Carrawburgh, 3½ miles from Cilurnum. A Roman well, at present furnished with a pump, will be observed before the camp is reached. The remains here are very scanty. The ramparts and gateways can clearly be made out. The guard-room of the west gateway has been uncovered, and a little to the south of this a barrack-room may be seen. Just inside the field dyke, on the west of the station, is the now famous Coventina's well, which appears to have been in the centre of a temple dedicated to Coventina, a goddess hitherto unknown in either Greek, Roman, or Celtic mythology. Lost sight of since Horsley's time, it was accidentally discovered a few years ago by some miners who were prospecting for lead ore. By Mr. Clayton's instructions it was shortly afterwards cleared, when a surprising discovery was made, for here were coins to the number of 16,000, ranging from the time of Marc Antony to that of Gratian, carved stones, altars, vases, Roman pearls, old shoes, fibulæ, and other relics of antiquity, in one indiscriminate mass. It would seem as if the military chest had on some occasion of alarm been thrown into the well for security. A sculptured stone, representing three water nymphs, which was found here, had formerly adorned the little temple. A coin struck in the fourth consulship of the Emperor Antoninus Pius, A.D. 145, to commemorate the exploits of Lollius Urbicus in Britain, appears in considerable number in the collection. Britannia is represented on the reverse as a disconsolate female sitting on a rock. She has no helmet, no sword, or spear. Her head is bent sadly forward, her standard is lowered, and her shield abandoned. The legend is Britannia. To circulate this coin in Britain, adds Dr. Bruce, was to add insult to injury. Procolitia covers an area of three acres and a half, and was garrisoned by the first cohort of Batavians.

Half-a-mile west is Carraw, a farm-house, once the summer retreat of the priors of Hexham, and half-a-mile south-west of this place are the remains of an earthen camp, called Brown Dykes. Near to Shield-on-the-Wall, a mile-castle, with gateway and northern wall very distinct, should be examined, and then a little further on the traveller should leave the road which bends to the left and make for the farm-house of Sewingshields, three-quarters of a mile distant. He will notice on the way how the vallum swerves so as to avoid the bold basaltic ridge up which the wall has been carried. This series of rugged crags, which will have to be followed all the way to Haltwhistle, is the great Whin Sill, "a name given to a sheet of dolerite, the outcrop of which stretches across Northumberland from Greenhead to a few miles south of Berwick, and which probably underlies almost the whole of the southern and eastern portions of the county. Of undoubted igneous origin, this flow of basalt has yet given rise to much contention among geologists, some arguing that it was a regularly interbedded trap, the mineralogical character of which alone distinguished it from the beds above and below, and others with—as it has since been proved—more reason, that it was a purely intrusive mass injected just as the ordinary dykes are, long after the deposition of the rocks amongst which it lies." The opinion expressed by Professor Lebour is that the intrusion took place at the close of the carboniferous period.

The farm-house of Sewingshields is built entirely of stones from the wall. The name is understood to mean "cottages by the fosse," from "seugh," fosse, and "shiels" huts. There is a steep "Shepherd's Pass" leading down through a cranny in the rocks to the plain where, a short distance from the crags, in a north-easterly direction, is the site of Sewingshields Castle. The date of its erection is unknown. In 1542 it belonged to John Heron, of Chipchase, and was then much delapidated. Exposed as it was to the raids of the thieves of Liddesdale and Tynedale on the one hand, and those of Gilsland and Bewcastle on the other, few could be induced to "aventure theyr lyves, bodies, and goodes in such remote houses where small relefe can come to them in theyr extreme necessyties." The state of the country was such that Sir Cuthbert Radcliffe, Deputy-Warden of the East Marches, appointed two watchmen to "stand at the Sewynge shealles cragge" from "sonne sett untyll the sonne aryse," in order to give warning in case any bands of borderers were seen.

Some years ago the walls were standing five feet high, but these and the vaults, which also remained, have been removed, and the site is now under the plough. Though this little patch of cultivation in the midst of the barren moorland is no longer rendered picturesque by the hoary ruins, yet there lingers around it an atmosphere of romance which the most matter-of-fact tourist must surely succumb to as he stands in this lonely region, tracing across those tall black crags, that assume such fantastic shapes, the wonderful wall of Hadrian, or listening to

> "Undescribèd sounds
> That come a-swooning over hollow grounds,
> And wither drearily on barren moors."

Sir Walter Scott has introduced the locality in the sixth canto of "Harold the Dauntless," where the old pele is referred to as "The Castle of the Seven Shields," and its desolation thus described :—

> "No towers are seen
> On the wild heath, but those that Fancy builds,
> And, save a fosse that tracks the moor with green,
> Is nought remains to tell of what may there have been."

A legend, which harmonises well with a theory recently advanced, that King Arthur was the Pen-Dragon of the Britons of Strathclyde, or the region between the wall of Hadrian and the wall of Antonine, has been preserved by Mr. Hodgson in his *History of Northumberland.*

"Immemorial tradition has asserted that King Arthur, his queen Guenever, his court of lords and ladies, and his hounds, were enchanted in some cave of the crags, or in a hall below the castle of Sewingshields, and would continue entranced there till some one should first blow a bugle-horn that lay on a table near the entrance of the hall, and then with 'the sword of the stone' cut a garter, also placed there beside it. But none had ever heard where the entrance to this enchanted hall was, till the farmer at Sewingshields, about fifty years since, was sitting knitting on the ruins of the castle, and his clew fell, and ran downwards through a rush of briars and nettles, as he supposed, into a subterannean passage. Full in the faith that the entrance into King Arthur's hall was now discovered, he cleared the briary portal of its weeds and rubbish, and entering a vaulted passage, followed in his darkling way the thread of his clew. The floor was infested with toads and lizards ; and the dark wings of bats, disturbed by his unhallowed intrusion, flitted fearfully around him. At length his sinking courage was strengthened by a dim, distant light, which, as he advanced, grew gradually brighter, till, all at once, he entered a vast and vaulted hall, in the centre of which a fire, without fuel, from a broad crevice in the floor, blazed with a high and lambent flame, that showed all the carved walls and fretted roof, and the monarch and his queen and court reposing around in a theatre of thrones and costly couches. On the floor, beyond the fire, lay the faithful and deep-toned pack of thirty couple of hounds ; and on a table before it the spell-dissolving horn, sword, and garter. The shepherd reverently, but firmly, grasped the sword, and as he drew it leisurely from its rusty scabbard, the eyes of the monarch and his courtiers began to open, and they rose till they sat upright. He cut the garter; and as the sword was being slowly sheathed the spell assumed its ancient power, and they all gradually sank to rest; but not before the monarch had lifted up his eyes and hands, and exclaimed—

> "O, woe betide that evil day
>   On which this witless wight was born,
> Who drew the sword, the garter cut,
>   But never blew the bugle-horn."

Terror brought on loss of memory, and the shepherd was unable to give any correct account of his adventure, or to find again the entrance to the enchanted hall. There are slight variations in this story, which is found in many parts of England and Scotland.

A slight connubial difference between the royal personages of the legend is associated with the highest points of two sandstone ridges to the north and a little to the west of Sewingshields. They are called respectively the King's and Queen's Crag. It seems that, according to the following legend, "King Arthur, seated on the farthest rock, was talking with his queen, who, meanwhile, was engaged in arranging her 'back-hair.' Some expression of the queen's having offended his majesty, he seized a rock which lay near him, and, with an exertion of strength for which the Picts were proverbial, threw it at her, a distance of about a quarter of a mile. The queen, with great dexterity, caught it upon her comb, and thus warded off the blow. The stone fell about midway between them, where it lies to this very day, with the marks of the comb upon it, to attest the truth of the story. The stone probably weighs about twenty tons."

Two miles north of Sewingshields, on the moors, is an upright stone, which also has its legend, as follows:—

"Cumming (or Kimmin), a northern chieftain, having paid one day a visit to King Arthur, at his castle near Sewingshields, was kindly received and presented with a gold cup, as a token of lasting friendship. The king's sons coming in, and hearing what their father had done, set out in pursuit of Cumming. They overtook him and slew him at this place, which has borne the name of Cumming's Cross ever since."

A quarter of a mile east of Sewingshields Castle, opposite the remains of a mile-castle, are the earthworks of an ancient British camp, with the foundations of rude circular dwellings still visible.

From the heights of Sewingshields the eye has a range over scenery of the most varied character, from the dreary stretch of waste and moss-land on the north to the fertile slopes on the south, with Hexham in the dim background nestling in a fold of the woody banks of the Tyne.

In the neghbourhood of Sewingshields may be found the ferns—

| | |
|---|---|
| Polypodium Dryopteris - - - | Oak Fern. |
| ,, Phegopteris - - - | Beech do. |
| Botrychium Lunaria - - - | Common Moonwort Fern. |
| Allosorus Crispus - - - - | Rockbrake, or Mountain Parsley Fern. |

and the flowers—

| | |
|---|---|
| Epilobium Angustifolium - - | Rosebay, Willow Herb, French Willow. |
| Listera Cordata - - - - | Heart-Leaved Tway Blade. |
| Lonicera Xylosteum - - - | Upright Honeysuckle. |
| Circæa Alpina - - - - - | Mountain Enchanter's Night Shade. |
| Orchis Bifolia - - - - - | Butterfly Orchis. |
| Orchis Conopsea - - - - | Aromatic Orchis. |
| Orchis Pyramidalis - - - - | Pyramidal Orchis. |
| Satyrion Viride - - - - | Frog Satyrion. |
| Salix Fusca - - - - - | Brownish Dwarf Willow. |

Proceeding westward along the top of the crags, the basaltic columns will be observed. One of these, about fifty feet high, called King Arthur's Chair, was mischievously thrown down some years ago. A narrow chasm in the rocks a little beyond is called Cat Gate, where, according to tradition, the Scots bored a hole under the wall large enough for a man to creep through. According to another supposition it was pierced by the Romans as a sort of sally-port. Continuing, an ancient cutting and earthwork of unknown antiquity, called the Black Dike, will be observed running past the Queen's Crag through a gap crossed by the wall. It is supposed to have been the boundary line between the kingdoms of Northumbria and Cumbria. A good view will now be obtained, to the north of the wall, of Bromlee Lough, which relieves the monotonous hues of the moorland with its silvery sheen. In its waters may be found the beautiful Nymphæa Alba, or White Water-lily.

According to tradition, a massive box of treasure was sunk in the lough by one of the ancient lords of Sewingshields, and subjected by him to a spell, that it should never be recovered save by the co-operation of "two twin yands (horses), two twin oxen, two twin lads, and a chain forged by a smith of kind (one who claims his descent in unbroken succession from six ancestors of the same trade as himself—he being of the seventh generation)." At a subsequent period some person, attaching credit to the legend, made an attempt to win the hoard of hidden gold in accordance with the requirements of the spell. The chain was attached, the horses and oxen urged forward by the young man, when, as the treasure-chest was moving towards the side of the lough one of the links in the chain broke, and with it the potency of the whole plan of recovering the lost treasure, which to this day lies hidden under the pale still waters. The failure is ascribed to a flaw in the ancestry of the smith who made the chain. Grindon Lough used to be a pleasant feature in the landscape to the south of the mural ridge, but it has recently been drained to a considerable extent.

The next point of interest is Busy Gap, a wide break in the ridge of basalt, about a mile from Sewingshields. This was the pass most frequently chosen by the freebooters of the Middle Ages when on their marauding expeditions to the rich valley of the Tyne, and hence it acquired an evil reputation. In Newcastle formerly, to call a brother burgess "a Busy Gap rogue" was to incur the censure of one's guild, as is attested by an entry in the books of the Company of Bakers and Brewers of Newcastle-on-Tyne. Camden, writing in 1599, calls it "a place infamous for thieving and robbing," and tells us that he dared not go near to take a full survey of the wall "for the rank robbers thereabouts," and Hutton, who made a survey of the wall when eighty years of age, says—"A more dreary country than this in which I now am can scarcely be conceived. I do not wonder it shocked Camden; the country itself would frighten him without the moss-troopers." The wall here being more than usually exposed, is not only strengthened with the fosse common in the low grounds, but has the additional protection of a rampart of triangular form to the north of it. Ascending the crags again, the vallum will be seen well-developed in the vicinity of the Moss Kennel farm-house. After passing a mile-castle and two other gaps, a descent is made into the valley of Knag Burn. Here there is a passage through the wall, which has originally been closed with double gates, and had a guard-room on each side. The purpose of this gateway has been to give access to an amphitheatre which is situated a short distance to the north of the wall at this point. It is 100 feet across, and about 10 feet deep, and has, no doubt, been furnished with wooden seats. Here the soldiery of Borcovicus relieved the monotony of their camp life by watching the gladiatorial combats of British captives. "Nettles," says Dr. Bruce, "may usually be seen growing in the bottom of it—a sure proof of human presence. Has the arena been soaked with human blood?"

Crossing the Knag Burn, the tourist follows the wall, which is here in good preservation, to *Borcovicus*, the modern Housesteads.

In no other station on the wall are the ruins so extensive and remarkable as in this one, the masonry of the surrounding ramparts and gateways being wonderfully perfect after the lapse of so many centuries.

Borcovicus, called by Stukeley, "the Tadmor of Britain," and by Dr. Bruce, with greater propriety, "the British Pompeii," derived its name from the neighbouring hill of Barcombe or Borcom, whence the Romans obtained large quantities of stone for their great work. It is in the usual form of a parallelogram with rounded angles, and was evidently built before the contiguous portions of the wall were commenced. Occupying a rocky eminence that slopes gently to the south, it covers an area of nearly five acres. The eastern wall, which is five feet in thickness, has been cleared, and the visitor to Borcovicus will thus have an opportunity of examining the massiveness of the Roman masonry as he proceeds to the East Gateway. The gates here, as at the Chesters and other places, have each consisted of two portals. In the southernmost guard-chamber a quantity of coal was found when the *débris* was cleared away in 1833. This had probably been stored there by some moss-trooper who had taken up his residence in one of the chambers of the camp. The holes in which the pivots moved, the stone against which the gates struck when they were closed, and the deep ruts caused by the chariot-wheels, should be noticed. From this gateway to the opposite one on the west ran the main street, or *via principalis*. Proceeding northwards along the inside of the east wall, a solid platform of masonry, evidently constructed for a catapult or balista, will be seen. The outside of the north rampart wall and the north gateway present one of the finest pieces of masonry on the line of the wall. The joints of the large square blocks forming its base are as close as ever. Near to the gateway is a large stone trough. What its purpose was is not known. One of the labourers employed in the excavations here gave it as his opinion "that the Romans used it for washing their Scotch prisoners in." Near to this trough is a round hearth formed of Roman tiles. When found it was covered with coal ashes and the scoriœ of iron. Dr. Bruce regards it as the remains of a smithy. From this gateway to the centre of the station ran the Prætorian street. On the west side are two large apartments—one 78 feet long and 18 feet wide, the other not quite so long, having at its west end a moss-trooper's kiln for drying corn. On the east side is a very large building, 147 feet in length and 30 feet in width. At its eastern end are several small chambers. One of them has been heated by the flues beneath the floor. Another contains a cistern or bath. Some of these large buildings, says Dr. Bruce, were no doubt the halls in which the public business of the district was transacted, and others were used as the residence of the prefect and his chief officers. The foundation walls of many other chambers, inhabited chiefly by the ordinary soldiers, remain, but there is little to be gathered from them as to the internal arrangements of the camp. The south gateway will repay examination. One of its guard-chambers has been utilised by some moss-trooper for his pele. The south wall of the station stands ten or twelve courses high. The finest and most complete of all the gateways is the west, eleven courses of masonry in height. At some period subsequent to its erection, the northern portion of the outside gate and the southern portion of the inside gate have been built up, thus rendering the entrance passage a diagonal one. The threshold has been worn by the tread of feet, and many projecting stones in the outside wall have been rounded and hollowed by the soldiers sharpening their knives or weapons upon them. The guard-chambers are in a state of good preservation.

The whole of the bank in front of the station is covered with the foundations of streets and houses, showing that the suburbs must have been very extensive. A little to the south, extending westwards, the hill-side has been scarped in flights of terraces, similar to the hanging vineyards seen in Italy and on the steep sides of Lebanon. The plain below towards the east was the burial-ground. Midway between the station and the turnpike-road is a small sandstone ridge, called Chapel Hill, from a belief that a considerable temple once crowned the summit. Many altars have been found here. Two of the most remarkable were discovered in 1883, and bear very elaborate dedications to Mars Thingsus and two goddesses named Beda and Fimmilena. A little to the west of Chapel Hill is the site of a semi-subterranean cave, discovered in 1822. It appears to have been devoted to the worship of Mithras—the Sun, or the Persian Apollo—and has doubtless been the scene of many of the abominable mysteries connected with the cultus of that deity. Three inscribed altars were found, besides the remains of several sculptured figures, and a tablet on which Mithras was represented coming out of an egg, and surrounded by a belt bearing the signs of the Zodiac. A beautiful bas-relief of the Goddess Victory was brought to light during the excavations of the station. Borcovicus was garrisoned by the first cohort of Tungrians. For some distance from Borcovicus the wall is in excellent condition. A quarter of a mile from the station are the interesting remains of a mile-castle, which has evidently more than once suffered from the devastations of the enemy, and been destroyed, judging by the *débris* on which the second floor was built. The springers of the arch of the north gateway are still in position. The north wall of the castle, identical with the great barrier, stands fourteen courses, or nine feet six inches high, and is the finest specimen of the mural masonry on the whole line. The wall now takes its course over Cuddy's Crag, across Rapishaw Gap, mounts the next height, from which it rapidly descends to Hot Bank. To the right is Greenlee Lough, one of the largest of the Northumbrian lakes, bounded on its north side by high and steep rocks. Near to its western margin is Bonnie Rig Hall, the shooting-box of Sir Edward Blackett. To the left, on the south of the turnpike-road, is Bradley Hall, now a farm-house, but once a place of importance, to judge from foundations of considerable buildings which may still be traced. Here Edward I., advanced in age and enfeebled in health, rested for a time on his last journey to Scotland in 1306. Crossing Milking Gap, where there are distinct traces of a mile-castle, the tourist ascends the heights above Crag Lough—a shallow little mere, whose waters are darkened by the reflection of the naked precipices of basalt above.

This lough is the habitat of the water-hen, and is often visited by flocks of wild ducks. Here may be found the different kinds of pondweed—*Potamogeton rufescens*, *P. perfoliatum*, and *P. pectinatum*; the yellow water-lily, *Nuphar lutea;* the reed mace, *Typha latifolia*, and other botanical specimens. In the crevices of the crags grow the mountain parsley fern (*Allosorus crispus*), oak fern (*Polypodium dryopteris*), beech fern (*Polypodium Phegopteris*), common moonwort fern (*Botrychium lunaria*). The Tyneside Naturalists' Field Club report the discovery, near the water's edge, of two beautiful fresh-water zoophytes, new to the north of England, with a few fresh-water shells; also among them *Phyla fontonalis*, *Planorbis albus*, and *Ancylus lacustris*, small in size, being dwarfed by their exposure in this elevated situation. A scarce little bivalve (*Pisidium niledum*) was also found. The skull-cap (*Scutellaria galericulata*), the intermediate bladderwort (*Utricularia intermedia*), intermediate and wild balsam (*Impatiens noli me tangere*), are occasionally found in the vicinity.

*Steel-Rig Gap* will soon be reached, where the traveller will notice the manner in which the courses of wall stones are stepped horizontally into the face of the ground. Hence the wall climbs a bold eminence, running along the verge of the cliff until it reaches *Castle Nick*, where the military way appears in very perfect condition, with the kerb-stones complete on each side. Here the remains of a mile-castle will repay examination. The walls are seven feet thick, and have six or seven courses of stone standing. The foundations of the interior apartments still remain on its western side.

Passing another gap, called the *Cat's Stairs*, *Peel Crag*, with its tall and precipitous basaltic columns, is next reached. In the valley by the side of the military road is a farm-house, which was once a famous inn, known as The Twice Brewed. It was a great resort for the carriers between Newcastle and Carlisle, whose appetites, as displayed here, made Hutton conclude that eating was the chief end of man. A little further along the wall-ridge are the remains of another mile-castle. The wall now ascends *Winshields Crag*, where it attains an elevation of 1230 feet above the level of the sea, the highest point throughout its course. From these crags the sails of vessels upon the distant Solway may be perceived on a clear day. To the north is a ridge of ground called Scotch Coulthard. When fugitive moss-troopers reached this point their escape was considered secure, for all beyond is waste and swire, where only they could find footing. Here, then, between the Wall and Scotch Coulthard, was the place where, if the fugitive could not make his heels, or rather the sturdy legs of his shaggy Scotch nag, save his head, he must turn at bay; and that many a fierce encounter has here been waged is evident from the numerous skeletons turned up wherever the ground is broken for drainage operations. The next depression in the ridge bears the uncanny name of Bogle Gap. The one succeeding it is Caw Gap, north of which is a lonely house called Burn Deviot, formerly the resort of smugglers and sheep-stealers, and now inhabited, it is alleged, by the spirits of the persons murdered there. Two large stones on the south of this gap, called the Mare and Foal, are said to be of Druidical erection. After passing Bloody Gap and Thorny Doors, a mile-castle of great interest is reached near the farm-house of Cawfields. The building is in the form of a parallelogram, with its corners at its lower side rounded off, and measures internally 63 feet by 49 feet. Its walls are eight feet thick and seven or eight courses of masonry high. The gateways, both on the northern and southern sides, are of large dimensions, consisting of massive blocks of freestone. The pivot-holes may still be seen. It is difficult to conjecture why this mile-castle should differ from the rest in having a gateway to the north, as it opens directly on to the edge of the crag, which is precipitous. A road leads from the vicinity of the mile-castle to Haltwhistle, nearly two miles distant. Crossing the Haltwhistle

Burn, and following the wall, the next object of interest is *Æsica*, or *Great Chesters*. This station covers an area of about three acres, but the remains are not very extensive. The ramparts and fosse are still clearly defined, and the southern and eastern gateway may also be identified. In the centre of the camp is a vaulted chamber, but in a dilapidated condition. To the south and east are traces of suburban buildings. The station was garrisoned by the second cohort of the Astures. The water supply to the camp was obtained from the head of the Caw Burn, 2¼ miles away, by means of an artificial water channel, three or four feet deep, which, on account of the nature of the ground, has had to wind about a good deal, thus lengthening out its course to six miles. Between this station and the next there is a fine stretch of the wall, exhibiting in its north face six or seven courses of facing-stones, and in some places as many as nine. It is reached soon after passing Cockmount Hill farm-house. The Nine Nicks of Thirlwall, so named from that number of peaks in the rocky ridge, next invite the traveller's attention. The highest of these is Muckle Bank Crag, 860 feet above the sea. The view opens out grandly to the west, where, in the extreme distance, may be descried the peaks of Arran ; to the south is the valley of the South Tyne, backed by heath-clad hills overtopped by the rugged form of Crossfell. Skiddaw also greets the eye across the wastes of Cumberland. To the north stretches the withered waste to which the eye has been accustomed for so many miles, and to the east lies the mighty basaltic ridge traversed by the wall.

At Walltown is a spring surrounded by masonry, called "King Arthur's Well." According to tradition, this is where Paulinus baptised King Egbert. In the crevices of the whinstone rock grow abundant patches of chives (*Allium schenoprasum*), which are said to have been planted by the Romans. Says Camden—"There continueth a settled persuasion among a great part of the people thereabout, and the same received by tradition, that the Roman soldier of the marches did plant here everywhere in old time for their use certaine medicinable hearbs, for to cure wounds: whence is it that some emperick practitioners of chirurgery in Scotland, flock hither every year in the beginning of summer, to gather such simples and wound-herbes ; the vertue whereof they highly commend as found by long experience, and to be of singular efficacy." Near the present farm-house stood the old castellated tower of Walltown, which formerly belonged to John Ridley, the brother of the martyr. Of his relatives here the bishop took farewell in the following affectionate terms :—"Farewell, my beloved brother, John Ridley, of the Walltoun, and you, my gentle and loving sister Elizabeth, whom, besides the natural league of amity, your tender love, of which you were said ever to bear towards me above the rest of your brethren, doth bind me to love. My mind was to acknowledge this your loving affection, and to have requited it with deeds and not with words alone." A little to the east, on a small hill, are the remains of an ancient camp. The wall over the "Nine Nicks" is in a good state of preservation. Sir Walter Scott, who was familiar with this part of the wall, may probably have gathered here the flowers which he "presented to a young lady with the lines—

'Take these flowers which, purple waving,
On the ruined rampart grew,
Where, the sons of freedom braving,
Rome's imperial standards flew.

Warriors from the breach of danger
Pluck no longer laurels there ;
They but yield the passing stranger
Wild-flower wreaths for beauty's hair.' "

With the Nicks the basaltic range disappears, and a descent is made through a more cultivated region to *Magna*, or *Carvoran*. This station is situated to the south of both vallum and wall, and was probably erected before them. The boundaries of the station, which enclose an area of three and a-half acres, are not very distinct. Some fragments of the north rampart, however, remain, and the north fosse can be traced. In the garden and premises of the neighbouring farm are preserved many interesting relics of Roman times, such as broken capitals, fragments of columns, mill-stones, and two altars inscribed to Belatvcadrvs, a local deity. The old Roman road—the Maiden Way—from the south, by way of Stanemoor and Alston, came up to the south-east angle of the station, and thence continued to Birdoswald and Bewcastle ; and the Stanegate, a direct Roman way, passed in front of it. The second cohort of the Dalmatians was stationed at Carvoran. Thirlwall Castle, which has already been described (page 172), may next be visited.

From Carvoran to Birdoswald the wall passed over a comparatively level tract, and was consequently more exposed to the attacks of the enemy. Aware of this, the Romans erected a third line of defence a little to the south of the wall, consisting of five camps, placed about half-a-mile apart. Crossing the railway, Wall-end is soon reached. Between this place and Chapel House the fosse of the wall is very large indeed. Its north bank is from fifteen to twenty feet in height. It appears again in a remarkably perfect state between Gap and the railway station, which stands on Rose Hill. Here was found a beautiful figure of a flying Victory. A little further on the wall crosses the Poltross Burn, which divides the counties of Northumberland and Cumberland.

# HEXHAM TO WARK.

Warden, 2 miles ; Chollerford, 5 miles : Humshaugh, 5½ miles ; Haughton Castle, 6½ miles ; Simonburn, 9 miles ; Wark, 12 miles ; Chipchase Castle (*via* Wark), 14 miles.

TWO miles west from Hexham Station the Tyne is crossed by a suspension bridge leading to WARDEN (A.-S. *weardian*. to defend), a sweet and retired little village, sheltering beneath a wooded hill in the midst of foliage, and commanding lovely glimpses of the two streams, with the richly-stained rocks above them. The old mill-dam here, of primitive construction, is very picturesque. The *Church*, dedicated to *St. Michael*, was rebuilt in 1765, and is in the early English style of architecture. The transepts are of early English date. The tower exhibits the characteristics of Saxon work, but is not thought to have been built much before the Conquest. The body of the church is largely constructed of stones from the Roman Wall. A Roman altar, bearing a figure supposed to represent Victory, and two small stone coffins, are preserved inside the building. Behind the vicarage-house are the traces of an ancient camp. In 1138, according to Prior John of Hexham, the greater part of King David's army rested at Warden on their way to Newcastle, after having raised the siege of Wark-on-Tweed.

Proceeding half-a-mile along the main road, a pathway will be found on the left leading to *High Warden*, from which a road by the side of a plantation conducts to the summit of the hill, half-a-mile or more away. Here are the remains of a British camp of considerable dimensions. It occupies an area of two acres, and has been defended by a rampart of unhewn stone, strengthened at a later period, perhaps, by ramparts of earth, with their corresponding ditches. The entrance to this rude stronghold has been on the east, and the approach to it flanked by stone ramparts. The remains of buildings may yet be distinctly traced within the lines, where several hand-mills or querns have been found. Nearly 200 yards to the north, a subterranean passage was discovered in the early part of the century, but, affording a refuge for foxes, it was filled up. Its use has not been conjectured. From this ancient fort there is an extensive prospect over the valleys of the North and South Tyne. Haydon Bridge, Langley Castle, the country around Corbridge, Dilston, Chollerford Bridge, Chipchase Castle, and Chesters, are all within view. Descending the hill to the east, the tourist will proceed northward along " Homer's Lane," having the beautifully-wooded gorge of the North Tyne on his right. On a small eminence opposite Wall Mill, about a mile from High Warden, there used to stand an unpretentious cottage, with low walls and thatched roof, inhabited by a kindly, inoffensive old man called Joseph Hedley, better known as "Joe the Quilter." From the 3rd to the 7th of January 1826 the lonely hut was observed to be closed, and nothing was seen of its aged tenant. At length the good people in the district became alarmed, and the door was burst open. In a small inner room the body of the poor quilter was found, with no fewer than forty-four wounds inflicted on the head, face, and neck, and the hands were dreadfully cut. Traces of the most desperate struggle were visible in the cottage, and from the fact of his clogs being found in the opposite lane, and the muddy state of his clothes, it is evident that he had at one time succeeded in making his escape from the house, fleeing in the direction of Wall Mill, about a quarter of a mile distant on the opposite side of the Tyne. All efforts to discover the murderer or murderers proved unavailing, and the tragic affair must remain wrapt in mystery. The only possible motive for the murder was considered to have been a hope of securing money, as it was foolishly believed that old Joe was rich, although receiving parish relief.

A little further, on the right-hand side of the road, is a curious old stone with a sword-blade carved upon it, probably one of the boundaries of the ancient Hexham Abbey lands. The road continues, for three miles or so, past Walwick Grange to the Chesters, and thence to Chollerford.

Half-a-mile north, on the west side of the river, is HUMSHAUGH, a healthy little village with many rural attractions. The name seems anciently to have been Hounshale, for so it is written in the *Iter of Wark* (1279). The *Church of St. Peter* was erected in 1818. There is a comfortable little inn at Humshaugh—the Crown. A path through the fields, for about a mile, leads to *Haughton Castle.* This fine mediæval stronghold is beautifully situated on rising ground overlooking the river, partly hidden in a grove of trees, among which the pine and larch predominate. A hundred years ago it was a mere collection of ruins, but the owner of it at that time, William Smith, Esq., put it into thorough repair, and the present proprietor, who bought it in 1862, has made considerable additions, adapting it to modern requirements.

Haughton is variously written in ancient documents Halvton, Haluton, Haluchton, and Halgton—that is, the *ton*, a homestead or hamlet on or near the low-lying ground; Norse: Haughland, by the river. The first recorded owner of the manor is Ranulph, the son of Huctred, who gave one-third of the vill of Haluton, in marriage, with his daughter to Reginald Pratt, Lord of Knaresdale, and Esquire of William the Lion, King of Scotland, to whom the lordships of North Tynedale belonged by grant of the English Crown. The grandson of this Reginald sold all his lands in Haughton and other possessions to William de Swyneburn, who was treasurer of Margaret, wife of Alexander III. of Scotland. It is to him that the castle, which dates from the middle of the thirteenth century, probably owes its erection.

"He was," says Dr. Charlton, "a powerful chieftain and often involved in disputes with his weaker neighbours, whose lands he seems to have been disposed to lay claim to at all seasons." For some centuries the castle was in the hands of the Widdringtons. When Wallis wrote, in 1769, it was in a state of partial dilapidation, and Hutchinson, writing a few years later, describes it as "chiefly dismantled, some few apartments only remaining habitable." The restorations were made in keeping with the ancient structure, the grim walls being left in their rough original state. The figure of the castle is that of a double square, with two parallel vaults of a simple construction running on the basement from end to end. It is immensely strong, the walls being for the most part eight feet thick, and, in one instance, eleven feet thick. Five square turrets crown the whole structure. Four newel stair-cases lead to the roof at the four angles. A large room in the upper storey was probaby the baron's hall. The recesses of the windows have arched ceilings. In one of the lower rooms a beautiful early English arch with nail-head ornaments has been built into the wall. The castle has evidently been burnt down to the height of about thirty-five feet—at what time is unknown. The lower part appears to be much older than the upper. The south front has been the most ornamental, though at present the north side, with its projecting garderobes and corbelling, is the most picturesque.

Among other interesting objects in the interior is a painting by the celebrated John Martin, representing a scene from the poem of "King Arthur," by the late Lord Lytton. In May 1878 Midhat Pacha, the great Turkish statesman, spent a week at the castle as the guest of Mr. Crawshay.

About three hundred yards from the castle are the ruins of the chapel which formerly stood outside the massive outer walls.

Haughton Castle has its legend, and it is to this effect:—Sir Thomas Swinburne, who was the lord here in the reign of Henry VIII., having captured Archie Armstrong, chief of the redoubtable clan of moss-troopers, cast him into a deep dark underground dungeon. Then being appointed with others to present before Cardinal Wolsey certain charges against Lord Dacre, the Warden of the East and Middle Marches, he set out on his journey to York, where he arrived in due course. On his way to the archiepiscopal palace it all at once flashed across his mind that he had given no instructions whatever with respect to the feeding of his prisoner in the dungeon of Haughton. Sir Thomas, who was a humane man, was horror-struck at the possible consequences of his neglect. This was now the fourth day of Armstrong's confinement, and during the whole of that time he might not have received either food or drink. Without waiting to see the Cardinal, Sir Thomas turned that instant the face of his horse northwards. At Durham his sore-spent steed dropped dead beneath him. Borrowing another, he galloped on at the utmost speed to Haughton, where he arrived by the middle of the night following the day on which he left York. Proceeding to the dungeon his worst fears were realised. The unhappy prisoner was found lying upon the steps descending from the floor of the vault, starved to death. In the agonies of hunger he had gnawed the flesh from one of his arms. In the dead of night shrieks of the most agonising kind were heard issuing from the dungeon, piercing and resounding through every room in the castle, which was henceforth haunted until the spirit of the famished moss-trooper was exorcised by means of a black-lettered Bible.

The scenery in the neighbourhood of Haughton is exceedingly beautiful. Along the stony bed of the river, grooved and worn by the action of chafing waters, the angler may often be seen flinging a line over some eddying pool or foaming rapid, with evident purpose to fill his creel. It may not be often his luck to land such a trout as that caught here in 1862 by the present proprietor, and preserved in the castle, which finny patriarch is said to weight four and a half pounds. The river is subject to rapid floods, called *spates*. Four hundred yards north-east from the castle, on the low-lying ground near the river, are the ruins of a paper mill, erected in 1788 by Mr. Smith, the owner of the castle, and interesting on account of its connection with a dishonourable act of England's greatest Prime Minister—William Pitt. Here were manufactured large quantities of forged French assignats, which were sent, as far as can be ascertained, with the Duke of York's unsuccessful expedition into Flanders in 1793-4. Mr. Magnay, the foreman of this mill, had a son in London, a wholesale stationer, and through him the whole affair was managed. One of the moulds for the forged notes, representing one hundred francs, has been preserved, and is now in the possession of one of Mr. Smith's descendants. The river is crossed by a primitive ferry-boat, which is worked by an overhead rope and pulley. As early as the reign of Henry II.—*i.e.* before 1189—an agreement was entered into between Ranulph de Halvton and William de Swyneburne respecting a ferry-boat to be maintained at their joint expense here, and from that time to the present the ferry has probably been plying to and fro uninterruptedly.

Three miles north-west from Haughton is the very ancient and charming little village of SIMONBURN, consisting of some rows of rustic cottages, the older ones thatched, the newer ones slated or tiled. In the centre is a large open space or village green. The name was anciently written Seismund or Symonde-burn, and is supposed to be derived from the famous Teutonic warrior, Sigmund, son of Volsung. The parish of Simonburn was once the largest in the county, extending from the Roman Wall to Liddesdale in Scotland, a distance of 33 miles, and occupying an area of 103 miles. It is now divided. The character of the inhabitants of this wild and extensive tract, and their need for spiritual admonition, may be inferred from the fact that it was not till the reign of George the Third that a writ could be served north of the wall. The bold, warlike, predatory inhabitants of North Tynedale maintained a kind of lawless independence, and continued their thieving exploits to a late period, for in the year 1701 safety was insured by County keepers, to whom a kind of protection-tribute was paid. George Pickering, a poet of local celebrity, was born at Simonburn in 1758. He was the author of "Donocht-head," a fragment of such poetical merit that Burns said he would have given £10 to have been the author of it.

The Parish Church, according to tradition, was founded by the disciples of St. Kentigern, surnamed Mungo, "the beloved," in the seventh century. Hard by, in the Rector's Dene, is the Holy Well, to which, for nearly twelve centuries, has been attached the name of St. Mungo's Well; it is, therefore, very probable that the church was originally dedicated to that saint. The Lych-Gate, through which it is approached, was erected in 1866 in memory of the late Lancelot J. H. Allgood, Esq., of Nunwick, by his "kindred, tenants, and friends," and is considered one of the finest in the county. Preserved in the porch are some fragments of a Saxon cross and other ancient carved stones. A peculiarity of the church is the descent from west to east. Tradition says that at one time there were steps from the nave down into the chancel. The hinge of the chancel gate is still there. The most ancient part of the present church is the chancel, 48 feet long by 19 broad, erected about the end of the twelfth century. The "Priests' door," on the south side, is a fine specimen of rich Gothic work. Near to it is a low-side window. A double piscina was discovered during the restoration of 1864. There are traces of a chantry in the south-east aisle, and some curious aumbreys in the vestry. A flat tombstone commemorates Giles Heron, of Wark. On the north side is the burial-place of Sir Lancelot Allgood, knight, and above it a mural tablet to the memory of other members of the Allgood family. The nave contains various monumental effigies representing the Rev. Cuthbert Ridley (rector 1604-1627), and his family; and also a beautiful white marble monument by Noble, in memory of Mr. and Mrs. Allgood, of Nunwick. Several stained-glass windows illumine the church, four of which are from the studio of Mr. Kempe, London, and are classed among the finest specimens of modern art. In making a grave under a pew in 1762 a very remarkable skull was turned up with the spade; on the back part of it was the figure of a large scallop-shell; at the orifice of one of the ears, the figure of a screw-like shell.

In the picturesque churchyard are two very fine sycamore trees. A small bright silver coin of Edward II. was found whilst opening a grave here in 1765.

One tombstone bears a quaint epitaph :—

"Tired of travelling through this world of Sin,
At length I'm come to Nature's common Inn :
In this dark place here, for to rest a Night,
In hopes t' rise, that Christ may give me Light."

Dr. James Scott, who obtained some distinction as a political writer by his letters, signed Anti-Sejanus, to the *Public Advertiser* in 1765, was a few years later appointed rector here. His curate was the Rev. John Wallis, the botanist and antiquary, whose *History and*

*Description of Northumberland*, published in 1769, is well known. The living of Simonburn was part of the property of James, Earl of Derwentwater. After his attainder it reverted to the Crown, and was given, with his other estates, to the Greenwich Hospital.

Following a lane leading west from the green for about half-a-mile, the tourist will come to a pretty dell, beyond which rises a steep hill, thickly overgrown with ash, fir, beech, and elm trees. A pathway ascends to the top, where are the remains of Simonburn Castle, defended on two sides by deep ravines. The northern end still stands finished above by embrasures and turrets. It is pierced by three windows, the centre one being divided by mullions and its arched head enriched with the dog-tooth ornament. Through the openings there is a beautiful glimpse of moory uplands, patched with vari-coloured fields and plantations and the blue hills beyond. The portion behind is much dilapidated, nothing being left but fragments of walls, a low doorway, and vault. It belonged to the Herons of Chipchase. In 1524 Sir R. Bowes recommended it as a suitable place for the residence of the Keeper of Tynedale, where he was to have "fifty horsemen always ready to ride." A belief long prevailed among the villagers that there was somewhere hidden within its walls treasure enough to buy all Northumberland; and in searching for it they almost demolished what was left of the old pele.

About a mile south-west of the village is the picturesque little waterfall called Teckitt Linn. It tumbles over a rocky ledge among lichen-coloured boulders, that are strewn around and beneath it in wild confusion. Over it hang steep cliffs, from whose moist crevices spring the bright green feathery ferns.

"Oh, 'tis a quiet, spirit-healing nook,"

where one may sit and dream of some beautiful Undine emerging from the glittering spray, watching the shy little water-ousel as he flits about, uneasy at an intrusion into one of his favourite haunts. Previous to reaching the fall the water runs on a natural stone pavement for a considerable distance, and in its vicinity is a curious grotto or cave, with a stone seat in it, and at one corner a cavity, resembling a cupboard. Here, tradition says, Wallis, the historian, used to compose his work. Having passed the fall, the water disappears under a large rock, and after pursuing a subterranean course for about a mile and a half, rises in a field near Nunwick Mill, and thence flows into the Tyne. The tourist will do well to follow the little wooded gorge from Simonburn to Teckitt, scrambling, in holiday fashion, amongst the mossy blocks of freestone which have fallen from the steep banks above. Teckitt farm was the property and residence of a branch of the Ridley family about the fifteenth century, and their arms still remain above the front door.

Half-a-mile east of Simonburn is *Nunwick Hall*, the seat of the Rev. James Allgood, an elegant structure of white freestone, situated in a beautifully-wooded park. It was built by Sir Lancelot Allgood in 1760. The prospect from the eastern terrace is exceedingly fine, embracing Chipchase on the one hand, and the vale of Simonburn on the other. Nunwick, as its name imports, was once a village, and a fine, but now hollow, ash tree, standing on the lawn 120 yards south-west from the hall, was one of a group on the village green which was subsequently enclosed in the park. Nunwick has good reason to be proud of its trees. Its beeches, especially, are worth seeing. One stately specimen, growing eighty yards south-west of the house, has a girth of 11 feet 10 inches at a height of 5 feet. Near the confluence of the burn, which runs through Nunwick Park, with the North Tyne, there formerly stood a Druidical circle, 90 feet in circumference, formed of five rude upright stones, 8 feet high. Four were standing in 1714, but at a later period they have been ruthlessly destroyed. A straight road leads west for three miles to the solitary limestone crags of Ravensheugh, on the moorland, whence the stone used in the erection of Nunwick was obtained. At the west end of the crag is a fine spring under a natural arch, shaded with ferns and fringed with water-cress.

Half-a-mile north of Nunwick is *Low Park End*, the residence of Mrs. Venables, from whose grounds may be obtained some very charming views of Chipchase and the woody glades of North Tyne. A pleasant drive, half-a-mile in length, connects this mansion with Park End, the seat and property of Thomas Ridley, Esq., J.P., beautifully situated among some fine groves adjoining the Tyne. One and a quarter mile from Park End the road, after crossing the Gofton and Wark's burns, enters the ancient village of

WARK.—Though a place of no great importance now, it was once the capital of North Tynedale, and boasts an antiquity reaching back to pre-historic times, as is evident from the existence of the Mote Hill on the south of the village near the river. Local legend asserts that this mound is in its present form partly artificial; that even women and children were compelled to contribute their quota of labour and carry "lapfuls" of soil to the top. Here the ancient Celtic inhabitants assembled in council to make the primitive laws affecting their little communities, and to discuss matters of justice and government. They would find it a strong place of defence, guarding the chief ford across the river. An altar which was found here would seem to imply that the Romans had occupied it to protect one of their cross roads which may be traced on both sides of the North Tyne. Here it was that, at a later period, the sessions of the Scottish Courts and the Courts of the Liberties of Tynedale were held. The Record Office preserves two valuable documents which give account of law proceedings here in 1279 in the reign of Alexander III., during the last period of Scottish occupation, and in 1293, in the reign of Edward I., when Tynedale had come under English rule again. From these ancient rolls we get a curious picture of the manners and customs of the period. The landed proprietors, country squires, clerks, and parsons seem to have been little better than the lawless people among whom they dwelt.

The tendency to relieve their neighbours of any superfluous cattle or goods they might possess, was evidently inborn and irresistible. One extract will suffice :—"William, the parson of Corbridge, was taken for a burglary in the house of Hugh of Burton, and was committed to prison at Wark, and convicted at the assize. But as the bishop of the diocese had no 'attornatus' there to claim his clerk, the said William was remitted to prison, from which he afterwards escaped, and fled to the church at Simonburn, where he was kept till he was claimed by Lambert, vicar of Warden, and taken to the prison of the Bishop of Durham, where he soon after died."

The Mote Hill was subsequently used as a guard-fort and as a post of observation for watching the movements of an enemy. A house was afterwards built upon it by the Radcliffes, to whom the manor of Wark belonged until it was forfeited by the rebellion of James, the last Earl of Derwentwater. This great earth-"Work"—pronounced in the dialect, Wark; Norse: virki, a mount, an entrenchment; Danish: värge, to defend—is said to have suggested the name of the town which sprang up around its base in Saxon and Danish times. Tradition tells that the streets and buildings of this ancient metropolis of Tynedale extended as far as Houxty Burn, and that in its midst stood the ancient church of "St. Michael of Wark," of which the ruined arches of an aisle still remained in the "Kirkfield," within memory.

The *Church*, dedicated to *St. Matthew*, was erected in 1815, and opened for service in 1818. It is a plain but neat edifice in the early English style, with a square embattled tower, and, unlike many of the older Northumbrian churches, has a very small chancel. The village contains an endowed school founded by Giles Heron, a poor pedlar, who died in 1684, having amassed by his industry and parsimony £800. His trustees purchased with the money the Tecket estate, which now produces about £200 a-year. As only a part of this sum goes to the maintenance of the school, the rest is distributed in charity among poor widows and others, and is called "Gilly's dole." The railway station is on the opposite side of the river, which is crossed by an iron bridge. Inns at Wark: Black Bull and Grey Bull.

> "From winsome Wark to Simonburn,
> The trouty streams are fine,"

sings the poet of anglers, Robert Roxby.

One of the pleasantest rambles from Wark is that up the Wark's burn. Half-a-mile up this streamlet, from the bridge which crosses the highway, is a curious "petrified cascade." A deposit of calcareous matter from the hard water dripping over a rock some fifteen feet high has solidified in the form of a nearly vertical rush of water. The geologist will examine with interest the outskirts of the coal-measures, as seen in occasional sections on the face of the scaurs, and the mountain limestone which here succeeds the coal strata. A short distance above the bridge is an interesting section displaying old Sigillaria stems in an upright position. After passing a sulphur well, the water of which possesses considerable medicinal power, and rivals that of

Gilsland, an interesting hamlet will be reached called *Rose's Bower*—probably derived from the Anglo-Saxon for a dwelling-place—distant from Wark about four miles. This so-called bower was formerly the pele or fortified residence of Anthony Milburn, a border chieftain. It is perched on the crags on the north side of the burn, and is cut off from the land on the west side by a deep dell, partly artificial, into which falls a small tributary of the Wark Burn over a romantic precipice. The remains of the ancient bower have been converted into a farm-house, which is now easily accessible from the north. A few old and weather-beaten trees on the top and sides of the rock afford some scanty shelter from the storms of winter. A little above Rose's Bower is the Linn, a remarkably wild and beautiful spot, where the mountain limestone forms an irregular but imperfect barrier to the waters of the burn. About a mile above the linn is a petrifying spring, trickling down the face of a scaur and encrusting the mosses and grasses in its course. Along the banks of the Wark's Burn may be gathered the brittle bladder fern *(Cystopteris fragilis)*, common spleenwort *(Asplenium trichomanes)*, beech polypody *(Polypodium phegopteris)*, and oak polypody *(Polypodium Dryopteris)*.

A mile from Wark Station, on the east side of the river, stands one of the most stately and picturesque of Northumbrian mansions, *Chipchase Castle*, the seat of Hugh Taylor, Esq. Striking as are the architectural features of the place, they are yet enhanced by the loveliness of the surrounding landscape, which is not to be surpassed in the whole valley of the North Tyne. The name is derived from the old-English word cheap, a market, wherein the produce of the locality was exposed for sale or barter (hence our Cheapsides and Chippings scattered over the country), and the Norman-French word *chasse*, a hunting-ground. Thus, the meaning of Chipchase is the "market" within the "chase," or hunting-ground of the lords of Prudhoe—the family of the Umfravilles, who held it as a detached manor of that important barony in the reign of Henry II. The village of Chipchase was a very ancient one, dating back to Saxon times, and continued to be inhabited to nearly the end of the last century. The foundations of two or three dwellings can be traced on the south side of the present park, close to the bridge that leads to the mill and the ancient ford of the river. A small fort was erected by the lords of Prudhoe for the defence of the village. It stood a little to the south of the present castle, where its rude foundations may still be seen. About the middle of the thirteenth century the manor was held under the Umfravilles of Prudhoe by Peter de Insula, to whom is ascribed the erection of the old Pele-tower, though Mr. Longstaffe, an authority on such matters, assigns a later date. In the fourteenth century the manor passed, by marriage, into the Heron family, so famous in Border history. Sir George Heron, keeper of Tynedale, High Sheriff of Northumberland in 1571, was slain in the Border fight called the "Raid of Reedswire," in July 1575. The Scots afterwards made presents of falcons to the prisoners, saying that the English were nobly treated, since they got live *hawks* for dead *herons*. In the reign of James I. the handsome manor-house was added to the old keep by Cuthbert Heron, who, for his loyalty, was created a baronet by King Charles II. in 1662. The last of the Herons of Chipchase was Sir Harry, who sold the castle and estate about the end of the seventeenth century. The ancient pele-tower is still retained in a good state of preservation as part of the present structure. It is thus described by the Rev. C. H. Hartshorne, in his *Feudal and Military Antiquities of Northumberland and the Scottish Borders*:—"The pele, properly so called, is a massive and lofty building, as large as some Norman keeps. It has an enriched appearance given to it by its double-notched corbelling round the summit, which further serves the purpose of machicolation. The round bartisans at the angles add to its beauty, and are set in with considerable skill. The stone roof and the provisions for carrying off the water deserve careful examination. Over the low winding entrance-door on the basement are the remains of the original portcullis, the like of which the most experienced archæologist will in vain seek for elsewhere. The grooves are also visible, and the chamber where the machinery was fixed for raising it, is to be met with, even as at Goodrich, where the holes in which the axle worked, and the oil-way that served to ease its revolutions, may be seen; but at Chipchase there is the little cross-grated portcullis itself, which was simply lifted by the leverage of a wooden bar above the entrance, and let down in the same manner." Through the openings between the corbels, stones and boiling water were thrown down on the assailants. There was discovered a few years ago in the thickness of the wall, on the third storey, a chamber, supposed to have been a chapel, used by the inmates of the castle in the time of the penal laws against Catholics Traces of the ordinary mediæval decoration may still be seen in the fragments of mural Gothic paintings on the walls of the third storey, or family chamber. Below this storey is the guard-room, where the men-at-arms were located; and on the ground-floor is the usual vaulted room, where the cattle were secured in time of danger.

The modern mansion, added to the old pele-tower by Cuthbert Heron, whose initials, with the date 1621, are cut in stone above the south entrance, is a beautiful specimen of the Jacobean style. The library, or "music-room," as it is called, is one of the most interesting apartments in the castle, on account of the richly-wrought cornice around the ceiling, and more especially on account of the elaborately-carved mantel-piece of black oak, representing "The March of Time, or the Four Seasons." The mansion contains several fine paintings by Millais, the Richardsons, and other masters.

The porch in the centre bay of the south front forms a very imposing entrance to the castle. On each side of the steps in the pediment of each column is a sculptured panel. That on the right hand bears the representation of a heron in a very conventional oak, and is said to symbolise the prosperous times of the Heron family. But it seems there was a local prophecy, that when the heron should be seen charging through a fence instead of flying over it, the extinction of the family was near at hand: and so, according to tradition, the last owner of the name is stated to have caused this ill-omened symbolism to be carved on the left-hand panel, before he parted with his last ancestral acres. There is another local tradition, that the Heron family will return to their ancient seat when the herons again resort to their old homes. If the right-hand panel represented the Herons in their "uplifted" condition of prosperity, it has been asked, might not the other panel represent that they have descended to their feeding-places to gather strength for another rise, when the time of adversity is ended?

A low subterranean passage has been traced from the level of the present cellar for a considerable distance southwards, beneath the carriage-drive at the front, towards the site of the ancient village of Chipchase. This mode of egress would no doubt be resorted to in case of siege, when the garrison found it necessary to escape, or to communicate with allies at a distance.

It is not strange that this grim old pele, which for so long had been the residence of lawless and quick-tempered barons, should have its gruesome legends. Tradition tells of an unfortunate knight, Sir Reginald Fitz-Urse, who was starved to death in one of the dark prison-chambers of the great keep, and afterwards haunted the scene of his sufferings, startling the passer-by with the clank of armour, mingled with the groanings of a dying man; and also of some other knight, whose name is unknown, killed in one of the intra-mural chambers, where he had vainly sought refuge from the murderous band who were pursuing him.

Chipchase is one of the places mentioned by tradition as the scene of the well-known story of the "Long Pack." Edward I. is said to have remained at the castle for one or two nights, on one of his journeys into Scotland. A mile to the north is Wark railway station, and adjoining it, an excellent inn, the Chipchase Arms.

# HEXHAM TO HALLINGTON AND WARK.

Chollerton, 6¾ miles ; Cocklaw Tower, 6½ miles ; Hallington, 12 miles ; Swinburn Castle (direct), 10 miles ; Barrasford (direct), 8½ miles ; Gunnerton, 10 miles ; Gunnerton Crags, 11 miles.

THE nearest road to Chollerford runs along the east side of the river, past St. John Lee, and through the quiet little village of WALL, the thatched and sandstone-slated cottages of which lie nestling beneath a furze-grown hill, said by Dr. Bruce to have been fortified by the ancient Britons.

A mile and three-quarters from Chollerford, by way of Low Brunton, is CHOLLERTON, a pleasant little village situated amidst cornfields and meadows. The *Church of St. Giles* dates back to early Norman times, though there is little of the Norman work about it now. It is a quaint-looking building, with a square embattled campanile tower surmounted by four pinnacles. The most interesting features of the church are—the monolith pillars of the arcade, the ancient font cut out of a Roman altar, the old organ built by Father Schmidt in the reign of Queen Elizabeth, and the monuments of some of the Umfraville family.

About a mile south-east of Chollerton, and a mile and a half north-east of Chollerford, is the ruined pele called *Cocklaw Tower*. It is considered to be a good example of a class of border keeps, less imposing than Haughton or Chipchase, but larger than many of its kind. Though built more for security than comfort, it yet shows a certain regard for the refinements of life in the traces of fresco-painting on the walls of the principal apartment where the family lived. It is said to have been the residence of the Erringtons from 1372 to 1567.

A mile and a quarter to the east of it is ERRINGTON, a hamlet on the Erring Burn, from which the celebrated Northumbrian family just referred to received its name. They were seated here in 1372, but soon after the reign of Elizabeth came into possession of Beaufront Castle, with which their name is more intimately associated

The Erring Burn is supposed by some to be the Denise Burn referred to by Bede in his description of the battle of Heaven Field.

A mile and a quarter north-east is the hamlet of BINGFIELD, with a small church dedicated to St. Mary. At a little distance from this place, within a few yards of the Erring Burn, is a minerai spring, the virtues of whose waters are said to be in no respect inferior to those of Gilsland Spa. Fish or worms put into it instantly expire.

Two miles and a half to the north is HALLINGTON, a village of considerable historical interest, for it appears not only from the similarity of name, but also from its position with regard to the Roman Wall, to be the *Halydene* of Saxon times, and the Halidew of a later period, where, according to Leland, some portion of the great battle between Oswald and Cadwallon was fought. "There is a fame," he says, "that Oswald won the battelle at the Haly dene, a two myles est from S. Oswaldes asche, and that Hallidew is it that Bede caullith Havenfield, and men thereabouts yet finde small wood crossies in the ground."

Near the village is *Hallington Demesne*, a white freestone mansion, the property and residence of Miss Florence Trevelyan-Trevelyan.

The *Hallington Reservoir*, belonging to the Newcastle and Gateshead Water Company, is a fine sheet of water, covering 142 acres, and having an average depth of 17¾ feet.

A fine view of this artificial lake, and the country bordering on the Watling Street, may be gained from an eminence a mile and a half to the east of Hallington, called Moot Law. On the summit is a square entrenchment with a hearth-stone in the centre, where fires were formerly kindled to alarm the country on the approach of an enemy. No more suitable post of observation could have been chosen than this hill, which commands so long a stretch of the Watling Street. From its name it may be inferred that the gemote, or court of the manor, was held here in feudal times, though some antiquaries affirm that the word mota, in old French *mote*, or motte, in its primary sense, means a mound cast up or escarped for the purpose of fortification.

Two miles north of Hallington is LITTLE BAVINGTON, a village which appears to have been the *ton* or settlement of the Bavingas, a Saxon clan, and in later times the property of the Shaftoe family, who were seated here as early as 1304.

Bavington Hall, the ancient residence of the Shaftoes, is now occupied as a shooting-seat by Lieutenant-Colonel Briggs, of Hilton Castle, Sunderland. It is surrounded by thriving plantations, and in front is a small artificial lake.

Two and a quarter miles west of Hallington is COLWELL, a small village situated near the intersection of the Watling Street by the Cambo Road. Here are the remains of an ancient chapel. A mile further west is *Swinburn Castle*, a beautiful stone structure in an extensive park, the residence of Dr. Murray. Near to the park is the rivulet—the Swin, or Swine Burn—which gave the name to the ancient family, who probably were in possession of the manor before the reign of Edward I. In 1695 it passed, by purchase, into the Riddell family.

Near the southern boundary of the park is a remarkable "Druidstone," or menhir, which is eleven feet in height, spreading out at the top like an open fan or human hand. There are one or two cup-markings upon it. It is called the Swinburn Standing-stone, and gives its name to the field just outside the castle-park. Near it are three or four tumuli, or burial-barrows, and a fine series of culture-terraces—for the limited growth of cereals used by the primitive hunters—all within the Swinburn Park. On the Reiver Crag, Oxhill, and Blue Crag, close to Swinburn, are some ancient camps.

Two miles north of Swinburn, up the Watling Street, is the *Colt Crag Reservoir*, belonging to the Newcastle and Gateshead Water-works Company. It covers an area of 258 acres. At *Little Swinburn*, a mile and a half to the north-east, are the remains of a Border tower, and at *Thockrington*, a similar distance beyond it, is a small church, built in Norman times, and still retaining portions of ancient work.

A mile and a half south-west of Swinburn is BARRASFORD, where the North British Railway Company have a station. It stands on Dalley Bank, the scene of a skirmish between the Yorkists and Lancastrians. The neighbourhood is very rich in memorials of the old Celtic inhabitants. Near to Barrasford School a solitary menhir was, till lately, visible as the only survivor of three stones of unknown antiquity, connected, perhaps, with the great "family-barrow" just above it, called the "Chip," or "Kiphill," from which five cists and their enclosed urns are said to have been removed more than fifty years since. "It is popularly believed," says the Rev. George Rome Hall, "that the series of stones which once stood here were located on the spot through a duel between two ancient giants, who, from their respective stations on the heights east and west of the river, hurled these Titanic missiles at each other, which clashed and fell midway—a legend closely resembling that of Brittany, which terms such great stones the quoits or *palets de Gargantua*." A large British burial-barrow stood on a lofty escarpment above the Barrasford Burn, and was excavated in making the railway cutting near the station. It contained several Saxon relics of considerable interest. Some follower of the renowned Hengist or Horsa, himself a chief of note, may have fallen here in battle, and been interred upon the site of a more ancient British hero's burial.

A little to the north is the village of GUNNERTON—the *ton*, or homestead, of Gunnar. An ivy-covered wall is the sole vestige of Gunnarton Tower. Beneath the hill on which it stands, in a fern-clad and moss-mantled hollow, is "The Lady's Well," or simply Margaret's Well, once probably a sacred spring. There are slight remains of an old chapel at Gunnerton. Half-a-mile further north, in the Dungill, or Dungeon Wood, is the very remarkable "Money-hill" of Gunnerton, situated on a promontory formed by the conjunction of deep ravines. It is an immense conical mound of earth, about thirty feet high, with concentric and flanking ramparts and fosses.

According to tradition, there is hid in this mound a hoard of treasure, guarded by a dragon, or some such unearthly monster. On the strength of this popular belief excavations have evidently been made at an early date, for when the "Money-hill" was carefully and completely opened a few years ago a fragment of a mediæval drinking-vessel was found—a relic, no doubt, of the former explorers. In the rocky channel of the little burn which runs through the dell are many curious perforations, called by the country people "Fairy Kirns."

To the east is the picturesque basaltic range called the "Gunnarton Crags,"—a portion of the great Whin Dyke, which extends in a south-westerly direction from Dunstanborough to Sewingshields. Here the botanist may collect, among many other basalt-loving plants, the pretty mountain pink (*Dianthus Deltöides*), crow allium (*Allium vineale*), rue-leaved saxifrage (*Saxifraga tridactylites*), and meadow saxifrage (*Saxifraga granulata*), stone rubus (*Rubus saxatilis*), mountain cudweed (*Gnaphalium dioicum*), shining cranes-bill (*Geranium lucidum*), knotted clover (*Trifolium striatum*), and brittle bladder fern (*Asplenium trichomanes*).

These crags, marked off by several gaps or fissures called heughs, into several isolated slopes and platforms, were the almost impregnable strongholds of the old Celtic tribes of North Tynedale. The remains of several of their camps may still be traced. Two of these are situated, one on each side of a deep pass called the Gunnar Heugh. The eastern one covers about an acre, its massive ramparts being formed of large blocks of the native whinstone only. It has within it some hut-circles, and outside, against the western rampart, are two oblong dwellings. To the south are outlying circular guard-chambers. The other camp is about ninety yards distant to the west. It lies on the gentle slope just under the highest outburst or "peak" of the whole range, which rises 576 feet above the sea-level. The early inhabitants of the district have wisely built this, the strongest of their fortified settlements, on the sunny hill-side, with natural barriers against an enemy on three sides. At the bottom of the Gunnar Heugh Valley there is a massive "cyclopean" wall, built, for the most part, close to the precipitous eastern side of the rocky ravine, thus forming a covered way to a spring a quarter of a mile distant.

The massive ramparts of the camp are built of unhewn unmortared stones, mingled with much earth, and average about thirteen feet in width. Upon these would probably be fixed a stockade or strong palisade of the trunks of felled trees and beams. Some of the whinstone blocks bear traces of fire.

The entrance or gateway of the ancient town has been in the south wall near the south-east angle, and from it a hollow way or street led into the interior of the camp, where may be seen the foundations of five circular huts, one square and one rectangular building. There is also an irregular oblong space or courtyard to the east of the hollow way, with an entrance midway, wide enough for the admission of a chariot. The usual form of British habitation is the circular one.

There was first a foundation-work of unhewn stones, on which, or against which, was raised a circular wall of wattled stakes, surmounted by a high-peaked roof of thatch. The door was of wattled or basket-work covered with skins. All the doorways of the hut-circles in this camp face the south-east, so as to catch the early morning sun. In most of these huts a portion of the space has been partitioned off, to form an inner chamber or recess. That the tastes of these rude aborigines was being influenced by the proximity of their Roman conquerors is shown in the relics which have been found in the huts, such as an iron armlet, iron ring, harp-shaped brooch of bronze, iron nails, and fragments of Roman pottery. Traces of terrace culture may be seen about two-thirds of the way down the south-fronting declivity of the crag. Fifteen yards from the entrance gateway an interesting discovery was made of an earth-oven. This was a stone-lined circular pit, having charcoal and ashes at the bottom, and bearing marks of the long-continued action of fire. This was the cooking and feasting place of the camp, and a mound close to had evidently been the kitchen-midden, as bones of animals in great number and variety were found in it. In the case of a successful attack of the town by an enemy, on the only assailable side, the vanquished would be driven over the tremendous precipice, and to judge from the number of human remains found amongst the crag-talus, such a disastrous occurrence has indeed taken place.

One mile north of Gunnarton Nick is the hamlet with the curious name of *Pity Me*, derived, it is suggested, from the British Beddau Maes, "field of graves." Here is an entrenched fort below the "Camphill." A walk of nearly three miles past the farm-house of Gunnerton Fell will bring the tourist to Chipchase, whence he may continue to Wark.

# BELLINGHAM SECTION.

## BELLINGHAM.

BELLINGHAM is a small market town, pleasantly situated on the north bank of the North Tyne, at the foot of some of the wildest and most barren fells in Northumberland. Its general aspect is dull and uninviting, the architecture of the buildings being bald and plain in the extreme. It has not yet escaped from the traditions of the turbulent old times, when the less attractive a town was the fewer temptations it offered to the lawless inhabitants of the Borderland.

Being in the direct route of the reivers and moss-troopers of Tynedale, Redesdale, and Liddesdale, when riding south upon their too frequent forays, it is not to be wondered at that there are no traces of mediæval grace or Jacobean elegance in this ancient town. From some valuable old records it appears the name was formerly written Bellinjham, thus confirming the local pronunciation, Bellinjum. The powerful family of De Bellingham, which, at an early period, was settled here, has quite disappeared from the district. The site of their fortalice was on the east side of the Hareshaw Burn, opposite to the railway station, where an artificial mound is still visible, and is at no great distance from the mill which the De Bellinghams held of the Scottish king, paying for it in 1263 the enormous rent of ten pounds sterling.

The *Church*, dedicated to *St. Cuthbert*, was built about the end of the eleventh century, and is in the early Norman style. It possesses a feature (almost unique in England) in the massive stone roof, which consists of hexagonal ribs about two feet ten inches apart, overlaid with heavy grey stone slabs. The necessity of such a ponderous structure will be evident when it is remembered that, according to tradition, the chancel (which has had a wooden roof) was twice burnt by the Scots during the Border wars. Another illustration of the unsettled condition of the country in olden times is seen in the extremely narrow windows of the nave, which could be made available for purposes of defence. From records preserved in the library of the Dean and Chapter of Durham, it appears that in 1607 the church was an institution not much patronised by the good folk of Tynedale. The communion was administered but once a year.

The font was broken, the bible, prayer-book, psalters, etc., were conspicuous by their absence, and the clerk could neither read nor write. A rude kind of justice was meted out in 1711 to William Charlton of the Bower, generally spoken of as "Bowrie," after he had killed Henry Widdrington of Buteland in quarrel. The body of the victim was buried before Charlton's pew-door in this church, on which account, it is said, Bowrie would never again enter the sacred edifice.

On the south side of the church, now forming a transept, is the chantry chapel of the De Bellingham family. It contains a piscina and a bracket for a statue, probably that of St. Catherine. In 1865 a Norman door was re-opened in the church. The churchyard forms a fine terrace above the river, and contains several incised and sculptured grave-covers. Just outside the churchyard wall may also be seen St. Cuthbert's, or "Cuddy's" well, which formerly was regarded with considerable veneration. It is referred to in the following legend, narrated by a monkish writer of the twelfth century. A self-willed young lady named Edda having persisted in finishing a new gown for the feast of St. Lawrence, although the holy day had dawned, found her left hand so contracted that she could not remove the costly stuff. All human aid being in vain, they betook themselves to the church to invoke the assistance of St. Cuthbert; and as they went thither they caused the sufferer to drink of the Well of St. Cuthbert. And during the whole of that night the parents and the girl lay prostrate in prayer in the church, and when it was about the small hours of the morning the figure of the saint arose at the altar, and, descending into the aisle, touched the contracted hand of the sufferer. The girl, terrified by the apparition, shrieked out, and her mother ("animâ ducta fœminea"), just like a woman, seized her daughter's hand between her own palms, and the miracle was left but half completed, for, though the cloth fell from her closed fingers, she could not open her hand. Thus they continued till the morning, when the priest at mass, having read the gospel, ordered all in the church to make a novena of nine "Our Fathers" for the recovery of the maiden, and, behold, she immediately recovered, and joyfully held up her healed hand before the assembled congregation. The saint appears to have rendered signal service to Sproich, the girl's father, on several occasions, and his favour must have been worth having in a time when men's minds were not very clear upon the subject of the rights of property.

The wool fair of Bellingham is one of the largest in the county. The Saturday following September 15th is the date of "Cuddy's Fair" (St. Cuthbert's), when the old custom is observed of "riding the fair," at the conclusion of which the charter is read. Muggers' Hill has received its name from the muggers or potters who attend the fairs, and always select that ground for the display of their wares. The river is crossed by a picturesque stone bridge, built in 1835. Hotels and Inns: Railway Hotel, Black Bull, Fox and Hounds, Rose and Crown, Temperance Hotel.

From Bellingham one of the most delightful walks is to *Hareshaw*

*Linn*, about a mile distant from the town. Just above the railway the tourist will climb over the shale heaps of the deserted ironworks, where he will have no difficulty in picking up any number of fossils. Then he follows the burn through a romantic glen of great beauty, the steep sides of which are clothed with luxuriant vegetation, save where the rock pierces the surface. Keeping to the narrow pathway which leads up and down amongst the trees and underwood, the lower fall is first reached, a perpendicular ledge of rock, some twenty feet in height, over which the stream breaks in two places. It forms a lovely little picture, in an exquisite setting of tree and fern and flower, and nothing can be more pleasurable than to linger on one of the mossy boulders that jut out from the bank above it, listening to the plash and murmur of waters. Half-a-mile further up is Hareshaw Linn proper.

> "With sudden dash and bound and splash,
> With rout and shout and roar and din,
> The brook, amaz'd, alarm'd, and craz'd,
> Is sprawling into Hareshaw Linn.
>
> 'Tween wooded cliffs, fern-fringed, it falls,
> All broken into spray and foam."
>
> —J. CLEPHAN.

The Linn is well described by Mr. Baker in his introduction to the *New Flora of Northumberland and Durham*:—"On the left a precipice rises up without break to a height of nearly 100 feet, one sheer wall of massive rock, brown and cool toward the base, with green mosses in the crevices. Higher up, where the sun sometimes catches it, bare brown and white, or yellow-stained with lichen, the summit clothed with ivy and bird-cherry, and waving branches of elm and rowan. The stream flows from an opening half-way down between this cliff and its counterpart on the opposite side, forming not a large waterfall, but one where nature has made the most of the volume of water she has had to work with. The tall, slightly overhanging side-cliffs of the glen converge crescent-wise towards the fall, and shut in a cool ravine, where such plants as woodruff, golden saxifrage, *Cardamine sylvatica*, and *Campanula latifolia* luxuriate, and where we may gather oak fern, beech fern, and *Trollius*, *Rubus saxatilis*, *Epilobium angustifolium*, and *Crepis succisæfolia*." Respecting this picturesque chasm in the richly-coloured sandstone rock, Professor Lebour says, "There is no better instance of the power of erosion (possessed by even such a little stream), or of the immensity of time required for the effects of that power to become appreciable, than this deep cleft of Hareshaw Linn, which the rushing of the water is continually, though imperceptibly, deepening."

From the Linn the tourist may proceed direct west to the road, half-a-mile distant, and follow it for a mile and a half to Bellingham; or he may clamber up the cliffs above the Linn, and strike across the fine bracing moors to the crags called "The Caller Hues or Heughs," and then afterwards gain the road a little below Hareshaw Dam.

# BELLINGHAM TO LEE HALL AND SHITLINGTON.

Lee Hall, 4 miles : Shitlington, 5 miles.

TWO miles and a half to the south of Bellingham, on the left-hand side of the road, is the Garret Holt British camp. A mile and a half further south is *Lee Hall*, the ancient seat of a branch of the Charlton family, one member of which, William Charlton of Lee Hall, who lived in the latter half of the seventeenth century, seems to have been of a very turbulent and fiery character. He is said to have been closely connected with an organised gang of horse-stealers, who made their raids on both sides of the Border. His feuds with Lowes of Willimoteswick, the county-keeper of South Tynedale, are still remembered in the district. After several narrow escapes from his bold and implacable enemy, Lowes was at length taken prisoner in a fight near Sewingshields, and conveyed to Lee Hall, where he suffered, it is said, the greatest indignities, having been actually fastened to the grate of the kitchen fire, with just enough length of chain to enable him to get his food at the table with the servants. He was subsequently rescued by Frank Stokoe, of Chesterwood.

Lee Hall is mentioned as the "probable scene" of the tragical incident narrated by the Ettrick Shepherd in his tale of the "Long Pack." The story tells how, in the year 1723, Colonel Ridley and his family being away in London, his country seat, on the banks of the North Tyne, was left in the charge of a maid-servant named Alice and two male servants. One afternoon, in the middle of winter, a handsome-looking pedlar called ; and after having been properly refused a night's lodging, asked permission to leave his heavy pack till the next morning. The request was granted, and the pedlar went his way, wishing Alice a good-night. Left alone, the girl could not help feeling uneasy about the pack, and after a while took up a candle to have a careful look at it. What was her horror to see it move ! She at once called in a fellow-servant, old Richard, who, however, assured her the pack was right enough. While they were talking, a lad named Edward, who herded the cattle, came in with a large old military gun named Copenhagen, and proposed to empty the contents of the barrel into the pack. This he accordingly did, with a hideous result, for a stream of blood gushed on to the floor, and a dreadful roar, followed by the groans of death, issued from the pack, where a man had been concealed in a very ingenious way. As it was quite evident that an attack would be made on the house by the man's confederates, a number of the colonel's retainers were called in to guard the house. About midnight it occurred to Edward to blow the thief's silver wind-call. In less than five minutes several horsemen came up at a brisk trot and began to enter the court-gate. Edward, unable to restrain himself any longer, fired Copenhagen in their faces. This was the signal for the other guns to fire, and when the smoke had cleared away four men were found to have fallen. During the night the corpses were removed by the robber-gang, and though large rewards were offered for the apprehension of any of the culprits, no one concerned in the affair was ever discovered.

About two miles west of Lee Hall is *Shitlington*, or, as it is written in old documents, *Shotlyngton Hall*, which superseded the old manor-house of another branch of the Charlton family. In 1528 it is recorded that a band of Border thieves, led by "Willie o' Shotlyngton" and others, rode a foray into the bishoprick of Durham, robbed many houses in the neighbourhood of Wolsingham, and carried off the priest of Muggleswick a prisoner. On their return the country rose in pursuit, and William Charlton was slain, and his body afterwards hung in chains at Hexham.

South of the hall is the wild and rapid *Houxty Burn*, and north are the *Shitlington Crags*.

# BELLINGHAM TO HESLEYSIDE AND FALSTONE.

Hesleyside, 1¾ miles ; Dally Castle, 4¾ miles ; Greystead, 5¼ miles ; The Bower, 6 miles ; Smales, 8¼ miles ; Stannersburn, 9 miles.

A MILE and three-quarters west of Bellingham, on the south side of the North Tyne, is *Hesleyside*, a beautiful modern mansion, situated on an eminence overlooking the river. The old tower which stood at the west end of the present building was probably erected towards the end of the fourteenth century by Edward Charlton, who held lands here in 1343. He was descended from that Adam de Charlton, who, as we learn from the *Iter of Wark*, A.D. 1279, successfully resisted the encroachments of William de Bellingham upon his lands at Hesleyside, possessed, as he proved, by his grandfather. From time immemorial the Charltons of Hesleyside had in their possession an ancient spur, six inches in length, which, according to a Border custom, was served up at dinner in a covered dish by the lady of the house when she wished to intimate that the larder was empty. The method of replenishing it was only too clearly signified. In one of Mr. W. B. Scott's series of historical paintings at Wallington this incident has been pictorially represented. During the unhappy struggle between Charles I. and his Parliament the Charltons espoused the Royal cause, and Edward Charlton, Esq., of Hesleyside, having raised a troop of horse for the king's service, was created a baronet in 1645. After the execution of the king, his estates were confiscated, but restored again by Charles II. The sympathies of the family were always with the Stuarts, and an illustration of this is seen in the existence of a "Priest's Hole" here, where, no doubt, many a hunted Jacobite found refuge. "At Hesleyside," says Dr. Charlton, "in the south front, built as late as 1719, but which is possibly a century older, there is a well-contrived concealed closet entered by a trap-door from a passage between two rooms. Air, but not light, seems to have been provided by making the opening behind some old carving affixed to the wall of the south front."

South of the hall, in some fine plantations, is the *Ladies' Linn*, a small cascade on the Hesleyside Burn. The old picturesque mill at the mouth of this burn boasts, according to Dr. Charlton, a considerable antiquity.

Three miles west, on the west side of the Chirdon Burn, stood *Dally Castle*, the few remaining stones of which are incorporated with a mill there. A mile further up the stream is "*The Boure*," or "Bower," long the residence of a branch of the Charltons. In 1524 it was in possession of one Hector Charlton, who cared as little for the maledictions of the church as he did for the threats of the law. William Frankelyn, writing to Wolsey, tells the Cardinal—"After the receipts of your Grace's sayd letter we caused all the chyrches of Tindaill to be interdicted, which the theves there temerariously disobeyed, and caused a Scots frere (friar), the sayd interdiction not withstanding, to mynistre them theyre communion of his facion, and one Ector Charlton, one of their capeteynes, resaved the parsonnes dewties and served them all of wyne." Another anecdote is recorded of this northern worthy, who is characterised as "one of the greatest thieves in those parts," not much to his credit. He being familiarly and daily conversant with Lord Dacre, did ransom two thieves who had been taken in Gilsland for twenty nobles of money, and suffered them to go at large, "which thieves and their friends have delivered and paid the said sum to the said Charleton with goods stolen from the king's true subjects."

At a later period the Bower was the residence of a noted character, William Charlton, generally spoken of by the sobriquet of "Bowrie." He was a rough, overbearing man, nearly always in trouble with either the government or his neighbours. The most prominent side of his character is well seen in the following quaint extract from a letter written by the steward at Hesleyside:—"Bowrry Charlton wass all wayes vearry a-Bousiffe and scornful man to my master—and would a made him foudelled and sould him deare Bargains, and abused him when he had done." The other and less prominent side may be inferred from a Jacobite letter, in which he is thus alluded to:—"Nothing would give me greater pleasure than to hear that our generous and worthy friend Bowrie is still able to bend a bicker. Long may he live to teem a cog and (while he disdains the little superficial formalitys of our modern gentry, or those who would be thought such) to receive his friends with the old undisguised and gentlemanlike hearty welcome." In an encounter with Mr. Widdrington, of Bellingham, on Reedswood Scroggs, consequent on a dispute about the qualities of a horse, he was unfortunate enough to kill that gentleman, whose body, as has been already stated, was buried in front of Bowrie's pew in Bellingham church. He was "out" in 1715 with the Earl of Derwentwater, who owned the manor of Hareshaw, and behaved, it is said, bravely at Preston, but it is not known when he was relieved. In 1745 he was imprisoned at the instance, it is said, of his friends, to prevent him joining the rising, which, like the previous one, proved so abortive. Dally Castle and the Bower may be reached by a track over the moorland from Greystead, connected by a suspension bridge with Thorneyburn station. Five miles higher up the Chirdon Burn, near Hope House, may be seen a succession of seven linns, or small waterfalls. It is in remote places like this lonely gorge, in the heart of the swelling moorlands, where the nest of the kestrel, it is said, may still be found, that one seems to be spirited away from modern ideas to participate in the wild and primitive life of the past.

About three and a half miles north-east of Hope House, following a track on the east of the Smale Burn, is the hamlet of *Smales*, two hundred yards from which the burn passes between precipitous rocks, sufficiently near to each other to render a leap possible, but yet a somewhat dangerous experiment. That the feat has been attempted is evident from the name, "Smales' Leap," or the "Smuggler's Leap," a name suggestive of days not very far distant, when the lawless spirits of North Tynedale followed a pursuit as congenial and perilous as cattle-lifting had proved to their ancestors. This interesting spot is about a mile from the mouth of the burn, close to which is *Ridge End*, one of the old fortified farm-houses, formerly owned and occupied by an ancient family of the name of Heron. Three-quarters of a mile north-west is the hamlet of *Stannersburn*—that is, the Stony Burn. The same distance further on is *Yarrow*, where, in 1858, there died an old lady named Sisterson, who was born in that place in 1761, and during her long life of ninty-seven years had never been more than six miles from her native place. Half-a-mile from Stannersburn, on the north side of the river, is *Falstone.*

# BELLINGHAM TO FALSTONE AND KIELDER.

**Charlton, 2 miles ; Tarset Castle, 3¼ miles ; Thorneyburn, 4½ miles ; Falstone, 8½ miles ; Kielder, 16 miles.**

TWO miles west, on the north side of the river, is *Charlton*, where, within the memory of persons still living, there stood an old pele, the ancient residence of the Charlton family. A mile and a quarter further on, near the confluence of the Tarset Burn with the North Tyne, is a green mound, whereon may be traced the site of *Tarset Castle*.

This ancient stronghold, which belonged to the Red Comyn, or Cuming, of Badenoch, assassinated by Robert Bruce in 1306, does not play a very important part in history. In 1526 it was occupied by Sir Robert Fenwick and eighty horsemen, who had been sent to apprehend one William Ridley, an outlaw, probably one of the Ridleys of South Tyne, concerned in the murder of Albany Featherstonehaugh. His presence there does not seem to have been agreeable to the Tindale men, whose sympathies were with the fugitive. A body of them, under William Charlton, of Bellingham, set upon Sir Ralph, "and not onely put him from hys purpose of attackinge the sayd Ridley, but alsoe chased the sayd Sir Rauff out of Tyndaill, to his great reproache." It is believed that on this occasion they burnt the castle down. It was never rebuilt. At the beginning of the century the walls were partly standing, of "about four feet thick, of the finest ashlar-work, and strongly cemented." It was defended by an outer wall, and a moat ten yards wide. "Its magnitude, strength, and antiquity," says Mackenzie, "have combined to impress the minds of the neighbouring people with the notion of its having been the dreadful habitation of a giant, and it is popularly believed that a subterannean road is cut out, even below the bed of the river, between this ancient stronghold and Dally Castle, which is distant about a mile to the south." Tradition asserts that along this passage carriages have been heard to rumble, and then seen to emerge from the other end, drawn by headless horses. To these grim old Border towers a further interest attaches on account of a romantic story lingering in the hearts of the people of the vales. At some remote period a feud existed between the lords of Tarset and Dally, who were both men of great stature and distinguished prowess. But as the whimsical god of love would have it, Gilbert of Tarset became enamoured of the fair sister of his rival, and, to complicate matters, the love was returned. Necessarily the interviews were stolen, and attended with considerable danger. On one occasion, however, the lovers were surprised, and a hand-to-hand conflict took place between the puissant lords of Tarset and Dally, in which the former was defeated, and had to seek safety in flight. Pursued by his enemy across the Tyne, he betook himself to the wild moors of Hareshaw, and had gained the highest point of the broken road which leads over that bleak eminence, when he was overtaken. Another combat ensued, and Gilbert of Tarset fell. A memorial was set up to mark the dark spot, and, from age to age, was known to the people in that neighbourhood as "Gibb's Cross." Inn: Tarset Inn.

About three miles north of the castle the Tarset Burn receives the Black Burn, which, tumbling over a high precipice, forms one of those small but pretty cascades so characteristic of our northern streams. Half-a-mile north of the confluence of the Black Burn and Tarset Burn are the remains of two old peles. About the end of the seventeenth century one of these strongholds was occupied by a powerful member of the Milburn clan, known as "Barty of the Comb;" the other, higher up the burn, by his faithful ally and fellow-reiver, Corbit Jack, or Hodge Corby. One morning when Barty arose, he found that his sheep had been driven away during the night by Scottish thieves. He immediately summoned Corbit Jack, and they set off in pursuit, but lost the track north of the Carter Fell. Barty did not relish the idea of returning empty-handed, and the two borderers having decided, after a short council, that the Leatham wethers were the best, made a selection and drove them off. They had got as far as Chattlehope Spout when they were overtaken by two of the sturdy Scots, and a hand-to-hand conflict took place in the long heather above the waterfall. Corbit Jack was slain, and Barty was wounded in the thigh; when, making one tremendous back-handed blow, he caught the slayer of his companion in the neck, and—as he expressed it—"garred his heid spang alang the heather like an inion." His first assailant tried to make off, but was cut down ere he had run many yards. Barty took both swords, lifted his dead companion on his back, and, in spite of his own wound, drove the sheep safely over the height down to the Combe, and deposited Corbit Jack's body at his own door.

With such men as these the Tarset valley was populated, and it is no wonder that Muckle Jock of Bellingham, a descendant of Barty of the Combe, should, at the beginning of the century, have more than once cleared Bellingham Fair with the Tarset and Tarret Burn men at his back, to the old border cry of

"Tarset and Tarret burn
Hard and heather bred
Yet—yet—yet."

A mile and a-half from Tarset is the moorland village of THORNEYBURN, and the same distance further west, between the railway and the river, are the remains of an ancient British fortification, the moat of which is still easily traceable. Near to it is an old pele called "Camp Cottage." A neat iron foot-bridge crosses the North Tyne here. Above the river are heathery crags covered with hardy trees, the remnants of ancient forests which once extended over the now bare fell-sides. Half-a-mile from Camp Cottage, occupying an elevated situation, is the hamlet of *Donkley Wood*, mentioned in the *Iter of Wark*, A.D. 1279, as being, in conjunction with Thorneyburne and Tarsethope, amerced in the sum of twenty shillings for decapitating a thief without awaiting the coroner's trial.

A mile and a half still further is FALSTONE. This rustic village, situated in the midst of green haughs and trees, forms a pleasing contrast with the bleak fells around it. The name is supposed to be derived from the Anglo-Saxon word *Fausten*, a stronghold; and evidences of its importance in early times are not wanting, for here was discovered the fragment of a Runic cross, bearing an Anglo-Saxon inscription—

> "Eomaer set this (cross) up for his
> Uncle, Hrœthbert—Pray for his soul,"

written on the one side in Roman uncial letters, and on the other, in Anglo-Saxon runes. From this circumstance the cross is said to be unique in England. "It is probable," says Dr. Charlton, "that the old Anglo-Saxon runes used in Pagan times were, at the date of the erection of this cross, fast disappearing before the influence of Latin Christianity introduced by St. Augustine and his followers; and hence, both the old form of writing and the new have been perpetuated on this solitary fragment." This valuable relic is now in the Museum of the Society of Antiquaries in Newcastle. A fragment of another cross, richly ornamented, rests against the wall of the church.

"The Hrœthbert of the inscription," says Dr. Charlton, "is equivalent to the Robert of our day, and the descendants of Robert would be Robertsons, or Robsons, which now, as of old, is the chief surname about Falstone. We think we have evidence here of the Robsons some twelve hundred years ago in the very district where, till lately, they held sway. Whether old Hrœthbert was the ancestor of the Wight-riding Robsons of the old play—'Honest men, save doing a little shifting for their living'—we will not say." The Robsons were often at feud with the Grahams or Græmes and Armstrongs of Liddesdale. There is a North Tynedale tradition that the Robsons once made a foray into Liddesdale, to harry the Grahams, and drove off a flock of their sheep down into the North Tyne. Unfortunately the sheep proved to be scabbed, and communicated the disease to the other sheep of the Robsons. Upon this the latter made a second raid into Liddesdale, and took seven of the most substantial of the Græmes they could lay their hands upon, and hanged them forthwith, with the warning that "the neist tyme gentlemen cam to tak their schepe they war no to be scabbit." Scotchmen are proverbially slow to see into a joke, and it is scarcely likely they would appreciate, under the circumstances, the grim humour of a remark like this. People required to have strong walls around them to indulge in pleasantries of this kind, and the peles of the Robson clan were not easily forced, at least so it would appear from the remains of one that has been incorporated with the laird's house nearly opposite the inn, and close to the church. The arched doorway, which apparently had led into the byre from the open, is now the centre of the building, and the byre itself, with its massive arched roof, forms the sitting-room. This pele may possibly have been a fortress from which the township derived its name.

The church is a small and plain building, with a castellated tower at the west end. On some of the older tombstones in the churchyard are carved the implements of the different trades pursued by those who lie beneath. The Presbyterian church was one of the first established in England. Falstone is chiefly visited by sportsmen and anglers, but it forms a splendid centre for those who love to visit the wilder scenes of nature, and can sing with Chatt, the Hexham poet :—

"Away on the hills I love to roam,
Where the winter-swollen streamlets foam;
Where the furious winds rush wildly past,
And the dark pines bend to the shrieking blast;
Where the curlew screams in its wild retreat,
And the fleet hare bounds from its lowly seat;
Where the moor-fowl crouch on their heathery bed,
And the restless plover wails overhead;
Oh! my heart leaps free, unfettered then,
Away from the crowded haunts of men."

Good accommodation can be obtained at the Black Cock Inn.

At *Ballen Mill*, near Falstone, there was born, in the last century, a man named Paterson, without hands or feet, who in every particular fulfilled the old Border prophecy, usually ascribed to Alexander Peden, the Cameronian seer, but probably of much greater antiquity :—

"Atween Craig-cros and Eildon tree,
A bonny bairn there is to be,
That'll neither have hands to fecht nor feet to flee,
To be born in England, brought up in Scotland,
And to gang hame again to England to dee."

Soon after his birth he was removed to Talnash Mill, near the head of the Teviot water, and while yet a child was taken back to England, where at Carlisle he died, aged seven years.

A mile north-west of Falstone is an ancient peat-moss, where the fossilised remains of ancient forests are still to be seen. The hill behind the village will abundantly repay the trouble of a climb for the fine views to be gained during the ascent.

At *Hawkhope*, nearly a mile to the north-west, are remnants of the rude old Border architecture. A mile further on are the *Belling Crags*, opposite to which the Whickhope Burn enters the Tyne close to Emmethaugh. "The greater Whickhope burn," says Palmer, "flows through a tree-studded valley, resembling that of the Trossachs, with birch and ash and tree-topped purple rocks, island-like, rising out of the long-grassed and ferny plain, where numerous cattle graze." By the side of the burn the stratified face of a small abandoned slate quarry is curiously stained by the iron in the water which drains through it from the moors. In this neighbourhood, again, extensive remains of the ancient forest exist. Professor Lebour says, "The largest and thickest stems known to me are to be seen in great numbers in the thick moorland capping, the fells immediately to the south of Shillingburn-haugh, in the fork between Whickhope Burn and the North Tyne river." In the next few miles the North Tyne receives a good many feeders. About two miles from the Belling Burn there is the Plashetts Burn, which comes "trotting," to use an expression of the Scotch poet, from the high moorland, forming a linn at Wanehope. Three-quarters of a mile north-east of Plashetts is Soney Rigg, where there is a circular ditch enclosing an area of about five yards in diameter, with seats on the outside cut out of the earth. It is called "Arthur's Round Table." Near Plashetts station is *Haw Hill*, where are the remains of a camp. On the other side of the river is another. Plashetts Colliery, where one of the oldest (geologically) seams of coal in the carboniferous rocks is being worked, lies hidden among the hills which feed the Belling Burn. The seam has an average thickness of four feet.

Higher up the stream than Plashetts, the Lewis Burn pours in from the moors on the south its contribution of peat-stained waters. Respecting this locality, Sir William Eure, writing to Cardinal Wolsey in 1536, says, "The rebels of Tynedale make some besyness in Tynedale, wher ther dwellings was, and in no place els they melle or dois hurt, ther abydings is a place called Lushburn Howles (Lewis Burn), a marvellous stronge grounde of woodes and waters." The next tributary is the Gowanburn from the north, referred to in the old song—

> "There's walth o' kye i' bonny Braidlees,
> There's walth o' youses i' Tine;
> There's walth o' gear i' Gowanburn,
> And they shall all be thine,"

a fact which accounts for the frequent raids into this valley.

A famous stream is next approached at a distance of two miles from Plashetts—the Kielder. Along its romantic "banks and braes" the birch, the pine, and the mountain ash form the appropriate accessories to the sparkling water. A pleasant path through the wooded vale leads to *Kielder Castle*, a castellated shooting-box belonging to the Duke of Northumberland, not much more than a hundred years old. It is beautifully situated on a green knoll ("Humphrey's Knowe"), not far from the confluence of the Kielder and North Tyne, and is in convenient proximity to the far-stretching moors, which abound in grouse. The story of the "Cowt of Kielder" has been told by Leyden in his well-known ballad, reprinted in the *Border Minstrelsy*. The young Cowt of Kielder being near the castle of his deadly foe, Lord Soulis of Hermitage, is decoyed, with his train, into the hall, to partake of some refreshment. He escapes the horrible death prepared for him by the treacherous Lord Soulis, and hews his way through the glittering lances of his foe's retainers. The brown man of the moors—a malignant fairy—rises up and tells Lord Soulis the secret of the Cowt's invulnerability. He wears charmed mail, and carries in his helmet the mystic "holly green and rowan leaves," which avail nothing against running water. Crossing the burn the Cowt stumbled, and the talisman was washed away, and his enemies coming up, held his head under the water until he was dead. The name "Cout, or Colt," was given to him on account of his strength and activity.

On the confines of Jed Forest and Northumberland is a huge heather-crowned fragment of rock, called the Kielder Stone, which is said to mark the spot where the ill-fated chieftain crossed the Border on this, his last expedition. According to a popular superstition of the district, it is unlucky to ride three times "withershins"—*i.e.*, contrary to the sun's course—around it.

> "Green vervain round its base did creep,
> A powerful seed that bore ;
> And oft of yore its channels deep
> Were stained with human gore.
>
> And still, when blood-drops, clotted thin,
> Hang the green moss upon,
> The spirit murmurs from within,
> And shakes the rocking-stone."

A short distance from the mouth of the Bell's Burn—a stream which enters the North Tyne a mile and a half up the valley—an irregular circle of stones, just outside a rude wall, enclosing what was once an ancient burial-ground, is pointed out as the Cowt's Grave. This quiet, romantic spot, rendered holy with the memories that always cluster round the site of an old chapel, is thus described in the ballad :—

> "This is the bonny brae, the green,
> Yet sacred to the brave,
> Where still, of ancient size, is seen
> Gigantic Keildar's grave.
>
> The lonely shepherd loves to mark
> The daisy springing fair,
> Where weeps the birch of silver bark,
> With long dishevell'd hair.
>
> The grave is green, and round is spread
> The curling lady-fern ;
> That fatal day the mould was red,
> No moss was on the cairn.
>
> . . . . . . . .
>
> Where weeps the birch with branches green,
> Without the holy ground,
> Between two old grey stones is seen
> The warrior's ridgy mound.

And the hunters bold of Keildar's train,
Within yon castle's wall,
In a deadly sleep must aye remain
Till the ruin'd towers down fall.

Each in his hunter's garb array'd,
Each holds his bugle horn;
Their keen hounds at their feet are laid,
That ne'er shall wake the morn."

Three miles up the Keilder Burn, half-buried in heather and fern, is a huge stone, said to be the grave of Brandy Leish, the brother of the Cout of Keilder; and some ruined walls beyond it are called "Brandy Leish's Walls."

The scene of the Ettrick Shepherd's beautiful and touching ballad of "Sir David Graeme" is laid in the neighbourhood of Keilder, and is full of exquisite local colour. The lady bemoans the absence of her lover, who had "sworn to meet her on St. Lambert's night, whatever dangers lay between."

"The day arrived, the evening came,
The lady looked wi' wistful e'e,
But O, alas! her noble Graeme
From e'en to morn she didna see.

An' she has sat' her down an' grat,
The warld to her like a desert seemed,
An' she wyted this, an' she wyted that,
But o' the real cause never dreamed.

The sun had drunk frae Keildar Fell
His beverage o' the morning dew;
The deer had crouched her in the dell,
The heather oped its bells o' blue.

. . . . . . .

The lady to her window hied,
An' it opened o'er the banks o' Tyne;
'An' O, alack!' she said, and sighed;
'Sure ilka breast is blythe but mine!'"

Her dove comes flying back to her with a diamond ring she had once given to her lover, and she once more begins to weep.

"When lo! Sir David's trusty hound,
Wi' humpling back, an' a waefu' eye,
Came cringing in an' lookit around,
But his look was hopeless as could be.

He laid his head on that lady's knee,
An' he lookit as somebody he would name;
An' there was a language in his howe e'e
That was stronger than a tongue could frame."

The sagacious animal does all in its power to induce the lady to follow it, and at last, with a fearful foreboding in her heart, she suffers herself to be led

"—— owre muirs an' rocks,
 Through mony a dell an' dowie glen,
Till frae her brow an' bonnie goud locks
 The dewe dreepit down like the drops o' rain.

An' aye she eyed the grey sloth-hound,
 As he windit owre Deadwater Fell,
Till he came to the den wi' the moss inbound,
 An' O but it kythed a lonesome dell."

There she beholds her lover dead, with a wound through his shoulder-bone, "an' in his brave breast two or three." There are several memorials of the primitive inhabitants of North Tynedale in the immediate neighbourhood of Kielder. Traces of camps may be seen at Bell's Hunkin, Raven's Hill, Hitchhill Wood, Camp Rigg, Lowey Knowe, and Hobb's Knowe, all within a radius of little more than a mile. To the north-east of Kielder towers the stern and dark-hued form of *Peel Fell*—1975 feet above the sea-level—the most westerly spur of the Cheviot range, "at the foot of which," says Hodgson, "North Tyne has its source, and runs in a most sluggish manner along a level plain, from which circumstance it is called Deadwater, until it joins Bell's Burn." This statement is not, however, accepted by the inhabitants of the district, who trace the source of the North Tyne to a spot a little further north, within the enclosure of the North British Railway Company, between the stations of Saughtree in Scotland and Kielder in England ; and the Deadwater they regard as the first of its tributaries. Near, but on the Scottish side of the Border, is a sulphur well, which, half a century ago, had a local reputation for the cure of scrofulous complaints. The long tract of land to the south is the Threapland, or debateable land, which led to so many disputes and contentions in the olden time. In 1552, however, the boundaries between the two countries were definitely fixed. They had been frequently altered during the preceding centuries, for in the time of St. Cuthbert, according to St. Bede, Roxburghshire formed part of Northumberland, and in the time of the Plantagenets, North Tynedale belonged to Scotland.

# BELLINGHAM TO BIRTLEY.

Redesmouth, 2 miles ; Clint Rocks, 3½ miles ; Birtley, 5½ miles.

TWO miles from Bellingham is REDESMOUTH, situated at the confluence of the Rede and North Tyne. It is a pretty hamlet, embowered in foliage. The road runs south to Countess Park, where are the remains of a British camp, placed on an extensive platform at the point of junction of two deep and wide ravines within a bowshot of the North Tyne. Its rampart walls, of massive blocks of freestone, unhewn and generally water-worn, enclose an area of about three acres. The main entrance is on the east side, from which a passage leads to a large and nearly circular enclosure in the centre of the camp. On each side of the south-western adit is a hut-circle. Half-a-mile to the south, overhanging the river, are the "Clint Rocks" and the beautiful fern-fringed ravines adjoining. On the weathered surface of some of the fallen masses of rock here are some curious outstanding "blebs," due to concretionary action. In this neighbourhood the dipper, kingfisher, and grebe have their quiet and secluded haunts. A mile to the south of Countess Park Camp is another valley-fort, "The Carry House Camp," commanded by an adjacent freestone escarpment on the east, but having a steep declivity on the west. It covers an area of about an acre. A number of hut-circles may be traced in the interior, the most of them being close to the western rampart, which is the best defended side. Many interesting relics have been discovered under the foundations of these rude dwellings, among which may be named a bundle of much corroded iron spear-heads, daggers, and knives ; a broken piece of a bronze buckle used for securing the harness and horse-trappings of some British chieftain's war-chariot ; also one of the rarely discovered *long swords* of iron, with a portion of its bronze-tipped scabbard. In the centre of the camp there was formerly a cist-vaen. The fence wall bisecting the camp is the boundary line between two ancient farm-holdings. On the hill above the camp are the well-defined terraced slopes for early cereal cultivation. These are associated in the popular memory, both with the encampment of an army in the "troublous times," supposed to refer to Edward the Third's first campaign against the Scots in 1327, and with "rig and reen" culture. Close to is the West Farm Camp, on a rounded eminence called "The Good Wife Hot" (Saxon : Holt), from which a hollow way has led down to several immense heaps of scoria called "Cinder Kiln Hills." These vast deposits of iron slag are of great antiquity.

Relics of mediæval metal-workers have been discovered here. It is generally believed, by antiquaries, that iron was smelted here by the early inhabitants of the district.

Half-a-mile north-east of the Carry House Camp is Birtley Shield's Dene Camp, on the verge of a deep precipitous ravine, protected by a massive rampart and fosse, and communicating by a hollow way of considerable depth with the neighbouring camps. A little to the east is the "Mill Knock Camp," occupying the summit of a lofty rounded hill, and covering an area of an acre and a half. It is elliptical in shape, and has been a fortress of some importance, commanding a prospect only limited by the Cheviots and the Crossfell range. A little to the south of it, and close to the chalybeate spring called the Birtley Holy Well, which issues from the perpendicular rock beneath a picturesque linn or waterfall, is a huge mass of rock, standing about twelve feet from the ground, and weighing several tons. It is popularly known as the Devil's Rock, from a wild tradition that, once upon a time, a demon, attempting to leap from its summit to the opposite bank of the river, a mile distant, fell short of his aim, and plunged headlong into the Leap Crag Pool, the deepest abyss in the whole course of the North Tyne, and was drowned—a catastrophe, says the Rev. George Rome Hall, unique in the annals of demonology. The truth of the legend is attested by the marks of footsteps which are still visible on the top of the rock.

Bending round from Pitland Hill for the distance of a mile and a half from the Mill Knock Camp and Birtley Shields Terraces, is a great limestone escarpment, which is indented in its entire length with innumerable rounded shallow pits, or ironstone delves, as they are called, whence the iron nodules were obtained for the smelting purposes referred to above.

The village of BIRTLEY, round which all these memorials of the ancient British inhabitants are grouped, is five miles and a half from Bellingham, and one mile from Wark. The *Church of St. Giles* was built about the end of the eleventh century, in the early Norman style of architecture. During the restorations in 1883-4 several curious incised tomb-slabs were discovered. The ancient piscina may still be seen in the chancel.

The Vicarage House occupies the site of the old pele, or castle of Birtley, or "Birkley," as it was formerly called, built by the Umfravilles in the latter part of the twelth century, to judge from the remains of Norman dog-tooth ornament and other architectural relics, and from the ruined walls of the tower still existing in the Vicarage garden. No historic notice can be found of this ancient stronghold, which, at a later period, was known as Birtley Hall. In the east face of the old castle wall are two stones with carved inscriptions, bearing the dates 1107 and 1611, with the initials J. H., supposed to be those of the ancient family of Heron. The Rev. George Rome Hall, an authority on Celtic antiquities, is the vicar here. Inns: Percy Arms, Shepherd's Home.

# BELLINGHAM TO SWEETHOPE LOUGHS.

Buteland, 3½ miles ; Waterfalls, 6 miles ; Sweethope Loughs, 7½ miles.

FOLLOWING the main road to Redesmouth, and crossing the river, let the tourist proceed eastward up the hill a little, turning south to Buteland, where there is a British camp overlooking the valleys of the Rede and North Tyne, and the Garret Hot Camp on the right bank of the latter river. It covers an area of an acre and a half, and, in addition to a strong rampart and fosse, is provided with a further defence, unique in the district, but not unusual in other parts of Northumberland, consisting of a second massive rampart projected like the arch of an ellipse on the eastern—the weakest side. From Buteland a cart-road runs eastward to the Watling Street, two miles distant. A quarter of a mile to the north of the point where the great road is intersected is Swine Hill, on the summit of which is a large Roman camp. Its ramparts are in an excellent state of preservation. Three-quarters of a mile to the north-west, on the limestone escarpment above the Steele Farm House, may be seen several of those terrace-lines for cereal cultivation which occur so frequently in various parts of the Birtley parish. Beneath them are innumerable ironstone delves. A great mound or hill of iron scoria also testifies to extensive smelting operations conducted here in early times.

Stretching across from the Watling Street to Sweethope Lough is the high ground called "Green Rigg," memorable as the rendezvous where the adherents of the Jacobite cause in Northumberland had arranged to appear in open arms against the House of Hanover in 1715. Here, on the 6th of October of that year, Mr. Forster, with several gentlemen, in number at first about twenty, met as appointed, but, thinking the place inconvenient, rode immediately to the top of a hill called the Waterfalls, about half-a-mile to the south. This elevation commands an extensive view down the Watling Street and the country all around, and thus they were able to discover any that came either to join them or to oppose them. They had not been long here, says Patten, before they saw the Earl of Derwentwater, who came that morning from his seat at Dilston, with some friends and all his servants, mounted, some upon his coach-horses and others upon very good useful horses, and all very well armed. The little army numbered about sixty horse, mostly gentlemen and their attendants, and after a short council had been held, they decided to march to the river Coquet, to a place called Plainfield. Thus was taken the first disastrous step in the ill-fated rising of 1715. On the top of this hill is an upright stone, known as the Derwentwater monument, and the country people still tell how, from the top of it, the luckless earl mounted his famous iron-grey steed to ride forth on the fatal expedition. Three-quarters of a mile to the south, west of the Watling Street, is Tone, formerly the residence of the Hodgshon family.

In the rising of 1715, says Dr. Charlton, the messages of Jacobites were carried by female equestrians—the two Miss Swinburnes of Capheaton and Miss Mary Hodgshon of Tone. Miss Hodgshon, he adds, remembered in after years General Forster's appearance at Hexham at the head of the English Jacobites, and the splendid way in which he managed his magnificent black charger; but, as she expressed herself, "That was all he was worth, for he was a pig-headed fool." The Tone Pitt Inn stands conveniently by the side of the road.

Near the waterfalls is the source of the Wansbeck, which expands a short distance away into the extensive sheet of water called Sweethope Lough, covering an area of 180 acres. The true bulrush abounds on its margin. Overlooking the lake are the wild and picturesque Wanny Crags, a cluster of huge sandstone rocks, known as Great Wanny, Little Wanny, Aird Law, and Hepple Heugh. They are all precipitous towards the west. In Great Wanny there is a long cleft or chasm which extends nearly parallel with the front of the rock, and is called "The Wanny-byer," probably from some tradition of its having been occupied as a den for wild beasts. The place is still frequented by foxes. The crags are luxuriantly covered with heather, and among the great disjointed masses of rock may be found various ferns, lichens, mosses, and hepaticæ. From the highest peak of the crags a magnificent view is to be obtained of the surrounding hills—Ottercaps, Hareshaw, Darna, Peaden, Simonside, and Darden, with the rugged crests of the Cheviots towering away to the north.

The praises of the "Wild Hills o' Wannys" have been glowingly sung by James Armstrong, a local poet, who lived for many years at Aid Crag.

> "High o'er wild Wanny's lofty crest,
> Where the raven cleaves the cloud,
> *An' gorcocks beck* around Aid Crag,*
> *Sae crousely† and sae proud,*
> *Gurlin'‡ through the glens o' Reed*
> *Wi' a weird and eerie strum,*§
> When around yon auld cot
> The winter winds they'd come."
>
> ["*Aid Crag.*"]

A walk of three miles east will bring the tourist to Kirk Harle, or he may turn north, up the Watling Street to Woodburn, and follow the Reed to Reedsmouth and Bellingham.

* To nod and cluck as a strutting cock does. † Briskly.
‡ Hurling with a moaning sound. § A low musical note like the tap of a drum.

# BELLINGHAM TO KIRKWHELPINGTON AND CAPHEATON.

West Woodburn, 4½ miles; East Woodburn, 5½ miles; Ridsdale, 7½ miles; Kirkwhelpington, 15 miles; Kirkharle, 16½ miles; Capheaton, 19 miles.

FROM Bellingham a road crossing the railway runs north-east to the Watling Street, about four miles and a half distant,

> "Where Rede upon her margin sees
> Sweet Woodburn's cottages and trees."

This is the village of WEST WOODBURN. A mile to the east, on a sandstone cliff at the mouth of the Lisle's burn, is *East Woodburn*, once the property and place of residence of the old and distinguished family of De Lisle, the site of whose house still goes by the name of the Hall-yards. Nearly two miles further east, up the prettily-wooded burn, is Lynnhead Waterfall, in a picturesque spot, surrounded with spruce-firs and other hardy trees. Crossing the valley of the Lisle Burn, at Whetstone House, near East Woodburn, is a crescent-shaped mound, which is believed to have been the actual terminal moraine of one of the last small glaciers of Northumberland. The materials of which it is composed are sub-angular (not waterworn) fragments of the surrounding rocks—sandstone of the carboniferous limestone series predominating.

Along the wild and craggy banks of the Rede and its tributaries many charming glimpses may be obtained of the verdurous loveliness that lies hidden in the folds of grim and barren hills. Half-a-mile from West Woodburn, on the opposite side of the river, is "the moated mound of Risingham," overgrown with the richest grass, where the foundations of the Roman station at Habitancum may yet be traced. The ramparts and fosse, with the south and west gateways, are all well defined. This large camp, which is, strange to say, not mentioned in the Notitia, covers an area of four acres and a half, and appears to have been garrisoned by the first cohort of the Vangiones, a people who lived on the west banks of the Rhine, near the ancient Moguntia, or, as it is now called, Mayence and Mentz. The fourth cohort of the Gauls also lay here, but probably only for the temporary purpose of assisting in building or repairing some part of the station. Some elaborately-sculptured slabs and altars have been found here, and in 1840 the foundations of some baths were laid bare at the south-east corner of the station. According to Camden, Risingham signifies "The Giant's Habitation" (from the German *Riese*, a giant), and he goes on to say "that the inhabitants report that god Magon defended and made good this place a great while against a certaine Soldan—that is, an heathenish prince. Neither is this altogether a vaine tale. For that such a god was here honoured and worshipped is plainly proved by two altar-stones lately drawne out of the river there. Out of the former of these we may, in some sort, gather that the name of the place was Habitancum." Magon, or Mogon, as the name is inscribed on one of these altars still preserved at Cambridge, seems to have been a local deity worshipped by the Cadeni, a tribe of the Vangiones.

About half-a-mile up the hill, near to Woodburn station, a road will be observed running through a plantation to Parkhead farm-house, near to which, on the face of a sandstone crag, there was formerly to be seen the famous figure of Robin of Risingham, or Robin of Redesdale, as it was called in the neighbourhood. The figure, sculptured in bold relief, stood about four feet high, and was attired in toga and tunic. He wore a Phrygian bonnet, and carried in one hand a bow, and in the other a hare—the symbols of a hunter. A square block or altar opposite to the knee, and a panel (twenty-nine inches long and twenty inches broad) above the head, seem as if they had been both intended for an inscription. Warburton, in the earlier part of the eighteenth century, spoke of the figure as the Soldan's stone. Horsley thought that it represented the Emperor Commodus under the figure of Hercules. Hutchinson assigns the sculpture to a later period, and endeavours to identify the figure with two historical personages, nick-named Robin of Redesdale—viz., an Umfraville who lived in the time of Edward III., and the Hilliard who murdered Earl Rivers, the father of Elizabeth Woodville. The character of the figure, and its proximity to the station of Habitancum, have led most antiquaries to regard it as the work of some Roman sculptor. Popular tradition, however, accounts for the existence of this "man in stone" in its usual romantic way. Long ago there lived in these parts two brothers, of colossal stature, who subsisted on the spoils of the chase. The one made his abode at Risingham and the other at Woodburn, and between them they cleared the country-side of game, and it became no easy matter to replenish the larders of both. As the supply of food was likely to be limited, the Woodburn giant administered a deadly drug to his companion, whose memory is said to be perpetuated by this rudely-carved monument. Sir Walter Scott alludes to the tradition in the following lines from "Rokeby":—

"Some ancient sculptor's art has shown
An outlaw's image on the stone;
Unmatch'd in strength, a giant he,
With quivered back and kirtled knee.
Ask how he died, that hunter bold,
That tameless monarch of the wold,
And age and infancy will tell
By brother's treachery he fell."

Some years ago the upper portion of this interesting sculpture was blown off with gunpowder by the farmer, and chiselled into gate-posts, to prevent, it is said, so many of the curious trespassing on his land. All that now remains is the lower part of the figure from the waist downwards.

About a mile to the south are the Ridsdale ironstone beds, interesting to geologists for the varieties of fossils that abound in them. Professor Lebour gives a list of nearly a hundred different specimens collected there, and preserved in the museum of the College of Physical Science at Newcastle. The manufacture of iron was commenced by Sir William G. Armstrong at Ridsdale in 1864, but the works were discontinued in 1879.

Seven miles east of Ridsdale is KIRKWHELPINGTON. This is a quiet country village, about a mile from Knowes Gate Station, pleasantly situated on a cliff above the river Wansbeck, which winds nearly half-way round it under high, steep, and picturesque banks. The scenery in the immediate neighbourhood is very varied and striking. On the north and west are bleak and swelling moors, and to the east and south rich meadows and stately parks. The place boasts a considerable antiquity, for in the time of King John we find Richard de Umfreville "making his whole court at Whelpingtun" witness to a grant to the monks at Kelso. The family of De Whelpingtun does not appear to have made any mark in history—the only member of any note being Robert de Whelpington, who was one of the burgesses in Parliament for Newcastle in 1412, 1422, and 1423, and mayor of that town in 1435 and 1438. The village in the olden times no doubt consisted of a number of the smaller kind of peles or fortified farm-houses arranged around the large green.

The *Church*, dedicated to *St. Bartholomew*, is an ancient but unremarkable structure, with a low square tower, strongly buttressed. It formerly had transepts, but these have been removed. The entrance is through a porch on the south. The recess of the inner doorway is decorated with two shafts, mouldings, and a drip-stone. Within the tower is a vestry under a stone arch. In the belfry the uppermost point of a zigzag arch appears, by which it has opened to the nave. On the north side of the chancel is the tomb of Gawen Aynsley (died 1750) and his wife Mary. Their excellencies of character are thus commemorated :—

> "Kind to their children.
> Humane to their servants.
> Obliging to their neighbours.
> Friendly, just, and courteous to all.
> Religious without superstition.
> Charitable without ostentation.
> Lovers and practisers of virtue."

The flourishing letters on the tombstone were engraved by Thomas Whittell, the author of "The Mitford Galloway." Attached to the churchyard wall, behind the tower, is a tablet to the memory of the

Rev. John Hodgson, the historian of Northumberland, who held the incumbency from 1823 to 1832, when he was promoted to the living of Hartburn. It was at Kirkwhelpington that he wrote the greater part of the work which has made his name famous. There is an excellent inn at Kirkwhelpington, The Board.

About one mile west by north of the village stood the village of *West Whelpington*, one of the sweet Auburns of Northumberland, now only a heap of ruins. It consisted of a strongly-built pele-house, and two rows of houses, enclosing a large village green, near the centre of which a small circle probably points out the site of its cock-pit.

A mile and a half south-east by east of Kirkwhelpington is *Little Harle Tower*, the residence of George Anderson, Esq. It is an imposing freestone structure in the early English style, with embattled towers and parapets, surrounded on all sides but the south by stately trees. The west tower is the most ancient, and in the survey of 1542 is described as "in good reparations." About 1865 the new square battlemented tower was added to the north-east, and the house otherwise enlarged and improved. It formerly belonged to the De Harles, passing successively into the hands of the Fenwicks and the Aynsleys. The mansion contains Carmichael's splendid picture, "Barge Day on the Tyne," and two of the finest existing specimens of Canaletti, which are of historic value as minutely portraying the procession of the Bucentaur. An interesting old chimney-piece, from Anderson Place, Newcastle, where Charles I. was confined as a prisoner, is preserved here. *Kirkharle Tower*, the ancient manor-house of the Loraines, which occupied a low and sheltered situation near the village, was demolished some years ago, with the exception of the east end, converted into a farm-house. Kirkharle formed one of the many manors included in the barony of Bolbeck, and was held, with other lands, by Sir Robert de Harle in 1365 A.D.; afterwards the property of the Strothers, it was conveyed by an heiress of the family, Joanna, on her marriage to William Loraine, whose ancestor Robert had come over with William the Conqueror. The fate of their grandson is commemorated by a stone pillar set up in the glebe ground, a little south-west of the church, bearing the following inscription:—"This new stone was set up, in the place of an old one, by Sir William Loraine, Bart, in 1728, in memory of Robert Loraine, his ancestor, who was barbarously murdered in this place by the Scots in 1483, for his good services to his country against their thefts and robbery, as he was returning from the church alone, where he had been at his private devotions." The *Church*, dedicated to *St. Wilfrid*, is evidently of some antiquity, though the mason-work of its oldest parts does not seem to be earlier than the time of Henry the Fourth, about which time it is said to have been in a state of great decay. It underwent a thorough restoration in 1885. Some of the epitaphs in the church relating to the Loraine family are quaintly amusing, as, for example, the following:—"Here lyes the body of Richard Loraine, Esq., who was a proper handsome man of good sense and behaviour:

he dy'd a batcheler of an appoplexy walking in a green field, near London, October 26th, 1738, in the 38 year of his age." The bell is dated 1732, and when being cast has had three silver coins of George I. inserted into it. This is a relic of an old superstition once current of having silver in bells.

KIRKHARLE is a snug and very small village, pleasantly situated on the Cambo road, and is chiefly notable as the birthplace of Lancelot Brown, the celebrated landscape gardener, who, from his common application of the word *capability* to the capacities for improvement in the feature and scenery of places where he was employed, received the name of "Capability Brown." This ingenious man first saw the light in 1716, and while yet a boy commenced his career as gardener to Sir William Loraine, exercising his peculiar gifts in the laying out of the grounds at Kirkharle Park. He afterwards entered the service of Mr. Shaftoe, of Benwell. In 1739 he left his native county for Stowe, where his talents soon brought him into notice, and he was appointed head-gardener at Windsor and Hampton Court. He also gained a considerable reputation as an architect, and was High Sheriff for Huntingdon and Cambridge shires in 1770. His death took place in 1783. Cowper has written somewhat satirically in his "Task" of the expensive improvements made by "th' omnipotent magician Brown."

Two and a half miles to the south-east is CAPHEATON, a truly Arcadian little village, consisting of a neat and comfortable row of model cottages, looking very picturesque with their carefully-trained roses and creepers clambering up the walls beneath low, quaint overhanging eaves. The prospect from the village is exceedingly beautiful, extending over a portion of the park to the lake, with its woody islets and girdle of majestic trees. The village is approached from the Newcastle and Otterburn road by "Silver Lane," so called from the remarkable discovery made by some labourers in 1745 of several Roman coins and a service of Roman plate, consisting of various vessels of silver. They kept the secret of this treasure-trove to themselves, and sold all the coins as well as some of the plate, after breaking it up. The following they presented to Sir John Swinburne, the lord of the manor:—One silver dish, entire, weighing twenty-six ounces; the bottoms of three others; three handles, ornamented with figures beautifully carved in relief; part of another carved handle; a figure of Hercules and Antæus wrestling; and a figure of Neptune, in a reclining posture, holding a trident in his right hand, and an anchor in his left. These, with a few fragments, which were recovered from a silversmith in Newcastle, to whom they had been sold, were presented by Sir John to the British Museum. The name Capheaton is derived from Caput Heton—*i.e.*, Head-heton—or, as in Latin deeds it is commonly called, Magna Heton, and Heton *major*, to distinguish it from Heton *parva*, now known as Kirkheaton.

The entrance gates to the hall, at the east end of the village, are curiously carved, one of the pillars exhibiting all the articles of the toilette—viz., mirror, pomatum pot, etc.

A little to the south of the present hall there formerly stood a large Border stronghold, which Leland speaks of as Huttun, "a faire castle, in the midste of Northumberland, as in the bredthe of it. It is a IIII or V miles from fenwicke pile, and this is the oldist house of the Swinburnes." Collins says it was "moated about and had a draw-bridge, and was a place of resort in the moss-trooping times, when the gentlemen of the country met together to oppose those felonious aggressors upon the goods and chattels of the country, having a beacon on its top, to alarm the neighbourhood." The Swinburnes are said to have been resident here since the latter part of the thirteenth century, Allan de Swinburne purchasing the castle from Sir Thomas de Fenwyke in 1274. They appear to have been a bold and vigorous stock. One member of the family, Sir Thomas Swinburne, with Lord Berkeley and Sir Henry May, captured fourteen French vessels that were carrying prisoners to their fleet in Milford Haven in 1405. In the struggle between Charles I. and his Parliament the Swinburnes espoused the Royal cause, and the estate held by William Swinburne, Esq., was sequestrated by the Parliament in 1639. The king, as a reward for his loyalty, granted a baronet's patent to his son, which, however, was never taken out. The early life of Sir John Swinburne, the first baronet, is highly romantic. "He was sent while a child to a monastery in France, where a Northumbrian gentleman of the Radcliffe family, accidently visiting the place, recognised in his face the features of the Swinburne family. On enquiring of the Monks how he came there, the only answer they could give was that he came from England, and that an annual sum was remitted for his board and education. On questioning the boy himself, it was, however, found that he had been told that his name was Swinburne, which, with the account of his father's death, and his own mysterious disappearance in Northumberland, induced the superior of the house to permit him to return home, where, in an inquest specially empanelled for that purpose, he identified himself to be the son of John Swinburne and Ann Blount, by the description he gave of the marks upon a cat, and a punch-bowl, which were still in the house."—*Hodgson.* He was created a baronet by Charles II. on account of his loyalty and zeal for the restoration. He married Isabel, daughter and heiress of Henry Lawson, Esq., of Brough, by whom he had twenty-four children, thirteen of them being daughters. He it was who demolished the old pele, and built in 1668, on a new site, a little to the east of it, the present mansion, after designs of Robert Trollop, the architect of Netherwitton Hall, and the old Exchange at Newcastle. Considerable alterations and additions have been made to the original structure. Trollop's Italian roof has been removed, and replaced with a covering of Westmoreland slate. The north front has been modernised, but the south still retains its ancient windows, its richly ornamented cornices, and its sun-dials. The original doorway, now walled up, is on each side of it appropriately adorned with sculptures emblematic of ancient charity and hospitality. The master of the house is represented receiving a poor stranger, who is drinking from a bowl. Above the ornamented jambs of the eastern doorway is a heraldic tablet, containing various quarterings of the builder and his ancestors. There is a large and well-assorted library at Capheaton, chiefly valuable for its extensive collection of French and Spanish literature. It is also very rich in topographical works. The pictures, principally hung on the walls of the central hall and the dining-room, are valuable and interesting. Among them may be noted, "Portrait of J. E. Swinburne"—*Gainsborough;* "Edward Swinburne"—*Gainsborough;* "Girl sitting on stile"—*David Cox, Sen.;* "Sunrise"—*Edward Swinburne;* "Julia Swinburne"—*W. Mulready, R.A.;* "Portrait"—*Gainsborough;* "A Landscape"—*J. Crome;* "Portrait of Charles I.," copied from *Vandyke;* "Hayfield"—*David Cox, Sen.* There are other pictures by Mulready, William Hunt, and others, and a good collection of old china.

"At Capheaton," says Dr. Charlton, "which was in the last century the great resort of the Jacobites and the residence of the chief of the Northumberland Catholics, there were no less than seven places of concealment in the old house. These were once accurately described to us by one who knew them all well, the late Sir John Swinburne, of Capheaton, who died just before entering on his ninety-ninth year. In the chapel, which was on the top of the house, there were two hiding-holes; the one opened at once by a side-door on to the leads, the other was closed by the picture above the altar, which, revolving on a pivot, would allow of immediate escape into the long, heavily timbered roof. In this roof itself was a third hiding-hole, most ingeniously contrived alongside of a chimney, and covered by the stone slating. When the lamented Lord Derwentwater was shut up in Preston, and had relinquished all hope of escape, he told his huntsman to take his favourite iron-grey horse, and, if possible, get through the barriers, then closely invested by General Carpenter, and to make his way to Dilston to secure the family papers. The huntsman found a spot in a side street where he could leap the barrier, and the gallant grey carried him by the hills to the east of Preston, and thence up the valley of the Lune, till he reached Dilston, late in the dark of a November afternoon. All the family papers were that night put into light carts, and before morning they had reached the friendly shelter of Capheaton. The removal was kept an inviolable secret, and the Government could never discover where the papers were concealed. About thirty years after Lord Derwentwater's death a mason was repairing the roof of the present house at Capheaton, when, in lifting one of the heavy stone slates with which the roof was covered, he observed, in the concealed closets above referred to, several boxes with coats of arms painted on them. He immediately gave information to Sir William Middleton, of Belsay, who raised his followers, and, on pretence of searching for arms, was led by the traitor to the place of concealment. The deed-boxes and papers were removed first to Belsay, and then to London; the Act of Parliament vesting the Derwentwater estates to the benefit of Greenwich Hospital had been safely carried, and from that day the Derwentwater papers disappeared. It was the opinion of our informant, who was himself personally acquainted with the betrayer of the secret hiding-place, that the whole of the papers were ruthlessly destroyed. There is yet remaining, in Capheaton, a secret chamber, which is entered from a closet in the room above the sitting-room, and is directly over the door of the apartment; at one time we believe that the secret of this hiding-hole was unknown to almost all Capheaton. It was shown to us by the late Sir John Swinburne about twenty-five years ago."—(*Society in Northumberland in the Last Century.*) The intimate relations existing between Capheaton and Dilston were not merely political. The Earl of Derwentwater was cousin to Sir William Swinburne, and his correspondence with Lady Swinburne, published in *Hodgson's History of Northumberland*, is exceedingly interesting on account of the glimpses it gives of the life and character of this amiable nobleman. The Swinburnes possess several relics and memorials of the unfortunate earl, among which may be mentioned a lock of his hair, and the wedding-ring of his countess, given to them by Lady Newburgh. The present owner of Capheaton is Sir John Swinburne, a retired commander of the Royal Navy.

A little to the west of the site of the old pele-tower are the ruins of an ancient chapel. There is a magnificent embowered walk from the hall to the lake. The trees around Capheaton are remarkably fine, and from their sheltered position retain their foliage late into the autumn, displaying a combination of gorgeous hues almost oriental in their magnificence. A few may be particularised:—Yew, about 300 yards west of house—girth, at a height of 5 feet, 7 feet 10 inches; height, 52 feet. Some fine healthy yews form part of an old avenue of which this tree is the most west and finest. Silver fir, south-east of house—girth, 11 feet; height, 104 feet. Silver fir, 250 yards north-east of house—girth, 12 feet; height, 103 feet—the west of two, which are very conspicuous from Wallington. Scotch fir, close to north-east corner of garden—girth, 8 feet 3 inches; height, 65 feet. Elm, 100 yards north-east of corner of garden—girth, 12 feet 2 inches; height, 113 feet. Flowering ash *(Fraxinus Ornus)*, 20 yards south of garden—girth, 5 feet 5 inches; height, 43 feet. Lime, east tree of a row in the park—girth, 10 feet 10 inches; height, 54 feet. The artificial lake, south-west of the village, already referred to, covers an area of about ninety acres, and is visited by large numbers of wild ducks and other waterfowl. Charming little glades open out on to this picturesque sheet of water. Within a short distance of Capheaton are the celebrated *Shafthoe Crags*, the wild and rugged grandeur of which form a singular contrast with the rich sylvan beauty of the neighbouring landscape.

# MORPETH SECTION.

## MORPETH.

THE ancient town of Morpeth, which is supposed to have derived its name from More-path, or the town on the path over the moor, owes its attractiveness more to its position than to its historical associations. The gently-moulded hills, all meadows, and pastures, and corn-fields to the summit; the clear, bright Wansbeck, that flows round three of its sides; the quaint-looking streets, with several of the old houses remaining; the profusion of trees; the lovely gardens that slope to the river, combine to make Morpeth an extremely picturesque town. Viewed from the railway as it lies nestling in the delightful valley of the Wansbeck, it forms a picture of rural quiet and well-being not easily surpassed in the north country—"more like a town in a dream than an actuality," says William Howitt. The town dates back to a very remote period, yet it is identified with few events of historical importance. It seems to have had its full share of the disasters during the troublous times, without any of the distinctions. First the Danes destroyed it, then the Normans, and finally the Scots. The place was occupied by the Scots under Lesley in 1644, who left a garrison in the castle. The little band of Northumbrian Jacobites, reinforced by seventy Scots horse at Felton Bridge, in the earlier stage of their disastrous rising, rode into Morpeth, and proclaimed the Pretender in the Market Place—"Mr. Buxton, the clergyman, taking on himself the office of a herald." Here it was, says Mr. Patten, they received their first disappointment in the affair of Newcastle, which they expected should open its gates to them. The great families associated with the borough were the Merlays, the Greystocks, and the Dacres. The present lord of the manor is the Earl of Carlisle, who obtained it through the marriage of one of his ancestors, Lord William Howard, the famous Belted Will, with Elizabeth, the heiress of the Dacres.

A slight sketch of the town, as it appeared in the sixteenth century, has been left us by Leland, who visited the place about 1540:—"Morpet, a market towne, is xii. longe miles from New Castle. Wansbeke, a praty ryver, rynnithe thrwghe the syde of the town. On the hyther syde of the ryver is the principall churche of the towne. On the same syde is the fayre castle stonding upon a hill, longing with the towne to the Lord Dacres of Gilsland. The towne is long and metely well buylded with low housys, the streets pavyd. It is a far fayrar towne than Alnwicke."

Morpeth was then at the height of its greatest prosperity, and though new streets have been added, the general contour of the place is much the same as when Leland wrote. Arms were granted to the town during the reign of Edward VI., in the year 1552; they bear the appropriate motto of "Inter Sylvas et Flumina Habitans."

On a woody eminence, separated from the railway station at Stobhill by the road leading to the town, stands all that remains of *Morpeth Castle.* This feudal stronghold was built shortly after the Conquest by William de Merlay, who had been rewarded with the barony of Morpeth for his service in crushing the revolt in Northumberland. Here, in baronial state, the lords of the manor resided, while the infant burgh on the other side of the river developed in the shadow of its lofty battlements. The part it has played in Northumbrian history is a comparatively unimportant one. During the sixteenth century it seems to have been much neglected, for, in 1644, it is described as being "a ruinous hole, not tenable by nature, far less by art." Yet such was its strength even then that a party of 500 Scots, who had been left to garrison it by the Parliamentarian general, Lesley, were able to sustain a siege of twenty days against an army of 2700 men, under the command of the Marquis of Montrose. The trenches thrown up by the attacking forces may still be seen to the west of the castle. A number of the cannon balls which were fired at the time were discovered in 1836 by some workmen, when clearing away a sandbank near the castle. The shattered walls were never repaired, and the ancient stronghold soon fell into hopeless ruin, so that nothing now remains of it but the gateway-tower, which is supposed to have been built in the fourteenth century by William, Baron Greystock. This interesting remnant, however, has been considerably restored, and is occupied by the local agent of the Earl of Carlisle. The extent of the old fortress is shown by the fragments of the massive outer walls, which enclose an area of eighty-two yards from north to south and fifty-three yards from east to west. The ruined castle of the De Merlays forms the subject of one of Turner's pictures, the famous artist having taken his view of it from the old bridge. To the north of the tower, facing the county prison, is the Ha', or the High Hill, a mound which resembles the Mote Hills at Elsdon and Wark, partly natural and partly artificial, where the rude councils of the Celtic tribes were wont to be held. The remains of a cairn, or tumulus, and fragments of an ancient arch and pillar, have been found upon it. Batteries may possibly have been erected there during the hostile operations against the castle. A little westward from the castle, and approached from the turnpike road, is the *Parish Church of St. Mary.* It is seated on an eminence called the Kirkhill, on the site of an earlier structure, of which some remains may be traced. Its architecture is chiefly that of the fourteenth century. The lower portion of the tower at the west end is Transitional work. The upper portion has evidently been renewed during the Decorated period, when other changes were made in the church, the chancel being re-built on a larger scale, and the two-storied sacristy added. The principal features of interest in the chancel are the canopied sedilia, the priest's door, the piscina, and the low-side window, through which the eucharist was administered to infected persons during times of plague, on the south side; the ancient aumbry, with its original hinges, on the north; and the two oblique slits—squints, or hagioscopes, as they are called—in the jambs of the chancel arch. The eastern window, composed of flowing quatrefoils, is filled with mediæval glass, depicting the tree of Jesse—a favourite subject with the old designers—restored by Wailes, in memory of John Bolland, sometime curate of the parish. The stained glass in the low-side window was given by Sally Tindale, an old woman who cleaned the church, in memory of her aged parents. In the west wall of the lower room of the vestry is a curious recess, pierced at its head with a quatrefoil opening, which looks into the north aisle of the church. Some persons suggest that the chamber may have been inhabited by an anchorite, and that this aperture was his medium of communication with the outer world, as there was no external door, and (at the time it was found) the north aisle did not extend up to the sacristy door. Others think it may have been a niche for a lamp or light. The author of *The Churches of Lindisfarne* is of opinion that it was a chauffoir, where the priests greased their sandals. "There are but few instances," he says, "of Decorated work of such richness, purity, and ripeness in the archdeaconry." Mr. J. R. Boyle thinks that the recess was a fire-place, and the quatrefoil opening simply a vent-hole for the smoke to escape from. The low-pitched roof of the nave belongs to the Perpendicular period. Near the eastern end of the south aisle is an arched recess for a tomb. Some effigies, one of them being that of a child, and a grave-cover are preserved in the church. A fine lichgate, erected in 1861, in memory of A. R. Fenwick, Esq., of Netherton, forms the entrance to the churchyard. The most conspicuous monument is a lofty cross, which, like the east window of the church, perpetuates the memory of the Rev. J. Bolland, late curate of Morpeth. The church walk is lined with yew trees, clipped in a conventional manner; behind them stands the old churchyard cross; the base and pillar are old but re-dressed. On the south side of the churchyard is a house, built in 1831, for watchers of the dead, whose function it was to prevent the graves being desecrated by the body-lifters, or resurrectionists, as they were called.

The road leading from the station to the town is bordered with magnificent trees, that render the approach from the south an exceptionally fine one. The stately building with castellated towers at the foot of the descent is the *County Prison*, built 1821, but now empty in consequence of the prisoners having been removed to Newcastle. The road crosses the Wansbeck by a strong and stately bridge of three arches, erected in 1831. An iron and wood foot-bridge, thirty yards above, rests on the piers of the picturesque old bridge, which was built previous to 1300, and was extremely narrow, and so steep as to be difficult and dangerous to loaded wagons. Two of the mail coaches, about sixty years ago, carried away the battlements of the bridge, and were thrown, with their passengers and horses, into the river. At the end of this old bridge, on the north side of the river, stood the *Chapel of All Saints*, where it was not only customary to hold services, but also to collect the duty which was charged for the repairing of the bridge. Within it were the chantries of All Saints, of the Virgin Mary, and of St. Mary Magdalene. Before the erection of the present Grammar School, the pupils of this ancient foundation met in a portion of the disused and ruined building, which has now been converted into shops, and an aerated water manufactory. The pointed arches on the outside and the belfry bear witness to the former religious character of the building. At the north-east end of the present bridge is *St. George's English Presbyterian Church*, erected in 1861 on the site of the ancient mill of Morpeth. In the centre of the town, at the junction of Bridge Street and Newgate Street, is the *Market Place*, having a quaint old-fashioned look about it. On its west side is the *Town Hall*, erected originally in 1714, on the site of the old Toll Booth of Morpeth, from a design by Sir John Vanburgh, who at the time was building the hall at Seaton Delaval. It has, however, been entirely rebuilt from the plans of Mr. R. Johnson, architect, of Newcastle, the restoration being completed in 1870. The facade is an exact reproduction of the former one, and the building, with its turrets and piazza of ornamented rustic-work, forms a decidedly picturesque feature to the town. On the spacious staircase is a marble bust of George W. F. Howard, seventh Earl of Carlisle and Viscount Morpeth, by Foley. In the Town Clerk's office may be seen the Town's Hutch—a large oaken chest, with seven locks, containing the charters, books, papers, and plate of the Corporation. Some of the documents have very curious seals attached to them. It is between three hundred and fifty and four hundred years old.

Adjoining the Market Place, in Oldgate Street, is an ancient-looking square stone tower, containing a capital peal of bells, and a clock which tradition says was brought from Bothal Castle, and is a very old one. It goes by the name of the *Clock House* or *Tower*. The lowest floor appears to have been used as a prison, or correction-house, till after 1800, and was the depository of the town stocks. At one corner of the tower stands the last survivor of several little stone figures which mounted guard there in quaint mediæval costumes. They have suggested a series of short tales, entitled, "The Watchmen of the old Clock Tower," by W. H. Short, of Morpeth. As the parish church is some distance from the town, this tower, with its peal, is found very useful for parochial purposes, and from its hoary belfry even yet

> "The curfew tolls the knell of parting day."

Approached by a fine avenue of limes from Newgate Street is the *Church of St. James the Great*, built 1844–46, from the designs of Benjamin Ferrey, F.S.A. It is a large and massive structure in the modern style of Norman architecture. The interior of the building is superbly decorated, and is lighted by several stained-glass windows, representing scriptural scenes, by Wailes. There is an elaborate fresco in the apse of the Incarnation of the Eternal Word, designed by the celebrated glass painters, John R. Clayton and Alfred Bell, of London, and executed by two of their artists, Messrs. Hewitt and Macdonald. It may thus be briefly described :—At the top of the semi-dome there is the Dove, the symbol of the Holy Spirit, by whose operation the Word was made Flesh ; immediately below which the Incarnate Son is represented in glory, with saints on each side. In the next stage below are represented—1. The Agony in the Garden ; 2. The Crucifixion ; 3. The Resurrection. In the arcade below is another series of paintings, illustrative of the early life of Christ. The three central compartments represent one subject—viz., the Nativity, with the Adoration of the Magi on one side, and of the Shepherds on the other. On the north side, the subjects are the Annunciation, the Visit of the Blessed Virgin to St. Elizabeth, and the Birth of John the Baptist. On the south, the Presentation of Christ in the Temple, the Flight into Egypt, and Christ among the Doctors. Below these again, between the pillars of green marble, there are seventeen single figures standing —David being in the centre, immediately under the picture of the Nativity. In addition to these frescoes there are also two fine oil paintings of "The Scourging" and "The Walk to Calvary."

Much of the old-fashioned character of Morpeth streets is due to its quaint hostelries. The old Grey Nag Inn, in Newgate Street, has still preserved its Elizabethan front during internal repairs, and the Queen's Head, Black Bull, and others contain many large and ancient rooms, with low ceilings and massive fire-places. It was at the Queen's Head Hotel that John Scott (afterwards Lord Eldon) and Bessy Surtees stayed on their way back from their runaway Scotch marriage. Over the fire-place of a large room here are the arms of the old Morpeth family of Pye in stucco. Adjoining the grounds of the Roman Catholic Church, in Oldgate Street, is a large house, the residence of the priest, which is said to have belonged to Lord Collingwood. Here the great admiral, when freed from official duties, delighted to spend his leisure and plant trees. On the opposite side of the street are the Collingwood Gardens. Oldgate Street is the most ancient part of the town.

At COTTINGWOOD, on a lofty site, about half-a-mile from the town, is the *County Asylum*, a large and commodious building of red brick, in the Italian style, with woods and gardens around it. It was opened in 1859, and has accommodation for 450 patients.

Below it is the *Free Grammar School* of King Edward the Sixth, founded in 1552. The present handsome building was built in 1858-9, from designs by Benjamin Ferry, F.S.A. The school bell belonged to the chantry of the Virgin, and is inscribed "Ave Maria gratia plena, dominus tecum." During the sixteenth, seventeenth, and early part of the eighteenth century, the school stood very high as an educational institution. In the latter part of the seventeenth century Charles, third Earl of Carlisle, and William, fourth Lord

Widdrington, were upon the scholars' roll. The friendship then formed between them as boys proved eventually very serviceable to the latter, for, after the failure of the Jacobite rising in 1715, it was chiefly the influence of the Earl of Carlisle which saved his old school-fellow from the scaffold.

Several eminent men have been associated with the town. William Turner, M.A. and M.D., the celebrated botanist and ornithologist, was born here early in the sixteenth century. His principal work is a history of plants, printed in three parts in 1551, 1562, and 1568, under the title of the *New Herball*, the first original botanical work published in English. He also wrote several works on divinity; and treatises on birds, fishes, plants, stones, metals, etc. In the library of the Mechanics' Institution, among several other rare books of Morpeth authors, is an interesting volume containing the first and second parts of the *New Herball* (black letter), published in 1551 and 1562 respectively, with the same writer's *Book of the Baths*, published in 1562. Thomas Gibson, the townsman and contemporary of Dr. Turner, acquired great fame for his attainments in physic, divinity, history, and botany.

The Rev. John Horsley, the learned antiquary, was probably born near Morpeth in December 1729. He subsequently became the minister of the Presbyterian Church in that town. The work by which he is chiefly rememberd is, *Britannia Romanæ; or, the Roman Antiquities of Great Britain.*

The Rev. Robert Morrison, D.D., the great Chinese scholar and missionary, was born at Bullersgreen, on the 5th January 1782. It is only recently that his birthplace has been removed. *The Dictionary of the Chinese Language* was his *magnum opus.*

There are some plots of unenclosed ground by the side of the river, called the High and Low Stanners (staners are the small stones and gravel on the margin of a lake or river), chiefly used as places of recreation. On the Low Stanners, to the east of the town, persons sentenced to death were at one time executed. Adjoining the Presbyterian Church, at the back, is a square plot of enclosed ground encircled with trees, known as the Terrace. It is provided with seats, and has a walk around it which makes a pleasant promenade in summer. During floods the river rises to a great height, sometimes sweeping over the wall of this little park and transforming the Stanners into a lake, so that the houses on the north side of the river and the Gasworks on the south, are frequently quite isolated. Morpeth Common lies on the south-west of the Parish Church, and is over 400 acres in extent. Pleasant walks abound in the neighbourhood of Morpeth, and the visitor will find some lovely paths through the woods above the river, either westward, past the "Ha' Hill" and the Castle towards Newminster, or eastward along "Bennett's Walk" and the Bore Hole Lane towards the Quarry Drift, and thence to Bothal.

The principal hotels and inns of Morpeth are: The Queen's Head, The Grey Nag, The Black Bull, Newcastle Hotel, Turk's Head.

# MORPETH TO MITFORD AND WALLINGTON.

Newminster Abbey, 1 mile; Mitford Castle, 2 miles; Meldon, 6 miles; Hartburn, 7½ miles; Scots Gap, 11 miles; Rothley Crags, 13 miles; Cambo, 12 miles; Wallington, 13 miles.

ABOUT a mile from the centre of Morpeth are the remains of *Newminster Abbey*, which may be reached by following the main road from Newgate Street, or by crossing the west bridge to the High Stanners, and following, first, a path by the riverside, called the "Lady's Walk," and then a lane called the "Lover's Walk"—an old avenue still shaded with a few large beeches. The ruins are beautifully situated on a green, triangular-shaped plateau, which is somewhat raised above the level of the river, and sheltered on three sides by the steep and wooded scaurs, called the "Abbey Banks." The surface of the field is broken up by the mounds of foundations still unexcavated. The situation of the abbey on the south side of the river corresponds with that of most of the castles of Northumberland, whose inmates were always solicitous to have a river between themselves and the Scots. A lovely view of the valley of the Wansbeck may be had from this sheltered spot, which is diversified with some fine trees of large dimensions, principally of the ash kind. The abbey, appropriately called "the first daughter of the holy church of Fountains," was founded in 1139, by Ranulph de Merlay, the lord of the manor, for a colony of monks from the newly-built house of Cistercians, which he had casually visited. There, "beholding the conversation of the brethren," he was, in the words of the old writer, "pricked to the heart, and under the inspiration of God, assigned a certain place in his paternal estate in order to build a monastery for the redemption of his soul." The plan of its buildings was almost identical with that of the famous Yorkshire abbey. A year had scarcely gone by since the foundations were laid

> "When Scottish raiders scoured the vale,
> Leaving a charred and bloody trail;" (*Chatt.*)

and the half-completed buildings of the abbey were among the ruins left smoking by the rude soldiery of King David. In order to repair the mischief as quickly as possible, Robert, the Abbot, offered free absolution to all who should assist in any way in rebuilding the desecrated pile, and he soon had the gratification of seeing the burnt walls rise again. As it was near the old north road from Newcastle, the abbey was favoured with many royal visits, which are represented as being exceedingly burdensome. Edward I., on January 5th, 1300, directed from it, by brief of Privy Seal, a commission to Lord St. John to receive the men of Annandale to the king's peace. Edward II. dated public documents from it during his visits to the north in 1310, 1314, and 1322; and Edward III. tested a mandate here on November 16th, 1334. In 1502, Margaret, eldest daughter of Henry VII., then affianced to James IV. of Scotland, on the 26th of July, was conveyed with a fair company to Morpeth, "and by the towne passed in fayr order, wher ther was much people; and so sche went to the abbay, wher sche was well recyved by the abbot and religyous revested, at the gatt of the church, with the crosse." The possessions of the abbey were valuable and extensive, comprising numerous lands on both sides of the Wansbeck, or in the adjoining district; vast tracts on the Coquet, including Kidland, lands in Kestern, Flotwayton (Flotterton), Bitelisden, Scharbirton, Stretton, etc.; two pits, or drifts, for extracting sea-coal; salt works near the mouths of the Blythe and Coquet; fisheries on the Tyne; houses in Newcastle; Chopwell on the Derwent; lands in Filton, Tolland, and Swinburn, in Chollerton parish; the advowson of Whelpington; peat moss at Edlingham, etc., etc. The value of their property has been estimated at £20,000 per annum of the present money. The destruction to their houses and land by hostile invasions often reduced the monks to extreme poverty. The monastery was dissolved in 1535, and its revenues distributed by the succeeding sovereigns among various persons. The abbey buildings appear to have been almost entirely destroyed immediately afterwards. There is a local tradition that this was done by a mob, and it is not unlikely that a more or less tumultuary gathering of professed thieves and robbers took part with the emissaries of the king in overcoming the resistance which the abbey seems to have made. All that now remains of this once magnificent house is the small archway of a door of the church, which stood on the north side of the conventual buildings. Hard by it is a venerable ash-tree, of vast bulk of stem, measuring 14 feet in circumference at 5 feet from the ground. In 1878 a portion of the site was excavated, when the foundations of the Chapter-house were laid bare. From the discoveries made, it appears that the Chapter-house was a finely-vaulted apartment, measuring 50 feet by 40 feet in the inside; its stone groining supported by four pillars; its western portion raised one or more steps, and with different mouldings in its groining; its floor paved in geometrical patterns; its windows, the form of which is yet uncertain, supplied with painted glass, and its walls and groining colour-washed, and marked as with joints by chocolate and white lines. A considerable part of the choir of the church was cleared out, and the site of the high altar disclosed. In the north transept were found four incised slabs, shattered by the fall of the groining, etc. One of the slabs had only a cross; a second had a cross and a pair of shears; a third a cross, and the words, "Joh'es de la Vale;" and the fourth a cross with the word "Tomas," and a surname, the only portion of which that could be deciphered was "sun." Here also was found a painting, in distemper, representing a nimbed saint in ecclesiastical vestments. It is executed in a rough and spirited manner, in lines of black and red, with a few touches of white, on three of the stones of a respond which fit together, and were found lying nearly as they had fallen. The face is the best preserved part, and is full of expression. Several stone coffins have been discovered, which may possibly have contained the bodies of St. Robert, the first abbot, and Ralph de Merlay, the founder, and other members of his family buried here. One of the coffins, used as a trough for cattle, is said to have contained the body of Meg of Meldon, and, according to another account, to have been the seat of her restless spirit. The cloisters, one hundred and two feet long, from east to west, and eighty feet wide from north to south, were situated on the south side of the nave of the church. The arrangements for the supply of water to the abbey were very elaborate. "Somewhat to the south-west of the abbey," says the Rev. J. T. Fowler, in his introduction to the *Chartularium de Novo Monasterio*, "and within the curtain-wall tanks of oak and lead lie buried; these were in connection with a fine spring of water. The great sewer for sanitary purposes, which also turned two or three mills, was an artificial water-course, taken off from the Wansbeck, about a mile and a-half higher up, where a weir, or dam, was put across. This water-course can still be traced through a considerable part of its length, and for some distance contains a briskly-running stream of surface drainage." This water, from the Wansbeck, is believed to have anciently filled a fish-pond near the abbey. One cannot but regret that so little remains of the magnificent house of the Cistercians, for since the dissolution of monasteries it has served as a quarry to the good people of Morpeth and the district, and nothing is now left but one small arch, and the foundations of the halls and cloisters, to remind the visitor of the once famous monks and their guests.

> "Gone are all the barons bold,
> Gone are all the knights and squires,
> Gone the abbot, stern and cold,
> And the brotherhood of friars;
> Not a name
> Remains to fame
> From those mouldering days of old."

The farm-house on the height to the south-east is called *Springhill*, and the ravine just north of the river is known as *Scotch Gill*—a name suggestive of Border raids, for down this defile the dreaded marauders used to come on their plundering excursions. The narrow road-way skirting the Abbey-field leads to the kennels of the Morpeth Foxhounds, through fields past the Abbey Mills, belonging to Thomas Ashton & Co., woollen manufacturers, and a path also takes through the Borough Wood to the ruins of *Old Mitford Castle*. The scenery that greets the eye of the visitor as he follows the road by the side of the Wansbeck westward is delightfully rich and varied, and almost justifies the enthusiastic statement of William Howitt, that "the valley from Morpeth to Mitford, about two miles in length, is one of the most lovely in England." The limpid waters of the Wansbeck flow over solid beds of sandstone, beneath a steep and wooded bank that in several places descends almost sheer to the edge of the stream. Near the village it receives from the north a considerable tributary, the Font, which is spanned by a fine old single-arched bridge.

The picturesque village of MITFORD, once a place of greater importance than Morpeth, now only consists of a few pretty cottages, a small reading-room, and a comfortable inn—the Plough. A building, once a snuff-mill, and, previous to that, a flannel manufactory, reminds the visitor of the former enterprise of this rural village. Mitford was one of the places burnt by King John in his northern depredations during 1216. The stone-fountain here was erected by Colonel Mitford on the supposed site of an old well which, according to a monkish writer, named Reginald, who lived in the reign of Stephen, was the scene of a strange miracle. The story runs as follows:—A monk who felt convinced that eyesight could be restored to a blind person by washing the eyeballs with a piece of the robe of St. Cuthbert steeped in the water of the well, drew a cupful and inserted the cloth. To the astonishment of all present the fabric, when drawn out, showed that water had not produced any effect upon it, as it was perfectly dry. On bathing the eyes of the blind person with the water the sight was restored, and the priest, who drank the water in order that it should not enter the well once more, was instantly cured of dysentery. The drinking-fountain that the rambler finds so useful nowadays is not at all a modern convenience, for, according to Bede, King Edwin, before A.D. 633, caused stakes with brass dishes suspended to them to be fixed near all public wells and springs, for the refreshment of wayfarers. On a wooded eminence directly overlooking the village is *Spital Hill House*, which occupies the position of St. Leonard's Hospital, founded by Sir William Bertram in the reign of Henry I.

Passing through the village, and up the steep bank as far as the Schools, the visitor must follow the road to the left, in order to reach the *Castle*, *Manor-house*, and *Church of Mitford*. After crossing the Wansbeck by a picturesque old bridge, embowered in trees, he beholds "a paradisal valley, a rich bit of English landscape poetry hidden from the world in a profound retirement of beauty and repose."

The *Church of St. Mary Magdalene*, which occupies a low and sequestered situation in the midst of luxuriant foliage, is an ancient stone building in the Norman and early English styles. By the munificence of Colonel Osbaldiston Mitford, it has been partly restored and rebuilt at a cost of £10,000. The chancel is early English, and has been recently provided with a beautifully-carved reredos. Its old sedilia and aumbry still remain. The frescoes above the chancel arch are the work of Mr. Thomas Bowman Garvie, a young Morpeth artist.

Under the range of lights, on the south side of the chancel, is a small lancet-headed splayed opening, called a low-side window. The fine Norman nave, fifty-nine feet in length, has been subjected to a good deal of renovation; the walls have been heightened to admit of clerestory windows, and a tower has been added. The interior would have been rendered more symmetrical if a north aisle had been built as well as the new south aisle. There is a pretty little chapel on the south side of the church, called the Mitford Chapel. In the vestry opposite, which goes by the name of the Pigdon Chapel, is preserved a curious old bell, said to have been cast 700 years ago. At the south side of the chancel is a fine Norman doorway, ornamented with the chevron and billet mouldings. In the chancel is a large mural monument of freestone erected over the tomb of one of the Bertrams (Bertram Reveley, of Throphill, nephew of Sir Bertram Bulmer), with his arms in a concave square moulding, underneath which is the following curious inscription, well cut in capitals :—

> "Here Lyeth Interred With-
> in This Molde, A Generous and
> Virtuous Wight, Whose
> Dewe Deserte Cannot be
> Told, From Slender Skil Unto
> His Right, He was Descended
> From A Race of Worshipful
> Antiquitie, Loved He was
> In His Life-Space, of High
> Eke of Low degree. Rest
> Bartram In This House of Clay,
> Reue'ley unto The Latter Day."

Below is his effigy, rudely cut in relief, and on the edges of the cover are these lines :—

> "Bartram to us so dutiful a Son,
> if more were fit it should for
> thee be done, who deceased
> the 7th of October, Anno Domini 1622."

The Rev. J. F. Bigge points out the similarity between this monument and one in Stamfordham Church. "The ornaments in both," he says, "are similar, and very probably have been designed and executed by the same lord." There are several tombs of the ancient Mitford family in the church. In the tower is a peal of eight bells, rung by machinery of a clockwork description. The bells are saucer shaped, and struck by wooden hammers, and the manner in which the mechanism plays a selection of hymns is said to be beautifully soft and harmonious. In the churchyard are two very aged yews. Within a short distance of each other are three abodes of the Mitfords:—the feudal castle, Jacobean manor-house, and modern mansion—significant memorials, as has been well said, of the changes which have taken place in society at different periods of our history. The ponderous ruins of *Mitford Castle* are seated on a lofty knoll on the south side of the valley, just above the Wansbeck, and being surrounded and, in some places, overgrown and half-hidden by trees, form a picture of the most romantic beauty. The circular keep, now shattered and crumbling, was raised upon an artificial mount, the chief elevation from the natural level being effected by arches of stone and vaults, which in ancient times were used as prisons, or places for concealment. A massive wall engirdled it at a distance of ten feet. The huge outer walls environing the hill serve only at present to shelter a thicket of hollies, and a quiet orchard that occupies the central courts. From the number of bones found in the south-west part of the courtyard, it has been supposed that the chapel stood there. The round-arched doorways on the south command a lovely, though limited, prospect, and the views that are framed by them of the picturesque old manor-house and church, with their background of orchards and gardens and river-banks, are pre-eminently beautiful. This mighty stronghold was built between 1150 and 1170 by William Bertram, the founder of Brinkburn Priory, and during the succeeding century and a half suffered considerably from the ravages of hostile armies. In 1215 it was seized by the Flemish troops of King John. The following year it was blockaded by Alexander II. of Scotland. In 1316-17 it was held by Sir Gilbert de Middleton and a company of bandits, from whom it was wrenched by Ralph, Lord Greystock. In 1318 it was captured by Alexander III. of Scotland, and dismantled. In 1323 it was dilapidated, having been destroyed by the Scots.

A little to the north of the castle, on the level ground near the church, is an interesting remnant of the old *Manor-house*, consisting of a battlemented tower, with large mullioned windows. Over the arched entrance are the arms of the Mitford family, with the date 1637 above them. An old font is preserved in the interior. A part of the old hall has been converted into a cottage for one of the servants of the estate, and is entered by an ancient porch supported on two stone pillars. This was the kitchen of the hall, and still preserves its large and stately fireplace, on the left-hand side of which is an appliance now very seldom seen, viz.: an old dog-spit wheel, or turnspit. The dog was put inside the wheel, which is composed of spokes, and subjected to a kind of tread-mill exercise. In order to preserve its balance the poor little animal had to keep replacing its front paws on a new spoke as the old one slipped downward with its weight. Thus the wheel went round, and the apparatus was worked which turned the roast. In the old orchard adjoining are several fine trees: acacias, maples, planes, silver firs, a medlar, old apple trees, etc. There is also a cedar of Lebanon, with a girth of eight feet at a height of three feet from the ground.

The river is crossed by a suspension bridge, giving access to the large and stately mansion of Colonel Mitford, which stands on the crest of a gently-sloping height in a finely-wooded park. It was built after designs by Dobson. Here is preserved an interesting relic from the old church, viz.: a stone with a Saxon inscription upon it, which antiquaries have not yet been able to decipher. On the south bank of the river, opposite to the hall, is a large sycamore, with a girth of nearly sixteen feet, and a height of over sixty feet; a splendid tree in full vigour.

The ancient Northumbrian family of Mitford were possessed of the villa and lordship, from which they derive their name, as early as the time of Edward the Confessor. At the Conquest, Sibil, the only daughter and heir of Sir John Mitford, was given in marriage by William the Conqueror to Sir Richard Bertram, one of his Norman adventurers. The estates were held by the Bertram family till 1264, when they were forfeited to the crown by Roger Bertram, who had appeared in arms against Henry III. at Northampton. In the reign of Edward II. the barony of Mitford was the property of Adomer or Aymer de Valence, Earl of Pembroke, the chief instrument in the capture of the famous Scotch patriot, Wallace of Craiggy, in 1305. On his third bridal-day he was slain at a tournament held in honour of his nuptials, and left a wife at once a maiden, bride, and widow. It is said that for several generations of this family a father never was happy enough to see his son, the proscribed parent being snatched off by the hand of death before the birth of his issue. The castle and manor became again the property of the Mitfords by a grant from Charles II. Several members of this family have distinguished themselves in the fields of literature and the law, among whom may be mentioned Mary Russell Mitford, authoress of *Our Village*; William Mitford, author of a History of Greece; John Mitford, Earl of Redesdale; Captain Meadows Taylor (by his mother's side a Mitford), author of *Confessions of a Thug*. Of this family, too, was the notorious "Drunken Jack Mitford," born at Mitford Castle, who, after having served with distinction under Hood and Nelson, sank into the lowest state of degradation through his intemperate habits. He had considerable literary ability, and was the author of a nautical novel, to some extent autobiographical, called *Johnny Newcome in the Navy*. The publisher of this work gave him a shilling a day until he finished it. Incredible as it may appear, he lived the whole of this time in Bayswater Fields, making a bed at night of grass and nettles. Two pennyworth of bread and cheese and an onion were his daily food; the rest of the shilling he spent on gin. Thus did he pass forty-three days, washing his shirt and stockings in a pond when he required clean linen. This miserable man died in St. Giles' workhouse.

Four miles west of Mitford is *Meldon Dyke Neuk*. A mile to the south, near to the railway station of Meldon, stands the early English *Church of St. John the Evangelist*. It contains the rudely-carved effigy of Sir William Fenwick (ob. 1652), the husband of the famous "Meg of Meldon." On the south side of the chancel is a piscina, and a short distance from it an aumbry in the thickness of the wall. One of its rectors was the Rev. Dr. Raine, the learned antiquary, under whom the church was restored. "His antiquarian lore," says Mackenzie, "proved neither stale nor unprofitable to him, for, in the prosecution of his studies, he discovered certain old manuscripts, from which he deduced his claims to the tithes—claims admitted to the fullest extent by the trustees of Greenwich Hospital." By Meldon old water-mill, which stood at the foot of Temple Bank, a little within the west wall of the park, and about one hundred yards below the dam of the present mill, Oliver Cromwell is said, by tradition, to have rested and fed his troops of horse, August 11th, 1651, on his return from Scotland. There was a border tower at Meldon in the reign of Henry VI., the property of the Fenwicks, but only the slightest vestiges remain. The manor of Meldon, granted by Elizabeth to Alexander Heron in 1598, was afterwards held by the Fenwicks, from whom it passed into the hands of the Radcliffes. Forfeited in 1715 by the Earl of Derwentwater, it was given to the Greenwich Hospital, and is now the property of John Cookson, Esq. Meldon Hall, a large modern mansion, is beautifully situated above the Wansbeck in a park containing some very fine and stately trees. Among the many valuable pictures in the house may be mentioned "The Fire-worshippers," by Vandyke, and "Portrait of Vandyke" by himself. One of the most popular of Northumbrian stories is connected with Meldon, and the mysterious doings of "Meg of Meldon" have diverted many a rustic fireside. This restless spirit, it is said, once animated the form of Lady Margaret, wife of Sir William Fenwick, of Wallington. She was the daughter of William Selby, a Newcastle money-lender, and from her father seems to have inherited a miserly disposition, which grew upon her with age, so that avarice became the ruling passion of her life. Among the peasantry, whom she oppressed and ground down, she had the reputation of being a witch, and was believed to drive between Hartington and Meldon along an underground coach-road. She had secret hiding-places for her treasure, and when she died it was said that her spirit was compelled to wander from hoard to hoard for seven years, then, after resting for a similar period, to begin the weary round again until the treasure was found and appropriated. The principal scene of her supernatural appearances was an old and deep draw-well near the south-east tower of Meldon, wherein she had hidden a bullock's hide of gold. She has been seen to cross Meldon Bridge as a large black dog and then assume the form of a lovely woman; others have watched her sitting upright for nights together in a stone coffin at Newminster. A bold countryman, so we are assured, was once in a fair way of getting this hoard, the only stipulation being that from the time he left his house till he returned to it again with the money he was not to utter a single word either to himself or to anybody else. Hodge, however, had no sooner hauled the treasure to the top than he forgot the conditions, and exclaimed, "There! all the devils alive can't help me getting it now." But, alas, he was mistaken; the instant the fatal words escaped his lips the bag slid into the well, and fell like a leaden weight to the bottom. One of the places where she had concealed her ill-gotten wealth seems to have been a house of considerable antiquity, afterwards the school-room of Meldon, for seventy or eighty years ago, as some children were romping about in it during the play-hour, the ceiling gave way, and a bag containing several pieces of gold dropped out, bursting in its fall, and causing a fine scramble among the fortunate youngsters. In a portrait of this famous lady, once hung in the gallery of Seaton Delaval, she was represented in the costume of a witch, with broad hat tied down at the sides over her ears, a stiff silk gown trimmed up to the elbows, and Vandyked ruff and sleeves.

A mile further westward is HARTBURN, a truly idyllic little spot, in the midst of rural scenery. It is situated on the west side of the Hart, above a charmingly wooded ravine, and consists of an old church, a vicarage, a school-house, and a few pretty cottages. Hartburn Church is a beautiful and interesting specimen of early English work. The name of the saint to whom it was dedicated has been forgotten. With its old square tower, plain-built nave and porch, and ivy-covered chancel, the building presents a very picturesque appearance from the outside. The inner doorway in the porch is enriched with dog-tooth ornament. The most curious feature about the church is the deflexion of the chancel towards the north. This part of the building retains several of its ancient features, for on the south side of it may be seen the priest's door, the sedilia, and two piscinæ, one considerably larger than the other, and the low-side window. One of the sedilia contains a marble slab, inscribed to the memory of John Hodgson, the well-known historian of Northumberland, who was for many years vicar of this place. He died in 1845, and his last resting-place here is marked by a simple epitaph—"John Hodgson, M.A., vicar of Hartburn, died 12th June 1845, aged 65." There are two beautiful monuments in the chancel. One is by Chantrey, and represents a full-length female figure reclining upon a couch of white marble beneath a stone canopy. It is a memorial of Lady Bradford, who died at sea, on her passage homewards from India, 14th February 1830. The other is by Ormiston, and represents two angels removing the grave-cloth from a recumbent figure, while Christ is addressing the sleeper in the words, "I am the resurrection and the life." It was erected in memory of J. H. H. Atkinson, Esq., of Angerton, eldest son of Admiral Sir Thomas Bradford, G.C.B. Several of the windows are filled with modern stained-glass, commemorating members of the Bradford family, the Rev. John Hodgson, and others. One of these, to the memory of Lucy, wife of Colonel Hugh Fitzroy, having for its design the figure of Faith, is a beautiful example of modern art. On the south side of the nave is a piscina, and at the west end stands the font on the ancient steps. The vestry forms the lowest stage of the tower, and is lighted by a window inserted during the Perpendicular period. Here may be seen a curious carving in oak, representing Eve offering the forbidden fruit to Adam. It came out of Angerton Hall, and was presented by Colonel Atkinson. The visitor will also examine with great interest the old collection-boxes, with the quaint carvings of grotesque figures upon them.

In the churchyard is buried Thomas Whittle, an eccentric and ingenious poet, who died April 19th, 1731. The poem by which he is chiefly remembered is the well-known ballad of "The Mitford Gallowa[y]." He was much employed in painting and engraving heraldic devices in the churches of the county. Some of his painting is to be seen at Hartburn. Almost opposite to the churchyard gates a pathway may be entered which leads through the meadows and beautiful woods of Angerton to Meldon. Permission will have to be obtained from Colonel Atkinson to take this delightful walk. The ivy-mantled tower at the west end of the village might be taken for an old pele-tower by a stranger, but it is not, having been built at the joint expense of Dr. Sharpe, who was vicar of Hartburn 1749-1792, and his parishioners. It contains apartments for the village schoolmaster above, and a parish stable below. Passing through a small wicket near the tower, the visitor enters a beautiful and romantic walk along the banks of the Hart, resembling very much that running along the Devil's Water from Dilston Castle. It was formed by Dr. Sharpe, who also cut a grotto of two compartments in the rock, and made a covered way from it to the river, for the convenience of bathers. Above the entrance are two niches, once containing statues of "Adam and Eve." One of these statues now lies prostrate in the grotto. The first chamber contains a substantial fire-place, but is now a cold and damp place, full of dead leaves and loose stones. The river at this point flows gently over a smooth pavement of rock, and is sufficiently deep for the purposes of swimming. A little lower down it passes into a deep pool, called "The Cobbler's Hole" by the village people, who imagine it to be fathomless. Among the sylvan glories of this lovely dene are two magnificent specimens of the silver fir *(Pinus picea)*—the king and queen of Hartburn. They stand four yards apart (north and south), and 450 yards north-west from the old castellated house just referred to, and thirty yards north of the river. The larger one measures, at a height of 5 feet, 11 feet 7 inches, and is 126 feet high; the other measures 10 feet 9 inches at a height of 5 feet. Mr. Selby, in his work on *British Trees*, says they were planted about the year 1755. One of them was nearly 140 (?) feet high in 1842. Hartburn is a station of the *Linnæa Borealis.* An old lane or bridle-road, called Hurpeth here, which bounds the vicarage ground on the west, is a part of the famous Roman road—the Devil's Causeway. The nearest railway stations to Hartburn are Angerton, one mile to the south, and Middleton, a mile and a half to the south-west. *North Middleton* is a little place of some interest, because there survived here until A.D. 1806 the pure Arian form of village-community, precisely as it is in Russia and India. *Angerton Hall* (the seat of Colonel Atkinson), designed by Dobson, is pleasantly situated, as might be inferred from the derivation of the name—Angerton (meadow-town)—about half-a-mile to the south of Hartburn.

From Hartburn the road runs westward for three miles and a half past the hamlet of *Hartburn Grange* to SCOTS GAP, a village that commemorates in its name an old Scottish raid. It seems the inhabitants of the district were accustomed in the olden times to drive their flocks for safety into an ancient night-fold, called the "Villain's Bog," about half-a-mile to the east. It is in a hollow, and was defended by a strong earthen dike, and was approached by a narrow avenue. Some moss-troopers, says tradition, attempted to rob this fortress, but the alarm beacon above Rothley being fired, the country-folk crowded from every quarter, and the lawless Borderers were driven back with great loss. The slain were buried near the scene of action, and a stone was set up at Scot's Gap, in memory of the affair. This relic, however, was destroyed when the adjoining highway was made. Scot's Gap was the scene of a terrible railway accident, in which four persons were killed and several wounded, on July 5, 1875. There is a Temperance Hotel and posting establishment here.

Two miles to the north are *Rothley Crags*, a bold range of picturesque rocks, which have been classified by Professor Lebour among the "Inghoe Grits." They are covered with a profusion of heather and bracken, and present an imposing front to the west. From the Rothbury road there is a fine view of these broad and rugged escarpments, with the huge boulders at their feet. Some artificial ruins of a castle, erected by Sir Walter C. Blackett, of Wallington, in the last century, crown the summit of the crags, and form a characteristically Northumbrian feature in the landscape. This imitation stronghold consists of a low square tower, flanked on each side with "a curvated wall, embattled and pierced with loop-holes, and terminating with a bastion." It commands a very extensive view of the surrounding country, and is itself a very prominent landmark, being 843 feet above the sea level. Near the castle are traces of an ancient earthen encampment. Nothing remains of the "lytle towre" of Rothley, built by the abbots of Newminster, which, in the year 1542, was said to be "in measurable good reparations." On another range of crags to the north is Codger Fort, a mere parapeted breastwork of unhewn stone, overlooking Rothley Lake.

The little village of ROTHLEY (Red-lea) lies to the south of the crags, and further to the south again, on the river Hart, is *Rothley Mill*, standing on the site of an older building, which was not only very picturesque, with its black water-wheel and heathery roof, but also very interesting on account of its romantic associations, for it was, if old tales are to be believed, the haunt of a family of fairies. According to Hodgson, Queen Mab and her train are said to have formed, out of the rock, the numerous circular basins which are still to be seen here in the bed of the Hart, and here they bathed every moonlight summer evening. The mill was their great council-hall, and the eye of the kiln their kitchen, where, in boiling their pottage, they burnt the husks of oats the miller laid up for drying the corn he had next to grind. This they took as payment for guarding and cleaning the mill, and rendering other useful services; but the miller, thinking them too extravagant, was determined to disturb them, and while they were preparing their supper one night, threw a sod down the chimney, and instantly fled. Before he could reach the verge of the glen he heard the cry, "Burnt and scalded! burnt and scalded! the sell of the mill has done it!" and the old mother of the family set after him, and just as he got to the stile going into Rothley, touched him, and he doubled up, was bow-bent, and a cripple, to his dying day. Another fairy-tale of the neighbourhood is recorded in Richardson's *Local Historian's Table Book*:—

"A widow and her little boy lived alone in a cottage at Rothley. One evening the child was sitting by the fire, when a beautiful little figure, the size of a child's doll, descended the chimney, and alighted on the hearth. 'What do they ca' thou?' said the little fellow. 'Ainsel,' the fairy replied, at the same time asking, 'And what do they ca' thou?' 'My ainsel,' answered the boy, and the two commenced to gambol together quite innocently until the fire began to grow dim; the boy then took up the poker to stir it, when a hot cinder accidentally fell upon the foot of his playmate; her tiny voice was instantly raised to a most terrific roar, and the boy had scarcely time to crouch into the bed behind his mother before the voice of the fairy mother was heard crying, 'Who's done it?' 'Oh, it was my ainsel!' answered the daughter. 'Why, then,' said the mother, as she kicked her up the chimney, 'what's a' the noise for? there's nyen to blame.'"

A mile west of Rothley is *Hartington Hall*, which, in 1542, is called "a strong bastell house of the inheritaunce of Sir John Fenwyke, in good reparaçons." Here it was that the miserly lady of Sir William Fenwick (Meg of Meldon) principally resided, and amassed her treasures. In the outbuildings of the farm-house of Kirkhill, close by, are the remains of Hartington Chapel. Several ancient gravestones, cut into quoins, are built up in the west end of the byre. Half-a-mile to the north is *Gallows Hill*, where the lords of Bolbeck probably had their gallows for the execution of criminals taken in this part of their barony. "Tradition tells of two brothers of the name of Reay, men of Cyclopean strength of stature, who farmed Gallows Hill, and in the twilight of a summer's morning, one of them, seeing a band of moss-troopers driving off their cattle, rose, ran after them, and attacked them single-handed; but before his brother could get to his assistance, the thieves had mastered him, and 'cut him into collops,' which his friends collected and carried home in a sheet."—*Hodgson.* Here is an outcrop of basalt, a part of the great Whin Sill stretching from Holy Island to Haltwhistle.

A mile south-west of Scot's Gap is CAMBO, formerly written Camhoe, a name signifying "the camp or fort on the hill." It is an exceedingly picturesque village, consisting of a fine Gothic church, a good inn, a school-room, reading-room and library, a large shop, once an old pele-tower, and several pretty dwelling-houses and cottages, with gardens in front, the whole forming a picture of rustic peace and beauty not easily surpassed in the county. Sheltered and half-screened by clumps of stately trees, the village forms a conspicuous landmark from every point of view, and commands some lovely and far-reaching views, especially along the well-wooded vale of the Wansbeck, and over the wilder country extending towards Rothbury and Elsdon. In the centre of the village is a granite drinking-fountain, with a large and grotesquely-ferocious dolphin carved upon it. Beneath is the inscription, "Futuri haud immemor oevi" (Not unmindful of future generations).

The *Church of the Holy Trinity*, which stands so prominently on the high ridge to the north of the village, was erected in 1842. It contains several memorials of the Trevelyan family. One of these, a stained-glass window representing the archangel Gabriel, was erected to the memory of Hannah More Macaulay, daughter of the great historian, and wife of Sir Charles Trevelyan. Several interesting early English grave-covers, removed from the site of the ancient chapel of Cambo, are preserved in the porch and vestry. One of them is ornamented in outline with the figure of a lady, whose feet rest on a dog—the symbol of fidelity; the others bear, mostly in relief, designs of floriated crosses, swords, and shears. In the churchyard is the memorial of the late Sir Charles Trevelyan, designed and executed by Mr. E. J. Physick, sculptor.

Launcelot Brown, the celebrated landscape-gardener, better known as "Capability Brown," received his early education at Cambo school. Two eccentric local characters were associated with the village—Thomas Whittle, the author of "The Midford Galloway's Ramble," and other comic productions of local interest (died 1736), and William Robson, a severe poetical satirist, author of several poetical pamphlets and miscellaneous essays, and the publisher of *The Poetical Works of the celebrated and ingenious Thomas Whittell.* He was the schoolmaster here, and kept a rhyming register of his scholars, extending over a period of nearly twenty-three years, and dealing with seven hundred and seventy-six names. He adopted a curious method of indicating the disposition and capacity of each individual by certain signs.

"The names distinguish'd by a star
Were the most docible by far;
And those with equi-distant strokes
Were second-handed sort of folks;
But where you find the letter B
A humdrum booby you will see;
And where an exclamation's set,
The rascals went away in debt."

This curious document is valuable as a parish record.

From Cambo a broad road, bordered with trees, leads down the slope to WALLINGTON. There are many mansions in the county architecturally more imposing and interesting than *Wallington House*, yet few have a situation more beautiful and romantic. Seated on a gentle eminence that is well protected on its north side by the high ground rising towards Cambo, it has a superb view over the rich valley of the Wansbeck. From the terrace on the south the richly-swarded lawn of the park slopes down to the edge of the stream, which is lined by magnificent trees, and crossed by a fine old bridge of three arches.

The hall itself is a large square building of white freestone, with little external ornament, erected by Sir William Blackett about one hundred and fifty years ago. It is now the seat of the distinguished writer and statesman, Sir George Otto Trevelyan. Incorporated with the mansion at its south-west corner is the lower portion of an ancient pele-tower, built, in all probability, by the De Strothers, previous to the reign of Henry VI. This consists of the basement storey of the southern wing—a vaulted chamber, fifty feet long and twenty broad, now used as a cellar, and the basement storey of the tower—an older room still, having an entrance into another vaulted chamber. At an early period this pele-tower seems to have passed into the possession of the Fenwicks, who added to it a Gothic manor-house, making this, according to Leland, their chief residence. "Show us the way to Wallington," a favourite local air, bears witness to the hospitable character of this ancient family.

> "Harnham was headless, Bradford breadless,
> Shaftoe picked at the craw,
> Capheaton was a wee bonny place,
> But Wallington banged them a'."

The old ballad, "Fair Mabel of Wallington," sings of the hapless fate of the lady of Sir William Fenwick, who died in child-birth, as five of her sisters had done before her.

> "There is a race in Wallington, and that I rue full sare,
> Tho' the cradle it be full spread up, the bride-bed is left bare."

Another old poem, entitled "Cheviot," contains a reference to the disposal of Wallington by Sir John Fenwick to Sir William Blackett.

> "Fair Wallington has been decreed by Fate
> To be the cap'tal of a large estate;
> The wine of Wallington old songsters praise,
> The Phœnix from her ashes Blacketts raise."

Allusion is made in the last line to the crest of the Fenwicks, which is a pun upon the name. The son of Sir William left his natural daughter, Elizabeth Ord, sole heiress to his immense property, on condition that she should marry his nephew, Walter Calverley, within twelve months of his decease. This union accordingly took place. The line, however, in spite of this arbitrary method of prolonging it, soon became extinct, Sir Walter dying without issue. His Wallington estate was inherited by his sister, who had married Sir George Trevelyan, and has remained from that time to the present in the Trevelyan family.

The large central quadrangle or court-yard in the interior of the building was transformed by Dobson, in the time of Sir Walter Trevelyan, into a beautiful and unique picture gallery, which has been much admired by such eminent men as Ruskin, D. G. Rossetti, and W. B. Scott. Dobson roofed over the space with globular, slightly obscured glass lights, which ensure all the year round an equable shadowless light, as long as day lasts, showing the decorations and paintings in an unexceptionable manner. Here, for once, the difficult problem of lighting picture galleries has been solved.

On the ground floor two sides of this great central loggia are divided by arches into eight panels or recesses, decorated with frescoes by William Bell Scott. They give a pictorial representation of Northumbrian history, the subjects chosen being typical of the various periods and states of society. The pictures in the series may thus be briefly described:—1. Building of the Roman Wall. In the background is seen Crag Lough. A cohort of Moors, Spaniards, and Germans are engaged on the works. In the foreground lie two Britons, too lazy to work. One of them is hiding the dice under his hand, on the approach of the centurion with his peeled rod. The other watches the simmering kettle. Over the fosse appears a party of the Caledonians, led on by a mad woman or priestess, annoying the labourers. Among the soldiers on the rampart will be recognised the well-known features of Dr. Bruce, the great authority on the Wall. 2. St. Cuthbert. This picture represents the visit of King Egfrid and Bishop Trumwine to the Farne Islands, to urge on St. Cuthbert the acceptance of the Bishopric of Hexham, which he had, till then, declined. The saint has been found in the act of digging up onions for his frugal dinner. Beside him stands a tame gander of the eider-duck species. The king presses the crosier upon him. The rude dress of the hermit, leaning upon his spade, forms a striking contrast to the rich attire of his petitioners. Sporting in the bright green sea beyond appear the sea-swallows and other birds of the islands. 3. Descent of the Danes. The promontory forming the background of the picture is Tynemouth Rock, with a little Saxon church upon it. The time is a spring morning, and the boats and galleys—the serpents and dragons, as they were called—approach out of the mist, taking the country by surprise. In the foreground the men of the place are rushing down to oppose the landing of the dreaded Northmen, and several fugitives hasten up the embankment to some place of security. Among them will be observed an old woman with her cat, her lint, and other valuables ; a young mother with her children ; and a priest with his mass furniture. 4. The Venerable Bede. The dying saint is represented on the floor of his cell, his head supported by affectionate young monks, that he might continue looking towards the place where he had been accustomed to say his daily prayers. One of his disciples has just finished writing from his dictation the last verse of the gospel of St. John. The acolyte is already lighting the candles. One is blown out by the wind from the open sea, the other is just lit. Other types of the change from one life to another may be discovered in the pigeon dying from the window, and in the distant ship. In the church the brethren are assembled to say the prayer for the passing soul. 5. The Spur in the Dish. The chief of the Charltons and his retainers are assembled for dinner, when the dame herself brings in a great trencher containing nothing but a spur. This is a practical joke to remind the Border chief that the larder needs replenishing, and they must "ride and reive" before another sirloin smokes in front of them. A monk on pilgrimage, who is a guest on the occasion, does not seem to comprehend the joke. There is, however, a mess of soup being brought in by a damsel. The room represented is in the castle at Newcastle, and the features of the astonished laird are those of the late proprietor of Hesleyside, Mr. W. A. Charlton. Several of the figures introduced are portraits of Armstrongs, descendants of a famous old moss-trooping family. 6. Bernard Gilpin taking down the challenge glove in Rothbury Church. The celebrated divine has arrived on Sunday morning at Rothbury, and observed a glove hanging on the wall of the church. Ordering the sexton to bring it to him, he learns, from the firm determination of that functionary not to touch it, the meaning of its appearance there. The two factions occupy the different sides of the church. A fight seems about to begin, when the good man steps down to interfere and prevent the feud. 7. Grace Darling and her father saving the survivors from the wreck of the steamer *Forfarshire* on the Farne Rocks, 7th September 1838. To the remains of the large steamer are seen clinging the eight survivors, with all the expressions of hope and fear depicted on their countenances as they watch Grace and her father straining through the boiling waves. The rain is coming down in torrents, adding to the gloom of the scene. 8. The Nineteenth Century—Iron and Coal, A.D. 1861. In the foreground is the Labour characteristic of the district, in the middle distance the Commerce, and beyond, the scientific result in the shape of Railway and Telegraph. Out of such materials as the High Level Bridge, the Quayside, an old fire-engine, an anchor, an Armstrong gun, whereon a child with her father's dinner waits till twelve o'clock, a loaded keel passing under the old bridge, etc., the artist has formed a striking and suggestive picture of the active life of our own day in the north. The figures are portraits of men employed at Hawks, Crawshay, & Co.'s, and Stephenson's works.

The pilasters dividing the pictures, and the solid piers corresponding to them on the two arcaded sides, are partially decorated with flowers and insects, mostly by the hand of the late Lady Trevelyan. One of these mural paintings, representing some ears of wheat, and barley, and corn-flowers, is especially interesting as the work of the great art critic, John Ruskin. The stone is of a very light-coloured close texture, very agreeable in tone, and the experiment of painting in ordinary oil paint upon them, without any preparation or "grounding," has been completely successful. Above are medallions containing portraits of celebrated men connected with Northumberland. These are—Hadrian; Severus; Abbot Alcuin, 804; Duns Scotus, 1307; Bishop de Bury, 1345; Bishop Ridley, 1555; Belted Will Howard,

1640; Sir John Fenwick, 1697; Lord Derwentwater, 1716; Lord Crewe, 1722; Sir Walter Blackett, 1777; Lord Collingwood, 1810; Thomas Bewick, 1828; Lord Stowell, 1836; and Lord Eldon, 1838; Earl Grey, 1845; George Stephenson, 1848; Sir Charles Edward Trevelyan, and Sir Walter Trevelyan. In the angles and spandrels of the upper series of arches are eighteen illustrations of the old ballad of "Chevy Chase." It is the history of a day and night, from sunrise to sunrise. The angle at which the last picture joins the first coinciding with the period of the morning, and the aspect of the sky in both. 1. The Departure, seen from the battlements. 2. Earl Percy parting from his Wife. 3. Knights Retainers trotting away: Heron, Lovell, Witherington, etc. 4. The Footmen and bowmen; dogs in leash. 5. The Sight of the Deer; watching from a distance. 6. The Hunting. The Leader of the Herd: a stag of ten. 7. The Battue; the archers posted for shooting. 8. Rear of the Herd; drivers following. 9. The "Brittling of the Deer;" cutting up the dead animals. 10. The Battle; the chiefwaiting; tidings are brought of the approach of the Scots. 11. The English bowmen advance, "A Percy! a Percy!" 12. The Scottish spearmen in closing, "A Douglas! a Douglas!" 13. The Douglas dies by an arrow; the Percy by a spear. 14. Death of the Witherington; end of the battle. 15. Next night and morning. A Leech extracting an arrow. 16. Women looking out for their husbands and brothers. 17. The Percy's body found by his wife. 18. The Return to Alnwick with the dead. This superb picture-gallery possesses an additional attraction in the shape of a fine group of sculpture by Thomas Woolner, R.A. It is a representation in marble of the civilization of England. The ideal aims of our modern life are shown by the mother's attempt to discipline the child's affection by making him say his prayers before permitting his caress. A striking contrast with this group is found in one of the basso-reliefs of the pedestal, representing scenes of ancient British life, where a mother is feeding her child with raw flesh on the point of its father's sword, and praying that the gods will make him so ferocious that he may destroy all his enemies.

The portraits at Wallington, embracing members of the Blackett, Calverley, and Trevelyan families, are very interesting; in some cases on account of the individuals represented and the stories connected with them, and in others on account of the artists who painted them. Of the former is that of Henry Calverley, painted in 1636. He was "my brat at nurse; my sucking beggar" of the "Yorkshire Tragedy"—a little drama generally printed amongst Shakespeare's works, but most likely written by one of his youthful imitators. Regarding the story, it is thus related in *Stowe's Chronicle*—"Walter Callverly, of Calverly in Yorkshire, Esquier, murdered two of his young children, stabbed his wife into the bodie with full purpose to have murdered her, and instantly went from his house to have slaine his youngest child at nurse but was prevented. For which fact at his triall in York hee stood mute, and was judged to be prest to death, according to which judgment he was executed at the castell of Yorke the 5th of

August 1604." Another is that of Joyce, the second wife of this Henry Calverley, and daughter of Sir Walter Pye. She is represented as holding a paper in her right hand, inscribed with the words :—

> "Silence, Walter Calverley,
> This is all I will leave W. C.
> Time was I might have given thee moe,
> Now thank thyself that this is soe,"

from which it would appear that, having some disagreement with her son, this portrait was all she left him. A third is that of Miss Sukey Trevelyan, by Gainsborough, originally painted with such a profusion of feminine adornment that Arthur Young made a satiric reference to it in his *Tour in Northumberland* as the "portrait of a hat and ruffles." This so annoyed Sir Walter Blackett that he got Sir Joshua Reynolds to paint out the offending finery, the outline of which may still be discovered by the careful observer. There are portraits by several other eminent artists—viz., Sir William Blackett and his wife, by Sir P. Lely; Sir Walter Blackett, by Sir J. Reynolds; Sir Walter Pye, by Cornelius Jansen; Mrs. Trevelyan, by Hopner. Other pictures are—"The Virgin, Infant Saviour, and St. John, with three Angels bearing lilies"—Lorenzo de Credi; "The Virgin and Child throned, with several standing figures"—Pietro de la Francesca; a portrait of a lady with an apple in her hand, and the Pyramid of Caius Cestius in the background, either by Raphael or Leonardo de Vinci. There is a magnificent collection of china at Wallington, arranged in cases, or in hermetically-sealed recesses, throughout the principal rooms. It includes many rare specimens of Nankin (*circa* 1465), Dresden, and Chelsea ware. In one case is a large election bowl, inscribed, "Let us drink success to Blackett and Fenwick"—a memento of the Newcastle election of 1741. The study contains some interesting memorials of Lord Macaulay—the bureau at which he wrote the whole of his *History of England*, his inkstands, and several volumes of the classical writers annotated and marked by him. In the dining-room there is a "Priest's Hole," a recess about eight feet long in the thickness of the wall, between the end of a cupboard and the fire-place. The drawing-room, originally the entrance hall, contains some beautiful decorations by a party of Italian artists employed by Sir Walter Blackett. Here is an exquisitely-embroidered screen, a large work of several panels, by Julia Calverley, eldest daughter of Sir William Blackett. The sculpture of the chimney-piece was done in the early part of last century by Sir Henry Cheere. One of the bedrooms is adorned with tapestry, the work of the deft and industrious lady refered to above. In the servant's hall is the curious sign-board of the "Rival Queens," from the old inn at Cambo, Queen Elizabeth being represented on one side, and Mary Queen of Scots on the other. In the passage is a marble bust of Lord Macaulay by Parkes. The clock-house in the court is by Paine, and is a very good architectural design. On the lawn in front of the house is an ancient fire-pan, in which the beacon was kindled on Greenleighton Hill. Some British querns, or hand mills, are lying near to it. The gardens to the east of the Cambo road, at some distance from the house, are very fine, and yield nearly every kind of fruit and berry. Overlooking them is a terrace-walk, adorned with several leaden statuettes by Sir Henry Cheere, representing Neptune, Flora, Perseus, Venus, the Burgomeister, and others. By the side of the footpath skirting the Chinese Pond is an upright, weather-worn block of stone, believed to be Druidical. It formed one of two monoliths that stood by a tumulus on Humlie Dod, near Shafthoe Crags, called "The Poind and his Man." Its companion is still in its original position. On the rockery close by are some fragments of figures and griffins from the City gate, Aldgate, London. The trees at and around Wallington are very tall and well drawn up. Some of the specimens have reached a considerable girth and height. A few may be mentioned. The measurements are taken at a height of five feet :—

Beech, by turnpike road, 100 yards east of stable-yard clock tower—girth, 11 feet 2 inches ; height, 113 feet.

Larch, on south-west side of Chinese pond, and 30 yards from it—girth, 9 feet 5 inches ; height, 102 feet. There is the stump of another larch, about 80 yards south of last, which was blown down some years since. It was then cut with a saw, when its rings showed it to be 135 years old.

Larch, at north-west end of Chinese pond—girth, 9 feet 11 inches ; height, 110 feet 6 inches.

Spruce, 100 yards from north-west side of Chinese pond—girth, 8 feet 8 inches ; height, 113 feet 6 inches.

Wych Elm, at end of garden pond—girth, 14 feet 10 inches ; height, 103 feet 6 inches.

Ash, a fine tree, 200 yards west of bridge over Wansbeck, and 50 yards north of river—girth, 16 feet 3 inches ; height, 72 feet.

Holly, on lawn, 100 yards west of house—girth, 6 feet 5 inches ; height, 45 feet 6 inches. A very fine, healthy, handsome tree, sweeping down to the ground.

A little over half a mile north-east of Wallington, in a locality that used to be known as Middleton Moss, an ancient swamp underneath Middleton Hill, there were found, on May 14th, 1879, some remarkable relics of the old British inhabitants—viz., fifteen axe-heads, four spear-heads, three sword blades, and three female armlets. They are all deposited in a glass case in the hall at Wallington. On the hill-top are the remains of a Celtic village, and near to it a small, but distinctly marked, Roman camp.

The nearest station to Wallington Hall is Scots Gap, two miles distant.

# MORPETH TO BOLAM AND SHAFTHOE CRAGS.

**Whalton, 6 miles; Bolam, 9 miles; Shortflatt Tower, 10½ miles; Harnham, 11 miles; Shafthoe Crags, 12 miles.**

THE road leading from Morpeth to Belsay runs through a rich agricultural district, and commands picturesque views of the country north of the Wansbeck. It branches off to the right from the Newcastle road just past the Parish Church.

Six miles distant, on the edge of a southern slope, is WHALTON, a good-sized village, consisting of well-built houses, having pretty little garden plots in front, and may yet, as in Mackenzie's time, be "considered one of the cleanest, neatest, and most pleasant villages in the county." The old Castle-houses, of which the village was formerly composed, have all disappeared since the Border reivers ceased to trouble the land, and there is little now to suggest the antiquity of the place except the *Church of St. Mary Magdalen.* The oldest part of this sacred edifice is the tall, narrow, round-headed tower arch, which is said to be of Saxon workmanship. The rest of the building is early English in style, and dates back to the thirteenth century. At the east end of the south aisle, by the side of the rich decorated window, is a piscina, marking the site of a chantry. Incorporated with the rectory is part of an old pele-tower, consisting of two vaulted apartments with strong arched roofs. In the inner one are the remains of a spiral staircase, which had formerly led to the upper rooms and battlements. In the grounds behind the house opposite is an interesting memorial of the times when the early Nonconformists were refused burial in the churchyards of the Establishment. It is a grave-stone bearing the following inscription: "To the memory of Mr. John Moore, of Whalton, who died in the year 1684, and, owing to the dissension of those times, was here interred. This stone, at the desire of the late Mr. John Moore, of Whalton, his grandson, was erected by his widow, Elizabeth Moore, December 7th, 1772." On the ridge of the high ground over which the road runs from Whalton to Morpeth, about three-quarters of a mile from the village, are two ancient British camps, supposed to have afterwards been occupied by the Romans. One of them, immediately behind the farm-house, called the Camp-house, covers about two acres of ground; the other, a little to the east and south-east on the opposite slope of the ridge, is much smaller, and goes by the name of the "Dead Men's Graves." Till recent years the villagers observed the custom, on the 4th of July (old Midsummer-eve), of kindling on the green a large bonfire, and then dancing around it and leaping through it—a relic of solar worship which has come down uninterrupted from Pagan times.

The principal inn is the Beresford Arms. The nearest railway station is Meldon, a mile and a half to the north. From Whalton there is a very pleasant walk of three miles, partly by road and partly by the fields, to Belsay. The same distance from Whalton to the north-west, past Riplington and Gallowhill, where, no doubt, many a bold moss-trooper received his "hempen caudle," is

BOLAM, once a little town, consisting of a castle, a church, rectory-house, and two hundred slated houses, enclosing a village green. It had a market and fair granted to it in 1305 by Edward I. *Bolam House*, the seat of Lord Decies, stands on the site of the castle, which, in its turn, had been erected inside an ancient British camp of great strength, oval in form. While every trace of the mediæval stronghold has disappeared, considerable remains of the earlier defences may be seen in the double vallum and ditch on the north, south, and west, and the single one on the east, with the round port-way through it. There is a heronry at Bolam, consisting of about thirty nests. The houses have gone, and the once populous town on the bol, or hill, is now but a name. One of the landlords of the old inn here—a Mr. Dallas—contrived, it is said, to follow the somewhat divergent callings of a licensed victualler and minister of the Presbyterian meeting-house at Belsay. The *Church of St. Andrew* is a building of great interest, for it is one of the few churches in the county erected in Saxon times. Restored and altered subsequently, it exhibits, in different parts of its structure, the various styles of English architecture. The remains of the original edifice consist of the tower at the west end, the north side of the nave, and a fragment of the north side of the chancel. The chancel arch, with its beak-head ornament and cushioned capitals, is Norman. The Transitional period between the Norman and early English styles is illustrated by the richly-ornamented doorway opening from the porch into the south aisle, and the arcade of clustered columns and round arches dividing this aisle from the nave. One of the double lights in the north side of the chancel belongs to the Decorated period, the other to the early English. On the south side of the chancel are sedilia with pointed arches, and a piscina; also an opening into the Shortflatt Porch, which contains two finely-carved tomb-slabs, and, in an early cusped-headed recess at the east end, a half-length effigy of a knight in armour, supposed to be that of Sir Walter de Bolam. In the tower arch is a specimen of late Transitional carving. The view from the churchyard towards Angerton, Rothley, and Wallington is one of exceeding charm and beauty. A pleasant footpath through the fields past South Stead farm-house leads to Angerton station, a mile distant from the church. The well-known Baptist minister, Joseph Angus, M.A., D.D., F.R.A.S., author of several hand-books to English literature and the Bible, was born at Bolam on the 16th of January 1816.

By the side of the road leading to Belsay, three-quarters of a mile from the church, is a large artificial lake, designed by Dobson in 1818 for the Hon. Charles Beresford. It is a picturesque sheet of water, with some pretty creeks, islands, and promontories, surrounded by trees and flowering shrubs, and frequented by several species of wild fowl. On old State Hill, at the head of the lake, is a circular British camp. Half-a-mile to the north of it, on Huckhoe, is another camp, eighty yards by seventy, with many traces near it of early occupation.

At the junction of the road from Bolam with that from Middleton, there is a footpath leading for half-a-mile through the fields to *Shortflatt Tower*, a picturesque old building, situated somewhat low, on the south side of a reedy brook called the Howburn, with a clump of trees for a background. Originally a pele-tower, crenellated in 1305, the property of the Raymes family, and afterwards of the Fenwicks, it has been enlarged and restored, and is now the seat of W. Dent Dent, Esq. The characteristic vaulted chamber of the lower storey remains unaltered.

A quarter of a mile to the south west is the quaint and interesting little village of HARNHAM, situated on a wooded eminence, which Wallis fancied bore some resemblance to "one of the fine towered hills in the pictures of Nicholas Poussin." The craggy knoll, with its tuft of trees, is a conspicuous object from the Newcastle and Otterburn road, and must have attracted the visits of many a "kindly Scot," *en route* for the Tyne. The position, however, of the old fortalice, called *Harnham Hall*, in the time of Henry the Fifth, and the little village which shared with it the crown of the hill, was a very strong one, the natural defences being, on the north and west, a range of precipitous sandstone rocks, and on the south a steep glacis and a morass. The neck of land on the east, connecting this glacis with the neighbouring ridge, was girt by a high wall, and at the end of the village was a strong iron gate within the memory of persons living in the time of Wallis. A few remains of the ancient fortalice may be seen behind the present manor-house. Originally a part of the barony of Bolbeck, and held by the Bolams and Bekerings till 1412, Harnham passed in 1667 into the hands of Major Babington, Governor of Berwick. His wife was Katherine, widow of Colonel George Fenwick, of Brinkburn, and daughter of Sir Arthur Haselrigg, both celebrated characters during the Commonwealth. To this lady the interest attaching to Harnham is mainly due. She was distinguished for her beauty, her portrait being inserted in the "Book of Beauty" of the period. So great were her personal attractions, that during her visit to Durham the people gathered in crowds to look at her, blocking up the narrow street. The magistrates, therefore, it is said, issued the strange order that when Dame Katherine Babington entered a cook's shop she might not eat sixpenny pies in public, but in a private room, that she "be not stared at of the people." The sympathies of both Major and Madame Babington were with the Puritans; and for four years Mr. Veitch, the well-known Covenanter, lived at Harnham, under the name of Johnson, preaching in a hall there to the scattered Independents of the district. So bitter was the lady's antipathy to the Established Church that she incited the son of a blacksmith at Bolam to pull Mr. Foster, the Vicar of the place, out of the pulpit, when he was ousted from his living, at the beginning of the Long Parliament, in 1643. On the return of the reverend gentleman, at the Restoration in 1661, he retaliated by excommunicating both the blacksmith and Madam Babington. Neither of them lived many years after this outburst of ecclesiastical displeasure, and the Vicar had the further satisfaction of refusing to bury the obnoxious Dissenters in consecrated ground. What became of the mortal remains of the blacksmith is not known. But Madam Babington, after remaining unburied ten days, while her husband was disputing with the ecclesiastical authorities respecting her interment, finally found a resting-place in a sepulchre or vault hewn out of the rock at Harnham. Several years after, the coffin, which rested on a stone shelf, was stolen by some faws, or itinerant tinkers, for the sake of its lead. The bones were scattered about, and lay exposed till they were buried a few years ago. The vault is situated beneath the terrace of Harnham Hall, in what is known as the "tomb-garden," and contains the following inscription:—

"Here lyeth the body of Madam Babington, who was laid in this sepulchre on the 9th September 1670.

> My time is past, as you may see,
> I viewed the dead as you do me;
> Or long you'll be as low as I,
> And some will look on thee.'"

A high parapeted wall shuts off from the world this quiet old garden, where the celebrated beauty of Harnham is fitly interred. Flowers, and green leaves, and other bright influences reconcile us to the presence of the tomb—"making one," in the words of Shelley, "half in love with death to be buried in so sweet a place." Several relics of the Babington family are still preserved at Harnham Hall, which is now occupied by Mr. J. C. Leighton. One is a tablet with the Babington arms painted upon it. The motto, "Foy est tous," was acquired by John Babington during the wars under Henry IV. in France. On his own petition he was one of six young knights sent on a perilous mission, and on leaving the royal presence he brandished his sword, exclaiming, "Foy est tous." The house occupied by Miss Leighton contains some paintings by the poet Whittle. The distance of Harnham from Belsay is two miles. A similar distance to the north-west are the celebrated *Shafthoe Crags*. These bold and weather-scarred rocks, which rise so picturesquely on the east of the Newcastle and Otterburn Road, belong to what geologists call the "Inghoe Grits"—course-grained sandstone and grit. The highest point is

697 feet above the sea level. According to some writers, the name is derived from the German *schaf*, a sheep, and the Anglo-Saxon *hoe*, a hill. Be this as it may, there is a pastoral charm about the crags and the surrounding country which carries the mind back to the simpler ages of the world. Shafthoe Crags are best approached from the south, for then one obtains a full view of the rugged escarpments which rise in broken, irregular masses from a steep slope covered with the fir, the birch, and the ash, and with an undergrowth of bracken and heath.

A huge isolated fragment of rock on the south side, projecting boldly from the brow of the crag, has its top hollowed out into several bason-like holes, the largest of which is called "The Devil's Punch-bowl." Whether natural or artificial it is difficult to say. It bears a striking resemblance to several round cavities in the granite rocks on the south coast of Tiree, which have presumably been formed by the action of pebbles swirled about by strong currents, though some antiquaries have not hesitated to assign to them a Druidical origin. On the occasion of the marriage of Sir William Blackett, of Wallington, on the 20th September 1775, the Devil's Punch-bowl was filled with such plenty of liquor as to be more than sufficient for the vast crowds of people who were attracted from the district round about by the illuminations on the crags. The bason is said to have been formed for this purpose, but the probability is, it was merely deepened or enlarged. Below this projecting stone is a rude cavern, called "Shafthoe Hall," which Hodgson considers to be the combined work of nature and art. "Is it not very probable," he says, "that this cavern and the Punch-bowl stone were a cave and a rock altar of that primitive heathen worship which prevailed all over the world from India to Britain; that the rock basons on the top of the altar were once consecrated to the mysteries of the Druidical Hu?" This supposition gains weight from the fact that the crags at this point form the south and west sides of a British camp, which, on its north and east sides, is defended by a double dyke and ditch. Mr. Hugh Miller, F.G.S., son of the celebrated geologist, entertains the same belief as that hazarded by Hodgson. In referring to what he calls "Pot-holes," or circular cavities formed by the action of the wind, rain, and sandy granules in certain rocks, he remarks on the difference between the Punch-bowl and the rest of the cup-like hollows. "The eye," he says, "may take a lesson here between the artificial and the natural. The natural are all lengthened in the direction of the slope. The artificial, although lying on the same slope, has not taken the cue, has been betrayed into no irregularities of form and shelves too deep." Another rock near the Punch-bowl stone bears the name of the "Piper's Chair." On the level ground below, near the steps leading from Shafthoe Hall, is an enormous mass of rock which has fallen from the crags. It has been split in two by the action of the frost, and is known in the district as "The Tailor and his Man." Further east, near the East Shafthoe farm-house, is the site of an ancient chapel, 66 feet long. It had a south transept, 14 feet square.

The lines of the fences of its burial-ground are still distinctly visible on the open ground. An incised tombstone found here is built up into one of the walls of the farm-house. It is beautifully carved with two crosses and a sword and shears. The road from East Shafthoe, by Shafthoe Grange, to Deneham, runs on the north side of the chapel, and formed the western extremity of a village of which traces can be seen in two long lines of foundations of houses, with a space for a broad street, or town green, between them. These lines may still be traced, running westward for 200 yards or more behind the mansion-house of the Shafthoes and Vaughans, through a thick grove of trees, towards the chapel. A small ornamental lake adjoins the bridle-path. The chasm on the north of the crags, through which passes the Scotch Street, or old road from Scotland, by Elsdon, to Newcastle, is called Sawter's, or Salter's, Nick. Here the smugglers of salt in the last century used to halt and lie concealed in their rapid journeys through the county, watering their horses at a well under the rocks close by. On the heights above, a little to the south, is a strongly situated British camp. The foundations of some of the hut-circles may be noticed inside it. Half-a-mile or so to the east are some other interesting memorials of the early inhabitants of Britain—viz., a rude stone pillar, standing beside a large tumulus. Formerly there were two of these monoliths, which went by the name of "Poind and his Man," but the other has been removed to Wallington. The one which remains is six and a half feet high, and nearly five feet square on the sides. The tumulus, the simplest and most ancient form of barrow, was opened by Warburton a hundred and seventy years ago, and found to enclose a stone coffin, or kist-vaen, blackened on the inside with smoke, and containing several pieces of glutinous matter. There was another relic of antiquity here, consisting of a pound, or fold, inclosed by two concentric circles of large sandstones set on edge. These have been removed to make fences, and nothing now remains but the traces of the foundations. Perhaps, as Hodgson suggests, the original name of these antiquities was the "Poind and his Men," from the pound-like form of this barrow, a name afterwards transferred to the two stones only; for our pound, or pind-fold, has its name from Pyndan—to shut up or inclose. Lord Wharton, in 1552, directs that one of the watches of the Middle Marches be kept at the "Poind and his Man." The great Roman Road, the Devil's Causeway, passed close by in a north-easterly direction.

*Shafthoe Crags* are three miles from Angerton Station. Let the tourist, after following the road on the south of the line through some plantations, leave it then for a footpath leading diagonally across a common. On gaining the road to Bolam, let him ascend the hill for a short distance, and take the first turn to the right, keeping straight on till the Crags appear in sight. The Druidical stone just described will be seen on the left of the road near a round hill called Humlie Dod.

# MORPETH TO NUNNYKIRK.

**Stanton, 6 miles: Netherwitton, 7½ miles; Longwitton, 9½ miles; Nunnykirk, 9½ miles.**

THE great North Road must be followed for about a mile. For half the distance the ascent from Bullersgreen is very steep, but when the summit of the ridge above Morpeth is gained, the view of the country-side opens out very beautifully. Taking the first turn to the left, a walk of a mile brings the tourist to *West Benridge*. Then there is another stiff climb for three-quarters of a mile past Benridge Hag to a junction of two roads. Keeping to the left for half-a-mile, he comes to the pleasant hamlet of *Pigdon*, picturesquely perched on the hill-side, and commanding an extensive view over the Nunriding woods and the valley of the Font. From Pigdon the road rapidly descends to the river, and for the rest of the way keeps parallel with it. After crossing two small burns, a cross road is reached, two miles from Pigdon.

The village on the hill-side, half-a-mile to the north, is STANTON (or Stonetown), once a place of considerable extent, the property of the Fenwicks, of Fenwick Tower. The old manor-house of the Fenwicks, which in the reign of Henry VI. appears to have been a pele-tower, is now partly occupied by a blacksmith. Its panelled rooms still bear the traces of former splendour. It was used for some time under the old poor law system as a parish workhouse. Veitch, the Covenanter, removed in May 1677 from Harnham to Stanton Hall, where he states "he found his lot fallen in none of the best places." He narrowly escaped being taken here on one occasion, but "got into a hole within the lining of a great window which had been made on purpose, for the whole room was lined about with wainscot." Being away from home on one occasion at Bousden, near Tweedmouth, under promise to stay a few days, he dreamt twice the same night that Stanton Hall was on fire. So strongly was he impressed by the dream that the next morning he altered his arrangements and set off home. "About a mile and a half from his own house, as he was going up a lane, he sees two men and three fine horses meeting him, the foremost of whom, when he perceived who it was, came riding fast up to him (it was Torwoodlee's man), saying, 'Sir, you are long looked for at your house,' which made him ask, 'What is the matter? is my wife and family well?' 'Yes,' says he, 'but there is a stranger longs to see you—viz., Argyle; and your wife and he have been sending about the country these two days to find you.' Then he saw that the dream was a clear call to bring him home."—*Memoirs of William Veitch.* Three-quarters of a mile to the north again, on the Lime-kiln flat, is *Clavering's Cross*, marking the spot where one of the Claverings fell in an encounter with the Scots.

From the point where the road branches off to Stanton, the tourist has a straight course of two miles to NETHERWITTON. A sweet and quiet spot is this little village, nestling amidst woods and pastures, in the centre of a valley where all the gentler charms of Nature seem to have been gathered together. Witton-by-the-Waters was it formerly called, and appropriately so, for it occupies the angle formed by the junction of the Font and the Ewesley Burn. Sheltered and shut in by high ridges of enclosed ground on the north and south, it still has that air of pastoral seclusion which so many of our villages have lost. The cottages are, in several cases, thatched, their walls covered with ivy or beautified with the blooms of the rose and the clematis. Around or in front of them are pretty gardens. In one of these stands a stone cross with the date 1698 upon it, a relic of times when most of the villagers were Roman Catholics. They used, says Mackenzie, to assemble in the evening and dance round it to the music of the Northumbrian bagpipes, while their aged friends sat around enjoying the sportive scene. On Sunday evenings they were joined by several of their neighbours in this joyous pastime. The cross on certain festival days was decked out with a profusion of flowers, ribbons, etc. It was restored in 1825. The ground whereon it stands was once a green or common. Near the picturesque old bridge which spans the Font, with two arches, is a large woollen mill. It was originally built and supplied with machinery for the manufacture of cotton, but the speculation was not successful. There is a small Temperance Hotel in the village. On the north side of the Font, among trees and shrubs, is the pretty little *Church of St. Giles*, approached from the village and the hall by lovely paths. Not a vestige remains of the ancient chapel which preceded the present structure. Near the pulpit is a full-length figure of a female in stone, discovered in digging for the foundations of the north wall of the nave. Roger Thornton, the munificent merchant-prince of Newcastle, was, according to Leland, born at this place. He purchased the manor of Witton in 1405, and built for himself a castle, which is stated to have stood on the site of the present gardens. The estate remained in his family till 1747, when it came to the Trevelyans by the marriage of Walter Trevelyan, of Nettlecombe, with the heiress of the Thorntons.

*Netherwitton Hall*, the seat of Thornton Roger Trevelyan, is a stately building of white freestone, built by Robert Trollop, the architect of Capheaton and the Old Exchange at Newcastle. The south front facing the road is pierced with as many as twenty-one windows. Above the door of the north front is a tablet with a weather-moulding round it, bearing the arms of Thornton and this inscription—"Anno Regis Edwardi Quinti" (In the year of Edward the Fifth). It was removed out of the old castle, and refers to some additions or repairs done to it in 1483. In the summer of 1651 Netherwitton was visited by Oliver Cromwell, and his army, consisting of nine regiments of foot, his horse guards, two regiments of dragoons and their baggage and train, "was quartered for one night upon the grounds of the Lady Thorneton." Two autograph letters from the great republican general to this lady are preserved by the family, the first granting her protection, the second ordering the sum of £95, 5s. 6d. to be paid to her in consideration of damage done to her estate by his army. According to tradition, Netherwitton was the hiding-place of Lord Lovat from the time of the battle of Culloden to his capture. The closet where he is said to have been concealed is in an upper room, and is eight feet long by three broad and ten high. It is one of those secret chambers called Priest's Holes, so common in the Catholic houses of the county. Lord Lovat's bed is now destroyed, but his chair is still preserved in the house. Among the pictures are two portraits of special interest—one of the Earl of Derwentwater, and another of his brother, Charles Radcliffe. The gardens to the west of the house are more useful than ornamental, and contain a large number of old fruit trees. A path leads from the gardens across a meadow to the *Newpark Wood*, where, immediately above the Font, are two of the largest oaks in Northumberland, named respectively the King and the Queen. They are about ninety yards north of the mill-dam. The King is 12 feet 11 inches in girth, and 82 feet high; the Queen 10 feet 11 inches in girth, and 78 feet high. The lower branches having decayed or been broken off, the rugged boles of these fine old trees appear to great advantage. Behind the old garden wall is a very remarkable stump of an oak braced together with iron clamps. It is now more or less a shell. It is about 20 feet high, and, at a yard from the ground, measures 22 feet 6 inches in girth. Nethrewitton is situated at about an equal distance from the stations of Angerton, Longwitton, and Ewesley—viz., four miles.

About a mile and a-quarter to the east is *Gallowshaw*, where the lords of Witton hung the felons caught within their manor. A quarter of a mile beyond it, at the head of a woody dene, is *Witton-Shields*, an old pele-tower of the seventeenth century. The letters N. T., over the south-west doorway, are supposed to be the initials of Sir Nicholas Thornton, and the figures, 1608, the date when the tower was built.

Two miles south-west is LONGWITTON, a long, straggling village, seated on a fertile and elevated ridge, traversed by the highway between Morpeth and Elsdon. It has once been a place of some importance, judging by the lines of many ruined cottages and garden walls on each side of the road.

*Longwitton Hall* is an ancient building with modern additions, sheltered on three sides with old forest trees, but open to the south, from which it overlooks the whole of the country between the Wansbeck and the Tyne. It is at present the seat of Ernest Percival, Esq.

From the hall there is a pleasant walk for nearly a mile through a woody dingle, called the Dene Burn, to the gardens, which are situated in a lovely and romantic spot on the banks of the Hart. A little to the east of them, in a wood, are the *Thruston Wells*, three in number, celebrated for their medicinal qualities. "A tremendous dragon, that could make itself invisible, formerly guarded the fountains, till the famous knight, Guy, Earl of Warwick, wandering in quest of adventures, came this way and waged battle with the monster. With words that could not be disobeyed, the winged serpent was commanded to come forth from his den and to keep his natural and visible form; but as often as the knight wounded him, and his strength from loss of blood began to fail, he glided back, dipt his tail into the well, and returned healed, and with new vigour, to the combat, till the earl, perceiving the cause of his long resistance, leapt between him and the wells, and in one furious onset stabbed him to the heart."—*Hodgson.*

Two miles north-north-west of Netherwitton, further up the valley of the Font, is *Nunnykirk Hall* (the residence of Captain Noble), an imposing stone building of great elegance and simplicity, with a fine prospect to the south. Extensive additions and alterations were made to the old mansion-house in 1825, from designs by Dobson. The scenery around the neighbourhood of the Font is very beautiful and romantic. Nunnykirk was granted by Ranulph de Merlay to Newminster Abbey, the abbot of which built a chapel, tower, and other edifices here. No traces of these now remain. Ewesley station is about a mile and a half distant. Two miles and a half to the north is *Wingates Spa*, once much resorted to for its chalybeate waters. The spring is in a lovely dingle a mile from Wingates, and is known as the Chirm Well. Since the opening of the colliery here the waters have almost ceased to flow. The picturesque little village of Wingates, on the top of a hill, commands one of the finest views in the county, embracing the vales of the Coquet and Font, the Simonside Hills, and an interesting part of the sea-board of Northumberland. There is a good temperance hotel at Wingates.

# MORPETH TO LONGHORSLEY AND WELDON BRIDGE.

**Longhorsley, 6½ miles ; Linden, 8 miles ; Weldon Bridge, 9 miles.**

THE Queen's highways from Morpeth to Wooler and Alnwick are straight, well-made, undulating roads, traversing a fine agricultural district.

Six and a half miles from Morpeth, on the line of the former, stands LONGHORSLEY, a large and straggling village on the ridge of high ground overlooking the vale of the Coquet. At the west end of it there is a massive old pele-tower, which formerly belonged to the Horsleys, and is now the property of the Riddells. It is the residence of the Roman Catholic priest. Adjoining it is the little chapel where he officiates.

*The Church of St. Helen* stands in a field called *Elleage*, about half-a-mile to the south of the village. Why built so far away it is difficult to conjecture. Of the old building, with its Norman arch and marble pillars, nothing now remains, as the church was entirely rebuilt in 1783. The east window is filled with stained glass, designed and executed in diaphanie by Mrs. Ames of Linden. The font is described by Mr. F. R. Wilson as "fantastically curious and barbarously painted." The communion table and rails are of black oak obtained from a peat-bog at Linden East Farm at the beginning of the century. The inns at Longhorsley are the Rose and Thistle and the Shoulder of Mutton. A mile to the north is Linden House, the seat of Henry Ames, Esq. A little over two miles from Longhorsley, in the valley, is WELDON BRIDGE, with its well-known Angler's Inn.

# MORPETH TO COCKLE PARK TOWER AND FELTON.

**Hebburn, 3 miles; Cockle Park Tower, 4 miles; Causey Park, 6½ miles; Bockenfield, 8¼ miles; Felton, 10 miles.**

THREE miles north of Morpeth, and half-a-mile east of the great post-road, lies the village of HEBRON, or HEBBURN, a place of some antiquity. The church which, in 1674, Dr. Basire found "most scandalously and dangerously ruinous: roof divided, under propt within with eight crutches, without with three; the seats all upturned or broken," was rebuilt in 1793, and contains nothing ancient except the chancel arch. A mile to the north is an ancient pele of great strength called *Cockley Park Tower*, now converted into a farm-house. It stands high on the farm, with the singular name of Bubbleymires, and is a conspicuous landmark for sailors. On the east front of the tower is a large stone tablet bearing the arms of Ogle quartering Bertram, with two collared and chained antelopes, the supporters of the lords Ogle, which show that the present building cannot be older than when Sir Robert Ogle, Knight, was made a peer of the realm. At the north-east and north-west corners of the building are round corbelled turrets with a machicolated parapet between them. The south-east corner contains a circular stone staircase. The upright tracery in the head of the great window on the north shows it to belong to the fifteenth century. The windows on the east, as well as those walled up on the west, are of the sixteenth. Two very curious old fire-places remain inside the tower. Cockle Park was the scene of a tragedy on 9th December 1845, when an old man named Robert Joicey was poisoned by his son. The young man, when apprehended on suspicion, admitted the crime, and was executed on the 18th March 1846.

Six miles to the north of Morpeth is the hamlet of *Causey Park Bridge.* Half-a-mile to the west is *Causey Park*, an old tower of the Ogles, built by James Ogle in 1586, as appears from a rude stone tablet bearing the date and his initials on two shields. There are in the body of the house two circular stone staircases. In the gardens is a curious dial, surmounted by a globe, and having the arms of the Lords Ogle on the one side, and on the other three sides the hemispheres, phases of the moon, and tables of the sun's rising and setting. A mile north from Causey Park Bridge, where the post-road which formerly went over the high ground past Helm-on-the-Hill is diverted to avoid the ascent, a branch road leads off on the right to *Eshott Hall*, the seat of Thomas Brewis, Esq. Half-a-mile north of it is the site of *Eshott Castle*, a mediæval manor-house, crenellated by Roger Maudut in 1310.

Eight miles and a quarter from Morpeth, a little to the right of the road, is BOCKENFIELD, once a place of considerable size. The foundations of many ancient buildings may still be traced. The village formerly possessed a market, given up, it is said, on condition that the inhabitants should ever be free of toll in Morpeth market. *Bockenfield House* is old. It belonged to the Heron family, whose crest is still to be seen on its front. Between the Herons and the Lisles of Felton there was long a bitter feud. Tradition tells how a Heron on one occasion fled to the church, but was overtaken by his adversary as he reached the porch, and slain. The murderer was captured in Kitswell Dene by the incensed villagers, and forthwith decapitated.

Ten miles from Morpeth, on the north side of the Coquet, is **FELTON.**

# MORPETH TO WIDDRINGTON.

**Longhirst, $2\frac{1}{2}$ miles ; Ulgham, 5 miles ; Widdrington, 8 miles ; Low Chibburn, 9 miles.**

ABOUT two miles and a half north of Morpeth is the pretty village of LONGHIRST. The church, whose handsome spire overtops the adjacent trees, was opened on the 14th September 1875. It is in the early English style of architecture, and was built at the sole expense of the late Rev. Edward Lawson. The windows are filled with stained glass.

*Longhirst Hall*, the seat of James Joicey, Esq., M.P., is a modern mansion, of fine-grained and warm-tinted sandstone, built in 1824 from designs by Dobson. The variety of outline and harmony of decorative detail are very effective. The house is approached by a projecting portico, graced with two beautifully-fluted columns, the capitals of which are original compositions of the architect. The Corinthian entablature, which is surmounted by a pediment, is continued round the principal building. The lower windows in the curving portion of the south front have architraves, friezes, and trusses, highly ornamented, and supporting cornices. The large entrance-hall, with its stately staircase and gallery, is decorated in the same chaste and elegant style as the exterior of the building. The conservatory is connected with the house by a cloister open to the south. The gardens, which are intersected by the Bothal Burn, are well sheltered, and of great beauty.

Two miles and a half north-east by north from Longhirst is ULGHAM, a small rural village, consisting of two rows of pretty stone and brick cottages, well set back from the road in little gardens, gay with pansies, irises, thrift, delphiniums, and peonies. Planted at intervals by the side of the main street are young poplars and laburnums. Fields slope down to the Line, which runs past under narrow and woody banks. The name has formerly been spelled in a variety of ways—as Huleham, Ullecham, Ulwcham, Elchamp, and Ougham. It is now pronounced, as if written, Uffham. In 1138, the part of the manor called Ulgham Grange was given by Ranulph de Merlay to the Abbey of Newminster, and there they cultivated a farm, not only to supply the house with corn and cattle, but also for profit. Another part was granted in 1294, or previous to that date, to the knights of the Hospital of St. John at Chibburn. *Ulgham Hall*, at the west end of the village, was probably the mansion-house connected with it. The presentments which appear in the Court Rolls of the manor are, many of them, very curious. One person, for instance. seems to have been a troublesome and hot-tempered neighbour:—"Thomas Hunter: for putting his cattell into the pasture before his neighbours." "The same Thomas, for disobeynge of the 'sworne man' [or constable appointed by the Court Leet], and saynge he was a bowtherly fallowe, and he respected him noe more than a dog—3s. 4d."

*The Church of St. John* has been quite rebuilt within recent years. The style is Norman. On the eastern gables of nave and chancel are floriated crosses. A carved stone is inserted at the east end of the north aisle, which one writer considers to be early Saxon. It is somewhat disfigured, but appears to represent a knight on horseback defending a lady from two birds. The original building was, doubtless, erected by the Cistercians, who invariably took care to attach a chapel to their granges. In the village there yet remain the steps, base, and part of the pedestal of an ancient cross, where, according to tradition, a market was held during the plague at Morpeth. There is also another tradition, that about the middle of the seventeenth century, on a Sunday afternoon in August, a number of armed men were seen lying in the lane leading from Ulgham to the park, while their horses browsed beside them. Some alarm was created, and the villagers secured their houses as best as they could. At the manor-house, unfortunately, all the men were absent. However, the women barred and blockaded the doors and windows, and sat up awaiting the result. About midnight the house was surrounded by the horsemen, and the inmates succeeded in repulsing them until assistance came. Little more than two hundred years have passed away since the country was thus insecure. Ulgham is the birthplace of Luke Clennel, the most celebrated of Bewick's pupils, who, as a wood-engraver and painter, gained a considerable reputation. The famous "Ulgham Oak" is about two miles north of the village, in the middle of the Park Wood. It is not easy to find. Crossing the little rivulet, the Line, we mount the ascent, passing on our left the farm-house of Ulgham Park, to the great plantation at the top of the hill. We follow the road round the end of it, and along its east side to the second gate on the left, close to the north-east corner of the wood. A very long glade runs west from this gate. We proceed along it till we come to the third opening on the left, and then turn down a glade running south, for a short distance, and on the left we shall see, surrounded by young pinasters, the object of our search—a mere hollow, rifted trunk, 21 feet 7 inches in girth, at a height of 7 feet from the ground. "A most weird, ghostly tree," says Mr. G. C. Atkinson; "more like a huge brown Druidical stone than a tree. No leaves! no bark! no life!" Grotesquely gnarled, almost from the very ground, with nothing of its large boughs left but the jagged stumps; blanched with age and stained with minute fungi, it seems, when contrasted with the young oak beside it and the pinasters around, like a grim old Burgrave of the Rhine in the midst of the modern race of men. In the old smuggling days a good deal of whiskey was manufactured in an illicit still beneath the shade of its ponderous branches. The village is two miles from Widdrington Station.

A mile and a half from the station, nestling beneath a high woody knoll, is the village of WIDDRINGTON, or, as it is written in the old documents, Wode-ring-ton—a name signifying the town surrounded by wood. The greater part of it has been rebuilt, and consists of a block of model cottages somewhat conventual in appearance. Of the old castle, crenellated by Gerard de Widdrington in 1341, nothing remains. Sir George Warren, a little more than a century ago, had the whole building pulled down, intending to erect another on its site. He had not fixed, however, on a design for the new building, and on requesting a friend to supply him with one, a view of the castle he had razed, taken in 1728 by S. and N. Buck, was presented to him as the best model he could have for the purpose. It seems as if a spirit, identified with the fortunes of the old Widdringtons, resented the removal of their ancient home, for just as the new mansion-house was nearing completion a fire broke out which reduced it to ruins. Once more the work of rebuilding was commenced, and a little to the south-east of the old site rose what has been described as "a slight, fantastical, insulated building, possessing neither grandeur nor convenience." This was destroyed in 1862, with the exception of the centre octagonal tower, which stands alone in a green meadow.

The first place in England where King James I. drew rein after leaving Berwick on April 8th, 1603, to assume the crown of the United Kingdon, was Widdrington. "Long as the miles were, his majestie made short worke, and attained Witherington, where, by the master of the place, Sir Robert Carey, and his right vertuous lady, he was received with all duty and affection: the house being plentifully furnished for his entertainment. Besides for scituation and pleasure it standes very delightful. His majestie having a little while reposed himselfe after his great journey, found new occasion to travel further; for as he was delighting himselfe with the pleasure of the parke, he suddenly beheld a number of deere neare the place. The game being so faire before him he could not forbear, but according to his wonted manner forth he went and slew two of them, which done, he returned with a good appetite to the house, where he was most royally feasted and banketted that night."—*Nichol.*

The little church, which at one time has been much larger than it is now, is an interesting specimen of fourteenth-century workmanship. The portion of the south aisle where the font stands has, probably, been the chantry of the Holy Trinity mentioned in old writings. It extends along part of the chancel, opening into it by a pointed arch. In the north wall of the chancel are two sepulchral niches. That to the east is pointed, and is curiously surmounted by the Widdrington coat as a finial. That to the west is segmental. In the flagging below it a very rude incised slab is inserted. These recesses are supposed to have contained effigies of Sir Gerard de Widdrington (d. *cir.* 1361), and Sir Roger de Widdrington (d. 1372). There is a large trefoiled piscina in the south wall. Above it is a small bracket. Above the north door of the chancel is an old tombstone with a cross and sword upon it; another forms the sill of a window. Widdrington gains its chief interest from the celebrated family who took their name from the ancient vill. Bertram de Widdrington was seated here in the reign of Henry II., but his claim to the possession of the manor was not altogether beyond dispute, for William Tasca challenged him to try his right by "wager of battel." Not, perhaps, till the time of the gallant squire who so distinguished himself at the battle of Chevy Chase did the family acquire its well-known reputation for valour. So long as the famous ballad still holds sway over the hearts of Englishmen, so long will Richard Widdrington be one of the most popular of heroes. His exploit is told in the following verse:—

"For Witherington my heart was woe,
That ever he slain should be;
For when both his legs were hewn in two,
Yet he kneeled and fought on his knee."

The heroine of Bishop Percy's ballad, "The Hermit of Warkworth," is a Widdrington, "Fair Isabel"—

"Young Bertram lov'd a beauteous maid,
As fair as fair might be;
The dew-drop on the lily's cheek
Was not so fair as she.

"Fair Widdrington the maiden's name,
Yon towers her dwelling-place;
Her sire an old Northumbrian chief,
Devoted to thy race."

The Widdringtons distinguished themselves by their loyalty to the Stuart family. Sir William Widdrington raised at his own expense a considerable body of troops for Charles I., and fought for the royal cause in twelve engagements. For his services he was rewarded, in 1643, with a peerage. His honours were short-lived, however, for he fell in 1651, in an encounter with the Cromwellian party at Wigan. Clarendon describes him as "one of the goodliest persons of that age, being near the head higher than most tall men, and a gentleman of the best and most ancient extraction in Northumberland, of a very fair fortune, and one of the four which the king made choice of to be about the person of his son, the prince, as gentleman of his privy chamber, when he first settled his family. His affection for the king was always most remarkable." The fidelity of his descendants to the cause of the Pretender was no less steadfast.

"Beneath Widdrington's walls
A loud trumpet calls
The valiant to rise for King James."

The summons was too readily obeyed, and William, fourth Lord Widdrington, with his two brothers, joined the disastrous rising of 1715. They were taken in arms at Preston, tried, and found guilty of high treason; and though their lives were spared, the attainder on their blood and property was preserved. The family, which for seven centuries had flourished in affluence and honour, was withered, and their estate passed to the Warrens, from whom it has come to its present owner, Lord Vernon.

A mile north-east of Widdrington is LOW CHIBBURN, where there still stands, in the midst of a richly-cultivated plain, an ancient preceptory of Knight's Hospitallers, supposed to have been founded by either the Fitz-Williams or the Widdringtons, in the early part of the fourteenth century. It formed a hollow square, and was defended by a moat and barmkin. The principal dwelling-house on the west was probably erected shortly after the dissolution of religious houses, by Sir John Widdrington, and was occupied in Elizabethan times as a pleasant mansion-house by the dowager ladies of the house of Widdrington. It is a long, low building of two storeys, having external chimneys at the south end, and others, in the centre, of great size. The windows in the second floor projected on corbels, the better to attack the assailants beneath. It is now let off in tenements. On the south side is the chapel, of excellent ashlar-work. It had an upper floor, a feature added at the same time, presumably, as the principal dwelling-house was built. Immediately over the arch of the south doorway are two escutcheons. Traces of a cross pattée, or cross, where the sides of the arms are curved inwards, doubtless for the knights of St. John, may be seen on one, and a quarterly coat, probably that of Widdrington, on the other. The piscina remains in the south-west angle. There is also in the chapel a corbel, or truss, rudely carved in oak, which may have been intended to represent the mitred head of a bishop, or possibly an angel, with a fillet round the forehead, ornamented in front with a cross. A grave-slab, with a floriated cross carved on it, now forms the threshold of the door leading from the courtyard into a stable. Some of the old wood-work still remains in this interesting home of the Knight's Hospitallers.

# MORPETH TO BOTHAL AND NEWBIGGIN.

Bothal, 3 miles; Sheepwash, 5 miles; Ashington, 4½ miles; Woodhorn, 8 miles; Newbiggin, 9 miles; Cresswell (direct), 10 miles.

THE Wansbeck may be followed the whole way from Morpeth to Bothal, a distance of three miles—by the road, as far as the Quarry Bank, and then by a sylvan path through the Lady Chapel Wood. The scenery, due to the harmony of wood and water, is of the most lovely character. Just past the massive railway viaduct, which spans the dene, is *St. Catharine's Well*. The water, slightly tinctured with iron, is of great purity. About half-a-mile further on, at a romantic bend in the river, is the *Lady Chapel*, built about the middle of the fifteenth century, by the first Lord Ogle, and dedicated to the Blessed Virgin. Here, in the sweetest seclusion, it lies nestling at the base of a craggy steep, overcanopied with foliage. Through a little grove of trees, which is as green underfoot as overhead, one hears the soft croon of the river, as it eddies along over the "rocky pavement and the mossy falls." Though still a ruin, the little chapel has been partially restored, the loose stones lying about having been replaced as far as possible in their original position. It measures internally 21 feet by 12 feet, and has been built of well-dressed freestone in the Perpendicular style. The roof was of stone, and consisted of slabs of freestone laid on huge ribs, as at Bellingham and Ladykirk. Many rare flowers grow near the ruins. Dr. Turner, the famous Morpeth botanist, speaks of orobanche as growing "in the north countre besyde Morpethe, where as it is called our lady of new chapillis flour." The lovely sylvan plant known as round-leaved winter green (*Pyrola rotundifolia*) also grows plentifully under the oaks here. On the west side of the chapel, under a pointed arch, is "Ye Jubilee Well," 1887. On the east side is the "Lady Well." Above it is an escutcheon cut out of the face of a huge sandstone rock and coloured. Close to it is carved the motto, "Fidelis Servus." Some years ago there was fastened to the overhanging roots, by a former curate of Morpeth, a large oblong board, bearing the following adaptation of "Bartram's Dirge"—

"Thei schot hym downe on ye Elsden rigg
Wher stands ye Headless Crosse;
Thei left hym swownen in hys bloude
In ye colde moor and mosse.

Thei made a beir of ye broken bough
  Of ye saugh and ye ashen gray,
And thei bore hym to ye Ladie Chapel
  And waked hym ther all day.

Hys leman cam to ye bonnie bower,
  And cast her cloke asyde ;
She tore her ling lang yellow hair,
  And kneeled at Bartram's syde.

She bathed hym in ye Ladie Well—
  His wounds baith depe and sair,
And she plaited a garland for hys breasts,
  And eke yen for hys haire.

Thei rowld hym in a lily shete,
  And bare hym to hys earthe ;
And ye Friars sung Sir Bartram's masse,
  When thei cam to ye kirkyarde garthe.

A Gray Friar stayed upon ye grave,
  And sang till ye morning-tide ;
And a Friar shall sing for Bartram's soul,
  While ye Headless Cross shall byde."

"The hero of the ditty, if the reciter be correct, was shot by nine brothers, whose sister he had seduced, but was afterwards buried at his request near their usual place of meeting, which may account for his being laid not in holy ground, but beside the burn." The ballad is said to have been taken down by Mr. Surtees from the recitation of an old woman, named Anne Douglas, who weeded his garden; but it is now believed to have been a production of the learned antiquary himself. The Bartrams were the early lords of Bothal. From the Lady Chapel the pathway goes undulating along the side of the ravine for a mile to Bothal Old Mill, affording the most picturesque glimpses of river scenery all the way. Here the river makes a magnificent bend, sweeping round one of the loveliest spots in Northumberland.

BOTHAL (Anglo-Saxon Bottell, an abode) lies in a quiet hollow, so sheltered that one approaching it by the road is unaware of its presence till close upon it. Above and around is the most luxuriant verdure. From the water's edge to the crown of the lofty ridge

"The ranks ascend
Shade above shade, a woody theatre
Of stateliest view."

The village is in every respect worthy of the beautiful surroundings, and forms a sweet picture of rural peace and contentment. The cottages are prettily and substantially built, with tastefully-planted flower-gardens in front. The Barony of Bothal was in the hands of the Bertrams prior to 1166, and remained in that family for two hundred years, when it passed by marriage into the possession of the Ogles. The property seems frequently to have been at the disposal of heiresses, for it was carried by marriage to Charles Cavendish, of Wellbeck, Notts, to John Hollis, Duke of Newcastle, to Edward, Earl of Oxford and Mortimer, and to William, Duke of Portland. It still belongs to the Portland family. *Bothal Castle* stands on the north bank of the Wansbeck, on a tongue of land formed by the river and the Bothal Burn. It dates back to the year 1343, when Robert de Bertram obtained from Edward the Third permission to "kernellate his manse at Bothal." The old fortress, in its perfect state, must have been very strong. It was defended by lofty walls (strengthened with buttresses and towers), which encircled the whole summit of the castle knoll, enclosing an area of nearly half an acre. Additional security was gained from the proximity of the river on the south and a moat on the east and west sides. The massive gateway, forty feet by thirty feet, remains in a good state of preservation, and is occupied by William C. Sample, Esq., agent of the Duke of Portland. On each side a semi-octagonal turret projects about fifteen feet to the north. Above the noble entrance arch is a very characteristic window of two lights, with a quatrefoil in the head between them. In the jambs of the entrance arch is a half-round portcullis groove. The vaulted roof of the roadway is supported on eight pointed ribs. Between them are openings through which molten lead or burning oil could be poured on assailants in possession of the archway. A shoulder-headed door on each side of the roadway leads to two vaulted chambers—an outer and an inner one, lighted by narrow slits. One of these four vaults has been the prison. A newel-staircase in the south-west tower leads up to the Great Chamber, above the archway, now divided into two apartments. From the Decorated window, on the south side, there is a view of the village and the valley beyond. The fine Perpendicular window to the east of it was removed from Cockle Park Tower. The drum-stair is capped by an umbrella vault of six large ribs, and six smaller ones branching out on a higher level between them. On the sides of the merlons of the battlements are to be seen the round holes in which worked the swing-shutters. "Archers could throw up one of these shutters, and take a shot at the enemy, and before the fire could be returned the shutter fell again." Some of the mason-marks at Bothal are similar to those on the barbican of Prudhoe. There are several escutcheons carved on the outer walls of the building, arranged in three series;—the first, of three shields, being on the three parapets immediately above the gate-way; the second, of seven shields, follows under a string immediately below the first; and the third, of four shields, at the same height as the second, is on the north-east face of the western tower. They appear in the following order, counting from left to right:—(1.) Thomas, Lord Wake of Lydel; Arms of England and France, borne by Edward III.; Edward the Black Prince as Duke of Cornwall. (2.) John de Coupland, or Gilbert de Aton; William, Baron of Greystock; Henry Percy II. of Alnwick; Robert Bertram; John D'arcy; Hastings or

Conyers; William de Felton, Lord of Edlingham. (3.) Delaval or Mauduit; Scargill; Roger de Horsley; John de Ogle. On the battlements are two stone figures; one on the merlon above the royal arms, in the attitude of sounding a horn; the other, on the western turret, in the act of lifting a stone as if to cast it down upon assailants. The fine gargoyles, two projecting from the north face of the turrets and two built into the new building on the west of the gate-house, deserve attention. In the year 1410 the castle, held by Sir John Bertram, sustained a siege of four days against Sir Robert Ogle, who sought to dispossess his younger brother of the property at Bothal, inherited in accordance with an entail made by his father. It was finally taken by assault. On the slope outside the castle is an orchard containing some fine old fruit trees. "Sempervivum, ivy, wall-flowers, also feverfew, pellitory of the wall, and the sambucus, or flowering elder," grow upon the ruined fragments of the walls. The arms of Ogle and Bertram, quartering Kirkby, which Grose found in the Lady Chapel, are preserved in the garden within the walls. The scene of "Lady Jean," a ballad by Robert White, is laid at Bothal. The poem commences by showing us the fair lady in tears at the prospect of wedding a man she does not love.

"I never lov'd Lord Dacre yet;
I dinna like him still—
He kens, though oft he sued for love
Upon his bended knee,
Ae tender word, ae kindly look
He never gat frae me."

She has sent word to her lover, Umfreville of Otterburn, to rescue her, and though her cousin reminds her of the long distance and the difficulties of the road, she is confident he will come, for

"Ah! weel I ken his heart is true;
He will, he must be here;
Aboon the garden wa's he'll wave
The pennon o' his spear."

Lord Dacre arrives, and the lady turns pale, and "totters like to fa'," when "List!" exclaims her cousin.—

"A bugle note!
It sounds not loud but clear.
Up! up! I see aboon the wa'
Your true love's pennon'd spear!'

An' up fu' quick gat Lady Jean,
Nae ailment had she mair;
Blythe was her look and firm her step
As she ran down the stair.

An' thro' amang the apple-trees,
An' up the walk she flew:
Until she reached her true love's side
Her breath she scarcely drew.

Lord Dacre fain would see the bride ;
He sought her bower alane ;
But dowf and blunkit grew his look
When Lady Jean was gane.

Sair did her father stamp an' rage,
Sair did her mother mourn ;
She's up and off wi' Umfreville
To bonnie Otterburne."

A bow-shot from the castle, half hidden in shrubberies, is the interesting little *Church of St. Andrew.* It is of fourteenth-century workmanship, and has been recently restored in harmony with its ancient character. Built, in the first instance, in the early English style, the church must have been entirely remodelled in the early Perpendicular period. The remains of the original building are the north arcade ; the chancel arch ; the chancel, with the exception of the eastern end ; the western gables, and the gable over the chancel arch, which stands isolated at its original pitch, looking down on a later and lower roof. The four arches dividing the nave and north aisle have plain ribs chamfered and labels terminating with carved heads, the easternmost being that of a bishop, the second of a king, and the third of a layman. The arches between the nave and south aisle are only three in number, and are much wider and plainer. On the south side of the chancel are three cusped-headed sedilia and a piscina, also a priest's door. The genealogy of the Ogles, of whom there were seven lords and thirty knights, is painted in tablets on the wall in old black letter. In the south-east corner is a low-side window, splayed as though a view, not of the east end, but of that part of the church about the rood screen, was desired from the exterior. In the north-east angle of the north aisle there is, too, a curious recess in the thickness of the two walls, high up from the ground, with splayed sides. What it was used for is not known. It is too high for an aumbry, and not regular enough for a niche. In the windows of the aisles is some beautiful ancient stained glass. Against the south-east pier of the chancel arch is a sixteenth-century altar-tomb, with two figures in alabaster upon it, representing, according to Mr. Longstaffe's reading of the heraldry, Ralph, Lord Ogle and Lady Margaret Gasgoine. The knight is in a coat of mail, and has a plain cross of St. George suspended by a chain round his neck. This head is supported on his crest (a bull's head), and his feet rest against a curled water-dog. The lady is dressed in a long robe and flowing mantle. Her head rests on a pillow, the tassels of which are held by two esquires. A small Italian greyhound nestles in her lap. A sword sheathed lies between these effigies. At the back of the tomb, in niches ornamented with tabernacle-work, is a shield, supported on the one side by a lion, collared and chained, and on the other by a monkey, tethered by the waist. In the wall, at the foot of the tomb, is a stone bracket bearing the Bertram arms. It was probably intended for a lamp. On the floor, at this end of the nave, there is a handsome tomb-slab, ornamented with a cross, a sword and a shield. During the restoration several fragments of cross-shafts, etc., of pre-Conquest date have been discovered; traces also of the Norman church have been found. The red-bricked Elizabethan house, with an octagonal tower on the south-west side, so beautifully situated above the river, is *Bothalhaugh*, the residence of the Hon. and Rev. W. C. Ellis. It was built in 1880,

From Bothal the road winds up a steep bank, shaded with trees, and takes a north-easterly direction, for a mile and a half, towards ASHINGTON, a large colliery village, somewhat less ugly than the majority of colliery villages, some of the later-built rows being comfortable and substantial, and even attractive.

A mile south-west of Ashington, and two miles south-east of Bothal, is SHEEPWASH, where the river Wansbeck is crossed by a good bridge of four arches. There was a church here in the olden time, dedicated to the Holy Sepulchre. Every vestige has long since disappeared. The only relic which has been preserved is the old font, now in Bothal churchyard. The old rectory still remains. On the south side of the river are beautiful market-gardens, a favourite resort of picnic parties during the strawberry season. Tea may be obtained at the house adjoining. On Sunday, September 15th, 1839, during the flood which caused so much damage, and was attended by such loss of life, the waters flowed into the second storey of some houses at Sheepwash. At high tide Sheepwash may be reached by boat from North Seaton; and the excursion up the river, between the finely-wooded banks, is an exceedingly pleasant one. Sheepwash—a corruption of "Ship-wash"—derives its name from the circumstance of small vessels ascending the river as far as the ford, or "wash," here. Michael Scott is said, by tradition, to have purposed bringing the tide as far as Morpeth, but his designs were frustrated by the cowardice of his assistant. After certain spells had been performed by the great wizard, this agent was to run from the neighbourhood of Camboise to Morpeth without looking back, and the tide would follow him. He accordingly set off, but had not proceeded far when the roaring of the waters behind him so excited his fears, that, forgetting the injunction, he cast a glance over his shoulder to see if the danger was imminent, and the tide immediately stopped, and has since that time advanced no further. The Morpeth and Newbiggin road passes the railway station at Hirst, and the old battlemented farm-house at Low Hirst—one of the ancient strongly fortified dwellings called peles, so common in the county—and continues on to

WOODHORN (*i.e.*, the Wood Corner), a small rural village, eight miles east by north of Morpeth, consisting of a few farms and cottages, and an old wind-mill, which is a conspicuous land-mark for sailors. Edward I. was at Woodhorn, December 19th, 1292. The venerable *Church of St. Mary* is a fabric of very great interest, for it contains examples of the earlier styles of ecclesiastical architecture. Founded by Saxon hands, it was at different times enlarged and altered during a period of five hundred years, from the date of its erection, and now stands as a precious monument of ancient piety. The remains of the early Saxon building are necessarily scanty; they consist of the piers and arch of the tower, the turret stair, and the return end of the nave on the north side. The Norman work is represented by the two round arches dividing the nave from the north aisle, with their sturdy columns and cushioned capitals, 7 feet 6 inches high. Facing them, on the other side of the church, are two other round arches resting on columns, 5 inches less in diameter, and 2 feet 2 inches higher. They belong to the Transitional period, as do also three walls of the tower. Examples of the early English style are seen in the graceful pointed arch of the south arcade, in the chancel and chancel arch. The richly moulded, delicate pointed arch of the north arcade was built when this style had reached its utmost perfection. The church was repaired in 1843, on which occasion all the exterior masonry, save that of the two lower stages of the tower, was replaced with new. All the windows belong to this "restoration." On the outside of the west wall of the tower are the arms of Widdrington and Ogle, and a male figure with its hands in a praying posture carved in high-relief on stone. The monuments and tomb-slabs, and fragments of ancient sculpture, preserved in the church, are exceedingly interesting. On the north side of the chancel is the effigy of an abbess carved in sandstone—a beautiful specimen of mediæval workmanship. The drapery, falling in exquisite folds around her, is admirably executed. Over her head is a canopy, carved at the top in high-relief, with a representation of the Resurrection. At her feet are two cherubs and the figure of a dog, the emblem of fidelity. Several fine monumental tablets, commemorating various members of the Cresswell family, are hung on the walls of the chancel. At the west end of the church stands the font. Near it are three pieces, —the head, base, and portion of the shaft—of a fine Saxon cross. Here are also several early English grave-covers, ornamented with various kinds of crosses, and, in one case, with a sword. Others of a more elaborate sculpture may be found in the porch.

In the vestry is a brass tablet, inscribed—

"AN ACROSTICK<br>
Epitaph on a vertuous Gentle-<br>
woman who died on Palm Sunday<br>
March 24th 1699<br>
A : skest thou Reader who lyes here<br>
N : o common corps then List & you shall here<br>
G : oodness rare meekness zeal pure chastitie<br>
I : nterred together in this Ground do lie<br>
B : ehold her acts whilst here she made abode<br>
S : he liv'd belov'd of men & died lov'd of God<br>
MRS. ANN RAILSTON."

There is an ancient bell inscribed—"St. Maria." The rectory of Woodhorn was formerly appropriated to the Priory of Tynemouth.

A mile from Woodhorn is NEWBIGGIN-BY-THE-SEA, a large fishing-village and popular watering-place, situated on a fine, broad bay that stretches in a magnificent sweep between two rocky promontories. Newbiggin was formerly a maritime town of some importance. As early as 1352 there was a pier on the north side of the harbour, for an indulgence of forty days was granted at that date to any who should assist in keeping it in repair. In the wars of Edward II. with Scotland, "Newbyggyng" was required to furnish a ship for naval purposes. Large quantities of corn used to be shipped at this port, and vessels of many tons burden rode in the harbour. The district seems to have been formerly much wooded, for, as some excavations were being made for sewerage purposes, a bed of peat seven feet below the superincumbent sand was discovered, with trunks of trees, hazels, and nuts embedded in it. Three bronze spear-heads, belonging to pre-historic times, were found, in making a cutting to the sea-shore, in June 1878. Edward II. was here for three days, on his way to besiege Berwick, 13–17th July 1319, and again on 8th September 1322.

On the bold rocky headland called Newbiggin Point stands the ancient *Church of St. Bartholomew*—a very conspicuous object for miles along the coast, and a useful landmark to sailors. This venerable edifice is much smaller than it formerly was, its side-aisles having been destroyed. The north and south walls have been built up to the old arches, which are finely moulded and enriched with labels. In these arcades, and in other parts of the church, are several grotesque corbel-heads. Two of these, all a-grin, salute the visitor on entering the porch. They appear on both sides of the chancel-arch, and must, one would think, awaken thoughts the reverse of solemn. One represents a lady, with a smug, half-humorous expression on her face; another a monk, with bushy eyebrows, distended nostrils, and grinning mouth; a third is a sharp, contemptuous face, with shut eyelids and compressed lips; and a fourth, a satyr-like, sensual face, with staring, prominent eyeballs, toothless mouth, and wrinkled cheeks. The east window, says Mr. Wilson, is one of the rare examples in this part of the country of five lancets grouped into a window without tracery. The sill of a window on the south of the chancel has been brought down to form sedilia, near which is a small piscina. In the porch are some very beautiful early English grave covers, ornamented with floriated crosses of exquisite workmanship. There are some curious epitaphs in the churchyard.

"Weep not for me, my dearest friends,
You all must surely die,
Time is uncertain, so prepare
To meet me here on high.

The rageing seas and stormy winds,
I was tossed to and fro,
But now I hope my God to find
At anchor here below."

"So frail is the youth and the beauty of men,
Though they bloom and look gay like a rose;

But all our fond care to preserve them is vain,
Time kills them as fast as he goes."

The churchyard here was once in a very neglected condition, owing to the ravages of the sea, several of the tombs being desecrated by the waves. Even yet fragments of human bones are lying about in the loose sand outside the churchyard wall. One would have been half inclined to think that Swinburne, who is of a Northumbrian family, had Newbiggin in his mind when he wrote that description of a crumbling churchyard in his poem, "By the North Sea," were it not known that it was suggested by a similar scene of desolation near Cromer.

"Tombs with poor, white, piteous bones protruded,
Shroudless down the loose collapsing banks,
Crumble, from their constant place detruded,
That the sea devours and gives not thanks.
Graves, where hope and prayer and sorrow brooded,
Gape and slide and perish ranks on ranks."

A thrilling scene in Mrs. Wasserman's little story "Ret" (*Gentleman's Magazine*, August 1886), is laid here. The heroine and her lover are seated beneath the crumbling banks, when a skull rolls down upon them, producing a somewhat sensational episode. To the north of the Point is Newbiggin Moor, a large and sandy common, where golf is very extensively played. Beyond it are "The Fairy Rocks." There is a station at Newbiggin, from which there is a branch line to Bedlington. The principal inns are the Old Ship Inn and the New Dolphin Inn.

Two miles to the north is *Linemouth*, a small hamlet, near the estuary where the Line enters the sea. Here it was that on August 8th, 1822, a large spermaceti whale, measuring 61 feet in length, and 37 feet 4 inches in girth, went ashore. It formed the subject of extensive litigation between Mr. Ralph Atkinson and Mr. Cresswell Baker, who both claimed the carcase, the one on the ground that it first of all landed on the foreshore belonging to the Manor of Newbiggin, the other on the ground that it finally rested on the Cresswell domain. The Admiralty however settled the dispute by seizing the oil and fixing their broad arrow on the bones. The skeleton is now preserved in the grounds at Creswell.

Two miles to the north again is CRESSWELL, a village of some size, inhabited amost entirely by fisher-folk. It is five miles and a half from Newbiggin by the road passing through Ellington, and nine miles from Morpeth. The *Church of St. Bartholomew* is a new edifice in the Norman style. The two inns which were formerly here have been removed. On January 5th, 1876, the Swedish steamer *Gustav* came ashore at Cresswell, but the crew wree rescued by the fishermen. One of the fisher girls, named Bella Brown, gained for herself a reputation for heroism on this occasion. She made her way along the beach this cold night in January to the next lifeboat station, to claim assistance for the shipwrecked people, and to accomplish this feat she was compelled to go ten English miles, wading through several bays by the way.

The family of Cresswell is a very old one, and was seated here as early as the reign of King John. A J. Cresswell, Esq., who built the present mansion-house, took the name of Baker on succeeding to the property of his wife's cousin, John Baker, Esq. The ancient manor-house of this family, built in the middle of the eighteenth century, has been pulled down, and nothing remains of it but the main doorway. The old pele-tower, reared in Edwardian times, still overlooks the magnificent links of Druridge Bay, and is one of the finest specimens of the fortified mansion-house in the county. It consists of the byre, vaulted with stone on the ground floor, and two rooms above, approached by a circular stone staircase. In the upper chamber is a *garde-robe* recess in the thickness of the wall. The north-east angle is surmounted with a turret, which commands a fine view of the German Ocean and the line of the coast, both north and south. In the inside of it is a rude inscription on the lintel, and two side stones of a window, supposed to read, "William Cresswell, brave hero." This hoary and picturesque old tower has its mysterious visitant. The White Lady of Cresswell was, according to tradition, the daughter of one of the old barons of Cresswell. Standing one day on the turret of the old tower, she had the terrible experience of seeing her lover—a Danish prince—slain on the sea-shore by her three brothers, and was so stricken with grief at the sight that she refused to touch food, and starved herself to death.

*Cresswell House* (Mrs. Cresswell) is a beautiful modern mansion, built from the designs of Shaw 1821-25. The stone of which it is constructed is an exceedingly fine sandstone, many of the blocks weighing as much as four, and even eight, tons, and so exquisitely chiselled that the joints between them are scarcely perceptible. Along the east front runs a stone terrace, 9 feet broad, with a parapet of pierced stone-work. In the centre of the west front a fine portico, having an elegant entablature supported by two fluted columns, admits to the entrance-hall, which is hung with tapestry. Separated from it by an enriched stone screen is a magnificent staircase, 38 feet long, 24 feet wide, and 29 feet high, the chief internal feature of the house. On circular pedestals at the commencement of the two first flights are bronze candelabra, and at the bottom of the second flight are casts of the celebrated Townley vase. Below the ceiling are three casts of the Metopes of the Parthenon, and a compartment from the frieze of this famous building ornaments each end. To the right of the hall and staircase are the billiard-room, drawing-room, library, and dining-room. The first of these, which is hung with tapestry, has a richly-moulded and coloured ceiling. The last contains a number of family portraits and a fine Japanese screen. Connected with the north front is a stately colonnade or open passage, with niches in the wall, opposite to each opening of the arcade, containing several ornamental vases and the busts of Agrippa, Antinous, Clytie, Commodus, Phocion, Pericles, Ajax, Ariadne, and others. This cloistral walk leads to the conservatory (70 feet by 22 feet), which contains some large tree-ferns and other exotic plants. Here, and on the rockery outside, may be seen some interesting specimens of the enormous fossil trunks known as sigillaria. They were obtained from the Boghall quarries on the sea-banks, nearly opposite the house, and were found in an alternating stratum of schist and somewhat soft kind of sandstone. The museums at Newcastle and Wallington Hall have been enriched with their finest specimens of sigillaria from the same spot. Magnificent avenues of evergreen shrubs form the most striking feature of the grounds. In the gardens is a rockery, formed of the enormous vertebræ of the whale which was stranded at Linemouth. From Cresswell northward sweeps the fine crescent-shaped *Bay of Druridge*, bordered with firm and beautiful sands. Here, at low tide, may be seen the remains of an ancient oak forest. The jaw-bones of the whale stranded at Linemouth form an archway to a field near Cresswell Hall. A mile to the south-west of Cresswell is Ellington, the ton or town of the Ellingas, or descendants of Ella. The gardens of Cresswell Vicarage here are celebrated for their collection of willows, one hundred and sixty varieties having been gathered together by the late vicar, J. E. Leefe.

# ELSDON SECTION.

## REDESDALE.

THE district known as *Redesdale* is a wild and monotonous stretch of dreary moorland, intersected by valleys and gorges which have been worn through the underlying rocks by swift-flowing rivers and burns, and by rugged cleughs and ravines rent in the sides of the hills by great natural convulsions. Its features are for the most part gently moulded and rounded, with no very salient prominences. Once covered by extensive forests that broke the force of the bleak winds, it is now almost treeless except for a few willows, birches, alders, and thorns on the margin of the streams, and an occasional clump of Scotch firs on the sterile slopes. There is considerable difficulty in rearing new plantations, as the sheep with which the moors are stocked find the young trees a pleasant addition to their limited bill of fare, and browse upon the tender bark and foliage. The colouring of the landscape, except in summer when the heather is in bloom, is tame and subdued in tone, chiefly composed of neutral tints varied by patches of green moss and purple-hued peat. Large tracks of the barren moor have been enclosed, and marshy land drained, during the last century, thus rendering them available as grazing-grounds for the rearing and feeding of cattle and sheep. The rich haughs along the valley of the Rede are beautifully green and fresh, but are liable to be inundated by the waters of the river during one of those rapid floods which occur after a few hours rain or thaw. Some tourists who have visited the district with imaginations stirred by the grand old ballads of "Chevy Chase" or the "Raid of the Redeswire," are apt to feel disappointed at the unromantic appearance of the vale, and "repelled," to quote the words of Dr. Johnson, "by the wide expanse of hopeless sterility" around it; while others know of no better tonic to the jaded mind than the sight of these austere landscapes, feeling a sense of exultation in wandering along the lonely sheep-tracks or wading through the wiry heather, content with the plaintive music of the curlew's note, and the simple beauty of the bog-asphodel, or the famous little sundew which Mr. Swinburne has celebrated in song. But the wild waste of heather and bracken, with its "sunny spots of greenery," forms a fitting background to the dark history of Redesdale, and owes much of the fascination it may exert over the tourist to its tragic memories of feud and foray, alas! too numerous.

Soon after the Conquest, Redesdale, with all its "royal franchises," possessed in Saxon times by Mildred, the son of Akman, was granted by William the Norman to Robert de Umfraville, or as he was known, Robert Cum Barba (Robert with the Beard), "to be held by the service of defending it from enemies and wolves with that sword which King William had by his side when he entered Northumberland." Conditions not at all easy to fulfil, as the Borders were in a state of continual turmoil, and the enemies to law and order were legion, while the crafty and ferocious quadrupeds seem to have been very difficult to extirpate from a district abounding in covers of scrub and heather, for in 1420 the barony was still retained on the same terms as in 1076. A rugged mass of rock called Wolf Crag, between Elsdon and Woodburn, has either been a haunt of these fierce animals or a favourite meet of the wolf-hunters in early times. In the reign of Henry V. so many complaints were made to the king by his faithful subjects in the northern counties of the murders and felonies and outrages committed by the thieves of Redesdale, "where the king's writ runneth not," that the Parliament, in 1421, found it necessary to enact that the provisions which had been made against similar crimes in Tynedale and Hexhamshire should extend to Redesdale—viz., that the process should be made against the offenders by the common law till they be outlawed, and their property within the franchise seized into the hands of the lord as forfeit, and without it, into the king's hands. A black picture of the life in this notorious district has been painted by Dr. Fox, Bishop of Durham, in his "Admonition against the famous thieves of Tynedale and Redesdale," issued in 1498. The majority of the inhabitants are represented as reivers and cattle-lifters, compounding for their offences by handing over a portion of the spoil to the venial officers of the crown, who, both for clanship's sake and for the benefits received, protected rather than punished the wrong-doers. The condition of the clergy affords a striking illustration of the proverb, "Like priest, like people." They are described as publicly and openly living with concubines, irregular, suspended, excommunicated, and interdicted, wholly ignorant of letters, so much so, that priests of ten years' standing did not know how to read the ritual. Some of them were even nothing more than sham priests, having never been ordained, and performed divine service not only in the authorised churches but in unconsecrated buildings. They administered the sacrament to their lawless parishioners, without compelling them to make restitution of their ill-gotten goods, and buried them in consecrated ground, against the laws of the church. The worthy prelate, in the much-needed mandate, charges the clergy to excommunicate all those men within their parishes who should presume to go from home, excepting against the Scots, armed in "a jack, a salet, or knapescul (helmet), or other defensive armour; or should ride a horse worth more than six shillings and eightpence; or should wear in any church or churchyard, during time of divine service, any offensive weapon more than a cubit in length."

The population was a great deal more than the land could maintain in honesty, but the government seem to have found it convenient to have, on the Borders, these warlike clans, whose function may be inferred from a letter of the Duke of Northumberland to Henry VIII., in which he promised "to lette slippe them of Tyndaill and Riddisdail for the annoyance of Scotland." The survey of 1542, writes Hodgson, in his *History of Northumberland*, describes the Redesdale men as living in sheels during the summer, and pasturing their cattle in the grains and hopes of the country south of the Coquet, about Wilkwood and Ridlees, or in the waste grounds which sweep along the eastern marches of North Tynedale. At this time they not only joined with their neighbours of Tynedale in acts of rapine and spoil, but often went as guides to the thieves of Scotland, in their expeditions to ravage the towns and villages between the Coquet and Wansbeck. To check these outrages, Sir Cuthbert Radcliffe devised a watch from sunset to sunrise at all passages and fords along the Middle Marches towards North Tynedale and Redesdale, that when the thieves of the north were seen descending, hue and cry might be raised for assistance to drive them back. Those amongst the dalesmen were most esteemed who soonest in youth began to practise themselves in thefts and robberies, for in these they delighted, boasted, and exercised themselves. They were divided into clans, each of which had rank and precedence, according to its numerical strength. That of Hall was the greatest and of most reputation, and next to it the Reeds, Potts, Hedleys, Spoors, Daugs, Fletchers, etc. So strong was the feeling which bound the several members of a clan together, that it was a difficult and dangerous task to bring a culprit to justice. Sir Robert Bowes, in a report prepared for the Marquis Dorset, Warden-General of the Marches in 1551, concerning the state of the Borders, gives prominence to this fact. "If," he says, "any trewe men of England gett knowledge of the thefte or theaves that steale his goods in Tyndalle or Ryddesdale he had much rather take a part of his goodes again in composition than to pursue the extremytye by the lawe against the theaf. For if the theaf be of any great surname or kyndred, and be lawfully executed by order of justice, the rest of his kynne or surname beare as much mallice, which they call deadly feade, against such as followe the lawe against their cossen the theaf as though he had unlawfully kylled hym with a sword, and will by all meanes they can seeke revenge there uppon." The common and discreet practice was for persons whose cattle had been driven off to treat with some of the chiefs of the clan who had committed the theft, and pay them a certain sum for the restitution of their property, and to prevent a recurrence of marauding visits, saufey money, or blackmail, was paid, even in Queen Elizabeth's reign, to these systematic robbers. Lesley, Bishop of Ross, describes very vividly the manner in which their cattle-lifting raids were conducted. "They sally out of their own borders in the night, in troops, through unfrequented byways and many intricate windings. All the daytime they refresh themselves and their horses in hiding-holes they had pitched upon before, till they arrive in the dark in those places they have a design upon. As soon as they have seized upon the booty, they, in like manner, return home in the night, through blind ways, and fetching many a compass. The more skilful any captain is to pass through those wild deserts, crooked turnings, and deep precipices, in the thickest mists, his reputation is the greater, and he is looked upon as a man of an excellent head. And they are so very cunning that they seldom have their booty taken from them, unless sometimes when, by the help of blood-hounds following them exactly upon the track, they may chance to fall into the hands of their adversaries. When being taken, they have so much persuasive eloquence, and so many smooth insinuating words at command, that if they do not move their judges, nay, and even their adversaries (notwithstanding the severity of their natures), to have mercy, yet they incite their admiration and compassion." "Such adepts were they in the art of thieving," says the biographer of Bernard Gilpin, "that they could twist a cow's horn, or mark a horse, so as its owners could not know it; and so subtle that no vigilance could guard against them. For these arts they were long afterwards famous. A person telling King James a surprising story of a cow that had been driven from the north of Scotland into the south of England, and, escaping from the herd, had found its way home, 'The most surprising part of the story, the king replied, you lay least stress on, that she passed unstolen through the debatable land.'"

So notorious was the bad character of the inhabitants of these northern vales, that the Incorporated Merchant-Adventurers of Newcastle, with a dim apprehension of the law of Heredity, made a bye-law in 1564, prohibiting any brother from receiving a person born in Tynedale and Redesdale as an apprentice; because "the parties there brought up are known, either by education or nature, not to be of honest conversation; and they commit frequent thefts and other felonys proceeding from such lewde and wicked progenitors."

This regulation continued to stand unrepealed till 1771. In the administration of justice this conception told very much against the accused, for Master Richard Crompton, "un apprentice de le common ley," as he styles himself in his work on the office and authority of a justice of peace, 1584, lays it down as a maxim that the country in which a man is born generally declares his natural inclination; for instance, if he were born or educated among the men of Tynedale or Redesdale, he ought to be the more suspected.

It was a long time before these predatory instincts died out. With the union of the two crowns, national rivalries and enmities ceased to exist, and peace and order began to be established in the lawless regions of the Borders. The calling of the moss-trooper was, therefore, gone, and his recrimination raids, instead of being encouraged, were now frowned upon by the authorities, and he was, therefore, obliged to lay aside sword, steel-jack, and head-piece, and begin to lead a more peaceful mode of life. For upwards of a century afterwards the wild Borderers continued to retain many of the characteristic traits of their ancestors, humorously described by the beggar in the "Dialogue both pleasaunte and pietifull" of Dr. William Bullein, as good, honest men and true, *saving a little shiftyng for their livyng, God and our Leddie help them*, silie pure men." One of the most beneficent influences exerted over this barbarous neighbourhood was the preaching of Bernard Gilpin, the Northern Apostle, as he was styled. "In this dreadful country," says his biographer, "where no man would even travel that could help it, Mr. Gilpin never failed to spend some part of every year. He generally chose the holy-days of Christmas for this journey, because he found the people at that season most disengaged, and most easily assembled. He had set places for preaching, which were as regularly attended as the assize-towns of a circuit. If he came where there was a church, he made use of it; if not, of barns, or any other large building; where great crowds of people were sure to attend him, some for his instructions, and others for his charity. Necessarily, the hardships he endured were very great, but his disinterested labours and kindly admonitions gained for him such an ascendancy over the hearts of these rough dalesmen, that, we are told, "he was little less than adored, and might have brought the whole country almost to what he pleased." The extent of his influence cannot be better illustrated than by the story which is told of the thief, who, having unwittingly stolen the reverend gentleman's horses, was so much terrified on hearing whose they were, that he instantly came trembling back and returned them, declaring that he believed the devil would have seized him directly had he carried them off, knowing them to have been Mr. Gilpin's. After the Union, the Borderers (with the exception of gentlemen of rank and repute) were prohibited from carrying armour or weapons, and keeping any horse, gelding, or mare above the price of fifty shillings sterling, or thirty pounds Scots, and there seemed to be every prospect of a more settled order of things in the unruly districts; but during the stormy period of civil war which shortly after ensued, when disorder reigned throughout the length and breadth of the land, the old spirit of the Border freebooters broke out again, as is but too evident from the accounts of moss-troopers' raids, which are to be found in the diaries and military reports of the time. Grey, in his *Chorographia*, published in 1649, thus speaks of their exploits and customs:—"These Highlanders . . . . come down from these dales into the low countries, and carry away horses and cattell so cunningly, that it will be hard for any to get them, or their cattell, except they be acquainted with some master thiefe; who, for some mony (which they call saufey mony), may help them to their stolen goods, or deceive them. There is many every yeare brought in of them into the goale of Newcastle, and at the Assizes are condemned and hanged, sometimes twenty or thirty. They forfeit not their lands (according to the tenure of gavelkind), the father to bough, the sonne to the plough. The people of this countrey hath had one barbarous custome amongst them; if any two be displeased, they expect no law, but bang it out bravely, one and his kindred against the other and his; they will subject themselves to no justice, but, in an inhumane and barbarous manner, fight and kill one another."

The people of Redesdale retained their unruly character for many generations after this period, and even as late as the beginning of the present century were noted for their wild and turbulent disposition, exhibiting a propensity for gambling, drinking, and cock-fighting, which involved the small lairds and tenant-farmers in difficulties, and swamped their little estates. The whole duty of a Redewater man used to be "to speak when he was spoken to, to drink when he was drunken to, and to go to kirk when the bell rang." He was rough and boisterous in his manners, unlettered and half-civilized, yet kind-hearted and hospitable, ready at all times to shake hands or break a head; he had a bite and a bottle for anyone, and was wont to say, "he would rather treat a beggar than lose good company." The population of this valley, about one-third of what it was in the reign of Henry VIII., is as peaceful, industrious, and law-abiding as any of Her Majesty's subjects, mostly engaged in sheep-farming and cattle-breeding, for which the high moorland pastures and rich valley meadows are peculiarly adapted. A slight tendency to poaching may, perhaps, be a last dying flicker of that predatory instinct which distinguished their marauding ancestors. The days of rapine and bloodshed have, happily, passed away, so far as these moorland wilds are concerned, for the schoolmaster, wielding a mightier power than ever the Lord-Warden of the marches possessed, has been, and still is, diffusing the light of civilisation throughout the length and breadth of this once neglected region, rendering a return of the bad old times impossible. To quote the words of the Redewater Minstrel:—

> "Sweet Redesdale, through thy winding glens
> No more shall hostile tumult roar,
> Wi' note forlorn, the bugle horn
> Shall echo from thy hills no more.
>
> No more shall ruthless flames devour
> The trembling shepherd's lowly shiel;
> No fierce moss-troopers burst the door
> That strongly bars the shelt'ring peel."

ELSDON is a small and straggling village, consisting of a church, fortified parsonage, an inn, a temperance hotel, and a few houses, chiefly situated on one side of a very large shelving green. Backed and sheltered by pastoral hills, with miles on miles of bleak moorland around it, the village still retains that old-world air of seclusion about it so much sought after nowadays by the dwellers in large towns. From the fact of its situation at the confluence of three small burns, it is said to have received its name Elsdon, a corruption of Elisden, Ellesden, or Ellesdene, as it used to be written, which means the valley of waters. Tradition, however, derives it from Ella, a Danish giant of marauding disposition, who had his stronghold on the Mote Hills. The place lays claim to a very high antiquity, and formerly had its weekly market on Tuesday, and an annual fair on the 26th of August, but both of these have long been obsolete, though the privileges of the last are still maintained by the yearly custom of riding the boundaries and proclaiming the fair in dumb show. The Court-leet of the extensive manor of Redesdale, an ancient Saxon institution in connection with the jurisdiction of a hundred or county-division, was held here until 1868, when it was abolished, and the business of the Court pertaining to the Regality transferred to the Quarter Sessions. In consequence of the long isolation of the village amid moors and morasses, remote from the enlightening influences of civilisation, many pagan customs and superstitions were observed till within a very short time ago. The Midsummer bonfires, through which cattle were driven to protect them from disease, were, says Dr. E. C. Robertson, burning only a few years ago on Elsdon green—their origin, in the worship of Baal, being forgotten. Well-worship continues to this day, and votive gifts, not so valuable as those showered into Coventina's Well, are still thrown into the clear spring waters. The cockpit and pinfold for stray cattle are still to be seen in the village. The antiquarian attractions of Elsdon are three :—The Mote Hills, the Church, and the fortified Rectory House. The *Mote Hills* are two remarkable mounds on the east side of Elsdon Burn, opposite to the Parsonage. They have evidently been large accumulations of drift, due to diluvial action, and shaped into their present form by the old Celtic inhabitants of the district, either as a rude stronghold or a place for the holding of tribal councils, and, perhaps, for the celebration of religious rites and ceremonies. The Romans are believed to have occupied them as a post of observation and as a place of sepulture, for several Roman remains have been found in them, one of the most important being a memorial tablet dedicated "to the god Matunus, for the safety of Antoninus Cæsar, born for the good of the human race." These two mounds, which are combined at their base, are partly separated by a deep moat or ditch, and vary a little in height. On the north and east sides they are defended by another moat, and on the south and west by natural declivities. The southern hill is 70 feet above the adjoining burn, and the nothern 63 feet. They are both fortified with massive earthen ramparts, the greatest width and height being in one case 40 feet and 12 feet, and in the other 60 feet and 15 feet. One writer, Thomas Arkle, Highlaws, Morpeth, whose opinion is of weight, considers that the beautifully level top of the northern hill is near to what, previous to the formation of the ditches and embankments, would probably be the natural surface of the ground; and he shows, by drawing the surface-line through the higher hill across the southern ditch, that about twenty feet of the top of the hill must have been raised by human agency. A work so stupendous would require twelve or fifteen thousand cubic yards of material, and it is believed this earth was taken out of the hollow in which the road from the High Mote House now goes down to Elsdon. From the remains of large and extensive camps and settlements in the neighbourhood, it is evident that the British tribes who inhabited the district were once very numerous and powerful, and Elsdon may possibly have been the Celtic capital, from the Mote Hills of which laws were promulgated and justice administered. The *Church* is an interesting cruciform structure, built about 1400, and dedicated to St. Cuthbert, whose body is said to have rested here a short time in 875, during the wanderings of the monks of Lindisfarne. It was erected on the site of a still earlier building, of which the only remnants are two pilasters in the west gable, of early Norman design —about 1100—and perhaps two small round-headed windows in the west ends of the aisles. Above the doorway into the church are two old grave-slabs which serve as lintels, one having a dagger carved upon it, the other a pair of shears. High up on the pillar nearest the porch are some deep scratches, which are supposed to have been made by the fierce bowmen of Redesdale in sharpening their arrows before leaving church. From other marks on the pillars near the door, it is supposed the warlike villagers of Elsdon were in the habit of whetting the edge of their swords on the consecrated masonry. In the north transept, called Anderson's Porch, from an ancient local family, are some monumental slabs, one with the Umfraville arms, a cross, with crosslets; another with a shield (a stag upon it), a cross, and sword; and others to former rectors and members of the Reed family. The most interesting object in this part of the church is an old Roman monumental tablet, brought from Bremenium (Rochester) in 1809. The inscription, much defaced, is thus translated by Hodgson, "Julia Lucilla saw that this stone was erected to . . . her very meritorious husband, who was an inspector under the surveyor of the Flaminian Way, and a pensioner under the surveyor of the public works. He lived 47 years, 6 months, 25 days." The pillar facing the pulpit bears some quaint coloured carvings of cherub heads. In the south transept, called Hedley's Porch, after a numerous clan of that name, is a piscina, and two incised slabs built into the wall, are to be seen. The chancel contains a tablet to the family of Reed, of Troughend, which, according to a statement on a scroll, has been seated in Redesdale for the last nine hundred years, also a monument to the Halls, of Whitelee, with coloured coat of arms and the usual emblems of mortality—skull (upside down), cross-bones, and hour-glass; and a monument to Mrs. Anna Eliz. Grose, daughter of the celebrated antiquary, Francis Grose, who died at Elsdon Castle, 1826. The sedilia for the ancient priests to sit in during service still exist in the chancel, and in the north wall are the remains of a low-side window, brought to light in forming a chamber for the harmonium. In the vestry is a box containing the skeletons of three horses'-heads, discovered inside the spire that surmounts the quaint little bell-turret during the restorations of 1877. These skulls, which are apparently those of two draught horses and one cob, nearly filled the small chamber, or cavity, prepared for them, and were piled against each other in a triangular form, the jaws being uppermost. Dr. Robertson, of Otterburn, thinks that the reason of these horses' heads being placed in such a strange position is to be found in the survival of some old Pagan custom, derived originally from the far east. After showing that the horse was once held in great veneration as an animal for sacrifice, on account of the qualities of strength, activity, and beauty, which it symbolized, and was also considered as the emblem of the sun, he goes on to say, "It seems to me to be within the pale of probability that, at the installation of the first church in Elsdon, the sacrifice of a horse, as an act of sanctification of the building, may have taken place. It was a sacrifice common in early times at the raising of buildings, and being in solemnity next to the human, what more likely than for it to be used by the half-savage and newly, and but partially, converted inhabitants of this wild district. And as the Gauls were described, not many centuries before, as fixing the heads of horses on high, as an act of worship and veneration for their gods, what more likely than that their kinsmen here should, even perhaps with the approval of the missionaries, show their veneration towards their newly-acquired religion, by fixing the heads of the sacrificed horses on the church. The practice thus commenced in faith would naturally be repeated with less and less belief in or understanding of its significance, as oft as a new church arose on the ruins of the old, until at last, in the fifteenth or sixteenth century, we find the rite still in practice, as shown by the preparation of a chamber in the belfry of the church, specially constructed to hold the horses' heads. Or the horses' heads may have been considered as emblems of Pagan sun worship, and the three heads of the animal so especially sacred to heathendom may have been raised aloft in the church tower, as a sign of the victory of the Triune God over Paganism, even as we at the present day hang up in our churches the banners gained in battle from a defeated enemy."

In 1810, during the removal of great accumulations of earth against the north wall of the nave, the bones of 100 or more persons were discovered, in double rows, with the skull of one row within the thigh bones of the other, packed in the smallest possible compass. These were evidently only part of a great interment which had once taken place, for in 1877 a large number of other skeletons in a similar attitude were found extending right under the north wall into the church, to all appearance the remains of young and middle-aged men. From the manner in which they were packed, it is inferred that they had been buried at one time, and that shortly before the erection of the nave, for the foundations of the north wall were found to be not so deeply laid as the other parts of the church, the builders evidently wishing to avoid disturbing the half-decomposed bodies. As the church was built about 1400, and the only battle of importance that took place in the district was that of Otterburn, there seems little doubt that many of the distinguished warriors, who fell on the memorable battle-field, were conveyed, as the ballad says, on "beeres of byrch and haysell graye," to Elsdon, and interred in consecrated ground.

In the churchyard are many examples of those quaint sculptures and epitaphs usually found in country districts. At the west end of the church, near to two stone coffins removed from the chancel, is a tombstone inscribed as follows :—

"Here lyeth Thos. Wilson, officer for the duty of salt, who died Mch. 16th, 1778, aged 51.

Surely pale Death could hardly
Find so good a man and friend so
Kind as these corps that here
Doth lie in hopes his soul is
Wrapt in joy."

*Elsdon Parsonage*, usually called *Elsdon Castle*, is one of the characteristic old Border peles, afterwards transformed into a rectory-house. "Cedant arma togæ," says William Chatto, "was the notice to quit served upon the warlike tenants of Elsdon town, when Cheviot Hills ceased to be the boundary between two hostile nations. The occupation of the Lord of Redesdale was gone, for there were no longer wolves in the country, nor enemies of the king to encounter within the four seas; and the Border rider, clad in a rusty steel jack, and armed with a long sword, stalked out, and the rector, having on a new cassock and a clean band, walked in, and hung up his goodly beaver in the hall, where the former tenant used to hang up his helmet." On a battlement of the south front is a shield bearing the arms of the Umfravilles, and above it a helmet surmounted with a cinquefoil for the crest, and supported by two wolves, each holding a sword upright. The inscription is "R. Dominus de Rede," probably intended for Sir Robert Umfraville, who died in 1436, though some read Sir Robert Taylboys. The first floor, formerly a "dark, damp vault," where the rector's cattle were housed at night, is now the drawing-room, 27 feet by 15 feet. A spiral staircase, in the thickness of the wall, leads to the roof, from which there is an extensive view of the vale of the Raylees and Monk burns, and the country opposite. Below, by the side of the burn, may be seen the haugh where the villagers used to practice archery, for which the men of Redesdale were famous. Some of the rectors were men of considerable note. The Rev. C. Dodgson, afterwards Bishop of Ossory, held the living from 1762 to 1765. He was succeeded by the Rev. Louis Dutens (or Duchillon), A.M., F.R.S., Historiographer to the King, and Honorary Member of the French Academy of Belles Lettres. He was the author of *Discoveries of the Ancients Attributed to the Moderns*, and *Memoirs of a Traveller now in Retirement*, and for a time held some post in the Embassy at Turin. The appointment of a foreigner was not viewed with much favour by his parishioners, who professed not to understand a single word of his discourses. He overcame the prejudice aroused against him by a pleasant and cheerful manner, and by a good-humoured joke he played on the principal members of his congregation. He invited them by word of mouth to dine with him on a certain day, and he professed to be very surprised to see them all when at the hour appointed they assembled to a man. One of them very warmly appealed to himself if he had not in person invited them to dine with him. "Oh, yes!" returned the clerical humorist, "oh, yes! my very goot friend, I did invite you, and you, and you to my dine; but you all say, every one of you say, you no understand one word I speak. Oh, ho! very goot! when I preach you from my pulpit you no understand my speak, but when I invite you to my goot dine, you very well understand!" The lesson was not lost, and the parishioners were conciliated. On the death of Mr. Dutens, in 1812, the living was presented to Archdeacon Singleton, grandson of the celebrated antiquary, Captain Francis Grose, well-known to lovers of literature as the person to whom Sidney Smith addressed a series of letters on the Ecclesiastical Commission. Cold Elsdon, as it is popularly called, has been made the subject of some good-humoured disparagement, and the visitor will read with amusement the impressions of the Rev. C. Dodgson and the Hexham poet, George Chatt, regarding the village and its inhabitants. "I am obliged," writes the former, "to be my own surgeon, apothecary, and physician, for there is not a creature of that profession within sixteen miles of this place. 'Tis impossible to describe the oddity of my situation at present, which, however, is not void of some pleasant circumstances. A clog-maker combs out my wig upon my curate's head by way of a block, and his wife powders it with a dredging-box. The vestibule of the castle is a low stable, and above it is the kitchen, in which there are two little beds joining to each other. The curate and his wife lay in one, and Margery, the maid, in the other. I lay in the parlour, between two beds, to keep me from being frozen to death, for, as we keep open house, the winds enter from every quarter, and are apt to creep into bed to one."

In another letter he goes on to say:—"Elsdon was once a market town, as some say, and a city according to others; but as the annals of the parish were lost several centuries ago, 'tis impossible to determine in what age it was either the one or the other. There are not the least traces of its former grandeur to be found, whence some antiquarians are apt to believe that it lost both its trade and character at the Deluge. Most certain it is, that the oldest man in the parish never saw a market here in his life. Modern Elsdon is a very small village, consisting of a tower, which the inhabitants call a castle, an inn for the refreshment of Scotch carriers, five little farm-houses, and a few wretched cottages, about ten in all, inhabited by poor people who receive the parish allowance, and superannuated shepherds. These buildings, such as they are, may be conceived to stand at very unequal distances from one another, in the circumference of an imaginary oval, the longer axis of which coincides with the meridian line, and is about 200 yards long; the shorter may be perhaps 100. In the centre of this supposed ellipse stands the church, which is very small, without either a tower or a spire; however, the west end is not totally void of ornamental superstructure. An Elsdonic kind of cupola forms a proper place for a belfry, and the only bell in it is almost as loud as that which calls the labourers to dinner at Sion. It may be heard at the castle when the wind is favourable. The situation of the village is such that, in descending a hill called Gallalaw on the south, it gives a person an idea of a few cottages built in a boggy island, which is almost surrounded by three little brooks: on the north by Dunsheeles Burn, on the east by Elsdon Burn, on the west and south-west by Whiskershiels Burn; the first runs into the second on the north-east part of the town, the second into the third on the south. There is not a town in all the parish, except Elsdon itself be called one; the farm-houses, where the principal families live, are five or six miles distant from one another, and the whole country looks like a desert. The greater part of the richest farmers are Scotch Dissenters, and go to a meeting-house at Birdhope Crag, about ten miles from Elsdon; however, they don't interfere in ecclesiastical matters or study polemical divinity. Their religion descends from father to son, and is rather a part of the personal estate than the result of reasoning, or the effect of enthusiasm. Those who live near Elsdon come to the church; those at a greater distance towards the west go to the meeting-house at Birdhope Crag; others, both Churchmen and Presbyterians, at a very great distance, go to the nearest church or conventicle in the neighbouring parish. There is a very good understanding between the parties, for they not only intermarry with each other, but frequently do penance together in a white sheet, with a white wand, barefoot, in one of the coldest churches in England, and at the coldest seasons of the year. I dare not finish the description for fear of bringing on a fit of the ague; indeed, the ideas of sensation are sufficient to starve a man to death, without having recourse to those of reflection. If I was not assured by the best authority upon earth that the world was to be destroyed by fire, I should conclude that the day of destruction is at hand, but brought on by means of an agent very opposite to that of heat. There is not a single tree or hedge-row within twelve miles to break the force of the wind; it sweeps down like a deluge from hills capped with everlasting snow, and blasts almost the whole country into one continued barren desert. The whole country is doing penance in a white sheet, for it began to snow on Sunday night, and the storm has continued ever since. It is impossible to make a sally out of the castle to make my quarters good in a warmer habitation; I have lost the use of everything but my reason, though my head is entrenched in three nightcaps, and my throat is fortified with a pair of stockings twisted in the form of a cravat. As washing is very cheap, I wear two shirts at a time; and, for want of a wardrobe, hang my greatcoat upon my own back. There is to be a hopping on Thursday se'nnight—that is a ball, the constant conclusion of a pedlars' fair. Upon these celebrities there is a great concourse of braw lads and lassies, who throw off their wooden shoes shod with plates of iron, and put on Scotch nickevers, which are made of horse leather, the upper part of which is sewed to the sole without being welted. The inhabitants are fond of a pastoral life, but have no taste for agriculture. The enclosed lands are only separated by a dry ditch and a low bank of earth. The sheep, as Milton says, at one bound would overleap all bounds. Quicksetts would grow, but the people are enemies to hedges, because the sheep would be entangled in them. The manner in which a herd (shepherd) lives upon the moors, especially in winter, would draw tears from your eyes when described in the most simple manner."

Chatt's poetical objurgation, "At Elsdon," is written in the same serio-comic vein :—

"Hae ye ivver been at Elsdon ?—
The world's unfinish'd neuk ;
It stands amang the hungry hills,
An' wears a frozen leuk.
The Elsdon folks like diein' stegs
At ivvery stranger stare ;
An' hather broth an' curlew eggs
Ye'll get for supper there.

Yen neet aw cam tiv Elsdon,
Sair tired efter dark ;
Aw'd travell'd mony a leynsome meyle
Wet through the varra sark.
Maw legs were warkin' fit ta brik,
An' empty was me kite,
But nowther love nor money could
Get owther bed or bite.

At ivvery hoose iv Elsdon
Aw teld me desperate need,
But nivver a corner had the churls
Where aw might lay me heed ;
Sae at the public-hoose aw boos'd
Till aw was sent away ;
Then tiv a steyble-loft aw crept,
An' coil'd amang the hay.

Should the Frenchers land iv England,
Just gie them Elsdon fare ;
By George ! they'll sharply hook it back,
An' nivver cum ne mair.
For a hungry hole like Elsdon,
Aw nivver yit did see ;
An' if aw gan back tiv Elsdon,
'The de'il may carry me.'"

The visitor who has fixed his quarters at the old-fashioned Crown Inn (dated 1729) will scarcely complain of Elsdon fare, nor will the prospect displease him when in summer the heather is in bloom and the trees between the castle and the Mote Hills are in leaf, or when in autumn the hills seem etherealised by the delicate rime that rests so lightly upon every blade and twig, and their gently-curving outlines appear so wonderfully distinct in the bright and limpid air. Elsdon is twelve miles south-west from Rothbury, twenty-nine miles north-west from Newcastle, and seven miles from Knowesgate station.

Three miles north of Elsdon, at a place called the *Raw*, are the remains of *Haws Pele*, the scene of a tragedy that caused more than the usual amount of excitement in the district. In 1791 there lived here an old woman named Margaret Crozier, who kept a small shop for the sale of drapery and other goods. Believing her to be rich, one William Winter, a desperate character, but recently returned from transportation, at the instigation and with the assistance of two female faws (vendors of crockery and tinwork) named Jane and Eleanor Clark, who, in their wanderings, had experienced the kindness of Margaret Crozier, broke into the lonely pele on the 29th of August 1791, and cruelly murdered the poor old woman, loading the ass they had brought with her goods. The day before the murder they had rested and dined in a sheepfold on Whiskershields Common, which overlooked the Raw, and it was from a description given of them by a shepherd boy, who had seen them and taken particular notice of the number and character of the nails in Winter's shoes, and also the peculiar gulley or butcher's knife with which he divided the food, that they were brought to justice. All of them were condemned and hanged at the Westgate, Newcastle. Winter's father and brother had in a former year been hanged at Morpeth. Winter's body was afterwards hung in chains, within sight of his victim's abode, at the Steng Cross (an ancient boundary-stone), near Harwood Head, two miles south-east from Elsdon, by the side of the road leading to Scots Gap. Long after the ghastly object had fallen piecemeal from the projecting arm of the gibbet, "Winter's Stob," as it was called, continued to be regarded by the rustics with superstitious awe.

According to the Rev. J. F. Bigge, toothache was formerly believed to be cured by rubbing the teeth with chips from the famous gibbet; and he states that pilgrimages used to be made from Stamfordham (and no doubt from other places as well) to this uncanny spot for pieces of the magic wood. The present gibbet, with the wooden head suspended from it, that meets the gaze of the traveller on this lonely moorland road, is of comparatively recent erection, standing, however, on the exact site of the old one.

An interesting excursion may be made from Elsdon to *Darden Lough* and the *Keyheugh*. After following the road past the Mote Hills to the top of the ascent, the visitor is not advised to take a short cut to the top of Darden Pike, as some rather difficult slacks have to be crossed. He should rather continue on to Billsmoor Park, and ask permission of the gamekeeper to ascend the hill from that point. An outcrop of a great Whinstone Dyke (Dolerite) will be noticed on the way. On reaching the summit, 1264 feet above the sea-level, a magnificent view of the scenery between Elsdon and Rothbury will be obtained. A number of old peles can be easily made out on the hill-side opposite, south of the bold and rugged hill called the Beacon. One of these is Haws Peel, where Margaret Crozier was murdered. The advantages of a position like Darden Pike as a post of observation are apparent; and the remains of an old watch-tower, seventeen feet in diameter, testify to the judgment of the ancient inhabitants. A similar one exists on Darden Rigg. Darden Lough, just below in the hollow formed by the two highest ridges of the moor, accounts for the derivation of the word Darden, from the British *dwr* or *dur*, water, and *dun*, a hill. In the dark, peat-stained waters of this lough, the roots and trunks of primeval birch trees may sometimes be descried. Leeches used to be caught here. In wandering round the lough it is necessary to be careful, as the soil, undermined by the water for some yards from the edge, has slipped a little towards the lough, thus forming large and deep cracks, which are sometimes concealed by heather, and liable to be passed unnoticed until the unwary traveller finds a leg suddenly disappearing. Half-a-mile to the east is another lough, somewhat smaller in size. Proceeding northwards, the tourist will come to a wild and picturesque ravine, strewn with enormous fragments of rock, and traversed by a moorland burn that in its rugged channel forms little cascades and pools of wine-coloured water. It is accompanied on its way by a long procession of birch trees, that lend a delightful sylvan charm to the harsh and sterile landscape. At the mouth of the cleugh is a romantic precipice of freestone rock, called the "Keyheugh" (Saxon: *Caeg*, a keyed or blocked place; and *how*, or *heugh*, a steep and rugged hill), referred to by the Redewater minstrel as a spot "where croaking corbies dwell." It is about sixty feet high, with huge fragments of rock at its base, fantastically arranged in the wildest confusion by the tremendous power of glacial action. At a little distance from the main precipice is the "Wishing Well," into which the young people of the district used to drop a pin, breathing at the same time the desire of their hearts, little thinking, perhaps, that they were observing a custom derived from Pagan times, when offerings were made to the deities presiding over fountains and springs. Cloven Crag, another local landmark, is about half-a-mile distant. From the Keyheugh a path above the burn leads to Midgy Hall, where the Grasslees Burn may be crossed, and the road regained. Should the tourist be going to Rothbury or Holystone, he will find a pleasant path leading through a plantation past *Whitefield House*, the residence of T. B. Riddell, Esq., J.P., to Swindon. If returning to Elsdon, he may extend his ramble by following the Keenshaw Burn for a mile or so; then strike across Elsdon Common to the old peles already referred to; and then proceed past Laingshill and High Carrick farm-houses, following the Monk Burn to the village. Fallowlees Lough and Chartner's Lough, where the rare *Nuphar minima*, least water-lily, is to be found, lie about six miles east of Elsdon, and may be visited from this point.

A mile and a half south-west of Elsdon is *Raylees*, where there may be seen a small Roman camp. Three miles, again, south-west of Raylees, on the way to Woodburn, is *Corsenside*, the church of which (*St. Cuthbert's*) contains a remnant of Norman times in the chancel arch (*cir.* 1100). A grave-cover forms the lower step of the doorway from the south porch, and another of rich design lies in the walk up to the porch. Close to the church is an interesting seventeenth-century farm-house.

# ELSDON TO OTTERBURN AND CARTER FELL.

Otterburn, 3 miles ; Elishaw, 5¼ miles ; Horsley, 7 miles ; High Rochester, 8½ miles ; Birdhope Crag, 8½ miles ; Bryness, 21¾ miles; Catcleugh, 14 miles ; Ramshope, 15½ miles ; Whitelee, 16½ miles ; Reidswire, 18½ miles.

TWO miles west is *Overacres*, a farm-house built on the site of an old mansion of the Howards, Lords of Redesdale. The only relics of its former greatness are the two piers of a gateway bearing the family arms, the date 1720, and a few ornamental carvings. Half-a-mile south-west is *Monkridge Hall*, an old seat of the De Lisles, now a farm-house. Half-a-mile to the north is Colwell Hill, where the remains of an extensive British camp are to be seen. It consists of two earthen ramparts, about eight feet high, protected by two ditches seven or eight feet deep. There are also faint traces of a hut-circle, fifteen feet in diameter. The situation is well chosen, on account of the wide view it commands. Half-a-mile west, on a lower height called Fawdon Hill, is another camp, believed by some antiquaries to be that occupied by the Scots on the evening previous to the battle of Otterburn. It is in shape an irregular circle of eighty yards, with one rampart varying from six to twelve feet in height. Just below the hill, on the east side of the Otter, is the farm-house of Girsonfield, in which are incorporated portions of the walls of a still older steading, the residence of the "fause-hearted Ha's" (Halls), who betrayed Percy, or Parcy (Percival), Reed, of Troughend, a keeper of Redesdale, to a band of moss-troopers of the name of Crozier, who slew him at Batinghope, near the sources of the Rede-water, as is graphically told in the old ballad.

A mile south-west is OTTERBURN, a small clean village, with good substantial houses and a comfortable inn, the Murray Arms, well-known to tourists. The banks of the Otter, from which the place derives its name, are luxuriantly studded with trees.

> " The Otterbourne's a bonnie burn,
> 'Tis pleasant there to be."

The *Church*, built after designs by Dobson, and dedicated to *St. John the Baptist*, was opened in 1857. It is a handsome stone building in the Decorated style, and contains some fine memorial windows. In the font is a carved stone brought from Hexham Abbey. There is a mill below the village for the weaving of woollen fabrics.

*Otterburn Tower* is a handsome modern structure, built by the late owner, Thomas James, Esq. The ground in front is prettily laid out in terraces. A small portion of the old pele-tower about the dining-room and library was incorporated in the present structure. The old Border stronghold was of great strength, for, according to Froissart, the Scots, in 1388, just before the battle of Otterburn, "attacked it so long and so unsuccessfully that they were fatigued, and therefore sounded a retreat." At the beginning of the fifteenth century it was in the possession of Sir Robert Umfreville. Not a century later it had passed into the hands of the Halls, once the most powerful among the clans of Redesdale.

One member of this family, who, on account of his eccentric humours and dissipated habits, was called "Mad Jack Ha'," was "out" with the Earl of Derwentwater in 1715, and taken prisoner at Preston. In his defence he alleged that while returning home from a Justices' meeting at Plainfield one tempestuous day he was surrounded by the rebels and compelled to accompany them. To all this his servant swore; but the Court, in directing the jury, said, "that if a man was seen with rebels, yet if it appeared that he had frequent opportunities of escaping, and did not do it, but continued by his presence to abet and comfort them, it was treason within the meaning of the law." When sentenced to die as a traitor he said, "God's will be done!" Reprieved five times, he was at last executed at Tyburn, and his estates were forfeited to the Crown. Readers ot Harrison Ainsworth's *Preston Fight* will remember the part this wild, reckless character plays in the novel. In the porch of the mansion are three Roman altars, brought from the station of Rutchester (Vindobala). One of them, elegantly carved, and bearing the representation of a man holding a bull by the horns, is believed to have been erected to Mithras, the Persian Sun God. There formerly stood on the haugh, between the village and the Rede, a huge cairn. It was removed in 1729, and after about sixty tons of stone had been carted away, a rude grave was discovered, containing charcoal and burnt bones.

One mile below the village, at Meadow Haugh, on the right bank of the Redewater, is the *Silvernut Well*, a sulphur spring, which here bubbles to the surface, and has, from a period of unknown antiquity, brought up, from a stratum lying below, hazel nuts slightly coated with sulphuret of iron. In the little wooded ravine which is traversed by the Otter the following wild flowers may be gathered:—Giant bell-flower (*Campanula latifolia*), yellow loose-strife (*Lysimachia vulgaris*), sea canary grass (*Phalaris arenaria*), hairy carex (*Carex hirta*), bearded wheat-grass (*Triticum caninum*), wood cranesbill (*Geranium sylvaticum*), wood betony (*Stachys Betonica*), great burnet (*Sanguisorba officinalis*), perennial mercury (*Mercurialis perennis*), water avens (*Geum rivale*), meadow-sweet (*Spiræa ulmaria*), square St. John's wort (*Hypericum quadrangulum*), marsh hawk's beard (*Crepis succisæfolia*), great wild valerian (*Valeriana officinalis*), and dog-roses, red white. The melancholy plume thistle (*Carduus heterophyllus*) is also very prevalent. *Trollius Europæus*, the globe flower, gilds the meadows in spring. Vipers are frequently killed on the moors. Otterburn is thirty miles from Newcastle, the road, before reaching the village, crossing a bleak and high fell called Ottercaps. The nearest railway station is Woodburn, five miles distant.

The battle which has made Otterburn so famous was fought August 19th, 1388, and is memorable as having taken place by moonlight. There is some dispute as to whether the site of the battle-field should be placed on the east or west side of the Otter. It is popularly believed to have been that benty upland which extends from the Fawdoun Hills for two miles westward to a ridge that runs down to the present public road through the valley of the Rede. The local name, Battle Croft, or Battle Riggs, commemorates the famous fight. The details of this hotly-contested conflict have been given by Froissart, the celebrated French writer, who obtained them from eye-witnesses of the engagement. Taking advantage of the distracted state of England, through the weak government of Richard II., James, Earl of Douglas, with an army of about four thousand picked men, entered England, and passing rapidly and secretly through Northumberland, penetrated as far into the county of Durham as Brancepeth, where they commenced their work of devastation, burning and plundering every place on their route. In returning they lay three days before the walls of Newcastle, which were defended by Sir Henry and Sir Ralph Percy, sons of the Duke of Northumberland. During one of the skirmishes which took place at the barriers, or wooden fortifications of grated upright palisades erected before the New Gate, Sir Henry Percy (the celebrated Hotspur) having challenged Douglas to single combat, was unhorsed by his adversary, and lost his spear and the silken pennon attached to it. The Scottish leader, waving the trophy aloft, exclaimed, "I will carry this token of your prowess with me to Scotland, and place it on the tower of my castle at Dalkeith, that it may be seen afar." "By God! Earl of Douglas," replied Sir Henry, "you shall not even bear it out of Northumberland; be assured you shall never have this pennon to brag of." With a taunting remark to come and seek it before the door of his tent, Douglas retired. Early the next morning the Scotch struck their camp and marched to Ponteland, which they burnt, after capturing and firing the castle. They then proceeded to Otterburn, and, marching a mile and a half up the valley, halted upon the eminence north-west of Holt-wood, above Greenchesters, where they made huts of trees and branches, and strongly fortified themselves. The nucleus of these defences was a British camp, of which considerable traces remain. They placed their baggage and servants at the entrance of the camp, which was partly concealed by trees, and the cattle they drove into the marsh lands bordering on the Rede. From their strategical position they had not only a good view up Redesdale, but also an open prospect to the south-east, the direction from which they would expect the approach of the English. The next day they assaulted the castle, but without success. In the meantime, Sir Henry Percy, eager to make good his threat, set out from Newcastle with 600 spearmen and 8000 infantry, arriving at night, when many of the Scots, who had laboured hard at the assault of the castle, were asleep, and others at supper. With that impulsiveness that gained for him the name of Hotspur, he at once decided to attack the enemy, though his men were weary with the long march. Raising the cry of "Percy! Percy!" the English broke into the camp, but, in mistake, directed their attacks against the quarters appropriated to the servants and camp-followers, thus affording time to the Scottish regular troops, who were acquainted with the ground and had settled their plans beforehand, to skirt the hill-side and fall upon their flank, returning the compliment of a surprise. The battle now commenced in right good earnest, amid the cries of "Douglas!" and "Percy!" which rang forth on every side, while the bright August moon shone on the dreadful scene of carnage. The Scots were vastly over-numbered, but were more fresh and vigorous, and, further, were better acquainted with the ground, "Cowardice," says Froissart, "was unknown, and the most splendid courage was everywhere exhibited by the gallant youths of England and Scotland; they were so closely intermixed that the archer's bows were useless, and they fought hand-to-hand, without either battalion giving way." Victory at first seemed to incline to the English, Douglas, seeing his men repulsed, seized a battle-axe with both his hands, and, to rally his men, dashed into the midst of his enemies, dealing blows around him with terrific force, till at last he was pierced by three spears, and borne to the ground, mortally wounded. When his friends reached him, they found him dying, with Sir Robert Hart, a valiant knight who had fought by him the whole day, lying by his side, covered with fifteen wounds, and his faithful chaplain, William de Norbenich, shielding him with a battle-axe. "Cousin, how fares it with you?" said Sir John Sinclair. "But so, so," replied he. "Thanks to God, there are but few of my ancestors who have died in their beds. I bid you, therefore, avenge my death; raise up my banner, and continue to shout 'Douglas!'; but do not tell friend or foe whether I am in your company or not; for should the enemy know the truth, they will be greatly rejoiced." Meanwhile, Sir Ralph Percy, like Douglas, had advanced too far into the ranks of the enemy and, being surrounded and severely wounded, had been forced to surrender to Sir J. Maxwell, a Scottish knight. The fact of Douglas's death was prudently kept back from his followers, who would else have been dispirited. The Sinclairs and Sir John Lindsay, obeying their dying leader's commands, raised his banner, and shouting the battle-cry of "Douglas!" soon gathered a compact body of their men together, who pushed their lances with so much courage that the English were repulsed, and, being reinforced by the Earls of Moray and March, renewed the battle with greater vigour than before. Sir Henry Percy was made a prisoner by Sir Hugh Montgomery, and a complete rout ensued, the fugitives being followed five miles from the scene of battle. 1040 English were taken or left dead upon the field, 1840 in the pursuit, and more than 1000 wounded. On the side of the Scots there were only 100 slain and 200 prisoners. The Bishop of Durham, who with 7000 men was advancing to the assistance of Sir Ralph and Sir Henry Percy, was met about a league from Newcastle by some of the fugitives, and informed of the disastrous fight. His army was so panic-stricken by the news that the Bishop could not retain 500 of his men together, and was obliged to return to Newcastle. He forthwith made an indignant appeal to the patriotism of the knights and squires of the neighbourhood, with the result that next morning, at sunrise, he had 10,000 men under his command. With this new army he set out once more in the direction of Otterburn. When about a league from the Scottish camp, the enemy, apprised by their scouts of his approach, began to play such a concert upon the horns, which each man slung round his neck, after the manner of hunters, "that it seemed as if all the devils in hell had come thither to join in the noise, so that those of the English who had never before heard such were very much frightened." The Bishop, however, advanced to within two bow-shots of the enemy, and observing how well they had chosen and fortified their encampment, decided not to risk an engagement, and so led back his hastily-gathered and undisciplined troops to Newcastle. The Scots then retired over the Border to Melrose, bearing with them the bodies of the Earl of Douglas, Sir Robert Hart, and Sir Simeon Glendinning, which were buried in Melrose Abbey, the banner of Douglas being suspended over his grave. Hotspur, as the price of his ransom, built the Castle of Penoon for his captor, Lord Montgomery. Sir Ralph Percy and other English knights were allowed to remain in Northumberland till they were cured of their wounds, on condition that, when able to endure the fatigues of the journey, they should surrender themselves in Scotland, or else remit the amount of their ransoms.

It is not so much historically that the battle of Otterburn is memorable as poetically. The deadly conflict would have been as little remembered as the siege of Troy would, had not the immortality of song been conferred upon it. Two ballads, the one Scotch, the other English, give their respective versions of the event, with those natural discrepancies between the two, which may easily be accounted for on patriotic grounds. The Scotch ballad, given in Sir Walter Scott's works, is undoubtedly the finer. It runs as follows :—

It fell about the Lammas tide,
   When the muir-men win their hay,
The doughty Douglas bound him to ride
   Into England to drive a prey.

He chose the Gordons and the Graemes,
   With them the Lindsayes, light and gay;
But the Jardines wald not with them ride,
   And they rue it to this day.

And he has burned the dales of Tyne,
   And part of Bambroughshire,
And three good towers on Reidswire fells
   He left them all on fire.

And he marched up to Newcastle,
And rode it round about;
"O wha's the lord of this castle?
Or wha's the lady o't?"

But up spake proud Lord Percy then,
And O but he spake hie!
"I am the lord of this castle,
My wife's the lady gay."

"If thou art the lord of this castle,
Sae weel it pleases me!
For ere I cross the Border fells
The tane of us sall die."

He took a lang spear in his hand,
Shod with the metal free,
And for to meet the Douglas there
He rode right furiouslie.

But O how pale his lady looked,
Frae off the castle wa',
When down before the Scottish spear
She saw proud Percy fa'!

"Had we twa been upon the green,
And never an eye to see,
I wad ha' had you, flesh and fell,
But your sword shall gae wi' me.

"But gae ye up to Otterbourne
And wait there dayis three;
And if I come not ere three dayis end,
A fause knight ca' ye me."

"The Otterbourne's a bonnie burn,
'Tis pleasant there to be;
But there is naught at Otterbourne
To feed my men and me.

"The deer rins wild on hill and dale,
The birds fly wild from tree to tree;
But there is neither bread nor kale
To fend my men and me.

"Yet I will stay at Otterbourne,
Where you sall welcome be;
And if ye come not at three dayis end,
A fause lord I'll call thee."

"Thither will I come," proud Percy said,
"By the might of Our Ladye!"
"There will I bide thee" said the Douglas,
"My troth I plight to thee."

They lighted high on Otterbourne,
Upon the bent sae brown;
They lighted high on Otterbourne,
And threw their pallions down.

And he that had a bonnie boy,
  Sent out his horse to grass;
And he that had not a bonnie boy,
  His ain servant he was.

But up then spake a little page,
  Before the peep of dawn—
"O waken ye, waken ye, my good lord,
  For Percy's hard at hand!"

"Ye lie, ye lie, ye liar loud!
  Sae loud, I hear ye lie;
For Percy had not men yestreen
  To dight my men and me.

"But I hae dreamed a dreary dream,
  Beyond the Isle of Skye;
I saw a dead man win a fight,
  And I think that man was I."

He belted on his gude braid sword,
  And to the field he ran;
But he forgot his helmet good,
  That should have kept his brain.

When Percy wi' the Douglas met,
  I wat he was fu' fain;
They swakked their swords till sair they swat,
  And the blude ran down like rain.

But Percy with his gude braid sword,
  That could so sharply wound,
Has wounded Douglas on the brow,
  Till he fell to the ground.

Then he called on his little foot-page,
  And said, "Run speedilie,
And fetch my ain dear sister's son,
  Sir Hugh Montgomery.

"My nephew good," the Douglas said,
  "What recks the death of ane?
Last night I dreamed a dreary dream,
  And I ken the day's thy ain.

"My wound is deep, I fain would sleep;
  Take thou the vanguard of the three,
And hide me by the braken bush
  That grows on yonder lilye lee.

"O bury me by the braken bush,
  Beneath the blooming brier;
Let never living mortal ken
  That ere a kindly Scot lies here."

He lifted up that noble lord,
  Wi' the saut tear in his e'e;
He hid him in the braken bush,
  That his merrie men might not see.

The moon was clear, the day drew near,
The spears in flinders flew,.
But mony a gallant Englishman
Ere day the Scotsmen slew.

The Gordons good, in English blood,
They steeped their hose and shoon;
The Lyndsayes flew like fire about,
Till all the fray was done.

The Percy and Montgomery met,
That either of other were fain;
They swappèd swords, and they twa swat,
And aye the blude ran down between.

"Now, yield thee, yield thee, Percy!" he said
"Or else I vow I'll lay thee low!"
"Whom to sall I yield?" quoth Earl Percy,
"Now that I see it must be so?"

"Thou sall't not yield to lord or loon,
Nor yet sall't thou yield to me;
But yield thee to the braken bush,
That grows upon yon lilye lee."

"I will not yield to a braken bush,
Nor yet will I yield to a brier:
But I would yield to Earl Douglas,
Or Sir Hugh Montgomery, if he were here."

As soon as he knew it was Montgomery,
He struck his sword's point in the gronde;
The Montgomery was a courteous knight,
And quickly took him by the honde.

This deed was done at the Otterbourne,
About the breaking of the day;
Earl Douglas was buried at the braken bush,
And the Percy led captive away.

The ancient ballad of Chevy Chase was founded on this battle, as is evident from a verse near the close—

"This was the hontynge off the Cheviat;
That tear begane this spurne;
Old men that knowen the grounde well yenoughe,
Call it the Battell of Otterburne."

The spot where it is said Earl Douglas fell is marked by a pointed pillar about twenty feet in height, raised on a circular pedestal of rough masonry, four or five feet from the ground. It rests on the socket of the original "Battle-stone," which, however, stood about one hundred and eighty paces north-east from the present cross. Standing at that distance, on the precise spot, a visitor to the battle-field has the modern cross on the line between him and the farm-house of Garretshiels. "Percy's Cross," as it is inappropriately called, is situated in a small plantation of firs near the road-side, about three-quarters of a mile from the village. In the chinks of the stone, at its base, grows the ivy-leaved toad-flax (*Linaria cymbalaria*), or mother of thousands—

> "The crevice flowers
> That sprinkle beauty o'er decay."

Two miles south-west of Otterburn, by the nearest road, is *Troughend Hall*, standing in a grove of trees, adjoining the Watling Street. It was built by Elrington Reed, who died in 1758. The old Tower of Troughend stood a little to the west of the present house, and its foundations, of very strong masonry, though overgrown with grass, are still traceable. At Troughend are some of the largest and oldest elm trees of the district. In a field to the north of the hall is an outburst of dolerite, called the Troughend Dyke.

Troughend was long the seat of the ancient family of Reed, which, in 1542, was reckoned the second clan of the dale in power and reputation. John Reed, "the Laird of Troughwen, the chief of the name of Reed, and divers of his followers," are referred to in an old report of the time as "a ruder and more lawless crew there needs not be; yet, if well tutored, they might do her majestie good service; but their practices are not to be defended." Something of the same unruly spirit seems to have characterised a later proprietor of Troughend, the celebrated Percival, or Percy Reed, for it is recorded against him that, failing to persuade the parson of Elsdon to remit the performance of a penance enjoined him, "he did break forth into violent and outrageous terms to and against the said Mr. Marrowe, and told him, 'He cared for never a priest of them all.' And at another time, upon the like occasion, unto the said Mr. Marrowe, the said Perceval Reed, in a disgraceful manner, did call him, 'Base priest and stinking castrel,' and did pull the said Mr. Marrowe by the beard, and uttered divers other reproachful words against the said Mr. Marrowe." He was condemned to make public acknowledgment of this offence in Elsdon Church, and to pay certain fines; but on the day appointed he feigned illness, and sent his wife to make excuses for him. He was a keen huntsman, and owed much of his influence among the wild Borderers to his successes in the chase. One incident connected with his favourite pursuit has formed the subject of a beautiful picture by Cooper, which, in its turn, suggested a touching poem by Sir Walter Scott—viz., the death of his favourite dog, Kieldar, accidentally killed by an arrow which he had discharged at a deer :—

> "And to his last stout Percy rued
> This fatal chance, for when he stood
> 'Gainst fearful odds in deadly feud,
> And fell amid the fray,
> E'en with his dying voice he cried,
> 'Had Kieldar but been by my side,
> Your treacherous ambush had been spied,
> I had not died to-day.' "

The important office of Keeper of Redesdale, held under the Warden of the Middle Marches, was conferred upon him; but the honour brought its peril, for in the exercise of his authority he came into collision with the lawless spirits of the district, who, in consequence, regarded him with no friendly feelings. The Halls of Girsonfield, and a band of moss-troopers, called Crozier, some of whom he had brought to justice, were especially incensed, and vowed to be revenged as soon as a favourable opportunity should present itself. Concealing their resentment, the Halls kept up the most friendly relations with their unsuspecting neighbour, all the time planning how to bring about his destruction. At last their arrangements were complete, and they invited him to join them in a day's hunting into Upper Redesdale. He unfortunately consented, and in spite of the fact of a loaf of bread being brought in with the bottom upward—still considered an unlucky omen throughout the North of England—and the warnings of his wife, who had had strange dreams the night before, he set out on his ill-fated journey:—

"'To the hunting ho!' cried Parcy Reed,
 And to the hunting he has gane,
And the three fause Ha's o' Girsonfield
 Alang wi' him he has them ta'en.

They hunted high, they hunted low,
 By heathery hill and birken shaw;
They raised a buck on Rooken-edge,
 And blew the mort at fair Ealyhawe.

They hunted high, they hunted low,
 They made the echoes ring amain;
Wi' music sweet o' horn and hound,
 They merry made fair Redesdale glen.

They hunted high in Batinghope,*
 When as the sun was sinking low,
Says Parcy then, 'Ca' off the dogs,
 We'll bait our steeds and homeward go.'

They lighted high in Batinghope,
 Atween the brown and benty ground;
They had but rested a little while,
 Till Parcy Reed was sleeping sound.

There's nane may lean on a rotten staff,
 But him that risks to get a fa';
There nane may in a traitor trust,
 And traitors black were every Ha'.

They've stown the bridle off his steed,
 And they've put water in his lang gun;
They've fixed his sword within the sheath,
 That out again it winna come.

* Batinghope is a lonely glen stretching westward from the Whitelee, whose little stream forms one of the chief sources of the Redewater.

'Awaken ye, waken ye, Parcy Reed,
Or by your enemies be ta'en;
For yonder are the five Croziers
A-coming owre the Hingin' stane.'

'If they be five, and we be four,
Sae that ye stand alang wi' me,
Then every man ye will take one,
And only leave but two to me;
We will them meet as brave men ought,
And make them either fight or flee.'

'We mayna stand, we canna stand,
We daurna stand alang wi' thee;
The Croziers haud thee at a feud,
And they wad kill baith thee and we.'"

The traitors abandon him to his fate, and the Croziers, riding up, salute their victim in the following words:—

"'Weel met, weel met, now Parcy Reed,
Thou art the very man we sought;
Owre lang hae we been in your debt,
Now will we pay thee as we ought.'"

They at once fell on the unarmed man, who, after feebly defending himself with the sheathed sword, sank, pierced with four wounds. The miscreants then stuck their daggers into his prostrate body, lopped off his hands, and left him with thirty-three wounds. When the dastardly deed became known, such was the abhorrence and contempt manifested towards the "fause-hearted Halls," as the three brothers were called, that they found it necessary to leave the district. The ghost of Percy Reed, it is averred, clad in his green hunting-dress, with his horn by his side and his gun over his shoulder, was long accustomed to revisit the glen of Batinghope, and flit along the banks of the Rede, between Todlawhaugh and Pringlehaugh.

"Oft by the Pringle's haunted side
The shepherd saw the spectre glide."

One of its favourite haunts was Todlaw Mill, and many persons going to the Presbyterian meeting-house at Birdhope Crag imagined they beheld the spirit of "the Laird of Troughend," in the form of a dove, perch upon a stone in the middle of the Rede, at Pringlehaugh; and if they made a bow or curtsy towards it by way of compliment, it very graciously returned the compliment. Once, however, a thatcher, on a roof at Wool-law, near Rochester, found courage to speak to the ghost, when he felt something like the wing of a bird whisk past his cheek, whereupon he came down the ladder, was seized with a cold shivering, and died through fright.

Two miles from Otterburn, past the "Percy Cross" and Shittleheugh Peel Tower, is *Elishaw*, a farmstead, that once was a village of some importance. Here, in mediæval times, there was a hospital, founded by one of the Umfravilles as a place of refuge and entertainment to travellers crossing the wilds of Redesdale, where inns were unknown. Many a scene of revelry and carousal used to be witnessed here, for Elishaw was a famous resort of faws, tinkers, and pedlars, and here they held their rustic races and merry gatherings. The eccentricities and doings of Wull Allan, the fisher and otter-hunter, Jamie Allan, the Northumbrian piper, and the hospitable Lord Cranstoun, of convivial memory, are still talked about in the district.

Faint traces of the Roman bridge, by which the Watling Street was carried over the Rede, may still be observed to the west of the present bridge. The haugh behind Elishaw, says Mr. Hardy, is the recipient of the floating rubbish that the Rede carries off from the upper country during floods. Hence it is said, when anything is amissing in that district, "You'll find it in the haugh anunder Elishaw."

A local proverb, "The lang gaunts o' Elishaw were heard 'm't coans o' Blakelaw," is now spoken of in deriding lovers' sighs, though it probably related in former times to some feud in which the people of Elishaw took terrible vengeance on the folks o' Blakelaw, a hill on the opposite side of the Durtree Burn.

A mile further on is HORSLEY, where there is a comfortable inn, the Redesdale Arms, a well-known house to anglers and sportsmen, who congregate here in large numbers during August and the following months. The *Church of the Holy Trinity*, standing close to a belt of firs, is an apse-ended building in the Lombardic style, and was erected as a chapel-of-ease in 1844.

To the westward is *Padon's*, or *Peden's*, *Pike*, so named from Mr. Alexander Peden (one of the most noted of the ousted Scotch ministers in the reign of Charles II.), who held conventicles on it among the wild Borderers. "The Rooken-Edge, sae wild and chill," towers a little to the north-west of it.

About a mile further up the vale is *Todlaw*, where, through a narrow cut in the rocky channel of the Rede, called the Todlaw Step, the confined waters rush impetuously.

A road branching off to the right leads to HIGH ROCHESTER, or *Bremenium*. This important station, which was designed to guard the mountain passes traversed by the Watling Street, covers an area of four acres and a half, and occupies a position of great strength, on account of the sloping character of the ground to the north, south, and west of it. Its weakest side, the east, was formerly, it is thought, defended by a marsh, which is now drained. To these natural defences an earthen rampart has been added, tripled on the south and east sides for still greater security. The camp was originally a large parallelogram rounded off at the corners, with a strong enclosing wall 14 feet in height and 17 feet in thickness, the outer portion built of large blocks of hewn freestone, the inner consisting of rubble-work. On the south and west sides there are sections of even more substantial masonry, being in the one case 20 feet, and in the other 28 feet thick. The wall, says Dr. Bruce, was probably increased in solidity at these places in order to give a base on which to plant the ballistæ and other engines of war. Several of the large rounded stones that were used for discharging at the enemy were found inside the camp. The western wall still stands upwards of nine feet above the foundation, and exhibits occasionally eight and even nine courses of facing-stones. In the thickness of the south wall two chambers have been found, entered from the inside of the station. That on the west side of the south gateway is in a good state of preservation. The masonry of the gateway is still, to a certain height, as perfect as when the Romans left. Extensive excavations were made in 1852 within the camp by the late Duke of Northumberland, and more recently by the Society of Antiquaries, but they have now been filled up again. The foundations of a large number of buildings were laid bare, and several interesting discoveries made. Elaborately-carved altars and tablets, coins, sculptured slabs, and fragments of statuary, testify to the high civilisation which must have been introduced into this desolate region. The arrangements for heating the buildings with hot air, draining the station, and supplying it with water were very elaborate, several hypocausts, conduits, and underground tanks having been discovered. The main streets varied in width from 10 to 14 feet, while the side streets were usually less than 3 feet wide. The station was garrisoned by the Varduli, who came from the north of Spain, and the Breuci, a people of Tannonia. Two pele-towers built of Roman masonry stand on the site of some of the camp buildings, forming links between the Roman era and our own. On the western side of the Sills Burn are the traces of three temporary Roman encampments, while on the opposite side of the river Rede, on the hill overlooking Birdhope, are extensive remains of an ancient British settlement. Half-a-mile across the heathery and grassy hill-side, on the west side of the Watling Street, a little to the south-east of the station, is a circular Roman tomb or cippus, believed to be the only example in England. It is ornamented in front with a small carving resembling the head of a fox, or perhaps of a goat. There were formerly three others, square in form, but they have been destroyed. The porch of the village school at Rochester is almost entirely built of stones from the neighbouring station, exhibiting the diamond broaching so characteristic of the Roman chisel. Here are also two of the rounded stones intended for "ballistæ." The bogs near Rochester are famous for cranberries. A mile up the valley is *Birdhope Crag*, a shooting-box of N. G. Clayton, Esq., on a rock covered with birch and fir trees. A stone built into the walls of the kennels bears the date 1682, and the letters M. H. A. M., probably the initials of some member of the Hall family who formerly owned the place. The old *Presbyterian Meeting-house* here, erected about the beginning of the last century, has many interesting associations, and was long the religious centre of the district. In the days of religious persecution the Covenanters used to hold their services in secluded spots among the hills. Lonely scaurs and rocks formed convenient meeting-places, and some of them are still called "kirks" to this day, as, for instance, Hool Kirk, Deadwood Kirk, Babswood Kirk, in the vicinity of Birdhope Crag, and Chattlehope Kirk, near Catcleugh.

The next hamlet is *Byrness* (probably a contraction of Buryness), four and a half miles distant from Birdhope Crag. According to Wallis, there formerly stood a Druid's circle here. The small chapel-of-ease at this place was built in an ancient burial-ground. A mile to the north-east is the "craggy Doure," a cluster of rocks on the grounds of Cottonshope. Doure Tarn is reached by a rocky staircase.

Two miles further on is *Catcleugh*. The old mansion of the Halls, who purchased Otterburn Tower after the attainder of "Mad Jack Ha'," has been converted into a farm-house, and is surrounded by some fine trees, particularly elms, which thrive well here. Three miles west, on the high moorland, is *Chattlehope Spout*, a waterfall 75 feet in height, but broken in its plunge by a projection of the rock. In summer it is often dry. In the rugged red sandstone cliffs above it the peregrine falcon used to breed, and the raven still makes its nest. Here it was that "Barty o' the Combe," and "Corbit Jack," who had been making a retaliatory raid across the Borders, were overtaken by two Scotch reivers. In the long heather above the waterfall the desperate encounter between them took place, which ended so fatally for three of the combatants. The farm-house of Chattlehope bears the date 1704, and is one of the oldest buildings in the district. The Ramshope Burn, which falls into the Rede through a deep gorge above Catcleugh, is celebrated for its jasper. The pebbles fall from the face of the crumbling rock into the stream below, and are sometimes beautifully polished by the action of the water. The colours are good—yellow, red, and a bluish white chalcedony, spotted with red—but the stone, although it takes a good polish, is much traversed by cracks. The scenery at the head of Redesdale is of a wild and monotonous character. Bleak and almost uninhabitable wastes stretch away from the bright green margin of the river, given up to the wild goats and hardy mountain sheep, the grouse, the moor-cocks, and birds of prey. At one time, to judge by the remains of birch, alder, and hazel-trees found in the peat mosses, they were covered by extensive forests, but now only a few stunted specimens remain to outbrave the mountain winds.

Four miles from Catcleugh, and thirteen miles and a half from Otterburn, is *Whitelee*, the last house in England on the road through Redesdale. On the stone-lintel over its front door is the appropriate inscription, "Pax sit huic domo intrantibus" (Peace to all that enter here), a welcome in striking contrast to the reception accorded to the "kindly Scots" a hundred years ago. The inn, which was a most convenient resting-place for travellers between Jedburgh and the lower parts of Redesdale to break their journey, has, unfortunately, been closed.

The men of Roxburghshire have long since given up the habit of sheep-lifting, yet they still occasionally make a poaching raid across the Border, sometimes in considerable numbers, and, as a consequence, come into collision with the water-bailiffs. A desperate affray took place one moonlight night in November 1886, near the Carter Bar, between a band of twenty-six poachers, armed with leisters, or salmon spears, and stable forks, and six representatives of the law, armed with truncheons and stout cudgels, when some hard blows and ugly wounds were given and taken. The poachers finally retreated, followed by the officers, who kept them in view by the light of the moon as far as Camptown, six miles from Jedburgh.

Two miles beyond Whitelee is *The Reidswire*, a neck of land from which the water falls one way into the valley of the Rede, and the other into Scotland. The highway runs over it. Being on the Border itself, it is not surprising that it should have been the scene of much bloodshed. Two Border skirmishes are recorded—one in 1400, when Sir Robert Umfraville gained a victory over the Scots, and the other in 1575, memorable as being the last encounter between the two nations previous to the Union. It began in this way:—The Wardens of the Marches on both sides of the Border were accustomed, it seems, to meet at stated times for the purpose of adjusting differences and settling disputes in an amicable way. On these occasions they handed over delinquents who had committed aggressions in the one territory or the other, and made pecuniary compensation for injuries done. Sir John Forster, the English Warden, and Sir J. Carmichael, the Keeper of Liddesdale, attended each by a party of armed followers, came together as usual at the Reidswire, and for some time the meeting proceeded peaceably. At length a dispute arose in respect of a notorious English freebooter named Farnstein, against whom a true bill of indictment had been found. Forster alleged that he had fled from justice. Carmichael considered this as a pretext to avoid paying compensation for the felony. Carmichael bade him "play fair," to which the haughty English Warden retorted with some insulting expressions respecting Carmichael's family. They also began to "fall into comparisons," each declaring that he did justice better than the other; whereupon the hot-tempered Tynedale men enforced their arguments with a flight of arrows. The origin of the dispute and its disastrous ending are well told in the excellent ballad, "The Raid of the Reidswire."

"Yett was our meeting meek eneugh
 Begun wi' merriment and mowes,
And at the brae aboon the heugh
 The clark sat down to call the rowes,*
 And some for kyne and some for ewes
Call'd in of Dandrie, Hob and Jock—
 We saw come marching ower the knowes
Five hundred Fenwicks in a flock.

* Rolls.

With jack and speir and bows all bent,
And warlike weapons at their will;
Although we were na weel content,
Yet, by my troth, we fear'd no ill.
Some gaed to drink, and some stude still,
And some to cards and dice them sped;
Till on ane Farnstein they fyled a bill,
And he was fugitive and fled.

Carmichael bade them speak out plainlie
And cloke no cause for ill or good;
The other answering him as vainlie
Began to reckon kin and blood;
He raise and raxed him* where he stood
And bade him match him with his marrows;
Then Tindaill heard them reasun rude,
And they loot off a flight of arrows."

With cries of "Comparisons! Comparisons! A Jedworth! A Tynedale!" the two parties rushed at each other, and a furious mêlée took place. On the English side, Sir George Heron, the Keeper of Redesdale and Tindale, with five other gentlemen of rank, were slain.

"Proud Wallington was wounded sair,
Albeit he be a Fenwick fierce;"

and Sir J. Forster, Sir J. Collingwood, Francis Russell, son of the Earl of Bedford, and others, were taken prisoners. On the Scottish side only one gentleman of rank was lost.

The English were chased three miles over the Border, and six hundred head of cattle were driven back into Scotland. The prisoners were taken to the Regent Morton, at Dalkeith, who detained them till their resentment had abated, and then dismissed them honourably for fear of irritating Queen Elizabeth, thus preventing a war between the two kingdoms.

It is very bleak on this lofty ridge, as may be inferred from the answer of an old carrier, who had been asked if he did not find it so: "Hoot, man, hoot; the very de'il himsel' wadna bide there half an hour unless he was tethered!"

The *Carter Fell*, from the Celtic *cart*, a height or hill, takes rank with Hedgehope and Simonside for the extent and magnificence of the views obtained from its summit. On one side of it springs forth the Rede, on the other the Jed.

* Rose and stretched him.

# ROTHBURY SECTION.

## ROTHBURY.

ON the north bank of the finest and most famous trout-stream in the county lies Rothbury, the capital of Coquetdale, and the centre of a district where the lovelier and the sterner aspects of Nature appear in close proximity. Enjoying the pure air of the hills and the moorlands, Rothbury, from its position in the deep and romantic gorge of the Coquet, is yet sheltered from the withering blasts. On the north a bold and picturesque ridge interposes between the little town and the wind-swept moors that stretch away to Thrunton Crags. On the east the vale seems closed by the wooded and heathery heights of Crag-end. Southward rise the gently-moulded slopes of the Simonside Hills. To the westward only is there an open prospect of any extent, and this embraces the richly-cultivated vale of the Coquet, with the high ground above Hepple and Holystone. The name of Rothbury is supposed to be derived from the Celtic word Rhath, signifying "a cleared spot." This derivation seems a plausible one, when it is remembered that a large and famous forest stretched from Thornhaugh on the east to Fallowlees on the west, a distance of seven miles, and from Coldrife on the south to the Park-house on the north, a distance of four miles. The town is referred to in the reign of Henry I. as Rodeberia, and during the three succeeding centuries the name passed through thirty or forty variations. The manor of Rothbury appears to have been in the possession of the Crown for nearly a century and a half after the Conquest. King John granted it to Robert Fitz Roger, Baron of Warkworth, in 1205. It reverted to the Crown in the reign of Edward III. Conferred by that monarch on Henry de Percy, it has been held by his descendants ever since. The two most stirring events in the history of Rothbury are the visit of King John in 1201, when he gave it a charter for a market; and the visit of the Prince and Princess of Wales in 1884. The aspect of the town on these two occasions would be as strongly contrasted as the character of the inhabitants. The people of Rothbury in former times were amongst the wildest and most uncivilised in the county. For fighting, gaming, and drinking they had a worse reputation than the inhabitants of Tynedale and Redesdale. Very little regard had the good folk of Rothbury for the laws, and their love of venison frequently led them into trouble. Even the worthy Rector himself seems to have shared in the poaching proclivities of his flock, for he, too, is stated to have been heavily fined for a breach of the forest laws.

Modern Rothbury consists of a long wide street, running east and west, generally called High Street, or Front Street, and two shorter streets—Rotten Row *(Route du Roi)*, or Bridge Street, and Church Street—branching off at different angles to the bridge. The appearance of the buildings is somewhat stern and severe, like that of all Border towns which have been exposed to the destructive raids of the moss-troopers. Though the ancient bastle-houses and peles have long since disappeared with the times which made them necessary, several of the older houses remain, with the dates of their erection cut on the door-heads. Every stone of the ancient fortress built by the Barons of Warkworth has quite disappeared The site, according to tradition, was the new cemetery, still known as the Haa' Hill. Near the church are the ruined walls of the "*Three Half Moons*"—an inn, which for three hundred years was associated with the fortunes of Rothbury. An apartment in this old hostelry was called the "Earl's Chamber," from a tradition that the Earl of Derwentwater had slept there on the night of October 6th, 1715, after having marched from Greenrig to Plainfield at the head of his small band of Northumbrian Jacobites.

The *Parish Church* is dedicated to "All Saints," and is supposed to stand on the site of a former Saxon edifice. The greater part of it was entirely rebuilt in 1850. The only portions of the venerable thirteenth-century building are the chancel, the east wall of the south transept, and the lofty chancel arch, which rises from massive piers. The semi-circular bracket on the north side of the reading-desk, enriched with the nail-head ornament, and the semi-octagonal pillar south of the pulpit, are also early English work. The three lancet windows arranged as a triplet in the east wall of the chancel, and the four eastern lancets in the south wall, as well as those in the east wall of the south transept (or Trewhitt porch), are all ancient, and mostly filled with modern stained glass. On the south side of the chancel is an early English piscina and a priests' door, with a square-headed trefoil arch. The reredos, erected in 1884, is composed of Corsham Down stone, alabaster and marble, in early English design. It has five trefoil-headed arches on marble pillars, four of which contain the emblems of the Evangelists. On the north side of the chancel is the Cartington Porch, now fitted up as a choir, vestry, and organ chamber. It communicated with the chancel by two semi-circular arches, which were built up in 1658 to prevent mischievous boys getting into the church, and to keep the cold winds from endangering the health of many old persons. The square embattled tower is seventy feet in height, and contains two bells, one of which is inscribed, "John Thomlinson, Rector of Rothbury, 1682."

The chief object of antiquarian interest in the church is the font.

Though the basin is dated 1664, the stem or pedestal once formed the lower part of the shaft of a Saxon churchyard cross, the remainder of which is preserved in the old Castle at Newcastle. This relic of ancient sculpture is of red sandstone, and curiously carved on its four sides. Some writers have traced a symbolical meaning in the rich ornamentation. According to the late Mr. Dickson, of Alnwick, it may represent three principal circumstances in the history of the world. On the south is portrayed an animal walking quietly amongst trees and foliage, and feeding upon the fruits of the earth, figurative of the peaceful and happy state of things before the fall of man. On the north side there are carved a number of nondescript animals preying and feeding on each other, showing the state of wickedness after that occurrence. On the east is seen the Saviour of the world, ascending up into heaven, and, underneath, are numerous heads of men looking upward in a suppliant manner. On the west side is the endless rope pattern, or the Saxon knot-work. The fragments at Newcastle, discovered during the restoration of the church in 1850, are the limbs of the cross and upper portion of the shaft. On one side of the former is a representation of our Lord, with the figure of an angel above him, with extended wings. On the other side are three well-carved figures, probably angels. The two ends are decorated with Runic knots. On one of the surfaces of the shaft is represented a figure with a crossed nimbus ; on a second, a figure restoring sight to a blind man; on the third, the well-known Dano-Saxon figure of the dragon or winged monster; on the fourth, a group of heads, probably the celestial choir. The perforations in the top of the limbs of the cross have been for the reception of candles, five lights being used during Saxon times in the consecration of churchyards and churchyard crosses. The fragments of several thirteenth and fourteenth century sepulchral slabs are built into the west wall of the porch. In the vestry is an ancient door-head of stone, bearing the inscription :—"Thomas Eansley, 1611." A mason's mallet, chisel, compass, and square, denote his trade. A stone slab, with a floriated cross carved upon it, stands at the chancel door. Bernard Gilpin, the Apostle of the North, as he was called, frequently preached in Rothbury Church. On one occasion it seemed as if two of the Rothbury factions, who had met in the church, would have come into conflict. They clashed their weapons, and were drawing near to each other, when Gilpin stepped down from the pulpit, and addressing the leaders, put an end to the fray for the time. On his return to the pulpit he spent the rest of the allotted time in pointing out the wickedness and folly of their barbarous feuds, and striving to reconcile the two parties. They promised to refrain from these hostile demonstrations so long as he remained in their midst. On another Sunday morning he observed a glove hanging up in the church, and was informed by the sexton that it was meant as a challenge to anyone that should take it down. Gilpin ordered the sexton to reach it to him, but, upon that functionary's refusal to touch it, he removed it himself, and put it in his breast. Before he concluded his sermon he took occasion to rebuke his hearers severely for these inhuman challenges. One of W. B. Scott's frescoes at Wallington Hall represents this scene. Gilpin gained an enormous influence over the wild and turbulent people of this district, so much so that his person was held in the highest veneration. One day, it is said, a thief had stolen his horses, but on learning afterwards whose they were, was so terrified at what he had done, that he instantly returned them, declaring he believed the devil would have seized him directly had he carried them off, knowing them to be Mr. Gilpin's. The only other church in the town belongs to the Congregational body. It was built in 1842. Rothbury possesses an excellent reading-room and circulating library, both of which are open to visitors on payment of sixpence per week. The library contains over three thousand volumes. The river is spanned by a fine old bridge of four ribbed arches. Three of them formed part of the original structure, erected, it is thought, in the fifteenth century. In a hollow, between the road leading from the bridge and the Coquet, are some remarkable mounds, or embankments, named in the ordnance map, "Holy Knowes," but locally called the "Hurley Knowes." They have evidently been thrown up by diluvial action, and may afterwards have been occupied by the old inhabitants of Rothbury for the purpose of defending the passage of the Scots' Ford in unsettled times. The North British railway station stands just above them. On this side of the river, but further westward, is the Haugh, one of the finest race-courses in the north of England. Here it is that the Coquetdale Steeplechase Meeting is annually held.

On the slopes of the hills above the town are numerous memorials of pre-historic times. Occupying an elevated platform to the north-west, near the Pennystane Quarry, is *Old Rothbury*, a circular camp, defended by a double fosse and rampart, with outworks on the south and east sides. The remains of a watch-tower in connection with the camp may be seen on the hill-top, about 500 yards to the east. In the vicinity are several tumuli and cist-vaens. Pennystanes, from which the quarry derives its name, were trimmed flat stones used as quoits before iron ones were frequent. Near to the camp is a deep recess beneath a huge overhanging cliff, known as "Cartington Cove," which, according to tradition, forms the entrance to an underground passage leading to Cartington Castle. On the surrounding rocks are several of those curious markings, which chiefly take the form of concentric circles, and are found only on sandstone rocks, and these confined to certain parts of the county. Other examples of them appear a little to the north on Chirnells Moor. Half-a-mile to the west, at Westhills, are the circular ramparts and ditches of another large camp. Near to it are several hut-circles. Below Old Rothbury is the "Beggar's Rigg," where the mendicants in the olden time waited to be admitted to the town. Tradition says it obtained its appellation thus :—"A gentleman, during the seventeenth century, and in a time of great scarcity, permitted the poor of Rothbury to pluck the peas which grew on the ridge, an offer gladly accepted ; but, wonderful to relate, at the time of reaping it was found to bear a most abundant crop." The hills around Rothbury used to be frequented by goats, and numerous visitors resorted to the town simply to drink the goats' whey, considered a remedy for certain ailments.

From the north end of the bridge a footpath follows the course of the river for half-a-mile or so, past a picturesque old corn-mill, to the Thrum.* This is a narrow chasm in the freestone rock which forms the bed of the river, and is somewhat similar to the "Strid" above Bolton Abbey in Wharfedale. Through this channel, which is about two yards wide and sixty yards long, the whole volume of the river is poured with the force and rapidity of a torrent. As the rocky sides of this gully were so close together, foolhardy persons were tempted to leap across, and several who had failed to clear the passage were drowned. It was, therefore, considered desirable, some years ago, to widen the channel by blasting the rock at various points. In one of Wilson's *Tales of the Borders*, Willie Faa, the gipsy king, is represented as leaping across the Thrum with the stolen heir of Clennel Castle, and leaving his pursuers behind. The old angler must have been a good hand at "drawing the long bow" as well as flinging the rod, who said, "About fifty years syne I mind o' seein' trouts that thick i' the Thrum below Rothbury, that if ye had stucken the end o' your gad into the water amang them, it wad amaist hae studden upreet." A little further east, by the roadside, is the famous *Reiver's Well*, a suggestive name to the student of Border history who recalls to mind some such passage as the following :—"Such adepts were they in the art of thieving, that they could twist a cow's horn, or mark a horse, so that its owners could not know it, and so subtle that no vigilance could guard against them."

Near this well is the principal entrance to *Cragside*, the beautiful and famous seat of Lord Armstrong. The mansion, begun in 1863, stands on a rocky platform above the Debdon Burn, and is reached by a winding pathway that, on its way, introduces the visitor to some charming bits of romantic scenery. It was designed by Norman Shaw, R.A., and is built in a composite style of architecture, partly Gothic and partly Elizabethan. The general effect of the building, with its numerous gables and corners, its red-tiled and high-pitched roofs, its overhanging eaves and grotesquely-carved gargoyles, its lofty chimneys and quaint-looking lattices, is highly picturesque, and harmonises well with the unconventional character of the surrounding landscape. The chief entrance is in the south front, through a fine Gothic doorway in the early English style. From the entrance hall a long corridor conducts to the *Library*, which, in addition to a choice collection of books, contains some valuable pictures by Turner, Müller, and Sir Edwin Landseer, and several vases and specimens of fine pottery. The *Dining-room*, on the right, a comfortable apartment with richly-panelled ceiling, has carved over the ingle-nook the quaint north-country proverb, "East or west, hame's best." The noble

* Thrums are the ends of the weft which the weaver cannot work closely up in warp of linen or canvas.

staircase is adorned with statuettes, rare Oriental vases, and old china. Several pictures hang on the walls. One is by D. G. Rossetti, "Margaret and her Jewels;" a second by H. H. Emmerson, "Faithful unto Death;" and a third by Sir F. Leighton, "Interior of a Mosque." The *Picture Gallery* is entered from the upper landing of this staircase. It contains, among others, the following pictures:—"The Bay of Gibraltar," by Ansdell; "A Driving Shower" and "Moorland Drovers," by Peter Graham; and "Jephthah's Daughter," by Millais. To the left is the small water-colour gallery, containing Turner's "Dunstanboro' Castle," and "Lucerne," with choice examples of the art of David Coxe, Copley Fielding, Birket Foster, Stansfield, Alf Hunt, and other masters. The *Drawing-room*, which is entered from the gallery, is situated in that part of the mansion known as "Gilnockie's Tower." It is a magnificent apartment, adorned with articles of virtu and art. A superb mantelpiece, of richly-carved marble, fills nearly the whole of one side of it. On a table, made out of the oaken piles of the Roman bridge at Newcastle, lies a beautiful album, presented to Sir William and Lady Armstrong, December 24th, 1885, by the inhabitants of Rothbury and neighbourhood. It is illustrated with sketches of local scenery by H. H. Emmerson. Hung round the walls of this room are several valuable paintings, among which may be noted—"A Storm in Autumn," J. Linnell; "Death of Raphael," O'Neil; "Chill October," Millais; "A Noble Lady of Venice," Sir F. Leighton; "Off the Maas," J. W. Turner; "The Cowslip Gatherers," George Leslie, R.A.; "A Flower Girl," John Phillips; "The Sleeping Beauty" (on vellum), by E. Burne Jones, R.A. Here are two rare specimens of the Keramic art, known as "The Hawthorn Vases." In a small recess opening from the drawing-room through a Gothic arch of beautifully streaked sandstone, is Sir David Wilkie's celebrated picture, "The Rabbit on the Wall." The electric light has been introduced into the house by the distinguished owner, who has utilised the power of a neighbouring burn to work the generating engine. Communication has been established, by means of the telephone, with *Trewhitt House*, a shooting-box of Lord Armstrong's, seven miles away, on the moors. A hydraulic ram, working night and day without attendance, supplies the house and gardens with water from an artificial lake higher up the ravine. A further application of hydraulic power may be seen in the conservatory, where fruit-trees growing in huge vases are made to move easily on pivots, so that each side in turn may receive its share of the sun's warmth; and the various plants, with the gangways on which they stand, may, if necessary, be wheeled into the open air. Visitors are not permitted to see over the house, unless they be professional or amateur artists. They are, however, allowed to explore the grounds on Thursdays, from ten A.M. to five P.M. Words are inadequate to describe the wonderful transformation which Lord Armstrong has made on the barren hill-side as it existed previous to 1863. Every natural advantage has been utilised by the great magician. Shrubs and trees that grow best in exposed situations have been planted among the boulders of Cragside with admirable results. Rhododendrons, azaleas, and other plants of rich-coloured bloom, with the native heather, bracken, and ling, soften and brighten the hard features of the landscape till it smiles again. The edelweiss of the Alps, the Swiss bridal flower, flourishes here, and on moist banks grows the Linnæa borealis. Along the hill-side various walks and drives have been formed, leading by easy ascents to the summit, which commands an extensive view of the whole district. On this elevated site is a huge boulder, called the "Sea Stone," deposited, no doubt, by some ancient glacier, which has left a record of its presence in the striations of the rocks all around. Near the "Lady's Walk" and the Black Burn there are six very perfect hut-circles joined in line together, and three others a short distance from them. To the east, beside a burn that runs down the bank from the Wolf's Fauld, is an illicit whisky-still, three yards in diameter. The two lakes, the waterfall, the fern grotto, with its profusion of rare and lovely fronds, the Italian garden, and orchard-houses, are all interesting sights to be seen by the visitor to Cragside. He will also find an exquisite pleasure in following the windings of the picturesque little ravine that is traversed by the Debdon Burn, pausing to watch the pretty cascades and pools with their mossy stones, and lingering in quiet romantic nooks, where, from the crevices in the rock, spring the male, the lady, the oak, beech, and broad buckler ferns. The beautiful grounds of Cragside presented a fairy-like appearance on the night of August 19th, 1884, when they were illuminated with ten thousand small glass lamps and several columns of coloured fire.

The hills and moors around Rothbury form happy hunting-grounds to the botanist, who, among other plants, will find the round-leaved sundew (*Drosera rotundifolia*), mountain everlasting (*Antennaria dioica*), petty whin (*Genista Anglica*), winter green chickweed (*Trientalis Europæa*), buck bean (*Menyanthes trifoliata*), cloudberry (*Rubus chamæmorus*), whortleberry (*Vaccinium myrtillus*), cowberry (*Vaccinium vitis-idæa*), crowberry (*Empetrum nigrum*), juniper (*Juniperus communis*), bog asphodel (*Narthecium ossifragum*), heart-leaved tway blade (*Listera cordata*), marsh andromeda (*Andromeda polifolia*), least yellow water-lily (*Nuphar pumila*), Wilson's filmy fern (*Hymenophyllum Wilsonii*), rock rose (*Helianthemum vulgare*). At a lower elevation in the valley grow the square-stalked St. John's wort (*Hypericum quadrangulum*), grass of Parnassus (*Parnassia palustris*), wood vetch (*Vicia sylvatica*), butterfly orchis (*Habenaria bifolia*), frog orchis (*Habenaria viridis*), sweet-scented orchis (*Gymnadenia conopsea*), marsh orchis (*Orchis latifolia*), broad-leaved helleborine (*Epipactus latifolia*), marsh helleborine (*Epipactus palustris*), mountain globe flower (*Trollius Europæus*), white meadow saxifrage (*Saxifraga granulata*), white briony (*Bryonia dioica*), hairy pepperwort (*Lepidum Smithii*), melancholy plume thistle (*Cnicus heterophyllus*), greater toothwort (*Lathræa squamaria*), winter green (*Pyrola media*), oak fern (*Polypodium dryopteris*), beech fern (*Polypodium phegopteris*). prickly shield fern (*Polystichum a. uleatum*), black maiden-hair spleenwort (*Asplenium trichomanes*), rue-leaved spleenwort (*Asplenium ruta-muraria*), mountain buckler fern (*Lastrea montana*), moonwort (*Botrychium lunaria*), adder's tongue (*Ophioglossum vulgare*).

Dr. John Brown, an author of considerable reputation in his day, was born at Rothbury, where his father was curate in 1715. His principal works are an essay on *Shaftesbury's Characteristics* (1751), and his *Estimate of the Manners and Principles of the Times* (1757). He also wrote "The Tragedy of Barbarossa," and is supposed to have assisted Avison in his *Essay on Musical Expression*. Bernard Rumney, a poet and musician of some note in his day, was born and died at Rothbury. He was one of the churchwardens of the church in 1662. His fame rests on the grimly humorous ballad of "Ecky's Mare," a poem which deals with the revolting circumstances of corruption in a spirit of realism not surpassed by Beaudelaire in "La Charogne. Rothbury is well provided with hotels. The principal ones are the County at the east end, and the Queen's Head at the west end, and the Turk's Head in the centre of the town, the Station Hotel near the railway station, and the Railway Hotel in Bridge Street.

# ROTHBURY TO SIMONSIDE AND FALLOWLEES.

**Whitton Tower, ½ mile; Lord-in-Shaw Camp, 2 miles; Simonside, 3½ miles; Fallowlees, 6 miles.**

FROM the south end of Rothbury Bridge a road leads up the rising-ground for half-a-mile to *Whitton Tower*, the residence of the rectors of Rothbury. It was built in the fourteenth century by a member of the Umfraville family, and formed one of a line of peles extending from Hepple to Warkworth. It is mentioned in a list of fortlets as early as 1416, and in the survey of 1542 is described as "a toure and a little barmekin, being the manc'on of the p'sonage of Rothbury, and is in good reparc'ons." The walls at the base are 11 feet thick, in the kitchen 9 feet, and towards the top 6 feet. The most characteristic part of the building is the ancient byre on the ground floor (now the cellar), in which the rectors secured their cattle from the depredations of the moss-troopers. It is a dungeon-like chamber, with a vaulted stone roof, and a deep well containing 18 feet of water. The first floor, also vaulted, is the rector's study. During some recent alterations on the second floor, in what must have been the private chapel of the rectors before the Reformation, the site of the altar and also the piscina were discovered. From the ground-floor a winding staircase leads to the summit of the tower, which has corner turrets of the usual type. Carved on the wall at the west side of the building are the arms of the Umfravilles. The modern portions of the rectory were added in 1784-5. The gardens and plantations around it enhance very much the picturesque appearance of this very interesting old Border fortlet. At the highest part of the grounds is a circular observatory, called Sharpe's Folly. It was devised by Dr. Sharpe, to give employment to the industrious poor during a season of scarcity. *Whitton Dene* is said to have been one of the haunts of the fairies in olden times. About a mile from Whitton this pathway crosses a heathery ridge, and to the right on another ridge is a small rock mysteriously marked with concentric circles. Westward of it is an open cist with the lid lying at the side. A little to the east of this cist is a curious line of small stones set on their edges. A second and similar row may be seen about half-a-mile to the south, and a third on the east of Garleigh Hill. East of the first line are some more circular-markings on a large rock adjoining some grave-mounds. These are all in connection with a large and interesting British settlement close by, which has been styled the Lord-in-Shaws (Lowerdean-shaws) camp. It occupies one of the westernmost heights of the Simonside range, a hill 879 feet high, and is of circular form, defended by three ramparts and a fosse. Within the central enclosure are the ruins of seven hut-circles. The walls of these primitive dwellings are about three feet high. Two watch-towers in connexion with this camp are situated on Garleigh Hill to the south-east, and three others on the three most elevated points of the Simonside range. From the west gate of the camp a hollow way, or ancient British road, leads down to the south-west in the direction of the old deer-park wall, twenty yards from which is a large rock covered with circular markings. To the Lordenshaws farm the pitmen bring up their bee-hives in July and August for the heather blossom. Sometimes a thousand will be placed here. The middle watch-tower on the Simonside range, 1026 feet above the sea, is very perfect, and has a very extended outlook. The flat stone on which the beacon lights were kindled may be seen lying on the south side. A mile or so to the west, and about a mile due south of Great Tosson, is a large rock on the side of the hill, having a shallow cavern inside it, roofed like a church, and capable of holding six or eight persons. It goes by the name of "Little Church." Right above it is the highest point of Simonside (A.-S. Simon's sete, or settlement),* 1409 feet above the sea. This dark and picturesque hill, which gives its name to the whole range, commands on a clear day a view of the whole coast of Northumberland, and is a conspicuous landmark to sailors. The scenery over which the eye of the spectator ranges from the summit of Simonside is characteristically Northumbrian, abounding in contrasts. Wastes of heather and bracken broken by fissured sheets of dark brown peat; sweeping uplands of coarse and withered-looking herbage; level haughs; corn-fields and pasture-lands; dells bristling with pinewoods; bare crags and green knolls, are the details of the picture. The rough sandstone of which the hills are composed is known to geologists as "Simonside Grits." Three-quarters of a mile to the south is *Selby's Cove*, an opening in the rock through which water has, doubtlessly, flowed at one time. At the south end of it are the ruins of an old farmhouse. The hill to the west is *Weather-head*, 1253 feet above the sea-level. From Selby's Cove a pleasant ramble may be had over the moors as far as *Chartner's* and *Fallowlees' Loughs*, where the black-headed gulls breed. From the former, which is a mile and a quarter to the south-west, issues the pretty rivulet, the Font. In its still and shallow waters a rare and small kind of water-lily grows secluded. "A plant found long ago by Sir John Trevelyan in Chartner's Lough on the Wallington Moors, and thence transported to Wallington, appears to agree with the North European *nuphar intermedium* of Ledebour, a sub-species not known elsewhere in Britain" (*New Flora of Northumberland and Durham*). In the marshes around thrives an elegant little shrub called by Linnæus *Andromeda Polifolia* (marsh

* NOTE.—The Simon of mythology was, it seems, a domestic brewer to King Arthur, identical with the German Sigmund, and very fond of killing dragons.

andromeda), for reasons which he has poetically explained in his *Flora Lapponica.* Three-quarters of a mile south-east by south of this sheet of water is *Fallowlees Lough.* Large heaps of slag found along the sides of Fallowlees Burn prove the existence of early smelting works. Half-a-mile south-east of the lough is *Fallowlees farm-house.* Fallowlees is interesting as the temporary abode of William Veitch, one of the outlawed Covenanters in the time of Charles II. Prevailed on by the Redesdale people, he removed his wife and two sons in creels from Edinburgh "into a village called Falalies, farming a piece of ground from Charles Hall, who was owner of that place and village within the parish of Rodberry in Northumberland." "But they were not well settled there, though in a moorish retired place," when their Roman Catholic neighbours, who abounded there, "did stir up the Lord Whiterington to mar some small meetings he had." The attempt to interfere with him failed, as he had procured a license to preach, and his enemies "went away with a great disappointment." The tourist may follow a sheep-track north for two miles past the ruins of Blackcock Hall to Selby's Cove, and thence strike north for Newtown, noticing on the way, near the Cowett Wells, a small British camp, about fifteen yards in diameter; or he may follow the windings of the Font to the Rothbury road (two miles), and proceed along it to Rothbury (five miles). If desirable, he may take the train at Ewesley Station, near which the river crosses the road.

# ROTHBURY TO TOSSON HILL.

Great Tosson, 2 miles ; Summit of Tosson Hill, 4 miles.

FOLLOWING the road westward from the County Hotel for half-a-mile, the tourist will cross the Coquet by the Captain's Bridge, and proceed past the woollen mill, where shepherds' plaids and similar fabrics are woven, to GREAT TOSSON, a hamlet of three farm-houses and a few cottages, with fine old ash and sycamore trees around them. In the centre is a square grey pele-tower in fairly good preservation. The pele and several of the cottages are roofed with sandstone slates, pinned, as was the custom, with sheep-shank bones. The walls are six feet thick. In one angle are the remains of the turret-stair. Here the lords of Hepple held their courts after their castle had been destroyed by the Scots. At the west end of the village, on the left, is *Burgh Hill Camp*, one of the largest strongholds of the Otadeni in the county, covering an area of over seven acres, and defended by a triple rampart. A mile to the south, at Ryehill, the Knights Hospitalers of St. John had a hospital, or house of entertainment for travellers, but no trace of it now remains. A mile and a half south-west of Great Tosson is *Ravensheugh*, a hill 1385 feet above sea level. Jutting prominently from the face of the hill are two large crags, called "Kate" and "Geordy." The summit of Tosson is rather more than half-a-mile from here. It rises 1447 feet above the sea level, and is the highest point of the Simonside range. The ascent is over several ridges, each with a craggy edge of gritstone, and across intervening terraces and hollows, filled with the three different kinds of heather. The botanist, on entering the open moors, will notice such flowers as whortleberry (*Vaccinium myrtillus*), crowberry (*Empetrum nigrum*), sheathing cotton-sedge (*Eriophorum vaginatum*), mat grass (*Nardus stricta*), waved mountain hair grass (*Aira flexuosa*), ferns like the bracken *Blechnum* and *Heath polypody*, and in the damper spots mosses like *Hypnum fluitans* (floating feather moss), *Polytrichum commune* (common hair moss), and *Sphagnum* (bog moss), ranging in colour from deep red to bright green, with pale green cushions of *Leucobryum* and *Aulacomnion palustre*, and amongst them round-leaved sundew (*Drosera rotundifolia*), bottle carex (*Carex ampullacea*), common cotton sedge (*Eriophorum angustifolium*), and the clustered sword-like leaves of the bog asphodel (*Narthecium ossifragum*). The Simonside hills are said, by tradition, to be haunted by a species of mischievous elves called the "Duergar." Many stories are told of their pranks. On one occasion, if popular testimony is to be believed, they set the huge wheel of Tosson water-mill a-going at night. Their favourite pastime seems to have been misleading travellers. One person, wandering in these treacherous solitudes, began to shout, "Tint! tint!" when a light appeared before him, at a short distance, like a burning candle in a shepherd's hut. With great care he approached, and found himself on the edge of a deep slough in a peat-bog. Throwing a piece of turf into the water, the light vanished, and as he shouted again, defiantly, "Tint! tint!" three of the elves, with hideous visages, approached, carrying torches in their diminutive hands. He betook himself to flight, and was followed by an innumerable multitude of the malevolent sprites, armed with little clubs. Charging the leader, he encountered no palpable form, and sank down in a kind of stupor to the ground, where he remained till the next morning. Another time a traveller was benighted in these parts, and perceiving a glimmering light, hastened towards it, and found what appeared to be a hut, on the floor of which, between two rough grey stones, the embers of a fire were still glowing. He had just seated himself on one stone, when a strange figure in human shape, not higher than the knee, came in and sat on the other. After remaining silently watching his diminutive companion till the fire went out and the morning broke, he perceived his danger. The roof and the walls of the hut were gone, and he was seated upon a stone sure enough, but it formed one of the higher points of a steep, rocky precipice. These fairies were not the only "uncanny folk" which the belated traveller might have encountered among these lonely hills during the earlier part of the present century, for in some quiet and secluded spot he might have dropped upon smugglers engaged in the manufacture of whiskey. One of their illicit stills, capable of making one hundred gallons of spirit per week, was discovered in 1840 by the Excise officers. It was most artfully constructed in a sort of cavern at the foot of the Tosson hills, on the north-east side. It was on a level with the ground, which the cover was made to resemble. There was a small hole for the ingress and egress of the smugglers, while a spring of water, running from the hills into the cave, served for the purpose of distillation.

# ROTHBURY TO ALWINTON AND COQUETHEAD.

Thropton, 2 miles; Flotterton, 3¾ miles; Sharperton, 6½ miles; Hepple, 5¾ miles; Harehaugh Hill, 6¼ miles; Holystone (*viâ* Sharperton), 7½ miles; Harbottle, 8½ miles; Alwinton, 10 miles; Usway Ford, 15 miles; Chew Green Camps, 20 miles.

THE Vale of the Coquet between Rothbury and Alwinton is a broad, bright, and sinuous fold of verdure, amongst bleak and high moorlands. The effects produced by the contrast are novel and picturesque, and the eye experiences an ever-varying pleasure in roaming from the rushy banks of the stream to the meadows and clumps of pines higher up, and from these again to the rolling sweep of heather, brown for ten months of the year, and purple for two.

Tourists, who do not care to follow the windings of the stream on foot, may get a lift in the rural post-gig, which has accomodation for a limited number of passengers, both on the outward journey and the return. The road along the Beggar's Rigg ascends gradually to *Wreighburn House*, which occupies the site of an old hospital, or religious house of entertainment, and descending a little, crosses the Wreigh Burn near its junction with the Coquet into

THROPTON, a considerable village, two miles west by north from Rothbury. At the west end of it is an ancient bastle-house, in good preservation. It is described in the survey of 1542 as a "lyttle towre of th' inherytaunce of Sir Cuth. Ratcliffe." The upper part is the residence of the farmer, while the arched vault beneath is still used for the housing of cattle as of old. The crosses which stood at the east and west ends of the village have disappeared. There are two inns—the Three Wheat Heads and the Cross Keys.

The Wreigh from Thropton to Netherton Burn foot is a favourite streamlet with the angling fraternity, who resort to it when the weather, both up and down the Coquet, is rough and impracticable for fishing purposes.

"There's braw, lang trouts aboon *Linn-shiels*,
Amang the scaurs they'll haud their screen;
De'il scale the byke frae *Redless-syke*,
Wi' wairsh moss-water, black an' lean!

At *Harehaughturn* and *Keengie-burn*,
They'll smell the weather i' the sky ;
On Carter-brow it's sleetin' now—
We'se cheat them a', an' up the Wreigh ! "
—THOMAS DOUBLEDAY.

A mile and three-quarters further on is another old village, FLOTTERTON, where, in 1416, Sir R. Ogill, of Hepple, had a "fortalicium." Flotterton House belongs to the Wealleans family. Half-a-mile to the north-east is *Warton*, the residence in former times of a famous race of warriors, who were the dread of the Scottish Borderers. Even so late as the middle of the last century, four brothers lived here of the name of Potts, who usually kept the peace at all public sports, when there was ill blood between the people of Coquetdale and Redesdale. From Flotterton there are two routes to Holystone. The nearest is by Sharperton, two miles and three-quarters distant. The road skirts Plainfield Moor, formerly a common, one of the mustering-centres of Coquetdale, and a rendezvous of the Jacobites in 1715. Here the Earl of Derwentwater, with his little troop of sixty horse, riding from the Waterfalls, were joined by a few more adherents of the Pretender from the district around Rothbury. At Sharperton is an old bastle-house, with the initials C.P.E.P., and the date 1675, carved on the door-head.

The other route is by Hepple. The road turns off to the south from the end of the village, and, at a distance of about a mile, passes on the left the small hamlet of *Caistron*, which was once in the possession of the priors of Newminster. It adjoins an ancient British camp (at present nearly obliterated), and to this circumstance may be traced the origin of its name—Caistron, or Cester-ton.

A mile south-west is HEPPLE. Here are the interesting ruins of a large pele-castle, the first of a line of towers which, extending to Warkworth, formed a barrier against the Scottish Borderers. The great arched vault on the ground floor, together with some shattered portions of the massive walls, overgrown with a profusion of grass and ragwort, bear witness to the great strength of this ancient hold of the lords of Hepple. Its present ruinous condition is said to have been the work of the Scottish moss-troopers. The picturesque fragments remaining narrowly escaped being demolished some years ago. Materials were required to build a neighbouring farmstead, and these, it was thought, might be obtained from the old castle ; but the workmen found it easier to cut stone from the hardest quarry than to separate the massive blocks from the cement in which they were embedded. The attempt was, therefore, abandoned, to the delight of antiquaries. The important barony of Hepple was, in the reign of Henry III., the property of "Joo Taylleboys," a descendant of the great Ivo Taillebois, Baron of Kendal, who traced his descent from Charlemagne. From this branch of the family, who assumed the name of Heppale, it passed by marriage into the hands of the Ogles. The lordship now belongs to Sir J. B. Riddell, Bart. Two noted Northumbrian characters are connected with Hepple—Robert Snowdon and old Will Allan. The former, who was born here, was a famous warrior in the stormy times preceding the union. When only sixteen years of age he fought and slew John Grieves, a celebrated Scottish champion, in a pitched battle with small swords, at Gamblepath, on the Borders. He was foully stabbed by a hidden foe while attempting to recover a favourite black horse which had been stolen. The latter, who resided here for many years, was a noted vermin-hunter and performer on the Northumbrian pipes. Many amusing anecdotes are told of this shrewd and original character. He was much attached to the Coquet, and composed two tunes—"We'll a' to the Coquet and woo," and "Salmon tails up the water," which he used to play with great zest.

About half-a-mile west of Hepple is an eminence called *Kirkhill*, on which there formerly stood an ancient chapel. Destroyed, it is said, by the moss-troopers, the remains were removed in 1760 to build the adjoining farm-house. In the chancel was discovered the tombstone of a lady, probably the wife of one of the lords of Hepple. It was much defaced, but fragments of a curious epitaph in rhyme, said to have been composed bv the lady herself, could be made out.

"Here lies . . Countess of . .
. . who died . . her age
. . . . . . . . . . .
. . . . . . . . . . .

I loved my lord, obeyed my king,
And kept my conscience clear,
Which Death disarmeth of his sting,
And Christians all endear.

My puissant posterity
Still the forlorn'd befriend;
Peace, pleasure, and prosperity
My tenantry attend.

. . . . . . .

There lay my head to Long Acres,
Where shearers sweetly sing,
And feet toward the Key-heugh scares,
Which fox-hounds cause to ring.

Farewell survivors in the gross!
When you behold my bust,
Lament your late liege lady's loss,
Then blending with the dust."

The bason and carved pedestal of the font are preserved at the farm-house here. About a hundred yards to the west of the spot where the chapel stood are traces of the village of *Old Hepple*, which was destroyed by the Scots during one of their incursions. There is a pleasant route through the fields, in a north-westerly direction, to Holystone. The first point of interest is a limestone quarry, half-a-mile distant, on the site of a large and strong hill-fortress of the ancient Britons, called Hetchester camp. It was 140 yards in length, and 90 yards in breadth, and was defended by four great ramparts. The excavations for stone which have been going on for so many years, have obliterated all traces of this remarkable entrenchment. The horns and bones of a large species of deer, and even human bones, have been frequently disinterred. Half-a-mile north-west again is *Wreighill*, a small hamlet on the south side of the Wreighill Pike, which rises to a height of 717 feet above the sea-level. A certain tragic interest attaches to this little spot on account of the calamities which have befallen it. On May 25th, 1412, which has ever since been called "the woeful Wednesday of the Wreck-hill," the whole village was destroyed and the inhabitants slain by the Scots in a raid of retaliation. Again, in 1665, the village was depopulated by the plague, which is said to have found its way into the place through the medium of a small package received from London by a Miss Handyside. First the young lady, and then the rest of the inhabitants, succumbed to the contagion, and Wreighill was again a scene of desolation. The bones of the victims to this dreadful visitation are still occasionally disinterred. The site of the old village is supposed to be indicated by some square enclosures near the hamlet; but these are more likely the remains of a Roman camp, guarding the road from Holystone past Sharperton. Wreighill has its celebrity in the person of George Coughron, a mathematical prodigy, who was born here on August 12th, 1752. His powers of calculation were indeed extraordinary, and during his brief career (he died in the twenty-first year of his age), he obtained no fewer than ten prizes for answering questions in fluxions alone. He challenged all the mathematicians of his time to answer the prize question in the *Gentleman's Diary* for 1772. His challenge was not accepted, and he gave the solution himself. The most difficult problems were submitted to his decision, and at the time of his death he held the appointment of calculator to the Astronomer-Royal.

Half-a-mile north-west of Wreighill is *Low Farnham*, where, on a slope above the river, several of the flint implements used by the old Celtic population were found. They consist of thumb-flints, or scrapers, knives, and arrow-heads, and, together with a tumulus in the adjoining field, seem to indicate the presence here of an outpost from Campville, or Hetchester camp. A mile further up the stream, past High Farnham, there is a foot-bridge connecting these farmsteads with Holystone.

A mile south of Hepple, behind Swindon Hill, is *Soldier's Fauld Celtic Camp*, one hundred yards in diameter, defended by a rampart seven yards high. A crag on the north, known as "Witch's Neuk," is said to have been the resting-place of Meg o' Meldon during one of her midnight flights.

The road to Holystone from Hepple crosses first the Coquet and then the Swindon or Harehaugh Burn, which joins the former a little lower down.

In the angle formed by the confluence is *Harehaugh.* The wide plain here used to be the scene of country sports. "The clattering cudgels' thud," says Chatto, in his *Rambles through Northumberland*, "is no longer heard falling fast and fiercely on heads and shoulders, at Harehaugh, below Halystone, which was the place where the two parties (the dalesmen of Reed and Coquet) were accustomed to meet for the purpose of fighting their cocks, and of having afterwards a sort of friendly *crowdy-main* among themselves, by way of a grand finale to the amusements of the day."

On *Harehaugh Hill*—a great triangular mass, which forms the converging point of the two valleys, is a large entrenched stronghold of the ancient Britons—one of the strongest in this part of the country. Defended by three massive ramparts, separated from each other by a deep fosse, its position was rendered still more secure by the presence of the Coquet on one side of the hill, the Woodhouse Burn on another, and the Harehaugh Burn on a third. On the outworks of the camp grows a profusion of the "petty whin," the "broad buckler fern," the "hard fern," and the "common bracken." There are several tumuli to the west of the camp.

On the north side of Harehaugh Hill, at Hepple Woodhouses, there is an old pele, or bastle-house, in an excellent state of preservation, now used as a byre. The arched vault, the spiral staircase, the stone spout above the doorway for pouring melted lead, etc., on assailants, and other characteristic features of these fortified dwellings, may still be seen. Carved on the door head appear the following initials and date :—

W.P.—B.P.—1602.
TAM.

James Allan, the celebrated performer on the Northumberland pipes, and a familiar figure at the old fairs and merry-meetings, was born at Woodhouses, in 1734. He was of gipsy descent, and possessed all the cunning and roguery of his race. Licentious and dishonest, his life was one long evasion of the law. Condemned to death for horse-stealing, his sentence was afterwards commuted to imprisonment for life, and he died in gaol in 1810. Innumerable anecdotes are told concerning this singular character and his marvellous achievements.

Many interesting memorials of the old Celtic population are to be found on the range of high ground to the left of the road leading to Holystone. At the foot of the "Beacon Hill" are five oblong stones, called the "Five Kings." They are a few feet apart from each other, in a straight line; one is thrown down, and lies at the base of the cliff. According to tradition, they are five brothers, who owned adjacent tracts of country. Possibly they may be connected in some way with the five grave-mounds on Holystone Common, a little to the north. The cairn, which gives this hill its name, is 988 feet above the sea-level. On Dews Hill a large barrow, or sepulchral mound, belonging to the brachy-cephalic, or round-headed Britons, was opened by Canon Greenwell in 1870, when several urns and other relics were obtained from it. It is sixty feet in diameter, and consists of a large circle in the centre, connected, by grooves or passages, with several smaller ones filled with graves. On another part of the hill is Dane's Cairn, or watch-tower. Crossing Holystone Common, where are the five large barrows already referred to, the road descends into

HOLYSTONE. or Halystane, as it is locally called, a place of some consequence in Saxon times, if we may credit the account of the wholesale immersions conducted by Paulinus. At present the aspect of the village is decidedly antique, and characteristic of the district. A number of irregularly-built cottages, many of them thatched and falling into ruins, and, to all appearance, constructed out of the materials of some ancient tower, the space enclosed by them partly transformed into little gardens; a small church and graveyard, an old water-mill, a farmstead, and inn; the whole clustering together on the north bank of a crystal stream, at the base of craggy hills, which rise on the west and south to a height of 800 feet. There was formerly a Benedictine Priory here, founded by one of the Umfravilles. The Sisterhood, which numbered from six to eight, had considerable possessions, some of their property being in Newcastle. At one time, however, they were so much impoverished by the incursions of the Scots that they were obliged to petition help from the Pope Nicholas IV., and the living of Alwinton was assigned to them. One of their patrons, Richard Umfraville, took holy orders, and became their chaplain and vicar. The remains of this Nunnery are very scanty, consisting of the end wall of a cattle-byre, in which the outlines of a pointed arch, built up, may be traced. Part of the site of the little Priory is occupied by the *Church of St. Mary*, restored in 1848-9. The lower portion of the walls of the nave are ancient, belonging to what is believed to have been a Norman structure. The original window-sills may still be seen *in situ*, about two feet beneath the new ones. Some fragments of carved stone-work, relics of the Priory. have been built into the walls. Three incised tomb-slabs are preserved in the south wall of the chancel. Two others may be seen in the churchyard, together with the base and socket of an ancient rood or church cross. Mungo's Well is called after St. Mungo, or Kentigern, a Celtic missionary. The principal attraction of Holystone, St. Ninian's, or "Our Lady's Well," is reached by following a footpath through the fields for a quarter of a mile north of the village. It lies in a little grove of firs not far from the junction of two Roman ways. The keys of the gate leading into the enclosure may be obtained at the Salmon Inn. Passing through a rustic arch, surmounted by a cross, the visitor approaches a large quadrangular bason, 39 feet by 24 feet, filled with water of the most crystalline purity. Through a bed of fine sand and gravel the spring bubbles up in numerous small jets, discharging about sixteen gallons of water per minute. The sides of the bason are lined with a wall of modern ashlar work, and, rising from the water, in the centre stands a tall stone cross, with an inscription upon it as follows:—"In this place Paulinus the Bishop baptized 3000 Northumbrians, Easter DCXXVII." On a board affixed to one of the trees is another inscription to the same effect, adding that the well belonged to the Nunnery in the village. The venerable bishop, however, was not at Sancta Petra (Holystone) on this Easter-day, but at Sancti Petri (St. Peter's Church), York. The tradition, though incorrect as to date, may still have some truth in it. At one end of the pool is a stone table, on which the British public has scrawled its names, and at the other a statue intended for Paulinus, clad in long flowing ecclesiastical robes. It was brought from Alnwick in 1780. Half-a-mile to the west of Holystone, adjoining the farm-house of Campville, are the remains of a large Celtic stronghold, defended by a double rampart and fosse. By the side of the Dove Crag Burn, which forms some pretty little waterfalls in the ravine hard by, is *Rob Roy's Cave*—a dim recess beneath a huge cliff, where the famous outlaw is said to have concealed himself. The spot is only accessible by a very narrow path, which may be entered opposite to the farm-house. A mile and a quarter further up the stream, at Dove Crag, is a very picturesque waterfall. Three-quarters of a mile north of Holystone is *Woodhall*, an old farmstead bearing the initials and date, E. H. F. H., 1650. From this point the road, which is bordered by thriving plantations, gradually descends to Harbottle, passing on the right *Clennell Hall*, the seat of Thomas Fenwick-Clennell, Esq.

HARBOTTLE, or, as it was written in 1244, Herbottel, is both a picturesque and historic little village. It lies on the south side of the Coquet, in a hollow, among craggy, heath-covered hills. The houses are quaint and comfortable in appearance, with gardens in front, and creepers or ivy around the doorways. The antiquity of the place may be inferred from the Saxon name Here Botl—the station or abode of the army. *Harbottle Castle* occupies the summit of a steeply-scarped hill, overlooking the river on one side, and the village on the other, and itself commanded by the stern and frowning hills around. It consisted of a quadrangular keep, a barbican, or entrance gateway, with a barmekyn, or enclosure for cattle, outside of it, and an inner and outer bailey, enclosed by curtain walls, which were strengthened by mural towers. The keep was defended by one fosse, and the whole enceinte by another, which was crossed by a draw-bridge. The principal remains of the keep, which stood on a conical point of the hill, on the south side, are two great masses of masonry. One of them hangs out of the perpendicular on the hill-side, while the other has slidden down the hill, and remains embedded in the ground at the bottom. The two baileys are overlooked by the keep, the inner one lying towards the north-west, and the outer one towards the north-east, and they are still divided from each other by a wall, partially ruined, running from the keep to the outer curtain wall. Of the inner ward, the draw-well still remains, and some portions of the curtain wall are standing on the south and west sides. The foundations of the domestic buildings may also be traced. On the north side are the fragments of a tower, where probably the postern was situated. Of the outer ward, the remains are few. Mounds of *débris* indicate the site of the barbican, which stood on the east side, but little is left of the stables, garners, and outer wall. The mound whereon the keep stands is supposed to have originally been a mote-hill of the ancient Britons. In Saxon times there was a stronghold here held by Mildred, the son of Ackman. This came in 1076 into the hands of Robert de Umfranvill, lord of Toures and Vian, otherwise called "Robert with the beard," who held the royal franchise of Redesdale by the service of defending that part of the country from enemies and wolves with that sword which King William had by his side when he entered Northumberland. For one of his descendants, Odenel de Umfraville, Henry II. built the present castle about the year 1160, as a protection to the wild district over which the lords of Harbottle held royal powers. Not long after its erection in 1174, it was taken by William the Lion in the course of that destructive raid into Northumberland, which ended so disastrously for himself at Alnwick. It was afterwards so strongly fortified that in 1296 the whole body of the Scots lay before its walls for two days, and were obliged to abandon the siege. In 1245 Harding, the historian, who is called "squier of the lord Umfraville," was resident at Harbottle Castle. Many a dismal sight must the dark dungeons of Harbottle have witnessed in these cruel times, for within them were confined the prisoners—and they would be very numerous—who were taken in the liberty of Redesdale. The castle had been so much ruined by the Scottish wars, that in 1336 Gilbert de Umfraville obtained permission to transfer them to his castle at Prudhoe. About 1436 the castle passed into the hands of the Tailleboys. It was for a long period the residence of the Warden of the Middle Marches. Henry VIII., in 1515, assigned this castle as a temporary abode for his sister Margaret, Queen-dowager of Scotland, after her marriage with Archibald Douglas, Earl of Angus. On the 7th of October she was admitted into the castle, and forty-eight hours afterwards gave birth to a daughter. And thus, says Mr. Tate, on the borders of the cheerless wastes of Redesdale was ushered into the world Margaret, Lady Douglas, who afterwards was the Countess of Lennox, mother of Lord Darnley, and grandmother of James I. of England. The castle in 1543 was in such a state of decay that the garrison could not remain in it without being in imminent peril from the fall of walls and timber. Part of it must have been kept in repair, for in 1599 Harbottle Castle was the scene of a rather singular case of unjustifiable imprisonment. The story which, with a few variations in regard to names and places, is celebrated in the ballad of "Christie's Will" in the minstrelsy of the Scottish border, is told in *Chambers's Domestic Annals of Scotland*, and runs as follows :—"A somewhat vindictive and violent young Scotchman, by name George Meldrum, of Dumbreck, having some grudge against a Mr. Gibson, afterwards Lord Durie, seized him as he was taking a ride by the waterside opposite Dundee, robbed him, and then with the assistance of two Border thieves carried him across the country through Edinburgh to Melrose. After dividing the money there, he conducted Mr. Gibson across the Border, landing him in the castle of Harbottle, which appears to have then been the residence of one George Ratcliff, and here the stolen lawyer was kept in strict durance for eight days. We may here adopt something of the traditionary story as preserved by Sir Walter Scott:—"He was imprisoned and solitary, receiving his food through an aperture in the wall, and never hearing the sound of a human voice save when a shepherd called his dog by the name of Batty, and when a female domestic called upon Madge, the cat. These, he concluded, were invocations of spirits, for he held himself to be in the dungeon of a sorcerer." How the poor captive was liberated is a matter for surmise. The castle fell rapidly into ruins after the Union, when the massive stronghold was less needed for the security of the district. It was finally dismantled by the Widdringtons to provide materials for the erection of the manor-house. In the centre of the village stands a beautiful fountain, erected in 1880 by public subscription, as a tribute to the memory of the late Mrs. Clennell. Harbottle is an exceptionally healthy place, the death-rate being only 4.7 per thousand, and mortality among children almost unknown. There are two inns—the Star and the Forster's Arms—and a well-known boarding-house, the Cherry Tree Cottage. A coach leaves every Monday and Saturday at 9.30 A.M. for Rothbury, returning from the Blue Bell at 3.50 P.M.

The Coquet, after encircling the castle, makes a curious bend, which is known as the "Devil's Elbow." Close to it, by the road-side, is the Presbyterian manse, past which there is a footpath leading up Harbottle Hill to the famous *Drake Stone*, a large block of stone of a reddish-grey grit, perched on the summit, about three-quarters of a mile from Harbottle. It is twenty-seven feet high, and visitors, though experiencing no difficulty in reaching the top, may sometimes find it no easy task to descend. The story is told that the inhabitants of Harbottle were surprised one summer morning at hearing a human voice bawling for assistance, and found it to proceed from a stranger on the Drake Stone, where he had passed a sleepless night. This huge boulder was the Draag Stone of the Druids; and the custom which prevailed till recent years, of passing sick children over the Drake Stone to facilitate their recovery, is probably a relic of ancient times, when they were passed through the fire on the same spot. About a hundred yards to the south-west is Harbottle Lough, a lonely little tarn, shut in on every side by ridges of grey gritstone crag, and surrounded by swamps of marsh cinquefoil (*Cormarum palustre*), common buck bean (*Menyanthes trifoliata*), smooth naked horse-tail (*Equisetum limosum*), and cotton grass; while sweeps of heathery moor, fragrant with gale and juniper, stretch away to the south in the direction of Redesdale. In summer time flocks of screaming sea-gulls may be seen wheeling round this elevated sheet of water. At *Harbottle Peels*, half-a-mile to the east of Harbottle, on the other side of the river, a remarkable cairn was opened by Canon Greenwell, and among other antiquities found was a food-vessel, which was, "with one exception, the most beautiful specimen of its class, both in fabric and ornamentation," that the learned Canon had ever met with. On the bottom of it was a cross formed by two transverse lines, with a series of dots along each side of the limbs.

A mile and a half from Harbottle and ten miles from Rothbury is the quiet and plain-looking little village of ALWINTON, which has been written Allington, Allenton, and Allonton. It is a favourite resort of anglers, and lies at the junction of two good trout-streams, the Coquet and the Alwine, on a sheltered flat by the water-side.

> "A region of repose it seems,
> A place of slumber and of dreams,
> Remote among the hills."

Here was formerly a hospital, subordinate to the nunnery of Holystone. There are two excellent inns in the village—the Rose and Thistle and the Red Lion. The *Church of St. Michael* is half-a-mile to the south, on a steep slope, and possesses a curious feature of interest in the separation of the nave from the chancel by a flight of ten steps. Originally a Norman edifice, it was subjected to many alterations in the early English period, and was restored in 1851. On the north side is the mortuary aisle of the Clennells of Harbottle, containing two massive altar-tombs. A portion of the south transept is the mortuary chapel of the Selbys of Biddlestone Hall. The ancient church was resorted to as a sanctuary. In the time of Gilbert de Umfreville, 1293, "Thomas de Holm, being taken within his franchise, escaped out of the prison at Harbottle, and fled to the church at Alwenton; but Simon Smart and Benedict Gley, porter of Harbottle, beheaded him at Simonseth, and hung his head up on the gallows at Harbottle." On the other side of the Coquet, half-a-mile from Alwinton, are the remains of Barrow pele. To the west of Alwinton some fine limestone scaurs rise from the edge of the stream, overhung with elm, birch, hazel, etc. "The sand beds of the Coquet," says Hodgson, "have been celebrated for their beautiful pebble-crystals, pale cornelians, chrysolites (?), and agates." The vale higher up is a narrow, grassy hollow, with a stony, unenclosed road. The most interesting point of the river is at Linn Shiels, two miles west of Alwinton. The name carries the mind of the tourist back to the sixteenth century, when, according to Bowes and Ellerker's survey in 1542, about the beginning of April, the old Borderers "were accustomed to take all their cattle into the high waste grounds towards the Borders, and build for themselves frail huts they call Scheals, and depasture their cattle in the valleys and hopes, as well as on the high grounds, till August, and this they call summering or shealing." Here, on the east, a precipice of porphyritic crag rises from the stream to a height of 100 feet above it. A little, however, below the horse-shoe shaped ravine, which is formed here, may be seen the interesting junction of the porphyry with the lowest formation of the carboniferous system—the Tuedian rocks. These dip towards the south east at a steep angle of inclination. The Ridlees Burn, which joins the Coquet just below, is almost coincident along its whole course with the line where the porphyry ceases. A mile north-west of Linn Shiels is *Shillmoor*, where the Usway Burn joins the Coquet. The tourist who wishes to walk on to Breamish Head and Cheviot must follow this streamlet past Fairhaugh to Uswayford, a shepherd's hut, five miles north, and to the west of a hill bearing the ominous name of "Bloody Bush Edge." Between Shillmoor and Windyhaugh, a distance of three miles, the eye has little to rest on except the rounded contour of the grassy hills, and the broken outlines of some porphyry crag, or the flashing runnels of the stream. As a type florula for one of our lower zone porphyritic crags, Mr. J. G. Baker has prepared an exhaustive list, the cliff selected being one between the above-named places. This list includes hairy rock-cress (*Arabis hirsuta*), common rock rose (*Helianthemum vulgare*), maiden pink (*Dianthus deltoides*), procumbent pearl-wort (*Sagina procumbens*), small upright St. John's wort (*Hypericum pulchrum*), Burnet rose (*Rosa spinosissima*), common Burnet saxifrage (*Pimpinella saxifraga*), foxglove (*Digitalis purpurea*), wood-sage (*Teucrium scorodonia*), field scorpion-grass (*Myosotis arvensis*), lamb's tongue (*Plantago lanceolata*). Half-a-mile from Windyhaugh, a little way after it has received the Barrow Burn, the Coquet flows between a narrow defile known as "The Wedder Loup." It was so called, says tradition, from the circumstance of a Border reiver having sprung fourteen feet across the cleft with a wedder on his back, and escaped from his pursuers. From another version of the story it would appear that the thief failed to cross it and fell into the stream below, where he was afterwards found with the legs of the sheep tied over his neck.

Five miles south-west of Windyhaugh, between the two forks of the Coquet, where the Watling Street crosses the Border, are the *Chew Green*, or, as they are locally termed, the *Makendon Camps*, at an elevation of 1436 feet above the sea-level. Two are of a large size, one containing 15 acres and the other 22. A third, which is in better preservation than these, covers an area of 6¼ acres. Beside the southern gateway of this camp is a peculiar circular flexure of the rampart, which is said to be characteristic of the camps of the ninth legion. Chew Green is believed to be the Ad Fines of the *Itinerary* of Richard of Cirencester. Surrounded by dark hills and monotonous moorland, the position of the Roman legionaries in this station must have been one of considerable hardship and discomfort. The old Roman road, before it reaches the camps, is called Kemmells, or Gammels Path. This was the rendezvous of the Wardens of the Middle Marches of England and Scotland when they met for the purpose of punishing offenders against the Border laws. As this road is referred to in old documents as Campaspeth, it is probable the place of meeting would be the Roman camps. Gamble Path, on the borders, was the scene of the hand-to-hand conflict in which Snowdon, a renowned Northumbrian swordsman, slew the celebrated Scotch champion, John Grieve. A mile to the south-east, on the line of this road, is the "Outer Golden Pot," and a mile distant, in the same direction, is the "Middle Golden Pot." These are pedestals which formerly contained columns of about ten inches in diameter, and are believed to be milliary pillars for the purpose of marking the distances on the Watling Street. Roy, in his *Military Antiquities*, speaks of five or more of these stones remaining between Redesdale and Chew Green, at somewhat less than an English mile distant from each other. Half-a-mile from the latter-named stone, on Foulplay Head, is a temporary camp of the Romans, and a little east of it is another square Roman camp, with earthen walls slightly rounded at the corners. Around this Border district extend the wastes of Thirlmoor, in which the beautiful Coquet takes its rise. The country to the west and north of Alwinton, bounded by the hills which form the dividing-line between England and Scotland, and by Cheviot, is one of the finest pasture-lands for sheep in the county. Of this tract the most famed portion is the lordship of Kidland, extending from two miles north of Alwinton to Cheviot. It consists of a number of conical-shaped hills, divided by lonely pastoral dales. Over the gently-swelling slopes, which are covered with a short, fine herbage, roam thousands of black-faced sheep of the Cheviot breed in perfect security. Very different was it three hundred years ago, when no one was willing to inhabit Kidland, even rent free. In later times Kidland was much frequented by smugglers, of whom many tales are told. The "Thieves' Rode" of the fourteenth century became the Salters Road of the eighteenth. About a mile north of Alwinton is *Clennell*, an old pele-tower modernised into a mansion-house. It is pleasantly situated among its patriarchal sycamores and ashes. Above the front door is the date of the old building 1365, though it is too much worn to be readily decipherable. The walls are in many places between six and seven feet thick, and in a dungeon below, now converted into a wine cellar, many a Border reiver is said to have been imprisoned and then taken out and hanged on the nearest tree. The manor gave its name to the ancient family of Clennell, which was seated here as early as the reign of Edward I. About three miles to the north is *Milkhope Hill*, on the south side of which are the traces of early entrenchments. Half-a-mile to the north are the ruins of the old *Chapel of Memmerkirk*, romantically situated at the foot of Cushat Law, the monarch of Kidland, a hill which rises to a height of 2019 feet above the sea-level. There is a story that the priest here, finding time hang heavy on his hands, employed himself in making bee-skeps. As he completed one a-day, it was easy to keep a record of the week and tell when the Sabbath day came round. On one occasion, however, he misplaced a skep, and when he should have been ready to celebrate the mass was hard at work, and naturally felt somewhat astonished at the arrival of his little congregation from the hills.

# ROTHBURY TO BIDDLESTONE AND ALNHAM.

**Snitter, 3 miles ; Trewhitt House, 5 miles ; Netherton, 6 miles ; Biddlestone Hall, 8 miles ; Alnham, 8 miles.**

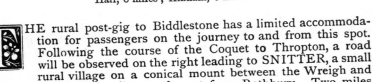

THE rural post-gig to Biddlestone has a limited accommodation for passengers on the journey to and from this spot. Following the course of the Coquet to Thropton, a road will be observed on the right leading to SNITTER, a small rural village on a conical mount between the Wreigh and Lorbottle Burns, three miles north-west from Rothbury. Two miles further on is *Trewhitt House*, a shooting-lodge of Lord Armstrong. High Trewhitt formerly belonged to the Claverings of Callaley, but was forfeited in consequence of their adherence to the Royal cause in 1652. To the north of the hall, on Robert's Law, are the remains of a circular Celtic camp.

A mile to the north-west is NETHERTON, a curious old village of one-storey houses and thatched cottages, wearing an aspect of comfort and repose. There are two small inns—the Phœnix and the Star.

A well-kept private road, about two miles in length, leads from the village to *Biddlestone Hall*, the stately mansion of the Selbys, which is built on the top of a gradual slope, and commands a fine prospect of the vale of the Coquet and the hills beyond. Behind it rise the stern, dark hills of Harden and Silverton, separated from the house by a deep and wooded dell, through which a moorland streamlet tumbles in a succession of pretty falls. Flourishing groves of oak and pine add to the picturesque surroundings of the place. Biddlestone is said to be the Osbaldistone Hall of *Rob Roy*. For more than six hundred years the Selbys have been seated at Biddlestone. The first of the name on record is Sir Walter de Selby, to whom Edward I. granted the lands of Biddlestone forfeited by William Vissard. The next Sir Walter, together with Sir John and Sir Gilbert Middleton, disclaimed the authority of Edward II., and took all the castles in the county with three exceptions. One affair in which he was concerned was peculiarly audacious. As the Bishop of Durham was escorting two legates from the Pope through his diocese, the three comrades in arms fell on the stately cavalcade at Rushyford, between Woodham and Ferryhill, rifled the Romish cardinals, and bore off the Bishop to Mitford Castle. In 1346 the bold Sir Walter was governor of Liddel Castle, and with the small force under him, resisted for six days the attacks of Robert Bruce and his army of 40,000 Scots. For this gallant defence he and his garrison were cruelly put to the sword. The present representative of this old family is Walter Charles Selby, Esq. From Biddlestone the tourist may either descend to Alwinton, two and a half miles distant, or follow a path over the fells to

ALNHAM.—This little village, which the natives pronounce Yeldom, is perhaps best approached from Netherton, *viâ* Screnwood. After descending the steep hill to the Aln, a road will be found on the left leading to the chief objects of interest at Alnham—viz., the church, the fortified vicarage, and the site of an old and extensive castle. These fully attest the antiquity of the village and its importance in former times. Alnham suffered much from the plundering raids of the Scots, and on October 10th, 1532, was burnt down by a band of these wild marauders. Nothing remains of Alnham Castle but the turf-covered foundations. These may be seen on a grassy knoll a short distance to the south-east of the church. The *Church of St. Michael*, which is said tc occupy the site of a small Roman station, is a compact little edifice, built during the Transitional period of English architecture. It was restored in 1870. The chancel arch is round, as are also the piers, but the capitals are early English. Of the transepts, the south one only belongs to the original structure. It is separated from the nave by an early English arch. Inlaid in the floor of the chancel are six tomb-slabs, ornamented with floriated crosses, the usual symbol of sex—the sword or shears. The font bears the date 1664, and has several heraldic devices on its bowl, which refer to the house of Percy. On a tomb-slab in the pavement close by is the curious epitaph of a Prendwick farmer, who was drowned in crossing the ford at Kelso. The vicar, Rev. W. D. Ground, is the author of *An Examination of the Structural Principles of Mr. Herbert Spencer's Philosophy* and *Ecce Christianus.* Adjoining the church is the vicarage, surrounded by trees and shrubberies. The nucleus of it is the strong pele-tower, referred to in the surveys of 1416 and 1542. On the Castle Hill, which towers up to the west, about half-a-mile distant, is a fine specimen of a Celtic camp, 100 yards in diameter. Close to the camp passes the old route of the smugglers—the Salters Road. At Hazelton Rigg the turbulent little "Rithe" dashes through a chasm which has received the name of "*Pigdon's Leap.*" A Border reiver named Pigdon, hotly pursued by his foes, sprang across the narrow gorge and escaped the threatened steel. Two miles east of Alnham is *Little Ryle*, where, in a farm-house, are the remains of an old pele or bastle-house, the ground floor having an arched roof of stone.

A good road through the well-wooded valley of the Aln may be followed to Whittingham, which is about three miles distant.

# ROTHBURY TO WHITTINGHAM AND LINHOPE.

Long Framlington, 5 miles; Cartington Castle (*viâ* Thropton), 3½ miles; Lorbottle, 4¾ miles; Callaley, 7½ miles; Whittingham, 9½ miles; Glanton, 11½ miles; Crawley Tower, 13 miles; Ingram, 16½ miles; Greaves Ash, 20½ miles; Linhope Spout, 21 miles.

THE tourist has several routes open to him. He may take the road to the east of Addycombe, which leads across the moors above Cragside, joining the North Road near Newton, or he may extend his journey by following the road past the Reivers' Well to Pauperhaugh, and proceed by way of Healey Cote to LONGFRAMLINGTON, on the North Road. This village will repay a visit. On the *Hall Hill*, near Heatherwick's Well, are the remains of a camp with triple entrenchments. As the eastern branch of the Watling Street passes a little to the west, it is probably a Roman camp. Here is also a small enclosure called the Evergreen, which contains the foundations of a fort, now covered with turf. The traces of platforms, on which cannons seem to have been planted, are visible on the south, north, and east sides. *Longframlington Church* consists of a nave, with an ancient porch on the south side, and a chancel. The chancel arch, supported by three slender detached columns on each side, the porch, and the doorway from it into the nave, are Transitional in style. On the south side of the chancel is one of the small original windows. To the east of it there was inserted, in the fourteenth century, a Decorated window of two lights, with geometric tracery in the heading. The village inn has the curious sign of the "Grand B" (Granby). A mile and a half to the north are the remains of an irregularly-shaped camp near the farm of Canada. On the banks of the rivulet close by are heaps of slag, or scoria. As the iron has been imperfectly extracted, it is thought that the smelting operations took place at a remote period, when the art of fluxing metals was little known. There is an old ballad connected with the moor, called "The Black Sow of Rimside and the Monk of Holy Island," which has, doubtlessly, given rise to the saying, "If ye were on Rimside Moor at twelve o'clock at night wi' a black sow by the tail, ye wadna be here to-night." This dreary waste was formerly much infested by highwaymen, who committed numerous outrages on travellers passing between Alnwick or Wooler and Morpeth. The road sweeps round behind Thrunton Crags, and enters Whittingham on the east side. The usual route to Whittingham is by way of Cartington.

Two miles from Rothbury, by way of Old Rothbury and West-hills, or three and a half by way of Thropton and Chirnells, are the picturesque ruins of *Cartington Castle*, consisting of what was probably the principal tower, and a portion of the east wall of the barmekin, situated on a woody knoll. The vaulted chambers underneath, with their barrel roofs of stone, are still in a good state of preservation. The remains of a smaller tower, with which the main tower was connected by a range of buildings, are still standing in the south-east corner of the garden. Cartington is mentioned in the list of Border fortresses drawn up in 1416, and described in the survey of 1542 as "a good fortress of two towres, and other strong houses . . . . in good reparacon." In 1644 the castle, which was held for the king by the Widdringtons, Selbys, Claverings, Horsleys, and other local families, was besieged by the Parliamentary forces. After a few hours resistance the garrison was overpowered, and the stronghold taken. Some years afterwards the castle was dismantled. The first recorded owner of Cartington was Ralph Fitzmain, the king's forester of Northumberland, who held it in 1154. It afterwards passed into the hands of the Cartingtons, Radcliffes, and Widdringtons, and is now the property of Lord Armstrong. Margaret, Queen of Scots, the widow of James IV., and wife of Angus, rested at Cartington, 16th November 1515, on her journey from Harbottle Castle, with her month-old daughter, Margaret Douglas, who was afterwards to become the wife of Lennox, mother of Darnley, and grandmother of James the First. On the brow of the hill, to the west of the farm, stands the so-called *Nunnery*, an alms-house for four Roman Catholic widows, founded, it is said, by Dame Mary Charlton, at the end of the seventeenth century. At the foot of Cartington Hill, on the south end, directly opposite to the telegraph poles, are the remains of two barrows opened by Canon Greenwell. Eastward, over the moor, across the height, and into the slack beyond, in the direction of Debdon House, is a small Druid's circle of nine large stones. About half-a-mile to the north, on the left-hand side of a moorland road, are two large stones called "Priest" and "Clerk," from their position, the one being a little below the other. On the highest points of these hills, above Cartington, are the remains of watch-towers, from which the Celtic inhabitants of the district could observe the movements of an approaching enemy. "The Dancing Green" at Debdon is a spot associated with the revels of the fairy-folk.

A mile and a quarter to the north of Cartington is LORBOTTLE, a small hamlet, which contains in the Saxon termination of its name the evidence of its antiquity. The ancient town of "Lowrebotell" was ravaged by a party of the Scots in 1532, and again in 1549, by another marauding band under the leadership of Mark Ker—

> "Mark Ker rode on, and Mark Ker rode on,
> And never a hoof or horn saw he,
> Till he came to the ford of Lorbottle burn,
> Where a dainty drove lay on the lea."

On Friday night, the 30th June 1648, a troop of weary cavaliers were destined to receive a somewhat unpleasant surprise at this little village, for, writes Major Saunderson, a Parliamentarian officer, "the first towne we fell into was Tossons, where wee took a liewtenant and sixe of his dragoons all in bed; the next towne was Lurbottle, where we tooke 60 horse and 60 men all in bed." About the beginning of the century some curious stories used to be told regarding the Lorbottle "cubs," or "coves." These are said to have been weak-minded persons, whose actions were decidedly peculiar. For instance, they could not tell when it was raining until they saw the drops falling on the surface of a pond called "Puddle," nor, when resting on a gate or fence, could they distinguish between their own limbs and those of their neighbours. They attempted to build a wall round the cuckoo, and so secure perpetual summer; and actually set off up the Long Crag with wain-ropes to haul down the new moon, imagining it to be a huge red cheese. The stories, as Mr. Dixon says, were probably fabricated to annoy certain of the inhabitants. A mile and a quarter to the north of the hamlet is *Lorbottle House*, in a pleasant situation, facing the south. It is protected on the east by a picturesque range of crags, called the Maiden Chambers. Half-a-mile to the north-west, on a fertile ridge, is *Dancing Hall*, a spot which, like Dancing Green, near Debdon, was formerly a haunt of the fairies. A mile and a half from Lorbottle is the once considerable village of

CALLALEY (*Caer-law-Ley*—the pasture near the camp-hill), now dwindled down to a few cottages. A magnificent avenue of beeches, through which the road to Whittingham passes, extends to the limits of the estate. On the low ground, to the west, among beautiful plantations and pleasure-grounds, is *Callaley Castle*, the seat of Henry Browne, Esq. It was erected about 1727. The tower at the west end is a portion of the ancient stronghold of the Claverings, described in the list of Border Fortresses of 1416 as "Castrum de Kaloule—Johis Claueveringe Chlr." It is the subject of a curious Northumbrian legend, which very probably had its origin in the apparent remains of extensive buildings on the castle hill. A lord of Callaley and his lady, so runs the story, once had a dispute as to the site of a new castle. He would have it built on a hill, she on the level ground below. However, in disregard of the lady's wishes, the foundations were laid on the top of the hill, and the walls began to rise. Not willing to be so easily set aside, the lady devised a scheme by which she might get her own way. A faithful attendant, dressed up like a boar, was to pull down nightly all that had been built during the day, and so awaken the superstitious fears of her good lord. The plan succeeded, and the work of destruction was set down to supernatural causes. Some retainers whom the lord had sent to watch the building came back to him with terror-stricken countenances. According to their report, a monstrous animal, of enormous power, had issued from the wood, and commenced to throw down the newly-reared masonry. Then, standing on the overturned stones, it had cried out, with a loud voice—

> "Callaly Castle, built on the height,
> Up in the day and down in the night;
> Builded down in the Shepherd's Shaw,
> It shall stand for aye, and never fa'."

Regarding the rhymes as an expression of the will of heaven, the lord abandoned the work, and built his castle low down in the vale, where a part of it still stands to commemorate the triumph of woman's wit. The chief internal feature of the present mansion is the great saloon, a magnificent chamber with a gallery at each end, decorated with highly-finished stucco-work. The Claverings, who for six centuries held the manor of Callaley, were descended from the "De Burghs," who traced their pedigree back to Charlemagne. From one member of this family, Eva, Baroness Clavering, who was four times married, were descended, in the short space of six generations, the following illustrious personages:—"A King of England, a Queen of England, a Duchess of York, a Duchess of Clarence, a Duke of Bedford, a Marquis of Montacute, an Earl of Westmoreland, an Earl of Northumberland, an Earl of Salisbury, an Earl of Kent, the celebrated Earl of Warwick, a Lord Latimer, a Lord Abergaveny, an Archbishop of York, and an Earl Marshal of England." The Claverings were well represented amongst the barons who compelled John to sign Magna Charta at Runnymede. At a later period they were among the most staunch adherents of the Stuart family, risking life and property for the Royal cause.

*The Castle Hill* is a detached mass of sandstone, rugged and somewhat conical in shape. Its sides are densely covered with pine and fir trees, and with a luxuriant undergrowth of brier and bracken. The summit, which is an irregular and broken plain of about two acres, is the site of a Celtic camp of the usual circular form, but modified to suit the inequalities of the ground. On the north side the escarpment of the hill is very steep, and there is but one rampart; there are two, however, on the other sides, and on the west side there is a third at a distance of about 100 yards down the hill. The fosse in some places has been excavated out of the solid rock. The principal features of interest about this hill-fortress is the inner rampart, which is formed of roughly-squared stones, built up with, and even bedded in lime. As the ancient Britons usually constructed their huge entrenchments of undressed stones and earth, it is believed that the Romans must have occupied this camp for a time. This supposition is strengthened by the fact of its being close to a Roman Way, and also commanding a view of the junction of Roman roads about two miles distant. There are two other camps, nearly obliterated, in the neighbourhood, one at the High Houses, the other at Rabbit Hall. Separated from the Castle Hill by a wooded gorge are the *Callaley Crags*, rising to a height of 919 feet above the sea-level. They, together with the Thrunton and Lorbottle Crags, are a continuation of a sandstone ridge which, after bounding the valley of the Till and Breamish at Doddington, Ros Castle, and Bewick, sweeps round by Beanley and Alnwick Moor to Thrunton, and thence in a southerly direction over the bleak upland moors of Northumberland. They are classed by geologists under the general term of "Simonside Grits." Very picturesque are these weathered crags, rising in bold escarpments from a steep slope strewn with boulders and fallen masses of rock. Flourishing plantations of larches and fir-trees, diversified with the beech, the birch, the bird-cherry, the wild cherry, and the mountain ash, extend all along the base and up the lower slopes of the crags; while on many a lofty ledge near the summit hardy individuals of the pine tribe have found a foothold. Amongst the ling and bracken with which nature has adorned the rugged sides and rocky shelves of the crags are innumerable "blaeberry bushes"—the bilberry, or whortleberry (*Vaccinium myrtillus*). These yield during the months of July and August an abundant crop of bright, black, bead-like berries, which are duly gathered by the people of the district. The rarer cowberry, or red whortleberry (*Vaccinium vitisidœa*), the cranberry, or marsh whortleberry (*Vaccinium oxycoccos*), and the black crowberry, or crawcrook (*Empetrum nigrum*), are also found growing here. Low down in the little patches of bogland on the plateau-like summit of the crags hide those strange, insectivorous plants, the round-leaved sundew (*Drosera rotundifolia*), and the common butterwort (*Pinguicula vulgaris*); while on the moors around wave the downy heads of the hare's tail, or cotton grass (*Eriophorum vaginatum*). In moist nooks and hollows among the woods, the sweet-scented mountain buckler fern, the male fern, and the graceful lady fern court the shade, mingling with beds of velvet bog moss (*Sphagnum*) of every hue, from the brightest green to the deepest crimson. The falcons which some years ago built their nests on Thrunton Crags have been driven away. A pool of water on Callaley Crag is a favourite resort of the dragon-fly. The slow-worm, lizard, and common adder are frequently met with in the open glades and among the rocks. From Callaley there is a winding footpath, which runs along the side of the ravine past a huge isolated mass of sandstone rising perpendicularly from the side of the hill, a considerable distance from the summit of Callaley Crag. Half-way up this upright block, on the east side, is *Macartney's*, or the *Priest's Cave*, a little oratory hewn out of the rock by a former chaplain of Callaley Castle. It has a well-formed Gothic entrance, and a window facing the east. To this quiet spot, it is said, he was accustomed to retire for meditation. Beyond the cave is a chasm in the range, by which an easy ascent of the crags may be made. There is a footpath along the top all the way to Thrunton. The view from the crags is one of the finest in Northumberland. It embraces not only the beautiful vale of Whittingham, with its fields and woods, its villages, halls, and hamlets, but the majestic forms of the Cheviot Hills on the one side and the wide-stretching moors on the other, with the dim outlines of the coast and the pale-blue sea beyond.

Two miles from Callaley, and nine miles and a half from Rothbury, is WHITTINGHAM, one of the most ancient and picturesque of north-country villages. Its name is of Saxon origin, and signifies either the "home of the Hewit" (*Hewiting-ham*), or the "dwelling in the white meadow" (*Hwit-ing-ham*). Beautifully situated on the flower-strewn banks of the Aln, in the centre of the most fertile vale of Northumberland, with the richest meadows and corn-fields around it, Whittingham retains the quiet old-world charm of rusticity which in the bright months of summer lures back the imagination to the fabled age of gold. The portion of the village on the north side of the rivulet, referred to in former times as "The Church Town," consists of the church, the vicarage, the schools, and a pretty row of cottages, raised above the road, and separated from it by well-trimmed flower-plots. That on the south side consists of an ancient pele-tower, the post-office, the court-house, the Castle Inn, and a number of small shops and cottages, built in a style of delightful irregularity. The river is crossed by two bridges, a neat stone bridge of four arches, and a small wooden foot-bridge, which seems to unite some cottage gardens on the one side with a shady grove of trees on the other. From the rich nature of the soil, and the sheltered position of the vale, the trees around Whittingham grow to a great height and size. At the east end of the village, near the Castle Inn, where the road turns south over Rimside Moor, is a fine old ash, 15 feet 6 inches in girth, and 85 feet in height.

Whittingham may claim to be considered a place of some historic interest, if the ancient chroniclers may be relied on. According to some authorities, it was the "Twyford near the river Alne," mentioned by Bede, where, at a great synod assembled in the presence of King Egfrid, A.D. 664, Cuthbert was chosen Bishop of Lindisfarne. More than two centuries afterwards, in A.D. 882, this famous saint, so we learn from the *Annals of Roger de Hoveden*, "appearing in a vision to Abbot Edred, commanded him to tell the bishop and all the army of the English and the Danes that, paying the price of his redemption, they must redeem Cuthred, the son of Hardicanute, whom the Danes had sold as a slave to a certain widow at Wintingham, and when redeemed they must make him their king. This was accordingly done, in the thirteenth year of the reign of King Alfred." The storm of civil war which broke over the country in the seventeenth century did not pass altogether by the little village. A letter in the State Papers narrates how on August 25th, 1640, about 400 horse ordered breakfast at Whittingham. They came from the Brandon Hills, singing psalms all the way. They behaved civilly, and paid for everything. Again, in the summer of 1648, Whittingham was visited by Cromwell's Roundheads, who captured there Lieutenant-Colonel Millet, with 200 horse. "Wee advanced on towards Branton," says Major Saunderson, in his report to head-quarters; "but finding that wee were cloyed with prisoners and horse and booty, wee retyred towards Whittingham, where Colonel Lilburne was labouring to rally into a firme body; for there appeared about Shawton four bodies of the enemies' horse, who had taken the alarme and got together; but all the rest wee took before they could mount."

What gives to Whittingham its chief interest in the eyes of antiquaries is the *Church of St. Bartholomew*, which stands on the site of a Saxon church, and still retains in its tower a portion of the original structure. Previous to the disastrous restoration of 1840, the tower, with the exception of its battlements, was almost intact, exhibiting the characteristic features of Saxon work in the long and short quoins and rubble walling, and in the rude baluster between the upper windows. As it then appeared, the tower is represented in Rickman's *Gothic Architecture*. The existing remains of the Saxon edifice may be seen in the lowest stage of the tower, as well as in the return angles of the nave on both the north and south sides. The tower rises straight from its foundations, without base or plinth. The quoins, or corner-stones, are arranged in a peculiar manner, a long upright block alternating with a short horizontal one much wider, and acting as a bond-stone to bind the rubble walling and keep it together. Notwithstanding that the storms of eleven centuries have broken over this old tower, the rubble masonry and the quoins, formed of the gritty sandstone of the district, are but little decayed. Inside the tower, nearly on a level with the belfry floor, above the basement, traces are visible in the east wall of the rude imposts and voussoirs of the tower-arch, much defaced and discoloured as if from the action of fire. The interior of the church is wholly in the early English style. The south aisle was probably erected in the thirteenth century, as the four arches dividing it from the nave belong to this period. The corresponding arches on the north side were built during the restoration of 1840, to replace some Norman arches of the twelfth century, which at this time were so ruthlessly taken down. At the west end of the south aisle is a small early English window, appropriately filled with stained glass representing St. Bartholomew, to whom the church is dedicated. The window next to the pulpit in the north transept, with the masonry below it, belongs to that period of early English architecture when the lancet began to be superseded by a combination of lights, and before the adoption of geometric tracery. The south transept was formerly the chantry of St. Peter, founded by one of the Eslingtons in the last half of the thirteenth century. The old piscina, beneath a trefoil-headed arch, may still be seen in the south wall. In the spandrels of the arches are the hatchments of the Ravensworth, Clavering, Atkinson, and Pawson families. A marble tablet preserves the memory of a young officer, Lieutenant Reginald Cyril Goodenough, who, at the early age of eighteen, fell before the Redan battery during the Crimean war in 1855.

The tombstones in the churchyard are, to a ludicrous extent, adorned with representations of the death's head, cross-bones, and hour-glass. An ancient stone cross, perhaps the boundary or churchyard-cross, stands on the wall near the east stile. Whittingham Church is supposed to have been founded in the middle of the eighth century by Ceolwulph, one of the kings of Northumberland, who, some years before he died, resigned his crown and retired into the monastery of Lindisfarne. This ancient religious house he richly endowed, one of his gifts to it being the town of "Hwitingham." The Vicarage used formerly to be a pele-tower, but this has been removed. There still remains, however, another of these Border castelets on the south side of the river, and very picturesque its grey walls look as they dominate the little cottages clustering around. In 1416 it was the property of William Heron, a member of the famous family who held Chipchase Ford and other castles. During the two or three centuries succeeding, it doubtlessly witnessed many a scene of violence and bloodshed. Now it is an almshouse, and a tablet over the doorway tells how, "By the munificence and piety of Lady Ravensworth, this ancient tower, which was formerly used by the villagers as a place of refuge in times of rapine and insecurity, was repaired and otherwise embellished for the use and benefit of the deserving poor, A.D. 1845." The basement of the building consists of the usual stone arched vault, with walls nine feet thick. An original doorway—a fine pointed arch—in the south wall, and a window in the east, prove it to be an Edwardian structure of the fourteenth century. Near the stone bridge, by the side of the road leading to Glanton, is an old house, having an outer flight of stone stairs. This was many years ago a noted hostelry, which bore the sign of "The Hole in the Wall." An elegant drinking-fountain stands by the roadside near the church.

Whittingham Fair is held on August 24th, and though not a celebration of such renown as when it was made the subject of the old ballad, is still the occasion of much festivity. At the east end of the village is the Castle Inn.

The railway station of Whittingham, on the new Alnwick and Cornhill Branch, is a mile and a quarter east of the village. Adjoining it stands the comfortable Bridge of Aln Inn.

Whittingham is the centre of the most delightful walks and excursions. A very enjoyable round of six miles may be made by way of the Thrunton Crags and Callaley. A road from the inn leads up the hill to Whittingham Lane, and thence to the foot of the crags, passing about two hundred yards to the right *St. Ninian's Well.* Going through a gate on the right, and skirting the edge of the wood for 880 yards, the tourist, by striking due east up the slope, will find, 220 yards from the footpath below and 110 yards from the top, *Wedderburn's Cave*, the retreat of a noted outlaw. Having made free with the flocks of the vale of Whittingham, he was, according to the tradition of the neighbourhood, pursued, and finally run to earth here. As no one could pass into the cave, through the small entrance, without being at the mercy of the desperate man, it was found necessary to make an opening in the top of the cave and shoot the delinquent from above. One can easily realise how secure was the retreat of this outlaw from the difficulty experienced in finding it. The letter V has been carved over the entrance, and so affords a slight clue. A footpath runs along the top of the crags, and may be followed to Callaley. From this place Whittingham may be reached, first by taking a footpath through the fields at the east end of the avenue, and then by following the road on to which it leads to the right.

A mile to the west of Whittingham is *Eslington Hall*, a country seat of Lord Ravensworth, built in 1720 on the site of an old Border pele-tower. It is an elegant building of polished freestone, with a terrace in front of it, standing in a low sheltered situation on the north bank of the Aln, and surrounded by picturesque gardens and shrubberies. On the south side of the river is a well-wooded park, stocked with a fine herd of fallow deer. A broad avenue runs through it from the east to the west lodge. One hundred yards west-north-west of the former stands a large silver fir, the finest of a group of nine. It is 14 feet in girth, and 130 feet in height. One hundred yards further in the same direction, close to the Aln, is a fine birch, 7 feet 6 inches in girth, and 60 feet high. Among the valuable pictures in the house are portraits of the Simpsons and Lyons, maternal ancestors of Lord Ravensworth, painted by Angelica Kaufman and Sir J. Reynolds. Nothing remains of the ancient stronghold of the Eslingtons, Heselriggs, and Collingwoods, which is noticed as early as 1336, and described in 1542 as in a good state of preservation. This tower was on one occasion stormed by the Scots, when several of the defenders were slain, Sir Cuthbert Collingwood, the owner, barely escaping with his life. In the north wall of the kitchen garden is a fine Jacobean doorway. "The Lady's Bridge," which spans the Aln near the present east lodge with one graceful arch, forms the subject of one of Bewick's woodcuts. The manor of Eslington was, in the time of Henry II. (1161), in the possession of Alan de Essington, and was held by members of his family till the middle of the fourteenth century. After passing through the hands of the Heselriggs and Herons, it became, in the reign of Henry VIII., the property of the celebrated family of the Collingwoods. A Scotch ballad preserves to us the character of one member of this family, Sir Cuthbert Collingwood, who, in the reign of Elizabeth, was taken prisoner at the Raid of the Reidswire—

"But if ye wad a souldier search
Amang them a' were ta'en that night,
Was nane sae worthie to put in verse,
As Collingwood, that courteous knight."

Among the Northumbrian Jacobites executed in 1716 for the part they had taken in the unfortunate rising of 1715 was another brave-hearted member of this family, alluded to in the ballad, "Lord Derwentwater's Farewell"—

"And fare thee well, George Collingwood,
Since fate has put us down;
If thou and I have lost our lives,
Our king has lost his crown."

From Eslington there is a gradual ascent of a mile and a half to *Great Ryle*, a large farmstead at the foot of a rounded heathery hill, called Chubden, 916 feet above the sea-level—a mass of porphyry protruding like a promontory from the Cheviot range. A pleasant round may be completed by returning to Whittingham, *viâ* Little Ryle. A tourist of antiquarian tastes will desire to explore the high moorlands towards Ingram, for the memorials of the old Celtic population are very numerous. There is a large camp on the north-east slope of Chubden Hill, defended by a double rampart. Within a distance of less than a mile, and chiefly in a north-west and north-east direction, are camps and fortifications on Old Fawdon Hill, Wether Hill, Gibb's Hill, and Castle Knowe. Fawdon Hill, according to a time-honoured tradition, was the royal residence of the Queen Mab of Northumberland and her elfin courtiers. From their porphyry halls in the hill-side the train of the tiny folk, clad in pea-green costume, might have been seen by some belated shepherd or rustic, winding their way to some velvety sward, there to dance and revel beneath the full-orbed moon. One very pleasant route from Whittingham to Ingram and the valley of the Breamish is through the fields to Howbalk, behind Glanton Pike, to the little village of Branton, across the Breamish, and then along its north bank to Ingram, the total distance being about five miles. A somewhat longer but more interesting route is by the Wooler road and Brandon. The road gradually ascends from Whittingham for two miles to

GLANTON, a large and picturesque village, commanding a fine view of the valleys of the Aln and Breamish. Here 180 Royalist troopers were taken prisoners in bed by Colonel Sanderson and his Roundheads in 1648. There are two inns—the Queen's Head and the Red Lion. One hundred and fifty feet above the village rises the conical hill of *Glanton Pike*. On this lofty site is the mansion-house of F. J. Collingwood, Esq., J.P., surrounded by plantations of pines and firs, and other hardy trees. Near the house is the observatory, well-known to students of meteorology. Near Glanton several interesting relics of the ancient Britons have been found. Instead of following the main road to Powburn, the tourist will find it preferable to leave the village at the east end, and descend the hill to Dean House, and turn to the left through Crawley Dene. On one side of the rapidly-descending road is a craggy steep rising sheer above it; on the other the little gorge, with its trees and ferns and wild-flowers, recently marred by a railway embankment. In the dene, the geologist will observe a section of the Tuedian, or lower carboniferous group of rocks. Passing the Glanton railway station, the road joins the Wooler turnpike near the Plough Inn. The Devil's Causeway—a branch from the Watling Street—passes through the garden of the inn. Half-a-mile to the east, on the high ground above the Breamish, is *Crawley Tower*, one of the oldest and most interesting of the Border peles. It occupies the east angle of a Roman camp, and appears to have been constructed out of the ruined masonry of the ramparts. The camp is 290 feet long, and 160 feet broad, and is surrounded by a fosse 30 feet wide, and an agger 20 feet thick. As the Devil's Causeway crossed the Breamish just below, this strong military station was, no doubt, intended to guard the passage and keep in subjection the tribes who occupied the numerous camps of the district. Crawley was anciently spelt Crawlawe, supposed to be a corruption of *caer*, a fort, and *law*, a hill. A mile north of Powburn, a branch road leads to the left at Brandon White House for another mile to the hamlet of *Brandon*, where there are the remains of an old chapel and disused graveyard. Three Celtic leaf-shaped bronze swords were found near the summit of a hill east of Brandon Farm.

A mile and a half further west on the south side of the river is INGRAM, a small and picturesque village situated on the narrow strip of level ground adjoining the Breamish. From its bright green haughs slope upward the gently-moulded hills that, covered with a short, fine grass, yield such excellent pasturage to sheep. From the numerous foundations of ruined houses which can be traced on the sides of the road, and in the neighbouring fields, it may be inferred that Ingram was once a much more populous place than it is at present. The base of its market cross still stands on the village green. Its name proves its antiquity. Ingéra-ham, the home of the "In yore folk,"—that is, of the people of yore, of the olden people of the land. On a low terrace above the river stands the ancient *Church of St. Michael*, which, with the Rectory close by it, is pleasantly girdled with elms. The sacred edifice has at one time been much larger, for, built up in the walls of the nave are the columns and arches of two arcades, proving the former existence of north and south aisles. The square low massive tower is worthy of notice, as a relic of the "troublous times," when strength was the first essential of a building, whether ecclesiastical or domestic. The windows are not such as would readily admit a moss-trooper, or even a missile. The lowest storey is simply lighted by arrow-slits, and the upper stages with a square-headed opening and lancets of the smallest dimensions. The large rough tower-arch—so rude, says Mr. Wilson, that it may possibly be a slight fragment of an earlier edifice—has been built up and reduced to a small modern doorway, which is the only entrance to the tower. The chancel arch and the two arcades are early English in style. Built up in the interior face of the east wall of the chancel is a fragment of an effigy of an ecclesiastic, consisting only of the feet, with a portion of the drapery, and angels holding candlesticks on each side of them. The bason of the font, which bears the date March 11th, 1662, is ornamented with heraldic devices, identified by Mr. Longstaffe as those of the Percy family. In the churchyard is a tombstone covering the grave of Mrs Allgood and her two sons, who were killed in the railway accident at Abbot's Ripon, January 21st, 1876. It is a rough unhewn fragment of a rock on which the deceased lady sat during her last stroll among the neighbouring hills. The hills around Ingram must, at an early period, have been very thickly populated, to judge from the numerous remains of camps, circular dwellings, and grave-mounds. To the north-east, on a green hill called Heddon, may be traced several lines of ancient terrace cultivation. From Ingram there is a gradual ascent westward to the summit of Brough Law, which has been strongly fortified by the Celtic population as an almost impregnable retreat in time of danger. Two high and massive ramparts surround it, the space between them being divided by cross walls. Inside the fort are traces of hut-circles. Brough Law is worth climbing for the view it commands of the narrow vale of the Breamish and the undulating landscape around it.

On one side of the hill the river is seen running due south and north, on the other, due west and east. From the summit to the stream the ground falls away in a very steep descent, covered with loose rolling stones, called glidders, or glitters. On Knock Hill, Ewe Hill, and Reaveley Hill, on the other side of the river, are various camps and tumuli. Two miles further up the valley is the farmstead of Hartside.

Near the foot of Hartside Hill there was discovered, in 1861, a small silver cross, inscribed on one side with the name of Acca, Bp. of Hexham, and on the other with the letters L. W. It is supposed to have been one of the crosses given to the Hexham pilgrims. Scattered over the Hartside Hills are several camps and hut-circles. Near to Linhope Farne, about four miles from Ingram, are the remarkable cyclopean remains of the Celtic oppidum, or fortified town, of *Greaves Ash*, covering an area of twenty acres. From the derivation of the name, Gerefa-folc-Ash (Greve's-folk-ash), or, as it may be rendered, "the burnt hamlet of the tributaries," it may be inferred that the Britons inhabiting the place in Saxon times were subject to the Greve, or Governor of the district, and had brought upon themselves in some way the calamity perpetuated in the name. This ancient town occupies a platform of level and rocky ground on the southern slope of Greenshaw Hill, and is in three divisions, which may be conveniently spoken of as the western, eastern, and upper forts. The first of these is the largest, and consists of a number of hut-circles, surrounded by two strong ramparts of unhewn blocks of porphyry. The outer rampart is from 10 feet to 12 feet in width, the inner one from 5 feet to 7 feet; their height would probably be 10 feet or 15 feet. The space between them is divided by cross walls into enclosures for cattle or horses. The antiquarian visitor will find the construction of these defences, and the methods adopted to give them stability, an interesting study. The facing-stones are large, and carefully fitted together. Stones of a smaller size fill up the interior of the wall. At intervals long and very large blocks are set upright, and at their sides flatter stones are built into irregular courses. In some parts courses of stones have been built across the breadth of the wall at right angles to its face, and this has been done, says Mr. Tate, so carefully that the places where it occurs have been mistaken for the sides of gateways. The chief danger seems to have been anticipated on the south side, for there the ramparts approach within 22 feet of each other, and are yet further strengthened by the insertion of a third rampart between them. Considerable skill in military engineering has been shown in the arrangement of the gateways. The entrance through the inner rampart is on the east, while that through the outer rampart, instead of being opposite to it, is thirty yards to the south, and is defended by an additional rampart.

Passing up the hollow way through the opening in the supplementary rampart, through the gateway in the outer rampart, and then through that in the inner rampart, the visitor will find himself among the ruins of the ancient dwellings. The foundations of eighteen of these are still visible. They are, for the most part, circular in form, varying from 11 to 27 feet in diameter, the usual size being between 16 and 20 feet. The floors are flagged and paved with small stones. In the masonry exposed on the south side of the inner rampart will be observed a conduit-like opening, 12 inches high and 14 inches wide at the bottom. This has been discovered to be a flue running through the whole breadth of the rampart into a hut on the other side, its purpose being to convey the smoke from a wood-fire lighted on a primitive fire-place hollowed out of the floor.

The Eastern Fort occupies higher ground than the western fort, and is connected with it by a massive rampart. One of the finest examples of a hut is here. From the north-east, corner of the fort a road leads through a well-formed gateway to the Upper Fort, 100 yards further to the north-east, on a high shoulder of Greenshaw Hill. Irregular in form, its greatest length is 220 feet from north to south, and its breadth from east to west 200 feet. In the interior are the distinct remains of fifteen hut-circles, most of them flagged and paved. There are also some large enclosures, one of which was found to be connected with a hut at a higher level by rude steps.

A quarter of a mile to the south on *Megrim's Knowe*, on the opposite side of the Breamish, are the remains of camps and hut-circles. Two miles to the south-east, on the high ground above the Breamish, is an important hill-fortress, called the *Chesters*. By striking due south from Hartside to the river, a ford will be discovered, giving access to a path which leads up the hill-side to the camp and the farm-house of the same name close by. The same arrangement will be observed in this camp as in others belonging to the Celtic tribes of the district—viz., a collection of circular huts and rectangular dwellings, surrounded by two great ramparts of circular form. During the excavations a green glass bead, supposed to have been the charm called by the Druids the Ovum Anguinum, was found.

From the Chesters, there is a footpath over the moorland to Great Ryle, joining the road that leads to Whittingham.

Three-quarters of a mile from Greaves Ash, up the deep and narrow gorge of the Linhope Burn, is *Linhope Spout*, the finest waterfall of the district. The little burn, which comes from the neighbouring hills, tumbles over a brown porphyritic crag into a deep pool fifty-six feet below. The rocky bason, fringed with fern and foliage, is about seven feet across, and fifteen feet deep.

# ROTHBURY TO BRINKBURN AND FELTON.

Pauperhaugh, 3 miles ; Brinkburn, 4½ miles ; Weldon Bridge, 6 miles ; Felton, 9½ miles ; Church of Guyzance, 11½ miles ; Acklington, 13 miles.

THE road past the Reiver's Well and Cragside continues along the hill-side like a terrace above the Coquet. After crossing the Black Burn, a singular mound will be observed on the left, resembling somewhat the mote-hills in various parts of the country. Three-quarters of a mile beyond is *Pauperhaugh*, sometimes called Pepperhaugh, where the Coquet is spanned by a picturesque stone bridge. The road over it leads to Brinkburn Station.

A mile and a quarter beyond, past some disused ironworks, is BRINKBURN. The visitor to this charming and romantic spot should, before proceeding to the Priory, call at the lodge, as the old man who acts as guide and keeps the key of the building resides there. The carriage drive has been formed on the edge of the steep scaurs above the river, and slopes in a gradual descent of half-a-mile to the ruins, the glimpses of river-scenery through the trees and shrubs being highly-picturesque. The Priory is situated on a narrow piece of low ground, around which the Coquet sweeps in the form of a loop—

"An ancient fabric awful in repose."

From the north wall of the building on the one side, and the south brink of the river on the other, rise beautifully-wooded slopes, so completely over-topping and concealing the ruins that one might be within a very short distance of them without suspecting the fact. A party of Scots were once in this predicament, if tradition may be believed. They had sought for it a long time in vain, with a view to plunder, and, quite baffled, were returning homeward, when they were arrested by the sound of bells, which the monks were ringing for joy at their departure. Turning back, they forced their way through the dense wood, and burst in on the brethren as they were assembled to offer up thanks for their deliverance. After pillaging the sacred edifice, they set fire to it, and departed, leaving the monks who had escaped to mourn over the blackened walls and smoking rafters. A similar story is told respecting Blanchland Priory.

*Brinkburn Priory*, according to Grose, was founded in the reign of Henry I., and dedicated to St. Peter by William de Bertram, baron of

Mitford, who endowed it with lands out of his wastes, and established there Black Canons, or Canons Regular, of the order of St. Augustine. Not much is known of the little religious community who lived here, "the world forgetting, by the world forgot." Of their magnificent Priory the remains are considerable, consisting of the *Church of St. Peter and St. Paul*, and the ruins of some of the monastic buildings. The church was partly restored in 1858, and is in an excellent state of preservation. It is a large cruciform edifice, 131 feet in length, having a nave of six bays, with a north aisle, transepts with aisles on the east, a chancel, and a low, square central tower, upborne on lofty and well-proportioned arches. "The richest Norman work," says Mr Wilson, "is here blended inextricably with the purest early English; and the fabric must be regarded as one of the most fascinating specimens of the transition from one to the other that there is in the country." This combination of styles is seen in the windows of the clerestory and triforium. There is little ornamentation inside the church, but its appearance, though plain and austere, is very impressive. In the south wall of the chancel is a slant-opening, through which strangers were permitted to view the celebration of the mass. A newel-staircase leads up to the belfry and roof of the tower. As interesting memorials of the past may be mentioned :—A double piscina, under a canopy of two pointed arches; an ancient font; a tomb-slab, ornamented with a cross-fleury, a mitre and crozier, to the memory of Prior William, Suffragan Bishop of Durham, who died in 1483. The doorway, on the north side of the nave, which first meets the gaze of the visitor descending the carriage-drive, is an exceedingly beautiful specimen of Transition work. It is round-headed, richly ornamented with the Norman fillet, chevron and beak-head carvings, as well as the early English quartrefoil flower, and surmounted by three trefoil-headed arches, on delicate shafts. Grotesque heads and figures appear between the mouldings. On the southern side of the nave, near the western angle, is another round-headed doorway, the capitals of which are entirely sculptured with the Norman knot-work, and the mouldings ornamented at intervals with large knots and bosses. The north arcade of the cloisters runs along this wall of the church; and the finely-enriched doorway, by which the monks entered the building from the quiet quadrangle, still remains to the east of the one just described. Another doorway, in the Transitional style, gives admission to the south transept. At the south end of this transept is an ivy-grown square building, with a Norman arch and groined roof, probably the Chapter-house. The rest of the monastic buildings have been removed to make way for the present castellated mansion-house, which has been built over the barrel-vaulted cellars of the Priory, and still contains some of the old walls. Near the east end of the church is a subterranean passage, or covered way, running for a short distance eastward. Scattered about the side entrance to it are several richly-carved stones, and an interesting sun-dial with many faces. During some excavations to the south-west of the church, in 1834-5, a copper jug of Edwardian character was found, containing nearly three hundred gold coins of Edward III., Richard II., and Henry IV. A portion of the lawn occupies the site of the monastic cemetery. A deep part of the river here bears the name of the "Bell Pool." The story runs that the Scots, during one of their raids, flung the bells of the Priory into it. Whoever succeeds in recovering them is assured by tradition that other treasures also will reward his efforts. This unreliable authority also states that on the hill opposite, where a bell was unearthed some years ago, Cromwell once planted his cannon and blew down part of the building. The beauty of Brinkburn did not escape the eye of Turner, who has given a charming view of the ruins in his *England and Wales.* East of the Priory is a picturesque water-mill, in which old portions of masonry are to be found. Near it may be seen, when the water is low, the piers of a Roman bridge, by which a branch of the Watling Street crossed the Coquet. In the field above the Priory are the remains of camps and the foundations of old habitations, probably Celtic, as several cistvaens, urns, etc., have been brought to light. A shady green spot in the precincts of Brinkburn is pointed out by a pretty tradition as the burial-place of the Northumbrian fairies. Their tiny forms are no longer seen in the moon-lit glade, but the flowers they loved still bloom plentifully beneath the shelter of green groves. Amongst these may be named the wood-basil, foxglove, throat-wort, woodruff, golden saxifrage, fig-wort, sweet-cicely, celandine, pellitory, toad-flax, St. John's wort, and barberry.

*Gawen's Field,* on the Brinkburn estate, receives its name from Gawen Redhead, a noted reiver, who was outlawed in the reign of Queen Elizabeth. His abode was a hollow oak tree, of such large dimensions that half-a-dozen calves are said to have been wintered in it at the beginning of last century. The railway station at Brinkburn is four miles from the Priory. From the lodge an undulating road, pleasantly bordered with trees, follows the course of the Coquet for a mile and a half to

WELDON BRIDGE. The Anglers' Inn here is a famous old hostelry of the posting-days, now chiefly patronised by members of the "gentle craft," and besung in their "Garlands":—

"At Weldon Bridge there's wale o' wine,
If ye hae coin in pocket;
If ye can thraw a heckle fine,
There's wale o' trout in Coquet."

*Weldon Hall,* long the family residence of the Lisles, is half-a-mile to the north-east. From Weldon Bridge there is a delightful walk along the winding banks of the Coquet past Elyhaugh (1¾ miles) to Felton (3½ miles).

FELTON is a charming little village, situated on a gentle declivity which rises from the north bank of the Coquet. Through the midst of it passes the great North Road to Alnwick. The scenery around it is as beautiful as any in the whole vale of the Coquet. It possesses all that rural grace and charm which spring from the harmony of lichened rock and running waters, hanging woods and sweeping meadows. Felton is associated with two or three historical events of some importance. Here the barons of Northumberland did homage to Alexander, King of Scotland, a defection which King John punished in 1216 by reducing the village to ashes. Here, on October 10th, 1715, the little band of Northumbrian Jacobites, on their way to Morpeth, were joined by "seventy Scots horse, or rather gentlemen from the Borders." The Duke of Cumberland and his army passed through, in 1745, on his way to Scotland. A little to the west of the village is the *Church of St. Michael*, an early English edifice dating from the thirteenth century, when it consisted of a chancel and nave. In the fourteenth century it was enlarged by the addition of the two aisles. The chancel, with its graceful pointed arch, belongs to the original building. The present porch is a continuation of the thirteenth-century doorway, which still possesses its old stone ribbing. In the east end of the south aisle is a fine early English window, the head of which is enriched with geometric tracery carved out of a single stone. Tradition states that it was brought from Brinkburn Priory. The low-arched priest's door in the south wall of the chancel has been built up.

Not far from the church is *Felton Park*, the seat of Hugh Andrews, Esq. The house is a handsome stone building, situated on gently rising ground in the park, amid very beautiful and extensive grounds. Attached to it is the *Roman Catholic Chapel of St. Mary*, built in the pointed Decorated style. The garden contains a fine collection of plants from Japan, remarkable for the peculiar and striking beauty of the leaves. There is a heronry in Felton Park of seventeen nests. The village has a small reading-room. The principal inn is the Red Lion. On the south side of the river is *West Thirston*, connected with Felton by a substantial stone bridge of three arches. Here is a comfortable hostelry, the Northumberland Arms. The nearest railway station is Acklington, three miles and a half distant by the road. Two miles north-west is *Swarland Hall*, the residence of James John Allison, Esq. It stands in a beautiful park, and was built about the year 1765. In front of the hall, and close to the road, is an elegant obelisk of white freestone, erected to the memory of Lord Nelson, in 1807. On the shaft is inscribed the famous signal to the fleet, "England expects every man to do his duty." The pedestal bears the following inscription :—"Not to commemorate the Public Virtue and Heroic Achievements of Nelson, which is the duty of England, but to the Memory of Private Friendship, this Erection is dedicated by Alexander Davison." At the west end of *Swarland* village are the remains of the Old Hall, built by the family of Heselrige, about the year 1640, on the site of an old pele. Two miles north-east of Felton, near the farm-house of Brainshaugh, are the ruins of the little *Church of Guyzance*, picturesquely standing on a sheltered haugh in a bend of the Coquet. These consist of the nave and part of the chancel, which are each about 30 feet long and 16 feet broad. According to Mr. Longstaffe, the general character of the building is Transitional. A striking example of this style may be seen in a capital, adorned with vertical strings of the nail-head ornament, at present used as the headstone of a grave. The piscina is decorated, and has probably had three basins. A tombstone, showing the lower portion of a cross carved upon it, has been built into the window at the west end. This ancient edifice is the *Church of St. Wilfred of Gysnes*, which was given to the canons of Alnwick by Richard Tyson, in the twelfth century. According to a popular tradition, there was a subterranean passage between Brainshaugh and Brinkburn. It may have been a secret footpath through the dense wood which, in early times, filled the vale of Coquet. Crossing the river by the ferry, a road will be found leading to Acklington station, which is a mile and a quarter from the ruins. The construction of a dam, eleven feet high, at Acklington, in 1776-78, is said to have been one of the causes why the salmon have left the Coquet. Frank Buckland describes the pain he felt, when surveying the Coquet, at seeing the vain attempts of the bull-trout to get up the weir. "In the space of one minute," he says, "I saw no less than twenty-seven fish make jumps, and in the next minute and and a half I counted thirty fish. Some actually leapt nine feet straight into the air, others jumped into the body of the waterfall, or dashed themselves against the solid wall, and fell back, half-stunned. Many had evidently given it up for a bad job, and were swimming about with their little black noses projecting out of the white boiling water, doubtlessly crying out, 'We can't get up, we can't get up! Cruel miller, to put this weir. Mr. Buckland, do what you can for us.' 'Wait a bit, my dear fish,' I said; 'the Duke of Northumberland is a kind man, and he is going to make a ladder for you. The plans are nearly ready, and you shall then jump for joy, and not for pain. In the meantime read this.' So I pinned a large piece of paper on the weir, which read thus :—

'NOTICE TO SALMON AND BULL TROUT!

'No road at present over this weir. Go down stream, taking the first turn to the right, and you will find good travelling water up stream, and no jumping required.—F. T. B.'"

# ALNWICK SECTION.

## ALNWICK.

ALNWICK ranks next to Newcastle among Northumbrian towns, both in regard to size and importance, but, unlike the great capital of the coal district, it has remained unaffected by the tremendous industrial changes of the century. Lying peacefully amid its pastoral hills, by the side of a river unpolluted by modern commerce, this ancient Border town still presents the plain and austere aspect which it wore when the great stage coaches passed through on their way from London to Edinburgh. In Newcastle, spite of its numerous relics of antiquity, one's mind is ever dominated by the potent Present, whereas in Alnwick, as in York or Beverley, for instance, it is ever under the spell of the dreamy Past. The quaint, irregular stone-built houses are touched with the sober hues of antiquity, and seem to take their character from the great baronial relic of feudal times. The history of the town is chiefly a record of

> "Old unhappy far-off things
> And battles long ago."

From the numerous traces of camps, circular dwellings, and burial-grounds in the neighbourhood, it is possible that the ancient Britons had a settlement here on the site of the castle. The waters of the river being then, as now, exceedingly "bright and clear," they called it A'lain or Aln. The Romans apparently visited the place, as some of their coins have been discovered. The Saxons, who had established themselves at Bamburgh, Whittingham, and other places in the district, were really the founders of the present town. They called it A'lain-Wick—the town on the clear water. As the Domesday-book did not include the northern counties, it is not known what was the name of the Saxon lord dispossessed of his lands at the Conquest in favour of Gislebert Tyson, the standard-bearer of the Conqueror.

Alnwick seems to have been a disastrous spot to the kings of Scotland, for, near the town, Malcolm Caenmore was slain in 1093, and William the Lion made prisoner in 1219. King John passed through in 1209 and 1213, and, during his devastating expedition to the northern counties, burnt the place to the ground in 1216. Henry III.

visited Alnwick in 1256. Edward I. was here on several occasions, between 1291 and 1298. Edward II. passed through in 1311, and Edward III. in 1335. The Scots made an unsuccessful assault on Alnwick Castle in 1327, and a century later burnt the town. In 1463 the Earl of Warwick took possession of the castle on behalf of Edward IV., but in 1464 it fell into the hands of Queen Margaret. Alnwick was occupied by both Royalists and Roundheads during the wars between Charles I. and his Parliament. It suffered severely from the plague in 1637, and also from the cholera in 1849.

The town of Alnwick lies principally on the south side of the Aln, on ground which slopes gently upward to the new railway station—one of the finest and most convenient of its kind on the North Eastern system. The first object which meets the gaze of the visitor entering Alnwick from the south is a fluted column, 83 feet high, surmounted by a lion, with stiff horizontal tail. This is the Percy Tenantry Column, or, as it is sometimes called, "The Farmers' Folly," standing on a green knoll, which has been planted with lilac shrubs and trees, and laid out in walks. It was erected in 1816 by the tenants of Hugh, second Duke of Northumberland, in grateful recognition of his liberality in remitting their rents during a period of agricultural depression. There is access to the gallery at the top by means of a winding-stair inside. Passing down Bondgate-without, an old house, with the sign of "The Plough," will be observed on the right. Over the lintel of the doorway is the following quaint inscription :—

> "That which your Father
> old hath purchased, and left
> you to possess, do you dearly
> Hold, to show his worthiness.
> M(atthew). W.(illoughby), 1714."

Right in front, blocking up the street, is a grim and weather-worn mass of masonry, popularly known as *Hotspur's Tower*. It was erected about the year 1450, by the second Earl Percy, and is an interesting relic of the time when Alnwick was a walled town, having its four entrances defended by strong towers. Like the Sallyport gate at Newcastle, this is the only one which has not succumbed to the exigencies of modern times. On each side of the central building projects a semi-octagonal tower, pierced with loop-holes. Above the arched gateway may still be traced the figure of the Brabant lion sculptured in relief on a recessed panel. Prisoners were formerly confined in its dark chambers. A side street to the left leads to the *Greenbat*, where stands *St. Paul's Church*, a large modern edifice in the Decorated style of architecture, built in 1846, and endowed by Hugh, third Duke of Northumberland. In the north aisle is a magnificent monument in white marble to the founder, by Carew. He is represented robed as a Knight of the Garter, with a ducal coronet on his head, and a lion couchant at his feet, lying on an altar-tomb of Caen stone, the sides of which are adorned with the Percy arms. The great feature of interest, however, in the church is the beautiful east window, which has been filled with richly-stained glass, to the memory of the third duke. The subject is Paul and Barnabas preaching to the Gentiles at Antioch. Designed by the late William Dyce, R.A., and executed at Munich by Max Ainmüller, this gorgeous window is rightly considered one of the finest specimens of the art of modern glass-staining. Passing down Bondgate-within from Hotspur's Tower, the *Market Place* is soon reached. On the west side stands the *Town Hall*, erected in 1731. Near to it, in the Corn Market, is *St. Michael's Pant*, a richly-carved Gothic structure, surmounted with figures of the saint and the dragon. On the south side is a heavy stone building, with arcades on the north and south, containing butchers' shops on the ground floor and the Assembly Rooms above.

In the centre of the Market Place may be seen, *in situ*, the large stone in which the old bull-ring was fixed. Towards the close of the last century as many as seven bulls were baited in the course of one winter, when thousands of spectators gathered to witness the cruel sport. The old Market Cross stands in the north-east corner of the Grass Market. At the junction of Bondgate with Narrowgate are two quaint-looking tenements, which, together, form the oldest house in Alnwick, dating from the early part of the fifteenth century. On a stone panel above the front entrance are carved two Percy badges—viz., a lion rampant, with a shield in its paws, standing between the horns of a crescent, on which is inscribed the motto, "Esperance." In the proximity of the Market Place are some of the quaint old hostelries—the Three Horse Shoes in Narrowgate, the Nag's Head in Fenkle Street, and the Grey's Inn in Clayport. In Pottergate, a continuation of Narrowgate, on the top of the rise, there stands a battlemented tower, with corner turrets, erected in 1768 on the site of an older one. It contains an ancient clock, removed from the Town Hall in 1772. Branching off to the north, at a right angle, is Northumland Street, where may be seen a considerable length of the town wall, five feet in height, with the remains of a corner tower. The walls of Alnwick were erected about the middle of the fifteenth century, being twenty and a half feet in height, six feet thick, and a mile in length. Northumberland Street opens into Bailiffgate, at the west end of which, on an elevated site, is the *Church of St. Mary and St. Michael.*

This venerable building was probably founded about the beginning of the fourteenth century. It took the place of an older church, of which the only remains are a few stones sculptured with the diaper pattern, built into the wall above the chancel arch, and the basements of round pillars, with plain mouldings, and a beaded ornament discovered buried within the church. The style of architecture, which, for the most part, characterises the church, is the Perpendicular. The interior is oblong in shape, consisting of a nave and chancel, both of which have north and south aisles. The earliest portion of the church is the arcade of the south aisle of the nave, which was added to the Norman fabric. Over it, projecting from the south wall, are four of the curiously-carved corbels which carried the first roof over the aisle. The north arcade was built a century later. The arches separating the chancel from its aisles spring from elegant octagonal piers, the capitals of which are elaborately sculptured with leaves and fruit and rich rope mouldings. Above the abacus of the south-west pier is an angel holding a shield, charged with the cross moline of Bishop Bek. The capital of the north-east pier displays on each of the eight faces of the abacus, instead of foliage, a crescent between lockets, the heraldic device of the fourth Earl of Northumberland. Above is an angel holding a shield, on which is a St. Catherine wheel. In the chancel aisles are three recumbent effigies. The oldest and most interesting is that of a female, supposed to be the Lady Isabella, widow of the last Vescy, Baron of Alnwick. She is represented reclining beneath a trefoiled canopy of the Decorated style, clad in a long-sleeved outer robe, over a tight-sleeved tunic, and wearing a veil over her face, and a wimple under her chin. At her feet is a dog, the emblem of fidelity. The other two are those of a layman and a monk; the first, under a trefoiled canopy, is attired in a short tunic, with a square purse attached to his belt; the second is robed in a flowing dalmatic over a tight-sleeved tunic, wearing on his head a close-fitting cap. The windows in the east and south walls of the chancel are filled with beautiful stained glass, to the memory of Algernon, fourth Duke of Northumberland. Those on the west represent Christ, with his Evangelists on the right hand and on the left; those on the south, eighteen scenes from our Saviour's life, the colouring of the whole being soft and harmonious. The basement of the tower is used as a baptistery. Here are two small statues, found buried in the north aisle in 1818; the one represents St. Sebastian, the other a king clad in a gown and cloak painted scarlet and crimson, standing on a square pedestal, on which are sculptured in relief the lion and antelope, badges of the house of Lancaster. In the vestry is an ancient oak muniment chest, with a hunting scene carved upon it, together with a number of grotesque animals, chiefly winged dragons. The tower is a massive, square embattled structure, with a crocketted pinnacle at each corner, and a step-buttress at each angle, continued to the parapet. The foundations are sunk as deep as thirty or forty feet below the surface. Two of the bells in the tower are ancient; one, which bears the inscription, "ADIVTORIO ✠ POPVLO ✠ DEI. MI ✠ CHAEL ✠ ARCHANGELE ✠ VENI ✠ IN ✠" (Michael the Archangel! come to the help of the people of God), belongs to the thirteenth century; the other, inscribed, "AVE ✠ MARIA ✠ GRACIA ✠ PLENA ✠ ORATE ✠ PRO ✠ AIA ✠ DE ✠ JOHANNE ✠ VALKA ✠" (Hail, Mary, full of Grace! Pray ye for the soul of John Valka), belongs to the fourteenth or fifteenth century. The most curious feature about the church is a turret at the south-east angle of the chancel, containing a winding stone staircase. There was formerly a chamber at this point, which may have been a look-out station in the time of Scottish invasion, or, as a writer has suggested, an occasional residence for one of the chantry priests who performed services at the altar of St. Mary. Over the outer doorway of the porch, on the south side, is a dripstone, carved with the Percy crescent and locket. A panel here bears some heraldic device nearly obliterated. It is said to be that of the De Vescy family. The windows in the aisles of the nave are filled with coloured glass, the whole series forming a great design of pictorial instruction. Those on the north side illustrate Childhood, Confirmation, Family Life, Death, and Resurrection; those on the south, Sacramental Life, Worship, and the Glory of the Resurrection. The central window at the west end is called the *Te Deum* window, from its subject, and is one of the seven erected to the memory of Algernon, the fourth Duke of Northumberland. In a small cusped window, at the west end of the north aisle of the nave, fragments of ancient glass have been preserved. There is a good deal of delicately-carved wood-work about the church, and numerous marble tablets adorn the walls. In the churchyard, on the north side of the church, are several carved and sculptured stones, which have been discovered—viz., the base of the Norman column, already referred to; several incised tombstones, one bearing a cross and sword; another, a cross and shears; and a third, beside the floriated cross, shears and a key; two fragments, one with a horse-shoe upon it, the other inscribed with the words, VXOR SIMOIS (the wife of Simon).

Not far from the church in Walkergate is a ruined wall, with a moulded doorway and mullioned window in it, being all that remains of *St. Mary's Chauntry-house*, where the two chaplains resided who served at the altar of St. Mary, in the parish church, and instructed "poor boys in the art of Grammar gratis." From St. Michael's Church the ancient street of Bailiff-gate, or Bailey-gate, the street of the bailey, conducts to the magnificent example of military architecture with which the name and fame of Alnwick is so inseparably connected.

THE CASTLE.—The original Norman fortress was doubtlessly begun by Ivo de Vescy, who became Baron of Alnwick a little after 1096, and was completed by Eustace Fitz-John. In 1135 it is described as a "munitissimum castellum," covering as large an area as the present one. After suffering a good deal from the assaults of the Scots, and the storms of two hundred years, it was restored and almost rebuilt by the first two Percies, between the years 1310 and 1350. Like the castle at Newcastle, it formed the base of military operations against the Scots, and was garrisoned by three thousand and thirty-seven men-at-arms, and forty hobelars—light-armed cavalry mounted on small ambling horses. The extensive alterations and additions made by Hugh, the first Duke, and Algernon, the fourth Duke of Northumberland, have given to the castle its present stately appearance. A feudal fortress, restored and inhabited, is not, perhaps, so picturesque an object as one in ruins, but the unbroken outlines of its massive walls and towers have a grandeur more impressive. It enables the student of history to comprehend the details of this formidable class of strongholds, wherein the northern barons were able to set even kings at defiance. Alnwick Castle does not owe so much to its situation as Bamburgh, Dunstanburgh, or Prudhoe. Occupying the summit of a small eminence above the river, and proudly dominating the town of Alnwick, it yet lies low when looked at relatively to the surrounding hills. The curtain walls, with their supporting towers and turrets, enclose an irregular triangular space of about five acres, in the centre of which is the cluster of rounded towers forming the Keep. The main entrance is on the west, and is guarded by a stern and massive *Barbican*, built by the first Lord Percy about 1350, and having the Percy lion and motto, "Esperaunce," sculptured above the outer gateway. Nothing more formidable than the defensive arrangements at this point could well be imagined, First there was a moat, then an iron-studded gate and gateway, defended by two turrets. Afterwards a small open court, surrounded on three sides by parapeted galleries, from which the assailants might be annoyed by combustible materials and arrows ; then another gateway, protected by a portcullis. On the battlements of turrets and gate-tower are a number of stone figures in a variety of attitudes, representing armed men repelling an attack. The Gatehouse is now the Porter's Lodge. Passing through the arched passage into an open swarded space, called the Outer Bailey, the visitor will do well to make, in the first instance, a tour of the walls, noticing in the lower part, at certain points, the old Norman masonry, distinguished by its wide-jointed ashlar-blocks laid in wavy lines, as if following the rise and fall of the ground. A long stretch of curtain wall runs northward, supported by a small tower, called the *West Garret* (Fr. *Guerite*, turret), and terminating in the *Abbot's Tower*, a bold battlemented structure of three stories, having a rib-vaulted chamber in the basement and a turret at the north-west corner, manned by stone figures of warriors. It was erected by the first Lord Percy, and, as its name would imply, was the residence of the Abbot of Alnwick Abbey, when his presence was required at the castle. In one of the upper rooms is a small geological museum, formed by the Duchess Florentia, consort of the third Duke. A short length of curtain wall connects the Abbot's Tower with a square tower, built about thirty years ago, when the Almoner's and Falconer's Towers, together with a considerable portion of the curtain wall, were removed in order to open out a view to the north from the windows of the Prudhoe Tower.

The first tower on the right of the Gatehouse is the *Garner*, or *Avener's Tower*. This is succeeded by the *Clock*, or *Water Tower*. An archway to the right admits to a large square, bounded on the north and west sides by the Stables, and on the south side by the spacious *Guest Hall*. Adjoining it are the Estate Offices and the Laundries. The *Auditor's Tower*, which is the next building, contains the Duke's private library, and a museum of Egyptian antiquities, collected by the Duke Algernon during his travels in the land of the Pharaohs. Several of the curiosities are of great interest, as, for instance :—A small Chinese bottle of porcelain for holding snuff, with an inscription signifying, "The flower opens to another year," proving the existence of commercial relations between Egypt and China at an early period ;

models of carpenters' tools of the time of Thothmes III., found in baskets deposited in a tomb at Thebes; painters' pallettes, still containing some of the colours; writing pallettes and tablets; small vase for holding stibium, or kohl, a substance used for increasing the brilliancy of the eyes; cosmetic boxes; large comb; metal mirror; necklaces; needle; glass pendants of ear-rings; daggers; walking-sticks; amulets; sandals; signets and finger-rings; lamp belonging to "Father Timotheos, Archbishop of the Thebaid;" altar of libations dedicated by Usertesen the 1st, of the twelfth dynasty; fragment of a bas-relief representing part of the victorious army of Thothmes III., which had overrun Palestine and Assyria; figures of various Egyptian deities. A very elaborate catalogue of the collection has been prepared by Dr. Birch, of the British Museum. Coming now to the archway of the Middle Ward, a work ascribed to the first Lord Percy, the Kitchens, with the Larders and Sculleries, will be observed on the right. This suite of buildings, completed in 1859, have walls of dressed ashlar and lofty groined roofs, and are no less remarkable for their perfect culinary arrangements than for their architectural grandeur. All the ingenious appliances of modern times have been utilised. The spits are turned by water power, and the various dishes are raised by means of hydraulic lifts to the end of a corridor, where they can be easily conveyed to the dining-room. Proceeding through the archway, the visitor enters the Inner Bailey, and, following the line of the curtain wall, passes in succession the *Warder's* or *Lion Tower*, built in 1860, the *East Garret*, a small tower, under which may be seen the ancient masonry of the De Vescy period, and the *Ravine* or *Record Tower*. From this point a walk leads along the top of the outer wall to the *Constable's Tower*, passing *Hotspur's Chair*, a turreted projection, built by the first Duke, and the site of a tower, popularly called the *Bloody Gap*, from a tradition that a party of Scots made a breach in the wall here, but perished in the assault. The Constable's Tower, the only part of the castle shown to the general visitor, is interesting from the fact that it has not been touched since the time when the first Lord Percy reared its massive walls between the years 1309 and 1315. Like the Abbot's Tower, it consists of three storeys, the lower one being vaulted. A newel staircase winds upward to the roof, which terminates in a gable turret on the parapet. The basement chambers contain fragments of sculptured stones found about the castle and Alnwick and Hulne Abbeys, and the upper ones various arms and accoutrements used by the Percy Tenantry Corps in the beginning of the present century, together with many ancient and curious weapons. The dress worn by Sir John Ross in the Arctic Regions, and a specimen of a primitive bicycle, will be examined with interest. A short wall connects this tower with the *Sallyport* or *Postern Tower*, a massive structure of the same date. A flight of steps descends to the vaulted chamber in the basement from which the Sallyport communicated with the grounds outside the castle. Here is a curious staircase in the walls, and a *garde-robe* in one of the external walls. The upper storey contains an interesting collection of ancient British, Roman, and Saxon antiquities. To the ancient British period belong a quantity of sepulchral pottery, consisting of ornamented cinerary urns, incense cups, food vessels and drinking cups; flint implements, such as celts, arrows, javelin-heads, chisels, scrapers, etc.; weapons of bronze—leaf-shaped swords, daggers, and spear-heads; slabs with curious circular markings upon them; bodkin pins, gold rings found at Blinkbonny, and gold beads found on Chesterhope Common. To the Roman period belong a number of sculptured and incised stones from various stations in the county—a beautifully-carved slab from Hunnum; an ornate altar to the Deæ Matres from Habitancum; richly-ornamented altars from Bremenium; the "Dream-altar" from Habitancum, so called from its inscription, translated as follows:—"In a dream forewarned, a soldier directed the wife of Fabius to erect this altar to the nymphs who are worthy of worship;" a tombstone from Chesterhope, near Habitancum, inscribed "to the divine shades Æmilianus, aged ten years;" two slabs from Bremenium, one bearing the figures of Mars and Hercules sculptured upon it, and the other, three nymphs at their ablutions; a tombstone bearing a representation of a horseman, found near the Oxclose, to the south of Cilurnum, with many others of great interest; a fac-simile of the celebrated silver plate known as the Corbridge lanx; an infant's feeding-bottle of Samian ware, and several sandals found at Bremenium; a miner's iron pick from lead workings at Snowbrook, near the summit of Plinlimmon, generally ascribed to the Roman times; a bronze enamelled vessel, familiarly known as the Rudge Cup, which was found in a well near a Roman building at Rudge Coppice, Wilts, and is interesting from the fact that round the rim is an inscription containing the names of five places connected with the Roman wall; objects from Pompeii, consisting of mural paintings in fresco, vessels of glass and bronze, lamps, and other articles of terra-cotta. To the Saxon period belong the beautifully-carved sepulchral cross discovered in 1789 in the ruins of Woden's Church, Alnmouth, an iron sword, spear heads, bronze fibulæ, and buckles and beads, etc. Among the mediæval and comparatively modern antiquities are several relics from the battle-fields of Hedgeley Moor, Shrewsbury, Flodden Field, Millfield, Towton, and Newburn; a bronze yetling, mortars, "knocking stones," curious andiron, and a great variety of minor antiquities; some ancient coins and seals of the Percies. A large and elaborate catalogue of these antiquities, with coloured illustrations, has been prepared by Dr. Bruce for the Duke of Northumberland. A broad terrace, commanding a pleasant view of the river and the country to the north, occupies the space between the Sallyport and new *Falconer's Tower.*

The *Keep* of the castle consists of a series of semi-circular towers grouped in the inner court. The moat which formerly surrounded it has been filled up, and the drawbridge removed. The entrance is between two lofty semi-octagonal towers four stories high, built by the second Lord Percy about the year 1350. On the battlements are several stone figures similar to those on the Barbican, and beneath them, under the string-courses, are the shields of the following families, who were connected in some measure with the Percies :—Tyson ; Eustace de Vescy ; Clifford ; Percy ; Bohun ; Plantagenet ; Warren ; Arundel ; Umfreville ; Thomas de Percy, Bishop of Norwich ; Neville ; and Fitzwalter. The central shield between the towers bears the coat of arms of Edward III.—viz., France and England quarterly.

Passing through the outer archway, and through a door on the right, a narrow passage in the wall may be followed to the *Prison*, a gloomy cell, still retaining in its walls the iron staples to which the prisoners were chained. Beneath an iron grating in the floor is a dark bottle-shaped dungeon, that requires no aid from imagination to set forth the sufferings of unhappy moss-troopers confined there. Traces of the castle built by Eustace de Vescy in 1140 may be seen in the ribbed roof of the entrance passage. An interesting Norman archway, enriched with the dog-tooth ornament, opens into the Inner Court. Beneath it passed King John, Henry III., and the first three Edwards, when they visited Alnwick. On the right, in an arched recess, is the wooden windlass of an ancient draw-well. Above it is the figure of a saint blessing the waters. Running round part of the court is a corridor on projecting arches and corbels, formed to give a separate access to the state apartments. At the base of the *Prudhoe Tower* a groined *porte cochère* covers the approach to the grand entrance.

A little may be said here concerning the alterations and additions which transformed the feudal fortress into a Roman palace. When the first duke came into possession of his Northumbrian estates, both Alnwick and Warkworth Castles were in ruins, and he was for some time undecided which to restore and make his ducal residence. He finally fixed on Alnwick. As Gothic architecture was not much understood at this time (1764), his architects spoilt the Edwardian character of the Keep. Algernon, the fourth duke, perceived the incongruities, and commenced in 1854 those restorations which, costing nearly a quarter of a million sterling, have made of Alnwick Castle one of the most magnificent seats in England. He built the Prudhoe Tower, in order to give greater elevation to the central part of the keep, and render the outlines more varied and majestic. After a consultation with the leading architects of the time as to the arrangements and decorations of the interior, he decided to adopt the style of the fifteenth century palaces of Rome, several of which he had visited. The outward restorations and general superintendence of the works were entrusted to Mr. Anthony Salvin ; the internal decorations to Commendatore Signor Luigi Canina, a celebrated antiquary and architect of Rome. The wood carvings were executed at Alnwick by English and Scottish workmen, under the direction of Signor Bulletti, of Florence. The works continued over a period of ten years, as many as three hundred artisans being employed.

The *Entrance Hall*, according to the scheme of the Italian

decorations, is treated with simplicity, its walls being of dressed ashlar work. From the inner hall a grand staircase leads upward to the first floor. The broad and stately freestone steps were obtained from the Rothbury quarries. Each step is 12 feet long, the block forming the landing stage being 12 feet square. The walls, panelled with coloured marbles and stuccos, and the high vaulted ceiling, decorated with delicately-tinted stucco, prepare the eye for the more sumptuous splendours of the state apartments. From the topmost landing a short flight of steps rises to the *Vestibule*, or Guard Chamber, as it is called, 30 feet square, with a flooring composed of a Venetian mosaic pavement, one of the first introduced into England. In four of the panels of a broad frieze round the room are pictures in oil by Francis Gotzenberg, illustrating the ancient ballad of "Chevy Chase." The subjects are—"The Departure," "The Repose before the Battle," "The Death of Douglas," and "The Death of Percy." Adjoining the Vestibule is the *Ante-room*, another richly-ornamented apartment, lined with damasked green satin, and hung with pictures by the early Italian masters—viz., Portrait of Giulio di Medici, a copy from Raffaelle—*Giulio Romano;* Allegory of a child decorating a skull with olive-boughs—*Schidone;* "Crying, Laughing, and Anger"—*Dosso Dossi di Ferrara;* "Adoration of the Shepherds"—*Lanfranco;* "Judith adorning herself before meeting Holofernes"—*Garofalo;* "Christ casting out the Evil Spirits at Capernaum"—*Garofalo.* The cabinet here was formed from the oak piles of the old Roman bridge at Newcastle.

On the left, occupying one floor of the Prudhoe Tower, is the *Library*, a large chamber (55 feet by 24 feet), containing upwards of 15,000 volumes, some of which are of great value. The shelves are inlaid with ornamental patterns in sycamore and limewood, while from the finely-carved ceiling stand out in bold relief allegorical devices of the arts and sciences. The walls are hung with family portraits. The three chimney-pieces of coloured marbles are adorned with busts of Bacon and Newton, by Professor Strazza, and Shakespeare, by Fabj Altini. To the right of the Ante-room is the *Saloon*, lined with yellow satin, and resplendent with decorations. The principal feature is the deep frieze painted on canvas by Signor Mantovani. The chimney-piece of white marble is ornamented with sculptures by Signor Taccalozzi. Two figures of Dacian slaves, by Signor Nucci, support the mantel-shelves. Among the pictures are—"St. Francis receiving the Stigmata"—*Ludovico Caracci;* "If the Blind lead the Blind," etc.—*Schidone;* Portrait of Guidobaldo II., Duke of Urbino—*Baroccio;* "Esther before Ahasuerus"—*Guercino;* "Burial of St. Stephen"—*Caravaggio;* "The Salutation of the Virgin," by *Sebastian del Piombo*—a fresco cut from the walls of the Church of Santa Maria della Pace at Rome by the French, and interesting from the fact that Michael Angelo drew the outlines out of jealousy, it is said, of Raffaelle. The figure of Joseph below formed part of the original picture. Portrait of Sebastian del Piombo (when forty-one years of age)—*Rosso Fiorentino;* "The

Daughter of Palma Vecchio with a Flute"—*Giorgione;* "Three Heads," by *Giorgione*—a picture from the Manfrini Gallery, and referred to by Lord Byron in the following lines :—

> "And when you to Manfrini's Palace go,
> That picture (howsoever fine the rest)
> Is loveliest, to my mind, of all the show;
> It may, perhaps, be also to your zest,
> And that's the cause I rhyme upon it so;
> 'Tis but a portrait of his son and wife,
> And self; but *such* a woman; love in life."

"Christ turning the Money-changers out of the Temple"—*Mazzolini da Ferrara;* "Six Heads of a Painter and his Pupils"—*Pordenone;* "Portrait of Pope Paul III."—*Titian;* "Henrietta Maria in her Bridal-dress," and "Algernon, 10th Earl of Northumberland"—*Vandyke.* The *Drawing-room*, which is entered from the Saloon by a double set of carved doors, is polygonal in form, and rich in colour and carving. A red satin damask, with yellow flowering, covers the walls. The frieze painted by Mantovani consists of cherubs and ornaments on a blue ground. The chimney-piece is of white marble, supported by female figures, copied from the antique canephoræ. Among the pictures in this luxurious apartment, which are of great value and beauty, will be found the following :—"St. Bruno"—*Francesco Mola;* "The Gods Enjoying the Fruits of the Earth"—by *Giovanni Bellini* and his pupil, *Titian*, the figures being by the former and the landscape by the latter; "Bacchus going to Ariadne after she had been abandoned by Theseus," a copy by *Nicholas Poussin* of *Titian's* "Bacchus," in the National Gallery; "Ecce Homo"—*Carlo Dolce;* "Andrea Del Sarto," painted by himself for Lorenzo de Medici; "St. Catherine and Mary Magdalene,"—*Raffaelle;* "The Virgin and Child, with St. Anne, St. Joachim, St. Joseph, Sta. Maria Salome, and St. M. Cleophas"—*Perugino;* "The Crucifixion"—*Guido Reni;* "The Holy Family," a copy from the Raffaelle at Naples—*Giulio Romano;* "A Harbour at Sunset"—*Claude Lorraine;* Portrait of Cardinal Antonio Barberine—*Carlo Marratti;* "St. John in the Desert"—*Ludovico Carracci* and *Domenichino.* The next apartment is the *Dining-room*, the walls of which are covered with a deep crimson satin damask, and hung with several of the family portraits. The ceiling consists of carved-work in yellow-pine, on a ground of American cedar, the natural colour of the wood being retained. In the central compartment are the armorial bearings of the Percy family. Running round the chamber, on a painted red ground, is a carved frieze by Mantovani. The chimney-piece of Sicilian marble is adorned with sculptured ornaments by Taccalozzi. Its mantel-shelf is supported by two figures—a Fawn, by Nucci, and a Bacchante, by Strazza. Adjoining this hall is a *Breakfast-room*, which was, till lately, the only relic of the gingerbread Gothic style of decoration adopted by the first duke. The ceiling having given way, its demolition was rendered necessary, and the room has recently been altered in accordance with the style prevailing in the rest of the building. In the Corridor which connects it with the Vestibule are several valuable pictures by artists of the last and present century:—"Northumberland House"—*Canaletto;* "Alnwick Castle"—*Canaletto;* "Westminster Bridge"—*Canaletto;* "Warkworth Castle"—*Richardson;* "The Gentle Shepherd"—*Sir David Wilkie;* "The Return from Deer-Stalking"—*Sir Edwin Landseer, R.A.;* "A Woodland Scene"—*T. Creswick, R.A.;* "A View on the River Teign (South Devon)"—*F. R. Lee, R.A.;* "The Caledonia and the Boyne chasing the French Fleet into Toulon"—"The Ramsgate Life-boat going to rescue the Crew of a Wrecked Vessel on the Goodwin Sands"—*Carmichael;* "The Life-boat returning into Ramsgate Harbour"—*Carmichael;* "A Boy with a Straw tickling an Old Man asleep"—*Goode;* The Duke of Wellington's Charger, "Copenhagen"—*Ward;* Napoleon's Charger, "Marengo"—*Ward;* Landscapes—*Marlow.* Contiguous to the Prudhoe Tower, on the west side of the Keep, is the *Chapel*, designed by Salvin, an oblong building, with high groined roof and lancet windows, filled with stained glass. The walls are adorned with mosaic work of coloured marbles, designed by Signor Montiroli, and similar in character to that round the shrine of Edward the Confessor in Westminster Abbey. At the back of the building is a gallery fitted up for the ducal family and their guests, approached from the Vestibule. The state bedrooms and dressing-rooms, which occupy the towers on the west and south, are decorated in the style of the cinque cento period with richly carved and gilded ceilings and sculptured white marble chimney-pieces. Among the pictures disposed in these rooms may be noted—"Venus Striving to Prevent Adonis from going to the Chase," by *Titian;* and "Christ Teaching in the Temple," by *Strozzi*, the Genoese ecclesiastic. In the wing extending from the Keep over the middle gateway to the block of offices is the *Duchess's Boudoir*, one of the most elegant and sumptuous apartments of the whole suite. The carved ceiling is exquisitely coloured and gilded. Below the cornice a beautiful frieze runs round the room, composed of fruit, flowers, masks, and conventional ornaments, painted on a dark ground by Moretti. The chimney-piece is of white marble, with panels of unique design, precious stones being inlaid in grounds of lapis lazuli and porphyry to represent birds and flowers. The walls are covered with satin damask of an orange tint, and hung with the following pictures:—"St. Catherine"—*Giotto;* "The Holy Family"—*Francesco Rossi del Salviati;* "The Magdalene Reading"—*Correggio;* "The Madonna Dei Garofani"—*Raffaelle;* "The Holy Family"—*Sebastiano del Piombo.* The Gardens occupy the rising ground to the north-east of the castle, from which they are approached through the Lion Gate. Broad walks, bordered with flowers, lead to the Conservatory, Vineries, Terrace, and Fountain. Visitors are admitted every Thursday, by the gardeners' entrance in Bondgate.

A brief account of the great historic house of Percy may interest the visitor to Alnwick. The name is derived, not from the incident connected with the death of Malcolm, as recorded by the old chroniclers, but from the little village of Percy, in Normandy. The line of William de Percy, who came over with the Conqueror, became extinct in the reign of Henry II. His heiress, Agnes, married Jocelyn de Louvain, and it is from this union that the Percies of Northumberland are descended. "As there never was a Duke," says Mr. Freeman, "so there never was even an Earl of Northumberland sprung from the male line of the Percy of Domesday." The first Earl Percy of Alnwick was Henry de Percy, a Yorkshire baron, who purchased the De Vescy estates from Bishop Bek in 1309. He rebuilt a large portion of the walls and towers of the castle. Henry, second Lord Percy, distinguished himself at the battles of Halidon Hill and Neville's Cross. Henry, third Lord Percy, was present at the battle of Crecy. His first wife was Mary Plantagenet, daughter of the Duke of Lancaster, and thus the brother-in-law of John of Gaunt. Henry, fourth Lord Percy, was advanced to the dignity of Marshal of England, and as such officiated at the coronation of Richard II. in 1377, being then created Earl of Northumberland. He took a prominent part in the deposition of this monarch, and for his services was made Constable of England by Henry IV. He gained the decisive victory of Humbledon Hill, and shortly afterwards rebelled against Henry IV. His son, Hotspur, was defeated and slain at Shrewsbury, and he himself found it expedient to surrender. After receiving a generous pardon from the king, he raised the standard of revolt again in 1409, but was defeated and slain at Bramham Moor. His eldest son, Henry, was the celebrated Hotspur, whose name has been immortalised by Shakespeare. At the battle of Otterburn (1388), he and his brother Ralph were taken prisoners and carried into Scotland. He maintained his reputation for valour at the battle of Homildon Hill (1402). Taking part with his father in his rebellion against the king, he was pierced through the brain by an arrow at the battle of Shrewsbury, and his body was afterwards drawn and quartered. The son of Hotspur, when only twelve years of age, was taken to Scotland by his grandfather. While there, his estates, which had been forfeited by the rebellion of his father and grandfather, were restored to him by Henry V., who thus attached the house of Percy to the interests of his own family. The wisdom of this act of generosity was seen in the results. The new Earl of Northumberland, as Warden of the East Marches, displayed great zeal and energy in the defence of the Borders, and, in 1455, fell fighting for Henry VI. at the battle of St. Albans. Four of his sons lost their lives in the Lancastrian cause—Thomas, Lord Egremont, who was slain at Northampton, 1460; Ralph, at Hedgeley Moor, 1464; Henry, who succeeded his father as the third earl, at Towton, 1461; and Richard, at Towton, 1461. "The Percy estates," says Mr. Tate, "attained their maximum of territorial extent under the third earl, and probably presented as large an area of productive lands as was ever held by a British subject." They were confiscated after his death, and conferred by Edward IV. on John Neville—Lord

Montague—who gained for his patron the battle of Hedgeley Moor. Henry, the fourth earl, who had been imprisoned in the Tower during his minority, was restored to the dignities and possessions of his family in 1469. He played a somewhat double part in 1485, for having first attached himself to the cause of Richard III., he basely deserted that ill-favoured monarch, at a critical moment, on the field of Bosworth. This act of treachery secured for him the favour of Henry VII., and he was appointed to several important offices. Being commissioned by the king to insist on the payment of a war-tax which the people of the north considered oppressive, he incurred so much odium that a mob broke into his house at Cock Lodge, near Thirsk, murdering him and several of his servants. Henry, the fifth earl, says Mr. Tate, "was a Percy-Lovaine of a new type, . . . more at home in gaudy shows than in battle-fields ; and he stands pre-eminent for the stately magnificence which he displayed, not only in the grandeur of his military equipment, but also in the semi-regal order of his household." He attended the Princess Margaret on her journey into Scotland to marry James the Fourth, and was present at the battle of Spurs in 1513. The life of Henry, the sixth earl, had in it a romantic element of a somewhat tragic character. He was the accepted lover of Anne Boleyn, and had obtained her good-will to marriage, when Henry VIII. interfered, through the instrumentality of Cardinal Wolsey, and the engagement was broken off, that the fair lady might be made a queen. Young Percy was induced to marry the daughter of the Earl of Shrewsbury, but lived unhappily with her. The loss of the object of his early love is said to have affected his character. He became reckless and extravagant, and plunged so deeply into debt that he bore the name of "Henry the Unthrifty," and was obliged to sell Poynings estate and other lands. Dying without issue, the earldom became extinct, in consequence of the attainder of his brother. It was, however, resuscitated in 1557 by Queen Mary, in favour of Thomas, son of the attainted lord, and he thus became the seventh Earl of Northumberland. He joined the rising of the north in the reign of Queen Elizabeth, for which act of rebellion he was outlawed, together with his countess. After hiding in the wastes of Liddesdale for some time, he was betrayed to the Earl of Murray, who, for a large bribe, gave him up to his enemies. He was conveyed to York, and on the 22nd of August 1572 beheaded as a traitor. Henry, the eighth earl, suspected of engaging with Lord Paget and the Guises in a plot for the liberation of Mary Queen of Scots, was committed to the Tower, where he is stated to have put an end to his life, being found dead in his bed with three pistol shots through his breast. Henry, the ninth earl, convicted of misprision of treason with respect to the Gunpowder Plot, in which his kinsman, Thomas Percy, took part, spent fifteen years in prison, where he enjoyed the society of Sir Walter Raleigh, and studied chemistry and astronomy. Algernon, the tenth earl, took an active and honourable part in the Civil War, and while in favour of the preservation of the monarchy, exerted himself to secure constitutional government and the rights of the people. His character has been admirably drawn by Clarendon. With Josceline, the eleventh earl, the male line of the Percy-Lovaines came to an end. The vast possessions of the family descended to the Duke of Somerset, who had married Elizabeth, the heiress of the ancient house. Through the marriage of her granddaughter, the estates passed to Sir Hugh Smithson, of Stanwick, a Yorkshire knight, who in his youth had been an apothecary in Hatton Gardens. He filled the office of Lieutenant-general of Ireland in 1763, and was created, on October 22nd 1766, Duke of Northumberland and Earl Percy. It was in his time that the castle was restored in the pseudo-Gothic style, which destroyed, to a considerable extent, its mediæval character. To Hugh, the second duke, the column of the Percy tenantry was erected. Hugh, the fourth duke, was styled "the magnificent," for the princely manner in which he restored the present castle and improved his vast estates. He distinguished himself very early in several naval engagements, having command of the *Caledonia* in the action with the French fleet off Toulon in 1815. He spent several years in travelling through Turkey, the Holy Land, Nubia, and Egypt, where he collected the numerous relics which form the museums at the castle. He expended large sums on the endowment of schools and churches, and the establishment of life-boat stations on the coast, besides contributing munificently to local charities. The present and sixth duke—Algernon George—was born in 1810, and for many years, as Lord Lovaine, represented North Northumberland in Parliament. Alnwick was the birthplace of James Catnach (b. 1792, d. 1840), and of Sir G. B. Airey, K.C.B., F.R.S., the late Astronomer-Royal (b. 1801).

To many visitors the natural beauty of the ducal parks and pleasure-grounds will afford more pleasure than the feudal grandeur of the old castle. They are thrown open to the public every Thursday and Sunday throughout the year. Tickets of admission for any other day can be obtained at the Auditor's Tower between the hours of ten and four o'clock. The lands on both sides of the river from the Lion Bridge to the Canongate Bridge are known as the *Dairy Grounds*, and are beautifully laid out with beds and walks of flowering shrubs and trees. The Dairy itself is a small picturesque building with projecting roof, and is well worth a visit. The floor is paved with encaustic tiles, and the shelves are of white marble. *Barberry Bank*, on the north side of the river, was formerly the property of the Radcliffes.

Crossing the bridge at the foot of Canongate, the park is entered at the Abbey Lodge. A short distance from it are the remains of *Alnwick Abbey*, which was founded in 1147 by Eustace Fitz-John and his wife Beatrice, daughter of Ivo de Vescy, for a colony of Premonstratensian canons. It was known as the Abbey and Convent of the Blessed Mary of Alnwick, and was the second house of the order established in England. The site of St. Norbert's first monastery, near Laon in Picardy, is said to have been shown to him by an angel in a dream; hence the place was called Premonstré, from *pré*, a meadow, and *monstré*, pointed out. This abbey at Alnwick also occupies a meadow, which, lying in a lovely bend of the river, and sheltered by a steep sandstone cliff on the south and west, and by the high lands to the north, would commend itself to the brotherhood as a desirable site for their house without any supernatural illumination. Very picturesque must the canons have looked amid these pleasant scenes, all clad in white cassocks and cloaks, with white felt hats on their tonsured heads. The history of the Abbey is an uneventful one. Under the immediate protection of the powerful lords of Alnwick, the canons would dwell in comparative peace and quietude. They displayed a magnificent hospitality, and are recorded to have entertained on one occasion upwards of a thousand guests. One of the priors, in 1304, wrote a curious Latin poem on Robin Hood, which is interesting from the fact of its being the earliest record of the name of the popular hero. A literary work which occupied the leisure of some of the canons was the Chronicle of Alnwick Abbey. Though full of anachronisms and erroneous statements, it is not without value to the historian. The original manuscript has been lost, but a copy is preserved in the British Museum. A relic much prized by the monks of Alnwick was the uncorrupted foot of Simon de Montford, which was preserved in a shrine of purest silver shaped like a shoe. The Chronicle of Melrose Abbey records a miracle performed by the precious member of the old warrior. A wealthy burgess of Newcastle, crippled by a painful malady, was instructed by a mysterious voice to proceed to Alnwick Abbey, where the foot of Simon de Montford would work for him a perfect cure. Not willing to leave such a remedy untried, he set out, and had no sooner caught a glimpse of the relic than he was at once restored to health and strength. At the time of the dissolution of religious houses in 1539 the number of canons was thirteen. During the succeeding centuries the ruins were used as a quarry by the builders of the neighbourhood, and now nothing remains of the famous Abbey but the massive gate-tower. This is of an oblong form, with small projecting turrets at the corners, built about the middle of the fifteenth century. The gateway passage runs through from north to south. Above the north doorway is a much-worn figure of an angel with outstretched wings. A little higher still is a canopied niche, now empty. The battlements project from the wall on corbels, forming machicolations through which an enemy below might be annoyed with boiling pitch or stones. Two shields on the merlons bear the De Vescy arms. On the south front there are similar escutcheons. In a niche above a window stands a figure of a Premonstratensian canon. The east front is the most elaborately ornamented. The armorial bearings of the Percies, adopted not earlier than 1385, appear over the low-pointed doorway in the centre merlon of the battlements, and high up on the walls of the flanking towers. The foundations of the various buildings of the Abbey have been laid bare, and the visitor may trace the ground plan of the church, chapter-house, cloisters, refectory, etc., by the paths of cement which have been laid on the bases of their walls. A very ancient yew hedge is supposed to be a remnant of the Abbey gardens. The "White Well," belonging to the canons, also remains. Following the course of the river for half-a-mile, and crossing it first by the Monk's Bridge, and then, a quarter of a mile further, by the Filberthaugh Bridge, a beautiful ravine is entered, where a succession of lovely and idyllic scenes are presented to the gaze of the visitor. A short distance from the bridge, by the side of the high carriage road leading to Hulne Abbey, is the celebrated "*Trysting Tree*," a gnarled and venerable oak, very hollow and much decayed. It must have been a great tree in 1624, as, at that time, it gave its name to the wood in which it stood. Being half-way between Alnwick and Hulne Abbeys, it was probably the meeting-place of the monks. The road by the river-side is hemmed in by steep banks and hanging woods, running through a fairy world of greenery. Half-a-mile up the glen is the *Lady's Well*, a spring of pure water by the wayside. A little to the east of it are several fine specimens of the silver fir (*Pinus picea*), some of which reach a height of from 108 to 114 feet. The girth of the tallest, at 5 feet from the ground, is about 14 feet 6 inches. Adjoining them, at a distance of 100 yards east of the well, is a *Pinus Douglasii*, which rises to the height of over 100 feet. On the opposite side of the river are some larches (*Pinus larix*) of great size and beauty. Among the flowers which grow so plentifully in the park are the hybrid avens (*Geum intermedium*), frog satyrion (*Habenaria viridis*), wood club-rush (*Scirpus sylvaticus*), scentless dame's violet (*Hesperis matronalis*), leafy spurge (*Euphorbia esula*), red valerian (*Valeriana rubra*), hedge calamint (*Clinopodium vulgare*), tooth-wort (*Lathræa squamaria*), hazel-leaved bramble (*Rubus corylifolius*), *Carex lævigata*, *remota*, *Pendula*, *Ampullacea*, and *Vesicaria*, common spleen-wort (*Asplenium trichomanes*), common hart'stongue (*Scolopendrium vulgare*), giant bell-flower (*Campanula latifolia*), herb Paris (*Paris quadrifolia*), hautboy strawberry (*Fragaria elatior*), wood melic-grass (*Melica uniflora*).

Half-a-mile further west from the well, on a small hill sloping to the river, are the picturesque ruins of *Hulne Abbey*. The house was probably built about 1240 by Ralph Fresborn, on a site given by William de Vescy. The circumstances connected with its establishment are somewhat romantic. According to one account, Ralph Fresborn, a Northumbrian knight who had taken the monastic vows, was discovered in a monastery on Mount Carmel by one of the crusading De Vescys, and permitted to return to England on condition that a Carmelite monastery should be established in his native country. The present site was fixed upon, it is said, on account of the great resemblance which the adjoining hill bore to Mount Carmel. According to another account, he was the person who visited the friars of Mount Carmel, and, struck with their piety and austerity of life, brought them away with him, and established them at Hulne, he himself being the first abbot. The Carmelite friars were called "White Friars," from the colour of their vestments. Their rules and discipline were very harsh and rigorous. Each friar had a coffin in his cell; he slept on straw, rising in winter at five, and in summer at six o'clock. Every morning he dug a shovelful of earth for his grave;

he crept on his knees to his devotions; he spent much time in his cell in long-continued silence or in prayer; he ate but twice a-day, never tasting animal food, and endured frequent fasts. Simple and austere as the friars were in their lives, their ritual services were distinguished by great splendour. A list of their sacred vestments, etc., has been preserved. It mentions robes of golden-knotted cloth interwoven with birds and leopards; robes and altar-cloths of bawdekyn—a rich material with web of gold and woof of silk; chasubles and dalmatics of embroidered samite in different colours, together with maniples, amises, copes, and stoles, several of these gorgeous vestments being adorned with gems. Their library was unusually large for the time, containing one hundred and fourteen manuscripts, chiefly of a theological nature. In addition to several copies of the Holy Scriptures, missals, psalters, and lives of the saints, were works by Bernard, Chrysostom, Gregory, Augustine, Anselm, Beda, Peter Lombard, Thomas Aquinas, Raymund, Goydfrydy, and Thomas de Chebyam. There were four treatises on grammar and logic by Bruto and Precian, and one on moral philosophy by Ysidorus. John Bale, a prolific writer, and author of *Illustrium Majoris Britanniæ Scriptorum*, a valuable repository of early British biography, is said to have lived and studied here for several years.

In approaching the ruins the visitor will observe that the surrounding curtain wall is tolerably complete, though it has lost the battlements along the top and most of its corner turrets. He will pass through a time-worn old archway on the south, overhung by the graceful tendrils of the ivy-leaved toad-flax, or mother-of-thousands. This entrance was guarded by a strong tower, the under storey of which is vaulted, and had been occupied by the porter of the convent. A winding stair leads up to the two upper storeys, which are at present in a ruined condition. To the left, against the curtain wall, are the secular buildings of the monastery in the following order:—the Guest Hall; Bakehouse, Brewhouse, Domestic Offices; Farmery; and the Maltkin, close to which is the modern entrance. North of the guest hall is the dwelling-house of the keeper of the priory, formerly the Strangers' Chapel. A little westward of it are the ruins of the mill-house, in which a quern, or hand-mill, still remains. To the north are the cloisters, surrounded by several of the monastic buildings. On the south side of the quadrangle are the remains of the Refectory, consisting of the east wall, in which may be seen a small door and a portion of the arch of a window. Adjoining this, on the right, is the kitchen, with a large fire-place and drain. On the east side is the Chapter-house, lighted by a large east window and by four large lancet windows in the south wall. On the west side are the ruins of a building, probably a chapel. There is also a modern tower in the pseudo-Gothic style, erected about a century ago, on the site of the Abbots' Tower. Near to it, standing by itself, is an embattled tower with vaulted under-storey, built by Henry, the fourth Earl of Northumberland, in 1488, as a place of refuge for the brethren during Scottish raids. It contains some fine tapestries representing events in the life of Constantine, from designs by Rubens. From the top there is a good view of the ruins and the lovely scenery around. In the curtain wall, near the tower, is the following inscription, much decayed :—

✠✠
"In the year of Christ Ihu MCCCCLXXXVIII.
This towr wos bilded by Sir hen Percy
The fourth Erle of Northūberlād of gret hōn & worth
That espoused Maud ye good lady full of vertue & bewt
Daughter to Sir Willm̄ Harbirt right noble & hardy
Erle of Pembrock whos soulis god save
And with his grace cōsarve ye bilder of this towr."

On the north of the quadrangle is the *Church*, remarkable for its great length in proportion to its breadth, the former being 118 feet, the latter but 20 feet. Most part of the south wall and some portions of the west and east ends still remain. There are five lancet windows with trefoil headings on the south. In the ancient sedilia is a mutilated figure of the Virgin and Child, belonging to the latter part of the fourteenth century. Several sepulchral slabs were discovered in the floor of the church in 1849, one of them ornamented with an incised cross of the Tau form. On the outside of the western gable is a monumental slab, brought from the old church of Alnmouth, bearing in relief a sculpture of a tree with a helmet on the top, a sword and bugle on the branches, and a shield on each side charged with the arms of Denom, the old lords of Meldon. The cemetery was to the north of the church. A door in the south wall opens into the sacristy, in which had been an altar and an oven for baking the holy wafer. The foundations of the pillars which supported the arcade of the cloisters have been exposed. Over the east and south sides of this arcade were the dormitories. A good idea of the garb of these Carmelite friars may be gained from two stone figures in the attitude of prayer, which are to be seen in the grounds. The ruins are rendered exceedingly picturesque by the trees, shrubs, and creeping plants which shade and cover them. Close to the east gateway are stone stairs leading up to the top of the wall, a pleasant resort of tourists. Half-a-mile north-east is the *Friars' Well*, from which there was a conduit to the Abbey. Crossing the river, below the ruins, by an ornamental iron bridge, and ascending the green slope to the right, an old road may be followed for some distance in a southerly direction, when, close to the Deer Park gate, a footpath will be found winding up *Brislee* or *Brislaw Hill*. On the summit, surrounded by plantations of pines and flowering shrubs, is *Brislee Tower*, an elegant structure in the pseudo-Gothic style, rising to a height of 90 feet. It was erected in 1781, by Hugh, the first duke, a medallion of whom appears above the lower balcony with the following inscription beneath it :—

"Circumspice !
Ego omnia ista sum dimensus ;
Mei sunt ordines,
Mea descriptio,
Multæ Etiam istarum arborum
Mea manu sunt satæ."

(Look around! I have measured out all these things; they are my orders, it is my planting; many of these trees have even been planted by my hand.) O. W. Holmes seems to have been struck with this inscription, for after mentioning in his *Autocrat at the Breakfast Table*, page 138, that Cyrus pointed out with pride and pleasure the trees he had planted with his own hands, he goes on to say, "I remember a pillar on the Duke of Northumberland's estate at Alnwick, with an inscription in similar words, if not the same. That, like other country pleasures, never wears out: none is too rich, none too poor, none too young, none too old to enjoy it." From the upper balcony, 66 feet from the ground, a fine view may be obtained of the lovely vale of the Aln on the one side, as far as Eslington, with the range of the Cheviots in the background, and on the other, the castles of Alnwick, Warkworth, Dunstanburgh, and Bamburgh, with the Farne Islands and the pale blue sea beyond. The key to the tower is kept in an adjoining cottage. The dreadful gale of 1881, in which the Tay Bridge was blown down, made great destruction among the pines of Brislee Hill, sweeping them down in great swathes. The botanist will find on the sides and summit of the hill red whortle-berry or cow-berry (*Vaccinium vitis-idæa*), bilberry or bleaberry (*V. myrtillus*), and chickweed wintergreen (*Trientalis Europœa*), in great profusion; also marsh violet (*Viola palustris*), common juniper (*Juniperus communis*), common crow-berry (*Empetrum nigrum*), green-ribbed carex (*Carex binervis*), butterfly orchis (*Orchis bifolia*), intermediate and common wintergreen (*Pyrola media and minor*), purple-leaved helleborine (*Epipactis latifolia*), mountain shield fern (*Lastrœa oreopteris*), with numerous mosses, lichens, and fungi, oak fern (*Polypodium dryopteris*), etc. By the side of the drive leading from the tower past the cottage will be observed, first, the "Long stone," a monolith which probably marked some ancient boundary, and then the "Nine-year-aud-hole," a large cavern in the sandstone cliff, containing two stone figures, one of them being that of a hermit. The drive eastward to Alnwick runs through the deer park, well stocked with fallow-deer—

"Dappled white and dun,
As if, being foresters of old, the sun
Had marked them with the shade of forest leaves."

Near the old Moor Lodge is an ancient cist-vaen, or stone coffin, of pre-historic times. The drive, after passing the "Stoney Peth Quarry," which supplied the stone for the recent restorations of the castle, terminates at the Forest Lodge. The road leading from the gateway to St. Michael's Church is called Ratten Raw—a name meaning the "King's Way," derived by some antiquaries from the Gaelic "Rathad'n righ," and by others from the French "Route du roi." Within the plantation, on the right hand side, is a large square block of sandstone on two steps, marking the place where, as an inscription copied from an older monument states, William the Lion, King of Scotland, was taken prisoner while besieging Alnwick Castle, 1174. An English force under Ranulph de Glanville, the author of our first legal treatise, and also a great soldier, after following the Scottish raiders from Prudhoe Castle, which they had unsuccessfully besieged, came upon the king and about sixty of his knights sitting down to dine. Thinking they were some of his own troops returning from a marauding expedition, he was taken by surprise, but, hastily arming himself, he mounted his grey horse, and, shaking his spear, exclaimed, "Now let it be seen who is a good knight." After gallantly defending himself for some time his horse was killed beneath him, and he was taken prisoner. Valorous deeds were also performed by the Scottish knights, but they were outnumbered and compelled to surrender or flee.

The antiquarian visitor will find much to interest him by crossing the Lion Bridge, built 1773, and proceeding along the North Road for a few miles. The picturesque old bridge itself forms the first object of attraction. An incident in connection with it has been preserved by Oliver Wendell Holmes in his *Autocrat at the Breakfast Table*, as an illustration of the strange fact that trivial things are often remembered when more important ones are forgotten. "I remember," he says, "the Percy Lion on the bridge over the little river at Alnwick—the leaden lion—with his tail stretched out straight like a pump handle—and why? Because of the story of the village boy who would fain bestride the leaden tail, standing out over the water—which breaking, he dropped into the stream far below, and was taken out an idiot for the rest of his life" (p. 245). The bridge is a prominent feature in Turner's magnificent picture of Alnwick by moonlight. Half-a-mile from the castle, on the left, are the ruins of *St. Leonard's Hospital*, founded between the years 1193 and 1216 by Eustace de Vescy for the soul of Malcolm, King of the Scots. It occupies a site in a field called "Radcliffe's Close," which formerly belonged to the lords of Dilston. The fragments left of the chapel give some slight idea of the building, which consisted of nave (22 feet by 27) and chancel (15 feet by 16) in the later style of Norman architecture. Foundations of the domestic buildings are traceable on the south side. Near the north side of the chapel is Malcolm's well, five feet deep, supposed to be the ancient spring of the chronicler, by the side of which the Scottish monarch drew his last breath. The traditional spot where he received his death-wound is a quarter of a mile higher up the hill, on the right hand side of the road, and is marked by a cross bearing an inscription—

"K. Malcolm's Cross<br>Decayed by Time<br>was restored by<br>His descendant<br>Eliz., Duchess of<br>Northumberland<br>MDCCLXXIV."

Part of the base and the upper limb of the older monument still remain in the plantation. In 1093 Malcolm III., who had been ravaging the northern parts of Northumberland, was encamped on the high ground here above the Aln, when he was suddenly attacked by the English forces under Robert de Mowbray, and slain by his godfather Morel. The English baron, it is said, had recourse to stratagem, and this has, no doubt, given rise to the monkish legend recorded in the chronicle of Alnwick Abbey. According to this romantic account, the constable of Eustace de Vescy (who, by-the-bye, did not gain possession of the barony till ninety-two years after), a knight named Hamund, rode out to the Scottish army bearing the keys of the castle on the point of his spear, as if in token of surrender. The king approached to receive them, but the wily Hamund pierced him in the eye, and then rapidly escaped across the river, at a spot which has ever since been called "Hamund's Ford." Two miles to the north, on a lofty hill, is *Highfarlaw*, or *Heffordlaw Pele Tower*, which belonged to the Abbey of Alnwick, and from its high position could give warning of approaching danger. It is a low square building of three storeys, only 24 feet 4 inches by 28 feet 9 inches, and is, as Mr. Tate observes, "but a poor specimen of a Border pele." The floor of the upper storey rested on stone corbels. In the east wall is a small niche under a trefoil canopy, occupied, no doubt, at one time by a statue. Sculptured panels on the east and south walls, bearing the Percy arms —a locket within the horns of a crescent—together with two crossed crosiers below them, fix the date of its erection between the years 1455 and 1464. Near the tower, on the crest of the hill, is a Celtic stronghold, overgrown with trees, oval in shape, and defended by two rampiers with a fosse between them. Two or three hundred yards to the south, on the slope of the hill, is another one, much larger, but nearly obliterated. Lower down the same hill, about a mile southward, is a third one—the camp of Black Chesters, covering an area of nearly two acres, and strongly fortified by two rampiers and a fosse. Trees have somewhat obscured the site, which is a commanding one, overlooking the valley of the Aln. From this point the road which skirts the Hulne Park may be followed to Alnwick, two miles and a quarter distant.

# ALNWICK TO RATCHEUGH CRAG AND CAWLEDGE DENE.

Denwick, 1 mile ; Ratcheugh Crag, $2\frac{1}{2}$ miles.

THE visitor, after crossing the Lion Bridge, will turn to the right into a park-like enclosure, called the "Pasture," and follow a footway which commands a good view of the castle to Denwick Bridge. Here a road to the left leads to the pretty little village of DENWICK, one mile from Alnwick, passing the remains of a cross in a field, called the "White Cross Howls," erected in memory of the victims of the plague who were buried there in 1665. From Denwick a lane runs eastward for a mile and a half to *Ratcheugh Crag*—an interesting outcrop of the "Great Whin Sill." The basalt has been intruded in two distinct eruptions among the stratified rocks, metamorphosing the shale below into porcelain jasper, and the limestone above into crystalline marble. The grand columnar masses which face the west rise to a height of over eighty feet, and are overhung with wood. On the summit is an observatory, commanding very extensive views of the line of coast and the valley of the Aln. One rock bears the name of *The Broken Stirrup.* Among the flowering plants and ferns to be found on the crags are—Greater meadow-rue (*Thalictrum majus*), sweet milk-vetch (*Astragalus glycyphyllus*), hairy violet (*Viola hirta*), shining cranes-bill (*Geranium lucidum*), common moonwort (*Botrychium lunaria*), common rock rose (*Helianthemum vulgare*), hornbeam-leaved bramble (*Rubus carpinifolius*), burnet rose (*Rosa spinossisima*), common burnet (*Poterium sanguisorba*), hairy rock-cress (*Arabis hirsuta*), rue-leaved saxifrage (*Saxifraga tridactylites*), early scorpion-grass (*Myosotis collina*), maiden pink (*Dianthus deltoides*), blue moor-grass (*Sesleria cærulea*), narrow-leaved oat-grass (*Avena pratensis*), downy oat-grass (*Avena pubescens*), wild oat (*Avena fatua*), crested hair-grass (*Aira cristata*), crow garlick (*Allium vineale*), black spleenwort (*Asplenium adiantum-nigrum*), common spleenwort (*Asplenium trichomanes*), wall-rue spleenwort (*Asplenium ruta-muraria*). The crags are not more than a mile from Longhoughton Station. Nearly a mile to the south, on the Hawkhill estate, some interesting traces of glacial action may be seen in the polished, grooved, and striated rocks of limestone lying below the boulder clay. A mile to the south again, on the other side of the railway, is the beautiful *Cawledge Dene*, which may be followed to the south road, and thence past the cemetery to Alnwick.

# ALNWICK TO EDLINGHAM.

**Edlingham, 5½ miles ; Freeman's Well (direct), 3½ miles.**

THE road leaves the town by Clayport Bank, on the top of which, to the left, is *Swansfield House*, the residence of Miss Cooke. In front of the mansion is a beautiful statue of "Peace." In the park, to the south, is an ornamental tower, built by Thomas Adams, Esq., on the Stonyhills. A little to the west of it, on the Camphill, where traces of ancient British entrenchments may be seen, is an elegant column, erected by the late Henry Collingwood Selby, Esq., to commemorate the policy of Pitt, the victories of Nelson and Wellington over the French, and the restoration of peace in 1814.

Through scenery which is chiefly of a moorland character, the road continues in a south-westerly direction to EDLINGHAM, an interesting little village of considerable antiquity, lying in a narrow green vale among the moors. Eadulfingham was given by King Ceolwulph to the monks of Lindisfarne. The *Church of St. John the Baptist* dates back to the middle of the twelfth century. Of the earlier edifice, built in Saxon times, the only remnant, according to Mr. Wilson, is the lintelled doorway, with its semi-circular tympanum at the west end of the nave. The enriched doorway opening into the church from the porch, the nave, rounded chancel arch, and chancel, are all Norman. The north aisle, and the four round arches which separate it from the nave, belong to a later period, just before the dawn of the early English style. In the south side of the nave is an early Decorated window, and near the entrance stands an early English font of octagonal form on two circular steps. One of the mural tablets is to the memory of the Rev. James Manisty, father of the present Judge Manisty. The ancient tower, with its massive walls and narrow arrow-slits of windows, is a stern memorial of the times when it was necessary to fortify even the church. It is surmised that the tower was sometimes used as a place of detention for captured moss-troopers, from the fact that the door could be fastened from the outside, the receptacle for the bar still being visible.

About 250 yards north-east from the church are the ruins of *Edlingham Castle*, a large pele-tower of the twelfth century. It was held in the reign of Henry II. by John, son of Walden, of the barony of Earl Patrick, for one soar-hawk, or sixpence. It is now in the possession of Sir John Swinburne, of Capheaton. While the lowest chamber has had the ordinary barrel-vault, so characteristic of north-country peles, the great hall appears to have had an elaborately-groined roof, the graceful arches springing from corbels in the angles. In the thick walls are deeply-splayed window recesses and seats. Besides the unusual groining, the hall possesses another feature of great interest—viz., its fire-place. The jambs are moulded into the semblance of columns, and on their rudely-carved capitals rested a remarkable lintel, which, instead of being a large oblong slab, as in other places, was formed of ten stones, curiously joined together by the method technically known as "joggling." A unique form of ornamentation was the result. This interesting relic has been allowed to fall into ruins. The outer angles of the tower are strengthened by huge buttresses, which, towards the top, are corbelled out into small overhanging turrets, called bartizans. A few fragments of the barmekyn, or walled enclosure, still remain. By the east side of the castle runs the Edlingham Burn, prettily wooded. In 1682–3 the little village was notorious as the residence of Margaret Stothard, a poor old woman known as the "Witch of Edlingham." The depositions of several persons against her are given in Mackenzie's *Northumberland*, and are of the most ridiculous character. The statement of John Mills, of Edlingham Castle, made on oath, is a fair sample of the rest. He stated that, lying awake one Sunday night, "he, the said informant, did heare a great blast of wind, as he thought, goe by his window, and immediately following there was something fell with a great weight upon his heart, and gave a great crye like a catt, and then after another in the same manner, and just as those was ended there appeared a light at his bedd foot, and did in the same light see Margaret Stothard, or her vission, to the best of his knowledge; so the poure of this informant's speech being taken from him at the tyme, and as soon as ever he recovered strenth to speake, he cryd out 'The Witch, the Witch!'" The reputed witch happily escaped the usual penalty inflicted on the ladies of the broomstick. There is a railway station at Edlingham, the first on the new Alnwick and Cornhill branch.

Half-a-mile to the south are two powerful springs, known as the "Senna Wells," a name derived by some authorities from the Saxon word "sainé" (health-giving). A mile to the south-east is the *Black Lough*, a small sheet of water in the wild moorlands, 700 feet above the level of the sea. It is surrounded by a peat bog, in some places 12 feet thick. At the bottom are the remains of an ancient birch forest. The tops of the trees are broken off, but the stumps are still standing, rooted in the sandy soil beneath the peat. A mile and a quarter direct east is the celebrated *Freeman's Well*, on the declivity of a high hill, called the Freeman's Hill. When dammed up, as it used to be, a sheet of water 100 feet long, from 6 feet to 15 feet broad, and from 3 feet to 5 feet deep, was formed, through which, on St. Mark's day, the 26th of April, the young candidates for the Freeledge were obliged to plunge and flounder, to the amusement of a crowd of spectators. Turf dykes built across, and straw ropes fixed from side to side, contributed to render their progress difficult and ludicrous. This curious rite of "going through the well" was a part of the ceremony of riding the boundaries of Alnwick Moor, a distance of fourteen miles, a ceremony observed by the freemen once a year. "Tradition has uniformly stated that King John, when hunting in Alnwick Moor, or Ayden Forest, as some part of it was anciently called, was laired in a bog, or quagmire, where the well now is, and was in consequence so enraged, that, as a punishment to the inhabitants of the town for their slovenliness, he took from the borough its charter, but was prevailed on to grant a new charter, with the condition that every burgess, on his admission to the freedom, should plunge through the same bog on the anniversary of the day on which Royalty stuck fast in the mire. The absurdity of this enactment accords with the character of a capricious and stupid tyrant; and the tradition is incidentally confirmed by the itinerary of King John, which states that he was at Alnwick in the year 1209, on the 24th day of April." This ancient but ridiculous custom came to an end on St. Mark's Day, 1853. From the well the boundary of the moor may be followed past St. Margaret's Green and a narrow rushy swamp, bearing the ominous name of "Cut-throat Letch," and by the west side of Swansfield Park to Alnwick, three miles and a half distant.

# ALNWICK TO BOLTON AND EGLINGHAM.

Lemmington Hall, 5 miles ; Bolton, 6 miles ; Shawdon Hall, 7½ miles ; Titlington, 7½ miles ; Beanley, 10 miles ; Eglingham (*via* Shipley), 7 miles.

A MILE and a half along the road that leads to Edlingham another road branches off to the right for a similar distance to the western edge of Alnwick Moor. By making a short digression of half-a-mile along the boundary wall, a magnificent view of the surrounding country and the distant range of the Cheviots may be obtained from the Cloudy Crags. The nearest route to these crags from Alnwick is along the park wall from the Forest Lodge. From the edge of the moor the road gradually descends past the beautifully-wooded grounds of Glen Allen to the main road from Alnwick to Whittingham. From this point there is a road to the left leading down Lemmington Bank, through which one of the deepest cuttings on the new Alnwick and Cornhill branch has been excavated. Forty-eight thousand cubic yards of solid rock had to be blasted away in order to form this narrow defile, which at one place is 48 feet deep. Half-way down the bank, at an elevation of 300 feet, is *Lemmington Hall*, a fine and pleasantly-situated mansion-house of the last century, now in ruins. It originally belonged to the Fenwicks, but is at present the property of W. J. Pawson, Esq., of Shawdon. Its east wing is an ancient pele-tower, mentioned in the survey of 1416 as the "turris de Lematon," a building about 53 feet square, with walls 6 feet 6 inches thick. To the south-west are signs of ancient terrace cultivation. A quarter of a mile to the north is a Celtic camp. The *Devil's Causeway* passes close by, and is supposed to have given the name to the place. "The appellation of leam was frequently applied by the Saxons to the remains of Roman roads, and wherever this word enters into the composition of a modern name some vestiges of a Roman way may be expected in the neighbourhood."—*Brockett.* A quarter of a mile westward from the point where the road to Lemmington branches off, the Edlingham Burn is crossed by the *Battle Bridge.* Here, according to tradition, a sanguinary conflict took place about the year 875 between the Saxons of Whittingham Vale and a band of Danes, who had pushed their way up the Aln from the coast, with the result that the former were defeated with great slaughter. Two miles further on is the Bridge of Aln, and a mile beyond that again, the delightful village of Whittingham.

A quarter of a mile, however, west of the bridge a road branches off to the right, and skirting the grounds of *Broom Park*, the seat of Major Bryan Burrell, crosses the Aln to the village of BOLTON, where, in 1225, Robert de Ross, Baron of Wark, founded a leper hospital, dedicated to St. Thomas the Martyr. The site is supposed to have been in a large British camp, called "The Guards," near the river. It was occupied by a master, three chaplains, thirteen leprous men, and lay brethren, who were to keep a good table, dress neatly, etc., out of their annual revenues, and apply the surplus to the relief of poor and helpless strangers. Bolton is noted as the place where, on September 5th, 1513, the Earl of Surrey was joined by the noblemen and gentlemen of the north of England, with their retinues, to the number of 26,000 men. In the little church the chiefs of the English army are said, by tradition, to have pledged themselves to conquer the Scottish king, or be left dead on the field. Four days afterwards the great battle of Flodden Field was fought.

*Bolton Church*—a chapel-of-ease of Edlingham—is a neat little edifice, restored in 1852, but contains little to interest the antiquary. The sole ancient fragment is the chancel arch, which is Norman.

On the north side of the road leading to Glanton, a mile from Bolton, is *Shawdon Hall*, an elegant mansion on the site of an old pele-tower, the seat of William J. Pawson, Esq. The park is finely wooded, some of the trees being of large size. The name Shawdon means the "tun," or dwelling, in the "Shaw," or wood. Eighty yards north-west of the house is "The Hangman's Oak," on which many a bold reiver may have expiated his evil deeds. This supposition receives colour not merely from the name of the tree, but also from the circumstance of human bones having been found near it. The girth of the tree is 9 feet 7 inches, the height 54 feet. A wych elm standing alone in the park, 150 yards south-south-east of the house, is called "The Big Elm." Its girth is 13 feet 5 inches, its height 69 feet. About a mile from the Hall, fifty yards north-west of a little bridge over the Shawdon Burn, is a very picturesque old oak, called "The King of the Forest," the finest of a grove of old native oaks which stand on the steep north slope of the burn. Its girth is 17 feet 6 inches, its height 68 feet. A curious oval orifice, six inches high by four inches wide, passes through the upper part of the bole from north to south. *Titlington Hall*, half-a-mile north-east from Shawdon, and a mile north-west of Bolton, contains several of the rich carvings, mantels, cornices, etc., which formerly decorated Lemmington Hall. It is the residence of William Hargrave Pawson, J.P. To the north-west is the rounded form of *Titlington Pike* (765 feet), a prominent feature in the landscape of Whittingham Vale. It is an offshoot of the Kyloe range, as is also *Jenny Lantern Hill* to the south-east. *Jenny's Lantern*, which gives the name to the hill, is an ancient look-out station built near a Celtic camp, where several querns, or hand-mills, have been found. Between Titlington Pike and Beanley plantation are the ruins of a Border stronghold, called *The Shepherd's Law*.

About two miles and a half north of Titlington, on the east side of the Breamish, is the village of BEANLEY (*ben*, a mountain, and *ley*, a pasture), at one time the residence of the Warden of the Marches. Near the highest point of the extensive sandstone ridge forming Beanley Moor are the remains of a strong Celtic fort, called the *Ringses*. It is circular in form, defended by three great rampiers of earth and stone, the outer one being in some parts twenty feet high and twenty feet wide. The inner area contains the foundations of a few circular huts. Traces of similar rude buildings may be seen a little to the west of the camp, together with several standing stones. Near to this ancient settlement some curious incised slabs have been found, with figures upon them, similar to those at Rowting Linn. A typical example is a groove passing through the circumference of a series of concentric circles.

Two miles north-east of Beanley, on the banks of a well-wooded burn, is EGLINGHAM, a pretty and ancient little village, much frequented during the summer season by anglers, the famous trout stream, the Breamish, being within an easy distance. Two inns, the Tankerville Arms and the Ogle Arms, afford good accommodation for visitors. "Eagwlfingham" was granted by King Ceolwulph in A.D. 738 to the Monastery of Lindisfarne. The name is said to signify the village with a church, from the British *eglys*, a church, and the Saxon *ham*, a hamlet. On the site of the early Saxon edifice is built *The Church of St. Maurice*. Of the ancient structure nothing remains, unless, as Mr. F. R. Wilson suggests, the present semi-circular chancel-arch be a fragment. The greater part of the church belongs to the seventeenth century, having been restored in consequence of the destruction caused to it by the Scottish army under Lesley. The fine strongly-built tower at the west end, however, is Edwardian; of the same date, probably, as the barbican of Alnwick Castle. The central stage of it has been finished as a chamber, and used, very possibly, as a retreat for the females of the village during Border frays. A small window in the east wall commanded a view of the services in the body of the church. There is a lancet-arched aumbry, or locker, in the north wall. One of the bells which originally belonged to the chapel at Bewick, and afterwards hung in the old pele-tower at that place, bears a German inscription, signifying "Anthony is my name, I was made in the year 1489." On the north side of the nave is a rectangular projection, known as the Ogle Pew, beneath which is the Ogle vault. Several of the windows are filled with stained glass. The font bears the date 1663. The vicars of Eglingham are also the archdeacons of Lindisfarne. A good anecdote of the old smuggling days tells how a former vicar received some rather startling information while crossing over from Bamburgh to the Farne Islands. One of the boatmen, hearing his name, said, "Ah, I knew Eglingham well by moonlight; you have a fine tithe-barn there, sir!" "Tithe-barn," exclaimed the vicar, "how do you know that?" "Many a time," replied the man, "I have slept there, and deposited kegs of whiskey. Why, sir, we always changed horses there!"

*Eglingham Hall*, the property of R. B. E. Ogle, Esq., is a fine modern mansion, with extensive gardens and pleasure-grounds. Incorporated with it, at the west end, are the remains of an ancient pele-tower of the Ogles. Cromwell is said to have visited the old manor-house on one occasion as the guest of Henry Ogle. The chamber where he passed the night, and the room where he quarrelled with his host before leaving the next day, are still pointed out. This Henry Ogle was one of the sequestrators of the lands in Northumberland for the Parliament, and deserves to be remembered for the part he took in the detection and exposure of the celebrated Scotch witch-finder—an infamous wretch, on whose information fourteen witches and one wizard belonging to Newcastle had been executed on the Town Moor, 21st August 1650. Coal is worked in the neighbourhood of Eglingham. The village is seven miles from Alnwick by the main road, passing *Shipley*, a decayed village, which, according to tradition, once possessed a weekly market and extensive works for the manufacture of war implements.

# ALNWICK TO SHILBOTTLE AND NEWTON-ON-THE-MOOR.

Shilbottle, 3 miles; Whittle, 5 miles; Newton-on-the-Moor, 6 miles.

THREE miles from Alnwick, by way of the Cemetery and Cawledge bridge, is the ancient village of SHILBOTTLE, situated on the summit and slope of a high cultivated ridge. It is referred to in early documents as "Schipilbodille." The trim cottages, with their red-tiled and blue-slated roofs, over-run, in some cases, with ivy; its kitchen and flower gardens; its newly-restored church, with massive battlemented tower; and its grey old turreted pele-house, now the vicarage, form the details of a pretty Northumbrian picture. From the churchyard there is a splendid view across a fine open country to Ratcheugh Crag in one direction, and to the sea-blanched towers of Warkworth Castle and the white gleaming lighthouse buildings of Coquet Island on the other. *The Church of St. James* was originally a small Norman building, and, as such, of considerable interest. It was rebuilt in the late Decorated style in 1875, when every care was taken to preserve such of the ancient features as could be retained—namely, the Norman doorway, the chancel-arch, the small narrow windows in the north wall, and the font. There is a beautiful little stained-glass window, by Mr. Kemp of London, representing the Baptism of Christ. A stone tablet to the memory of Captain Widdrington, of Newton Hall, formed part of the court of the Lions in the Moorish Palace of the Alhambra. The nucleus of the vicarage is an ancient pele-tower, mentioned in the list of Northumbrian castles and peles of 1416 as being held by the Duke of Bedford. Two trefoil-headed windows give light to the upper storey, and two lancets to the one below. The turrets are pierced with narrow loop-holes. On the side next to the churchyard is inserted a panel, inscribed with a verse taken, probably, from an old tombstone at Melrose Abbey.

> "The earth goeth on the earth
> Glistring like gold,
> The earth goes to the earth
> Sooner than it wold.
> The earth builds on the earth
> Castles and towers,
> The earth says to the earth
> All shall be ours."

There is a Mechanics' Institute and Reading-room in the village. The principal inn here is the Percy Arms.

On the skirts of Shilbottle Moor, nearly two miles to the south-west, is WHITTLE, concerning which there is told an interesting story of the moss-trooping days. Mark Ker, of Cessford (ancestor of the Dukes of Roxburgh), having a grievance against the Earl of Northumberland, sent word that he would come within three miles of his house and give him a light to dress by at midnight. Accordingly, with a band of thirty light horsemen from Teviotdale and the Merse, he rode forth one October day in 1522 to the little village of Whittle, intending to burn it down. A simple circumstance prevented him from carrying out his purpose. He had neglected to bring flints and tinder, and all the fires of the village being out, not a spark could be obtained. The baffled Borderers, however, stabbed a poor woman who was with child, saying, "Where we cannot give the lord lyght, we shall do this in spyte of hym." By this time beacons were blazing on the hill-tops around them, and the countryside was raised; but the Scots got away in the darkness. By way of reprisal, the Earl of Northumberland "let slip" one hundred of the best horsemen in Glendale, who burnt Coldingham and other places, bringing off twenty-three prisoners, sixty horses, and two hundred cattle. They intended, *God willing*, to have burnt Kelso also, but were prevented by the breaking of the day.

During some blasting operations at the Whittle Quarries in April, 1856, a block of limestone was split open, and in the middle of it was found a live toad immured in a cavity just large enough to receive it. When exposed to the air, the reptile breathed a few times, stretched out its feet, and then died.

Three miles south-west of Shilbottle, descending the ridge, is the small rustic village of NEWTON-ON-THE-MOOR. *Newton Hall*, the seat of Major S. F. Widdrington, J.P., is a little to the south of it.

# ALNWICK TO WARKWORTH.

**Lesbury, 3 miles ; Alnmouth, 5 miles ; Warkworth, 7½ miles ; Morwick, 9 miles ; Amble, 9 miles.**

THREE miles east-by-south of Alnwick, by the undulating road running, first on the south, and then on the north side of the river through Hawkhill, is LESBURY, a long and straggling village snugly embosomed in trees, consisting of a church, vicarage, hall, inn, two farm-houses, a large corn-mill, and about forty-six cottages. It probably had its origin in Saxon times, when the chief thane of the district lived here in his burgh, or fortified dwelling. A hall-mote, or manorial court, was held in Lesbury at an early period.

*The Church of St. Mary* is an early English edifice, founded in the beginning of the thirteenth century on the site of a Saxon building which was granted to Alnwick Abbey in 1147 by Eustace Fitz-John. It was restored in 1854 under the direction of Mr. Salvin, and now consists of a nave, chancel, and north aisle, the latter formed by an arcade of four arches running the whole length of the church. A square tower at the west end, with corbelled-out parapet and pyramidal roof, sustains the ancient character of the building.

Two of the vicars of Lesbury have claims to remembrance. The first is Patrick Mackelvyan, A.M., instituted August 26th, 1609. This famous centenarian, though very quarrelsome and litigious, was, at any rate, faithful in the discharge of his pastoral duties, for when the plague visited Lesbury in 1665, and several of the inhabitants had to be removed to tents on the neighbouring moor, the aged vicar was assiduous in attending to their spiritual and bodily welfare. His name has been rescued from oblivion by Fuller, who says of him "that, being a hundred and ten years old, his hair came again as a child's, of flaxen colour ; that he had three teeth cut within two years, which were not then come to perfection ; that, whereas forty years before he could not read the biggest print without spectacles, there was then no print nor written hand so small but that he could read it without them ; that he was as strong as he had been twenty years before ; that he preached and prayed an hour and a half without any notes, and was very hearty and cheerly at that age, but stooped much. Being asked how he preached so well with so few books, and was so cheerly with so few acquaintances, he answered, 'Of friends and books good and few are best.'" His age has been somewhat overstated. He was born in Galloway in 1568, and died in 1659. The other vicar of note is the Rev. Percival Stockdale, born at Branxton, October 26th, 1736, died at Lesbury, September 14th, 1811. He tried his fortune in the army, the world of letters, and the church. As an author he enjoyed some reputation in his own day. He wrote poems, sermons, political pamphlets, memoirs, criticisms, and essays, his largest work being *Lectures on the Poets*. He dedicated his autobiography to his friend Miss Porter, authoress of *Thaddeus of Warsaw*, who paid a visit to Lesbury, dating several of her letters from the Vicarage. He is supposed to have been the original of the eccentric Belfield in Miss Burney's *Cecilia*.

A mile and a half to the south-east of Lesbury, and five miles east of Alnwick, on a narrow strip of rising ground, between the river Aln and the sea, is ALNMOUTH, the ancient port of Alnwick, now one of the most popular of Northumbrian watering-places. Very picturesque does it look when viewed from the railway, with its long, meandering street of dwelling-houses, villas, and cottages, surmounted by the elegant spire of St. John's Church. The town itself has great attractions, and is, besides, within an easy distance of many lovely rural and pastoral scenes and places of historic interest, like Warkworth, Alnwick, and Dunstanburgh. On the smooth, firm sands, or the far-stretching breezy links, where golf, cricket, and tennis are played during the summer months, the visitor in search of health will soon realise the benefits of the sea-side. An admirable description of Alnmouth, disguised under the name of Redburnmouth, will be found in an article, entitled "Winter in a Northumberland Watering-place," which appears in *Blackwood's Magazine*, for June 1876.

Bilton Junction, the nearest railway station, is a mile distant from the village, but conveyances meet all trains. There are three inns—The Schooner, the Red Lion, and the Hope and Anchor, together with several good boarding-houses. Alemouth, or Yellmouth, is the local pronunciation of Alnmouth.

Though the name does not appear in ancient documents till the twelfth century, the place had evidently an existence in pre-Norman times. First, there was the settlement of the ancient Britons—a rude camp which still may be traced on the east side of the present road, about two hundred yards from the north end of the village. In shape it is an irregular quadrangle, 90 yards by 70 yards, with an entrance at the north-west angle. The *Beacon Hill* would no doubt be used then, as in later times, for a look-out station. *Marden*, the name of the neighbouring farmstead, is thought to be derived from *mare* and *dun*, the sea-camp or fortress. To the Saxon Vikings Alnmouth must have been a place of some consequence, on account of its situation at the mouth of a tidal river. That they erected a church here is proved by the discovery of the shaft of a Saxon cross, in 1789, on the Church Hill. This interesting relic is 2 feet 10 inches in height. One face represents the crucifixion, the figures of Christ, the two thieves, and two executioners being sculptured in low relief. The other face, filled with characteristic knot-work, bears the inscription, "Myredeh meh wo"—that is, Myredeh me wrought. As the name of Eadulf appears on one edge, it is supposed that the cross was erected to this Northumbrian king, who was slain at Bamburgh. Alnmouth shares with Whittingham the honour of being the Twyford of Bede, where, at a great Synod held in 684, Cuthbert was chosen Bishop of Lindisfarne. The supposition that Alnmouth was the place referred to is supported by the fact that close to the hill on which the old church stood there were two fords, one called the Low Ford, leading through Woden township, by the Low Ford Lane to Warkworth, the other leading by High Ford Lane to the village of Lesbury, and so on to Alnwick. In the fourteenth century the ships of "Alemuth" were frequently required for the defence of the kingdom, and in the troublous times preceding the union, the burgesses of the town were compelled to "keep, upon their own charge, one good sur watch upon the Wallop-hill, as well by daye as by nighte, and also to have ther two beakens of wood sett upon the said hill, the same to be made for fyer pannes to hang therein, for warning of the countrye as opportunity shall serve by land or by sea, over and besides the night and neghborly watche aboute the towne." In the eighteenth and early part of the nineteenth century Alnmouth had a considerable trade. Wallis, in 1769, says—"The principal export is corn kept in large granaries, the largest, perhaps, in the county. They import Norway timber and goods from London, Holland, and other places. A new ship of nearly three hundred tons was built and launched at this port on Wednesday, 13th March 1765, supposed to have been the first ever built at it." As many as eighteen vessels are said to have been in the harbour at the same time. Most of the granaries have now been converted into large dwelling-houses, which are not without a certain picturesque incongruity. Though commerce has left the little town, it still employs about forty men and sixteen cobles in the fish trade. During the war with France, in the eighteenth century, several naval encounters took place off Alnmouth.

On January 6th, 1744, the *Thomas and Margaret* of Sunderland, and a brigantine from Berwick, were taken by a privateer, after an engagement of five hours, in which Captain Turner's vessel, the *Thomas and Margaret*, was thrice boarded.

On April 4, 1747, a Berwick sloop was captured by a privateer.

On August 22nd, 1756, a French privateer, "a long dogger that appeared to be full of men," took a fishing smack belonging to Berwick, freighted with salmon, off Alnmouth, "in sight of a great number of the inhabitants."

On August 15th, 1779, an exciting sea fight, which lasted two hours, and was witnessed by a large number of persons on the shore, took place between two French privateers, one of eighteen and the other of twenty-four six-pounder guns, and the *Content*, a man-of-war of twenty guns, with the result that the Frenchmen were compelled to flee with all the sail they could make. The *Greenlander*, a consort of the *Content*, for some reason or other, took no part in the engagement, but ran in close to the shore. Great alarm was felt lest the French should attempt to land, and a body of volunteers, with two mounted cannon, arrived from Alnwick Castle.

On September 23rd, 1779, Paul Jones, who had been cruising about the coast of Northumberland the whole day, appeared off Alnmouth at six o'clock, and at eight took a brig. He then continued his course south, after firing a cannon shot at the old church. The ball missed, but grazing the surface of a small field east of Wooden Hall, struck the ground, and rebounding three times, rent the east end of the farmstead from bottom to top. It weighs 68 pounds, and is in the possession of Roger Buston, Esq., of Buston, a country house about a mile and a half south-west of Alnmouth.

The river formerly flowed to the south of the Church Hill, which was connected with Alnmouth by a narrow ridge of land, but in 1806, a breach having been made in this sea-worn isthmus, the Aln changed its course, and has since entered the sea on the north side. The *Church Hill*, covered with blown sand and overgrown with coarse bents, is a spot of much interest to antiquaries, for upon its summit stood the old Saxon church dedicated to St. Waleric, and the later Norman edifice of *St. John the Baptist.* The rent and tottering walls of this thirteenth-century church, which in 1738 had fallen into ruins, were blown down by a great gale on the Christmas day of 1806, and all that now remains to indicate its site are a few tombstones of the last century. It was sometimes known as Woden's Church—not because it had been dedicated to the Saxon divinity, but on account of its position near the township of Wooden, or Walden—a name similar in derivation to weald. The present church of *St. John the Baptist*, in the centre of the village, a neat edifice designed by Mr. Matthew Thompson, of Newcastle, was consecrated and formally opened on the 7th of November 1876. In the salt-marshes grow the marsh-samphire (*Salicornia herbacea*) and the sea-aster (*Aster tripolium*), and on the links may be gathered the sea-pearlwort (*Sagina maritima*).

A little over three miles south of Alnmouth is the ancient town of WARKWORTH, around which cluster so many historical and romantic associations. Seated on a steep declivity, almost encircled by the lovely Coquet, it presents to the north a very picturesque aspect, with its plain-fronted but substantially-built houses ranged on each side of a broad street leading up to the grand baronial castle of the Percies. Being within a short distance of the sea, and having some of the most lovely river scenery in the county close at hand, it is not surprising that Warkworth should be a very popular holiday resort. Good accommodation is provided at the Sun Hotel, the Hermitage Hotel, and the Black Bull Inn. The railway station is a mile and a half to the west. The Saxons early established themselves in a stockaded stronghold on this elevated peninsula, the mouth of the river covered by the Coquet Isle affording a convenient harbour for their long chiules. "Wercewode" was one of the five villages conferred in 737 by King Ceolwulph on the monastery of Lindisfarne, of which he became an inmate, and

"For cowl and beads laid down
The Saxon battle-axe and crown."

In 1174 a division of William the Lion's army burnt the town, committing many cruelties on the inhabitants. General Forster and his little army of Jacobites arrived at Warkworth on the 7th of October 1715, and rested for the Sunday there. Service was held in the church, and then the Pretender was proclaimed as King of Great Britain and Ireland "by Mr. Forster in disguise, and by the sound of trumpet, and all the formality that the circumstances and place would admit. It may be observed that this was the first place where the Pretender was so avowedly pray'd for and proclaimed as King of these realms."—*Patten.* Before entering Warkworth, the Coquet must be crossed by a quaint, many-angled bridge of two arches, rebuilt in 1379. It was formerly embellished with a pillar bearing the Percy arms. At the south end are the remains of a small tower and gateway which defended the passage. A lane leads to the right, past the site of a chantry founded in the reign of Henry III. by Nicholas de Farnham, Bishop of Durham, to the *Church of St. Lawrence*, a venerable structure, erected on the site of the Saxon church of King Ceolwulph. During the restorations in 1860 the angles of this earlier building and a length of walling, four feet thick, were discovered. A Saxon cross, rudely carved with knot-work on both sides, is preserved in the recess of the south wall of the chancel. The Saxon church was the scene of a terrible massacre in 1174, when a division of William the Lion's army, under Earl Duncan, put to death more than a hundred—another account says three hundred—men, besides women and children, who had taken refuge in the sanctuary and the vicarage. After this defilement and probable destruction of the building, the present church was erected. Examples of the various styles of English architecture may be found in this interesting edifice. The north wall of the nave and chancel are late Norman; the tower belongs to the Transitional period, and the spire to the Decorated; the vestry is probably an early English erection; the south aisle and porch were added during the Perpendicular era. The features most worthy of special notice are—the Norman windows of the nave; the original groining of the chancel, and the Norman triplet filled with modern stained glass at the east end, and the chancel arch with its singular and perhaps unique fan ornamentation; the old staircase for the ringer of the Sanctus bell, at the north-east angle of the nave; the cross-legged effigy of a knight in the south aisle, supposed to represent Sir Hugh de Morwick, who gave the common of Warkworth to the burgesses; and a curious window in the vestry, composed of three narrow slits, through which, it is believed, an anchorite, inhabiting the chamber, communicated with persons outside. The porch is well peppered on the outside with bullet marks. Within it is laid the opening scene of Mr. Walter Besant's story, *Let nothing you dismay*, the hero of the narrative having to do penance in a white sheet before the congregation entering the church.

The Northumbrian Jacobites, during their short stay at Warkworth in October 1715, attended the church. Mr. Buxton, the chaplain of the little army, conducted the service, as Mr. Ion, the incumbent, declined to pray for the Pretender as king. "Buxton's sermon," says

Patten, "gave mighty encouragement to his hearers, being full of exhortations, flourishing arguments, and cunning insinuations, to be hearty and zealous in the cause." In the vestry is the prayer-book which was used by Mr. Buxton, as an inscription on the margin of a page of the Calendar informs the reader. The present vicar is Canon Dixon, the author of *The Church of England from the Roman Jurisdiction; Mano, a Poetical History of the time of the close of the Tenth Century; Historical Odes and Poems*, and other works.

The road from the church and the road from the bridge meeting at the ancient market-cross, enclose a triangular space which was formerly called the Nova Villa, or New Town. Crowning the steep ascent above the river, its grandly picturesque outlines, visible from far and near, is the *Castle.*

"Warkworth," says Mr. Freeman, "of less historic fame than Alnwick, is in itself a more pleasing object of study. It stands as a castle should stand, free from the disfigurement of modern habitation." The original structure, reared on the site of the old Saxon stronghold of King Ceolwulph, is believed to have been built by Roger Fitz-Richard, to whom Henry II. granted, in 1158, the manor of Warkworth. William the Lion, according to the old chronicle, "coming to Warkworth" (in 1173), "did not deigne to stop there, for weak was the castle, the wall, and the trench." It must have been very much strengthened shortly afterwards. King John was here on February 2nd, 1213. The castle, reverting to the Crown in the reign of Edward II., was conferred by Edward III. on the second Lord Percy of Alnwick, from which time, to the middle of the fifteenth century, it was the principal residence of this great Northumbrian family. This was the home of the gallant Hotspur, and to his connection with the massive pile is due very much of the romantic interest which attaches to Warkworth. Worthy, indeed, are these grim walls, to have been touched with the glamour of Shakespeare's genius. Here is laid, scene iii. act 2. of "Henry IV.," in which Lady Percy questions her husband as to the reason of his abstraction.

"Some heavy business has my lord in hand,
And I must know it, else he loves me not."

Hotspur ungallantly will not tell her his secret, but, his thoughts dwelling on the plot against Henry IV., replies—

"Away, you trifler! Love? I love thee not;
I care not for thee, Kate: this is no world
To play with mammets, and to tilt with lips."

In the introduction to Part II., Rumour, after the battle of Shrewsbury, in which Hotspur is killed, approaches Warkworth, saying—

"Thus have I rumour'd through the peasant towns,
Between the royal field of Shrewsbury
And this worm-eaten hold of ragged stone,
Where Hotspur's father, old Northumberland,
Lies crafty-sick."

Again, scene iii. act 2, Part II., is laid at Warkworth, before the castle, the persons represented being the Earl of Northumberland, Lady Northumberland, and Lady Percy. Henry IV. himself laid siege to the castle in 1405, but at the seventh discharge of his artillery, the constable capitulated. In 1567 the castle was in a ruinous condition, and in 1672 part of the materials of the keep—the lead and timber, etc.—were carried away by one Joseph Clarke, by permission of the Countess of Northumberland, to build himself a house at Chirton. Baron Warkworth, one of the titles of the Duke of Northumberland, was first conferred on Algernon Seymour, Duke of Somerset, October 3rd, 1749.

The present entrance to the castle is by the postern gate, on the west side. On the left, at the north end of the great quadrangular space, enclosed by the walls, stands the *Donjon*, or *Keep*—the most perfect portion of the castle—on an artificial mound, which raises it above the level of the other buildings. It was re-built on the site of an earlier one, by the son of Hotspur, between the years 1415 and 1454. The plan is somewhat peculiar, and may be roughly described as a square, with a semi-hexagonal tower, projecting from each side, the whole structure being surmounted by a lofty exploratory turret. Several shields, supported by knights or angels, are displayed on the outer wall. "This keep," says Mr. Freeman, "a work of the Percies, of the second line, is a good study of the process by which the purely military castle gradually passed into the house fortified for any occasional emergency." The details of the interior have been planned with great skill. Not only are the various chambers lofty and well-lighted, but they are arranged in the best possible manner for the convenient working of a large domestic establishment. The entrance in the south turret, approached by a flight of steps, was very strongly protected, for the besieged, by raising a trap-door as they would a drawbridge, could confront the bold intruders at the threshhold with a deep pit, over which it was necessary to cross in order to reach the heart of the building. On the ground floor are the Hall, the Guard Chamber, with a deep, dark bottle-shaped dungeon beneath its floor, the cellar and several vaulted chambers for the safe-keeping of stores or water tanks. The Grand Staircase leads up to the Vestibule, a large chamber furnished with stone seats for the use of the attendants. To the right is the great Baronial Hall, or Banqueting-room, with its tall oriel lighting the dais, and the three arched doorways at the lower end, communicating with its kitchens and buttery, and the apartments in connection with them. Adjoining it is the apsidal *Chapel*, still containing its piscina and broad trefoiled sedilia. It is lighted by three tall traceried windows at the east end, which command a very extensive sea-view. By means of "squints" on the south side, members of the household detained in the side apartments could watch the celebration of the mass. Several of the smaller chambers are in a good state of preservation. Two of them have been fitted up with antique furniture and tapestry by Algernon, the fourth duke, and assist the imagination in picturing the domestic life of the feudal barons of Warkworth. Running from the top to the bottom of the keep, through the centre of the various floors, is an open space called a "lantern," or impluvium, which gave light to several of the rooms, and carried away the rain-water from the roof. Descending to the court-yard, the visitor will see before him the foundations of an unfinished collegiate church, among which are the moulded bases of several piers. It is not known who the founder was. The masons' marks, which may be traced on every stone, differ from those in the keep. The Great Hall attached to the curtain wall was built in the Transitional period. A kind of aisle was formed on the east side by a row of pillars, of which the bases of two remain. Near these remains is the *Lion Tower*, which derives its name from the sculptured figure, on a stone shelf, of a "portentous lion, of a race certainly now extinct, with a vast frill round his neck by way of mane, the quaint ugliness of his features being mellowed by the touch of time." This tower was built between the years 1461 and 1489, by Henry Percy, fourth Earl of Northumberland. He married the daughter of William Herbert, Earl of Pembroke, and thus it happens that the badge of this family, a bascule or swing used in fortifications, appears among the armorial bearings of the Percies and Lucies, that adorn the front of the tower. Here are preserved two objects of interest, the baptismal font of the castle chapel, and a huge, round blue stone, connected with which there is the following tradition. One night a custodian of the castle had the good fortune to dream three times in succession that in a certain part of the castle area there lay hidden beneath a blue stone an untold treasure. He communicated the secret to a neighbour, and allowed two or three days to pass over before testing the truth of his strange dream. When, at last, he proceeded to the spot indicated, he found a deep trench there, and upon the edge of it a blue stone, which he had not previously noticed. Clearly he had been forestalled, and his feelings of chagrin may easily be imagined. It is stated that the family of the "early bird" became suddenly rich, and that years afterwards there was found in the river a large kettle supposed to have contained the golden pieces desposited under the blue stone. Beyond the Lion Tower is a small chapel showing delicate additions of Decorated date. Attached to it is a turret surmounted by a tall spire, bearing the curious name of Cradyfargus. A newel-staircase in the interior leads upward to a groined dome. The first floor of this tower of Cradyfargus opened immediately from the Great Chamber, which Mr. Bates considers, with its mural stairs and chambers, to be practically the germ of the present castle. Near the middle of the court-yard is the draw-well by which the castle was supplied with water. On the south side of the quadrangle is the principal entrance, a strongly fortified gateway, having on each side of its pointed archway a heavy tower, supported by peculiar many-angled buttresses. A picturesque object is this ruined stronghold, with its quaint-looking machicolations, corbels, and narrow loopholes. The gateway exhibits Transitional work, and probably owes its erection to Roger Fitz-Richard. It was defended by a portcullis and drawbridge. Traces of the moat are still visible. The outer walls, which in some places reached a height of 35 feet, enclose an area of 5 acres, 17¾ perches. "The loop-holes in the eastern tower," says the Rev. C. H. Hartshorne, "are very remarkable. Within they are totally unlike any others I remember to have seen in England or on the continent." Warkworth Castle has engaged the pencils of both Turner and T. M. Richardson.

For about a mile westward from the castle, as far as Warkworth Mill, there is a charming walk, overhung with the leafy branches of the chestnut, beech, elm, and other stately trees, which grow so luxuriantly in this "happy valley." A flower-strewn meadow intervenes between the footpath and the Coquet, which ripples gently past at the base of wooded slopes and richly-weathered crags. Who can wonder at the angler, as he follows the windings of his favourite river through scenery so beautiful, expressing his raptures in words like the following:—

"The Coquet for ever, the Coquet for aye!
The Coquet the king o' the stream an' the brae;
From his high mountain throne, to his bed in the sea,
Oh! where shall we find such a river as he?
Then blessings be on him, and lang may he glide,
The fisherman's home and the fisherman's pride;
From Harden's green hill to old Warkworth sae gray,
The Coquet for ever, the Coquet for aye!"

The salmon (*Salmo salar*), once so numerous in the Coquet, is now rarely captured, a circumstance due, as some think, to the erection of a weir at Acklington in 1778, or, as others think, to the rapid increase of the bull-trout (*Salmo eriox*), who destroy the fry of the former. Half a mile up the river, on the north side, is the famous *Hermitage*, which may be reached by pleasure-boats from the landing below the castle hill, or by the ferry from the opposite bank. This remarkable little oratory, cut out of a solid freestone rock, twenty feet in height, is quite unique in England. To find anything like it one must travel to the rock-hewn churches of Brantôme and St. Emilion. Its sylvan surroundings are as beautiful as the story connected with it is romantic. Trees, shrubs, ferns, and mosses give to this famous spot it dreamiest charm in the eyes of the modern pilgrim. Spenser must have had a similar scene in his mind when he penned that lovely stanza, so applicable to this famous retreat on the banks of the Coquet.

"A little lowly hermitage it was,
  Down in a dale, hard by a forest's side;
Far from resort of people, that did pass
  In travel to and fro; a little wide
  There was an holy chapel edified,
Wherein the hermit duly wont to say
  His holy things each morn and eventide;
Thereby a crystal stream did gently play,
Which from a sacred fountain welled forth alway."

Built up against the side of the rock is an apartment about eighteen feet square, the walls being of ashlar-work. It contains a fire-place six feet wide, and is believed to have been the kitchen of a chantry priest, who resided here at a later period. Opposite to the entrance in which may be seen the remains of bolts and hinges, is a doorway, giving access to a seat in the rock outside overlooking the river. A flight of seventeen steps leads up to the Hermitage. A quaint little porch, with a stone seat on each side of it, forms the entrance. Above the doorway will be noticed a mutilated piece of sculpture representing a rood. On the inner wall, over the entrance, is the following much-faded inscription in the old English character:—Fuerunt mihi lacrymæ meæ panes die ac nocte ("My tears have been my meat day and night"). The three chambers of the Hermitage are known as the Chapel, the Confessional, and the Dormitory, and have evidently been constructed just before the middle of the fourteenth century. The architectural skill shown in carving them is remarkable. The first chamber entered is the chapel, 20 feet in length, and not more than 7½ feet in height and width. The beautifully-groined ceiling is divided into three compartments, each with its central boss, the graceful arches springing from pilasters of a semi-hexagonal form. At the east end, slightly raised above the level of the floor, is a stone altar, with a recess, or niche, behind it for holding the pyx. To the right, on an altar-tomb, in front of a two-light window, is the recumbent effigy of a lady with upraised hands, her feet resting against what some have thought to be a bull's head—the crest of the Widdrington family, and others a dog—the emblem of fidelity. At the foot of this monument kneels the half-length figure of a hermit, under a trifoliated ogee arch, his right hand supporting his head, his left hand laid on his breast, as if in sorrow. A much-defaced piece of sculpture on the shaft between the two window-lights has been conjectured to represent a hovering cherub. Besides the two openings just referred to, the south wall is further pierced with a quatrefoil window, in the niche of which is a lavatory. A traceried lattice near the altar admits the light into the next chamber.

This is an inner chapel, or aisle, five feet wide, known as the Confessional, from the fact of its stone altar having been cut down, so as to assume in one part a rude resemblance to a seat. Close to it is a holy-water stoup, opposite to which is an aumbry. Over the door leading into this chamber is a shield bearing the sponge, nails, crown of thorns, and other emblems of the crucifixion. The third chamber was the dormitory of the recluse. It has four narrow windows opening into the principal chapel, and one looking out to the Coquet on the south. A gallery, or cloister, commanding a pleasant prospect of the river, has been destroyed by a fall of rock. On the summit of the cliff was the hermit's garden, all traces of which have disappeared before the growth of trees and underwood. The visitor can now judge of the truth of Bishop Percy's description in his ballad, "The Hermit of Warkworth"—

"And now attended by their host,
The hermitage they view'd,
Deep hewn within a craggy cliff,
And overhung with wood.

And near a flight of shapely steps,
All cut with nicest skill,
And piercing through a stony arch
Ran winding up the hill.

There, deck'd with many a flower and herb,
His little garden stands,
With fruitful trees in shady rows,
All planted by his hands.

Then, scoop'd within the solid rock,
Three sacred vaults he shows;
The chief a chapel neatly arch'd,
On branching columns rose.

Each proper ornament was there,
That should a chapel grace;
The lattice for confession fram'd,
The holy-water vase.

O'er either door a sacred text
Invites to godly fear;
And in a little 'scutcheon hung
The cross, the crown, and spear.

Up to the altar's ample breadth
Two easy steps ascend;
And near a glimmering solemn light
Two well-wrought windows lend.

Beside the altar rose a tomb
All in the living stone,
On which a young and beauteous maid
In goodly sculpture shone.

A kneeling angel, fairly carved,
Lean'd hovering o'er her breast;
A weeping warrior at her feet,
And near to these her crest."

The Rev. C. H. Hartshorne ascribes the formation of the Hermitage to the third Earl Percy of Alnwick; Mr. Longstaffe, to his son, the first Earl of Northumberland.

The tradition preserved in the ballad is this:—Sir Bertram, Lord of Bothal Castle, loved the beautiful Isabel, daughter of the neighbouring Lord of Widdrington. The lady held back a little, for

"That heart, she said, is lightly priz'd
Which is too lightly won,"

and determined to put the constancy of her lover to the test. So, as he was feasting with Lord Percy at Alnwick, he received a splendid helmet, by the hands of her maiden, who presented it with these words—

"Sir Knight, thy lady sends thee this,
And yields to be thy bride,
When thou hast prov'd this maiden gift
Where sharpest blows are tried."

Lord Percy at once decided to make a raid into Scotland; so, on the day appointed, young Bertram rode away from Alnwick under the earl's banner. In a desperate encounter with the Scots he performed many valiant deeds.

"The vigour of his single arm
Had well-nigh won the field,"

when a Scottish battle-axe cleft open his "precious casque," inflicting a serious wound. He was saved by his friends, and borne off the field to the castle of Wark. Isabel, blaming herself as the cause of her lover's sufferings, resolved to atone for her foolish pride by nursing him. Accompanied by two tall yeomen, she set out on her journey, but near the Cheviots was taken captive by a Scottish chieftain, who had formerly aspired to her hand, and who now carried her off to his stronghold. Bertram, on his recovery, started with his brother in search of her, one going north, the other west. Having discovered the place of her confinement, he was awaiting an opportunity of rescuing her, when one night he saw his lady descend a ladder of ropes, assisted by a youth in Highland garb. Blind with jealousy and rage, he followed them, and with the words, "Vile traitor! yield that lady up," drew his sword and attacked the stranger. The lady, recognising his voice, cried out to him to stay, as it was his brother, but the warning came too late—the fatal blow had been struck. Isabel, flinging herself forward to avert it, was also pierced in the breast. From her dying lips the unhappy Bertram learnt the story of her capture and rescue by his brother. Filled with remorse and anguish, he gave away his possessions to the poor; and, after hewing out this hermitage, retired from the world to spend the rest of his days in penitence before the effigy of his lost love.

On the rocks near the Hermitage is the flood-mark of 9th February 1837, at a great height above the normal level of the stream.

A mile and a half west by south of Warkworth is *Morwick Hall*, an old seat of the Greys, now the residence of James Dand, Esq. The grounds are laid out with much taste, their beauty being enhanced by the proximity of the Coquet. A fine tulip tree, a large acacia, and a number of old yews will attract notice. In the garden is a vault belonging to the Grey family. It contains an old monument, brought, it is said, from Warkworth. The barony was held at an early period by the powerful and wealthy family of De Morwick. In a narrow and picturesque bend of the river is *Morwick Mill*, where several of the incidents in Mr. Walter Besant's *Let Nothing You Dismay* are supposed to take place. Near to it, 1000 feet to the east, on the face of a perpendicular sandstone rock, overlooking the Coquet, are several incised figures, chiefly spiral in form, and differing in certain particulars from those discovered at Old Bewick, Routing Linn, and other places. They are from ten to fifteen feet above the level of the river, and may be observed from a boat. The rocks are covered with impressions of lepidodendrons. The banks here are beautifully wooded, and gay with the following flowers :—Red campion (*Lychnis diurna*), wood geranium (*Geranium sylvaticum*), mountain speedwell (*Veronica montana*), wood sanicle (*Sanicula Europœa*), wood-loose strife (*Lysimachia nemorum*), giant bell-flower (*Campanula latifolia*), great water horse-tail (*Equisetum telmateia*), great pendulous carex (*Carex pendula*), betony (*Betonica officinalis*), wood-ruff (*Asperula odorata*), axillary clustered carex (*Carex axillaris*), frog satyrion, or orchis (*Habenaria viridis*), pimpernel (*Anagallis arvensis*), etc.

A mile and a half south-east of Warkworth, on a steep acclivity at the mouth of the Coquet, is AMBLE, a small and rising seaport town, which owes its rapid development to the coal-trade. The importance of the site must early have been recognised, judging by the numerous remains which have been found of the primitive inhabitants. A cist containing a perfect skeleton was opened in 1858, about fifty yards north-east of Cliff House and twenty yards from the end of the south pier. Several more cists and urns were again discovered in 1883-4, in a quarry near the town. It is supposed the Romans, too, had an encampment in the neighbourhood, from the fact of a broken altar, inscribed, "To the Campestral mothers by the first Cohort," having been found at Gloster Hill. The tithes of Amble were granted to the monks of Tynemouth by William the Conqueror.

There was formerly a small Benedictine Monastery here, subordinate to the Priory of Tynemouth. In the little chapel connected with it a man did penance as late as 1765. All that remains of this religious house now is a ruined wall with a Gothic window. The monks had the privilege of collecting toll from ships passing up the river. A harbour, in all probability, existed here as far back as 1326. The present harbour was constructed at the enormous cost of £180,000, and is principally used by the Radcliffe and Broomhill collieries for the shipment of their coals. *The Church of St. Cuthbert*, a small edifice in the early Decorated style, was built in 1870, from a design by Mr. R. J. Johnson. Amble is the terminus of a small branch line from Chevington Junction. There are several inns, the principal being the Wellwood Arms and the Dock Hotel. A quarter of a mile north-west of Amble is *Gloster Hill*, where there is yet standing the gateway of the old manor-house, burnt down on Sunday, January 7th, 1759. Lions' claws are carved on the two stone piers. In a field, a little to the south-west, the fragment of the Roman altar already referred to was turned up by the plough in 1856. The names—

Temple Hill, Chester House, and Street Head, all in the parish, favour the idea that a line of Roman road ran in this direction from the interior to the Coquet mouth. To the south is the small fishing village of HAUXLEY, containing some old cottages, one of which bears the date 1600. Running out from the point are the Bondicar Rocks.

Nearly opposite to Amble, a little over a mile from the mainland, is COQUET ISLAND, a low and level strip of land about sixteen acres in extent, its northern and southern extremities running to very fine points. Geologically, it is part of the Northumberland coal-measures, composed of sandstone resting on thin strata of coal and shale. A small Benedictine Monastery existed here as early as A.D. 684, for this was the place where Elfleda, the abbess of Whitby, and sister of Ecgfrith, King of Northumbria, had an important interview with Saint Cuthbert. The aim of the princess was to prevail on the recluse to accept the bishopric offered to him by her brother. She succeeded in obtaining a reluctant promise to the effect that, if he could render the State better service, he would not refuse the unwished-for dignity. There was a Hermitage on the island at some distant period, for, buried at Tynemouth, lies Henry, the hermit of Coquet Isle. The remains of the Benedictine cells are incorporated with the keeper's house. In 1567 the island was resorted to by coiners as a "place of secretness" for making experiments in stamping "hard hedds." The most important event in connection with the island took place in 1643, during the Civil Wars. "The Scots," so writes Colonel Curset in an old tract, "have taken the isle of Cocket, and the garrison thereof, with seventy commanders and other common souldiers, seven peices of ordnance, and all their ammunition, and have placed a garrison of their owne men therein." On the ruins of the old tower has been erected a lighthouse, which, being whitewashed, is visible from a great distance. The first light was exhibited on 1st October 1841. The rocks are very dangerous to vessels. The *Catherine* of Sunderland was wrecked on the north end of the island on November 4th, 1821. The crew of nine men clung to the rigging for hours, in sight of an immense number of people on the mainland, who, for want of a lifeboat, were compelled to listen to their cries without being able to render assistance. The ship went to pieces in the night, and the poor fellows were all lost. The island, with the exception of a small garden attached to the keeper's house, is in pasturage, the scanty vegetation being plentifully interspersed with ragwort, "unprofitably gay." A feature of the island used to be the rabbit warrens. Some Angola rabbits, introduced by the Duke of Northumberland, increased by thousands, and soon overran the place. They were destroyed after the building of the lighthouse. Terns, gulls, and other sea-birds frequent the place in great numbers.

# ALNWICK TO LONGHOUGHTON AND CRASTER.

Longhoughton, 4 miles ; Boulmer, 5½ miles ; Howick Hall, 8 miles ; Craster, 9½ miles ; Proctor Steads, 10 miles.

FOUR miles east by north of Alnwick, by way of Denwick, is LONGHOUGHTON, a quiet agricultural village, consisting of an old and interesting church, and a few pretty cottages scattered along the side of the road, their trim gardens brightened with well-assorted flowers. Roses flourish well on the stiff loamy soil here, and many varieties have been cultivated with success in the garden of Longhoughton Hall.

The *Church of St. Peter* has little architectural beauty, but is, nevertheless. an interesting link between the present and the far-distant past. The greater part of the building belongs to the time of Henry I. The stilted Transitional chancel arch is of a rude type, having neither column, capital, nor moulding, but springing from an abacus that is carried along the wall on each side as a string-course. The arch between the nave and the tower, formed of plain rounded mouldings, is also Transitional in character. To the same architectural period belongs the tower, a low massive structure, 23 feet by 22 feet, with walls 4 feet thick. In the absence of a strong pele-tower within the vill of Longhoughton, it doubtlessly served as a place of refuge for the inhabitants during Scottish raids. That it was used for this purpose is borne out by Clarkson in his survey of 1567. "The chirch and steple is the great strengt, that the poor tenants have to drawe to in tyme of warre ; wherefor it is ever needfoull the same be for that and other causes kepid in good reperations." During the early English period the south aisle was added to the nave, as is evidenced by the gracefully-pointed arches with their clustered columns. The ancient workmanship is seen in the masonry at the west end and a part of the south side of this aisle. A cusped-headed window of two lights at the east end of it, and the adjoining buttress at the south-east angle, are of Decorated date. Crowning the east wall of the church is the old Market Cross of Longhoughton, which, after being lost for many years, was discovered buried up in a smuggler's grave. Several years ago the church suffered from a great fire. The register of the parish is remarkable for some curious entries made by the Rev. George Doncan, vicar from 1696 to 1719. Not content with recording the marriage or death of his parishioners, and the birth of their children, he has summed up in a descriptive phrase—Latin or English—the character of the persons concerned. Very low must have been the moral and religious condition of the people of Longhoughton in the eyes of their not very charitable pastor. They little knew that there was "a chiel amang them takin' notes," who would hand down their characters to posterity in terms like the following:—*Profanus* (profane); *ambo valde impii* (both very impious); *nequissimus homo* (most worthless man); *omni modo nequam* (in every sense worthless); *very nequissimus* (worthless in a superlative degree); *malus malorum* (vile of the vile); *malus filius mali patris* (a bad son of a bad father); *valde ignorans et obstinatus peccat* (a very ignorant and obstinate sinner); *infelix valde nuptiis* (very unhappily married); *viles ebriosa peccat* (a vile, drunken, female sinner); *improbus Hibernicus miles* (a dishonest Irish soldier); *triste ignorans et prophanus peccat* (a sadly ignorant and profane sinner); a quack and warlock doctor; a very brutish and wicked fellow; obstinate, ignorant, and wicked; a wicked knave and a Dissenter; brutish and profane; a Janus tergiverse whig. Those worthy of commendation are comparatively few. They are described as "a very serious good man;" a knowing good man; a serious, sensible, and good day labourer; *valde probus* (very upright); *filia piæ matris et uxor probi maritis* (daughter of a pious mother, and wife of an upright husband); *honestus homini sed prophanus Deo* (honest towards man, but profane towards God); *probus et honestus* (upright and honest); best of wives; an old innocent and fortunate fisher (a bachelor); a very good churchman. His last record is kindly: *valde pius et probus* (very pious and upright).

The celebrated Ratcheugh Crags (already described) are about a mile to the west. Longhoughton railway station is close to the village.

A mile and a half east by south of Longhoughton is the small fishing village of BOULMER, the principal resort of smugglers from Yetholm, Morebattle, Crailing, Jedburgh, and all parts of Bamburgh, Coquetdale, and Glendale wards in the olden time. As many as twenty or thirty of them, mounted on horseback, would come to Boulmer for gin, and carry it to the centre of the county and the wilds of Coquetdale, not without many hair-breadth escapes and lively encounters with the excisemen. Numerous are the dare-devil exploits recorded of Wull Balmer, Jock Melvin, Ruthor Grahamshaw, Laird Cranstoun of Smailham, and Wull Faa of Kirk Yetholm, the gipsy king. The first of these famous smugglers is alluded to in the old song.

> "Blind Wull Bawmer o' Jethart,
> His grips are no guid to come in;
> He felled a' the gaugers i' Jethart
> When comin' frae Boomer wi' gin."

Though this illicit traffic has now ceased, smuggled goods, such as silks and casks of spirit, are sometimes dug up on the coast, having been deposited there in bygone times, and forgotten by their owners. The scene here forms a characteristic picture of the Northumbrian coast: the little cluster of red-tiled and blue-slated cottages; the gaily-painted fishing-boats drawn up on the beach, or lying in the little harbour; the curving line of low cliffs and sand-hills; the grey beds of sandstone stretching out to sea, smooth-washed, or shaggy with sea-weed, and the shallow lagoons among them tenanted by heron-gulls, plovers, and lapwings.

Two miles and a half to the north of Longhoughton, and a mile and a half east of Little Mill Station, is *Howick Hall*, the seat of Earl Grey. This noble mansion, built in 1782 from the designs of Mr. Newton, of Newcastle, is situated in a well-wooded park at the head of a lovely dene, and commands a prospect of exceeding beauty, the green and dark tints of the foliage around it contrasting with the pale blue and purple hues of the ever-changing sea beyond. The little "Turris de Howyke," mentioned in the list of castles in 1416, was taken down when the present building was commenced. The internal decorations, which were chiefly renewed in the time of the second earl, are of classic elegance, and in fitting harmony with the general character of the house. The outer hall contains a striking marble statue of the second Earl Grey, by Campbell. It was presented to Countess Grey by the friends of the earl on his retiring from office in 1834. Another piece of sculpture here is by Lough, and represents "David with the Sling." In the inner hall are two large pictures by Northcote—"The Disobedient Prophet," and "Daniel in the Lion's Den." Several valuable pictures and portraits adorn the walls of the principal rooms—namely, The Drawing-Room: "Rotterdam"—*Sir A. Calcott;* "Nymph Bathing"—*Martin;* "Virgin and Child with a Cross"—*Schidone;* "Lady Mary Wood as a child"—*Thompson;* "The Library of Holland House, with portraits of Lord and Lady Holland, and Mr. Allen"—*Leslie;* The Library: "Curran"—*Lawrence*; and the late "Earl Grey," by *Lawrence;* "Dr. Franklin," of special interest from the fact of its being taken from his house in Philadelphia during the War of Independence by the ill-starred Major André, aide-de-camp of the first Earl Grey; the "amiable spy," as Charles Lamb calls him, whose effigy in Westminster Abbey has more than once been mysteriously mutilated; "The Emperor Napoleon," painted during the Hundred Days, and procured for Lord Grey by Sir Robert Watson. The bees on the frame were taken from the Emperor's throne. Breakfast-Room: "The late Countess Grey, with Lady Durham and Lady E. Bulteel, as children"—*Lawrence;* "Jupiter in Infancy"—*Thompson;* The Dining-Room: "The Last Sleep of Argyle—*Northcote;* "The Grey Family"—*Thompson;* "The first and second Earl Grey"—*Lawrence.*

The gold timepiece in the library was given to Mr. Albert Grey by the Queen on the occasion of his marriage. Adjoining the hall are fine flower-gardens and conservatories. "No family in the north of England," says Raine, "has, in the course of the centuries through which the line of Grey can be traced, afforded so great a variety of character. It has had its warriors and its statesmen, its authors and its divines. It can boast of an ancestor made immortal by Shakespeare—the treason disappears before the wand of the magician—it can boast of a churchman who, like a second Bernard Gilpin, lived a life of the most disinterested liberality and the most unfeigned piety, and who died the death of a saint, leaving behind him a good name; and, to come to the present time, it can boast of a statesman whose name will descend to posterity as the chief promoter of the most important political change which has been effected in the British Constitution for many a century." This distinguished member of the family was the second son of General Sir Charles, afterwards Earl Grey, and was born at Falloden on the 13th March 1764. He fixed his residence at Howick on the 17th July 1801, by the kindness of his uncle, at that time owner, and on the anniversary of that day, forty-four years later, he there breathed his last. "How he loved the place," writes his son, the Hon. Charles Grey; "with what reluctance he at all times left it—and with what delight he ever returned to it, his letters abundantly testify. And had he not a right to love a place, as it may in truth be called, of his own creation? Where, with the exception of the few old trees about the house and garden, and in the glen leading to the sea, there is scarcely one which is not of his own planting—where there is not a walk or an improvement but of his laying-out—and where he could look round on the comfort and happiness of all about him, with the proud satisfaction of feeling how much he had himself contributed to them." It was while staying at Howick that Monk Lewis wrote his ballad of "Sir Grey the Seeker."

Not far from the hall, on the edge of the wooded ravine, is *The Church of St. Michael*, a highly-ornamented structure in the Norman style, erected in 1849 by Henry, third Earl Grey, on the site of two former buildings—one the early mediæval edifice, the other a Greek temple, built in 1746. In the chancel is a beautiful marble tomb, with a rich Gothic canopy of caen-stone above it, to the memory of Charles, the second Earl Grey, and Mary Elizabeth, his countess. Upon the sides of this monument are canopied niches with sculptured figures in them. On the walls are some marble tablets, and on the floor some tomb-slabs to the memory of other members of the Grey family. A former rector of Howick was Dr. Isaac Basire, chaplain to Charles I., a singular character, who was ousted from his living during the Protectorate, and led an adventurous life as a missionary among the Greeks, Arabians, and Egyptians.

An ornamental bridge crosses the burn, and affords a communication with the most beautiful portion of the Howick grounds. This is a long dene of a mile and a half in length, winding down to the coast. It is watered by a little sparkling burn, and well-wooded with beeches, elms, and firs, the moist banks being overgrown with herb mercury, the lesser periwinkle, and other training plants. The pathway through it was a favourite one with the second Earl Grey. "The walk down the glen, known as the 'long walk,'" to quote again the words of the Hon. Charles Grey, "and that along the sea-shore, have seemed to me to deserve especial mention, not only as giving in fact a character to the place, but as the round which, each Sunday in succession, weather permitting (and it must indeed have been a bad day that kept us at home), my father would take with his family."

In the central part of the dene is a well-sheltered Pinetum, remarkable for the number of specimens of the *Araucaria imbricata* found together. Among the conifers of Howick are specimens of *Abies Canadensis* (hemlock spruce of North America), *A. Douglasii*, *A. Menziesii*, *Cedrus deodara*, *Cedrus Libani*, *Cephalotaxus Fortunei*, *Cryptomeria Japonica* and *elegans*, *Cupressus Lawsoniana*, *Cupressus macrocarpa*, *Picea nobilis*, *P. Nordmanniana*, *P. pindrow*, *P. pinsap*, *P. Webbiana*, *Pinus austriaca*, *Pinus insignis*, *Pinus Genevensis*, *P. Excelsa*, *Thinopsis borealis*, *Cupressus noatkaensis*, *Thuja gigantea*, *Th. Menziesii*, *Occidentalis*, *Argentea* and *Pendula*, and *Wellingtonia gigantea*.

In a pasture-field about 300 yards north-west from the mouth of Howick Burn are the remains of a circular camp, 60 yards in diameter. It had occupied the summit of a gravel mound, which slopes abruptly to the wooded dene. Several pieces of broken spears and swords, and some Roman coins have been found here.

On the sea-banks to the north of the burn, above the cliffs, *Hippophæ rhamnoides*, or sea buckthorn, grows plentifully. Here also occurs the rare bristly ox-tongue (*Helminthia echioides*). Near Howick boat-house the high tide in 1849 laid bare a submarine forest, consisting of a number of oak, fir, alder, and hazel trees, some lying prostrate and others still rooted and having short upright stems. Hazel nuts were also found. The sandstone rocks on the Howick coast are hollowed into picturesque caverns. One of these is known as the "Rumbling Churn." Further north a good section of the calcareous division of the mountain limestone is exposed. On the cliffs the *Asplenium marinum* may be gathered. At *Cullernose Point*, about two miles north of Howick Burn, there is a striking outbreak of the great Whin Sill. The rude semi-columnar basaltic mass, rising to a height of 120 feet, and a section close by of the mountain limestone formation of Northumberland, with its alternating beds of limestone, sandstone, shale, and coal, will be observed with much interest by the geologist. At this point the Whin Sill leaves the coast and runs across the country in a south-westerly direction.

Three-quarters of a mile further on is the fishing village of CRASTER. Here is the large herring-curing establishment of Messrs. Cormack & Son, where the process of preparing the fish for the markets may be seen in its various stages. Three-quarters of a mile to the west is *Craster Tower*, the seat of J. W. Craster, Esq., pleasantly situated among trees, with fine views of the sea through chasms in the rocks that intervene between it and the coast. The nucleus of the building is an ancient pele, constructed of basalt. The characteristic vaulted chamber is now used as a cellar. The family of Craster is a very old one, dating from before the Conquest. William de Craucestr' is stated to have held the estate in 1272. Craster is two miles east of Little Mill Station.

A short distance to the north of the Tower is the hamlet of *Dunstan*, near to which is a group of buildings of some extent, called *Proctor Steads*, or *Dunstan Hall*. The oldest part is an ancient pele, which was formerly used as a watch-tower in advance of Dunstanburgh Castle. It measures 18 feet 8 inches by 14 feet 9 inches on the outside, and consists of four stages. The basement storey belongs to a very remote period, one portion of it exhibiting, according to Mr. Longstaffe, an approximation to the long and short work of Saxon times. The walls of this part of the building, four feet in thickness, and the vaulted chamber, are built entirely of basalt. The superstructure is of freestone, the Edwardian ashlar-work indicating that it was erected about the same time as Dunstanburgh Castle. The corbels supporting the machicolations by which the entrance was defended still remain on the east side. Adjoining the tower is an early hall of considerable interest. In the seventeenth century the west end of it was much altered, and a porch at the same time thrown out to the north. The east gable, however, is in its original state. On the lintel of the doorway are the letters J. P., and the date 1652. The material for building this wing is supposed to have been obtained from the ruins of Dunstanburgh Castle. Proctor Steads is the reputed birthplace of the most famous of the schoolmen—John Duns Scotus. The authority for this statement is a note at the end of one of his own manuscripts in the library of Merton College. "Here endeth the lecture of . . . John Duns, who was born in a certain hamlet of the parish of Emylton, called Dunstan, in the county of Northumberland, belonging to the house of the scholars of Merton Hall, in Oxford." This remarkable man, who was born in the latter half of the thirteenth century, received his education in the house of the Grey Friars at Newcastle, and became a monk of that order. He continued his studies at Oxford, and in 1304 was appointed professor and regent in the University of Paris. Such was the dialectical ingenuity he displayed in his defence of the doctrine of the Immaculate Conception, that he won for himself the title of "Doctor Subtilis." His great opponent in this controversy was Thomas Aquinas, and their respective followers were called the Thomists and Scotists. In regard to philosophy, he held that there was no true knowledge of anything knowable apart from theology as based upon revelation. The "Evangelical Doctor" maintained, on the other hand, that reason and revelation were two independent sources of knowledge. The works of Duns Scotus are numerous, the most important consisting of questions and commentaries on the writings of Aristotle, and on the sentences of Lombard. He died of apoplexy on the 8th of November 1308. A portrait of this learned divine hangs in one of the rooms at Proctor Steads.

# ALNWICK TO ROCK.

Rennington, 4 miles ; Rock, 5 miles.

NEARLY four miles north-east by east of Alnwick, by way of Denwick, is RENNINGTON, a small and pretty village, well-sheltered, with a flat, fertile country around it, dotted with farm-houses. Part of the village lies on the lower ground by the side of the Alnwick Road, and part on the gentle slope of a hill, which is crowned by a large farmstead surrounded by trees. Most of the cottages have gardens in front of them, gay with a profusion of London-pride, southern-wood, pansies, and stocks. The little inn even has its triangular plot of flowers. The *Church of All Saints*, standing on a slight elevation, begirdled with trees, was built in 1831, on the site of an ancient Norman chapel. A new chancel, vestry, and north aisle were added in 1865. A handsome vicarage adjoins the church, with ivy-covered out-buildings. The nearest station to Rennington is Little Mill Station, about a mile distant by the footpath through the fields.

A mile to the north, on an eminence in the midst of rich and romantic scenery, is the charming village of ROCK, lying just outside the gates of Rock Hall, and, like Capheaton, looking on a small ornamental lake. It consists of a single row of modern stone cottages, very neat and picturesque with their weather mouldings and quaint little dormer windows, and roses clambering up the wall around the doorways. In front of them is a lawn-like village green, and behind are small kitchen-gardens, well-stocked with currant and gooseberry bushes, and backed by a row of sycamore and chestnut trees set in a well-trimmed hedge. At one end is the school-room ; at the other the church. A large farmstead, with barns, stables, and byres, and a rustic smithy, complete the remaining details in the picture. The Mid or Middle Hall, supposed to have been erected by Mr. John Salkeld for his eldest son, was taken down in 1855. The school-room, which stands on its site, preserves, built up in its walls, two relics of the ancient building—a sundial and a square stone, bearing the Salkeld initials T S | | A S, and the date 1623. The *Church of St. Philip and St. James* is a Norman edifice, with modern additions. The richly-ornamented west door, with portions of the mason-work in its vicinity, up to the string-course, part of the side walls, and the beautiful round-headed chancel arch, are remnants of the original building. The windows on the south side belong to the early English period. The apse and north aisle are modern. The present north wall, though removed from its former site, is really a part of the old church, for when it was taken down it 1866 the sound stones were carefully marked, especially those of the Norman windows, and re-used in their previous order. The blending of the grey and reddish facing-stones gives to the outer walls a very pleasing effect. On the north wall of the chancel is a monument to Charles Bosanquet, by Jedward, of London, and on the floor beneath it a tomb-slab engraved with a foliated cross and two-handed sword. On the north wall of the church is the memorial brass of Colonel John Salkeld.

From the church an avenue of fine chestnut and lime-trees leads to *Rock Hall*, the seat of Charles B. P. Bosanquet, Esq., J.P., looking very picturesque with its ivied walls, heavy mullioned windows, and battlemented roof. Incorporated with it is an old tower, which, according to the late proprietor, was founded in the time of Stephen, though much altered and enlarged in the time of Elizabeth. It was burnt down on May 15th, 1752, and remained in ruins till 1819, when it was restored by Mr. Charles Bosanquet. The house contains many valuable pictures, among which are the following :—"Virgin with the Child rising from a Couch," part of the celebrated picture in the Louvre, said to be a duplicate by *Raphael*, and signed with his name ; "The Virgin and the Child Reposing"—*Schidone;* "The Saviour at the Last Supper"—*Carlo Dolce;* "The Infant Saviour and St. John playing with a lamb"—*Rubens.*

In the early part of the thirteenth century the manor was held by William de Rok under William de Vescy. It has been in the hands of the De Tughalles, De Swynhoes, Lawsons, Salkelds, and Proctors. The arms of the Salkelds appear over the head of the low door in the east front, and also on three sun-dials, which are placed on the different sides of the building. Colonel John Salkeld, of Rock (b. 1616, d. 1705), lived a somewhat eventful life. At the age of twenty-seven he killed Mr. John Swinburne, of Capheaton, near the gates of Meldon, under circumstances which induced the jury at the inquest to return a verdict of wilful murder. He escaped in some way the penalty of his deed, and, according to his epitaph, "serv'd King Charles y^e 1st with a constant, dangerous, and expensive loyalty as volunteer, captain and collonell of horse ; and for his service of his king and country, he took in Berwick-upon-Tweed and Carlisle, which was a rice (rise) to the warr of '48. He afterwards served in Ireland under King Charles and King James y^e 2nd, as Lieutenant-Coll. He was Justice of y^e Peace 35 years, and (aged 89 ; he departed this life June the 2nd, 1705." Another deed of blood is recorded against a Mr. John Fenwick, of Rock, who basely stabbed Mr. Ferdinando Forster, after he had fallen on the ground during a duel at the White Cross, Newgate Street, Newcastle. Not so fortunate as Salkeld, he was tried and executed 25th September 1701. Christon Bank Station, about two miles distant, may be reached from Rock by following the road north for a short distance, then continuing along a cart-track down a field, turning to the right in the next, and following a footpath through three or four more fields, past Christon Bank Farm.

# BAMBURGH SECTION.

## BAMBURGH.

THERE is no part of the United Kingdom more stimulating to the imagination than the district of which Bamburgh is the centre. Firstly, on geological grounds, for the masses of columnar basalt there, standing out grimly above a wild sea, and the displaced strata around them, are monuments of the fiery forces that in remote ages rent the earth's crust. Secondly, on historical grounds, for "at Bamburgh, above all," in the words of Mr. Freeman, "we feel that we are pilgrims come to do our service at one of the great cradles of our national life;" and again, "round Bamburgh and its founder, Ida, all Northumbrian history gathers;" while in the neighbouring island, appropriately styled "Holy," was generated that spiritual force which was to revolutionize the religious thought of our Saxon ancestors. Thirdly, on legendary grounds, for the lonely Farnes have their legends of St. Cuthbert, and Spindleston Crags and Dunstanburgh Castle have their respective legends of the "Laidley Worm" and "Sir Guy the Seeker." In addition, there are the stories of female daring and devotion, of which Grace Darling and Grizzel Cochrane are the heroines.

Bamburgh, once the royal city of Bernicia, is a quiet and pretty sea-side village, on a gentle slope running up from the shore, and consists, for the most part, of two rows of well-built and flower-decked cottages, which diverge from each other at the upper end, leaving a considerable space, now occupied by a flourishing grove of trees. At the west entrance stands the church; at the east the mighty, rock-based castle. Some cottages, called the Windings, lie between the main body of the village and the life-boat station.. In one of them lived, until recent years, the sister of Grace Darling. The heroine herself was born at Bamburgh, in a house which stood opposite to the churchyard, on the left-hand side of the road leading to Belford. The castle gardens also form an attractive feature to the village. The country around is beautiful and richly cultivated. Bamburgh, on account of its unrivalled situation and varied associations, is one of the most popular of Northumbrian pleasure resorts; and its hotels, the Lord Crewe Arms and the Victoria, are among the most comfortable in the county. It is three miles and a half north-east of Lucker Station, and four miles and three-quarters east of Belford. The past importance of the town of Bamburgh may be gathered from the fact that it sent two members to the twenty-third Parliament of King Edward I., and in Edward III.'s time contributed one vessel to the expedition against Calais. Its history is that of the castle. "Wreckers" were very numerous on the Bamburgh coast in the olden time. In 1472 the magnificent barge of the Bishop of St. Andrew's—the *St. Salvador*—laden with rich merchandise from Flanders, was wrecked on this coast, and the Bamburghers fell on the cargo and plundered it, and, further, kept the Abbot of St. Colomb, who had escaped from the disaster, a prisoner, until a ransom of £80 sterling was paid. Again, in 1559, other Scotch vessels were similarly treated. It is said that a common expression in the mouths of Northumbrian fisher-folk used to be, "Let us pray for a good harvest this winter"—signifying many shipwrecks. In *Chambers's Domestic Annals of Scotland* is an account of a curious sea animal thrown ashore at Bamburgh in 1544:—"At the seaside at Bamburgh there was nae kind of fish ta'en by the space of twa year; but the sea made ane great routing and horrible noise, which was by (beside) custom and use. So it chancit, at the hie spring (tide) that ane terrible beast was casten in dead, of the quantity (bulk) of ane man. Nae man could devise ane thing mair terrible, with horns on the head of it, red een; with misshapen face, with lucken (webbed) hands and feet, and ane great rumple hinging to the eird. It consumit and stinkit sae, that in short time nae man nor beast might come near it; but all the country about saw it before, and sundry took great fear and dreadour for the sicht of it a lang space after. It was callit the Sea-devil. Witness the Laird of Mow." During the fierce election contest of 1826 a duel was fought between the rival candidates, Mr. Lambton and Colonel Beaumont, on the sands near Bamburgh, but fortunately the affair ended without bloodshed.

BAMBURGH CASTLE, "with its main outline hardly marred, stands on a site which is all but the noblest by nature, and which surpasses the sites of all other Northumbrian fortresses in ancient and abiding historic interest."—*Freeman.* This is an isolated mass of the great Whin Sill, 75 feet thick, resting on beds of sandstone and shale. The massive curtain walls, of the same material, and the lofty towers and turrets, rise from the very brink of the black, precipitous crags, and seem, as it were, to form an integral portion of the rock itself. The vast accumulations of sand on the east side diminish the effect of the lofty cliff, which rises to a height of 150 feet from the level of low-water mark. A more impregnable stronghold could not well be imagined. For rugged strength and barbaric grandeur, it is the king of Northumbrian castles. From nearly every point of the compass its majestic outlines are visible. To the mariner plying between the Elbe and the Tyne, it is the most conspicuous landmark on the north-east coast. Standing before this towering mass of masonry that—

"From its tall rock looks grimly down,"

it is desirable to recall to mind the most interesting facts of its history. Some antiquaries are of opinion that the Romans had a military post here, and the discovery of three Roman denarii give a slight colouring to their supposition. The earliest reference to Bamburgh appears in the *Anglo-Saxon Chronicle*, where it is stated that Ida, shortly after beginning his reign in A.D. 547, "built Bamburgh, which was at first enclosed by a hedge, and afterwards by a wall." This monarch, the founder of the Northumbrian kings, struck such terror into the Celtic people of the district that his name has descended to us in their language as Ida "Flamdwyn," or the "Flame-bearer." As the present keep was not founded till five hundred years after his death, it is by a poetical license that Sir Walter Scott speaks of "King Ida's fortress huge and square." Till the seventh century, Bamburgh was known, according to Nennius, as "Dinguvaroy," apparently its ancient British name. Ethelfrith gave the town to his queen, Bebbab, and called it after her name, "Bebbanburch." St. Aidan, who had a small church and bed-chamber not far from the royal city, was sometimes a guest at the king's table. One Easter-day, Bede tells us, he was so much struck with the magnanimity of King Oswald, in sending the viands provided for himself to some beggars outside the gates, that he seized the royal hand and blessed it, saying, "May this hand never grow old." If saintly legends are to be believed, this prayer was answered, for Bede assures us that the hand and arm, which had been severed from the king's body in battle, were treasured in a silver casket in St. Peter's Church, at Bamburgh, and remained there undecayed in his days. A miracle even greater than this is stated to have been worked by the saintly Bishop a few years later, when the ruthless Penda, King of the Mercians, the slayer of Edwin and Oswald, laid siege to Bamburgh, A.D. 651. This heathen warrior, so often victorious, had destroyed all the villages in the neighbourhood, and piled up a quantity of planks, beams, wattles, and thatch against the outer walls, with the intention of burning the city. Saint Aidan, who was at the time in the islet of Farne, saw the flames and smoke carried above the city walls by the boisterous wind. Raising his hands and eyes up to heaven, he exclaimed, "Behold, Lord, how great mischief Penda does." Which words were hardly uttered, when the wind, immediately turning from the city, drove back the flames upon those who had kindled them, so that some of them being hurt, and all frightened, they forbore any further attempts against the city. Twelve days after the death of King Oswin, Aidan died at Bamburgh. He was staying at the king's country house near the city, when he was seized with an attack of illness so suddenly that a tent had to be hastily stretched against the western wall of the little timber church, and there, lying upon the ground, his head resting upon a log which served as a buttress to the church, he breathed his last on the 31st of August 651. In 652 Penda again marched as far as Bamburgh, and burnt both church and village. In 705 Eardulph, who had usurped the throne of Northumbria on the death of Alfred, laid seige to the castle, at that time held by Berthfrid, a zealous adherent of the late king, and the guardian of the young prince Osred. During a vigorous sally made by the garrison, the pretender was taken, and afterwards beheaded. Alred, the tyrant, fled hither from York, where he had been deserted by his family and nobles. Bishop Cynewulph was imprisoned by Edbert in the castle for thirty years, 750-780, for his supposed protection of Offa, a prince of the royal blood, who had taken refuge at Lindisfarne. The years 933, 995, and 1015, were disastrous to Bamburgh, for the Danes stormed and pillaged the castle, leaving it in a ruinous condition. . In 1095 Bamburgh sustained a siege which is memorable because of a romantic incident in connection with it. Mowbray, Earl of Northumberland, having rebelled against William the Second, and suffered several reverses, retired before the royal troops to this, his strongest fortress. The king, finding it impregnable, determined to reduce the garrison into subjection by cutting off supplies. He, therefore, erected against the walls a wooden fort, or tower, called a "Malvoisin," or evil neighbour, and leaving a strong garrison, drew off the main body of his army southward. Force having proved of little avail against the castle, a resort was made to stratagem. Mowbray was deceived into believing that the garrison of Newcastle were prepared to surrender the town into his hands. He, therefore, stole out, as he supposed, unperceived, from his fastness, with a retinue of thirty horsemen, but, finding himself pursued, he fled to the church of St. Oswin, at Tynemouth. The rights of sanctuary were ignored by his enemies, who endeavoured to drag him forth from the sacred precincts. For six days the earl and his followers defended their place of refuge. At last, sorely wounded, he was taken prisoner. As the Countess Matilda still held out against the besiegers, the Red King took the captured earl to a spot in front of his castle, and threatened to put out his eyes if she did not surrender at once. A woman could have little difficulty in choosing between two such alternatives, and so the Countess Matilda threw open the gates, and the garrison capitulated. David of Scotland, together with Eustace Fitz-John, who had been dispossessed of his honours by Stephen, marched on Bamburgh, and made an attack on the castle. They forced the outworks, which had but a short time before been erected, and put to the sword a hundred of the defenders. King John was here on the 13th, 14th, and 15th February 1201, and again on the 20th January 1213. In 1296 Edward I. summoned John Baliol to renew his homage here, and on his refusal to do so, entered Scotland with a great army. Hither fled in 1312 the minion of Edward II.—Piers de Gaveston—to escape for a while from the vengeance of the incensed nobles. David Bruce was confined here after the battle of Neville's Cross, previous to his removal to London in 1347, and Bamburgh was one of the three castles at which his ransom was appointed to be paid in 1358. The Earl of Murray also was "a prisoner of war in the king's prison" here in 1355. The great convention between the King of England and Edward de Baliol, King of Scots, dated January 20th, 1356, was entered into at Bamburgh. Edward III. was still at the castle on 30th January and 8th February of the same year. In this monarch's reign the keep and other buildings underwent a thorough restoration. During the wars of the Roses, Bamburgh was chiefly in the hands of the king's party. In 1463 four of the Lancastrian lords—the Duke of Somerset, the Earl of Pembroke, the Lord Ros, and Sir Ralph Percy, with a garrison of three hundred men, held the castle for two months against a force of 10,000 men, under the Earls of Worcester and Arundel, Lord Ogle, and Lord Montagu. On Christmas eve they, however, capitulated. In 1464 Sir Ralph Grey surprised the castle, which was then in the custody of Sir John Astley, and regained it for the queen. He was himself shut up within its walls soon after the battle of Hexham Levels. Being excepted from the general pardon, his position was a desperate one, and he offered a gallant resistance. Severely injured by the fall of a tower, he was taken up for dead, and his garrison, losing heart, surrendered to the Yorkist generals, the Earls of Warwick and Montagu. Little was done in the succeeding reigns to restore the dilapidated walls of the castle, which, after the union of the two kingdoms, ceased to be of very great importance. In the time of Elizabeth, Sir John Forster, Warden of the Marches, was governor of the castle, which, together with the Manor of Bamburgh, was granted to his grandson by James I. Some of the later members of this family, Sir William Forster and his sons, William and Ferdinando, ran through their splendid inheritance by reckless extravagance, and their estates were sold by order of the Court of Chancery to pay their debts. These were purchased by Lord Crewe in 1704 for £20,679, 10s., and conveyed to him by deed, dated 15th and 16th May 1709. After the payment of all debts and charges, there remained over for the co-heirs—Lady Crewe and her nephew, Thomas Forster, afterwards notorious as the Jacobite general of 1715—the sum of £1028, 15s. 7d. only. This Lord Crewe, says Mr. G. T. Clark, "was neither a brilliant political nor ecclesiastical character, and there was nothing in his life became him like the leaving of it, since he then founded the Bamburgh Trust." On this account his name will ever be associated with the royal stronghold. Born on the 31st January 1633, at Stene, Nathaniel Lord Crewe, at an early age, was advanced to positions of great honour. His handsome person and agreeable manners, combined with great abilities and "remarkable diligence," recommended him to Charles II. He was promoted in 1671 to the see of Oxford, and translated in 1673 to the rich bishopric of Durham. Bishop Crewe's youth had been urged to the king as an objection to his appointment to Durham. Charles replied, "He would mend of that fault every day." He was equally in high favour at the court of James II., and furthered, to the detriment of his own fame, some of the measures of that monarch inimical to the liberties of the church and the kingdom. During the reign of William III. his political power and influence were much curtailed, but his private fortunes continued to prosper. On the accession of Queen Anne he regained his former ascendancy at Court, but experienced another reverse in the reign of George I. "If he received any attention from the Crown, it was only (says Mr. Surtees) such as might, without any compromise of principle, be paid to his age and reverend appearance." He died on the 18th of September 1722, at Stene, in the eighty-ninth year of his age. Besides making a grant to several hospitals during his lifetime, Lord Crewe, by his will, dated 24th June 1720, founded those princely charities which have made his name so famous. After directing how the greater portion of his property was to be applied, he left the residue to be devoted to such charitable purposes as his trustees might consider desirable. It is under this clause of his will that the Bamburgh Charities have been established. The subsequent manner in which these benefactions have been administered is due entirely to one of the trustees, Dr. John Sharp, Archdeacon of Northumberland. He restored the castle, which had fallen into decay, and bequeathed a sufficient sum for the maintenance of the buildings, so as to leave the original trust unfettered. The principal portion of the large and valuable library was his gift. The large income at present derived from Lord Crewe's estate is applied to the augmentation of small livings, the building of churches and chapels, the support of schools, the relief of distressed persons, and especially to the maintenance of the Bamburgh Charities. These comprise a surgery and dispensary for the poor, and schools, to which the children of parishioners are admitted and taught free of charge. Furthermore, thirty-four girls, selected by the trustees, between the ages of seven and nine, are received into the castle, and clothed, fed, and educated till they reach the age of sixteen, when they are provided with an outfit and placed in service. Certain of the charities were established by Archdeacon Sharp in the interest of mariners on the dangerous north-east coast. During fogs a gun is fired at intervals from the castle, and a bell rung. On every stormy night men are sent to patrol the coast for eight miles, the length of the manor, to bring notice of any shipwreck. A look-out is also kept from the east turret for vessels in distress. Apparatus for rendering assistance to vessels on the rocks and saving life is always in readiness at the castle. Persons shipwrecked upon the coast are provided with food, lodging, and the means of returning to their homes. Drowned persons are buried at the expense of the charity. A lifeboat is maintained, and aid can be summoned in case of shipwreck from Holy Island or North Sunderland, by a recognised code of signals. A coble, constructed on the principle of Lionel Lukin's "unimmergible boat," was in use at Bamburgh before the launching of the Shields boat. With these few facts relating to the past history and present purpose of Bamburgh before him, the visitor will now proceed to examine the details of this once important stronghold.

The main entrance, or barbican, is on the south-east, and is reached by a winding road leading up the steep embankment on the south. A narrow passage, cut through the solid rock and hemmed in by high walls, conducts to the inner Bailey. It will be seen, at the outset, that this approach to the Keep was guarded in the strongest manner possible. There were, firstly, the outer and inner gateways—the one defended by a portcullis and fosse, the other by machicolations, and then a massive round tower commanding the whole. Admission to the castle area may also be gained on the north-west side by means of the Postern or Sallyport Gate—a narrow aperture in the wall, approached by a flight of steps. An area of eight acres is enclosed by the great battlemented walls, that, with their massive towers and bastions, present such imposing outlines. The central space is known as the inner Bailey, and is surrounded by the buildings of the charities. Within it stands the great rectangular Norman Keep, which is earlier in date than the Keep at Newcastle, though, as is proved by the character of the moulding of the fine string-course around its base, not earlier than the latter part of the reign of Henry I. The walls are of enormous strength, being 11 feet thick on the front, and 9 feet thick on the other sides. The stone with which they were built was quarried at North Sunderland, three miles distant, and so small are the blocks that it is conjectured they were carried on the backs of men or horses. The roof was originally no higher than the top of the second storey; it has now been raised to the battlements. The idea put forward by Mr. G. T. Clark, that a Norman Keep was not so much a place of residence as a depository for stores, and a refuge of the garrison in the last resort, seems to receive confirmation from the fact that the principal chambers are without chimneys, and must have been warmed, if warmed they were, in a very primitive fashion. The only fire-place in the Keep was a grate in the middle of a large room, supposed to have been the guard-room. The floor, which is supported on arches, retains in the centre the marks of fire, some of the stones having been burnt red. The entrance to the Keep is on the ground floor through a small round-headed doorway. The Entrance-hall is a gloomy chamber, for the light is only admitted through the door or narrow loopholes. Hanging on the walls are two huge chains, formerly used for raising sunken vessels. They are familiarly spoken of as "King Ida's Watch-chains." Here may also be seen the sedan chair of Archdeacon Sharp, and a genealogical map of the kings of Scotland from the earliest period. In a vault opening from the hall is a remarkable draw-well, 150 feet deep, having been cut out of the solid rock, of which 75 feet is of hard whinstone, and the remainder red and white sandstone. It is of great antiquity—much older than the Norman castle—for Simeon of Durham, a monk who wrote about the year A.D. 1129, in describing Bamburgh, under date A.D. 774, says—"There is in the western side, and in the highest part of the city, a fountain hollowed out in a marvellous fashion, and the water of which is sweet to drink and most limpid to the sight." For many years its existence had been forgotten, but in December 1770 the mouth was uncovered during some alterations. By means of candles let down the shaft on a wooden cross, the visitor is enabled to see the clear water gleaming at the bottom. There is a draw well of a similar kind, though of later date, at Beeston Castle in Cheshire. The wicked queen of the ballad, who changed her step-daughter by witchcraft into a loathly worm, is said, by tradition, to lurk at the bottom of this well under the form of a gigantic toad, and is doomed to appear every seven years. In the *Servants' Hall* are two portraits—one of Lord Crewe, and the other of the old man who discovered the well in 1770. A mural staircase, as at Carlisle and Chepstow, leads to the upper storeys. On the first floor is the *Court Room*, in which are four pieces of tapestry, brought from the Deanery of Ripon about the year 1788. They are said to be of Gobelin manufacture, and illustrate several incidents in the life of Justinian:—1. Justinian consulting with his counsellors about the framing of his code. 2. Approaching the temple and shrine of Janus, with manumitted slaves proclaiming, after one of the victories of Belisarius, eternal peace. 3. His coronation. 4. Hunting scene, in which his dogs are poisoned. The chamber also contains some old and curious furniture, a rare and valuable collection of engravings, and portraits of Lord and Lady Crewe (over the fire-place), the Venerable Archdeacon Sharp (over the doorway), the Rev. Sir George Wheeler, Dr. John Sharp, Archbishop of York, Thomas Sharp, D.D., and others. The most interesting of these portraits is that of Lady Crewe, daughter of Sir William Foster of Bamburgh. She is represented with blue eyes, light hair, and delicate features, the expression of her face being sweet and amiable. Lord Crewe was fifty-eight years of age when he first paid his address to the beautiful Dorothea—viz., in 1691; but she rejected his suit on the ground that she was too young. When the first Lady Crewe died, in 1700, the aged bishop lost no time in renewing his addresses to his former love, with such success that he was united to her only four months afterwards. She died in 1715.

Another large chamber, which is vaulted, and occupies the entire length of the Keep, is called the *Armoury*. It contains a great variety of old weapons—swords, halberts, guns, pistols, etc. Two pictures on the walls here will attract attention—"Bamburgh Castle by Moonlight," taken in 1863 by the great local marine painter, J. W. Carmichael; and "Bamburgh Castle in 1788," by G. Sykes. There is also a rare engraving here of the last Earl of Derwentwater. Over the fire-place are the richly-emblazoned arms of Lord Crewe. In the *Old Banqueting Hall*, now partly used as a kitchen, is to be seen the gallery of the minstrels. On the wall of the staircase, near the entrance to the library, is a framed sonnet on Bamburgh Castle, by the Rev. William Lisle Bowles, A.M. The sonnet is in the poet's handwriting, and bears his signature. It runs as follows:—

"Ye holy towers, that shade the wave-worn steep,
Long may ye rear your aged brows sublime,
Though, hurrying silent by, relentless Time
Assail you, and the winter whirlwinds sweep!
Far, far from grandeur's blazing crowded halls,
Here Charity hath fix'd her chosen seat,
Oft list'ning tearful when the wild winds beat

With hollow bodings round your ancient walls;
And Pity, at the dark and stormy hour
Of midnight, when the moon is hid on high,
Keeps her lone watch upon the topmost tower,
And turns her ear to each expiring cry;
Blest if her aid some fainting wretch might save,
And snatch him cold and speechless from the grave."

The *Library*, established in 1778, and supplemented in 1792 by the collection of Archdeacon Sharp, consists of about four thousand volumes, principally of a theological and historical nature. It comprises some of the best editions of the classics, some old breviaries, and several curious tracts and pamphlets. The chief rarity is an illuminated missal of great beauty, brought hither from Sarum. This library is divided into two sections, the "old" and the "modern"—the former being kept in that part of the building now occupied by the charity children, and the latter in the upper of the two large rooms of the Keep. The walls of this apartment are hung with the following portraits:—General Thomas Forster, the incompetent leader of the Jacobites in 1715; Dorothy Forster, his devoted sister, who contrived his escaped from Newgate, the heroine of Mr. Walter Besant's interesting novel of the same name; Lord Crewe; and Mrs. Boult Sharp. The habitable rooms of the Keep are occupied by one of the trustees and his family, or by those persons to whom the trustees may let them. The passages in the upper part of the building are exceedingly narrow. In one of these was found upwards of fifty iron arrow-heads, rusted together into a mass. A mural staircase ascends to the north turret. The view from the summit in all directions is grand and varied, and probably the finest in the north of England. To the east are the Farne Islands, twenty-five of which can be seen at low water; to the north-west is Holy Island, and beyond it, the old border-town of Berwick, backed by the faint outlines of the grey Scotch hills; to the west is an undulating stretch of fertile country, sprinkled with villages and hamlets, and in the distance the rounded Cheviots; to the south is Dunstanburgh Castle, and beyond it a rugged coast-line, winding in and out from point to point as far as Tynemouth Priory, which terminates the prospect.

The ancient *Chapel of St. Peter*, founded in the reign of Henry II., probably on the site of the first ecclesiastical edifice reared in Northumberland, crowned the south-east point of the castle's area. For many years it lay buried beneath a great accumulation of sand, which was removed in 1773. The remains show that the chapel was about 100 feet in length, with a chancel 36 feet long and 20 feet broad. The altar did not stand at the east end, but in the centre of the apse. The font, which is richly carved, is still preserved in the Keep. A very ancient burial-ground was laid bare by the strong south-westerly winds which prevailed in 1817, about two hundred yards south-east of the porter's lodge. On the north and north-west of the castle are remains of some very old outworks, which ran round the ridge of the cliff. The battery platform, which looks towards the sea, was built by

Archdeacon Sharp. The structure at the north point of the rock is the castle windmill, where barley, oats, and peas were formerly ground for the poor in the district. In former days, when the castle was neglected and ruinous, "The Wandering Shepherdess," the sad spirit of a lady of rank and fortune, who had been crossed in love, is said to have tended her sheep on the hill. The castle is open to visitors daily, at a nominal charge, from 2 to 4 P.M., Sundays excepted.

At the head of the village stands the *Church of St. Aidan*, a large cruciform edifice, with a low square tower at the west end. It was built during the reign of Henry II., in the early English lancet period, and is, according to Mr. Longstaffe, a remarkable example of a double church, comprising the churches of SS. Oswald and Aidan, which Henry I. endowed at Bamburgh. The boundary line Mr. Longstaffe would fix at the pillar with the ornamental capital on the north side of the nave. One part would be the cell which Henry I. made subject to Nostel Priory, near Pontefract; the other part was the parish church. Of the Saxon structure, which was built for Aidan between the years 635-52, and where, in a wooden cell at the west end, he breathed his last, there is not a remnant. The church is entered through a porch on the south side. Very impressive is the view of the interior from beneath the groined roof of the tower, which opens to the nave and aisles by three pointed arches upon impost mouldings. The nave is good work of a peculiar local type, of what might be called the Transitional style of about 1170. The two arcades, each consisting of four graceful arches, which spring from circular columns, lead the eye onward to the richly-decorated chancel. A peculiarity in the plan of the church is the deflection towards the south of the chancel arch, and of the arch between the nave and south transept. Similar deflections, according to some authorities, are believed either to represent the drooping position of Christ's head upon the cross, or to mark the point in the horizon at which the sun rose on the day of the tutelary saint. At the west end of the north aisle is a very beautiful marble monument, erected by the late Mrs. Sharp to commemorate various members of her family. It is supposed to have been one of the last works of Sir Francis Chantrey, and represents a female figure, with a cross on a pedestal, and a bust of Dr. Sharp. In the north transept is the effigy of Grace Darling, by Mr. Raymond Smith, which was placed, in 1844, under the canopy in the churchyard, but suffered so much from exposure to the weather that it was removed to its present position in 1885, a new, but exactly similar effigy, by the same sculptor, being given by Sir William G. Armstrong. At the chancel arch is a carved oak rood-screen. The chancel is of unusual length, 62 feet by 21 feet, and more elaborate in its architectural details than the rest of the building. It is fitted with oak stall-work, and surrounded by an arcade of lancet arches—eight on the south side, four on the north, and three on the east being pierced as windows. Most of these are filled with Flemish stained glass, the designs of which represent Christ, the four Evangelists, and some of the Apostles. The old ritual arrangements consist of a piscina under a pointed arch, and a large aumbry on the north side, and another piscina under a trefoiled arch, with three ascending sedilia with cusped heads on the south side. Besides these there are other features and objects of interest: on the north side, a lychnoscope, or low-side window, usually found on the south side—a narrow trefoiled opening, through which persons afflicted with the plague could receive the communion; a mural tablet to the memory of Sir Claudius Forster, to whom the castle was granted by James I.; a marble monument, with an inscription by Dorothy, Lady Crewe, daughter of Sir William Forster, of Bamburgh, to the memory of her brothers William, John, and Ferdinando ("she being the only one remaining of the family"), "as a last respect that could be paid them for their affection to the church, the monarchy, their country, and their sister, A.D. 1711;" and the helmet, breast-plate, sword, and glove of Ferdinando Forster; on the south side, the cross-legged effigy of a crusader in armour, popularly called Sir Lancelot du Lake, under a low-arched, mural recess, and another lychnoscope; on the south side of the chancel arch a remarkable hagioscope, or squint, consisting of a square aperture filled with pierced stone panelling. The lancet in the pillar between the nave and south aisle is of modern date, filled with stained glass. The windows of the nave and transepts, with one exception, belong to the Decorated period. The most interesting feature, probably, in connection with the church is the early English crypt beneath the chancel, supposed to have been the residence of a recluse. For many years its existence had been forgotten, but in 1837 some steps were discovered leading down to it from the floor of the chancel. The entrance from the outside is a pointed doorway in the south wall, and is reached from the churchyard by descending a flight of stairs and proceeding along a short passage. This little underground hermitage, known in later times as the *Death House*, or the *Forster Vaults*, consists of two chambers. The first one entered is the larger and more finished of the two. It has a groined roof, and is lighted by three narrow lancet windows—two in the east wall and one in the south, immediately above a piscina. An iron staple, to which a lamp was no doubt suspended, may be seen in the roof. At the east end, on a stone shelf, formerly rested the coffins of William Forster, died 1700; Ferdinando Forster, died 1701; General Thomas Forster, died 1738; Dorothea Forster, died 1739; B. Forster, of Adderstone, died 1765. They have now been buried in the ground. An old sun-dial, fragments of tombs, a broken cross, and other relics lie on the floor. The second chamber, opening out from the first, is long and narrow, with an arched roof, and a small window at the east end. Around three of the persons buried here—Ferdinando, Thomas, and Dorothea Forster—a romantic interest has gathered. Writers of fiction like Mr. Harrison Ainsworth, Mr. Walter Besant, and Mrs. Hibbert-Ware have reproduced in their novels and stories the leading events in the history of these members of the Forster family.

Ferdinando Forster is chiefly remembered on account of the tragic circumstances of his death. He was a member of Parliament for the county, and on August 22nd, 1701, had been dining at the Black Horse Inn, in Newgate Street, Newcastle, with the Grand Jury of Northumberland, when Mr. John Fenwick of Rock, with whom he was at feud, came in, singing a favourite partizan song, having the refrain, "Sir John Fenwick's the flower among them." An altercation took place that led to the parties meeting subsequently, near the White Cross, to fight a duel. In drawing his sword Forster slipped and fell on his back, and Fenwick stabbed him through the heart—an act of treachery which he expiated on the scaffold, near the same place, on the 25th of the following month. General Forster was the general of the Jacobite army in 1715. He was an incompetent leader, but not a traitor, as the old ballad declares. He was condemned to death for his participation in the rebellion, but escaped from Newgate by the assistance of his devoted sister Dorothy. This amiable north-country heroine, then in her twenty-ninth year, rode up to London behind a blacksmith of Adderstone named Purdy, and used every means to effect the liberation of her brother. Finally she procured an impression of the key of his prison. With the false key thus obtained Forster set himself free, and so well was the escape concerted that in twenty-four hours he was safe in Calais. His sister gave out that he had died shortly after this, and a mock interment took place at Bamburgh, the coffin being filled with sawdust. The Jacobite leader, however, lived till 1738, when his body was actually brought from France and conveyed to his ancestral home.

A little to the west of the church is the beautiful monument of Grace Darling, designed by Mr. Raymond Smith, of London, and presented to the trustees of Lord Crewe by Mrs. Catherine Sharp. The heroine is represented with hands crossed and an oar by her side, reposing under a Gothic canopy within sight of the islands rendered famous by her deed. The effigy, through the generosity of Sir W. G. Armstrong, has been renewed, as the old one had suffered much from exposure to the weather. A few yards from the monument is a plain tombstone marking the last resting-place of Grace Darling, her parents, and brother. A broken column commemorates the Rev. G. Morell Mackenzie, who, when the *Pegasus* struck on the Goldstone in July 1843, gathered the passengers around him on the deck, and prayed aloud with unfaltering voice as the vessel slowly sank, till the last drowning cry was stifled by the waves. In the churchyard rest the remains of Prideaux John Selby, Esq., the eminent ornithologist.

A little to the south-west of the churchyard, near the farm-house called Bamburghfriars, is a small portion of ivy-covered masonry, which is all that remains of the Augustinian Friary founded here in the latter part of the reign of Henry III. Of the monastery of Friars' Preachers (a collegiate foundation), and the Hospital of St. Mary Magdalene, which existed here at an early period, there are no traces. The old manor-house of the Forsters, now a farm-house, is near the church, facing the Grove.

# BAMBURGH TO BUDLE AND SPINDLESTON.

**Budle Bay, 1½ miles ; Spindleston Heughs, 2½ miles.**

A NARROW road called the Wynding leads down from the village to the Lifeboat-house, which was built in 1882. From this point northward for some distance the coast is composed of dunes, or hillocks of blown sand, where hound's-tongue (*Cynoglossum officinale*) and henbane (*Hyoscyamus niger*) grow plentifully. Half-a-mile along are the "low-lying and beautifully exposed *Harkess Rocks*, displaying," says Professor Lebour, "almost every vagary to which the igneous rocks are subject." Fragments of the sedimentary rocks are embedded in the trap, and have undergone, in some cases, considerable change from contact with the molten mass. A good section may be seen along the "Stag" rock. This is perhaps one of the best localities in Britain for the study of metamorphic phenomena, as such an extensive area of rock is exposed. Three-quarters of a mile further on, along a footpath skirting the heathery Kitling Hill, is Budle Bay, a deep inlet, famous for its cockles. Here some well-known shales of a reddish-brown colour, abounding in the shells of the fragile *Posidonia* will be examined with interest by the geologist. On the south side of the bay, which is overlooked by the Budle Hills, are some large disused granaries. From the coast-guard station here a footpath runs through the fields to the main road, which may be followed for a mile to the right past the village of Budle to the Waren Mills. Here the little river Warn enters the great Budle Bay. Warnmouth, long since devoured by the waves, was a town of considerable importance, and one of the most ancient ports of Northumberland, for a charter was granted to the borough by Henry III. A lane to the south, half-a-mile in length, leads to the *Spindleston Heughs*. They may be soon reached from Bamburgh by proceeding along the Belford Road for three-quarters of a mile to the top of Galliheugh Bank, and then following a footpath to the left past Shada plantation in a south-westerly direction. The celebrated ballad of the "Laidley worm of Spindleston Heugh" (*laidley*, loathsome ; *worm*, old term for serpent) was first printed by the Rev. Robert Lambe, Vicar of Norham, ostensibly from an ancient MS., as a song made by the mountain bard, Duncan Frasier, living on Cheviot, A.D. 1270." According to the legend, the Princess Margaret, daughter of the king of Bamburgh, was transformed by her wicked stepmother, by means of witchcraft, into a "Laidley Worm," from envy of her beauty. Great was the terror that prevailed in the district.

"For seven miles east, and seven miles west,
And seven miles north and south,
No blade of grass or corn would grow.
So deadly was her mouth.

The milk of seven streakit cows,
It was their cost to keep;
They brought her dayly, whyche she drank
Before she wente to sleepe.

At this day might be seen the cave
Where she lay faulded up,
And the trough o' stone—the very same,
Out of which she did sup.

Word went east, and word went west,
Word is gone ower the sea,
That a Laidley Worm in Spindleston Heugh
Would ruin the North Countree."

The story reaches the ears of Margaret's brother, "The Childe Wynd," who, concerned about the safety of his sister, determines to return home. He called together his "merry men all," and

"They built a ship without delay,
With masts of the rowan-tree,
With fluttering sails of silk so fine,
And set her on the sea.

They went on board; the wind with speed
Blew them along the deep;
At length they spied a hugh square tower
On a rock high and steep.

The sea was calm, the weather clear,
When they approached nigher;
King Ida's castle well they knew,
And the banks of Bamburghshire."

The queen, looking out of her bower window, saw the gallant ship approaching, and sent her witch-wives to sink it; but their spells were of no avail against the rowan-tree (mountain ash) mast, and they returned baffled. She then sent a boat of armed men to board the ship, but Childe Wynd drove them away, and afterwards secured a landing on Budle sands. The worm was at first disposed to be restive, but on Childe Wynd laying his berry-brown sword on her head, she broke into supplications—

"O quit thy sword, unbend thy brow,
And give me kisses three;
For though I am a poisonous worm,
No hurt I'll do to thee.

O quit thy sword, unbend thy brow,
And give me kisses three;
If I'm not won ere the sun goes down,
Won shall I never be.

He quitted his sword, and smoothed his brow,
He gave her kisses three;
She crept untill the hole a worm,
And came out a fayre ladye."

Wrapping his sister in his mantle, Childe Wynd proceeded to the castle, and thus addressed the pale and trembling queen—

"'Woe be to thee, thou wicked witch,
An ill death mayst thou dee;
As thou hast likened my sister dear,
So likened shalt thou be.

For I will turn thee into a toad,
That on the ground doth wend;
And won, won, shalt thou never be,
Till this world have an end.'

He sprinkled her with three drops o' the well
In her palace where she stood;
When she grovelled down upon her belly,
A foul and loathsome toad.

And on the lands near Ida's towers,
A loathsome toad she crawls;
And venom spits on everything
Which cometh to the walls.

The virgins all of Bamburgh town
Will swear that they have seen
This spiteful toad, of monstrous size,
Whilst walking on the green.

Nor dwells a wight in Bamburghshire
But swears the story's true;
And they all run to Spindleston,
The rock and cave to view."

Some commentators see in the "Laidley Worm" a personification of the Paganism that once prevailed in Northumbria, and in Childe Wynd the purer faith by which it was overcome; or, the worm represents the Danes, and the Childe the Saxons. The worm of Sockburn, near Bishop Auckland; the "wode worm of Wormiston," near Linton, in Roxburghshire; the dragon of Wantley; the worm of Lambton, near Fatfield, are legends of a similar nature to the "Laidley Worm." The hole and trough of the "Laidley Worm" were on the north side of the south hill, but they have been destroyed within recent years by the opening out of a quarry. The only object to remind the visitor of the legend is a detached upstanding pillar of whinstone at the side of the pass. This is the "Spindlestone" on which the hero of the ballad is said to have hung the bridle-rein of his horse as he prepared himself for approaching the den of the worm in the marshy hollow farther up. The crags which form part of the great Whin Sill are bold and picturesque, presenting in places, where the huge pillars have been shattered and rent, the appearance of a ruined castle. Ivy, elder, spindle tree, dog-roses, and honeysuckle have taken root in the crevices, hanging gracefully over the face of the rocks. The principal plants along the edges of the cliffs are—Streaked field garlic (*Allium oleraceum*), white horehound (*Marrubium vulgare*), in quantity; knotted clover (*Trifolium striatum*), and wood hawkweed (*Hieracium sylvaticum*). This is a great resort of birds, especially of redstarts. Jackdaws also take up their head-quarters here. A striking mass of rock on the south side of the West Hill bears, at a distance, a fancied resemblance to an Egyptian sphinx, and is called the *Cat Crag*, from having been, at no very remote period, the resort of the wild cat. The highest point of the crags, 243 feet above the sea-level, is crowned by the rude remains of a British camp, so accommodated to the irregularities of the area that the precipice forms one of the ramparts. It is in two divisions. The easternmost, much the larger, is defended by a double wall, the westernmost by a single wall and a ditch, which communicates with a hollowed way descending the back of the hill towards the Waren. Adjoining the entrance to the smaller section of the camp is an oblong guard-chamber. From this commanding site the eye may sweep round a circuit of great beauty and extent—from Bamburgh Castle to Holy Island and the Lammermuir Hills, in one direction, and from Dunstanburgh Castle to the Edlingham Hills, Ras Castle, and the Cheviots in the other. A quarter-of-a-mile to the south-east, on the slope of Crook Hill, are the remains of another camp. The distance from the crags to Bamburgh, by way of Glororum, is about two miles and a half. The pedestrian may add another mile to his tour by following the Waren from the crags past Spindleston Mill to *Bradford*, which derives its name from the *broad* shallow *ford* across the rivulet. The old mansion-house exhibits traces of great antiquity. A panelled stone preserved in its walls is pronounced by Mr. Raine to be Roman. An eminence hard by is said to have been a place of execution for the lords of Bamburgh. There is an ancient British barrow upon it, which, in 1817, was found to contain several skeletons, and also some rudely-ornamented sun-baked urns. A road, a mile and a half in length, leads from Bradford to Glororum.

# BAMBURGH TO LUCKER AND ELLINGHAM.

**Lucker, 3½ miles; Warenford, 5 miles; Twizell House, 5½ miles; Ellingham, 7 miles; Preston Tower, 8 miles; Falloden, 10 miles.**

THREE miles and a half south-west of Bamburgh, passing the hamlet with the strange name of *Glororum*, or *Glow'r-o'er-him*, is the small village of LUCKER, where there was at one time an ancient chapel. Near the place was found a small glazed Roman lamp, with projecting lip. Other Roman antiquities were discovered six feet beneath the surface in a peat bog at Adderstone, a little to the west—viz., twenty-two copper and brass coins, ranging in date from the time of Hadrian, A.D. 117, to Postumus, A.D. 267, a portion of horse furniture, and an apothecary's scale and beam, all contained in a small oak box, fastened by copper nails. *Adderstone Hall* is the residence of Steven Sanderson, Esq. The old manor-house was the seat of the ancient family of the Forsters. It was an Adderstone blacksmith who accompanied Dorothy Forster to London, whither she went to contrive the escape of her brother, the Jacobite general. A mile and a half south-west of Lucker is *Warenford*, formerly a considerable village, now dwindled into insignificance. Westward of it is *Twizell House*, the beautiful mansion of the Rev. Edmund Antrobus, M.A., J.P. For the greater part of the present century the hall was a place of interest to lovers of natural history as the seat of Prideaux John Selby, Esq., whose splendid *Illustrations of British Ornithology* and *History of British Forest Trees* have given him a well-merited reputation. The figures of the birds, in at least two hundred of the two hundred and twenty-eight plates in the first elaborate work, were sketched by his own hand, from specimens in his valuable ornithological museum at Twizell. He was born in Bondgate, Alnwick, on 23rd July 1788, and died at Twizell House 27th March 1867. Much of the beauty of the grounds around the hall is due to his taste in planting. The romantic little dene, through which the pretty Waren Burn tumbles fantastically, is overhung with trees, and well set with flowers and shrubs.

Four miles to the south-east is *Ellingham Hall*, the seat of Sir John de Marie Haggerston, which stands in a low and sheltered situation by the side of Tughall Burn. The old Northumbrian family of the Haggerstons was much attached to the Stuart cause. In 1745 the baronet of the day sent his coach and horses to convey the

Duke of Cumberland from Belford to Berwick, but took care to bribe his coachman to overturn the vehicle in the way. And in the same year, when the work-horses of the baronet were required to assist in forwarding the baggage of the troops, they could not be found. They are said to have been concealed at Haslerigg, in Northumberland, an estate belonging to the family. The *Church of St. Maurice* is a handsome cruciform edifice, rebuilt in 1862. A fragment of early English masonry is preserved in the chancel. The original building must have been Norman, as it was founded by Randulph de Guagy in the twelfth century. On the east wall of the south transept is a marble tablet, inscribed as follows:—"Here lies the body of Sir Carnaby Haggerston, Bart., a Gentleman of uncommon Erudition, clear and penetrating wit and solid judgment, of an extensive and well-guided charity to the Distressed, universal Benevolence to all men, and adorned with every Christian and Social virtue. He died July 17th, 1756." A mile to the south-east is *Preston Tower* (Mrs. Baker-Creswell), situated on a hill, with a fine prospect over the surrounding country. At the west end is an ancient Border pele. A mile to the north is *Chathill Farm*, where there was a fairy ring, round which the children of the neighbourhood delighted to gambol. There is a railway station at Chathill. Two miles to the south-east of Preston is *Falloden Lodge*, from which a magnificent avenue, a mile in length, leads to *Falloden Hall*, a large red brick mansion, the seat of Sir Edward Grey, Bart., M.P. Here was born, on the 13th March 1764, the second Earl Grey, whose name is so indissolubly connected with the passing of the Reform Bill and Catholic Emancipation. There are some remarkably fine trees around the house. Two silver firs, 11 feet 9 inches and 10 feet 9 inches in girth, at a height of two feet from the ground, are referred to by Mr. Selby in his *British Forest Trees*, page 481. The Grey family has a private station at Falloden.

# BAMBURGH TO BELFORD AND BEAL.

Waren Mills, 2 miles; Outchester, 3 miles; Belford, 5 miles: Middleton Hall, 6½ miles; Grizzy's Clump, 9½ miles; Kyloe, 10 miles; Beal, 12 miles.

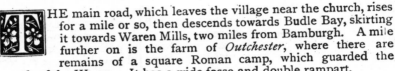

THE main road, which leaves the village near the church, rises for a mile or so, then descends towards Budle Bay, skirting it towards Waren Mills, two miles from Bamburgh. A mile further on is the farm of *Outchester*, where there are remains of a square Roman camp, which guarded the mouth of the Waren. It has a wide fosse and double rampart.

A mile to the west is Belford Station, and a mile beyond that again is the small town of BELFORD, which lies on a gradual slope, sheltered on the north-east by a wooded ridge. It is an exceedingly quiet place, with quaint reminiscences of the past in its irregular streets and plain grey houses of stone. In the olden times the houses were covered with heather and sods, and the place, being liable to be burned by the Scots, was very poor. It was sacked by these northern raiders in the reign of Henry II. In the reign of Charles I. (1639) it was in a state of declension. "Belfort, nothing like the name either in strength or beauty, is the most miserable, beggarly town, or town of sods, that ever was made in an afternoon of loam and sticks. In all the town not a loaf of bread, nor a quart of beer, nor a lock of hay, nor a peck of oats, and little shelter for horse or man."—*Court and Times of Charles I.*, vol. ii., p. 285. There is a tradition that on one occasion the town was visited by the plague, and the bodies of the dead were buried in their wearing apparel on Belford Moor. Fragments of the dresses have been dug up there by people who attempted to disturb the tombs, in hope of finding coins in the pockets. The cross stands in the old market-place, but the market has become obsolete. The "Castrum de Beleford," which existed as early as 1416, is now *West Hall Farm-house*. The old moat may still be traced. On the 23rd May 1722, David Graham, the eldest son of the Duke of Montrose, was created Earl and Baron Graham of Belford, no doubt from some connection with the manor. The *Church of St. Mary* was rebuilt in 1827, on the site of an ancient chapel, and is almost entirely modern. The masonry of the chancel, however, is ancient. In 1879 there was discovered incorporated with it a Norman arch of thirteenth-century workmanship, which had been plastered up, the pillars that supported it having been hewn away. On the inner side of it there is a piece of dog-tooth carving. The principal hotel in the town is the Blue Bell.

*Belford Hall* is a large stone mansion, designed by Payne, and altered and enlarged by Dobson. It is the seat of G. D. A. Clark, Esq. The door, studded with large-headed nails, admitting to the grounds, came from the old or west hall. In the verandah is the upper portion of a Roman quern. The entrance-hall contains some curiosities and cases of stuffed birds. A pair of bronze spurs, of the time of Henry VI., discovered, together with some human remains, in one of the moats of the old Belford castle, are preserved here. Among the paintings in the drawing and sitting rooms are a couple of Morland's, several sea-views by Carmichael, and two excellent views, by Richardson, of Holy Island Priory and Bamburgh Castle. The trees in the park are stately and well-grown, especially the elms, Spanish chestnuts, ashes, and beeches. Near the turret-pond are two specimens of *Quercus Ilex*, which are considered to be the finest in the north of England. The pride of the place is a tall, upright Spanish chestnut, measuring, close to the ground, 13 feet 4 inches. On what is called the turret crag there is a small prospect tower. Here the maiden pink (*Dianthus deltoides*) grows wild. Beneath is an excellent fernery. From the park a private walk leads to *Belford Crags*, a portion of the great Whin Sill, which, commencing at Kyloe, sweeps round by Detchant to Belford, and after bending north to Easington, curves away to Spindleston. On the *Chapel Hill* may be traced the foundations of an ancient chapel, which was dedicated to St. Mary. It has been fortified, or enclosed, by some high mounds, but these may be more ancient. Two hundred yards to the south of it is "Our Lady's Well." To the north of the chapel, on the highest part of the crags, is an oval camp of the ancient Britons, with strong ramparts. It commands a good view of the coast from Berwick to North Sunderland, with Lindisfarne, Bamburgh Castle, and the Farne Islands. A little to the north is *Derry Camp*, square in form, on the north-west side of Chesters Hill. Below, embosomed in woods and pleasure-grounds, is *Middleton Hall* (John T. Leather, Esq.), about a mile and a half from Belford. The house is new, and contains some richly-carved mantel-pieces and side-boards, and valuable cabinets. The ceilings are superbly decorated with geometrical designs. Some of the wood-work is by Signor Bulletti. Two iron bullets, extracted from the wreck of the old house, and a bronze celt, are preserved in the lathe-room. Three miles and a half further north, a little past the hamlet of Buckton, by the roadside, is *Grizzy's Clump*—a solitary plantation of fir trees, walled round, famous as the scene of Grizzel Cochrane's daring exploit. In July 1685 Sir John Cochrane, of Ochiltree, made prisoner in the rising under the Duke of Argyle, was under sentence of death in the Tolbooth Prison, Edinburgh, for the part he had taken, along with Sir Patrick Hume, of Polwarth, in the political troubles of James the Seventh's reign, but hopes of pardon were entertained through the intercession of the king's favourite counsellor, who had received a bribe of five thousand pounds from Sir John's father, the Earl of Dundonald. To obtain a brief respite, the condemned man's daughter, "Bonny Grizzy," at that time eighteen years of age, formed the daring resolve to rob the London mail of the warrant for her father's execution. She made her way to the abode of her old nurse, who lived four miles from Berwick, on the English side of the Border, and borrowed a suit of that good dame's foster brother. Thus disguised, she proceeded to a small public-house on the outskirts of Belford, where the postman usually put up. No opportunity presented itself for obtaining the warrant here, so withdrawing the charges from the man's pistols while he slept, she rode forth to a lonely spot on the high road, between Belford and Berwick, and awaited his coming; finally accomplishing her purpose in some such way as described in the following verses of the ballad—

"The red sun went down o'er the sea,
And the wind blew stiff and snell;
And as it shot by Grizzy's lugs,
It sounded auld Cochrane's knell.
'But downa despair, 'tis a kittle carle,'
Said Cochrane's bonny dochter.

The larch and the tall fir shrieked wi' pain,
As they bent before in the wind;
And down there fell the heavy rain,
Till sense and e'en were blind.
'A lang night 'tis ne'er sees a day,'
Quoth Cochrane's undaunted Grizzy.

The warlocks are dancing threesome reels,
On Goswick's haunted links;
The red fire shoots by Ladythorne,
And Tam wi' the lanthorn fa's and sinks.
On Kyloe's hills there's awfu' sounds,
But they frighted not Cochrane's Grizzy.

The moonbeams shot from the troubled sky,
In glints o' flickerin' light;
The horseman cam skelping thro' the mire,
For his mind was in affright.
His pistol cocked he held in his hand,
But the fient a fear had Grizzy.

As he cam' fornenst the Fenwicke woods,
From the whin bushes shot out a flame;
His dappled filly reared up in affright,
And backward over he came.
There's a hand on his craig, and a foot on his mouth,
'Twas Cochrane's bonny Grizzy.

'I will not tak thy life,' she said,
'But gie me thy London news;
No blood of thine shall fyle my blade,
Gin me ye dinna refuse.'
She's prie'd the warrant and away she flew,
With the speed and strength o' the wild curlew."

The delay thus occasioned proved useful to the friends of Sir John, who, by untiring efforts, succeeded in obtaining his pardon. The heroine afterwards married John Ker, of Moristoun, and a tombstone in Legerwood Church, near Earlstoun, states that she "died 21st March 1748, in the 83rd year of her age."

To the west of the road lie the *Kyloe Hills*, which form the northern termination of the great Whin Sill. Very picturesque are the rugged and pillared crags, rising to the height of 500 feet above the sea-level. They are well wooded and covered with bracken and ling. The basalt overlies a thick sandstone, which boldly crops out of the west end of the crags, and is called the *Collier Heugh Crag*. Here are to be found the rare two-flowered linnæa (*Linnæa borealis*) and angular Solomon's seal (*Convallaria polygonatum*); also the rare ferns, forked spleenwort (*Asplenium septentrionale*), alternate spleenwort (*Asplenium Germanicum*), brittle bladder fern (*Cystopteris fragilis*), and Tunbridge filmy fern (*Hymenophyllum Tunbridgense*). Strongly situated on a high rocky platform is an ancient British camp with a double rampart. Remains of two other camps exist a mile or so to the south-east on *Buckton Moor*. The view from the crags is very beautiful and extensive across the clear blue sea to Holy Island, the Farnes, Bamburgh, and Dunstanburgh. On a hill at West Kyloe, a mile to the north, is the *Church of St. Nicholas*, which, with its embattled tower, forms a conspicuous landmark to sailors. It was rebuilt in 1792, on the site of an old Norman chapel, which, erected sometime between the years 1082 and 1145, was dependent on the Priory of Holy Island. The name Kyloe itself is said to mean "the church on the hill," from the Celtic *cil*, a recess or retreat, designating the secluded places of Druidical worship, and applied to the cells or chapels of Christian missionaries, and the Saxon *how*, a hill. At East Kyloe, three-quarters of a mile from the church, is *Kyloe Pele-tower*, the ancient residence of the Greys, which was inhabited till 1633. The upper storey is in ruins, but the lower one is in a good state of preservation. A pointed archway, on the south side, gives admission to a vaulted chamber, 23 feet by 17 feet, lighted by two narrow, long slits. The walls are eight feet thick. Remains of machicolations may be seen at the west side, in the stone corbels, terminating in rudely-carved heads. Two miles to the north, on the main road, is the Plough Inn, three-quarters of a mile from Beal.

BEAL was formerly spelt Behill, and is supposed to have been the place where the Monks of Lindisfarne obtained their honey. It is also said to have been the residence of the beautiful Irish princess and virgin, St. Bees (or Begogh), who took the veil from the hands of St. Aidan, and afterwards, as the abbess of a flourishing nunnery, became celebrated for her piety. There are some old dwellings in the district. Beal farm-house (once the mansion of the Selbys) bears upon it the initials, W. M., and the date 1674. Another old steading is dated 1690. Beal is the best starting-point for Holy Island.

# BAMBURGH TO DUNSTANBURGH.

**Monk's House, 2 miles ; North Sunderland Sea-Houses, 3½ miles ; Beadnell, 5½ miles ; Newton-by-the-Sea, 8 miles ; Embleton, 10½ miles ; Dunstanburgh, 12 miles.**

TWO miles from Bamburgh, by the road which runs behind the barren links, is *Monk's House*, a great resort of visitors during the summer months, part of it forming St. Cuthbert's Inn, and part of it being let in lodgings. Monk's House formerly belonged to the monks of Lindisfarne. A pretty tradition tells how a Viking, wrecked on the Seal Rock, just off shore, was rescued by a mermaid, who swam with him to this point on the mainland. On the right, after passing this place, will be seen *Shoreston Hall*, pleasantly situated in well-wooded grounds.

A mile and a half from the Monk's House is the fishing village and seaport of NORTH SUNDERLAND SEA-HOUSES, a malodorous place, where fish-curing is extensively carried on. There is a small harbour here, which is being very much improved, and also a lifeboat station. The piers, commenced in July 1886, will be, when completed, 875 feet and 874 feet long. Lime is the principal article of trade, and the kilns are built close to the harbour for convenience of loading. There is a small inn, the Bamburgh Castle. This is the usual place of embarkation for the Farne Islands.

Half a mile to the south-west is NORTH SUNDERLAND, where formerly stood an ancient pele-tower. It was removed in 1832-3, when the present church was built. Several large silver coins, of the reigns of Elizabeth, James I., Charles I., James II., and Queen Anne, were found at the time. The *Church of St. Paul*, an uninteresting little edifice in the Norman style, was opened for service on June 9th, 1833.

A violent display of public feeling took place in 1844 against a Dr. Belaney, who had for some years lived in the place, and was well known in the north of England in connection with the revival of falconry. Committed to trial on suspicion of poisoning his young and lovely wife, and her mother, Mrs. Skelly, he was acquitted, much to the surprise of the North Sunderland people, who believed him guilty. On his return they assembled in front of his house, called "The Grotto," carrying an effigy; and this so incensed him that he fired a pistol amongst them, and then made his escape by the back of the premises. The mob thereupon sacked the house, and then set fire to it.

Half-a-mile to the south-east of the Sea-houses is *Snook Point*, where, in August 1844, a very singular place of concealment was discovered in working a limestone quarry upon the sea-coast. The entrance was small. The cave was neatly flagged out, and had a clay pipe, or conduit, communicating with a hut or cottage above, for the conveyance of air or sound. Being in the neighbourhood of Dunstanburgh and Bamburgh castles, which were the last strongholds of the Lancastrians in the north of England, it is believed to have been a retreat of the intrepid Queen Margaret. Here she took refuge for a time, when she fled with her son, Prince Henry, to the sea-coast, after the battle of Hexham.

A mile and a half to the south of North Sunderland is BEADNELL, or, as the fisher-people call it, Beadlen, a good-sized fishing village, planted down on the flat, green, sandy sward, about a quarter of a mile from the sea, and sheltered by a belt of trees. Beadnell Square, a collection of cottages under a continuous quadrangular roof, lies between it and the rocky shore. The occupation of the villagers is well seen by the drawn-up cobles, the outspread nets, the lobster-pots lying about in heaps, the sheds, constructed of old fishing-boats as receptacles for the yarns and lines and other fishing-gear, and the big cauldrons, with stumpy chimneys, for heating the tar. In the centre of the village stands the *Church*, rebuilt about the middle of the eighteenth century. Its spire, relieved with an open panelled stage, is a conspicuous landmark. The public-house here has at one time been a small pele, having walls 6 feet and 8 feet thick. The vaulted basement storey is now used as a beer-cellar. The rocks here form an interesting study to the geologist. A section along the coast, from Ebbe's Nook to Annstead Bay, of nearly a mile and a half in length, exhibits a fine series of rocks belonging to the Mountain Limestone formation. Thick sandstones and limestones, shales, with ironstone and coal seams, are intercalated with each other, and these strata are traversed by a lead vein and a basaltic dyke. There are in this section eighteen different coal seams, and fourteen different limestones. Most of the latter are of a bluish colour, and yield good lime and many fossils characteristic of the Mountain Limestone formation—fishes, mollusks, corals, etc.—especially in the thicker sills and in the calcareous shales connected with them. The bold headland of Ebbe's Nook is of magnesian limestone, thirty feet in thickness, of a buff colour, and forms a narrow point running into the sea, about a quarter of a mile. Here were discovered in 1853, the remains of an ancient *Chapel*, which had for a long period been buried in a sand-drift. It consists of a chancel, nave, and an apartment on the west, either a vestment room or the lowest stage of the tower. The masonry is of coarse rubble work. Portions of the walls at the east and west ends are, curiously enough, cemented with clay instead of lime. A low stone seat ran along the north and south walls of the nave. The piscina, of a rude form, still remains inserted in the south wall. The chapel, which must formerly have stood at a much greater distance from the sea, is supposed to be of thirteenth-century workmanship, occupying the site of a chapel erected in the seventh century by, or in memory of, the Saxon princess Ebba, sister of Oswald, King of Northumbria.

Two miles and a half to the south, along the links of Beadnell Bay, which are overgrown with the ragwort and rest-harrow, is NEWTON-BY-THE-SEA, which, in the words of Mr. Walter White, is "not pretty or pleasing, but exhibits itself to the sea as a village of pantiled cottages and stables along three sides of a square, where only the public-house has an upper storey." Like Beadnell, it is almost entirely occupied by fisher-people. *Newton Point* is a fine striking headland.

A mile and a quarter to the south-west of Beadnell is *Swinhoe*, which gave its name to an ancient family. A mile beyond it is *Fleetham*, where is an old pele-tower; and a mile and a quarter south of it are the remains of an ancient chapel of great antiquarian interest. Mr. Raine writes of it—"*The Chapel of Tughall* was, I doubt not, immediately built on the spot where the body of St. Cuthbert rested for the night on its being removed from Durham to Lindisfarne. From its present remains, I know of no ecclesiastical structure in all Northumberland which has pretensions to higher antiquity. One single feature is sufficient to prove this. The nave and chancel are separated from each other by a Norman arch, slightly ornamented; and the latter is not only semi-circular, but coved overhead, curving to the top of the dividing arch, so as strictly to resemble a large oven." According to the visitation books, the people of the district must have formerly been a turbulent lot, for one person is presented for striking the minister of Tughall on the head with his dagger; a second, for firing a pistol into the midst of the congregation coming out of church; and a third, for riding into the church during service on horseback.

Two miles and three-quarters to the south of Tughall is EMBLETON, an irregularly-built village lying chiefly under the ridge of a hill which shuts out the sea-view. *The Church of the Holy Trinity* is a venerable-looking edifice in the patronage of Merton College, Oxford. It was built about 1320 on the site of a Norman church, and has undergone two restorations—one by Mr. Dobson of Newcastle in 1850, when the Falloden aisle was added, and the other by Mr. F. R. Wilson in 1867, when the chancel was rebuilt. The most ancient portions of the building are the tower and the arches dividing the nave from the aisles. The former, which bears a close resemblance to the tower of Ponteland Church, also under Merton College, is supported on Edwardian stone-ribbed arches, and exhibits, in its pierced battlements, a unique feature in the north of England. The latter are ornamented with a species of dog-tooth ornament, which Mr. Longstaffe regards with great interest as an instance of "local style" in architecture. The porch, which was added in the Perpendicular period, contains several sculptured tomb-slabs of the fourteenth and fifteenth centuries. Covering the vestry-table is an old altar-cloth, with a beautiful though faded needlework border, representing the story of the Prodigal Son. A large collection of groats, ninety-four in number, ranging from Edward III. to Edward IV., was found, in three rows, set edge-up, in the churchyard, at two feet from the surface, some years ago. The vicarage, erected at three different periods, has attached to it an ancient pele-tower, the Turris de Emylton, described as existing c. 1416. Parker, a cousin of Steele the essayist, was vicar here in the reign of Queen Anne. He contributed to the *Spectator* the letter in No. 474, of date September 3rd, 1712, describing, in no flattering terms, the boisterous manners and insipid conversation of the north-country gentlemen. He was also the author of the celebrated, "Cure for a Scold." The Rev. Mandell Creighton, Professor of Ecclesiastical History at Cambridge, editor of the *Historical Review*, and author of *The History of the Papacy from the period of the Reformation*, was vicar here from 1874 to 1884.

Embleton was the birthplace of Mr. W. T. Stead, the influential editor of the *Pall Mall Gazette*. An interesting memorial of Sir Andrew Barton, the famous Scottish sea-captain, and the hero of a well-known Elizabethan ballad, was discovered on the sea-shore at Embleton some years ago. A heavy sea washed away the loose sand covering a sandstone rock, near low-water mark, on which was inscribed, in Roman capitals, the name, "Andra Barton." Sir Andrew was killed in a naval engagement with Sir Edward Howard, who, according to the ballad, was directed where to find the dreaded knight by Henry Hunt—a merchant belonging "to the Newcastle that stands upon Tyne." King James of Scotland insisted upon satisfaction for the death of Barton, and capture of his ships; and the affair was, in a great measure, the cause of the battle of Flodden. There is a good inn at Embleton, the Hare and Hounds. The nearest station is Christon Bank, a mile and a half distant. From the village there is a pleasant walk of a mile and a half to Dunstanburgh Castle, following a lane by the side of the Embleton Burn to Dunstan Steads, and thence continuing southward along the links, where the burnet rose (*Rosa spinossima*) and bloody cranesbill (*Geranium sanguineum*) grow very abundantly. Before reaching the ruins, the *Saddle Rock*, an outcrop of limestone of a remarkably strange shape, which afterwards dips away under the basalt, may be examined.

*Dunstanburgh Castle*, to quote Mr. Freeman, "surpasses all other Northumbrian castles in the grandeur of its site, and it alone abides as a castle should abide in all the majesty of a shattered ruin." It is seated on the dark-pillared crags of the Whin Sill, which is here about 40 feet in thickness, and which overlies beds of sandstone, shale, and coal belonging to the Mountain Limestone formation. Many of the fissures in the basalt are filled with metamorphosed shales and sandstone, and it is in these patches that the various coloured quartz crystals called "Dunstanburgh diamonds" are found. The great natural feature of these rocks is a deep perpendicular chasm called the "Rumbling Churn," which has been formed by the crumbling away of a column of basalt of somewhat softer nature than the rest. Into this gully the waves, during a storm, rush with tremendous force, rolling the big black stones around it, and spouting up columns of foam to a great height. Here the geologist will notice, nearly enveloped in the basalt, a mass of limestone which has been converted into white crystalline marble. The bed of limestone under the whinstone has been hollowed out so as to form an almost continuous cavern, hence Scott's reference to "Dunstanborough's cavern'd shore" is a just and appropriate one. Dunstanburgh, though by far the largest castle in Northumberland as regards area, played but a small part in history. Four historic personages, all of them canonized, have, however, been connected with it—St. Simon de Montford, St. Thomas of Lancaster, St. Henry VI., and Queen Margaret. From the traces of a rough stone rampart to the south of the castle, and from the affix "burgh," it is supposed that Dunstanburgh was a tribal centre of the ancient Britons. The idea of raising a fortress on these impregnable cliffs must have been in the mind of Simon de Montfort, the great Earl of Leicester, when he purchased the barony of Embleton in 1257. Dying in arms against the king, his estates were forfeited, and granted by Henry III. to his younger son, Edmund Crouchback, Earl of Lancaster. The elder son of this nobleman was concerned in the decapitation of the favourite, Gaveston, and while still unpardoned by the king, commenced, on the 7th May 1313, with no very loyal intentions, it may be supposed, the building of this stronghold on a scale of great magnitude. Three years afterwards, however, in 1316, he obtained from Edward II. a license to crenellate or fortify his mansion at Dunstanburgh. Convicted in 1322 of having had "secret dealings with the Scots," he was executed, and his estates were confiscated. They were afterwards restored to his brother Henry, and continued in the hands of the House of Lancaster till the Wars of the Roses. During these troublous times Dunstanburgh was taken and retaken no less than five times, and as artillery was used in these successive sieges, the castle was much shattered. In 1538 "Dunstunburght" was reported to be "a very reuynus howse, and of smaylle strengthe." King James I. granted Dunstanburgh to Sir William Grey of Wark on 6th February 1625, and it continued the property of his descendants till Lord Tankerville sold it to the Eyre Trustees in 1869. The castle occupies the north end of the basaltic ridge, which is washed by the sea on the north and on the east, and is cut off on the west and south-west by low, swampy ground. The area enclosed is about ten acres. The southern portion of the ridge was the outer Bailey or Barmekyn—a space of fifteen acres, partly defended by the escarpment of rocks and partly by a rampier, and here cattle might be kept and corn grown. The main entrance was originally on the south, through a vaulted archway, in which the groove for the portcullis may yet be seen. Above the outer door was a gallery resting on corbels, which are carved with the lion of England, an escallop, and two fleurs-de-lys. The Great Gatehouse was at an early date converted into a keep, the ends of the archway being built up, and a new entrance made in the curtain wall about twenty yards to the north. This gatehouse consists of a central block of masonry, two storeys in height, with a semi-circular tower on each side, surmounted by a square turret resting on corbels. The building, when complete, was eighty feet high. The vaulted basement storey of each tower was occupied by the guard. Over the door to the large room in the western tower is an enormous lintel of one stone, seven feet long. The south wall, of which a great portion is still in good preservation, was defended by four towers. The first projects over the castle ditch in bold corbelling; the second is three storeys in height, with double, narrow, pointed windows, and the remains of a newel-stair, from which passages lead off to latrines in the thickness of the wall; the third is small, with the vault of its basement formed of huge flags resting on a single rib; the fourth is the Margaret Tower, which stands on the pillared rock overlooking the Rumble Churn. Here, according to tradition, the heroic but unfortunate queen took refuge for some days, finally escaping in a fishing-boat from the narrow, rocky cove beneath it. The tower is of three storeys, the lower one vaulted with flat stones resting on two massive ribs. The first floor had a seated window-recess, with two lights to the north, and a passage with a latrine in the north-east corner. "No better example," says Mr. C. J. Bates, "perhaps, exists of the utter inability of the mediæval mind to appreciate the romantic scenes in which, for practical reasons, the buildings of those centuries were often placed, than the way in which the east side of the Margaret Tower, commanding a scene of singular majesty, was wholly devoted to latrines." A little to the north of the second tower are the remains of a rough-walled building, standing east and west, and generally assumed to have been the chapel. In the courtyard behind the Gatehouse is the draw-well (now partly filled up), which has been cut through the solid basaltic rock. The only other towers that have not been referred to are on the west side. One is completely in ruins; the other is the Lilburn Tower, built probably by John Lilburn, constable of Dunstanburgh, about 1325. "Nothing," says Mr. Freeman, "can well be conceived more striking than the Lilburn Tower, a Norman keep in spirit, though far later in date, rising on the slope of the wild hill, with the tall basaltic columns standing in order in front of it 'like sentinels of stone.'" The walls are six feet thick, and through them, on the east side, runs a mural passage as a continuation of the walk round the parapets of the ramparts. Immediately beneath the tower to the north a postern, with a round arch of the Decorated period, opened on to a footpath which led down the steep escarpment towards Embleton. At the foot of the Gatehouse towers the common mallow (*malva sylvestris*) grows plentifully. Dunstanburgh Castle has been painted by Turner and T. M. Richardson, and other artists of more or less note.

Around these desolate ruins, so remote from the movement of modern life, there has gathered a romantic legend, retold in rhyme by M. G. Lewis, as "Sir Guy the Seeker;" by James Service of Chatton, as "The Wandering Knight;" and by William Gill Thompson, as

"The Coral Wreath; or, the Spellbound Knight." In the latter poem there is a considerable deviation from the original story. Lewis's ballad tells how Sir Guy the Seeker, while sheltering in the castle during a storm, was accosted by a "ghastly wight" with flaming hair.

> "'Sir Knight! Sir Knight! if your heart be right,
> And your nerves be firm and true,
> Sir Knight! Sir Knight! a beauty bright
> In durance waits for you.'
>
> 'That mortal ne'er drew vital air,
> Who witnessed fear in me;
> Come what come will, come good, come ill,
> Lead on, I'll follow thee!'
>
> And now they go both high and low,
> Above and underground,
> And in and out, and about, and about,
> And round, and round, and round."

They mount a winding stair to a brazen door, the bolt of which was a venomous snake, enter a vast hall draped with black and lit by a hundred lights, wherein

> "Of marble black as the raven's back,
> A hundred steeds stood round;
> And of marble white by each a knight
> Lay sleeping on the ground."

At the end of the room, in a tomb of crystal, is the captive lady, with tearful eyes and suppliant hands, guarded by two gigantic skeletons.

> "That on the right holds a falchion bright,
> That on the left a horn."

Sir Guy is told by the wizard that the fate of the spellbound beauty depends on the choice he makes between the sword and Merlin's horn. After much hesitation he pressed the latter to his lips, but at the sound of the shrill blast the hundred horses stamped, the hundred knights sprang to life, while with the taunt of the wizard,

> "Now shame on the coward who sounded a horn
> When he might have unsheathed a sword,"

thundering in his ears, he sank down senseless, and awoke the next morning to find himself stretched in the ruined gateway. Rousing himself, he commenced a fruitless search among the ruins, which was to last for ages. The pale yellow and red quartz crystals, called "Dunstanburgh diamonds," are supposed to form part of the immense treasure with which the imprisoned lady will reward her deliverer.

# BAMBURGH TO HOLY ISLAND.

**Holy Island (via Budle), 5 miles; (via Easington), 8 miles.**

THE nearest route from Bamburgh to HOLY ISLAND (five miles) is by way of the links to Budle Water, which may be waded or crossed by the ferry-boat at the Granaries, then along the dreary Ross Back sands—the resting-place of many a stranded barque—to a long sandy spit, called the Law, separated from the island by a channel half-a-mile wide. A boat is sure to be in attendance at the Beacons to ferry over the pedestrian, whose progress all the way from Budle Point has been watched with interest by the fishermen, with an eye to business. The fare usually charged for the single passage is 2s. In the channel, between this point and the island, there is a valuable oyster-bed, belonging to the Earl of Tankerville. One winter the tide sank so low that the oysters were laid bare, and destroyed by the frost. In the following year, however, the bed was renewed by oysters from the Forth.

The route from Belford is about six miles, by way of Easington (the *ton* where the Æscingas or family of Æsc settled in Saxon times) and Elwick, to the Law. The route from Beal (three miles and a half) is the nearest, and the one most frequently taken by tourists. There is, first, a country-road to be followed for a mile to the shore, then a wide waste of plashy sands, uncovered for six hours and a half each tide, from two hours after ebb, to two hours and a half before flood, to be crossed, keeping to the circuitous line of barnacle-crusted stakes, to avoid quicksands. The fact of the island being accessible from the mainland twice a day was recorded by Bede eleven hundred years ago, and expressed in verse by Sir Walter Scott, in "Marmion"—

> "For with the flow and ebb, its style
> Varies from continent to isle;
> Dry-shod, o'er sands, twice every day,
> The pilgrims to the shrine find way;
> Twice every day the waves efface
> Of staves and sandall'd feet the trace."

The pilgrim of the present day is recommended to put off the modern substitute for sandals, and walk across barefooted, as there is more mud than sand near the shore, and, in addition to many a good-sized runnel to be crossed, there is the Low, a streamlet nearly half-a-mile from the land, forming the boundary of Holy Island. A very striking and unusual spectacle was witnessed on the sands on Thursday, the 11th

August 1887, when the Catholics of the north of England commemorated the twelfth centenary of St. Cuthbert, by a pilgrimage to his island-home. A number of priests, in the habit of their order, and secular clergy, wearing cassock, cotta, and biretta, together with several thousands of pilgrims, English, Irish, Scotch, and foreign, marched barefooted under their religious banners, in a solemn procession across the sands, reciting the fifteen mysteries of the rosary, and singing such hymns as "Faith of our Fathers," and "Hail! Queen of Heaven." On arriving at the island, the procession, headed by cross-bearer and acolytes, moved towards the venerable ruins of the Priory, where Holy Mass was celebrated.

Exclusive of a narrow spit of land, which extends for about a mile in length to the west-north-west, the island is about six miles in circumference, being about two miles across from east to west, and from north to south. A considerable portion of it is under cultivation, and produces early crops of wheat, beans, and potatoes; the rest consists of barren sandhills, held together by the creeping roots of the sea lyme-grass, the sea mat-grass, rushy wheat-grass, and sea carex, and is overrun with rabbits. The rocks of which the island is composed are limestone on the north and south, and sandstone on the north and east. Through these strata has been intruded a vertical mass of basalt, known as the *Lindisfarne Dyke*, which crosses the south part of the island from west to east, metamorphosing the limestone and shale contiguous to it. The island formed part of the ancient territory of Lindisfarne, after which it was called. The name, according to Mr. Ralph Carr-Ellison, is derived from the Anglo-Saxon *Lindesfarēna Ealand*—Island of the Pilgrims of the Lind, that is, of the Linn, or slake. The present name was given to it, says Prior Wessington, in consequence of the sacred blood shed upon it by the Danes.

The history of the island began with the year A.D. 635, when St. Aidan—an Irish monk from Iona, who had accepted the invitation of King Oswald to teach the new faith to the Northumbrians—made it the seat of his episcopacy. His choice of this place was probably due to three considerations—its security, insulated by the tide twice a day; its proximity to Bamburgh, the royal residence; and its resemblance to his beloved Iona. Here, as from a "spiritual citadel," he commenced the difficult task which had baffled his predecessor, Corman, teaching the plain and simple rudiments of Christianity, and leaving the abstruse and mysterious doctrine until his hearers were able to grasp them. Whenever, through his imperfect knowledge of the Saxon tongue, he failed to make himself understood, Oswald was at hand as a ready interpreter. His success was such that 15,000 persons are said to have been baptised by him in the space of seven days. A small church or oratory would, no doubt, be founded here by Aidan, for the little community of monks on the island. This humble edifice, thatched with the coarse bents of the links, could not long withstand the brunt of the storms and the brands of the wild sea rovers. The first Bishop of Lindisfarne died at Bamburgh on the 31st of

August 651, his head resting against the wooden buttress of the church he had built. Truly, as the present Bishop of Durham observes, "not Augustine, but Aidan, is the true apostle of England."

Finan, another monk from Iona, succeeded Aidan, and rebuilt his church. Two kings were baptised by him—Peada, King of Mercia, and Sigbert, King of the East Saxons. In his time arose the dispute in the northern churches as to the proper time for the observance of Easter. He died in 661. Colman, also from Iona, was the third bishop. Having been defeated at the Whitby Synod in regard to the question just referred to above, he resigned his bishopric, and retired to Iona in 664. Tuda, his successor, in less than a year was struck low by the plague. After his death considerable changes took place in the bishopric, and the see was removed from Lindisfarne to York. Ceadda, during the absence of St. Wilfrid, who had gone to France for consecration, was appointed in his stead, but resigned on the return of that prelate, three years afterwards. Wilfrid made York his episcopal seat, and continued for some years to exercise spiritual jurisdiction in the diocese of Northumberland. He quarrelled with Theodore, Archbishop of Canterbury, and was compelled to resign his see, which was then divided. Eata, a pupil of Aidan, was, in 678, installed as the fifth bishop of Lindisfarne, but, on the further dismemberment of the see, effected a change with Cuthbert, the newly-appointed bishop of Hexham, and retired to the famous abbey. Cuthbert, the sixth bishop, who had formerly been a prior of the monastery under the abbacy of Eata, began his pastoral oversight of the see in 685. After labouring here for the short space of two years, he returned again to his secluded oratory on one of the Farnes, where he died within two months, a victim to his own austerities. He was buried in a stone coffin at the right side of the altar at Lindisfarne. For a year after Cuthbert's death, Wilfrid, Archbishop of York, exercised episcopal authority over the diocese, and then choice was made of Eadbert, 688, in whose time the body of St. Cuthbert was disinterred, and found uncorrupted. He died in 698, and was succeeded by Eadfrid, chiefly remembered for his caligraphy, as exemplified in a remarkable copy of the gospels in the Vulgate, preserved in the Cottonian collection of the British Museum, where it is described as "The Durham Manuscript." He wrote the text, Æthelwald, his successor, supplied the illuminations, which are still brilliant beyond conception. Bilfrid bestowed upon it a cover of silver and gold, bedecked with precious stones, and a while after, Aldred, a priest of the house, added an interlineary Dano-Saxon version, with marginal notes. This beautiful example of the art that flourished on this lonely island, after many vicissitudes, formed one of the treasures of the Priory from its re-construction in 1093, to the dissolution. After the death of Eadfrid in 721, an interval of three years elapsed, and then in 724 Ethelwold, Abbot of Melrose, though formerly a monk in the church of Lindisfarne, was appointed to the vacant see. During his episcopate, Ceolwulph, King of Northumbria, exchanged his purple robe for the cowl of a monk, and retired to the monastery of Lindisfarne, which he endowed with many valuable possessions. Cynewulph, tenth bishop of Lindisfarne, installed 740, had the misfortune to offend King Edbert by giving protection to Offa, a prince of the royal blood, who, for some unexplained reason, had taken refuge at the High Altar of Lindisfarne. Thrown into the royal prison at Bamburgh, the Bishop lingered there for the long period of thirty years, the spiritual concerns of his diocese being attended to in the meantime by Friothubert, Bishop of Hexham. Cynewulph was succeeded in 780 by Higbald. This prelate was compelled in 793 to flee from the sacred isle before the piratical Danes, who plundered the church of its silver and gold, and murdered several of the monks. After his death, the see was successively held by Egbert, 803-821; Heathured, 821-830; Ecgred, or Egfrid, 830-845; Eanbert, 845-858; and Eardulph, 854-900. With Eardulph, the sixteenth bishop of Lindisfarne, this line of saintly men came to an end, for in 875 the Danes, after plundering the monastery of Tynemouth, proceeded to Lindisfarne, and nothing was left to the monks but flight. Hastily placing the body of St. Cuthbert into a wooden coffin, together with several precious relics—the head of St. Oswald and the bones of Bishops Aidan, Eata, Eadfrid, Ethelwold, and others—they took their departure from the spot, endeared to them by so many sacred memories, never to return. Their desertion of the island is said by Reginald to be due to the report of a monk left behind, who, miraculously hidden in the vacant shrine of St. Cuthbert by a hollow cloud, heard the Danes threaten a speedy return. The church and monastery were reduced to ruins, in which state they were destined to remain for over two hundred years. For the space of about a year Lindisfarne was again to give refuge to the remains of St. Cuthbert, and that was in 1069, when the Conqueror marched north to punish the inhabitants of Northumberland for their resistance to his authority. The monks of Durham, concerned about the safety of the saint's relics, fled with them by way of Jarrow, Bedlington, and Tuggall, and on the fourth evening appeared on the strand opposite to the island. The tide was high, the night dark and stormy, and the prospect before the weary monks was not encouraging, when, as the ancient chronicler relates, behold! a miracle. The waves parted, and the track over the sands was bare before them. The bones of the celebrated saint were taken back to Durham in April, 1070, and though more than once disturbed, have at last found a final resting-place. Bishop Carileph granted, in 1082, the ruined monastery and church to the Benedictine monks of Durham, who shortly afterwards established a colony in the island. Ten years later, in 1093, they laid the foundations of a Priory and Church, of which there are such interesting remains at the present time, the architect being a monk of Durham, named Ædward. The stone used was chiefly sandstone, brought over from the mainland—Goswick—of a warm, red tint, but not suited for exposure to the wild winds of the north-east coast. The church was completed, dedicated, and opened about A.D. 1120, and no material alteration was made in size or form until about 1440 or 1450, when the apse at the east end of the chancel was taken down, the chancel lengthened, and made oblong in shape. As late as 1750-1780 the centre tower was standing. Except on one occasion, when William de Prendergast and his Scottish borderers plundered the bake-house and brewhouse, the Priory did not, like Hexham, Brinkburn, and Hulne, suffer from the visits of sacrilegious moss-troopers. The monastery fell with the smaller ones in the time of Henry VIII. (1541), and was used, together with all its adjacent buildings, as "The Queene's Majestie's storehouse" (1560). It was finally unroofed in 1613 by Lord Walden, who took away the bells, the lead, and everything worth laying hands on. "The ship, with manie persons therein, was drowned and sonke into the sea, even sone after their goeinge from the iland; whereof the wronge doers (if God shall so touch their hearts) may and will make use." The Crown has still possession of the ruins.

The *Priory Church*, in its plan, bears a remarkable resemblance to Durham Cathedral, the arrangement of the bays in couples, divided by piers, alternately cylindrical and compound, being peculiar to these two places among English churches. "Lindisfarne," says Mr. C. C. Hodges, "was not a model of Durham on a smaller scale, nor yet a copy of it in any sense, but an adaptation of the same design to a church of lesser magnitude." The alterations to the original building have been comparatively so few, that the ruins are especially interesting, as showing what a Benedictine Church of the twelfth century was like. The church was cruciform, the chancel terminating in an apse, and the transepts also being semi-circular at their eastern ends. The edifice was vaulted with stone, and surmounted by three towers, one in the centre and two at the west end. The principal entrance is a beautiful round-headed doorway, enriched with the zigzag ornament. Having been covered up with rubbish till 1821, it is in a good state of preservation. On each side of it are the remains of a Norman arcade. Above it, in the interior of the church, is an open gallery of five arches, one of them pierced as a window, to throw the light of the afternoon sun into the nave. The *Nave*, 100 feet in length, had north and south aisles, which were separated from it by arcades of six round arches each. None of these now remain on the south side, and only two on the north. The cylindrical columns of the nave—three on each side—were covered with a surface ornament of a remarkable and somewhat unusual character, consisting of a sunk moulding, which traversed the pier in spiral, zigzag, vertical, and double spiral lines, the latter forming lozenges. Ornamentation of a similar design may be seen in the nave of Durham Cathedral. Springing diagonally over the centre of the cross from a rudely-carved corbel is an arch of singular beauty, decorated with the zigzag moulding, and locally known as the "Rain-bow." It is 44 feet from the ground, and was one of the two groins which supported the central tower. As already stated, the chancel was extended about the middle of the fifteenth century from 35 feet to 50 feet in length, and the new east end made rectangular, instead of apsidal. The foundations of the Norman apse were laid bare in the year 1821, on the removal of some rubbish. At the same time was discovered the original pavement, consisting of glazed bricks, resting on a substratum of lime. The lower portion of the walls in the west end of the chancel is believed by Mr. Hodges to have belonged to a pre-conquest church, firstly, because the plaster which still remains on the walls goes down 18 inches below what was the floor level of the Norman church, and seems to have been left unbroken and undisturbed by Ædward; and secondly, because the stone used is of a different kind and colour from that in the rest of the building. In the south wall of the chancel is a trefoil-headed piscina. Between the chancel and the apse of the south transept there is a curious passage, only wide enough to admit one person at a time, cut through the wall immediately behind the pillar. The pointed window of three lights in the north aisle was inserted about the year 1340. Fragments of Saxon crosses and other relics of the ancient church are preserved in a building adjoining St. Mary's churchyard. One fragment, built up in the staircase of the north-west tower, has carved upon it, in basso-relievo, a nondescript animal, with a head like a dog, and ending in a long, snaky, and intertwisted tail. Recent excavations have laid bare the foundations of the various monastic buildings.

Immediately to the south of the nave is the little *Cloister-garth*, about 16 yards square. West of it was the *Dormitory* of the monks, raised upon low groined arches, some of which are still standing. East of it was the *Chapter-house*, which was connected by a slype, or vaulted passage, with the *Cemetery*, a small plot of ground on the south side of the chancel, now called the Sanctuary-garth. South of the south transept was the *Calefactory*, a vaulted building in four bays, divided into different sections by cross-walls. In the building next to the Calefactory was the *Parlour*, where merchants exhibited their wares, and where the monks conversed with each other. On the south side of the Cloisters was the *Fratry*, or Dining-room. West of this building was the *Lavatory*. Adjoining the west wall may be traced the *Kitchen*, *Buttery*, and *Bakehouse*. The great oven has been discovered. Between these buildings and the wall of the nave is a building where all the joinery and mason-work was done. The walls are of excessive thickness, to deaden the sound, and prevent it passing through and disturbing the monks. The Outer Court, where the monks had their garden, orchard, stables, etc., was surrounded by a high battlemented wall. The principal entrance was on the west side. *The Prior's Hall*, at the north-east angle, is a building of great strength, and was probably the stronghold of the monks. Its large fire-place and chimney, and the greater part of its massive walls, are still standing. Among the coins, etc., found during the excavations, was a medal of the Reformation period, having a representation of the Pope on one side of it, and of the Devil on the other.

Sir Walter Scott has thrown the spell of his genius around the picturesque ruins, but the tragical story of "Constance of Beverley" has no foundation in fact. Readers of "Marmion" not troubled with antiquarian scruples may still picture to themselves the black-robed and stern-featured judges in the damp "vault of Penitence," with the statue-like form of the beautiful but frail nun before them, may hear the blind Abbot's sentence, and the shriek of the maiden immured alive in the awful niche, while the bell tolls for the welfare of a parting soul.

"Slow o'er the midnight wave it swung,
Northumbrian rocks in answer rung;
To Warkworth cell the echoes roll'd,
His beads the wakeful hermit told;
The Bamburgh peasant raised his head,
But slept ere half a prayer he said;
So far was heard the mighty knell,
The stag sprung up on Cheviot Fell,
Spread his broad nostril to the wind,
Listed before, aside, behind,
Then couch'd him down beside the hind,
And quaked among the mountain fern,
To hear the sound, so dull and stern."

The description of the Priory Church, as it rose before the eyes of the nuns, is a very fine verbal sketch:—

"A solemn, huge, and dark red pile,
Placed on the margin of the isle.

. . . . .

In Saxon strength that Abbey frown'd,
With massive arches broad and round,
That rose alternate, row and row,
On ponderous columns, short and low;
Built ere the art was known,
By pointed aisle and shafted stalk,
The arcades of an alley'd walk
To emulate in stone.
On the deep walls the heathen Dane
Had pour'd his impious rage in vain,
And needful was such strength to these
Exposed to the tempestuous seas.
Scourged by the wind's eternal sway,
Open to rovers fierce as they,
Which could twelve hundred years withstand
Winds, waves, and northern pirates' hand.
Not but that portions of the pile,
Rebuilded in a later style,
Show'd where the spoiler's hand had been;
Not but the wasting sea-breeze keen
Had worn the pillar's carving quaint,
And moulder'd in his niche the saint,
And rounded, with consuming power,
The pointed angles of each tower;
Yet still entire the abbey stood,
Like veteran worn and unsubdued."

Turner's view of Holy Island represents it under peculiar atmospheric conditions, the ruined Priory Church being seen in light, the castle and sea darkened by an oncoming storm.

A little to the west of the ruins is the *Parish Church of St. Mary*, which, for the most part, is of early English workmanship. Remains of an earlier structure, built shortly before the year 1145, may be seen in three of the four arches separating the nave from the north aisle. These are round-headed, resting on columns of red stone. Two chamfered ribs of each arch are built of red and white stone in alternate courses—an arrangement both novel and pleasing. The south arcade was built in the early Decorated or Geometric period. The arches are pointed, resting on octagonal piers. The chancel is early English, forty-nine feet in length. Here may be seen two ancient aumbries, one on the north side, and the other at the south-east angle, also an ancient tomb-slab having a cross, a blank inverted shield (mitre-shaped), and a sword carved in relief upon it. A piscina in the south aisle marks the site of the chantry of St. Mary and St. Margaret. On its north and south sides the church is lighted by windows of Decorated character. The tombstone of Sir William Reed, of Fenham (d. 1604), within the altar rails, is inscribed with the quaint motto, "Contra vim mortis non est medicamen in hortis." The walls are hung with memorial tablets to members of the Askew and Haggestone families, and others. The inscriptions on many of the tombstones in the churchyard commemorate those who have been drowned at sea, and remind the visitor that he is in a "seaboard parish." One tombstone records the death of Captain James Lilburn, of H.M. sloop *Goshawk*, who was "cut off" in attempting to "cut out" vessels lying in the harbour of Malaga, 1812.

A group of cottages would, at an early period, spring up under the shelter of the sacred walls for the accommodation of the dependants and work-people of the Priory, and of the pilgrims to the shrine of St. Cuthbert, and it is probable there was a considerable population here in the olden times. The present *village* has little to recommend it, from an artistic point of view. The houses are plain and primitive in style—several of them with white-washed walls and thatched roofs—occupied by fisher-folk and others engaged in the working and burning of lime. There is a commodious reading-room. The principal inns are the Crown and Anchor, Northumberland Arms, and Iron Rails. In a square, formerly the market-place, is a beautiful cross of stone twelve feet high, rebuilt, as the inscription upon it states, by H. C. Selby, 1828. It was designed by Mr. Dobson, and stands on the pedestal of "St. Cuthbert's Cross," erected by Bishop Æthelwold. This ancient socket was called the "Petting-stone," and newly-married people were formerly made to leap over it for luck, a marriage being said to prove unfortunate if the bride was unable to stride across it. The islanders, who, at the present day, display so much heroism in the saving of life, were, in the seventeenth century, redoubtable "wreckers;" so, at least, one may gather from *Blakhal's Brieffe Narration*:—"He (the Governor) told us how the common people ther do pray for shippes which they see in danger. They al sit down upon their knees, and hold up their handes, and say very devotely, 'Lord, send her to us; God, send her to us.' 'You,' said he, seeing them upon their knees, and their hands joyned, do think that they are praying for your sauvetie, but their myndes are far from that. They pray not God to sauve you, or send you to the port, but to send you to them by shipwreck, that they may gette the spoil of her. And to show you that this is their meaning,' said he, 'if the ship come wel to porte, or eschew naufrage, they gette up in anger, crying, the devil stick her, she is away from us!'" The little harbour curving inward, on the south side of the island, is a safe anchoring-ground, except during heavy gales from the westward, having 22 feet of water on the bar at high tide, and 8 feet at low tide. During the herring season it forms a picturesque and busy scene. To the west of it is the *Heugh Hill*, a basaltic ridge 45 feet in height, at one end of which are the remains of a square building, called "The Chapel," and at the other, the ruins of a small fort, built in 1675. To the east of the basin is another outbreak of the same whinstone dyke—a conical eminence of columnar formation, rising to a height of 105 feet, and forming the most striking feature of the island. Its ancient name was *Beblowe*. Occupying the entire summit is the *Castle*, which was probably erected about the year 1539, when it was ordered that "all havens should be fensed with bulworks and blocke-houses." It was out of repair in 1544. Sir Robert Bowes in 1539 recommended that the lower part be strengthened with bulwarks. Several of the garrison, to the number of thirty, seem, from the church records, to have died of the plague in 1639. In 1643 the fort was held for the king, but soon after it fell into the hands of the Parliamentarians. The capture of the castle by two Jacobites, Launcelot Errington and his nephew, Mack, in 1715, forms a somewhat romantic incident in connection with the place. This event took place on the 10th October of that year, when it happened that five out of the seven men composing the garrison were absent. The facts are these:—Launcelot Errington—the master of a Newcastle brigantine at anchor in the harbour—after a visit to the castle, for the ostensible purpose of getting shaved by the master-gunner, who practised a little as a barber, returned shortly afterwards, accompanied by his nephew, and once more gained admission, on the pretence of having lost the key of his watch. Pistol in hand, they accosted the astonished barber with the words, "D—— you, the castle is our own!" A struggle ensued, in which the gunner and the sentinel who had come to his aid were violently thrust out of the castle. The two bold Jacobites signalled to the mainland for reinforcements, but none came, and they were made prisoners the next day by a party of soldiers from Berwick, who had come to retake the fort. Their escape from Berwick gaol by burrowing under the foundations, depositing the earth removed in an oven, and their subsequent adventures, concealed for nine days near Bamburgh Castle in a pea-stack, are even more romantic than the capture of the castle. Errington afterwards kept for many years the Salutation Inn, at the head of the Flesh Market, Newcastle, and died, it is said, from grief, on hearing the news of Culloden.

The castle is now occupied by coastguardsmen. It is approached by a gradual ascent on the south side, and commands a magnificent view, not only of the whole island itself, but of the coast from Bamburgh to Berwick and St. Abb's Head. In the harbour below is kept a life-boat by Lord Crewe's trustees, which, on a signal from Bamburgh Castle, puts off to sea. On the east side of the island is Sheldrake Bay, bending round to Emmanuel Head, a green bluff protected by large boulders.

The interesting limestone caverns, on the north of the island, have been destroyed by "the utilitarian aggressor." Seals used to be very plentiful on the island, and were killed in large numbers. There is a fine lough in the north-east corner, covering an area of about six acres. *Equisetum limosum* (smooth naked horse-tail) grows in great abundance at the east end of it.

About one hundred yards west of the Heugh is *St. Cuthbert's Isle*, or *Hobthrush*, a basaltic rock of about half-an-acre in extent, covered with grass, and rising in its south-west corner to a height of 12 feet above high-water mark. It is accessible, at low tide, along a ridge of weed-covered boulders. Here are the remains of the small chapel of *St. Cuthbert in the Sea*, which has been 24 feet long, and 13 feet broad, and contained images of St. Cuthbert and St. Thomas. Raine thinks it probable that a lamp was kept burning here during the night for the benefit of mariners unacquainted with the harbour. According to tradition, it is on one of the rocks there that at night-time

> "St. Cuthbert sits and toils to frame
> The sea-born beads that bear his name,"

using the opposite rock as an anvil. They are the fossil joints of the stems of encrinites, or stone-lilies, and, when single, are called trochites, and when several are united, entrochites. They are about the size of the seeds of the mallow, of a dark leaden colour, with a brownish speck in the centre, and were formerly much used for rosaries. *Statice limonium* (the sea-lavender) grows plentifully on St. Cuthbert's Isle. The botanist, in his rambles through Holy Island, will find not only the interesting sea lungwort, or oyster-plant (*Mertensia maritima*), but several other attractive wild-flowers—*Silene inflata* (bladder campion), *Silene maritima* (sea campion), *Fumaria officinalis* (fumitory), *Malva sylvestris* (common mallow), *Ononis arvensis* (rest-harrow), *Trifolium procumbens* (hop-trefoil), *Epilobium hirsutum* (greater willow-herb), *Achillea millefolium* (yarrow), *Carduus lanceolatus* (spear-plume thistle), *Myosotis arvensis* (field scorpion-grass), *Anagallis arvensis* (pimpernel), *Armeria maritima* (thrift), *Cynoglossum officinale* (hound's-tongue), *Erythræa littoralis* (dwarf centaury), *hyoscyamus niger* (henbane), *Glaux maritima* (black saltwort, or sea glaux), *Asperugo procumbens* (German madwort), *Arenaria peploides* (ovate sandwort), *Salicornia herbacea* (glasswort, or marsh samphire), *Cakile maritima* (sea-rocket), *Samolus Valerandi* (water pimpernel, or brook-weed).

# BAMBURGH TO THE FARNES.

**Sea-houses, 3 miles. [Distance from Sea-houses.] Farne Island, 2 miles; Stapel Island, 3½ miles; Wawmses, 4 miles; Longstone, 5 miles.**

THE usual place of embarkation for the FARNES is the little harbour at the Sea-houses, North Sunderland, about three miles south of Bamburgh. Here a boat may be secured for fifteen shillings. In addition to this charge the boatmen expect to be provided with refreshments, solid and liquid. With a fine day and a smooth sea, no excursion can be more delightful. The time usually taken from leaving to returning to the port is about six hours, though, of course, this depends on the length of the stay made on the islands. A pass has to be procured at Bamburgh Castle to visit all the islands. The Farnes, which are chiefly naked rocks, vary in number from fifteen to twenty-five in number, according to the state of the tide. They are from one and a half to five miles eastward from the coast, the nearest point being Monkshouse. From ancient documents, it appears that the names of the various islands were almost the same in the twelfth century as they are to-day. The Farnes were among the most ancient possessions of the Church in Lindisfarne, and passed, in the course of time, to the Priory and Convent of Durham. At the dissolution of the monasteries in 1536, Henry VIII. bestowed them upon the Dean and Chapter of Durham. The Outer Farnes are under the control of the Ecclesiastical Commissioners; the Inner Farnes are the freehold property of the representatives of Archdeacon Thorpe, and now leased by them to the Farne Islands' Association. The first island to be visited is two miles and a quarter from the harbour, separated from it by the Fairway, and is the largest and most historical. This is the *Farne*, or as it is most commonly called, the *House Island.* Its name, applied to the whole group, is said to be derived from the Anglo-Saxon *Fárena éalande*, signifying "Islands of the Pilgrims," which superseded, probably in the time of St. Cuthbert, the earlier British appellation of *Inis Medicante*, or *Medcaut.* The island is of an irregular quadrangular form, with an area at low water of sixteen acres, eleven of which are almost entirely bare rock. It presents, on the west and south sides, a range of black, precipitous cliffs, of rudely columnar basalt, rising to a height of about 80 feet. Long and deep fissures run through the hard whinstone. One on the north-west is called the *Churn*, and extends from the sea into the island for some distance, being partly bridged over with rock, and having an opening upward at the farther end. When a gale is blowing from the north, the water at half-tide is driven with such violence into this chasm that a column of foam is forced up to a height of 90 feet, distinctly seen from Monkshouse or Bamburgh. Another fissure on the north side is known as *St. Cuthbert's Gut.* There are two lighthouses on the island, one on the south-west and the other on the north-west, the former very conspicuous from the land, with its long reach of white-washed wall, and its three houses for the accomodation of the lighthouse-keepers. The High Lighthouse, 43 feet high, was erected in 1766, and has a revolving light on the catoptric, or reflecting system, visible fifteen miles. The Low Lighthouse is an octagonal tower, 27 feet high, built in 1810, and shows a fixed light, visible twelve miles. A fog-horn, which can be heard twelve miles off, is sounded in thick weather, as soon as the keepers lose sight of the Pinnacles. The landing-place is on the eastern side, where the ground falls with a gentle slope to the water. Small and desolate as the island is, it yet possesses associations of the greatest historic interest. Here it was that Aidan sought rest from the active life at Lindisfarne and Bamburgh, and, as saintly legends tell, beat back, by his prayers, the flames from the royal city on to the host of the ruthless Penda. Not St. Aidan so much as St. Cuthbert is remembered in connection with this lonely isle, for hither came the austere Prior of Lindisfarne in 676 to carry on the conflict with his "invisible adversary" more remote from the eyes of men. On his arrival, he constructed for himself, not far from the landing-place, a rude cell, circular in form, consisting of two chambers—one for prayer and meditation, the other for domestic purposes. The outer walls, which were not much higher than a full-grown man, were of unhewn stones and turf, the former, in some instances, so large that, as Bede narrates, the saint had to have angelic aid to raise them to their places. The roof was of rough pieces of timber, thatched with bents. By excavating the solid rock, he sunk the floor of his cell below the surface, that he might behold nothing but the heavens above him, and so keep his eyes and thoughts from wandering. Nearer to the water's edge he built a larger house, or hospitium, for the accommodation of the pilgrims and monks who visited him. He raised crops of barley from the barren soil by means which were then regarded as miraculous; and he caused, it is said, two wells to flow where fresh water was never seen before. Here he continued for nine years to practise the misguided austerities which established his fame. A memorable scene (represented in one of W. B. Scott's frescoes at Wallington) was witnessed here in 685, when King Egfrid, the Archbishop of Canterbury, and the whole synod, which had been sitting at Twyford on the Aln, sailed over from the mainland, and on bended knees entreated the solitary anchorite to accept the bishopric of Hexham. He refused at first, but their prayers at length prevailed, and he consented to leave his sea-girt home. By mutual arrangement with Eata he obtained a more congenial diocese, thus fulfilling the prediction of his friend and master, Boisil, that he, "the poor shepherd boy, the monk of Melrose, the Prior of Lindisfarne, and the anchorite of Farne, would one day wear the mitre, and hold the pastoral staff as Bishop of Lindisfarne." After two years of active work he began to yearn once more for the quiet of his island retreat, and so threw aside his episcopal dignities, and returned to his hermit life. Two months of rest only were allowed to him, and then he was seized by a mortal illness. The account of his sufferings in these last days, as narrated by Bede, is very pathetic, and one can scarcely read it without a feeling of pity for the misguided recluse, left without friend or attendant for five days and nights to struggle with a painful malady, having nothing but a few onions to gnaw at during the whole time. He lingered for some days, and died after receiving the sacrament from the Abbot Herefrid. His body was conveyed to Lindisfarne, and buried on the right-hand side of the altar. The example of so famous a man as St. Cuthbert was followed by a number of monks, who kept up the reputation of the island for sanctity. The first was Ethelwald, a monk of Ripon, who lived here from 687 to 699. He was succeeded by Felgeld, for whom Bishop Eadfrid rebuilt the oratory. After his time Elwin took up his abode in the sea-girt oratory, and when, shortly afterwards, Bartholomew of Durham left his convent to become a hermit of Farne, there was for a while a great jealousy and misunderstanding between the two. By-and-by, Elwin retired, and left Bartholomew in sole possession. The saint was then joined by Thomas, the ex-Prior of Durham, who had resigned his charge in 1163, in consequence of the tyranny of Bishop Pudsey. The two quarrelled, but after a time lived together amicably till the death of Thomas. Bartholomew died about the year 1193, having lived forty-two years on the island. The last of the hermits was Thomas de Melsonby, Prior of Durham, who, in opposition to the wishes of Henry III., was elected Bishop of Durham by the monks, and, dreading the resentment of the king, took refuge here in 1244, where he spent the remaining two years of his life in austerities and devotion. About 1255 the convent of Durham established two monks, styled respectively the Magister, or Custos, and his Socius, on the island, and the Hermitage became known as the House of Farne. The Rolls of its receipts and expenses, preserved in the Treasury at Durham, are exceedingly interesting and instructive. A book recording the religious feelings of a monk located here about the year 1350 or 1360, is preserved in the Library at Durham, and is known as *Farne Meditations*. The monks were driven out of this House of Farne at the dissolution of monasteries, about the year 1538. They had become very lax in their habits during the fifteenth century, for two masters were dismissed in the first half of the century for their disorderly mode of life, while a third, John Kirke, in 1461 was severely rebuked for several offences, but especially for "haunting a womanse house over oft a for-noon."

There are no remains on the island earlier than the year 1370. On the site of the Hospitium of St. Cuthbert, near to the landing-place, stands an old building, described in Speed's Map as a "Fishe House."

On the brow of the hill is the little *Chapel of St. Cuthbert*, built in 1370, and restored by Archdeacon Thorpe in 1848. It consists of a nave only thirty-six feet long, with oak fittings. Service is usually performed in it twice a-year, in the summer months, when the congregation, composed of the lighthouse-men and visitors, generally numbers thirty persons. In the south wall may be seen one of the original windows. It is formed of two lights, with trefoil headings, under a pointed arch. To the same decorated Gothic style also belongs a small doorway at the south-east end. The Chapel contains a monument to the memory of Grace Darling, the heroine of the Islands. On the north and west are traces of old buildings in connection with the chapel. Some relics of the past are lying on the grass in front of the chapel—a large stone coffin, probably Master Sparowe's (d. 1429 or 1430), though commonly regarded as St. Cuthbert's, two smaller coffins, and a tomb-slab, having sculptured upon it a floriated cross and sword. Close by are the ruins of another small chapel, dedicated to St. Mary. A little towards the north, on the brink of St. Cuthbert's Gut, is *Prior Castell's Tower*, a square building, having the character of a Border pele, with thick walls, a vaulted under-storey, stone stairs, and a small, narrow, round-headed doorway. It was erected about 1500 for defence, and was used in the reign of Elizabeth as a fort. From the time of Charles the Second until the present lighthouse was built a coal-fire beacon was kindled every night on its summit, as a warning to mariners. Some of the rooms have been panelled with old carved oak from Durham, and fitted up as an occasional residence for the representatives of the Dean and Chapter of Durham. A curtain wall formerly ran from this tower to the two chapels, between which was a transverse building, with a doorway in the centre, leading to the enclosed courtyard.

The island, in 1855, supported twelve sheep, but at present no animals are kept on it. The abundant growth of the pretty white-flowered sea-campion (*Silene maritima*) is said to have caused the disappearance of several of the more nutritive grasses. Among the plants growing on the light and peaty soil, the rarest is, perhaps, the Danish scurvy grass (*Cochlearia Danica*). The sea-glaux, or saltwort (*Glaux maritima*), spreads along the sea-margins, while the small bugloss (*Lycopsis arvensis*), and other bright-petalled flowers, are welcome bits of colour in the midst of the wind-swept herbage.

Eastward of the Farne, and separated from it by a shallow channel, are the *Wedums*, or *Wide-opens*, and the *Noxes*. These form one island at low water, being connected by a long ridge of rolled stones, called the "Bridges." The Wedums were regarded with dread by the hermits as the haunt of the demons whom St. Cuthbert had banished from Farne, a former stronghold of theirs. According to Galfrid of Coldingham, the author of the *Life of St. Bartholomew*, "The brethren, when enjoying their rest after labour, have seen them on a sudden, clad in cowls, and riding upon goats, black in complexion, short in stature, their countenances most hideous, their heads long—the appearance of the whole group horrible. Like soldiers, they brandished in their hands lances, which they darted after the fashion of war. At first the sight of the cross was sufficient to repel their attacks, but the only protection in the end was a circumvallation of straws, signed with the cross, and fixed in the sands, around which the devils galloped for a while, and then retired, leaving the brethren to enjoy victory and repose." The only tenants of the Wedums at the present day are rabbits, rats, and sea-fowl—the malignant demons, and the spirits of shipwrecked sailors who were formerly buried here, having long since disappeared. *Cakile maritima* (the sea-rocket) is found on these islands. Nearly a mile north-westward from the Farne are two well-known rocks, the Swedman and Megstone, The Staples Sound, a channel one mile wide, separates the inner from the outer group of islands. Though deep enough for the largest ships, the passage is rendered dangerous by the presence of the Ox Scars, and especially of the Crumstone—a basaltic reef washed over by every high tide, chiefly interesting as the breeding-place of the Great Seal (*Phoca barbata*). It was in making for this channel that the *Pegasus* struck on the Goldstone. The outer group of the Farnes is famous for the number and variety of the sea-birds that breed there. Mr. Hancock mentions the names of fifteen species—viz., the ring-dotterel, oyster-catcher, lesser black-backed gull, herring gull, kittiwake gull, Sandwich tern, common tern, Arctic tern, roseate tern, cormorant, shag, eider duck, guillemot, puffin, and razor-bill.

The *Stapel Island* is of basaltic formation, fissured in all directions, and for the most part bare of all vegetation. Standing apart at a distance of twelve feet from the tall black cliffs, on the south, are three detached columns of basalt, about forty feet high, called the Pinnacles. Formerly there were four of them, but one was thrown down during a violent storm. Multitudes of chattering and screeching sea-birds, fluttering their wings and jerking their heads up and down with ceaseless movement, occupy the flat summits of these pillars, while multitudes more are wheeling gracefully through the air, or swimming in the sea. These are mostly guillemots (Welsh, *Çwilaug*, whirling about), and kittiwakes (so-called from their well-marked cry, "Kitty-week"), who deposit their eggs on narrow ledges and projections sometimes not more than a hand's-breadth in width. The reason they do not roll off is due to their shape—conical, with straight sides. The young birds seem instinctively to feel their perilous situation, where the least movement would precipitate them into the waves beneath, and it is observed that they seldom change their position or attitude in the nest till they become newly-fledged, and able to provide for their own safety. Thousands of eggs are gathered from May till the first of July, and sold, many being sent to London. To secure them is sometimes a task of no little danger, the bird-keepers having to pass from one to the other of the pillars by means of a narrow board laid across their summits. In this colony of birds will be noticed a singular-looking gull, with a short thick bill—the puffin, or sea-parrot, as it is sometimes called. North of Berwick it is known as "Tammie Norrie." A quaint rhyme alludes to its grotesque appearance—

"Tammie Norrie o' the Bass
Canna kiss a young lass."

The puffin generally breeds in the burrow of a rabbit, if it can find one, dispossessing the lawful owner by means of its powerful beak. Separated from the Stapel by a narrow channel, dry at low tides, is the *Fosseland*, or, as it is now called, the *Brownsman*, where the bird-keeper has his residence. Here is also an old tower, which formerly served as a lighthouse. Sheep were at one time kept on the island; but the grasses they fed on are disappearing before the unchecked growth of the sea-campion. The sea-fowl are here very numerous, especially the sea-pie, the puffin, and the sea-swallow, or common tern; the Sandwich tern and the roseate tern are less abundant. Among the plants on the Brownsman, the rarest are—*Chenopodium botryoides* (many-clustered goose-foot), *Cochlearia Danica* (Danish scurvy-grass), *Orchis latifolia* (marsh orchis), and a beautiful double variety of *Silene maritima*.

To the north are the *Wawmses*, remarkable as the chief breeding-place of the cormorant. Mr. Walter White's description of the feathered occupants of the *North Wawms* is exceedingly graphic:—"The eider-duck breeds here, contrasting in its quiet habit with the noisy tribes that haunt the islet, and retaining still the gentleness with which, as the monkish chroniclers tell us, it was first inspired by St. Cuthbert, who loved the eider-duck above all other sea-fowl, and trained it to build near his oratory. As for the gulls, the puffins, and sheldrakes, their cries, as they hovered above our heads, were well-nigh deafening; and it was curious to see how they rose at our approach, and settled down once more as we advanced, so that we had a flock of birds always behind and before us on the ground, and one attending us with wild shrieks in the air. Anon, we saw a range of black objects sitting, as it seemed, on thick cushions, and were aware of a noisome smell of fish. They were cormorants on their nests; and as we came nearer, one after another flapped its wings, rose suddenly, and flew circling over us, now and then sweeping down, on a sudden, close to our heads, and mingling their harsh croaking cry with the general din. The nests are conical mounds of sea-weed, about two feet in height, built up on the ledges of rock, and on these the birds sit a-straddle, as a man on horseback, the eggs being laid in a slight hollow on the top. . . . In some of the nests I saw portions of fish newly caught, and the base of every one was bestrewn with small fish of various kinds, for the most part in an offensive state of decomposition, which, combined with an overpowering smell of guano, renders long observation of domestic economy among the cormorants a nauseous kind of pleasure." The presence of these voracious birds in the Tyne seems to have been resented by the Municipal Authorities of Newcastle in the olden time, for in 1561 they paid fourpence for two cormorant heads, and in 1654 two shillings for three.

To the east of the Wawmes are two islands, the *Big and Little Harcar*, whereon are large colonies of birds—gulls and eider ducks, with a few of the oyster-catcher. It was on the west side of the Big Harcar that the *Forfarshire* was wrecked on the 5th September 1838, when forty-three persons perished. In the narrow gap into which the ill-fated vessel drifted, there yet lies the half of one of the ponderous working-beams at the bottom. To the north-east of this memorable spot is the *Longstone*, a bare and fissured reef not four feet above high water mark, and, consequently, during storms swept over by drifts of foam. With the exception of the Navestone, a sunken rock much dreaded by sailors, it is the most seaward of the islands. Conspicuous upon its eastern side is the tall, red lighthouse, eighty-five feet high, from the lantern of which there is a good prospect over the islands and the adjoining mainland. It was erected in 1826, and is furnished with a revolving light on the dioptric, or refracting system, visible eighteen miles. In this isolated tower, so beaten by the waves in great storms that the keepers and their families have to retreat to the upper chambers for shelter, Grace Darling lived for the greater portion of her brief life ; and from this rock she and her father went forth to the rescue of the nine surviving passengers of the *Forfarshire.* The story of this disaster, and the heroic deed of the Darlings, is as follows :—The *Forfarshire*, a steamer of three hundred tons burden, left Hull for Dundee on the evening of Wednesday, the 5th of September 1838, with forty-one passengers on board, and a crew of twenty-two men. When off Flamborough Head the fires were nearly extinguished, owing to a leak in the boilers, and the progress of the vessel was much retarded. In this state she passed through the Fairway, and struggled with the storm until off St. Abb's Head, when the engines became useless, and sails had to be hoisted to prevent her driving ashore. The vessel, however, soon became unmanageable, and drifted with the tide, through a dense fog, in a southerly direction, till she struck with tremendous force on the Harcar rocks at three o'clock on Friday morning. Eight of the crew and one passenger took possession of one of the boats, and succeeded almost miraculously in getting clear of the rocks through the only available outlet. They were picked up by a Montrose sloop about eight o'clock on Saturday morning, and carried into Shields. Scarcely was the boat out of sight before a mighty sea struck the vessel, separating it into two parts, and the stern, quarter-deck, and cabin, with the majority of the passengers and crew, were swept away through a powerful current called the Piper Gut, whilst the fore part of the vessel remained fast on the rock. The captain stuck to the wreck till washed overboard with his wife in his arms, and both were drowned. The survivors got on to a small rock, and their sufferings were very severe. Here, benumbed with cold, they were compelled to hold on with the utmost tenacity, for heavy seas broke over them at intervals, and the force of the gale was such as to strip the clothes off their limbs. The most painful incident of this terrible night is that of Mrs. Dawson holding, in the agonies of despair, her two children, a boy of eight and a girl of eleven, grasped in each hand long after the buffetings of the waves, which drove them to and fro, had deprived them of existence. About seven o'clock the next morning the miserable survivors were descried from the lighthouse huddling together on the rock, and Grace Darling and her father determined to make an effort to rescue them. The boat was launched with the assistance of Mrs. Darling, and the intrepid lighthouse-keeper and his daughter, who knew well how to handle an oar, rowed through the furious sea towards the shattered wreck.

"And the nine who clung despairing
All that wild and dreadful night,
Heard a cry of help come ringing
Through the air with morning light.
Little marvel that the maiden
Seemed to them an angel bright."—R. S. WATSON.

The scene of the disaster was reached at length, and five of the sufferers were relieved from their uncomfortable position. Darling and two of the rescued men returned in the coble, and succeeded in bringing the other four to the Longstone. The old man, some years afterwards, told Mr. Walter White that "he did not know how they should have got the boat back to the lighthouse against the tide, had not some of the men whom they saved been able to row." Attempts have been made, not only by the ill-natured fisher-folk, but recently by writers in the London press, to detract from the fame of Grace Darling, by showing that the brave deed she performed was not attended with so much peril as is generally supposed; but anyone standing on this foam-swept island, and witnessing the sea during a storm, will certainly not underrate the courage of the Darlings, but rather repeat the fine apostrophe with which Wordsworth concludes his somewhat laboured and inadequate poem :—

"Shout, ye waves!
Pipe a glad song of triumph, ye fierce winds!
Ye screaming sea-mews in the concert join!
And would that some immortal voice, a voice
Fitly attuned to all that gratitude
Breathes out from flock or couch, through pallid lips
Of the survivors, to the clouds might bear—
(Blended with praise of that parental love,
Beneath whose watchful eye the maiden grew
Pious and pure, modest and yet so brave,
Though young, so wise, though meek, so resolute)
Might carry to the clouds and to the stars,
Yea, to celestial choirs, Grace Darling's name."

The survivors from the wreck—five of the crew and four passengers—were kindly entertained and tended by their preservers during the three days and nights they were storm-stayed on the Longstone. George and William Darling, with three other young men, put off from North Sunderland, and reached the wreck at ten o'clock. Such, however, was the fury of the gale, that they could not return, and had to stop in the old barracks on the Longstone two days and nights with scant provisions, no beds, and no change of clothes. When the story of the wreck and the subsequent rescue became known, a thrill of enthusiasm passed through the length and breadth of the land, and Grace Darling's praise was on all lips. In the full blaze of popular admiration she displayed as much good sense and firmness as she did heroism, and maintained the same reserve and simplicity which had always characterised her. Presents were showered upon her by the great and powerful, and public subscriptions to the amount of £700 raised for her. She was offered £20 a-night to appear at the Adelphi, in a scene of the shipwreck, merely to sit in a boat, and had various offers of marriage, but she steadily declined to leave her island-home. William Howitt, who visited her at the Longstone, was much impressed with her unassuming demeanour. "Grace Darling," he says, "as perfect a realisation of Jeanie Deans, in an English form, as it is possible for a woman to be. She is not like any of the portraits of her. She is a little, simple, modest young woman, I should say of five or six and twenty. She is neither tall nor handsome, but she has the most gentle, quiet, amiable look, and the sweetest smile that I ever saw in a person of her station and appearance. You see that she is a thoroughly good creature, and that under the modest exterior lies a spirit capable of the most exalted devotion."

The life of the heroine was destined to be cut short prematurely. Only two years after the event which made her so famous, symptoms of consumption began to show themselves, and she was compelled to quit the Farnes for the mainland. Change of air and scenery at Wooler and Alnwick failed to check the fatal disease, and she died at Bamburgh on the 28th of October 1842, in the twenty-sixth year of her age. The character of William Darling, the father of the heroine, and partner with her in the deed of mercy, is equally worthy of admiration. In his log-book, describing the wreck of the *Forfarshire*, appears this simple statement—"Nine persons held on by the wreck, and were rescued by the Darlings." He died in May 1865 at Bamburgh. A brother of Grace Darling is still living. Many artists have attempted to represent the heroic deed of the lighthouse-keeper's daughter with more or less exaggeration and inaccuracy. The most faithful record of this incident on canvas is a picture by Mr. Robert Watson, the son of a lighthouse-keeper on the Farnes, who visited the Longstone a short time after the rescue, and made drawings of the coble, of Grace Darling, and her father and mother, and of what remained of the wreck. "Carmichael," says a writer in the Newcastle press, "saw Mr. Watson's picture in the studio, and immediately went and made what became a more famous painting of the same subject. Carmichael, however, made the sea a little too terrifying."

Two miles south-west of the Longstone is the *Goldstone*, the rock on which the *Pegasus*, a Hull steamer, was wrecked on July 20th, 1843. Six persons only were picked up by the *Martello*, floating about on pieces of timber, much exhausted. Forty-nine were drowned. From some cause not ascertained the steamer was quite out of her track, and there seems no excuse for the disaster, as the evening was calm and the sea smooth.

# WOOLER SECTION.

## WOOLER.

THE Wooler district has recently been rendered easy of access by the opening out of the line between Alnwick and Cornhill. It is a pastoral and agricultural region, comprising the most famous of Northumbrian hills—the Cheviots—and most of the Northumbrian battle-fields—Flodden, Piperden, Homildon Hill, Hedgeley Moor, Millfield, and Geteringe. The remains of the ancient British settlements and camps are very numerous and perfect, while the mysterious rock sculpturings at Rowting Lynn, Doddington, and Old Bewick give to this neighbourhood a unique interest in the eyes of antiquaries. The memorials of mediæval times are somewhat scanty, but this may be accounted for by the unsettled state of the Borders till a very late period. Ford, Chillingham, and Coupland castles have been modernised, but Etal and Hebburn are still eloquent of the past. Few streams are dearer to the angler's heart than the Till, the Glen, the Colledge, and the Breamish, and few localities more favoured by naturalists than the valleys through which they run. The artist will find around the Cheviots many bits of primitive Northumbria to engage his pencil, and the lover of poetry, scenes of romantic beauty, immortalised by the genius of the old ballad-writers, and the greater minstrel who sleeps at Dryburgh.

WOOLER, the capital of this hilly district, is a quiet and small rural town, with little of the picturesque about it, delightfully situated on a slope above the Wooler water. The houses are plain and unattractive, few possessing gardens in front. The principal streets converge towards a market-place. A drinking fountain, eighteen feet high, erected in 1879 to the memory of William Wightman, serves as a market-cross. Few events of any importance are associated with Wooler, which, in early feudal times, belonged to the family of Muschampe. The name has apparently undergone several changes, for it is written in the *Testa de Neville*, Willove. On Thursday, the 26th October 1715, the Northumbrian Jacobites, under General Forster and the Earl of Derwentwater, strengthened by a party of Scots under Viscount Kenmure, arrived in Wooler. "Here," says Mr. Patten, "they rested all Friday, where I, with some men which I had inlisted, joyned them, and was kindly entertained by the chiefs. Here Mr. Errington brought them an account of the Highlanders being also coming to join them, and that they were advanced to Dunse. On this news they marched for Kelso." The king's forces, under General Carpenter, also occupied Wooler on the 27th of the month. The town was almost destroyed by fire in 1722, and, again, in 1862. Wooler, like Rothbury, was much visited by invalids during the last century for the "goat's whey cure." The pure air and water from the Cheviots, and the many attractions of the neighbourhood, still render the town a favourite resort of persons in delicate health. In few districts is the death-rate so low as in Glendale. The principal events which break the monotony of life in Wooler are the weekly markets held on Thursdays; the fairs for cattle on the first and third Thursdays in January and February, and on the third Monday in May (Whitsun Bank Fair), for sheep, cattle, and horses; and the hirings for servants on the 4th of May and the 17th of October. On this latter day there is also a fair for sheep, cattle, and horses. An occasion of some interest to the town is the celebration of the Cheviot games in August. The *Castle*, or *Tower* of Wooler stood on a circular mound above the river, near the church, and was evidently built at an early period, for in 1254, in an inquisition taken on the death of Isabella de Ford (daughter of the last of the Muschampes), it is described as "a certain waste-fortress, not of any value." Little is known of the part it played in the history of the Borders. Its strategical importance was recognised by Sir Robert Bowes in his survey of 1542, who very strongly urged its repair. It does not seem as if the recommendations of Sir Robert Bowes were acted upon, for the castle remains in ruins. The tradition that Oliver Cromwell destroyed the castle on his way into Scotland in 1650 has no foundation. The only remains of the tower are several huge fragments of masonry, overthrown, apparently, by the force of gunpowder. Four shattered masses lie prostrate on the ground; two on the top of the hill, where the foundations are still traceable, a third half-way down the declivity, and a fourth at the bottom, whither it has rolled from its exalted position. The walls have been 6 feet to 8 feet thick. An ancient-looking building in Cheviot Street, known as the *Old Workhouse*, has evidently been one of the Border bastle-houses.

The *Parish Church of St. Mary*, at the north-east of the Market Place, is a plain stone edifice of no architectural interest, erected in 1765, near the site of the old thatched one, which was destroyed by fire in 1722. It has a tower, but neither chancel, aisles, nor porch.

The *Catholic Church of St. Ninian*, at the western extremity of West Street, contains a fine stained-glass window, representing in its four compartments several of the Northumbrian saints. The Presbyterian body have three places of worship in the town.

Wooler is nine miles west of Belford, the nearest station on the main line. There is good accommodation for visitors at the Tankerville Arms, better known as Wooler Cottage, the Black Bull Hotel, and the Red Lion Hotel. Wooler is the birthplace of the Brothers Dalziel, the celebrated engravers on wood. George was born in 1815; Edward, in 1817; and John, in 1822.

In the immediate neighbourhood of Wooler are several objects of antiquarian interest. 1st. *The Whetting Stone*. This is a block of sandstone, whereon the inhabitants of Wooler are said to have sharpened their weapons in the time of war. It forms part of a fence-wall between the upper and lower turnpikes, and separates the farms of Wooler Cottage and Burn House. 2nd. *The Wishing or Pin Well*. This may be reached by skirting, on the east, the hill called Horsdean, on which the statute fairs for sheep and cattle are annually held, and proceeding along the first lane branching off the road to the right, towards Earle, for a quarter of a mile, when, turning to the right through a gate, and crossing a field, the well will soon be discovered by following up the clear bright rill produced by the overflowing water. It lies, enclosed by a few smooth stones piled together, at the base of a long narrow ridge protruded between Kenterdale and Horsdean hills, and separated from them by deep rocky ravines. Formerly on May-day a number of the inhabitants of Wooler, both young and old, marched in a formal procession to the well, dropping in the crooked pin and wishing their wish, quite unconscious of the fact that this custom was a relic of the well-worship of Pagan times. 3rd. *The King's Chair*, a mass of porphyry exposed in the cliff overlooking the Pin Well. It formerly bore a rude resemblance to a seat, and obtained its name from the tradition that a king once sat upon it watching through an opening in the hills a battle fought on the lower grounds to the south. 4th. *Kettles Camp*, sometimes called Maiden Castle, or Greenside. This remarkable entrenchment is just behind the King's Chair, occupying the whole summit of the hill, and enclosing an area of from three to four acres. It is somewhat quadrangular in form, being defended by four rampiers on the north side. Roman coins and a broken sword were found here some years ago. The place is called the Kettles from the pot-like cavities in the surrounding ravine. In these hollows are old folds and hut-circles of the ancient Britons. A footpath running northward past the camp to a cottage called the Wadhouse leads into Wooler by Ramsay's Lane. 5th. *Cup and Saucer Camp*. This hill-fortress lies a little to the south-west of Humbleton Mill, and half-a-mile north-west of the Kettles. It is but half-a-mile from Wooler Market Place, and may be reached by way of Ramsay's Lane. It crowns the summit of a conical-shaped hill which rises abruptly about 300 feet above the level of a deep ravine, and resembles not a little the mote hills of other parts of the country. Surrounded by a rampier of stone and earth, which is yet in some parts three feet high, the camp must have been a very strong one. A hollow in the centre of the area is called the "cup," intended probably for the chief of the clan, while the rest of the camp—the "saucer"—was occupied by the common people. A pretty little waterfall, called the Linns, is formed by the Humbleton Burn, just above the mill. Near the turnpike road at Wooler Cottage the beach and bank of the ancient lake once covering Millfield Plain are very conspicuous. It is about forty feet high.

# WOOLER TO LANGLEEFORD AND CHEVIOT.

**Earle, 1¼ miles; Middleton Hall, 2 miles; Langleeford, 5 miles; Cheviot Cairns, 8 miles.**

THERE are three routes to the top of Cheviot from Wooler. That by way of Langleeford is the most popular, the distance being eight miles—viz., five miles to the farm-house, and three miles thence to the summit. Leaving Wooler by Cheviot Street, and proceeding along the road for three-quarters of a mile, the tourist will take the first turn to the right, and follow a lane for half-a-mile to the village of

EARLE, formerly known as "Yardhill," or "Yerdhill," "Eardle," etc.—a name still traceable in the local pronunciation, "Yer-ill." Two or three farm-houses, the mansion of the late Charles Selby, surrounded by trees, and several labourers' cottages, are grouped picturesquely beneath a bracken-covered hill. Traces of ancient husbandry are numerous in the vicinity of Earle. Nearly all the top and middle face of the hill, forming the cover called Earle Whin, except the declivity of Earle Dene, have been cultivated on the ridge and balk system. Several hut-circles and old walls have been discovered here. From Earle a footpath passes over a slight hill to Skirl-naked, three-quarters of a mile distant. A short detour may be made by way of *Middleton Hall*, the seat of G. P. Hughes, Esq., pleasantly situated amid gardens and plantations on the rising ground above the Wooler Water. When Sir Robert Bowes made his survey in 1542, "the towneshippe of Mydleton Hall" had in it "two stone houses or castells, the one of th' inheritance of Robert Rotherforde, and th' other of John Rotherforde." These buildings have since disappeared. One was probably the old hall, which stood at the bottom of the present pleasure-ground, where there are two spreading sycamores. The foundations of the other are to be seen in the adjacent field. The hall formed part of the splendid possessions of the Derwentwater family, and was confiscated on the rebellion of the last earl, and given to the Greenwich Hospital. In the garden there is preserved a clipped and pyramidal-shaped beech, overgrown and encircled by the sweet-scented honeysuckle plant and a white rose-bush. The three were planted by two ladies of the Derwentwater family, who resided in the hall after the ruin of its former owners—the Radcliffes. In the hall are preserved the antlers and head of a large specimen of the *Cervus elaphas*—one of the most perfect specimens in Great Britain—discovered while draining Cresswell Bog, near Middleton. This bog was about four acres in extent, and marked the site of a small lake which was formed in the Boulder Clay period. In the marl, deposited to a depth of eight feet, have been found skeletons of the red deer, teeth of the boar, and great numbers of fresh-water shells of species still living in the district. A bed of peat above the marl, two to four feet in thickness, contained, embedded in it, the prostrate trees of hazel and birch, and also hazel nuts.

From the ascent above Middleton Hall the tourist will gain his first view of Cheviot and Hedgehope—"recumbent guardians of the great lone moorland." Below is the moorland glen—one of the most charming on the Borders—which has to be followed to Langleeford. Through it runs a splashing streamlet, fringed with patches of gorse and belts of natural wood—birch, oak, alder, thorn, and mountain ash. This is the Wooler Water, or, to use the older name, Caldgate Burn. Above the woods on each side rise heathery hills, steep and rugged, with great rocks standing out here and there as abrupt as ruined castles. From the shepherd's house called "Skirl-naked" the track descends the slope of "Armer Brae" to the point where the Care Burn joins the Wooler Water. On the left is the "Slack," where may be seen a miniature representation, in its broken tiers of pillared rocks, of the chasm behind Cheviot, known as the "Henhole." The opposite hill, with its steeps of blue glitters, is Hartheugh. On the south-east side are the ruins of a shepherd's cottage called Switcher-down, once, it is said, the residence of a witch. From the foot-bridge the track runs in a south-westerly direction by the side of the burn. On the right is Snear Hill (sneer: snifter), its highest peak being appropriately named Cold Law. On the eastern end of the hill may be seen traces of the twisted ridges, balks, huts, tombs, folds, etc., of the ancient Britons. One of their dividing fences, called by the shepherds "the awd dike," crosses the point of the Snear nearest the Care Burn, and may be followed up the steep heathery acclivity of Brand's Hill. Near the bottom of the glen are a few juniper bushes. The white bloom of the hawthorn, which grows very abundantly on the dry gravelly soil of the vale, forms a pleasing contrast with the waste around. Above the cottage of Langlee is a camp with several hut-circles. A cluster of cup-shaped cavities in the bank farther on appear to have been used as places of concealment by the smugglers of modern times. Extending circuitously round a high bank adjoining the Pebble, or Hawsden Burn, are the ruins of a Celtic town, the boundary wall of which skirts the present main road. "The huts," says Mr. Hardy, "are closely clustered and in good preservation, some of them remaining still, as the natives would leave them when unroofed, with their causewayed floors exposed, and they require no excavation to bring their form to light. I thought I could trace in some a raised platform inside round the walls. A British road passes slant through amongst them, and they ascend well up the hill-face. They are copiously supplied with springs." The Diamond Burn receives its name from the quartz-crystals found along its course. Proceeding onward up the glen, a conspicuous crag of blue porphyry will be observed on the ridge to the left. This is named the Housy Crag, or House of Crag. On the south side of it are two boulders (one of them partially suspended over the cliff), which belong to the well-marked porphyry of Hedgehope, and are supposed to have been deposited in their present position either by an iceberg or a glacier during the remote ice-age. Further evidence of glacial action is found in the terminal moraines near the outlet of the Rae (or Roe) Burn to the south-west. The farmstead of Langleeford, which lies sheltered behind a small plantation of pines, is a convenient resting-place for tourists ascending both Hedgehope and Cheviot. Langleeford is mentioned in 1552 in connection with the Border night-watches. It is an attractive picture amid the moorland wastes, and one who has been wandering for some time on the hills and suddenly drops upon it will agree with the lines—

> "Hedgehope and Cheviot are pleasant bits of ground,
> But such a place as Langleeford is rarely to be found."

A traditional interest attaches to Langleeford as the place where Sir Walter Scott made a short stay during the autumn of 1791, embuing his mind with the legends, history, and scenery of the neighbourhood. "Behold a letter from the mountains," he writes to his friend, William Clerk, of Edinburgh, "for I am very snugly settled here, in a farmer's house about six miles from Wooler, in the very centre of the Cheviot Hills, in one of the wildest and most romantic situations which your imagination, fertile upon the subject of cottages, ever suggested. And what the deuce are you about there? methinks I hear you say. Why, sir, of all things in the world—drinking goat's-whey—not that I stand in the least need of it, but my uncle having a slight cold, and being a little tired of home, asked me last Sunday evening if I would like to go with him to Wooler, and I answering in the affirmative, next morning's sun beheld us on our journey, through a pass in the Cheviots, upon the backs of two special nags, and man Thomas behind with a portmanteau, and two fishing-rods fastened across his back, much in the style of St. Andrew's cross. Upon reaching Wooler we found the accommodation so bad that we were forced to use some interest to get lodgings here, where we are most delightfully appointed indeed. To add to my satisfaction, we are amidst places renowned by the feats of former days; each hill is crowned with a tower, or camp, or cairn, and in no situation can you be near more fields of battle: Flodden, Otterburn, Chevy Chase, Ford Castle, Chillingham Castle, Copland Castle, and many another scene of blood are within the compass of a forenoon's ride. Out of brooks with which these hills are intersected, we pull trouts of half a yard in length, as fast as we did the perches from the pond at Pennycuik, and we are in the very country of muirfowl. . . . My uncle drinks the whey here, as I do ever since I understood it was brought to his bedside every morning at six by a very pretty dairymaid. So much for my residence; all the day we shoot, fish, walk, and ride; dine and sup upon fish struggling from the stream, and the most delicious heath-fed mutton, barn-door fowls, poys (pies), milk-cheese, etc., all in perfection; and so much simplicity resides among these hills, that a pen, which could write at least, was not to be found about the house, though belonging to a considerable farmer, till I shot the crow with whose quill I wrote this epistle."

Two miles further up the valley is *Harthope Linn*, a succession of pretty waterfalls overhung with native wild wood and fringed with ferns.

The Cheviot range of hills is composed of several varieties of porphyry and syenite, which have been upheaved in a cool and consolidated state through the stratified rocks in two different periods—viz., that succeeding the Cambro-Silurian era, and that succeeding the Tuedian era. The hills, which are chiefly conical in form and covered with grass, extend from Branxton on the north to Ridlees Hill on the south, about twenty-two miles; and from Branton on the east to Bloodylaws on the west, nearly twenty-one miles; the area in Northumberland being about two hundred, and in Roxburghshire about one hundred square miles. The steep slopes and uplands of these hills are tenanted by hardy flocks of "Cheviot" sheep, which retain much of their wild nature, and depend wholly on natural instinct in seeking their daily food. "The flock or *hirsel* on a large farm forms itself into three, four, or more divisions called *cuts*, each keeping to its own range of pasture, and feeding gradually upwards to its resting-place for the night near the top. If a stranger or other unusual object interrupts the even tenour of their way, the first to perceive the intruder stamps with its foot and utters a sort of hiss, on which the whole *cut* takes the alarm and runs off, but always keeping upwards."—*Sir Walter Elliot.*

Cheviot itself is a broad-backed mountain with a flat top, rising to a height of 2676 feet above the sea-level. Snow generally lies upon it during half the year, and in severe winters has been known to remain in the highest ravines from September to July. The sides are covered with bracken, heather, and grass; the summit with peat. The name Cheviot, according to Mr. Ralph Carr, is derived from two Celtic words —*Chefnau*, ridges; and *od*, snow—and hence is equivalent to snow-fells. The distance from Langleeford to the top is about three miles. The ascent, though not steep, is toilsome. For a certain distance it is facilitated by the track made by the sledge, a very rude vehicle used in conveying peat from the heights for the shepherds' stock of winter fuel. Climbing upward over a tract of ordinary moorland, and leaving the gaunt cone of Hedgehope on the left, the flat summit of the mountain presently comes in view, still far above. The heather grows less and less luxuriantly towards the summit, the vegetation for the last few hundred feet being so stunted as to resemble a great soft mossy carpet. Strewn broadcast on it lie patches of the dark grey rocks—porphyry, dolerite, and granite. The summit is a desolate-looking tract of treacherous moss-hags and oozy peat-flats, traversed by deep sykes and interspersed with black stagnant pools. Among the coarse wiry bents and bog-mosses grow several mountain plants—the cloud-berry or mountain bramble (*Rubus chamæmorus*), whose scarlet berries, becoming yellow when they ripen, are scattered over the waste like gems ; the red whortle-berry or cow-berry (*Vaccinium vitis idæa*), the crow-berry (*Empetrum nigrum*), the bilberry (*Vaccinium myrtillus*), cotton grass (*Eriophorum angustifolium*), cow-wheat (*Melampyrum montanum*), rigid carex (*Carex rigida*), and three species of club-moss. The highest points are marked by heaps of stone called the eastern and western cairns. An hour and a quarter will suffice to reach the former from Langleeford. The modern tourist laughs at the fears experienced by Daniel Defoe when ascending the mountain in 1728. He was accompanied by a guide and "five or six country boys and young fellows." "As we mounted higher," he writes, "we found the hill steeper than at first, also our horses began to complain, and draw their haunches up heavily, so we went very softly. However, we mov'd still, and went on till the height began to look really frightful, for I must own, I wished myself down again. . . . We were the more uneasy about mounting higher, because we all had a notion that when we came to the top we should be just as upon a pinnacle, that the hill narrowed to a point, and we should have only room enough to stand, with a precipice every way round us ; and with these apprehensions we all sat down upon the ground and said we would go no further. When, however, our guide perceived our mistake, he assured us there was room enough on the top of the hill to run a race if we thought fit, and we need not fear anything of being blown off the precipice as we had suggested ; so, he encouraging us, we went on and reach't the top of the hill in about half-an-hour more."—*A Tour through Great Britain.* The view from the summit on a bright clear day is magnificent, embracing the whole sea-board of Northumberland and the hilly country between the Tweed and Coquet.

There are two great rents or chasms in the flanks of Cheviot—the Bazzle on the north and the Henhole on the west. They are famous hunting-grounds for the botanist, who will find in their rocky recesses or in their vicinity the star saxifrage (*Saxifraga stellaris*), the cut-leaved or mossy saxifrage (*Saxifraga hypnoides*), Alpine epilobe (*Epilobium Alpinum*), chickweed epilobe (*Epilobium alsinifolium*), dwarf cornel (*Cornus suecica*), green spleenwort (*Asplenium viride*), teeth fern (*Cystopteris dentata*), curled or parsley fern (*Allosorus crispus*), floating sweet grass or Balfour's pea (*Poa Balfourii*), serrated winter green (*Pyrola secunda*), black willow (*Salix nigricans*).

*Henhole*, especially, is a wild and picturesque chasm, several of the great crags on each side rising precipitously to a height of 250 feet, or thereabouts. Long trains of glitters or loose stones give a rugged character to the steep slopes. From the summit of Cheviot a peaty burn splashes down from ledge to ledge for nearly 1500 feet, forming pretty waterfalls, fringed with ferns and mosses, and issuing from the dreadful gorge as the Coledge Burn. This cleft is, according to tradition, one of the haunts of the Northumbrian fairies. In the days of old, it is said, a party of hunters, when chasing a roe upon Cheviot, were allured into the Hen Hole by the sweetest music they had ever heard, and could never again find their way out. The final scene of a ballad in Fred Sheldon's *Minstrelsy of the English Border*, "Black Adam of Cheviot," is laid in this wild ravine. The poem narrates how the hero—a notorious freebooter called the "Rider of Cheviot"—burst in upon a wedding-party at Wooperton, when the bridegroom was away to fetch the priest, stripped the jewels from the women, then ravished and stabbed the bride. Wight Fletcher, the bridegroom, returning, is just in time to hear "Black Adam's laugh o' scorn." Stripping off the bride's kerchief, all stained with blood, he vows to be revenged on the cruel reiver, and then a terrible chase begins. Black Adam, however, reaches the chasm, and, by a desperate leap of seven yards or more, succeeds in gaining his lair—a cave in the side of a steep cliff. Then

"He held a stane in baith his hondes,
  And swore so save his sowl,
If Fletcher lap, to gar his bodie
  Into the stream to roll.

'Ise try your brag, ye mean caytiff,'
  Quo' Fletcher, and lap the sheugh;
Black Adam wi' ane heavy pash,
  Bluid frae his forehead drew.

The blow it struck him off his feet,
  Or ere he gained the bank;
He gave Black Adam a ghastly paik,
  And back Wight Fletcher sank.

But as he slippit oure the edge,
  He clutched at his enemie,
And hung oure yonder fearful steep,
  Wi' ae grip o' Adam's knee.

'Unloose thy gripe, thou Wight Fletcher,
  And I will spare thy life;'
The youth smiled grimly on his foe,
  A warsling in the strife.

They tottered on the varra brink
  O' that precipice so high;
Black Adam clung unto a rock,
  For he feared sic death to die.

And now their scowling een were close,
  And they fand each ither's breath;
And every struggle Black Adam gave
  Was nearer till his death.

The rock it slippit frae Adam's clutch,
  As he wrenchit bane and limb;
Fingers o' iron and nerves o' steel
  Wight Fletcher kept on him.

Loud and lang Black Adam shrieked,
But naething Fletcher said;
And there was neither twig or branch
Upon their rocky bed.

Slowly right owre then they fell,
For Fletcher his hold did keep;
A minute and their twa bodies
Went crashing doune the steep.

There was a splash as the waters flew
Half up the rugged dell;
The torrent rushed and the water gushed,
But a' was dethely still."

The peregrine falcon is frequently seen among these pinnacled crags. In a bank of clay near Henhole were found some massive mountings of cast bronze harness and horse-trappings of a late Celtic period. The rocky peak above the chasm is crowned by Auchhope Cairn, which marks the boundary between England and Scotland. Half-a-mile to the south-east of the cairn, at a height of 2300 feet above the sea-level, is the *Hanging Stone*—a rock which derives its name from the circumstance of a packman being strangled by his pack slipping over the edge and tightening the strap round his neck. The great *Forest of Cheviot*, which formerly covered the lower slopes of the hill, was chiefly on the side fronting Scotland, and the remains of it may be seen in the oaks and birches along the Colledge Valley. "The Scottes," we are told in the "Survey of Waste Lands, 1542," "as well by nighte time secretly, as upon the daie tyme with more force, do come into the said forrest of Chevyott dyverse tymes and steale and carry awaie much of the saide wood, which ys to them a great proffyte for the mayntenance of their houses and buyldinges, and small redresse can be had by the lawes and customes of the marches." From the Hen Hole the tourist may complete a very delightful, though perhaps a long, round by following the Colledge to Kirknewton, and continuing by way of Akeld and Humbleton to Wooler. A shorter route would be to follow, first, the Colledge to Fleehope, and then the Lambden Burn to Goldscleugh, proceeding thence by way of Broadsthruther and Rea's Stead to Wooler. Some tourists may prefer to go by this route to Cheviot, making the ascent from Goldscleugh. They leave Wooler by Ramsay's Lane, and follow a pathway running to the west of the Kettle's Hill and Earle Whin Cove to the farm-house of Rea's Stead. They then continue by a track known as Hell-path, with Hart-heugh on one side and Watch Law on the other, to Broadstruther, and thence to Goldscleugh. There is a third route, by way of Kirknewton and Heathpool, along the Colledge Burn to Fleehope, and up the Lambden Burn to the Bazzle, by the east side of which the ascent is easily made.

# WOOLER TO HEDGEHOPE.

**Langleeford, 5 miles ; Hedgehope, 6 miles ; Threestone Burn Antiquities, 6½ miles.**

THE tourist will proceed to Langleeford farm-house, as directed above, and ascend the hill from this favourable point. The ground at first is very spongy and treacherous, and great care has to be used to avoid the patches of bright green moss. Scattered over the face of the hill are several trees and whin bushes. A curious natural phenomenon was witnessed by Mr. Hardy, one autumn, in ascending Hedgehope, while the sun was shining in the west and some light mists were creeping across the hollow, almost obscuring the Housy Crag. Turning round, he perceived a gigantic shadow of himself projected across the interval, with a halo encircling the head. The hill is conical in shape, so that the tourist, from the cairn at the summit, 2348 feet above the sea-level, has a better view all round this part of the county than he could have from the loftier but flat-topped Cheviot. The position of the hill at the "head of the small vales"—Linhope, Harthope, and Calderhope—is supposed to have suggested to the Saxon settlers the name "Head-gehofa," or "Heafod-gehopa." Between Hedgehope and the adjoining hill of Great Standrop there is a syke, near which a Highlandman, named "Black Rory," had his whiskey-still, over fifty years ago. A green spot near it is called "Rory's Gair"—*gair* being a small strip of green ground among heather or ferns. The tourist who likes a stiff walk may proceed from Hedgehope southward, along the sheep-tracks between Great Standrop and Dunmoor Hill, and follow the Dunmoor Burn to its junction with the Linhope Burn, where there is one of the largest waterfalls in the district—*Linhope Spout*. He may then continue along the side of the ravine to the interesting Celtic town of Greaves Ash and the valley of the Breamish, returning by way of Ingram, Branton, and Percy's Cross to Wooler. A mile and a half north-east by east of Hedgehope Cairn are the remains of a Druidical Circle, standing on flat peaty ground, to the north of Threestone Burn, and about 400 yards west of a farm-house. It may be visited by way of the Long Crag from Langleeford, from which it lies a mile and a half to the south-east. Situated in the midst of wild moorland hills, this temple of the ancient Britons inhabiting the valley of the Breamish possesses a singular interest to the antiquarian tourist as a memorial of a "creed outworn." It is elliptical in shape, having a circumference of 340 feet, and a diameter of 112 feet from east to west, and 96 feet from north to south. The monoliths are of the porphyry rock of the district, and for many years were eleven in number. A local tradition that there was a twelfth somewhere, with a hoard of gold underneath it, led a tenant of a neighbouring farm to dig round the circle, when he discovered two others, thus making the total number thirteen—an unlucky number, which accounts for him finding no treasure. The stones vary in size from 21 inches to 5 feet 5 inches in height. The three largest are lying prostrate on the ground. The bulkiest is 3 feet 9 inches in height, and 10 feet in girth, weighing, it is calculated, about two tons. Five of the stones still maintain their upright position. A flint knife was discovered in the circle, and may have been used in the sacrificial rites. The tourist will find it desirable, in order to complete the round, to follow the burn to Ilderton, and proceed by the road to Wooler. On Dunmoor Hill are the grand ice-rounded Cunion Crags, or Chieftain Rocks, as they were called by the ancient Britons. It is difficult to imagine that 2000 years ago these hills were thickly-populated, as they must have been, to judge by the numerous memorials of our primitive ancestors and the place-names of the district, and that across these moors ranged the red deer and other pre-historic animals, with the wild cattle whose descendants are to be seen in Chillingham Park. The solitude is complete, and the aspect of the landscape wild and cheerless. Were it not for the bold, black-faced moorland sheep, these wastes would look desolate indeed. The very birds that make their homes here seem to have caught in their songs something of the melancholy of the scene.

> "How wild the lonely moorland music floats
> When clamorous curlews scream with long-drawn notes,
> Or, faint and piteous, wailing plovers pipe,
> Or, loud and louder still, the soaring snipe;
> And here the lonely lapwing hoops along,
> That, piercing, shrieks her still-repeated song,
> Flaps her blue wing, displays her pointed crest,
> And cow'ring lures the peasant from her nest."

# WOOLER TO HEDGELEY MOOR.

Wooler Haugh Head, 1½ miles; Lilburn Tower, 3 miles; Ilderton, 4½ miles; Roddam Hall, 6 miles; Wooperton, 6 miles; Percy's Cross, 7 miles.

CROSSING the stone bridge over the Wooler Water, the road runs by the east side of the stream to *Wooler Haugh Head*, a mile and a half from the town. Here the English army lay encamped for two days before the battle of Flodden, and from this place Surrey sent a letter, dated 7th September 1513, to the Scottish King, upbraiding him with breaking his promise to meet the English forces on a certain day (September 9th), and offering to give him battle on Millfield Plain next day. A little to the west, on the other side of the stream, is *Cresswell Bog*, where several skeletons of red deer were found about 1830. A mile and a half further south, on slightly rising ground, is *Lilburn Tower*, the seat of Edward John Collingwood, Esq., an elegant mansion in the Tudor style of architecture, built in 1829 from the designs of John Dobson. Beneath it, through a pretty dene, runs the Lil (or little) Burn, which gives its name to the place. The grounds are very picturesque, and several of the trees surrounding the house have attained a great height. A short distance to the south-west of the house are the ruins of the old Border tower of the Lilburns, who were seated here during the reign of Edward II. From this family was descended Colonel John Lilburn, familiarly called "Free-born Jack," who distinguished himself during the reign of Charles I. and the Commonwealth by his disinterested efforts in the cause of popular liberty, subscribing himself on one occasion as "An honest and true-bred free Englishman, that never in his life feared a tyrant, or loved an oppressor." The estate came into the hands of the Collingwoods in 1793, and is now their principal seat. The old crest of the family being a stag under a tree, is an emblem of the name. Anciently all beasts and birds were familiarly called by some Christian name, as, for instance, Robin Redbreast, Tom-tit, etc. In this way the stag was called *Colin*, and a tree represented *wood*. Connected with the crest is an old prophecy, which runs—

"The Collingwoods have borne the name
Since in the bush the buck was ta'en;
But when the bush shall hold the buck,
Then welcome faith, and farewell luck."

To the east of the pele, and nearer the mansion, are the remains of an old chapel (a dependant on Eglingham), in which, notwithstanding its ruinous condition, several members of the Collingwood family have been baptised. Occasional interments still take place in the adjoining graveyard. At the west side of the township of East Lilburn, on the east side of the high road, there used to be a heap of stones, which the credulous of the district attributed to the agency of the devil; but in 1768 this "apronful of stones" was removed, and there was found beneath it the base and fragments of a cross, with four rows of steps. In Armstrong's Map it is called "Fair Cross." An ancient British grave, containing numerous human remains, was opened in 1883 on Lilburn Hill Farm. A mile and a quarter further south, by the side of the main road, is a tract of common land called "Plea Piece," a favourite camping-ground of the gipsies. Here it was that in 1811 a journeyman mason, named Kay, was brutally murdered. The assassin exchanged shoes with his victim, and flung over the adjoining wall the body, which was subsequently discovered by a shepherd's dog. The guilty person escaped, but suspicion fell on a tramp of weak intellect, who used to hold out his hand and exclaim—

> "Here's the hand, but where's the hammer
> That killed John Kay on Lilburn Aller?"

A quarter of a mile along the main road from the bridge over the Lilburn, a road branches off to the right for a mile to the village of ILDERTON, which is seated on a hill-top at the edge of the bleak moorlands stretching away to Cheviot. The *Church of St. Michael* was rebuilt during the Georgian period, and retains nothing of the ancient edifice except two stages of the tower, which is Transitional in character. At the eastern extremity of the churchyard is a mausoleum of the ancient family of Roddam. The railway station of Ilderton lies to the east, near the Wooler road. South-west is *Ilderton Dod*, on the east side of which is a rectangular camp. West of it, on the north side of the Three-stone Burn, are some Druidical remains of great interest, three miles from Ilderton. A quarter of a mile south-east is *Roseden Edge*, a ridge between Ilderton and Roddam, on which are the remains of an ancient British camp, octagonal in form, defended by two earthen ramparts, and a deep fosse seven yards wide, with an inner wall of rough unhewn stones. The inner area is about sixty yards in diameter. Foundations of hut-circles may be traced in the interior. There are remains of an oblong outer-work at the north-east part of the camp, and near it, vestiges of a hollow way running towards the north. About sixty years ago two rudely-fashioned urns belonging to the Celtic period were found here. There is a tradition of a battle having been fought on Roseden Edge, and this is supported by the discovery of a brass spear, together with broken armour.

The hamlet of *Roseden* is a quarter of a mile to the east, and a mile to the south-west of it is *Roddam Hall* (the seat of John Roddam Roddam, Esq.), a mansion rebuilt about 1776 by Admiral Roddam. The grounds and gardens are of considerable extent, their beauty being heightened by contrast with the bleak moorlands around. Roddam Dene, below the house on the north, is a very lovely and romantic dell, with a peat-coloured streamlet splashing through it. The steep banks, which are covered with fine ash and sycamore and other woodland trees, gain a rich tinge from the presence of some thin beds of red sandstone, with the conglomerates of porphyry pebbles and brick-red clay and sand beneath. The flora of the dene includes the rare plant, black bitter-vetch (*Orobus niger*), alternate-leaved golden saxifrage (*Chrysosplenium alternifolium*), melancholy plume-thistle (*Carduus heterophyllus*), the wood-vetch (*Vicia sylvatica*), star saxifrage (*Saxifraga stellaris*), meadow saxifrage (*Saxifraga granulata*), wood scorpion-grass (*Myosotis sylvatica*), wood melic-grass (*Melica uniflora*), giant bell-flower (*Campanula latifolia*), soft-leaved hawkweed (*Hieracium molle*), wall hawkweed (*Hieracium murorum*), prickly shield-fern (*Polystichum aculeatum*), white stone-crop (*Sedum album*). The charms of this dene have been sung by the poet Story, who lived for a time in the neighbourhood.

The family of Roddam is one of the oldest in England, and was seated in Northumberland in Saxon times. This antiquity is attested by an old writer, John Major, who states that when Robert Stewart, Earl of Fife, was devastating the north of England, during the reign of Richard II., there was brought to him an ancient charter, containing the following curious grant:—

> "I King Athelstan
> Giffis heir to Paulane
> Odam and Roddam
> Als gud and als fair
> Als ever tha myn ware
> And yair to witness Mald my wife."

And this simple rhyming conveyance he used afterwards to recite from memory as a contrast to the prolix documents of later times. This royal grant is recorded in Saxon characters upon an old pedigree of the family, but differs slightly from the former version :—

> "I, King Athelstan, give unto thee Pole Roddam,
> From me and mine, to thee and thine,
> Before my wife Maude, my daughter Maudlin, and my eldest son Henry,
> And for a certen truth,
> I bite this wax with my gang tooth,
> So long as muir bears moss, and cnout grows hare,
> A Roddam of Roddam for ever mare."

The Roddams had formerly considerable influence, and were allied by marriage with the principal families in the county. They were, says Leland, "men of faire landes in Northumberlande about Tylle river, ontyl one of them, having to wife one of the Umflaville daughters, killed a man of name, and thereby lost the principale of 800 markes by yere; so that at this time Roddam, or otherwise Rudham, of

Northumberland, is a man of mene landes." The most distinguished members of this family were Sir John Roddam, who was slain at the battle of Towton in 1491, and Robert Roddam, Admiral of the Red, who died in 1803, aged 83 years, having spent a long and adventurous life in active service, performing innumerable feats of daring and heroism. With him the direct line of the Roddams came to an end. The name was assumed by a kinsman, W. Stanhope, Esq.

A mile to the east of the hall is the village of WOOPERTON, situated a short distance from the main road, on a ridge which forms the high ground of Hedgeley Moor. The station of Wooperton is close to the road. A quarter of a mile to the south-east is the site of the battle of Hedgeley Moor, which was fought on the 23rd of April 1464, between the Yorkists, under Sir John Neville, Lord Montagu, Warden of the Eastern Marches, and the Lancastrians, under Sir Ralph Percy and the Lords Hungerford and Ros. At the first onset Lords Hungerford and Ros deserted, either from treachery or fear, and Sir Ralph Percy was left to bear the whole brunt of the battle alone. Bravely did he maintain his ground for a time, but his little army, weakened by defection, was at length compelled to give way, and the day was lost for King Henry. Sir Ralph was mortally wounded, and fell, exclaiming, "I have saved the bird in my bosom"—meaning, says Hall, that he had kept his promise and oath to his sovereign. The consciousness that he had saved his honour, when his colleagues had disgraced themselves by flight, may have prompted the exclamation. He may also have felt a warrior's pride in thus atoning for his own unfaithfulness to Henry VI. A writer in the *Archæologia Æliana* contends that the dying lord meant that he had kept in his own breast the secret of Queen Margaret's hiding-place, near North Sunderland. The hero, on receiving his death-wound, is said by tradition to have made a bound of twelve yards. Those who disbelieve the story may see in a little enclosure of firs and shrubs, quite close to the road on the west side, the two upright stones which mark the distance.

Half-a-mile to the south, on the east side of the road, is *Percy's Cross*, standing, protected by an iron railing, behind a row of cottages not far from the railway. It is a square sandstone pillar, with the edges cut off, having the badges of the Percy family sculptured upon it—crescents, lucies, and fusils on the four principal sides, and lockets on the truncated corners. As it stands at the edge of the Devil's Causeway, and resembles the "Golden Pots," near Coquet Head, General Roy is of opinion that it was originally a Roman "milliary pillar." Formerly the inhabitants of the neighbouring villages were accustomed to assemble annually at this Cross to play at football, cudgels, and other rustic games. At *Percy's Well*—a spring which issues not far from the Cross—Sir Ralph is said to have quenched his thirst in the heat of battle. The fight has been celebrated in two ballads—"The Battle of Hedgeley Moor," by Frederick Sheldon, and "The Legend of Percy's Cross," by James Service.

# WOOLER TO CHILLINGHAM AND OLD BEWICK.

**Weetwood, 2 miles; Fowberry Tower, 3½ miles; Chatton, 5 miles; Chillingham, 6½ miles; Hebburn Tower, 7½ miles; Old Bewick, 9½ miles; Blaw-weary, 10½ miles.**

LEAVING Wooler by the wooden bridge, let the tourist follow the road, which runs in a north-easterly direction, to Weetwood Bridge, two miles distant. He will have to his right Weetwood Moor and Whitsunbank Hill. Here it is that the "Whitsun-Tryste," or great annual fair for cattle, horses, and sheep, is held on the third Monday in May. Sir Walter Scott's grandfather is related to have attended this fair to purchase a flock of sheep with the sum of £30, lent to him by his old shepherd. While the shepherd was going from drove to drove for a suitable *hirsel*, the master recklessly bought with the money a high-mettled hunter which had struck his fancy. The purchase, however, turned out more fortunately than could have been expected, the horse being sold a few days afterwards for double the original price, and the farm stocked in earnest. Many remains of the ancient British period are found on this hill. On the north side of the hill, two hundred and fifty yards south-east of Weetwood Bridge, is *Weetwood Camp*, in which have been found a quern of porphyry, a stone trough, and three round artificially-formed stone balls, about three inches in diameter, supposed to have been used for some game. Several of the sandstone rocks on the summit and the higher parts of the hill have been marked by the Celtic inhabitants with those mysterious figures of concentric circles which have puzzled antiquaries so much. At least thirty-two figures have been discovered, connected, it is surmised, with tumuli and cist-vaens. On the north bank of the Till, not far from the bridge, is *Weetwood Hall*, the property of the Rev. L. S. Orde, and the residence of George Culley, Esq. From the bridge the road ascends a moory hill for a quarter of a mile, then turns round sharply to the south-east. Half-a-mile from the bend a road branches off to the left to *Fowberry Tower*, a modern mansion, situated in a well-wooded park, the property of George Culley, Esq. It stands on the site of an old Border pele, the barmkyn, or outer enclosure, of which may still be traced by the foundations of its massive walls. The manor gave its name to a family of some note in the troublous time. Fowberry was plundered by the Scots in 1532, in the course of a retaliatory raid.

For half-a-mile more the road runs south, then turns to the east for a mile and three-quarters to CHATTON. Chatton is a pretty agricultural village of some antiquity, situated near the Till, and consisting of a number of cosy-looking cottages, with gardens in front, a plain modern church, school-house, reading-room and library, and a comfortable inn, the Percy Arms. Edward I. was here from the 13th to the 16th of August 1291, and on the 14th of December 1292. Chatton suffered much in the fourteenth century from the inroads of the Scots and the ravages of the plague. In 1352, out of twenty-seven bondagia eleven lay waste and uncultivated, and out of thirteen cottages eight were tenantless. There were two pele-towers here in 1416 and 1542. One was occupied by the clergyman of the parish, and is incorporated with the present vicarage.

The *Church of the Holy Cross* is a building of little architectural interest. Founded in the twelfth century, it became ruinous about the middle of the eighteenth, was rebuilt 1763-1770, and restored in 1844. There are some good stained-glass windows in the church to the memory of Algernon, Duke of Northumberland, and the Rev. M. Burrell. On the north side of the church a stone coffin was discovered on the 6th March 1814, containing the remains of a human body, which is supposed to have been one of the followers of Robert Bruce, who had fallen in 1318, during an invasion of Northumberland, and, being under excommunication, was buried in the least hallowed part of the churchyard. There were also found, at the same time and place, a steel spur, one of Bruce's silver pennies, and the fragments of a helmet which had probably belonged to the deceased warrior. Near the village is *Chatton Park*, the residence of John Marshall, Esq., M.D. A mile and a half to the east is *Chatton Law*, rising to a height of 603 feet above the sea-level. At the western extremity there is an ancient British camp, small and circular, defended by three rampiers. In the central area is a sandstone rock, with six rudely-carved circles upon it. Two hundred yards to the east are others of these mysterious figures, remarkable for their great size and geometrical forms, one of them being thirty-six inches in diameter, and composed of seven concentric rings, with a peculiar curved elevation or crown at the top.

A mile and a half to the south of Chatton is the village of CHILLINGHAM, formerly called Chevelingham, which is merely a part of the outbuildings of the castle, the trim little cottages being occupied by the workmen on the estate. On the roadside is a handsome fountain, erected to the memory of the Rev. William Dodd, M.A. A broad carriage drive, a quarter of a mile in length, branches off from the road to the antique and beautifully-situated *Church of St. Peter*, which was founded in the thirteenth century. Enclosed within the modern porch is the original Norman doorway, with its characteristic ornamentation. Affixed to the north wall of the nave is a rudely-carved slab to the memory of Robert Charnockle, stewart, of Ford, Lord Grey, who died 1691. The font originally belonged to the church at Ancroft, and bears on its basin the date 1670.

In the south aisle of the chancel, which contains the seats of the Tankerville family, is a magnificent altar-tomb, with the effigies of Sir Ralph Grey and his lady, Elizabeth Fitzhugh of Ravensworth, resting upon it. It is beautifully-carved in the style of the Perpendicular period. Shields, supported by angels, and bearing heraldic devices, and niches containing the figures of north-country saints and persons of distinction, are the chief ornaments. The knight, who is dressed in a red tunic, is a powerful-looking man, with a somewhat elongated face, prominent nose, and large lips, the upper-one fringed with a well-trimmed moustache. The lady's face is thin and sharp, with slightly open lips and narrow, sloping forehead, and a head-dress of the high Flemish style of Edward II. She is habited in loose, flowing robes, and wears a ring on her left hand. On the wall above the tomb is a full-length standing figure supporting the family helmet and crest. Beneath it are representations of angels carrying to heaven the souls of the deceased, and above it are two pinnacles, and a marble tablet of more modern workmanship, bearing the family motto, "De bon vouloir servir le Roy," not older, apparently, than the reign of Elizabeth. Two of the headstones in the churchyard contain quaint inscriptions—

"My friends, go home,
And cease from tears
I must lie here
Till Christ appears."

"Consider this as you pass by—
As you are now so once was I;
As I am now so must you be,
Prepare yourselves to follow me."

The vicarage stands in the midst of flower-gardens close by. Opposite to it is the North Lodge, from which there is a short winding drive to Chillingham Castle.

Situated in a richly-wooded park, about half-a-mile to the east of the river Till, which murmurs through the valley below, *Chillingham Castle* is not excelled by any mansion in the county for the beauty of its surroundings. Designed by Inigo Jones at a time when the Italian style of domestic architecture had somewhat superseded the Elizabethan, it is quadrangular in form, consisting of four strong Border towers of the fourteenth century, connected by seventeenth-century buildings, and surmounted by embrasured parapets. The castle is four storeys high in the wings, and three in the central portion. The spacious court-yard contains on its south side a picturesque portico, balustraded, and ornamented with the effigies of Alexander the Great, Julius Cæsar, Charlemagne, Godfrey de Bouillon, and others of the nine worthies. Under the balcony is preserved the famous "Toad-stone," an oblong slab of freestone, in which a live toad is said to have been discovered immured in a small cavity. The stone, which is 5 feet 6 inches in length, 2 feet 4 inches in breadth, and 1 foot 3 inches in thickness, was afterwards used as a chimney-piece, and for many years was lost sight of. In the Steward's Room close by there is a rude painting of the toad. Figures of lizards, snakes, frogs, etc., are worked into the frame. Underneath are two Latin incriptions, generally attributed to Dr. Cosin, who was made Bishop of Durham in 1660, though there is much diversity of opinion among antiquaries as to the authorship of them. These verses, as rendered by Lord Ravensworth, run as follows :—

"Ho ! Stagyrite !
If you wish for something more wonderful
Than your own Euripus,
Come hither !
Let the tides flow and ebb, and be he moonstricken
Who robs Trivia of her (due) honour.
Lo ! for you something novel, which Africa bears not,
Nor Nile, on his sandy shores ;
(To wit) fire and pure flame,
Yet without vital air.
Out of the dark recess of the cleft rock
As much as you see, the hands
Of the midwife stone-cutter gave light
To a live toad."

This room also contains a curiously-carved chimney-piece, representing "Susanna and the Elders." From the court-yard, a long flight of stone steps leads up to the Dining-hall, which has a fine prospect over the pleasaunce and the wooded slopes of the park. It is adorned with numerous trophies, armour, weapons, heads of deer and wild cattle, and skins of magnificent foreign animals, and contains some valuable pictures. Among these latter are portraits of Charles I., Charles II., James II. ; Lord Bacon, by Cornelius Jansen ; The Earl of Arlington, by Lely ; Judge Jeffries, by Sir G. Kneller ; Lord Treasurer Burleigh, Lord Middlesex, Antonine Marechal de Gramont, Duchess of Cleveland, Duke of Monmouth, Charles, third Earl of Tankerville, and Alicia, his Countess, Charles Augustus, fifth Earl ; and Charles, the sixth, and present Earl, by Sir Francis Grant. This noble apartment also contains three celebrated pictures by Landseer—"The Bull and Wild Cattle in Chillingham Park," "A Group of Red Deer," and "The Dying Bull." This last-named picture depicts an incident in the life of the present lord, who, when a young man, was attacked in the park by a wild bull, and might have been killed, had not one of the keepers brought the infuriated brute to the ground by a well-aimed shot. Landseer admired this picture so much, it is said, that he had it in his studio for twenty-five years, and only parted with it when the other two pictures were sent to Chillingham. The Drawing-room has a rich coved ceiling, with pendants, and its walls are hung with several fine pictures, among which may be mentioned, "The Prisoner of Chillon," by Hurlstone, and "Dunstanborough Castle." Here may be seen a piece of old China, said to have belonged to the unhappy Marie

Antoinette, and a beautiful screen, hung with miniatures and enamels. The furniture is in the antique style, harmonising well with the character of the building. On the north-east side of the castle is the old Baronial Prison, lighted only by a narrow slit in the thick wall. The unhappy prisoners confined here have left a record of their captivity in some rudely-cut letters and some rows of long and short lines scribbled upon the walls. A trap-door in the floor gives access to a dark dungeon, or oubliette, similar to that at Alnwick. Chillingham had formerly, according to tradition, its mysterious visitant in the shape of a "Radiant Boy." Since the bones of a child were discovered in the walls of one of the bed-rooms and buried in the churchyard, it has ceased to appear. The manor of Chillingham was held in feudal times, under the barony of Vescy, by the Huntercombe family. It subsequently passed into the possession of the Greys, of Wark. Sir William Grey was, in 1623, raised to the peerage as Lord Grey of Wark. He died in 1674, and was succeeded by his son, who in 1695 was created Viscount Glendale and Earl of Tankerville. On his death in 1701 these titles became extinct, but were revived in 1714, in Charles Bennet, Lord Ossulston, who married the heiress of the family. From this nobleman the estates have descended in a direct line to the present owner. Henry III. was at Chillingham Castle on the 5th of September 1255, and sent from this place a safe-conduct to Alexander III., King of Scotland, and his queen, on their coming to meet him at Wark, or some other place on the Marches. In 1872 the Prince and Princess of Wales were the guests of the Earl of Tankerville, from October 15th to October 18th.

The Gardens, with their pretty flower-plots, are generally to be seen on any day, and are well worth a visit. Several exotic plants bloom gaily among those of native growth. Among these is one of recent introduction from Japan—the *Primula Japonica*. The black spleenwort (*Asplenium Trichomanes*) grows everywhere in the walls—a proof of the antiquity of the place. The American grounds contain some magnificent monarch walnut trees, and two curiosities—the plum-pudding tree, and a remarkable lime, beehive-shaped. In the pasture, 200 yards south of the school-house, is a gnarled and very old oak, 20 feet 7 inches in girth, at a height of 4 feet from the ground. It is a monstrous dwarf, consisting almost entirely of stem, and appears to have been originally two trees, which stood in close proximity to each other and coalesced. Another famous tree is the "Summer Tree"—an English elm standing near the lodge, adjoining the entrance to the castle. A beautiful avenue of limes extends from the west lodge to the castle. To the east of the castle is a deep and ferny little dell, through which runs the Chillingham Burn, fringed with unusually fine alders. Eastward of this dell the ground gradually rises, till, from "Charley's Knoll," the castle appears to be quite in a hollow. The Park, which is said to have been enclosed in the thirteenth century, contains about 1500 acres of broken and undulating ground, where pasture, thicket, glen, and moorland combine to form a landscape at once wild and picturesque. The highest part, a craggy ridge—called Ros or Ras Castle, from the Celtic *rhos* (moist-land) or *ros* (a promontory), and *castell* (a fortress)—is crowned by a double-rampiered Celtic camp. The view from the summit is very extensive, ranging from Alnwick on the south to Cheviot and Hedgehope on the west, Berwick and the Scottish hills on the north, and to Holy Island, with Bamburgh and Dunstanburgh Castles, on the east. In the times of Border warfare there flared forth from Ros Castle one of the most important beacons in the county, to the maintenance of which all the villages between the Tweed and the Aln contributed. Chillingham Heronry—the only one in North Northumberland—is located partly in a thick plantation called "Fox's Knowe," about half-way down from the summit of Ros Castle hill, and partly in the Hart Wood, a little to the north-east. The birds wing their way to considerable distances during the day in search of food—to the Cheviots and the valleys of the Till, Tweed, and Aln, and to the sea-coast, a distance of from fifteen to twenty miles. About 1500 acres of the park are allotted to the wild cattle and the red roe and fallow deer. This part is wild and rugged, consisting of fine, open feeding-grounds, dense thickets and woods, and extensive bogs, fringed with alders. It is to the wild cattle that Chillingham Park owes its wide reputation. They are supposed to be the descendants of the aboriginal herds which roamed in the great Caledonian forest. From the stand-point of comparative anatomy they are declared to be the purest type of the gigantic fossil, *Bos primegenius*, much diminished, however, by "in and in" breeding. The "great wood" of Chillingham, referred to in a document dated 1220, was probably one of the last retreats to which they were driven by the increase of population. In its tangled recesses they were able to breed in comparative security until the park was enclosed, when they were preserved by the Norman barons for the purposes of the chase, or as a curious remnant of an ancient stock. The herd is generally kept up to eleven bulls, seventeen steers, and thirty-two cows, or sixty in all. An admirable description of the cattle and their habits is given in Bewick's *History of Quadrupeds*, by Mr. Bailey, a former bailiff of the Tankerville family. "Their colour," he says, "is invariably white, muzzle black; the whole of the inside of the ear, and about one-third of the outside, from the tip downwards, red; horns white, with black tips, very fine, and bent upwards. Some of the bulls have a thin, upright mane, about an inch and a half or two inches long. The weight of the oxen is from thirty-five to forty-five stones; and the cows from twenty-five to thirty-five stones, the four quarters. The beef is finely marbled, and of excellent flavour. From the nature of their pasture, and the frequent agitation they are put into by the curiosity of strangers, it cannot be expected they should get very fat; yet the six-years-old oxen are generally very good beef; from whence it may be fairly supposed that in proper situations they would feed well. At the first appearance of any person they set off at full speed and gallop to a considerable distance, when they make a wheel round and come boldly up again, tossing their heads in a menacing manner. On a sudden they make a full stop, at a distance of forty or fifty yards, looking wildly at the object of their surprise; but upon the least motion being made, they again turn round and gallop off with equal speed; but forming a shorter circle, and returning with a bolder and more threatening aspect, they approach much nearer, when they make another stand and again gallop off. This they do several times, shortening their distance and advancing nearer, till they come within a few yards, when most people think it prudent to leave them. The mode of killing them was, perhaps, the only modern remains of the grandeur of ancient hunting. On notice being given that a wild bull would be killed upon a certain day, the inhabitants of the neighbourhood came in great numbers, both horse and foot. The horsemen rode off the bull from the rest of the herd, until he stood at bay, when a marksman dismounted and shot. At some of these huntings, twenty or thirty shots have been fired before he was subdued. On such occasions the bleeding victim grew desperately furious from the smarting of his wounds and the shouts of savage joy that were echoing from every side. From the number of accidents that happened, this dangerous mode has been seldom practised of late years, the park-keeper alone generally shooting them with a rifled gun at one shot. When the cows calve, they hide their calves for a week or ten days in some sequestered situation, and go and suckle them two or three times a day. If any person come near the calves, they clap their heads close to the ground, and lie like a hare in form to hide themselves. This is a proof of their native wildness, and is corroborated by the following circumstance that happened to the writer of this narrative, who found a hidden calf, two months old, very lean, and very weak. On stroking its head it got up, pawed two or three times like an old bull, bellowed very loud, retired a few steps, and bolted at his legs with all its force. It then began to paw again, bellowed, stepped back, and bolted as before; but, knowing its intention, and stepping aside, it missed him, fell, and was so very weak that it could not rise, though it made several efforts. But it had done enough; the whole herd were alarmed, and, coming to its rescue, obliged him to retire, for the dams will suffer no person to touch their calves without attacking them with impetuous ferocity. When any one happens to be wounded, or grown weak and feeble through age or sickness, the rest of the herd set upon it and gore it to death." Other interesting particulars respecting the cattle are supplied by the Earl of Tankerville in a paper read before the British Association at Newcastle in 1838. "They have, pre-eminently, all the characteristics of wild animals, with some peculiarities that are sometimes very curious and amusing. They hide their young, feed in the night, basking or sleeping during the day. They are fierce when pressed, but, generally speaking, very timorous, moving off on the appearance of anyone, even at a great distance. Yet this varies very much in different seasons of the year, according to the manner in which they are approached. In summer I have been for several weeks without getting a sight of them, they, on the slightest appearance of anyone, retiring into a wood, which serves them as a sanctuary. On the other hand, in winter, when coming down for food into the inner park, and being in contact with the people, they will let you almost come among them, particularly if on horseback. But then they have also a thousand peculiarities. They will be feeding sometimes quietly, when, if anyone appears suddenly near them—particularly coming down the wind—they will be struck with a sudden panic, and gallop off, running one after another, and never stopping till they get into their sanctuary. It is observable of them, as of red deer, that they have a peculiar faculty of taking advantage of the irregularities of the ground, so that on being disturbed, they may traverse the whole park and yet you hardly get a sight of them. Their usual mode of retreat is to get up slowly, set off in a walk, then a trot, and seldom begin to gallop till they have put the ground between you and them in the manner that I have described. In form they are beautifully shaped—short legs, straight back, horns of a very fine texture, thin skin, so that some of the bulls appear of a cream colour; and they have a peculiar cry, more like that of a wild beast than that of ordinary cattle. With all the marks of high breeding, they have also some of its defects. They are bad breeders, and are much subject to the *rush*, a complaint common to animals bred in and in, which is unquestionably the case with these as long as we have any account of them. When they come down into the lower part of the park, which they do at stated hours, they move like a regiment of cavalry in single files, the bulls leading the van; as in retreat it is the bulls that bring up the rear. Of their tenacity of life, the following is an instance:—An old bull being to be killed, one of the keepers had proceeded to separate him from the rest of the herd, which were feeding in the outer park. The bull, resenting this, made a rush at the keeper and got him down. He then tossed him three times, and afterwards knelt upon him, and broke several of his ribs. The only other person present being a boy, no assistance could be given. However, a deer-hound was let loose, who attacked the bull, and, by biting his heels, drew him off the man, and eventually saved his life. The bull, meanwhile, never left the keeper, but kept continually watching and returning to him, giving him a toss from time to time. In this state of things, and while the dog, with singular sagacity, was holding the bull at bay, a messenger came up to the castle, when all the gentlemen came out with their rifles and commenced a fire upon the bull, principally by a good marksman behind a fence 25 yards distant; but it was not till six or seven balls had actually entered the head of the animal (one of them passing in at the eye) that he at last fell." A similar incident to that just narrated is described by William Air Foster in his "Chillingham Bull Hunt":—

"From flank to shoulder, at a blow he ripped the courser's side:
The blood in torrents gushing ran upon his snow-white hide,—
The piercing cry rose loud and high, as stretch'd upon the plain
The charger lay, the bull at bay, blood dropping from his mane.

Like streaming tide, through nostrils wide he breathes with slaver'd jaws,
And throws aloof, with polish'd hoof, the green sward as he paws;
The wrinkles on his brawny neck lie stretch'd along the crest,
Like wreaths of snow they stand below against his massive chest.

His brow is lower'd, his knee is bent, his tail is tossing high,—
His horns are set, their points of jet are level with his eye;
The rider lies before him, from out the saddle thrown,
The bull is bending o'er him, like thunder loud his tone."

It is said that when Bewick was making his drawing for his celebrated "Chillingham Bull," the leader of the herd gave chase to him, and that the artist only escaped from the bull's fury by climbing a tree, where he completed his sketch, very much to his own satisfaction, while the animal kept bellowing and pawing the ground below. Landseer also, when making sketches for his pictures, was tracked by some of the herd, and was glad to take refuge in the forest as fast as he could. The present Earl of Tankerville, when a young man, was attacked by a bull as he was riding through the park. His pony was gored under him, and he would probably have shared the same fate had not one of the keepers shot the enraged animal as it was about to renew its charge. The Countess of Tankerville was in the park at the time, and saw the peril of her son. A tree is now planted on the spot where the young heir of Tankerville had so narrow an escape. During winter the cattle are not nearly so wild, and will follow the hay-cart for the forage which is flung out to them. In a storm, or when unusually alarmed, they seek the shelter of a thicket known as "Robin Hood's Bog," the traditional site of the first of the race. Here the calves are hidden for a week or ten days after birth. On the 17th of October 1872 the Prince of Wales celebrated his visit to Chillingham by shooting the king of the herd. Some difficulty was experienced in getting within gunshot of the noble beast, which took up his position in the centre of the herd. However, with much manœuvring, he was separated from the rest, and the Prince, concealed in a hay-cart about seventy yards distant, succeeded in sending a bullet into his head, about six inches from the base of the horns, severing the spinal cord. In a well-known local poem, by Mr. Robert Elliott, "A Pitman gan te Parliamint," this exploit is referred to in a vein of good-natured satire—

"He's a warrier, ye knaa, and the papors are full
Iv a tarrible encoonter he had wiv a bull!
He slowtered the bull, but his critics will say
That the Prince was cuncealed in a bundle iv hay;
An' thit it was ne feat at a' te lie hid
An' slowter the bull in the way that he did;
But some fokes are selfish, an' winna hear tell
Iv ony greet feats unless dune be thorsel."

The wild cattle may be seen on Tuesdays and Saturdays, but no one is allowed to enter the park unless accompanied by the keeper. From the castle there is a footpath through the park past the "Yaxes

Plantation" to *Hebburn Tower*, an old bastle-house, now in ruins, once the seat of the Hepburn family The vaulted chamber on the ground floor, and the newel staircase leading up to the rooms in the higher storeys, may yet be seen. "Lord Hepburn," a ballad by Fred Sheldon, which appears in his *Minstrelsy of the English Border*, illustrates very powerfully the lawless character of the old times, when such buildings as the "old bastle" were necessary for the protection of life and property. To the east rise the *Hebburn Crags*, on one of which are the remains of an ancient British camp. A thicket near Hebburn Bell is still pointed out as the place where a party of Nonconformists used to assemble in secret and hold their services before the passing of the Toleration Act in 1688. The tourist who wishes to return to Wooler by way of Lilburn will proceed, in the first instance, from the West Lodge down a broad and shady road for half-a-mile to the Newtown Bridge, and thence for half-a-mile more to the hamlet of *Chillingham Newtown*, noticing on an eminence in a field to the south of it a quaint-looking pillar, called "The Hurl-Stone"—a corruption, probably, of "Earl's Stone." According to a local tradition, some persons once exploring the subterranean passage which is said to extend from the Caterane's Cave on Bewick Moor to the Henhole on Cheviot, had got as far as the Hurle Stone when their lights went out, and they heard above them strange voices repeating, amid the trampling of horses' feet, the elfin rhyme—

> "Hup, hup, and gee again!
> Round and round the Hurle Stone."

Terror-stricken, they retraced their footsteps through the darkness to the mouth of the cave as fast as possible.

Two miles and three-quarters south from the West Lodge is the little village of OLD BEWICK, situated high beneath a heath-clad hill, with a fine prospect over the slopes of Hedgeley Moor and the valleys of the Breamish and Till. The name is said to be derived from the Norman *beau*, fine, and the Saxon *wick*, village. The manor, anciently called Archi Morel, was holden in Saxon and Norman times under the king's castle of Bamburgh. It formed part of the dowry of Matilda, the daughter of Malcolm, King of Scotland, and wife of Henry I., and was conveyed by her, about 1107, to Tynemouth Priory, a cell of St. Alban's. In 1253 the place was of sufficient importance to have a weekly market granted to it by Henry III. Part of the ancient market-cross was found a few years ago in a field a little to the north-west of the monument erected by the road-side to the "memory of John Charles Langlands, 1874." A short way up the lonely glen to the north of the village is the little Norman *Chapel of the Holy Trinity*, which was probably built between the years 1110 and 1120 by the monks of Tynemouth. During the Decorated period a window was inserted in the nave, and another in the apse, which at the same time was made to appear, by means of ingenious corbelling, square instead of round above a certain level. The Cromwellian troops, under Lesley, did much damage to the little edifice, which, however, was repaired in 1695 by Ralph Williamson, the lord of the manor. Early in the last century the roof was blown off by a great gale, and the chapel remained for a long time a picturesque pile of ruins. It was restored in 1866-7, and though of necessity some new work was added, every ancient fragment, Norman and Decorated, was carefully preserved. The interior of the chapel has a hoary charm, which cannot but impress the visitor as he scans the "silvery grey" walls with their weather-softened masonry, and the beautiful arches of the chancel and apse, one beyond the other, with their massy mouldings and billet ornamentation. On the north side of the chancel is a recumbent effigy under a Decorated canopy, said to be that of Matilda, wife of Henry I. Among the relics of the past which have been found here are two small bells and two fine tomb-slabs (one of them that of a child), richly ornamented with a floriated cross, etc. In the churchyard are many old headstones. Nothing remains, but the foundations, of the old pele-tower which Sir Robert Bowes, in 1550, recommended to be repaired, "for it standeth in a fyte place for the defence of the countrye thereabouts, and is able in tyme of warre to contayne fifty men in garrison." The Alnwick and Wooler road passes over the site. Immediately above the village to the east is Bewick Hill, rising to a height of 773 feet above the sea-level. A huge mass of sandstone projecting from the escarpment of the hill is called from its appearance the "Hanging Crag," and an ancient prediction that

> "As long as the Hanging Crag shall stand
> There'll aye be a Ha' on Bewick Land,"

seems to be verified, for a family of the name of Hall still reside at Bewick. Bewick Hill is crowned by a large and perfect specimen of a Celtic hill-fortress, to which the tribe inhabiting the valley of the Breamish and the adjoining hills would resort in time of danger. In shape it resembles two horse-shoes placed side by side. The defences consist of four great rampiers, high and wide, abutting on to a steep escarpment, which has been itself strengthened by a low wall. Two of these huge engirdling mounds of unhewn stone and earth are still wonderfully perfect, the fosse between them being in one part upwards of 20 feet in depth. Within the camp may be traced the foundations of circular huts similar to those at Greaves Ash. The most remarkable feature in connection with the Bewick camp is the series of incised circles which appear on the surface of five sandstone blocks. A stone within the camp near the outer rampart and eastern entrance contains five figures, one of which resembles the impression of a horse's foot. Another stone, about 20 yards northward of this, and close to the rampart within the camp, has two figures, one of them somewhat spiral in shape. Six figures are traceable on a large block about 30 yards eastward of the camp, the largest of them being 10 inches in diameter. A fourth block, about 100 yards from the camp, is engraved with two circles. The chief group of these curious markings, however, appear on a quadrangular-shaped rock, rising, where highest,

4½ feet above the ground at a distance of 100 yards eastward of the camp. In spite of the wasting storms of twenty, and it may be thirty centuries, twenty-seven figures are still discernible when the stone is viewed by the light of the evening sun. The principal character of these figures is a series of concentric circles cut into the surface of the rock around a cup-like hole, from which proceeds a hollow line or duct. By being much connected with each other they have a curious maze-like appearance. Passing nearly horizontally along the south and east sides of the stone may be seen a number of shallow pits, having some symbolic connection with the other markings. Lower down the hill, on a gentle slope facing the south, are the remains of an ancient British village or oppidum. The chief fortlet is circular, and about one hundred and twenty feet in diameter. A mile to the north-east is *Blaw-weary*, a shepherd's house, romantically perched on an outcrop of sandstone, with a sheep-pen enclosed by walls of rock, fifteen feet high, and a garden, approached by winding steps cut out of the solid rock. A quarter of a mile to the south-east is a small but very perfect camp of the ancient Britons, overlooking the deep ravine of the Harehope Burn. Two hundred yards to the south of it are the Corbie Crags, 30 feet high, where the raven and peregrine falcon used to build. A short distance from these rocks, poised high up on the hill-side, are some fine large masses of sandstone known as "The Grey Mare and Foal." A number of goats roam about these rocky hill-sides. On *Langside Moor*, stretching away to the south-east, are accumulations of scoriæ, the refuse of primitive iron-smelting operations. A mile and a quarter north-east of Blaw-weary is *Cateran Hole*—a narrow fissure in the sandstone rock on the north side of Cateran Hill. It tends towards the west for nearly forty yards. From its name it is supposed to have been the haunt of a freebooter. A popular tradition asserts that the cave is connected with the Henhole on the north side of Cheviot by a subterranean passage running beneath the Hurle Stone. On the moors around Old Bewick are found—common trientale, or chickweed winter green (*Trientalis Europæa*), sweet gale (*Myrica gale*), cranberry (*Vaccinium oxycoccus*), climbing fumitory (*Corydalis claviculata*), frog satyrion or orchis (*Habenaria viridis*), bog pimpernel (*Anagallis tenella*), common moonwort (*Botrychium lunaria*), lesser club-moss (*Lycopodium selaginoides*), grass-of-Parnassus (*Parnassia palustris*), common buck-bean (*Menyanthes trifoliata*), Tunbridge hymenophyll (*Hymenophyllum Tunbridgense*). From Old Bewick the tourist may return to Wooler by way of the one-arched bridge near Bewick Mill, where the river changes its name from Breamish to Till, according to the old rhyme :—

"Foot of Breamish and head of Till,
Meet together at Bewick Mill."

The nearest station to Old Bewick is Hedgeley.

# WOOLER TO HUMBLETON AND THE VALLEY OF THE GLEN.

**Humbleton, ¾ mile ; Bendor Stone, 2 miles ; Akeld, 2¾ miles ; Yeavering, 4¼ miles ; Kirknewton, 5¾ miles ; Heathpool, 8 miles ; Henhole, 12½ miles ; Paston, 9¾ miles ; Mindrum, 10½ miles ; Piperden, 12¼ miles.**

A QUARTER of a mile northward, along the main road, a pathway to the left, near the Highburnhouse, leads off for half-a-mile to the once considerable but now almost deserted village of HUMBLETON. The village-green is covered by a duck-pond, and the dwellings that bordered it have crumbled to a few broken walls. On the foundations of the old pele-tower grows an elder bush. Barley waves over the site of the old graveyard in what is called "The Chapel Field." The headstones which were standing at the beginning of the century have been broken up by the good housewives of the neighbourhood for sandstone to clean their hearths with. The decline and subsequent decay of this "English Auburn," as it has been appropriately styled, are due to the gradual absorption of the small freeholds here into the estates of the great land-proprietors. To the west of the village rises *Humbleton Hill* to a height of 977 feet above the sea-level. It is chiefly remarkable for the artificial terraces or "baulks" on which the ancient Britons cultivated their scanty crops. There are three successive tiers of them, 20 feet to 30 feet apart. The summit is encircled by ancient fortifications of the usual rude and massive type. Traces of hut-circles, earthen walls, sheep or cattle folds, and burial mounds are found all around the lower slopes. The Celtic population of these hills seems to have been very large. To the west of the Humbleton Camp, and separated from it by rugged ravines, is Harehope Camp, at the head of a deep craggy-sided hollow called Monday Cleugh, which winds around the south-west of Standrop Hill. An ancient wall protects the base of the promontory on which the camp is seated. The camp is approached from the north-west by a wide road of great length, bordered by earthern ramparts. The camp is square in form, with the angles rounded off, and is defended by huge walls six feet high or more, two on the west and three on the north. An additional mound, more remote still, further strengthens the north side, and encloses numerous folds and hut-circles. The entrance crosses the walls obliquely, and is protected by an inner guard-chamber. There have not been many buildings within the camp, as the central area is supposed to have been intended more as a place of security for cattle than for habitation.

Though hidden in a gap between hill-tops the camp yet commands a far prospect, standing in a line with the camps on the Kettles Hill, Humbleton Hill, and Yeavering Bell. On the east side of Standrop there is another camp overlooking Akeld fields. On the north side of Humbleton Hill, about two miles from Wooler, is the *Bendor Stone*, standing in a field called the Redriggs, not far from the Black Bull Inn. It commemorates the *Battle of Homildon Hill*, which was fought on Holyrood Day (September 13th), 1402. In draining this field human skulls and bones, and the skeletons of horses were turned up for a considerable distance. The account of the battle is as follows:—Archibald, Earl of Douglas, surnamed Tine-man—*i.e.*, Lose-man, from his frequent reverses—having made a raid of retaliation into Northumberland as far as the Tyne for the defeat sustained by the Scots at Nesbit Moor, was returning towards the Tweed, laden with plunder, when he found that the Earl of Northumberland and his son Hotspur, with his deadly enemy, the Earl of March, were posted near Millfield ready to dispute his progress. He at once took up a strong position on the slopes of Homildon or Humbleton Hill. The English thereupon occupied the ridges of a neighbouring hill. Harry Percy (or Hotspur) was about to charge up the hill of Homildon when the Earl of March caught his bridle and advised him to begin the fight with his archers. This advice was taken, and the English bowmen advanced to the base of the hill and shot upwards with terrible effect, whole ranks being swept down by the dreadful shower of English arrows. At length a spirited knight named Swinton exclaimed, "O, my brave countrymen! what fascination has seized you to-day that you stand like deer to be shot, instead of indulging your ancient courage and meeting your enemies hand-to-hand? Let those, who will, descend with me, that we may gain victory, or fall like men." Adam Gordon, between whom and Swinton there existed a deadly feud, was so affected by these stirring words that he fell on his knees before the speaker, begged his pardon, and desired to receive the honour of knighthood from "the boldest and wisest of that order in Great Britain." The ceremony performed, Swinton and Gordon rushed down the hill with only a hundred followers, it is said. The English archers, however, fell back as their enemies advanced, keeping up an incessant discharge of arrows which no armour could withstand, and the desperate valour of the little band led them to their death. A complete rout of the Scots ensued. Of the ten thousand who followed the banner of Douglas eight hundred remained dead on the field, and five hundred more, it is said, were drowned in the Tweed. Douglas himself received five wounds, one of which deprived him of an eye. He was made prisoner, together with Murdach, the son of the Duke of Albany, the Earls of Moray and Angus, two barons, eighty knights (among whom were some Frenchmen), and many other persons of rank. Livingston of Calendar, Ramsay of Dalhoosie, Walter Sinclair, Roger Gordon, and Walter Scott were in the number of the more illustrious slain. The whole affair was decided by the English archers alone.

Three-quarters of a mile from the Black Bull Inn is AKELD, once a village of some consequence, now a large farmstead with a few labourers' cottages. The earliest reference to Akeld in the Pipe Rolls is A.D. 1177. The old pele-tower mentioned in the Border Survey of 1542 is still in a good state of preservation. The lowest chamber is vaulted with walls 4½ feet thick. A grass-grown patch of ground, about an acre in extent, open to the road leading to Kirknewton, is the site of the old graveyard. On the opposite side of the road is the *Chapel Field*, where it is supposed a chapel formerly stood. Rising behind the village on the south is *Akeld Hill* (hill of fire), 986 feet above the sea-level. Among the glitters on the north side of it a bronze sword was picked up many years ago. There is a railway station at Akeld.

From Akeld a road runs westward along the wild and romatic valley of the Glen to the village of YEAVERING, a mile and a half distant. The early name of Yeavering was Ad-gebrin. It had the distinction, in Saxon times, of being a royal residence of the Northumberland kings, and is thus alluded to by Bede in his account of the missionary labours of Paulinus :—" Paulinus, at a certain time coming with the king and queen (Edwin and Ethelburga) to the royal country seat, which is called Adgefrin, stayed there with them thirty-six days, fully occupied in catechising and baptising, during which days, from morning to night, he did nothing else but instruct the people, resorting from all villages and places, in Christ's saving word ; and when instructed, he washed them with the water of absolution in the river Glen, which is close by. This town, under the following kings, was abandoned, and another was built instead of it, at a place called *Melmin* (now Millfield)." A long, low quadrangular cottage at *Old Yeavering*, nearly a mile further west, and a little to the south of the road, is said, by tradition, to have formed part of King Edwin's Palace. The masonry is certainly of a very rude type, but there is nothing to show that it belongs to so early a date as the seventh century. The walls are five feet thick, built of porphyry blocks, but not in regular courses, and seemingly without lime. Squared oak posts pass perpendicularly through the middle of the walls, giving stability to them, and supporting the roof. Old doorways and windows, with squared headings, are traceable. It may have been a rude pele-tower, though not of the common type, which has a vaulted chamber on the ground floor. In a field between new and old Yeavering is a large upright stone, commemorating the battle of "Geteryne" (as the place was then called), fought on Magdalen-day, 1415, when Sir Robert Umfraville, called Robin-mend-the-Market, commander of Roxburgh Castle, and the Earl of Westmoreland, Lord of the Marches, with a small force of 140 spearmen and 300 bowmen, defeated a party of 4000 Scots, killing 60, taking 160 prisoners, and chasing the rest for twelve miles over the Borders. A plantation above the road east of the Yeavering is said to be haunted by an apparition known as "The White Lady." In draining a field adjoining it, immense quantities of horses' shoes were dug out, relics, it is conjectured, of the stampede after the fight at Humbleton. To the south of the village is *Yeavering Bell*, rising to a height of 1182 feet above the sea-level. In shape it is a cone, truncated at the top, the rocks composing it being porphyry, dolerite, and syenite. No other hill in the Cheviot range commands such a magnificent prospect over the romantic Borderland as Yeavering Bell. Famous hills, plains, rivers, castles, villages, pele-towers, and battle-fields lie stretched like a beautiful picture before the delighted gaze. What gives, however, to this hill its chief interest are the remains of pre-historic times which are yet to be seen on the summit and the grassy slopes. The summit is encircled by a rude and massive wall, now much broken down. It was originally about 10 to 12 feet in breadth, and 7 or 8 feet in height, constructed of unhewn blocks of porphyry without lime. There are four gateways, the principal one being that on the south, which is 12 feet wide, and has been defended by a guard-house of an oval shape. There is an additional wall, crescent-shaped, at both the east and west ends of this fort. The area enclosed is about twelve acres in extent, somewhat oval in form. The ground, which is comparatively level, rises, however, at the eastern end, where the rock protrudes through the soil about 20 feet above the general level. This naturally strong position has been taken advantage of by the ancient Britons. They have surrounded it by a ditch 5 feet deep, cut, for the most part, out of the rock, and by a low rampier about one foot in height. Within this fortlet, at its very highest point, is a small oval enclosure 13 feet in diameter from north to south, and 10 feet from east to west. When antiquaries believed that the remains on Yeavering Bell were those of a primitive temple consecrated to the worship of the sun, they placed in this excavated chamber the Druidical altar. Mr. Tate, however, has shewn their theories to be untenable. The foundations of about a dozen circular pit-dwellings may be traced in the great fort, their usual size being from 24 to 30 feet in diameter. Charred wood, fragments of coarse pottery, flints, oak rings or armlets, the upper stones of querns, and a round jasper bali, were discovered during some recent excavations. Lower down the hill, towards the east, are the remains of several fortified dwellings containing hut-circles with stone-flagged floors. In one case the wall is built of large upright blocks with smaller stones between. These fortlets yielded to the excavator a flint javelin head, two hones, a small perforated stone, fragments of a peculiar kind of pottery covered with a yellow glaze, etc. In a hut-circle on Swint Law—an eminence a little to the east—a fragment of an armlet was found. This was formed of green and blue glass, with white and yellow enamel running through it. An iron instrument, probably a rude spear-head, was discovered. Mr. Tate draws an interesting parallel between the strongholds of British and mediæval times. The great forts encircling the hill-tops were the impregnable castles which served as a temporary refuge during a hostile invasion, while the fortlets lower down were the pele-towers round which clustered the rude dwellings of the common people. There are numerous barrows on Worm Law, Swint Law, and other small elevations, some of them being guarded, as it were, by large upright stones. About a mile southward of Yeavering Bell is *Tom Tallon's Crag*, an outbreak of porphyry on the crest of a ridge. Near to it, on a high hill looking westward to Newton Tors, was a large cairn called "Tom Tallon's Grave,' or "The auld wife's apronfu' o' stanes." Tradition has not preserved for us the origin of the name. One half of this mound was carted away previous to 1837, and out of the remainder a wall was constructed in 1859, five feet high, two feet two inches wide, and one thousand yards in length. The stones were found to have been heaped over a cist-vaen of the usual kind.

A mile and a half to the west of Yeavering is the quiet and pretty pastoral village of KIRKNEWTON, resting amid a few trees at the base of cone-shaped hills near the confluence of the Colledge and the Glen. The scenery around is very wild and stern. To the south rise the Newton Tors, 1762 feet above the sea-level, and beyond them is the bulky form of Cheviot itself. The village was too near the Borders to escape the disastrous visits of the Scottish moss-troopers, and a passage in Sir Robert Bowes's report on the state of the Borders in 1550 refers to their exploits here :—"At Est Newton there ys a lytle toure, and a stone house joyned to the same, the walls of which stone house ys so lowe that in the last warres the Scotts wan the same stone house and sett fyre on yt, and had thereby almost burned the toure and all." Life then was very precarious ; very different from what it is now, judging by the inscriptions on the gravestones which record the death of persons at the great age of ninety-seven, one hundred and two, and even one hundred and nine years. The *Church of St. Gregory*, which was rebuilt in the time of Charles II. (*circa* 1670), and restored under Dobson in 1860, stands on the site of a Norman edifice. The base of a Norman buttress and part of the foundations of the early building were laid bare by Mr. F. R. Wilson during some excavations in 1857. Fragments of the ancient billet and lozenge ornaments are built up in the south wall. The chancel is a very remarkable one, being, it is supposed, the vaulted chamber of a pele or store-house built out of the ruins of the Norman church. The spring of the chancel arch is only two feet nine inches from the floor. At right angles to it on the south is a smaller but similar chamber, supposed to be an ancient chantry, now called the Burrell Vault. Here may be seen the old piscina, and a tomb-slab of the twelfth or thirteenth century. Attached to the wall behind the reading-desk is a curious piece of sculpture representing the Virgin and the Magi, which Mr. Wilson considers to be a caricature, as the wise men appear incongruously attired in kilts. The font is panelled in lozenges, and bears the date 1663. Built up in the wall of the tower on the outside is a child's coffin-lid with a floriated cross upon it. A gravestone on the left-hand side of the approach to the church has carved upon it a head with a skull suspended from its mouth, and cross-bones, hour-glass, etc., below. On Gregory's hill, above the village on the south, are the remains of a camp. There is a railway station at Kirknewton—a good starting-point for tourists wishing to ascend Cheviot from the romantic Henhole. Three-quarters of a mile west, at the head of a long pass among the hills, is *West Newton*. Here grow the dwarf elder (*Sambucus ebulus*), corn bell-flower (*Specularia hybrida*), and pennycress (*Thlapsi arvense*).

From this place a road runs south, skirting the base of Heathpool Bell, to *Heathpool*, a lonely hamlet, consisting of a few shepherds' cottages, perched on the high ground above the Colledge Burn, and overlooked on the east by the smooth green slopes of the Newton Tors. Here are the massive ivy-covered ruins of a pele-tower, which shares with Dunstan Hall the distinction of being the oldest building of its class in Northumberland. The walls are of great thickness, the porphyry blocks composing them being of prodigious size. Sir Robert Bowes describes it in his survey of the Borders in 1550 as "a lytle stone house or pyle which ys a greate releyffe to the ten'nts thereof." This is supposed to be the castle alluded to by Bishop Percy in his ballad of the "Hermit of Warkworth," where the heiress of Widdrington was imprisoned by her captor, while the heart-shaped camp, or enclosure, on the opposite side of the river, marks the spot where she fell, pierced by the sword of her hapless lover. Below Heathpool, in a deep and narrow glen, overhung with pine trees, is *Heathpool Linn*, a series of small cascades and black pools. Lord Collingwood had a small estate at Heathpool in right of his wife, a daughter of J. S. Blackett, Esq. He was raised to the peerage by the title of Baron Collingwood of Caldburne and Hethpoole, in the county of Northumberland. His correspondence reveals a curious solicitude about the planting of trees on the hill-sides here. The disappearance of the oak from our forests made him fearful lest he should not be able to find material for the building of his ships, and wherever he could find a place to put it in he planted an oak. "I wish," he says, writing to Lady Collingwood, March 21st, 1806, "some parts of Hethpoole could be selected for plantations of larch, oak, and beech, where the ground could be best spared. Even the sides of a bleak hill would grow larch and fir. You will say that I have now mounted my hobby; but I consider it as enriching and fertilising that which would otherwise be barren. It is drawing soil from the very air." Again, in December 20th of the same year, he writes—"It is very agreeable to me to hear that you are taking care of my oaks, and transplanting them to Hethpoole. If ever I get back I will plant a good deal there in patches; but before that can happen, you and I shall be in the churchyard, planted under some old yew tree." Lord Collingwood's gnarled old oaks may yet be seen on Harrowbog, about three-quarters of a mile south of Heathpool, on the east side of the stream. The valley of the Colledge is remarkably rich in memorials of pre-historic times. The Celtic population must have been very great, to judge from the numerous fortifications, hut-circles, and baulks on the slopes and summits of the adjacent hills. The extraordinary terraces, or "baulks," as they are locally called, which occur at Heathpool will be observed with much interest by the antiquary. "Similar terraces," says Mr. Tate, "are seen in the valley of the Breamish, but those on the Colledge are more marked, distinct, and numerous. White Hill, near the farm-house, is terraced to its summit. These terraces are generally flat, but some are slightly convex; they are smooth, and resemble carriage drives cut out of the hill-sides: they are not quite horizontal, nor are they all parallel; some run into each other, and, in such cases, one or two other terraces are intercalated for a short distance. Their breadth is from 10 feet to 42 feet, usually it is about 20 feet; they rise above each other by nearly perpendicular steps, which vary in height from 2 feet to 15 feet, generally it is from 4 to 5 feet. I counted sixteen of these terraces rising in succession above each other on this hill; but other higher hills in the district are terraced in a similar manner up, I estimated, to the height of 1000 feet above the sea-level; and these high-terraced hills seemed in the distance like the gallery of a great amphitheatre with benches cut out of the hill-sides. The want of horizontality and parallelism shows that these terraces have not been formed by the action of water; nor do I know of any natural agent which would produce them; evidently, indeed, they are the work of art—ancient terraces, I believe, of cultivation for the growth of corn, most probably dating backward to a very early period, as they are associated more or less with ancient British remains. They have been used for the purpose even to the middle of last century. Two reasons would lead to the adoption of this method at an early period—less mechanical power would be required to form ridges along the side of the hill, and the heavy rainfalls of the mountainous regions would be less liable to wash away the soil from ridges that were horizontal, than from those up and down the hill." A rough cart-track runs undulating along the ridge and scaur on the west side of the Colledge. Little Hetha, Great Hetha, and Sinkside Hills on the right are all crowned with circular camps. A mile and a half from Heathpool is the farm-house of *Whitehall*. The burn close by is luxuriantly fringed with fern and flower. An amber-coloured, fairy-like pool, under an old holly tree, forms a very pretty picture. Above the steep bank are the remains of primitive habitations. Half-a-mile further on is a remarkable camp, crowning an alluvial hillock which rises from the level ground near the stream. It consists of a number of chambers, enclosed by a massive rampart of unhewn stone. Half-a-mile beyond it is the farm-house of *Southern Knowe*, near which the Lambden Burn joins the Colledge. Half-a-mile further south is Fleehope, and three-quarters of a mile beyond this farm again is Mountholy. From this point it is worth while diverting the gaze from the towering heights of Cheviot in front, to the prospect behind, with its lovely combination of harmonious curves. There lies the long, deep, rounded glen, with its heather and bracken-covered slopes, and the Colledge winding its way at the bottom like a thread of silver; while in the far distance a gently-moulded ridge, surmounted by the dome-shaped peak of a more remote hill, strides across the opening, intercepting the view, its graceful outlines merging into those of the hills at the head of the glen. On Fawcett Shank, east of Mountholy and the flanks of Cheviot, the traces of early occupation are exceedingly numerous. Circular forts, clusters of hut-circles, look-out posts, ancient roads and walls, etc., indicate this as a very important British oppidum. A mile and a half up the valley from Mountholy is the great chasm in the side of Cheviot called the Henhole. Cheviot may be ascended from this point, and the return to Wooler made by way of either Goldscleugh or Langleeford.

From West Newton the Wooler and Kelso road takes a north-westerly direction, following the course of the Bowmont Water.

Two miles from Kirk-Newton is the small pastoral village of KILHAM, at the base of Kilham Hill (1108 feet). To the north-east of it, on the north side of the river, is *Howsdon*, a fine grassy hill, celebrated by the Northumbrian poet Story in one of his prettiest lyrics. "Its base," he says, "when I kept sheep upon it in my boyish days, used to exhibit a perfect forest of bloom." Two miles further west is the hamlet of *Paston*, in a pleasant and fertile vale, which contrasts with the bleak hills around. *Paston Hall* is the seat of Beauchamp Prideaux Selby, Esq. Paston Hill (755 feet) is crowned by a large circular camp. On its south side is Paston Lake, a small sheet of water. South again is Harelaw (915 feet), which appears from its name (*here*, an army, and *law*, a hill) to have been one of the military stations of the early inhabitants. There are traces of a circular entrenchment upon it, defended by a double rampier and fosse. The hill gives its name to a hamlet at its base, which is associated with a dark incident in the history of the Percy family. Thomas, the seventh Earl of Northumberland, after his ill-advised rebellion in 1568, was obliged to seek safety in flight. According to one account, he is said to have "skulked in some poor cottages at Harelaw among the Grahams, who were notorious robbers, and that one of them, Hector Graham, for a bribe, delivered him to the Earl of Murray. For this inhospitable deed the fierce Borderers, who respect their own laws of honour, wished to have Hector's head, that they might eat it among them for supper. Dr. Percy's account, gathered from Border songs, is a little more romantic. When the earl reached the Borders, he was seized, stripped, and maltreated by thieves; but at length he found an asylum in the house of Hector of Harelaw, an Armstrong, who, under considerable obligations to him, had pledged his honour to be true. Hector, like a faithless wretch, betrayed, for a sum of money, his noble guest, in January 1570, to James Stewart, the Earl of Murray. Retribution followed this treachery. Hector, before this, was rich, but soon afterwards he sunk into poverty, and his infamous conduct gave origin to a proverb. 'To take Hector's cloak' is applied to the man who betrays his friend."—*Tate.* There is a road over the Borders from here to *Yetholm*, the seat of the gipsies. Two silver coins—one of Hadrian

(A.D. 120), and another of Faustina the younger, wife of Marcus Aurelius (A.D. 175)—have been found on Bowmont Hill.

A mile to the west of Paston is the village of MINDRUM. Here are the ruins of an old chapel. In the disused graveyard there are still a number of headstones standing. Here is one of the stations on the new Alnwick and Cornhill Branch. A mile north-east of Mindrum Mill is *Downham*, behind which is a hill with a circular camp. Still further, in the same direction, is another on Moneylaws hill. Several Roman coins have been discovered in the neighbourhood. A mile and a half north-west of Mindrum Mill, approached by Piperdean Lane, is *Piperdean*. The Presson Burn flows through it, and near it is Presson farm-house. This is the site of a Border skirmish, unimportant in its results, yet of considerable interest to lovers of English literature, for some of the incidents connected with it seem to have formed the groundwork of the ballad of "Chevy Chase." The accounts of this battle vary in their details. According to Boethius, Henry Percy, the second Earl of Northumberland—it is uncertain by what authority, whether his own or the king's (it was a regency at that period)—made an incursion into Scotland in 1435 with a force of 4000 men. He was met at Piperden by an equal number of Scots, under the leadership of William Douglas, Earl of Angus, Warden of the Middle Marches, Adam Hepburn of Hailes, Alexander Ramsay of Dalhousie, and Alexander Elphinstone, and, after a short and sharp conflict, defeated. The English lost Henry Cliddesdail (Clennell of Clennell), John Ogle, Richard Percy, and about 400 men. Three hundred were made prisoners and conducted into Scotland. On the Scottish side there fell Alexander Elphinstone, and with him two knights and two hundred soldiers. Bower, who gives the date of the battle as September 10th, 1436, states that the number of the English captured was one thousand five hundred, among whom was Sir Robert Ogle, junior, and that "out of either kingdom there fell not over forty men of little note." Pinkerton, who fixes the date as September 30th, 1435, and not 1436, says nothing about the Earl of Northumberland. "An infraction of the truce happened on the part of England. Sir Robert Ogle, the younger, in support of one of the rebels against James, entered Scotland with a considerable force, and ravaged the country about Halton and Paxton. After a conflict in which about forty men were slain, Ogle was defeated and made prisoner with most of his followers by William, Earl of Angus, Hepburn of Hailes, and Ramsay of Dalhousie." The Earl of Northumberland was at this time Warden of the East Marches, and Sir Robert Ogle, junior, from the later accounts, broke away without authority. The Ogles were men of note on the Borders, the older one being sometimes Governor of Roxburgh and Berwick Castles. By the side of the road between Hagg and Moneylaws is a monument, erected A.D. 1878, in front of the house in which the Rev. Ralph Erskine—one of the founders of the Scotch Secession Church—was born, 1685.

# WOOLER TO FLODDEN FIELD.

**Ewart Park, 4 miles ; Coupland Castle, 4¾ miles ; Millfield, 6 miles ; Flodden Hill, 7¾ miles ; Site of Battle, 9½ miles ; Branxton, 10 miles.**

FOUR miles north of Wooler, by the road running past the Bendor Inn and Akeld, is *Ewart Park*, the seat of Sir Horace St. Paul, Bart. Two ancient swords, a compound of brass and copper, were discovered in the park in February 1814, buried perpendicularly, as if they had been thrust down for concealment. The Glen, which curves round the southern boundary of the park, falls into the Till a little to the east. In this angle, forming the south-east corner of Millfield Plain, King Arthur, according to Nennius, is said to have achieved one of his great victories over the Saxons. A Saxon fibula was found here, and is now in the possession of the proprietor of the mansion. Three-quarters of a mile to the west, on the north bank of the Glen, is *Coupland Castle*, the seat of Matthew T. Culley, Esq., J.P., built during the first part of the seventeenth century. When the Survey of Border towers and castles was made in 1552 there was "no fortress or barmekyn" at Coupland. The fact of such a stronghold being raised sixteen years after the union of the two kingdoms is a remarkable proof of the unsafe and unsettled state of the Borderland at that time. The oldest portion of the existing castle consists of two strong towers, containing eleven rooms, and a remarkable stone cork-screw staircase. The walls are in some places 6 or 7 feet thick. At the corners of the castle are "pepper-pot" turrets, the only other examples south of the Tweed being at Dilston and Duddo. Carved on a long stone chimney-piece, in what is called the "Haunted Chamber," are the initials of George and Mary Wallace, with the date 1619—the date probably of the erection of the castle. The Wallace family were the old proprietors of Coupland.

This place gave its name to an ancient family, of whom were John de Copeland, one of the twelve English knights appointed to settle with the Scottish Commissioners the Border disputes in 1248, and Sir John de Coupland, who took David of Scotland prisoner at Neville's Cross in 1346. Above the castle, on the west, rises Lanton Hill (683 feet), conspicuous on which is an obelisk erected by Sir William Davison, of Lanton, to the memory of his father, Alexander Davison, Esq., of Swarland Park, and his brother, John Davison.

Two miles north of Coupland Castle, and six north-east of Wooler, is MILLFIELD, a pleasant agricultural village, once the residence of the Saxon kings of Bernicia. The royal palace at Yeavering, says Bede, was neglected for a new one built "in a place called Melmin, but at this day Millfield." Not a vestige of this ancient building remains at the present day. Ancient British remains have been found at Millfield—leaf-shaped bronze swords, and a very large urn, 15 inches in height, ornamented with the common zigzag pattern. General Monck lay at Millfield on December 21st, 1659, where he received a deputation from the citizens of Berwick favourable to the restoration of Charles II. John Grey, Esq., the eminent agriculturist, resided at Millfield Hill previous to his appointment as agent to the Greenwich Hospital; estates and here his daughter and biographer, Mrs. Josephine Butler, well known for her advocacy of great social reforms, was born.

*Millfield Plain*, the bed of the great Glendale Lake in pre-historic times, was the scene of one of the minor battles between the Scots and English, which proved an ill-omened prelude to the battle of Flodden Field, a month later. On the 13th of August 1513, Lord Home, at the head of 3000 horsemen, was returning from a raid of retaliation, in which he had burned seven villages, when he was suddenly attacked by Sir William Bulmer, of Brancepeth Castle, with 1000 archers and men-at-arms, who had been laid in ambush, concealed by the wayside among the tall broom of Millfield Plain. The Scots, taken by surprise and encumbered with spoil, were able to make but a weak resistance. Hundreds were swept down by the terrible flight of arrows before they had even seen their foes, and the rest were thrown into confusion. Five or six hundred were killed and 400 taken prisoners. The victors lost but sixty. The road through Millfield was afterwards called by the Scots, in allusion to this disastrous fray, "The ill-rode." The plain seems adapted by nature to be the scene of some great conflict, and here it was that the Earl of Surrey wished to give battle to James IV. of Scotland. It is supposed to have been the bottom of the great Glendale Lake of pre-historic times. The depth of clay at Ewart Park exceeds seventy feet.

Two miles north of Millfield, and eight from Wooler, is the lodge called the *Linthaughs*, from which there is a broad carriage-drive, bordered with trees and shrubs, right round Flodden Hill. This "high ridge, which frowns o'er Milfield Plain," was occupied by James IV. and his army on September 8th, 1513, in the expectation that the Earl of Surrey would lead his forces across the level ground on the south. The summit is crowned by an ancient British camp, within which the king fixed his tent. On the north-east side of the hill is "Sybil's Well," made famous by Sir Walter Scott in "Marmion."

"Behold her mark,
A little fountain cell,
Where water, clear as diamond-spark,
In a stone basin fell.
Above, some half-worn letters say,
Drink, weary pilgrim, drink, and pray,
For the kind soul of Sybil Grey,
Who built this cross and well."

Here, according to the poem, Lord Marmion died, uttering the words, "Charge, Chester, charge! On, Stanley, on!"

"They dug his grave e'en where he lay,
But every mark is gone;
Time's wasting hand has done away
The simple cross of Sybil Grey,
And broke her font of stone.
But yet from out the little hill
Oozes the slender springlet still.
Oft halts the stranger there,
For thence may best his curious eye
The memorable field descry;
And shepherd boys repair
To seek the water-flag and rush,
And rest them by the hazel bush,
And plait their garlands fair."

Three-quarters of a mile south-west of the camp on Flodden Hill is a clump of firs marking the site of the "King's Chair," where King James IV. of Scotland sat watching the movements of the English army. To the north-west is Branxton Hill, which, with the valley below, forms the site of the battle of *Flodden Field.*

This great and decisive conflict—the last and most sanguinary struggle between the two nations—had its origin in a number of petty grievances, which had been accumulating for some time. The desire to strike a crushing blow at England had long been present in the heart of Scotland, and when, in 1513, Henry VIII. invaded the territory of the Scottish allies—the French—a favourable opportunity for doing so seemed to have presented itself. In the short space of three weeks 100,000 men, fully equipped and accoutred, with provisions for forty days, assembled on the Borough Moor, near Edinburgh. With this formidable host James IV. crossed the Tweed near Coldstream, on Monday, the 22nd of August 1513. The principal reason he assigned for invading England was to obtain satisfaction for the death of Sir Robert Kerr, Warden of the East Marches, who was slain at a Border meeting, about 1508, by the bastard Heron and two other Englishmen, named Lilburn and Starhead; and for the death of Andrew Barton, whom the Earl of Surrey's sons, Edward and Thomas, had attacked as pirate and killed at sea in 1511. The king's real object, however, was to oblige Henry VIII. to abandon the war which he was then carrying on against Louis XII. in Flanders. According to Pitscottie, James was largely influenced by a romantic appeal made to his gallantry by the French queen, who sent him a ring off her finger, with 14,000 French crowns to enable him to raise "an army and come three foot of ground, on English ground, for her sake." The castles of Wark, Norham, and Etal were besieged and quickly taken by the Scots. In the meantime the Earl of Surrey, who had been entrusted by Henry with the defence of the kingdom during his absence, summoned the gentlemen of Northumberland to meet him, with their retainers, at Newcastle, and advanced northward with such forces as he had gathered together at Pontefract. On the 30th of August he reached Durham, where he received the celebrated banner of St. Cuthbert from the Prior, and on the same day he arrived at Newcastle, where he was met by Lord Dacre, Sir William Bulmer, Sir Marmaduke Constable, and many other noblemen and gentlemen of the northern counties. At Alnwick he was joined by his son, Thomas Howard, Lord Admiral, with 5000 men, whom he had brought with him by sea. From this place he sent a challenge to the Scottish king, offering to give him battle on Friday, the 9th of September. At the small village of Bolton, which he had fixed upon as the general rendezvous for his army, Surrey received an answer from the Scottish king accepting his challenge. On the 6th Surrey moved to Wooler Haugh, while James, after assaulting Ford Castle, and partly overthrowing it, took up a strong position on Flodden Hill. The Scottish army was much reduced by desertions, several of the Scots having returned home with their booty, and the king was advised by his more experienced counsellors not to risk a battle. James considered that his honour was pledged to meet Surrey on the Friday, and harshly told the old Earl of Angus, Archibald Bell-the-Cat, that "if he was afraid he might go home." Angus, it is said, shed tears on hearing the scornful reproof, and quitted the field, leaving his two sons to fight and lose their lives under the banner of a king who had so unfeelingly insulted him. Surrey, after having tried different plans to induce James to meet him on Millfield Plain, but without success, broke up his encampment, and crossing the Till near Weetwood, proceeded behind the high ground to the southward of Doddington to Barmoor Wood, where his army encamped on the Thursday night. The Scots would find it difficult to account for this movement of the English on the north side of the Till, in a direct line for the banks of the Tweed. No sooner, however, had the fatal day arrived when the two armies were to meet, in accordance with the challenge given and accepted, than the unexpected manœuvre was explained. The English vanguard, with the artillery and heavy baggage, was seen passing over the bridge at Twizel, while the rear-guard was crossing the Till higher up by the Willowford, a little to the north of the village of Crookham, and by the Sandyford to the east of it. The spectacle, as seen from Flodden Hill, is thus graphically sketched by Sir Walter Scott—

"From Flodden ridge
The Scots beheld the English host
Leave Barmoor Wood, their evening post,
And heedful watched them as they crossed
The Till by Twizel Bridge.
High sight it is, and haughty, while
They dive into the deep defile;
Beneath the caverned cliff they fall,
Beneath the castle's airy wall.
By rock, by oak, by hawthorn tree,
Troop after troop are disappearing;
Troop after troop their banners rearing,

> Upon the eastern bank you see.
> Still pouring down the rocky glen,
> Where flows the sullen Till,
> And rising from the dim-wood glen,
> Standards on standards, men on men,
> In slow procession still,
> And sweeping o'er the Gothic arch,
> And pressing on in ceaseless march,
> To gain the opposing hill."

James has been accused of military incapacity in throwing away the opportunity of attacking the English during their passage of the Till, but unjustly, for there were many reasons why he should maintain his strong vantage-ground on Flodden Hill. The skilful generalship of Surrey, however, soon compelled him to abandon this position. Seeing that the English were evidently about to occupy the adjoining eminence of Branxton Hill, and so place themselves between him and his country, James issued orders to have the camp fired, and, under cover of the great smoke raised, the Scots silently descended the hill and seized the neighbouring ridge. The two divisions of the English army met at Branxton village. The two armies were about equal in number, each containing about 30,000 men. The disposition of both was also much the same, a centre and two wings, with a reserve force in the rear. On the English side the centre, placed near Branxton Vicarage, was under the command of the Earl of Surrey, assisted by Sir Philip Tilney and Henry Lord Scrope of Bolton; the rear was protected by a body of 2000 horse, in two divisions, drawn up in and around the village of Branxton, under Lord Dacre, assisted by the bastard Heron. The right wing, in two divisions, placed to the south-west of the church in the fields leading to Moneylaws, was commanded by Admiral Lord Howard, assisted by his brother, Sir Edmund Howard, and Sir Marmaduke Constable. It was hid from the rest of the English army by Piper's Hill. Behind were the baggage-wagons to protect its rear. The left wing, stationed on the fields south-east of the village leading to Mardon, was under the command of Sir Edward Stanley, assisted by Sir Henry Molyneux and Sir Henry Kirkley. The whole line would extend considerably more than a mile and a half in length. On the Scottish side the centre was commanded by the king, with the reserve, under the Earl of Bothwell, in the rear a little to the south-east. The right wing, stationed on the gentle slope of the eastern end of Branxton Ridge, was under the command of the Earls of Lennox and Argyle. The left wing was in two divisions, the one nearest the king being under the Earls of Crawford and Montrose; the other, on the sloping part of the hill, looking towards Wark, being composed of the wild and undisciplined Highlanders and stout Borderers, under the Earl of Huntley and Lord Home. The battle began about four o'clock in the afternoon of Friday, the 9th of September, with cannonading on both sides. The English were superior in artillery, and their ordnance seems to have been better served. The master-gunner of the Scots was killed, and his men were driven from their guns. Little harm was done to the English ranks, as the shots were discharged over their heads. After this preliminary flourish the struggle was carried on at closer quarters. The Earl of Huntley and Lord Home, with part of the left wing of the Scots, who fought on foot with "long spears like Moorish pikes," fell upon part of the English right wing under Sir Edmund Howard with a fury that was irresistible. Sir Edmund was three times beaten down; his banner was brought to the dust; his lines were completely broken, and part of his men fled in the greatest disorder. The fugitives are said to have been a party of Cheshire men, who were dissatisfied at being separated from the rest of their countrymen under Stanley and placed under the command of a Howard. At this critical moment a band of north-countrymen, led on by John Heron, the bastard, and Lord Dacre with the reserve coming up, checked the further progress of the Scots. Lord Home, however, managed to maintain his ground, and kept possession of it throughout the day and night, guarding the numerous prisoners taken on the field, amongst whom was Sir Philip Dacre, brother of Lord Dacre. The Lord-Admiral, being hotly engaged with the Scottish division under the Earls of Crawford and Montrose, and finding himself hard pressed, sent the Agnus Dei that he wore at his breast as a token to his father, requesting him to bring forward his division in all haste. Surrey immediately advanced, and was encountered by the Scottish centre, led gallantly on by James himself. The battle was now tremendous, and when the Earl of Bothwell came up with the reserve to the support of the king, the victory for a while inclined to the Scottish side. The scale was soon turned in an unexpected way. The English left wing, assailed by the Scottish right, received the half-naked clansmen with so terrible a discharge of arrows that they lost their discipline, and, flinging away shield and target, in a wild frenzy rushed tumultously on the ascending ranks. Staggered at first by the fierce onslaught, the hardy bowmen and stout pikemen from Cheshire and Lancashire, quickly closing their ranks, drove back their assailants with great slaughter, and forced their way to the top of the ridge. Elated with victory, Stanley gave the word to charge the Scottish centre in the rear, and a terrible carnage took place at the southern base of Piper's Hill. The king, with a devoted band of nobles—the flower of his army—was hemmed in on every side. With a desperate courage he struggled with the combined forces of Surrey, Stanley, Howard, and Dacre, contesting every inch of ground, till at length, with his hands hacked to pieces, his head gashed with a bill, and his body pierced with arrows, the gallant king fell amid the dead bodies of thirty of his faithful nobles. Graphically has Sir Walter Scott depicted the closing scene of the fight:—

"The English shafts in volleys hail'd:
In headlong charge their horse assailed;
Front, flank, and rear, their squadrons sweep
To break the Scottish circle deep,
  That fought around their king.

But yet, though thick the shafts as snow,
Though charging knights like whirlwinds go,
Though bill-men ply the ghastly blow,
  Unbroken was the ring;
The stubborn spearmen still make good
Their dark impenetrable wood,
Each stepping where his comrade stood,
  The instant that he fell.
No thought was there of dastard flight;
Link'd in the serried phalanx tight,
Groom fought like noble, squire like knight,
  As fearlessly and well.'

The conduct of Lord Home is difficult to explain at this crisis in the conflict. According to Pitscottie, when urged by the Earl of Huntley to advance to the assistance of the king, he answered, "He does well that does for himself. We have foughten our vanguards, and have won the same, therefore, let the lave do their part as well as we." His wild Borderers, being joined by marauders from Tynedale and Teviotdale, stripped the slain and pillaged the baggage of *both* armies during the night, which separated the combatants, and when day dawned Home's banner was seen hovering near the left flank of the English, while another body of Scots—apparently the remnant of the centre—appeared in front, occupying a hill as if to renew the contest. Surrey brought his artillery to bear upon them, and they were dislodged; but even then they seem to have retreated very deliberately, and Lord Home's people carried a rich booty and a considerable number of prisoners across the Tweed. Lord Dacre found seventeen pieces of cannon deserted on the hill-side, among which were the seven beautiful culverins from Edinburgh Castle, called "The Seven Sisters." Not until the Saturday morning, when the scattered bands of the Scots learned the death of the king, could the issue of this hotly-contested battle be said to be no longer doubtful.

The loss of the Scots, according to the most moderate calculation, amounted to 8000 or 9000 men; but this number included the very prime of their nobility, gentry, and even clergy. Besides, the king and his natural son, Alexander Stuart, Archbishop of St. Andrew's, there were slain twelve earls—Crawford, Montrose, Lennox, Argyle, Errol, Athole, Morton, Cassilis, Bothwell, Rothes, Caithness, and Glencairn; to these must be added fifteen lords and chiefs of clans, amongst whom were—Sir Duncan Campbell of Glenorchy, Loughlan Maclean of Dowart, and Campbell of Lawers; and conspicuous in the sad list are the names of George Hepburn, Bishop of the Isles; William Bunch, Abbot of Kilwinning; Lawrence Oliphant, Abbot of Inchaffray; the Dean of Glasgow; La Motte, the French agent, and most of his countrymen. "Scarce a family of eminence in Scotland," says Sir Walter Scott, "but has an ancestor killed at Flodden, and there is no province in Scotland, even at this day, where the battle is mentioned without a sensation of terror and sorrow." There is something very pathetic in the death of the Earl of Caithness, who, though under sentence of outlawry, presented himself on the eve before the battle, accompanied by three hundred young warriors, and submitted to the king's mercy. James, touched by this mark of attachment, granted an immunity to the earl and all his followers. The parchment on which it was inscribed, said to be preserved in the, archives of the Earls of Caithness, was cut out of the head of a drum, and still bears the marks of the drum-strings. The body of the king was discovered by Lord Dacre, and identified by his chancellor, Sir William Scott, and his sergeant-porter, Sir John Forman, and other Scottish prisoners. It was conveyed to Berwick, where it was embalmed and enclosed in lead, and afterwards, secretly, among other things, sent to Newcastle, from which place Surrey took it with him to London, and placed it in the Monastery of Sheen, near Richmond. The Scottish people, by whom the king was greatly beloved, could scarcely believe that he had fallen ; and several romantic stories got abroad that the king had escaped from the field, and crossed the Tweed in the twilight with four horsemen, afterwards journeying to the Holy Land to pray for the souls of his slaughtered nobles. The loss on the English side was so heavy that Surrey was in no condition to follow up his advantages. The number who fell could not be less than 5000, among whom, it is interesting to remark, there was hardly any one of note belonging to the English nobility. A large number of the dead were buried on the the west side of Piper's Hill. The spot is marked by a stone erected by J. Collingwood, Esq. Others were interred in consecrated ground.

The village of BRANXTON is chiefly interesting on account of its connection with the battle of Flodden. On yet another occasion the Scots were to have good reason for remembering this little place. On Trinity Sunday, the 21st June 1524, a party of 500 Scots, who had plundered some merchants going to Berwick fair, were attacked here by the young lord of Fowberry, at the head of 100 horse, and defeated, 200 of them being taken prisoners. The *Church of St. Paul* was rebuilt in 1849 in the Norman style of architecture. Only one fragment of the ancient structure remains, and that is the chancel arch, which is of the period recognised as Transitional. Percival Stockdale, author of *Ximenes*, a tragedy, and *Lectures on the Poets*, etc., was born at Branxton. A road runs eastward from Branxton to the Blue Bell Inn, on the main road, a mile and a quarter distant.

A little to the east of this point is the quiet and picturesque little village of CROOKHAM. *Ford* is two miles beyond to the south-east. The railway station to Flodden Field is Cornhill, four miles and a half distant. The tourist will proceed along the road running east as far as *Pallinsburn*, noticing in a field on the left, before reaching the House, a Border "Gathering Stone," locally known as "The King's Stone," and, when near the east lodge, will follow a path to the right, crossing what was, in 1513, a dangerous bog, to Branxton.

# WOOLER TO FORD AND ETAL.

Ford, 8½ miles ; Etal, 10 miles.

THE shortest route to Ford from Wooler is to proceed along the Kelso road as far as the Black Bull Inn (two miles), then follow the road branching off to the right past Glenlee-Ford and Akeld Steads to Ewart Park (one mile), and thence to Redscarbridge (two miles and a quarter). From this point there is a steep ascent of a mile and a half to *Kimmerston*, a pretty hamlet, with a few of the old thatched cottages still remaining. *Broomridge*, a little to the north-east, has been thought by some antiquaries to be identical with Brunanburg, where King Athelstan defeated Anlaf the Dane ; but it is now pretty well established that the battle was fought at Brough, near Hull. A mile and a half from Kimmerston is *Ford Castle*, the famous seat of Louisa, Marchioness of Waterford, situated amid beautiful grounds on a considerable eminence above the Till, with a delightful prospect over the valley as far southward as Wooler, and of the pine-clad heights of Flodden and the high green Cheviots beyond. The greater part of the building belongs to the years 1761-4, when Sir John Hussey Delaval made considerable additions to the towers of the mediæval fortress which were then standing. As these were of the ginger-bread Gothic style of that period, the Marchioness of Waterford found it desirable, in 1861-3, to carry out some extensive alterations, which restored the castle to something of its ancient grandeur. The entrance is in the south front, in the centre of a semi-hexagonal projection, on each side of which is a wing jutting out from a square turret, and forming a spacious court-yard. On the west side of the area, in front, is an old square tower, which supports a turret-like superstructure for raising the flag-staff above the generally flat sky-line of the building. The old Border stronghold was built about the year 1287 by Odenel de Forde. His daughter and heiress married Sir William Heron, who thus became possessed of the manor. He obtained, 1338, a license from Edward III. to crenellate his mansion-house of Ford. This nobleman was a very influential personage in his day, being captain of the castles of Bamburgh, Pickering, and Scarborough, also warden of the forests north of the Trent, and High-Sheriff of Northumberland for eleven successive years. Sir William Heron's stronghold, when thus fortified, would prove a doughty guardian of the district around, overrun as it was by the marauding Scots. The importance of Ford in military architecture consists in its being the earliest example, between the

Tees and Tweed, of a quadrangular building, with a square tower at each corner (an arrangement afterwards followed at Chillingham in 1344, and at Lumley in 1393), with an outer bailey added to the south. Ford was taken and demolished in 1385 by a party of Scots under the Earls of Fife, March, and Douglas. The story told by Pitscottie that James IV. of Scotland, after crossing the Tweed in 1513, wasted his time in dalliance with Lady Heron at Ford, instead of following up the advantages he had gained on English ground, is entirely without foundation. While he was besieging Norham and Etal, Lady Heron was far away, beseeching Surrey to make such stipulations with James as would secure the safety of her castle and the freedom of her husband. The result of her intercession was that Surrey wrote to the Scottish king offering to give up Lord Johnstone and Alexander Hume if he would spare Ford. James, disregarding these overtures, burnt down the stronghold previous to taking up his position on Flodden Hill—a proceeding which must be characterised as very unchivalrous, if he were, as the historians state, enamoured of the fair châtelaine. On the death of Sir William Heron in 1536 the manor and castle passed into the hands of Thomas Carr, of Etal, who had married the heiress of the Heron family. The castle had been partially restored when Sir Robert Bowes visited it in 1542, but a great part of it was still in ruins. Further injury was done to the castle in 1549, when a party of Scots, under the command of D'Esse, a French general of great military skill, battered down some of the walls with four field-pieces. The governor, Thomas Carr, driven with his garrison into one of the towers, offered such a stubborn resistance that the besiegers were obliged to retire, leaving it unreduced. Ford subsequently became the property of the Blakes and the Delavals. From Lord Delaval the estate passed to Susan, Marchioness of Waterford, daughter of Lady Tyrconnel.

The most interesting part of the castle is the north-west tower, a remnant of the fourteenth century fortress. A room in the upper storey, approached by a stair in the thickness of the wall, contains a fine modern chimney-piece adorned with the arms of Scotland, and inscribed with the somewhat dubious legend—

King . James . ye 4th .
of . Scotland .
did . lye . Here . at Ford Castle
A.D. 1513.

An old-fashioned bedstead and some good tapestry of the early part of the seventeenth century give an air of antiquity to the chamber. From the windows there is a magnificent view over the field of Flodden. In the basement of the tower is a vaulted chamber, popularly styled the "Dungeon." A straight stair leads down to it, covered by a trap door, which is apparently original, as, when shut, it forms the floor of a passage between two pointed doorways.

Several masons' marks of the fourteenth century are visible on the four-ribbed arching of the roof. A small trefoil-headed slit in the north wall admits, by a long shaft, the only light penetrating into this gloomy vault. The north-east tower has, beyond its general outlines, only preserved a wide newel stair leading to the first floor. The Library, Drawing-room, Labyrinth-room, and other apartments, are superbly decorated, the ceilings especially being worthy of notice for their beautiful tracery and ornaments in imitation of carving in wood. Many of the windows have stained glass, pictured with family armorial bearings. In no other private mansion in the kingdom is there, perhaps, to be seen such a valuable collection of antique furniture, curiously carved oak cabinets and cupboards, and old china. Lady Waterford's boudoir is hung with silk, beautifully embroidered with figures of birds. Two of the bed-rooms are in yellow satin, one of them being that in which the Queen of Holland slept. The pictures include portraits of Lord and Lady Delaval; their grand-daughter, Lady Tyrconnel; her cousin, Lady Audley, daughter and co-heiress of the second Lord Delaval; Admiral Delaval; Sir Francis Delaval; Thomas and Rhoda Delaval; the Duchess of Cumberland, by Sir J. Reynolds; and Sir Ralph and Lady Milbank, parents of Lady Noel Byron. Several of the paintings on the walls of the Library are by the Marchioness of Waterford herself. A curtain wall, with a curious semi-circular moulding running along it, extends from King James' Tower and past the Flagstaff Tower to a corner turret, now fitted up as an armoury. The lower part of it contains ancient masonry. The grounds, flower-gardens, and terraces adjoining the castle are exceedingly beautiful, and command from every point delightful bits of pastoral or sylvan landscape. Just outside the principal entrance is an elegant fountain, surmounted by the figure of St. Michael, erected in memory of Henry, Marquis of Waterford, who died 1859.

A sweeter little village than FORD could hardly be imagined outside of Arcadia. It is seated on a gentle slope between the gates of the castle and the highway, a broad carriage-drive edged with turf-banks passing through it. The cosy-looking, red-tiled cottages, half-hidden in foliage and flowering tendrils, are approached through the prettiest and trimmest of gardens, and with the attractive little school-room and idyllic post-office, present a picture of rural peace and retirement. The walls of this school-room have been decorated by the Marchioness of Waterford with a series of frescoes, illustrative of the lives of good children. The order of the compartments is as follows:—

1. Cain and Abel. In the medallions, Adam and Eve. Ornaments, apple in flower and fruit.
2. Abraham and Isaac. In the medallions, the angel and the ram. Ornaments, brambles of the thicket.
3. Jacob and Esau. In the medallions, Isaac and Rebekah. Ornaments, oak-leaves.

4. Joseph and his Brethren. In the medallions, the Chief Baker and Chief Butler. Ornaments, sheaves of corn.
5. Moses in the Bulrushes. In the medallions, Moses and Aaron. Ornaments, bulrushes,
6. Samuel lent unto the Lord. In the medallions, Eli and the child Samuel. Ornaments, grapes, corn, and olives (the first-fruits).
7. David the Shepherd. In the medallions, Saul and David. Ornaments, vine.
8. Josiah made king at eight years of age. In the medallions, Huldah and Hilkiah. Ornaments, the cutting down of the groves.
9. The Three Children. In the medallions, Daniel and the Hand on the Wall. Ornaments, tree in life and death.

The whole end of the room is covered with a large fresco of Christ blessing little children. The faces represented are those of children in the village. In the Visitor's Book, which is kept by the schoolmaster, may be seen the autographs of W. E. Gladstone, Sir Edwin Landseer, Earl Grey, Augustus J. C. Hare, Lord Stratford de Redcliffe, the Earl of Shrewsbury and Talbot, Dr. Lightfoot, Earl Cowper, Earl Brownlow, Coutts Lindsay, Earl of Gainsborough, Earl of Home, Duke of Buccleuch and Queensbury, Princess Christian of Schleswig-Holstein, the Duke of St. Albans, the Dean of Westminster and Lady Augusta Stanley, Lord Redesdale, William Landells, D.D., Earl Granville, Richard Doyle, Sophia, late Queen of the Netherlands, Sir Stirling Maxwell, Lord Armstrong, Lord Houghton, Earl of Warwick, Hamilton Aidé, Canon Greenwell, Professor Huxley, Earl of Crawford and Balcarres, Mandel Creighton, Stopford W. W. Brooke, General Probyn, Sidney Herbert, Professor Fairbairn, Sir Charles Trevelyan, James Wylie, D.D., the Duke of Teck, the Princess Mary Adelaide Victoria Mary Teck, Sir Walter Phillimore, and those of many other distinguished persons, amongst them being, in a bold, legible hand, that of "Charlie Beresford." There is no inn in the village, but a coffee-room has been provided by the Marchioness of Waterford for the convenience of visitors. A reading-room, with library attached, has also been established, and in connection with it is a recreation ground. *The Church of St. Michael* stands by the side of the Belford Road, a little to the south-west of the village. It was restored in 1853, but the work was executed with such good taste that the antique charm of the building has not been destroyed. The quaint bell-tower, containing three niches for bells, belongs to the ancient edifice, and was as picturesque a feature in the landscape in 1513 as it is now. Several wall-flowers add their floral grace to it. The roofs are covered with ornamental tiles; the interior is rich and impressive. There is an arcade of three arches on each side of the nave, that on the south being part of the original fabric. The east end of the south aisle was a small chantry, the piscina of which still remains. Here are the low pall-covered tombs of Lord Frederick FitzClarence and his only daughter. The chancel, which is paved with small tiles in mosaic, is reached by three steps, and lighted by a richly-decorated window filled with stained glass. A few years ago there was discovered in the church a fragment of an effigy, on which could be traced the letters—"Quondamdnatrix." In the churchyard, to the south of the church, is a monumental slab, ornamented with a floriated cross, and also with what appears to be the Northumbrian small-pipes. Another tombstone bears the date 1586.

A mile and a quarter from the church, by the side of the Berwick road, is *Ford Forge*, built in 1769, once famous for the manufacture of spades; and three-quarters of a mile beyond is the picturesque little village of

ETAL, which may fairly dispute with Ford the honour of being the loveliest village in Northumberland. The small, low, grey-walled cottages are less trim and dainty than those of Ford, but, being quaintly thatched, have that peculiar air of antiquity about them so attractive to the modern tourist. Beneath the overhanging eaves, around the doors and windows, climb the rose, the Virginia-creeper, and the clematis, with other festooning plants; while in front are little green-railed gardens, stocked with hardy, old-fashioned flowers and cottage herbs. At the upper end of the village, surrounded by fine plantations, is *Etal House*, built by Sir William Carr in 1748, and enlarged in 1767. It is the residence of James Laing, Esq. Within the grounds is the beautiful little *Church of the Blessed Virgin Mary*, built and endowed by the Right Honourable Lady Augusta FitzClarence in 1850, in memory of her husband and only child. The style of architecture adopted is the Decorated, and the walls, constructed of bands of red rubble, alternating with courses of cream-coloured ashlars, are rich and warm-tinted in tone. The chancel and sanctuary are richly decorated, the roof being radiant with gold and blended colours. Separated from the chancel by two pointed arches is the FitzClarence Mortuary Chapel, forming part of the south aisle. It contains the family vault. Traceried windows, filled with stained glass, add to the sumptuous effect of the interior.

At the lower end of the village, on the verge of a steep bank overlooking the river, are the ruins of *Etal Castle*, an Edwardian stronghold of the Manners family, who held the manor from the barony of Wooler previous to 1179. Sir Robert de Manners obtained from Edward III. a license to crenellate his mansion-house at Etal in 1341. The arms of this valiant ancestor of the ducal house of Rutland—viz., *or, two bars azure, a chief gules*—may be made out above the gateway. The castle was built by the same masons who, two years before, had erected the castle of Ford for William Heron. To reach the castle in former days it was necessary to cross a drawbridge, pass through an archway defended by a portcullis, and along a narrow passage commanded by battlements on the four sides, and under the gate-house. This entrance-tower is still standing—an interesting specimen of feudal military architecture. In front of it are two guns that once belonged to the ill-fated *Royal George*. On each side projected a high turret, connected together by a bretèsche, or pent-house, with loop-holes in it, attached to the wall above the gateway. Besides the strong gate and portcullis, four bars, nine inches square, worked backwards and forwards in holes cut in the wall on the east side. In the gateway-passage one of the soldiers of the guard has carved an elegant *fleur-de-lys* to while away the time. The gateway is flanked by guard-chambers, 24 feet by 6 feet. The western one has a fine arched roof with five ribs, a curious fire-place with an external chimney, and in the north-west corner a *garde-robe*, approached by a few steps. A narrow staircase, defended by iron bars sliding out from the walls, conducts to the apartments in the upper storeys. One of these, immediately above the groined archway, is lighted by handsome mullioned and traceried windows. From this gateway a massive curtain-wall, five feet in thickness, the battlements of which rested on projecting corbels, runs to a tower at the south-east corner of the castle-area. The basement storey is finely vaulted, and serves as a cellar for the adjoining manse. At the south-west corner of the quadrangle is the donjon, or keep—a tall, square, ivy-covered building, with only the four walls remaining, and these fast crumbling away. The basement storey was strongly groined. On the next floor is a very large fire-place, probably that of the kitchen. Above are two other tiers—one, the great hall ; the other, the sleeping apartments. The newel-stair, and a set of small rooms opening out into it, can be pretty well made out at the north end. The windows are small and arched, of only two lights, and transomed. The ends of the huge oak beams which supported the different floors may still be seen in the putlog-holes. The remains of *garde-robes* are numerous. Etal was one of the castles destroyed by James IV. previous to the battle of Flodden. It has never since been restored. Above the castle are visible the ruins of an old bridge across the Till ; the foundations are of a triangular form, the apices pointing up the river. It was doubtlessly over this bridge that the captured Scottish artillery was conveyed to Etal the day after the battle of Flodden. Cannon-balls, similar to those occasionally unearthed on the field of Flodden, have been found among the ruins of the castle. Along the beautifully-wooded banks of the Till there is a long, romantic carriage-drive continued as far as Tindle-house and Tiptoe Rocks. A quarter-of-a-mile down the river from Etal Mill, on a moist and verdurous site in the woods, a little to the left of the drive, are the mossy ruins of *St. Mary's Chantry*, founded by Sir Robert de Manners about 1346-7. When the site was uncovered some years since, a human skull was turned out, in which a wren had built her nest. Adjoining the chantry is *St. Mary's Well*, a spring of cool, clear water. Two miles and a half north-west of Etal, on the right bank of the Till, is "Big Nichol," a tall crag, situated between Tiptoe Mill and Tiptoe Throat, as the channel of the river is called at this point. There is a comfortable, old-fashioned inn at Etal—the Black Bull. The nearest railway station is Cornhill, five miles to the east of the village.

# WOOLER TO DODDINGTON AND LOWICK.

Cuddy's Cove, 2 miles; Doddington, 3 miles; Rowting Linn, 6 miles; Fenton, 5 miles; Barmoor, 7¾ miles; Lowick, 8¼ miles.

THREE-QUARTERS of a mile along the Wooler and Berwick road is the hamlet of the *Turvelaws*, and a mile further on the Doddington bridge crosses the Till. A few yards beyond, a road branches off to the right to Weetwood, and a quarter of a mile eastward of this point, projecting from a steep hill-side, will be observed a prominent mass of red sandstone, 20 feet high, in which is a small cavern called *Cuddy's Cove*. On the scalp of this rock, where it dips into the hill, and on its perpendicular western face, are some curious archaic markings of various forms. The moory hill rising above it is *Dod Law*. Behind the gamekeeper's cottage, which stands conspicuously on its brow, is a remarkable double camp, the two parts being nearly contiguous. It is defended by a huge rampier and a very deep fosse. Several hut-circles can be traced in the central area. The primitive inhabitants of these high moorlands have left many traces of their presence in the remarkable rock-sculptures around their entrenchments. Within six yards to the northward of the principal camp a figure formed of three concentric circles around a cup appears on the surface of the outcropping rock. Only thirty yards eastward of this camp is a rock, 16 feet by 8 feet, covered with figures differing considerably from the common type. They are rudely quadrangular in form; one of them consists of three concentric squares around fourteen hollows. To the northward, less than half-a-mile, and less than that distance eastward of Doddington, there are two figures on a grey gritty sandstone cropping out midway up the hill. A quarter of a mile eastward of the camp are two groups of large circles. Within a short distance of the Dod Law camp are three other camps—one, half-a-mile to the east, near which are three standing stones, the remains of a Druidical circle; another, a mile to the south-east and half-a-mile from Horton; and a third, a mile north-north-east, called the *Ringses*. This last-named camp is a very strong one, defended by three great rampiers formed of earth and stone. Steep escarpments on the west and south render it yet more secure. On the north side is an additional semi-circular wall enclosing a large area. The interior of the stronghold contains the foundations of several hut-circles and enclosures. Less than a quarter of a mile eastward of the camp are five groups of rock markings containing sixteen figures. On *Gled Law*, a platform of rock breaking out of the south-west escarpment of Dod Law, and ranging from north-west to south-east, seven groups, comprising thirty-six figures, are traceable. One of these is thirty-nine inches in diameter, and has eight concentric circles, a central cup, and three radial grooves.

Half-a-mile to the north-west of Dod Law Camp is DODDINGTON, three miles from Wooler. It is a quiet and quaint little village, irregularly built, and spread over a larger area than is usual with north-country villages of the same size. It occupies a comparatively low site, beneath the heathery sandstone ridge, which protects it from the north and east winds. Through the wide green haughs to the south of it winds the Till. Doddington was no doubt founded by the Saxons, and from a very early period belonged to the Barony of Alnwick. The importance of the place may be gathered from a tradition that on the occasion of a Doddington man dying at Belford, forty lairds of Doddington, each riding his own horse, went over to attend the funeral. The village in 1734 does not seem to have impressed visitors, for George Mark, in his Survey, says—"It is remarkable for its largeness and badness of its houses, and low situation, and perhaps for the greatest quantities of geese of any of its neighbourhood, and is distinguished from all the rest of the county, except Branxton, for having the chapel covered with heather and straw." A weekly cattle-market was once held here. In the centre of the village is a large pele-tower, a good example of one of the latest fortified houses. It was built in A.D. 1584 by Sir Thomas Grey, of Chillingham and Wark, as may be seen from the stone panel inserted in the wall of its battlements. There were three storeys above the great chamber on the ground floor, approached by a spiral stone staircase built on the south side. The roof is now covered with red tiles, and has a battlement on the north and south. A little to the south-west of the village is the *Church*, an early English edifice of considerable interest, restored and enlarged in 1838. There was a previous chapel here, probably built at the instance of the monks of Holy Island, before the Norman conquest. A curious feature in this church is the arch in the centre of the nave, dividing it into two portions. The westernmost division is used as a mortuary chapel of the family of Sir Horace St. Paul. The font placed here bears the date 1723. The easternmost division only has a north aisle, of which the three pointed arches, on octagonal pillars, are good examples of the early English architecture of the thirteenth century. On the south side of the chancel is a fine stained-glass window, representing "Christ blessing the little children." There is a watch-house at the south-east corner of the churchyard, built in 1826, when the "resurrectionists" were abroad. By the side of the main road is the *Dod Well*, an ancient spring, enclosed in 1846, and surmounted by a massive cross of Calvary. There was a song current in the village in days gone by, the burden of which was—

"The bonny Dod Well and the yea-pointed fern."

This fine old fern is thought to have been the *Osmunda regalis*.

The nearest railway station to Doddington is that of Wooler.

By the main road Lowick is five miles and a half from Doddington. If the road be followed, the tourist should see, in a cultivated field called High Chesters, on the right-hand side of the road, about half-a-mile from Doddington, one of the most remarkable of the incised stones of the district. It juts out from the hill-side, and its whole surface, nine feet by seven feet, is covered with thirty figures, chiefly of the ordinary type of concentric circles, though there are some of an oval horse-shoe and pear shape. By taking another route, by way of Hetton Hall and Howburn Grange, *St. Cuthbert's Cave*—or *Cuddy's Cave*, as it is sometimes called—may be visited. It is a short distance east of the farm-house, on the southern slope of a hill, and is said to have been one of the retreats of St. Cuthbert when absent from Lindisfarne. Rudely carved initials, and dates on the stones of which it is composed, prove it to have been, for a very long period, a place of interest. The ruins of the fortified manor-house of the ancient lords of Howburn were standing within living memory. There is a third route to Lowick, past Fenton House and Rowting Linn. A new road has been made along the wooded base of a high ridge behind Fenton House. This mansion, the residence of the Hon. F. W. Lambton, J.P., was built by the late Earl of Durham, 1871-5. It forms, with its ornamented façade of polished freestone, its tall tower, its extensive grounds, gardens, and artificial lake, an attractive feature in the landscape. The *Hamlet of Fenton* (the town in the fens) lies lower down the slope, two miles west from Doddington. It was pillaged and burnt by the Scots, under the Earl of Bothwell, in 1558. In a field called the Kirk Close it is supposed that the mother church of Wooler formerly stood. The old burial-ground is quite neglected. The last interment took place in 1842. Until very recently the foundation of an old pele-tower might have been seen in the garden of the farm-house. At *Fenton Hill*, a mile north, are the remains of a camp. Close to where the road past Fenton Hill joins another one from Kimmerston is *Rowting* (bellowing) *Linn*, a pretty waterfall in the ravine traversed by the Broomridge Burn, three miles from Doddington. There is a bridge over the ravine near the junction of these roads, and the linn is a few yards below it. The clear, amber-coloured water from the moorlands glides along the rocky channel, beneath overarching boughs, to the edge of a small precipice, thirty feet high, when it tumbles over into the linn, or pool, at its base, making a further fall lower down. Very picturesque are the worn and pitted sandstone cliffs on each side, overhung with trees and adorned with ferns that spring from the moist crevices. In the woods around are found the sweet-gale (*Myrica gale*), hart'stongue (*Scolopendrium vulgare*), the swallow willow (*Salix caprea*), the purple small-reed (*Calamagrostis lanceolata*), the tufted aira (*Aira cæspitosa*), the bay willow, (*Salix pentandra*), and the common heath (*Calluna vulgaris*). The high ground on the north is crested by the Goat Crags. On the other side of the road crossing the glen is an ancient British camp, which occupies an angle formed by the bend of the streamlet. It is defended on the north and west sides partly by deep gullies, and on the other sides by four immense rampiers and intervening trenches. A supplementary rampier encloses a large area on the south, within which is a great mass of sandstone rock, 60 feet long, 40 feet broad, and 10 feet above the ground on the south side, remarkable for the great number of symbolic figures carved upon it by the ancient Britons. Of these, fifty-five are traceable on its northern and western slopes, and five on its southern slope. Most of the figures are of the common type, consisting of concentric rings round a cup-like hollow, from which proceeds a groove, passing through all the circles to the outside. Some of the circles have two or three grooves issuing from them. One figure resembles a recessed Gothic archway; another a horse-shoe. One singular figure has nine grooves radiating from the top of the outer circle. "Some of the compound figures are peculiar, one resembling a plant with stem, branches, and floral heads; another—two circles united by a groove—a pair of spectacles." No difficulty need be experienced in finding this incised rock, as it is but a few yards from the gate opening out from the Kimmerston and Barmoor Road. Nearly a mile to the north-westward, on Hunter's Moor, are some other incised rocks. Near them are several ancient barrows. These ancient sculptures belong to the Celtic race, and are at least 2000 years old. They have been chipped out with rude tools of flint or basalt, or possibly bronze. It is thought that these figures are symbolical, most probably of religious ideas. "Some of the groups of the concentric circles," says Mr. Tate, "may show their idea of the motion of the heavenly bodies, and the radial lines might set forth the 'influence and ability of the immortal Gods,' as extending through and beyond the orbits of the heavenly bodies; the plant-like figures might enable them to expound 'the nature of things' as seen in vegetation; possibly the grooves, passing from the centre of one system of circles to another, might symbolise the passage of a soul from one state of being into another, and a higher state. And, in addition, I cannot but think that one of the chief uses of these sacred stones was for magic and necromancy." It is not improbable they may have been connected with the obscene Phallic worship once so prevalent among primitive peoples.

From Rowting Linn the road runs for two miles over tke bleak high moors before it reaches the Berwick road. Then, half-a-mile north from the point of junction, is the village of BARMOOR. Here it is said that the Lord Wardens of the Marches assembled, in 1417, with an army of 100,000 men, to chastise the Scots for dispersing a body of English near Roxburgh. The Scots, who had just crossed the Border, retired on hearing of the approach of this formidable army. *Barmoor Castle*, the residence of Edmund Meade Waldo, Esq., is built on the site of an old pele-tower of the Muschampe family

*Barmoor House* is the residence of Mr. Sitwell. About two miles north-west is *Woodend Wood*, where the English lay encamped the night before the battle of Flodden. From Watch Law Hill they observed the movements of the Scots on the opposite ridge. A mile east of Barmoor is

LOWICK—the "village on the Low." It consists of a few farm-houses and cottages, three churches—Anglican, Catholic, and Scotch Presbyterian—a Primitive Methodist Chapel, two good schools, and three inns—the White Swan, the Commercial, and the Black Bull. The nearest railway station is Beal, four miles and a half east.

The *Church of St. John the Baptist* stands on the site of a Norman Chapel, built about the year 1145 by the monks of Lindisfarne. It consists of four walls, with a small saddle-backed tower at the west end. Over the door is a tablet inscribed, "This chapell rebuilt An Dom 1794." The only relic of the ancient edifice is one of the window capitals built in the east wall of the graveyard. It is recorded that while the Prior of Durham was hearing mass here in the olden days, Sir Alan de Heton, lord of Howburn, impounded his palfrey, took possession of the churchyard, and sent no less than seven men to give the prior's servant a thrashing before the gates, besides committing other outrages. At the time when the body-snatchers were causing alarm throughout the county, extraordinary precautions were taken to protect the newly-buried bodies at Lowick, wooden spiles being driven into the ground to the level of the coffin lid, and iron bars fixed across them. Much historical interest attaches to the Scotch Presbyterian congregation, which dates its existence from 1662, and is therefore one of the oldest Nonconformist congregations in England.

According to tradition, Lowick Moor was the scene of the midnight gambols of the "Lady of Barmoor" who, by magic, transformed herself into a wondrous white hare. This legend forms the subject of a ballad in Sheldon's *Minstrelsy of the English Borders*.

# BERWICK SECTION.

## BERWICK-UPON-TWEED.

THE historic town of BERWICK-UPON-TWEED, picturesquely seated at the apex of the rudely-triangular county of Northumberland, may be considered as the capital of the romantic Borderland which Sir Walter Scott and the old ballad-writers have invested with so enduring a charm. In the neighbourhood are ruined castles, "old in story," the sites of great battles, places of literary and legendary interest, picturesque abbeys, charming villages, and beautiful scenery. The country north of the Tweed does not come within the scope of this work, hence the Berwick section, dealing merely with the country south of the Tweed, must, necessarily, be a small one. The town of Berwick, as seen from the top of the Royal Border Bridge, creates a favourable impression on the mind of the stranger ;—a compact and picturesque little town, with battlemented walls around it, sloping up from the north bank of the river, which is connected with the south bank by a quaint old bridge of fifteen arches. At the west end are the fragments of a strong castle, which at one time defended the town from the English, and at another from the Scots. At the east end is a long, curving pier, which guards it from the encroachments of the sea. Few vessels at present visit the port of Berwick, for commerce has hitherto refrained from defiling the fair banks of the Tweed with factories and foundries. As in the case of many other old towns, Berwick looks best at a distance. When viewed at closer quarters, the streets, with the exception of one broad thoroughfare, which, like a main artery, runs through it from west to east, are found to be narrow and cheerless, the cramped and plain-fronted houses having a look of Calvinistic hardness and austerity about them. Architectural embellishment of even the simplest kind has been scrupulously avoided. A visitor to Berwick in 1888 can scarcely say what Monsieur Jorvin said in 1762—"So that by walking over Berwick I discovered it to be one of the greatest and most beautiful towns in England." Yet, while walking along these confined, irregular streets, and gazing upon these tall and red-tiled buildings, and the many fragments of ancient masonry cropping out amongst them, memory will be busy reviving scene after scene of historic or tragic nature once witnessed in the grey old town.

Berwick was to the English and Scots, on a small scale, what Alsace and Lorraine are to the French and Germans—a constant source of contention and bitterness; and between the two it experienced more of the calamities of Border warfare than did any other town or village in the north. After such vicissitudes, it is not surprising that the energies of the town should have been crippled, and that while other and newer boroughs have developed with mushroom-like rapidity, she should have settled down into that condition of "masterly inactivity" so characteristic of towns with a famous past. An attempt has been made within recent years to beautify the town by planting trees on Bank Hill and in various parts of the walls and along Gillies Braes. A brief account of the history of Berwick will prove of service to the visitor before commencing his rambles through the town.

Berwick was most probably founded by the Saxons, very shortly after they had gained a foothold on English ground, for the bold sea-rovers would naturally choose the most prominent sites near the coast for their early settlements. Its name, Bere, or Bar Wic—corn or grain port—indicates its commercial character at this time. The accounts of the early chroniclers respecting the vicissitudes of Berwick previous to the Conquest are not very reliable. It would seem that Donald and Gregory the Great, with their bands of Picts and Scots, had taken and sacked the rising burgh, and that the Danes also had paid some predatory visits. Duncan, who succeeded Malcolm to the Scottish throne, is said to have fitted out in Berwick harbour eleven ships with which to oppose the usurper Macbeth. The town was plundered by the mercenaries of William the Conqueror. The really first authentic notice of Berwick is a charter of Edgar, King of Scotland, conferring the town, with its churches and possessions, on the see of Durham. In the succeeding reigns Berwick became the chief seaport of Scotland, and was created by David I. a royal burgh, being represented in the "Court of the four Burghs." The castle here, together with other Scottish strongholds, was delivered up to Henry II. by William the Lion as a pledge of his good faith in fulfilling the conditions of his release. Richard I., however, in 1189, freed the Scottish king from his allegiance and subjection to the crown of England, on payment of 10,000 merks, and restored the fortresses of Berwick and Roxburgh. The town was taken in A.D. 1214 by King John, who perpetrated the most barbarous cruelties on the helpless inhabitants. On his return from a raid into Scotland he lodged in Berwick for a night, and next morning burnt down the town, setting fire himself to the house where he had found entertainment and rest. Rebuilt on a larger scale before A.D. 1216, Berwick reached the height of its prosperity during the reign of Alexander III. (1247-1286). It was then, according to the Lanercost chronicler, "a city so populous and of such trade that it might justly be called another Alexandria, whose riches were the sea and the waters its walls." The wealth of the town may be gauged from the fact that the customs of Berwick in 1287 amounted to about £2000, while those of the whole of England only produced a little over £8,000. A great convention, consisting of the chief barons and prelates of England and Scotland, presided over by Edward I., was held here on August 2nd, 1291, to consider the rival claims of Bruce and Baliol to the crown of Scotland. On the 17th November 1292 the deliberations were brought to a close in the great hall of the castle, when Edward I., in the presence of a distinguished assembly, declared the result to be in favour of John Baliol. The new-made king took his oath of allegiance to the English monarch, but in 1296, on account of certain alleged grievances, broke into open rebellion and invaded Northumberland. Edward advanced northward to inflict a terrible vengeance. The first blow fell on Berwick. About 7000 of the inhabitants were massacred without distinction of age or sex. The rude soldiery sacked the mansions of the prosperous merchants, plundered the churches, and then stabled their horses in the sacred edifices. A body of Flemings, who had done much to develop the trade of the town, made a gallant resistance in the "Red Hall of Commerce" until the place was set on fire, and they perished in the flames. Here Edward I. received the homage of the Scottish nobility on the 24th of August 1296, in the presence of an English Parliament assembled for that purpose. Berwick was re-peopled with English traders and the remnant of the Scots who had sworn fealty to their new king; but was evacuated by them in 1297, on the approach of Sir William Wallace. The castle, however, held out until relieved by an immense body of foot and horse. In 1305 an arm of the Scottish patriot, who had been basely betrayed by Sir John Menteith, was exposed in some prominent position at Berwick. A barbarous punishment was meted out here to the Countess of Buchan, who had crowned Bruce at Scone. She was shut up for four years in one of the turrets of the castle, her cell being a cage of strong lattice-work, which exposed her to the mockery and scorn of the passers-by. For nine months, during 1310-11, Edward II. made Berwick his head-quarters, whence he harried the border counties of Scotland. In 1313 the magnificent army of 100,000 men which he had assembled for the purpose of relieving Stirling Castle marched through Berwick to their doom at Bannockburn. The defeated monarch passed through the town on his way to the south. The Scots made an attempt to surprise Berwick in 1315, but were unsuccessful. In 1318, however, Bruce gained possession of the town, through the treachery, it is said, of Spalding, one of the sentinels at the "Kow Gyate." Edward made a determined attempt to regain the town in the summer of 1319. His land-forces assaulted it on one side, while his navy attacked it from the side of the river. So gallantly was it defended by Bruce's son-in-law, Walter Stewart, that the siege had to be raised, and for fifteen years Berwick remained in the hands of the Scots. Here, in 1328, Joan de Turribus, sister of Edward III., was married, with great rejoicings, to Prince David. Great hopes were founded on this union, and the fair princess, who brought with her the Ragman Roll, and all the records carried off by Edward I., received the appellation of "Make-peace." On the death of Robert Bruce, Edward III., disregarding this alliance and the treaty made at Northampton in 1328, found a pretext for invading Scotland, and began his campaign by laying siege to Berwick, which, in view of such a contingency, had been fortified and strengthened in every possible way. After a blockade of three months, during which the sufferings of the inhabitants were very great, the garrison agreed to capitulate on certain conditions, if not relieved before a given date. Sir William Keith, the governor, set out to communicate the terms of this treaty to Douglas, who was besieging Queen Phillipa in Bamburgh Castle. During his absence, Edward is stated to have cruelly put to death the two sons of Sir Alexander Seton, the deputy-governor (at the time prisoners in his hands), since their father would not surrender the town to him. The place where this tragedy was enacted is a knoll on the Tweedmouth side of the river, still called "Hang-a-Dyke-Neuk." In the meantime Sir William Keith agreed with Lord Archibald Douglas to try the issue of a battle. On July 19th, 1333, the two forces met at Halidon Hill, two miles and a half north-west of the town, and the Scots were defeated with a loss of 14,000 men according to the Scotch, and 35,000 according to the English historians. The immediate surrender of Berwick followed as a natural result. Edward encouraged the English merchants to settle in Berwick and develop its trade, granting them several important privileges and immunities. In 1355, while Edward was in France, a party of Scots, under cover of the darkness, landed on the north side of the town (Greenses Harbour), and scaling the walls near the "Cowgate," surprised the garrison and captured the town. They were unable to take the castle, and on the approach of Edward in January 1356 with a large army, prudently retired from the town, after having first destroyed the walls and defences. In 1377 a band of desperate Borderers—only eight in number, it is said—entered the castle stealthily by night, killed the governor, Sir Robert Boynton, and overcame the garrison. Joined by about forty confederates, they held the stronghold for eight days against 7000 English archers and 3000 cavalry. The tower was burnt during a raid of the Scots in 1384. In 1404 the Earl of Northumberland engaged to deliver up the castle and town to the King of Scotland, Robert III. After the battle of Shrewsbury, Henry IV. marched north, and laid siege to the castle, which was held by Sir William Greystock on behalf of the rebel earl. A cannon of large bore was used for the first time against the walls at this siege, with such effect that the garrison were soon suing for terms. After the death of the Earl of Northumberland at Bramham Moor, a portion of his body was exposed at Berwick. An unsuccessful attempt was made by the Scots in 1422 to gain possession of Berwick. During the Wars of the Roses, however, Henry VI. delivered it up to James of Scotland, in consideration for the promise of help against the Yorkists. For twenty-one years the Scots held this key to their kingdom. A futile effort was made by the English to retake it in 1480; but in 1482, when an army of 22,000 men, led by the Earl of Northumberland and the Dukes of

Albany and Gloucester, came against it, the town surrendered without offering any resistance. Lord Hailes was prepared to hold the castle with the small force at his command; but not receiving the aid from Scotland which he expected, he was obliged to give up the stronghold. From this time forward Berwick, which had changed masters no less than thirteen times in the space of three centuries, remained in the possession of England, ceasing to be a source of contention between the two nations. In 1502 the Princess Margaret, daughter of Henry VII., stayed two days at Berwick on her way to Lamberton Kirk to be married to the young King of Scotland, James IV. After the battle of Flodden, in 1513, the dead body of the royal bridegroom was brought to Berwick to be embalmed and removed to the south. In 1560-65 the present fortifications were built at an enormous expense. On March 27, 1603, James I., on his journey to assume the crown of the United Kingdom, passed through Berwick, and was accorded a loyal welcome. Berwick during the Commonwealth was surprised in 1648, and taken possession of by Sir Marmaduke Langdale, with 1000 foot and 800 horse. Cromwell came to the neighbourhood shortly after, and found the Royalists had evacuated the town. He returned here in 1650, when on his way to Dunbar. General Cope retreated to Berwick after the battle of Prestonpans, and the Duke of Cumberland passed through it on his way to Culloden. Though included in all the county histories as part of Northumberland, Berwick forms a county of itself, having been so constituted in the reign of William IV. The fact of it being nominally independent of both England and Scotland is accounted for by the humorous as follows:—During the temptation, while the Evil One was showing to the Holy One all the kingdoms of the earth, he kept Berwick hidden beneath his thumb, wishing to reserve it as his own little nook. The Liberties of the borough, commonly called "Berwick Bounds," containing an area of nearly eight square miles, extend to the north and west, and form the north-east extremity of England. At the north end of the bounds is *Lamberton Toll*, where runaway couples were formerly married. It was also a notorious depôt for smuggled goods. The two principal sources of the trade of Berwick are the exportation of grain and the salmon fishery, for which it has long been famous. The town is the head-quarters of the Berwick Salmon Company, Limited, which occupies most of the stations on the neighbouring coast, and for some miles up the river. The fish are mostly sent to the London market. Salmon-fishing at Berwick begins February 15th and ends September 14th. The visitor to Berwick no sooner enters the railway station than he is on historic ground. This castellated building stands on part of the site of the old castle. The *Great Hall*, in which Edward I. declared his decision in favour of Baliol, corresponds as nearly as possible with the site of the platform of the station. Not much is left of the old castle. There is the western flanking wall (the White Wall of early times), with the base of the Water Tower, by the river-side; and there are the remains of two other towers still standing a few feet above ground—one, an octagonal tower in the garden of Castle Vale House; the other on the west side of the site of the castle, and adjoining the western wall before it begins to descend to the river. A flight of steps, once covered over and battlemented, leads down to the *Water Tower.* The appearance of this stronghold may be gathered by a description of the ruins in 1762 by Monsieur Jorvin:—"It is environed on one side by the ditch of the town; on the other side by one of the same breadth, flanked by many round towers and thick walls, which enclose a large palace, in the middle of which rises a lofty keep or donjon, capable of a long resistance, and commanding all the environs of the town." From the Water Tower a strong chain, in ancient times, passed to the opposite shore, preventing the enemy's boats proceeding up the river.

Berwick is bi-sected in one direction by Castlegate, High Street, or Marygate, and the Wool Market; and in another by Sandgate, Hide Hill, Church Street, and Wallace Green. Branching off from these main thoroughfares are several smaller and less imposing streets. In so ancient a town as Berwick there is a remarkable absence of old historic buildings. Not a trace remains of the four convents belonging to the Red, the Black, the Grey, and the White Friars, nor of the three ancient hospitals and churches of Saint Nicholas, Saint Lawrence, and Saint Mary. The site of the Hospital of Saint Mary is preserved by the name—"Magdalen Fields." Tradition identifies it with the site of the farm-house in these fields. Some interesting remains of the Edwardian fortifications still enclose the Castlegate suburb and the fishermen's quarter, known as the "Greenses." They lie a little north by east of the railway station, and include a portion of Lord Soulis' Tower and the Bell Tower. The latter, though perhaps of later date, is an interesting relic of ancient times. From its lofty turrets a watch was kept, so that the garrison and town might be apprised of the approach of an enemy. The signal of alarm was given by the ringing of a bell. According to tradition, there was a covered way between the tower and the castle. Of the four storeys only three remain. Over the entrance door on the west may be traced the arms of England—three lions rampant.

At the north side of the Parade stands the *Church of the Holy Trinity*, the oldest ecclesiastical edifice in the town, built 1648-52, and restored and enlarged in 1855. The materials of which it is constructed were obtained from the outside walls of the old castle—an application of the *lex talionis*, for the old parish Church of Saint Mary's was taken down and appropriated to the building of a new wall and fortifications near its site. The church is quadrangular in shape, built in the Italian style. Being without a tower or bell-turret, and having the walls of the nave carried above the roofs of the rest of the building, it has a somewhat singular appearance. Several stained glass windows and carved oak fittings relieve the Puritan plainness of the interior. There are two arcades of fine semi-circular arches, resting on slender round pillars. The panelled oak pulpit is Elizabethan. It belonged to the old Parish Church at St. Mary's Gate, and was sold July 10th, 1657. John Knox is stated, by tradition, to have preached from it when in Berwick, A.D. 1548. Nearly opposite is the last resting-place of one of Cromwell's friends and officers, "Colonel George Fenwicke, of Brinkburn House, Governor of Berwick in the year 1652," who, so the epitaph runs, "was the principal instrument of causing this church to be built, and died March 16, 1656. A good man is a public good." The stained glass in the west window was brought from the chapel of the Duke of Buckingham at Canons Park, and part of it is stated to be of Flemish workmanship. It represents the Crucifixion in the centre, with the Baptism on the left, and the Ascension on the right. There is a fine altar-piece. A bier, removed from the old church, and dated 1620, is still used at the cemetery. The present *Church of St. Mary*, in Castlegate, is modern, having been built in 1858 in the early English style of architecture. The *Scotch Presbyterian Church*, in Hide Hill, called the "Low Meeting," or "Knox's Church," dates from 1719, and the *United Presbyterian Church*, in Chapel Street, from 1756. There are three churches in the town belonging to the English Presbyterians. They are situated in Wallace Green, Church Street, and Bank Hill. The other places of worship are—the *Roman Catholic Church*, in Ravensdowne; the *Wesleyan Methodist Chapel*, in Walkergate Lane; the *Baptist Chapel*, in Castlegate; and the *Primitive Methodist Chapel*, in College Place.

The *Town Hall* of Berwick, blocking up the lower end of High Street, occupies as inconvenient a site as the Town Hall of Newcastle. Designed by Mr. Joseph Dodds, a burgess of the town, it was built between the years 1754-61. The principal features are the portico and steeple. The former consists of four Tuscan columns supporting a handsome pediment, on which are engraved the arms of the town. The latter, rising to a height of 150 feet, is a graceful combination of three orders of architecture—the Tuscan, Doric, and Ionic. The belfry contains a peal of eight bells. Curfew is rung every night, except Sunday, at eight o'clock. The ground-floor of the building is a market for poultry, eggs, and butter. The upper storey is used as a lock-up. Outside may be seen the old town stocks. The *Barracks*, situated on the Parade near the Parish Church, were erected in 1719.

"Wallace" Green, according to tradition, is the spot where the arm of the Scottish hero was buried after having been exposed for some time in Berwick. In High Street, opposite to Eastern Lane, is the *Scientific Institute, Museum, and School of Art*. The Reading-room is open from 7.30 A.M. to 10 P.M. Non-members have the privilege of using it on payment of one penny per visit. The Museum, open on Wednesdays and Saturdays from 12 A.M. to 4 P.M., and during the winter on Saturday evenings from 6 o'clock, contains a good collection of moths, birds, fishes, and animals; the botanical collection of Dr. Johnson, of Berwick; ancient British sepulchral urns; leaden balls found in the old castle walls, on Flodden Field, and Halidon Hill; broad-sword from battle-field of Bothwell Bridge; an old deed dated 1568; printing press and violin, with other relics.

Berwick is one of the few remaining walled towns in the United Kingdom, and its ancient ramparts, reconstructed in the reign of

Queen Elizabeth, form the chief promenade of the town. The circuit is one mile three furlongs. That of the older walls was two miles. To the north and east they are formed of earth faced with stone. The following is the order of the various bastions and batteries, starting from the south-west corner of the wall, near the Scotch Gate:—Meg's Mount Demi-bastion, Cumberland Bastion, Brass Mount Bastion, Windmill Mount Bastion, King's Demi-bastion, Fisher's Fort, and Bramham's Battery, which defend the entrance to the harbour. In the former is a Russian gun, a trophy of the Crimean war. The Saluting Battery and the Flank Battery complete the defences on the river front. The cannon were taken from the walls at the general peace, and are now in Edinburgh Castle. From this point to the bridge are the quay walls. The gates remaining are the Scotch Gate, bestriding Castlegate; the Cowport Gate, leading from the Parade to the Magdalen Fields; the Ness Gate, leading from Ness Street to the pier; the Shore Gate, leading from Sandgate to the Quay. There is a delightful walk by the river-side, along the New Road, past the Lady's or Conqueror's Well, and beneath the Royal Border Bridge. A fine breezy promenade is the pier, extending nearly half-a-mile south-east from the north bank of the river's mouth. It was erected in 1810 at a cost of £40,000. At the end is a lighthouse. Remains of a rude breakwater, built in the reign of Elizabeth, to prevent the accumulation of sand-banks at the mouth of the river, may be seen on the rocks to the north of the present pier. The channel between the pier and Spittal Point is only 30 feet broad. There is a pleasant walk northwards along the coast past the Greenses Haven, which is much resorted to by bathers. Several caves, which are known as the Singing Cove, the Burgesses' Cove, and the Smugglers' Cove, have been hollowed out of the soft red sandstone cliffs by the waves. The ancient *stone bridge* of fifteen arches over the Tweed was completed in 1634, having taken over twenty-four years to build. It is 1164 feet in length and 17 feet wide. At its north end formerly stood, till 1825, the English Gate, with its guard-house, the entrance to the borough from the south. The timber foundations of an older structure, destroyed by a great flood in 1199, and afterwards re-built by William the Lion, are said to be visible at low tide about eighty yards higher up the river.

A quarter of a mile from the old bridge is the *Royal Border Bridge*—a magnificent railway viaduct of twenty-eight semi-circular arches, designed by Robert Stephenson. It was begun on the 15th of May 1847, and opened by the Queen and Prince Albert on the 29th of August 1850. The total length of the bridge is 2160 feet, and its greatest height from the bed of the river 126 feet 6 inches. The total cost of bridge and embankment was £207,000. The principal hotels and inns in Berwick are the Red Lion (High Street), King's Arms (Hide Hill), Hen and Chickens (Sandgate), Royal Hotel (Castlegate), Black Swan (Castlegate).

# BERWICK TO BEAL.

Spittal, 1 mile; Richardson's Stead, 2½ miles; Ancroft, 5 miles; Cheswick House, 5 miles; Haggerston, 7 miles; Beal, 9 miles.

NOT quite a mile from Berwick, on the south side of the river, is TWEEDMOUTH, a large and not particularly attractive village, which shows more industrial activity than its venerable neighbour, having ironworks, saw mills, docks, etc. Founded at an early period, the village was used by the English kings as a base of operations against Berwick. King John in 1204 began to erect a castle here; but William the Lion, after having twice obstructed the work, razed the walls to the ground. In 1277 the English and Scottish commissioners met here to settle the vexed question of the line of demarcation between the two kingdoms; but in consequence of the attitude assumed by the English, the conference was abruptly broken off. Edward I., while at Tweedmouth, summoned a parliament, which met on the site of Parliament Street. "Two lytel towers" are mentioned by Sir Robert Bowes, in his survey of 1542, as being "at Twedemouthe foranenst Barwyke." A great annual event here is the "Tweedmouth Feast," held on the third Sunday in July. The *Church of St. Bartholomew* stands close to the Tweed, on the site of an old Norman chapel. It was built in 1780, in the style which has been called "Carpenter's Gothic," and was enlarged by the addition of a chancel and vestry in 1866. In the churchyard lie buried John Mackay Wilson, author of the *Tales of the Borders*, and James Stuart, a well-known Border character, who died April 14th, 1844, at the great age of 115. He claimed to be, in the words of William Howitt, "the descendant of Scotland's ancient kings, the son of a general of a former century, the grandson of the lady of Airlie, the spectator of Culloden and Prestonpans, the soldier of Bunker's Hill and Quebec." Some of his pretensions have been demolished by Chambers; but it is admitted there was a certain amount of truth in the story of this remarkable man, who was, furthermore, possessed of such extraordinary strength that he once carried for a short distance a cart loaded with hay, the united weight being a ton and a half. Another centenarian is buried near—Thomas Bell, of Spittal, died 26th November 1791, aged 105. At the east end of Tweedmouth is *St. Cuthbert's Well*, where the saint is said to have baptised a number of Pagans during one of his journeys. At the north-west side, close to the Royal Border Bridge, is the famous knoll, called *Hang-a-Dyke-Neuk*, where Edward III. is said to have barbarously put to death the two sons of Sir Alexander Seton, deputy-governor of Berwick, under circumstances already narrated (p. 541). There is a fine ballad in Sheldon's *Minstrelsy of the English Border*, entitled, "Seton's Sons; or, the Beleaguering of Berwicke." According to this version of the story, it was Lady Seton who would have given up the keys of the town sooner than sacrifice her sons. To the entreaties of this lady, Sir Alexander replied, "Wyth Chryst blessynye, altho they hang my sons, I wolde keep goode fayth wyth the Scottish Kynge and barre out Yedwarde." "Duty," she says, "is natheless hard to thole, but feeling it mair." Honour wins the day, and preparations for the tragic scene are made—

"They biggit a gallows on hangie-dyke-neuk,
And the hangman came there betyme;
The cock crow'd loudly o'er the muirs,
'Seton's sonnes, 'tis matin pryme.'

The trumpets sounded out oure the Tweed
Wi' a blast o' deadly sound;
Auld Seton and wyfe gaed up on the wa's,
For theyre sonnes to death were bound.

They kent the tread o' their gallant bairns
As they cam forth to dee.
Richard, he mounted the ladder fyrst,
And threw himself frae the tree.

William, he was his mither's pride,
And he looked sae bauldly on;
Then kyst his brither's lyefless hands,
When he fand the breath was gone.

. . . . . . .

He leaped from aff the bitter tree,
And flauchtered in the wynd;
Twa bonnie flowers to wither thus,
And a' for yae man's mind!

. . . . . . .

Oh! there was a shriek rose in the air,
So wylde, so death-lyke gien;
A mother's wail for her gallant bairns,
Such sight was seldom seen.

It called the grey gull frae the sea,
For he wist his mate had spake.
Never a mither in city walled,
Wi' a heart that wad'nt break."

In the old Poor-house, the site of which is now occupied by a rag-store, two skulls were long preserved as those of Sir Alexander Seton's two sons. *Tweed House*, which immediately faces the bridge, was formerly a posting-house of considerable importance, and is referred to by Smollett in *Humphrey Clinker*. Matt. Bramble, one of the characters, dates from Tweedmouth a letter which he commences—"I have now reached the northern extremity of England, and see, close to my chamber-window, the Tweed gliding through the arches of that bridge which connects this suburb to the town of Berwick." There is a tradition of some king having lodged at this inn. The new Dock at Tweedmouth, having a water surface of between three and four acres, was constructed in 1871, at a cost of £66,000. It has accommodation for sixteen ships. The principal hotels are the Station Hotel and the Union Hotel. The Thatch-house Tavern possesses some of the punch-bowls and ladles used by the workmen when building the old bridge in 1634.

Half-a-mile or so from the station, along the Belford Road, is the *Cemetery*, which is formed of about nine acres of land formerly called "The King's Quarry." Before reaching it, Billendean Road branches off to the left to SPITTAL, a good-sized fishing village, which derived its name from a Leper Hospital founded here by Edward I. It has for some years been rising into favour as a popular watering-place, and the old-fashioned cottages are being replaced by better-class houses and villas. The sands being smooth and firm, are very suitable for bathing. The fishermen here were formerly much addicted to smuggling, and Spittal was one of the most noted places on the coast for the landing of contraband goods. In the old houses were secret holes and nooks made to stow away an entire cargo. In some instances the soil underneath the kitchen floors was entirely removed so as to form places of concealment for the kegs of brandy and gin and the bales of tobacco. At the north end of the village is *Spittal Hall Farmstead*, which bears on its walls the initials and date, T. S., 1754. It is supposed to stand on or near the site of the old Leper Hospital, the cemetery of which would seem to be indicated by a plot of ground close by, where human remains have been frequently unearthed. Spittal Church was built in 1867, in the early English style. The other places of worship are St. Paul's English Presbyterian Church, rebuilt 1878; the United Presbyterian Iron Church; and the Christians' Meeting-house. At the south end of the village is the *Spa Well*, a mineral spring much resorted to for its medicinal properties by persons with scorbutic and similar complaints. Spittal, like Tweedmouth, has its annual feast. The principal hotels and inns are the Roxburgh Hotel, Blenheim Hotel, Spittal Hotel.

Two miles and a half from Berwick, or a mile and three-quarters from Tweedmouth Station along the main road, passing over Sunnyside Hill, is RICHARDSON'S STEAD. Here is *Scremerston Church*, built 1842 in the early English style, and dedicated to St. Peter. The village is one mile and a quarter further south. It was destroyed by the Scots in 1386, and plundered again in 1528. The foundations of a tower or fortalice mentioned in 1416, and described in 1542 as "a greate old toure much decayed," may be traced in a field on the north side of the village. Coal seems to have been worked here at an early period. From an old minute-book belonging to the corporation of Berwick, it appears that the inhabitants were "very farr abused and evill intreated by such naughtye fellowes and servants as have the charge of the coale pitts of Skrymerstone" by giving "half a measure for holl," and "serving countrymen and Scottesmen before any of the garrisons of the town." When the plague visited Scremerston in 1667 the sick were taken down to the links on the sea-side, where huts were erected from the bent growing thereon, for their reception. The manor of Scremerston formed part of the estates of the unfortunate Earl of Derwentwater, and was forfeited in 1715 by his rebellion. On the 14th February 1884 a live frog was found embedded in the solid rock (carboniferous limestone) of the "Lowdean" workings of the Scremerston quarries, thirty-one feet below the surface of the surrounding ground. When discovered by the workmen it was in a torpid state, with closed eyes, and fell over on its side as if dead, but in a few minutes revived and assumed a squatting attitude. It was taken care of, and lived till 3rd May 1885.

From Scremerston a road branches off for two miles to ANCROFT, a long, straggling village, lying on a gentle slope in the midst of a fertile and well-cultivated country. It was formerly a place of greater size and importance than at present, and the foundations of the old houses are still visible in a field south-west of the church. A colony of "cloggers" seem to have settled here at an early period. In the time of Queen Anne they were employed in making boots for the army. When the plague visited Ancroft in 1667 many of the inhabitants fell victims to it. They were carried out to an uncultivated field which adjoins the brae on the Wooler road eastward, and laid under little bowers of broom, and when they died, their bodies, and the yellow flowered canopy above them, were burnt. Hence the field is to this day called the Broomie-huts. *Ancroft Church* was built by the monks of Holy Island shortly before the year 1145, at which time it consisted merely of a nave and chancel. In Edwardian times the present massive pele-tower, three storeys high above the groined ground-floor, was added to the west end of the church. At the same time additional strength was given to the south wall of the nave, by the erection of a bold projecting buttress still to be seen there. Reference is made in the survey of 1542 to the "lytle fortresse nere unto the church." In 1869-70 the nave was lengthened and widened, and the old Norman chancel destroyed. The only ancient masonry now standing is at the west end, with the tower, and a fragment of the west end of the south side of the nave. The small bell in the tower originally hung in John Wesley's Chapel, London. There is a small inn at Ancroft, The Lamb.

A mile and a half south of Scremerston, on the east side of the great post-road, is *Cheswick House*, the seat of Major-General Sir William Crossman, K.C.M.G., M.P. Of the "lytle toure at Cheswyke" in 1542, not a trace remains. The village was destroyed by the Scots in 1400. Oliver Cromwell visited Cheswick on his way to Scotland in 1648, and on the 18th of September of that year dated a letter thence to the Earl of Loudon. From the beach at Cheswick the red sandstone was obtained for building Lindisfarne Priory. According to an old rhyme, Cheswick contributed an important article to the larder of the monks—

"From Goswick we've geese, from Cheswick we've cheese,
From Bukton we've venison in store;
From Swinhoe we've bacon, but the Scots have it taken,
And the Prior is longing for more."

Several ancient British barrows have been opened on Cheswick Links. In one was found a spear-head.

Two miles and a half south-west is *Haggerston Castle*, the property of Captain Leyland. The Haggerston family were seated here at an early period. Within the walls of their manor-house King Edward II., in 1311, received the homage of Thomas, Earl of Lancaster, for the earldom of Lincoln. License to crenellate his mansion was obtained by Robert de Haggerston from Edward III. in 1345. It was described in 1542 "as a strong tower in a good state of repair." In 1618 a fire destroyed most of the building; a large square tower was left standing, and this was incorporated with a mansion built by Sir Thomas Haggerston some time before the year 1777. His son, Sir Carnaby, in 1805 pulled down the old tower, and erected on its foundations the western wing of the present hall. The Haggerston family boasts of a long and uninterrupted pedigree. The first baronet obtained his patent from Charles I. for his devotion to the Royal cause. His descendants were warm adherents of the Stuart dynasty. The Haggerston family were always true to the old faith, and their private chapel, dedicated to Our Lady and St. Cuthbert, still remains attached to the house. Two miles and a quarter by the road from Haggerston, passing, on the right, *Lowlyn*, the residence of Lieutenant-Colonel Rowley R. C. Hill, is Beal Station, the nearest point for visiting Holy Island.

# BERWICK TO ETAL AND CORNHILL.

**Duddo, 7½ miles ; Etal, 10 miles ; Pallinsburn House, 12 miles ; Cornhill (*via* Etal), 15 miles.**

THE broad and undulating road from Berwick to Etal, which passes over high moors and through richly-cultivated fields, commands an extensive prospect over the beautiful vale of the Tweed. Passing Unthank (A.-S., *Thenung*—duty or service, hence Unthank, land held without service being rendered), and Camphouses (four miles,) near which are the remains of three ancient British camps, the first place of interest is *Duddo*, (*Dod*, a round topped hill, and *hoe*, a height), an old village seven miles and a half from Berwick. Standing on a hard red and white freestone escarpment, close by the road, are the remains of the ancient pele-tower of the Lords of Tillmouth, which was destroyed by the Scots a few days before the battle of Flodden. The tower is in a very ruinous condition, the walls being cracked and shattered, and though buttressed up in parts, threaten soon to topple to the ground. The foundations are believed to have been undermined by the working of coal seams beneath them. The view from this point embraces the Eildons, Lammermuirs, the Merse, Hume Castle, Penielheugh, the Cheviots, the fertile plain of Millfield, and Flodden Hill. Separated from the ruins by the road is the *Church of St. James the Great*, built in 1832 from the designs of Bonomi, but now disused. The new church of *All Saints*, consecrated in 1880 by the Bishop of Durham, is about a mile to the east.

On Grindon Rig, a mile to the north-west, are the *Duddo Stones*, five in number, one of them lying prostrate on the ground. They are from 5 to 10 feet high, red in colour, and deeply furrowed, and form part of a circle, 40 feet in circumference, enclosing an ancient British burial-place. Several sepulchral urns have been removed from cairns in the vicinity of these monoliths.

A Border skirmish took place on Grindon Moor, a mile and a half north-west of Duddo, in 1558, between a troop of Scottish marauders, consisting of one thousand horse and a contingent of foot, and a party of English under the Earl of Northumberland and his brother, Sir Henry Percy, in which the former were defeated and driven over the Tweed.

Two miles and a half from Duddo, and ten miles from Berwick, is the charming little village of ETAL, with its ruined castle and ornate church.—(Page 531.)

Two miles west is *Pallinsburn House* (the seat of Watson Askew, Esq., J.P.), a handsome modern mansion, overlooking the famous battle-field of Flodden. It contains a very large and magnificent picture of the "Adoration of the Shepherds," by *Bassano;* also the flag under which the Grenadier Guards fought at Waterloo. In the "Kaim Bog," a lake which lies just below the house near the public road, the Roman missionary, Paulinus, is said to have baptised some thousands of his Northumbrian converts. It is one of the inland breeding-places of the black-headed gulls, and in the spring-time myriads of these snowy sea-birds may be seen, whirling in graceful flights above their nests on the marshy borders and islets of the lake, or following the ploughmen in the neighbouring fields. A remarkable geological feature at Pallinsburn is the "Kaim," a detrital ridge, chiefly composed of rolled shingle from the rocks of the Silurian series of Greywacke, and supposed to have been formed by the currents of the sea when it covered the northern counties in primeval times.

A mile to the west, in a field north of the road, is an ancient Border Gathering Stone, called "The King's Stone," from a mistaken belief that it was set up by Surrey to commemorate the battle of Flodden. Two miles beyond it is CORNHILL, a small agricultural village of a single street, situated, as the name implies, in the midst of rich corn-lands. *The Church of St. Helen*, built 1840, and enlarged by the addition of a chancel in 1866, stands on the site of an ancient chapel-of-ease to Norham. In the churchyard is a curious Latin epitaph, of which the following is a translation—"Alas, who shall now retard the scythe of death? James Purdy, at the bridge of Twizel, was an excellent old man, although not exempt from diseases. He died on the 4th day of December 1752, aged 81 years, and, together with Jane, his wife, and Eleanor, his grand-daughter, lies under this stone. But passenger, if thou hast a good heart, perhaps thou mayest live. Samuel, the son of James, survives, and is healthy, and exercising the profession of his father, under his paternal roof. If thou seekest health—Go thither!" Nothing remains of the ancient tower of "Cornell," which was destroyed by the Earl of Fife in 1335, rebuilt by the Swinhoes, and taken by the French General D'Esse, at the head of a troop of Scots in 1549. It was standing in 1560. Its site is believed to be occupied by the ancient hall of the Collingwood family—a picturesque building in the Elizabethan style, standing upon a fine terraced lawn, at the end of the village street. About a mile north-east, by the side of the river, nearly opposite to the old ford of Lennel, are the grass-covered remains of another pele-tower, called "Castleton Nich," built about 1121, and frequently taken during the Border wars. A mile north-west of the village, the Tweed is crossed by a noble bridge of five arches (built 1763), famous in the history of run-away marriages. In the toll-house, at the Scottish side of the river, "dukes, lords, marquesses, colonels, right honourables, peers, ploughmen, and hinds have been tied fast for life by the hymeneal blacksmith"—(*Sheldon.*) Many romantic incidents have occurred here. A celebrated statesman, who had eloped with an heiress, on being overtaken by the guardian of the lady at Cornhill, rose from his seat and shot the near leader of his pursuer through the head, thus gaining time to dash over the bridge and get married before the guardian could arrive. A short distance south of the church is "The Bathing-well Plantation," where, on the banks of a little stream, there formerly stood a small Bath-house. Here grows, in great profusion, the butterbur (*Petasites vulgaris*). Other flowers are: wood scorpion-grass (*Myosotis sylvatica*) and sand garlic (*Allium arenarium.*) *St. Helen's Well*, in the haugh below, was formerly esteemed for its medicinal properties, said to be beneficial in cases of scurvy and gravel. Not far from the well, on what is known as Camp Field, or Kippie Hill, are the remains of ancient British entrenchments. Half-a-mile below Coldstream Bridge is an outbreak of basalt, known as the Cornhill Dyke, cutting perpendicularly through beds of the Tuedian formation. It is traceable, in a direction east by north, a distance of seven miles, intruded also through the mountain limestone beds. There is a very comfortable hotel and posting-house at Cornhill—the Collingwood Arms.

# BERWICK TO NORHAM AND CARHAM.

East Ord, 2 miles; Horncliffe, 5¼ miles; Velvet Hall, 4½ miles; Norham, 7 miles; Twizell Castle, 10 miles; Cornhill, 13 miles; Wark, 15 miles; Carham, 16¾ miles.

THE road from Berwick to Kelso runs, for the most part, but a short distance from the Tweed. Many places of historic interest and much beautiful scenery lie along its route. Two miles from Berwick is the village of EAST ORD, half-a-mile north-west of which are the remains of an ancient British camp, situated on Canny Bank, above the Canny Burn. Two miles west of this point the Tweed, which here sweeps round in a fine curve, is crossed by the Union Chain Bridge, a graceful structure, erected by Captain S. Brown, R.N., in 1820. Its total length between the points of suspension is 432 feet, its width 18 feet, and its height above low water 69 feet. The piece of ground lying in the bend of the river was the site of King Charles the First's camp, A D. 1639. A copy of Hollar's "Mapp of King Charles, his camp or leaguer, at the Birks, near Berwick, May, June 1639," is given in the *Proceedings of the Berwickshire Naturalists' Field Club*, volume v. The Birks farm-house stands just beyond the southern line.

Three-quarters of a mile to the south of the bridge is the pretty village of HORNCLIFFE, which has a small Presbyterian Chapel and inn (the Fishers' Arms). A thatched cottage at the lower end, now divided into two, is said to have once been occupied by Oliver Cromwell, when his army crossed the Tweed by the ford, and encamped on the opposite side. *Horncliffe House*, which commands a wide view over the Merse, is the beautiful residence of Thomas Allan, Esq. *Horncliffe Dene* is a favourite haunt of botanists, and is represented in a well-known wood-cut in Johnston's *Botany of the English Border*. The finely-wooded banks, and the steep scaurs overhung with ivy and honeysuckle, are no less attractive to the general visitor; the old mill forming a picturesque feature in the lovely scene. Velvet Hall Station is a mile south-east of Horncliffe. A mile to the north-east of it are *Longridge Towers*, the residence of Hubert E. H. Jerningham, author of *Norham Castle*, *Life in a French Chateau*, *To and From Constantinople*, and translator of the lives of *Sixtus V.*, by Baron Hübner, and *Lord Byron*, by Countess Guiccioli.

Half-a-mile south-east of the railway station, a stone in an old garden marks the site of an ancient chapel and cemetery.

Two miles south-west of Velvet Hall Station are the ruins of

*Norham Castle.* This grim old Border stronghold, so celebrated in history and song, occupies a high rocky platform, on a steep and thickly-wooded cliff, defended by the Tweed on the north, by a ravine on the north-east, and by a deep fosse on the south and west. The castle-area was divided into upper, or inner, and outer wards, and surrounded by a thick curtain wall, strengthened by polygonal bastions. The defences of the inner ward were exceptionally strong. In addition to the embattled wall, there was a broad and deep ditch on two sides of it, extending from the eastern ravine to the northern slope. At the north-east corner stands the *Keep*, a massive rectangular building of red sandstone, measuring at its base about 64 feet north and south, by 56 feet east and west, the walls being 12 to 15 feet thick, and 90 feet high. Of the four fronts, the south and west are the best preserved. In the latter are two pointed doors, one leading into the south chamber of the keep, the other into a well-stair, which ascends in the wall to the summit, and terminates in a raised square turret—a marked feature in every view of the ruins. A large round-headed door, at the first floor level, approached by an outer stair, now removed, was evidently the original main entrance to the keep. The basement floor was divided, east and west, by a party wall, into two chambers; the northern one, probably the dungeon, having a groined stone roof; the southern one, divided into two rooms, being barrel-vaulted. Above the basement storey were four other floors, the second one containing the Great Hall. "Considering the thickness of the walls," says Mr. G. T. Clark, "the absence of mural chambers and galleries in this keep is remarkable." The kitchen, the hall, and the chapel were built against the north curtain-wall, of which the ruins are still standing. From the south-west angle of the keep the curtain-wall may be followed westward to a nearly rectangular bastion tower—the "little Bulwark" of 1551. The castle-well remains in the north-east corner of the ward. Very little is preserved of the defences of the outer ward—a part of the castle which was intended to be used as a retreat by the villagers in the event of a Scottish raid. What there is consists of the remains of the Lower Gatehouse—a rectangular Norman structure 40 feet long by 20 feet broad. The passage beneath it is, for the most part, fifteen feet wide at each end, and in the centre, however, it is reduced to twelve feet by gate-piers: these carried round-headed ribs to stiffen the barrel-vaulting of the roof. Attached to the north-east angle of the gatehouse is a portion of the curtain-wall, rebuilt in the Decorated period on the Norman foundations. Three of the deep recesses which pierced it remain. They are each eleven feet broad, and splayed to a loop, designed, it is conjectured, to flank the approach from the town to the outer gate. Further east is another portion of the curtain-wall, forming part of the southern defences of the outer ward. Between two of the polygonal bastions upon it are six curious round-headed arches, the purpose of which can only be surmised. They have a span of twelve feet, and spring from square piers about three feet or four feet broad. The masonry of five of them is rough, and was intended to be covered with earth. The most western of these arches is of ashlar, and is considered by Mr. G. T. Clark to have been a gateway intended to facilitate the entrance of the villagers and their cattle during a raid. Beyond these arches and bastions the curtain makes a sharp turn, and proceeds northward to cross the ditch and join the keep. Ruined as the castle is, sufficient is left to enable the visitor to picture this "Queen of Border Fortresses," as it has been called, in all its mighty strength and grandeur. Sir Walter Scott's famous description of the stronghold at sunset, as given in the opening lines of "Marmion," is no less graphic than beautiful—

"Day set on Norham's castled steep,
And Tweed's fair river, broad and deep,
And Cheviot's mountains lone;
The battled towers, the Donjon Keep,
The loophole grates, where captives weep,
The flanking walls that round it sweep,
In yellow lustre shone.
The warriors on the turrets high,
Moving athwart the evening sky,
Seem'd forms of giant height:
Their armour, as it caught the rays,
Flash'd back again the western blaze,
In lines of dazzling light."

At the door of the keeper's house are several cannon-balls, both iron and stone. One of them, eighteen inches in diameter, is said to have been discharged from "Mons Meg." Norham Castle was founded in 1121 by Bishop Flambard, in order to prevent the predatory incursions of robbers and the sudden irruptions of the Scots. The remains of his work may be seen in the south-east corner and the whole east side of the keep, which was 10 feet to 20 feet lower than at present. The castle was taken by David, King of Scotland, in 1136, and, again, in 1138, when it suffered much injury, and is said to have been dismantled. Bishop Pudsey, in 1154, restored the ruined stronghold, rebuilding the western half of the keep. King John was here four times between 1209 and 1213, and on one of these occasions negotiated a treaty with William the Lion. In 1215 the castle was besieged without success for forty days by Alexander, King of Scotland. This king, with Pandulf, the Pope's legate, and Stephen de Segrave, met here in 1219 to settle disputes between the two kingdoms. In 1291, during the proceedings initiated to settle the claims of Baliol and Bruce to the Scottish crown, Edward I. resided at Norham, while the Scots were quartered at Upsettlington, now Lady Kirk, on the other side of the river. In 1318 the Scots blockaded Norham for twelve months, and, again, shortly afterwards, for seven months; but the garrison under Sir Thomas Gray made a gallant resistance. An incident occurred during the first siege which Bishop Percy has woven into his ballad of "The Hermit of Warkworth," and which probably brought before the notice of Sir Walter Scott the name of Marmion. It is thus narrated by Leland:—"Aboute this tyme there was a greate feste made yn Lincolnshir, to which cam many gentelmen and ladies ; and emonge them one lady brought a heaulme for a man of were, with a very riche creste of gold, to William Marmion, knight, with a lettre of commaundement of her lady, that he should go into the daungerust place in England, and there to let the heaulme to be seene and knownen as famose. So he went to Norham ; whither, withyn four days of cumming, cam Philip Moubray, gardian of Berwike, having yn his bande 140 men of armes, the very flour of men of the Scottisch marches. Thomas Gray, capitayne of Norham, seyng this, brought his garison afore the barriers of the castel, behynde whom cam William, richely arrayed, as al glittering in gold, and wering the heaulme his lady's present. Then sayd Thomas Gray to Marmion, 'Syr Knight, ye be cum hither to fame your helmet. Mount up on yor horse, and ryde lyke a valiant man to your foes even here at hand, and I forsake God if I rescue not thy body deade or alyve, or I myself wyl dye for it.' Wherapon he toke his cursore, and rode emong the throng of ennemyes, the which layed sore stripes on hym, and pullid hym at the last oute of his sadel to the grounde. Then Thomas Gray with al the hole garison lette prik yn emong the Scottes, and so wondid them, and their horses, that they were over throwen, and Marmyon sore beaten was horsid agayn, and with Gray pursewid the Scottes yn chace. There were taken fifty horses of price, and the wemen of Norham brought them to the foote men to folow the chace." During the siege two fortresses were raised against the castle—one at Upsettlington, a little below Ladykirk, and another at Norham Church. The outer ward was taken and held for three days, but as no impression could be made on the inner ward, the Scots retired. In 1322 the castle was taken, but recovered by Edward in person, after a siege of ten days. In 1327, the night of the coronation of the new sovereign, it narrowly escaped being taken by treachery, but the plot was frustrated by Thomas Manvers, then captain. During the reigns of Henry IV., V., and VI., Norham was well maintained, and played a part in all the great transactions on the Border. In 1497 the castle was besieged by James IV., but was held by Bishop Fox for sixteen days, until relieved by Surrey. On August 23rd, 1513, King James made another attempt to take it. On this occasion "Mons Meg" is said to have been brought against the massive walls. At the end of two days the barbican was in ruins, and the outer ward taken by assault. On the 29th, Sir Richard Cholmeley, not being relieved, surrendered. There is a tradition—not a very reliable one—that the castle was won through the treachery of one of the inmates, who advised the king to descend from Ladykirk Bank to Gin Haugh, a flat ground near the river, and thence to throw down the north-east corner of the wall with his cannon.

"So when the Scots the walls had won
And rifled every nook and place,
The traitor came to the king anon,
But for reward met with disgrace.

"'Therefore for this thy traitorous trick
Thou shalt be tried in a trice;
Hangman, therefore,' quoth James, 'be quick;
The groom shall have no better price.'"
—*Ballad of Flodden.*

A field north-east of the castle, called "Hangman's Land," is supposed to have been the scene of this execution.

After the battle of Flodden Bishop Ruthal repaired the damage done by the Scots, and generally strengthened the fortress, dismantling his castle of Middleham for materials. About 1530 the Scots appeared before Norham, but the castle was saved by the valour of Archdeacon Franklin, who had a special coat of arms assigned to him by Henry VIII. for this service. The importance of the castle was emphasised by Sir Robert Bowes in 1542:—"That castle standeth marvellously well for the defence and relief of the country, as well from incourses of ennemys in time of war, as from thefts and spoils in tyme of peace; for it standeth upon the utter frontier, and upon a fray made, or any other warning given by fire beacon, or otherwise, the inhabitants of that castle, or a garrison of horsemen lying there, may be in the way of any enemies that shall pass into Scotland between Berwick and Wark, or between Wark and Teversheugh." He reported the castle to be "in muche decay," and its outer walls to be "old, thynne, and weake." The day of Norham, however, was past. A fray took place in 1557 in the space between the bridge and the iron gate. As late as 1583 it was still used as a place of defence, but not being kept in order, gradually sank into ruin. Norham Castle must have had a considerable attraction for the stern reformer, John Knox, for within its rude walls dwelt Margery Bowes, daughter of the governor, and grand-daughter of Sir Ralph Bowes, of Streatlam—a lady whose acquaintance he had made while stationed at Berwick in 1549 and 1550, and who eventually became his wife. Dr. George Carleton, Bishop of Chichester, who wrote the life of Bernard Gilpin, was born here while his father was keeper of the castle.

At the foot of the castle cliff, on the north side, is the *Monk's Well*, the waters of which, according to tradition, had the power of bestowing on barren wives the blessings of maternity. To the south of the castle is a broad and level platform, on which may be traced the remains of a Roman camp, and the less regular banks and ditches of some of the besiegers of the castle.

Below the castle, to the south-west, is the ancient village of NORHAM, which consists of one long, wide street, with a fine open green in the middle of it. The cottages are small and plain, tenanted by agricultural labourers and those employed in the salmon fishery. In Saxon times it was known as Ubbanford, or Upper-ford, from the fact of it commanding one of the two great fords across the Tweed, and was conferred by King Oswald on the See of Lindisfarne. Here, about 830, Bishop Ecfrid built a church, to which he removed the remains of the king and Saint Ceolwulph. By 1082 the vill had assumed the name of Norham (the northern-home of the see), and, as the capital of the district of Norhamshire, became the place where the bishops of Durham exercised a special jurisdiction, and where they held their exchequer. Gospatrick, created Earl of Northumberland by William I., and, on his rebellion and flight into Scotland, created Earl of Dunbar by Malcolm, died here, and was buried in the church porch. Norham suffered greatly from the depredations of the Scots, and was burnt by them in 1138 and 1356. The village had a market in olden times, and still has its market-cross, the lower portion of which is ancient. At the west end of the village is the *Church of St. Cuthbert*, built by Bishop Flambard, probably about the same time as the castle, on or near the site of the former Saxon edifice. On the 10th of May 1290, Edward I. sat on his throne in Norham Church, and opened the convention summoned to consider the claims of Baliol and Bruce to the Scottish crown. In 1318 the Scots, during the siege of the castle, converted the edifice into a place of strength, and in 1551 a treaty between the two kingdoms was signed within its walls. Much of the Norman work was destroyed during the restorations which took place in 1617, 1846, and 1852. Still there are sufficient remains of the fine old twelfth-century building to indicate its architectural character. These are :—The round-headed arches between the nave and the south aisle, with their tall, cylindrical columns ; the stately chancel-arch, with its three-shafted piers ; and the five round-headed and deeply-splayed arches in the south wall of the chancel, connected by a continuous label carved with zigzag. The aisles, vestry, and tower are modern. The south-east window of the chancel, and the great east window, belong to the Decorated period. On the north side of the chancel, close against the arch, are the remains of a low-side or leper window. The east end of the church originally terminated in an apse, the commencement of which is still visible. The church contains two beautiful recessed and canopied tombs, one on the south, and the other on the north side of the chancel. The former is of exquisite fourteenth-century workmanship, and supports on its slab the cross-legged effigy of a knight, clad in mail. Puritan hands have, unfortunately, destroyed much of the carving on the sides, and removed the little figures from the corbelled brackets. The latter is modern, in the Norman style, and was erected to the memory of Dr. Gilly, author of *The History of the Waldenses*, whose effigy, sculptured by Lough, reposes on the tomb-slab. Behind the reredos, on the south side of the chancel, is a large early English piscina. The bell in the tower is inscribed, "Anthony Bartlet made me 1670." The black oak fittings and reredos are from Durham Cathedral. In the churchyard are some Saxon stones, carved with interlaced ornament, piled up into a pillar on the spot where they were unearthed some years ago. They are fragments of crosses, and one of them contains the upper part of the figure of a saint giving his blessing. Close by are the foundations of the Proctor's house. The principal inn at Norham is the Victoria Arms. Norham railway station is half-a-mile to the south-east.

On the opposite side of the river are the picturesque woods of Lady-Kirk and the church, with a stone roof, built by James IV. in performance of a vow made when nearly drowning in the Tweed. Reginald of Durham tells a story concerning a pool in the river below, called Pedwell. A boy named Haldene, who was receiving instruction from the priest, threw the keys of the church into the river, hoping to get a holiday. His master, in consequence, was unable to officiate in the church as usual, and received a visit from St. Cuthbert in the night, reproaching him for the neglect. He pleaded the loss of the key. "Go," said the saint, "to-morrow, early in the morning, to the Pedwell site on the Tweed, and tell the fishermen you will give them any price they ask for the first fish they catch." This he did, and a salmon with distended stomach was caught. Full of confidence in St. Cuthbert, the priest put his hands in the mouth of the fish, and there found hanging to the upper jaw the lost key of his church. There is a pleasant walk by the river past Norham boat-house, overhung with bold rocks, to *Newbiggen Dene*—a deep and bosky glen, through which meanders the Rutchey Burn. A branch road, three-quarters of a mile long, connects Norham Station with the Kelso turnpike. Two miles south-west of this point is *Twizell Castle* (A.-S., *Twislung*—store-house), a huge and melancholy pile of ruins, standing on a beautifully-wooded cliff above the Till. It was begun in 1770 by Sir Francis Blake on a very extensive scale, and though the work was in progress for forty years it was never completed. The lower apartments are vaulted, and at each corner are circular towers. The magnificent gallery measures 90 feet by 22 feet. From the ruins the material was obtained for building the house of Tillmouth Park. The old pele-tower that formerly crowned the hill "was suffered to stand only that it might be buried in the centre of the present fabric."—*Raine*. In the hollow below, the "sullen Till" is crossed by the famous *Twizell Bridge*, over which the English vanguard marched on its way to the battle of Flodden. It is a lofty semi-circular five-ribbed arch, 90 feet 7 inches in span, and 46 feet 2 inches high, built during the sixteenth century by a lady of the Selby family. Half-a-mile west, along the north bank of the stream, is *St. Helen's Well*, a petrifying spring, celebrated by Scott, for

> "Many a chief of birth and rank,
> St. Helen, at thy fountain drank."

It bubbles up beneath a tall rock 20 feet high, and is not easy to find, on account of the accumulations of earth and marshy overgrowth. Another name for it is "The Wishing-well," for St. Cuthbert was believed in olden times to grant the desires of his votaries who drank the waters thereof. Near it is an ancient burial-place of the Selbys. There is a charming walk west of the bridge for a mile through the woods and tangled brakes on the south side of the Till to the confluence of the river with the Tweed. The character of the two streams is well described in a popular rhyme, which Mr. Ruskin, speaking in "The Two Paths" of "the stern and measured meaning in every syllable" of Scotland's great poets, cites as "a bit of first-rate work"—

"Tweed said to Till,
'What gars ye rin sae still?'
Till said to Tweed,
'Though ye rin wi' speed,
And I rin slaw,
Whar ye droon ae man,
I droon twa!'"

In the middle of a field, near the meeting of the waters, is a roofless and neglected chapel, rebuilt by Sir Francis Blake, during the last century, on the site of the domestic chapel of the early lords of Tillmouth, which was dedicated to St. Catherine. Much of the ancient masonry is incorporated with the present structure. It was to this spot that the heroine of Scott's "Marmion" fled for refuge after the battle of Flodden—

"'Oh! lady,' cried the monk, 'away!'
And placed her on her steed,
And led her to the chapel fair
Of Tillmouth upon Tweed.
There all the night they spent in prayer,
And at the dawn of morning, there
She met her kinsman, Lord Fitz-Clare."

A stone coffin, 9 feet long, 4 feet wide, and 15 inches deep, formerly stood beside it, in which the remains of St. Cuthbert are said, by tradition, to have floated down the Tweed from Melrose. The legend is referred to by Sir Walter Scott in "Marmion"—

"Not there his relics might repose;
For, wondrous tale to tell!—
In his stone coffin forth he rides,
(A ponderous bark by river tides);
Yet light as gossamer it glides
Downward to Tillmouth cell."

"It was," says Gough, "a stone boat, of as fine a shape as any boat of wood," and was capable, not only of floating, but of carrying the body of the saint, if not exceeding twelve stones in weight. A neighbouring farmer, having designs upon this interesting relic as a useful trough for pickling beef in, the saint, so runs the story, came in the night, and broke it to pieces. One portion of it afterwards went to repair the pig-sty of a farmer at St. Cuthbert's. The other was removed to Tillmouth Park.

Half-a-mile from Twizell Bridge, a road branches off by the lodge of Tillmouth Park to the east, for a mile and three-quarters, to *Old Heaton*, where, on a hill, defended by the river on the north and a burn on the east, are the ruins of a castle of the Greys—a family who were settled here at an early period. The scenery around is very beautiful. The castle was dismantled by the Scots previous to the battle of Flodden, and was in ruins when Sir Robert Bowes visited it in 1542. Part of the keep is standing. The vaulted chamber is used as a stable, and the floor above it as a granary.

A mile south-west of Twizell Bridge, on the right-hand side of the road, is a square entrenchment called "Haly Chesters."

Two miles further south is the village of *Cornhill*, from which a road running close to the river for two miles, conducts to WARK, a small and ancient-looking village of about ninety low thatched houses, built in a very irregular manner. There are about forty freehold properties in the village, held by the descendants of the keepers of the old castle. They have all houses and portions of land, with the right to pasture cows on the common. The Earl of Tankerville is the lord of the manor, and a Court-leet is held in the school-room every three years. There is an old churchyard here, in which may be traced the foundations of St. Giles' Church. Extending from the east end of the village westward towards Carham for about seven-eighths of a mile is a remarkable detrital ridge, called the *Kaim*. It is about 60 feet in height, and 150 feet in width at the base, rising, where undisturbed, to a sharp ridge of two or three feet in breadth at the top. A road intersects it, called "Gilly's Nick." Two great natural agencies are supposed to have been at work in forming this interesting mound. Icebergs or glaciers, in the first instance, have deposited their burden of boulders and gravel, and the currents of an ancient sea have laid them in a series of strata, thus forming the present ridge. The boulders and pebbles have travelled a considerable distance from the west. There is greenstone from the Tweed at Maxton, or Merton; basalt from Hume Castle; greywacke from the Lammermuirs to the west; conglomerate from the neighbourhood of Hawick; and dark porphyry from the Eildon Hills. The belief that this ridge was raised by human agency may have given rise to the name Wark, or Werk—*Anglicè*, wark. It was certainly, after Bamburgh, one of the earliest fortified places of which Saxon annals make mention. About the middle of this ridge, west of the village, are the remains of the once famous *Castle of Wark*, "the honour of Carham," as it is called in old MSS.—one of the most important of the Border fortresses. It was erected during the early part of the twelfth century, by Walter Espec, who obtained a grant of the manor of Carham from Henry I. Its vicissitudes commenced at a very early period. In 1135 it was taken by David I., but restored to England in the beginning of 1136. The next year David once more laid siege to the castle, but was unable to reduce it. The year following, Stephen made Wark the base of his depredatory excursions into Scotland. After his retreat, David once more besieged the castle, and only took it after a lengthened blockade. The dismantled fortress remained in the possession of the Scots till 1157, when it was restored to England, and rebuilt by Henry II. King John set fire to the town and castle of Wark in 1216. In 1255 Henry III. resided here for some time with his queen. Sir William Wallace invaded England in 1297, and there are traditions of his presence at Wark. Edward I. kept the festival of Easter in 1296 at Wark, and hence marched a great army against the Scots. He was here again four years before his death. Edward II. mustered here his vast army for Bannockburn. Robert Bruce took the castle in 1318. In 1342 Sir William Montague, the governor, with forty horsemen, sallied out, and attacked the rear of King David the Second's army, who were returning from England laden with plunder. They captured a hundred horses that were bearing the spoils. Incensed at this attack, David led his army against the castle, and invested it. The governor, passing by night through the enemy's line, conveyed the intelligence to Edward III., and he at once marched northwards to relieve the garrison. The Scots retired but six hours before the English van appeared. The Order of the Garter is said to have been instituted here by Edward III., about the year 1349. It is ascribed to the following romantic incident:—At a court ball held in the castle Lady Salisbury had the misfortune to drop her garter. The king gallantly picking it up, presented it to her, and seeing some of his courtiers smile, turned round upon them with the memorable words, "Honi soit qui mal y pense," adding "Shortly you shall see that garter advanced to so high an honour and renown as to account yourselves happy to wear it." In 1385 the castle was taken by storm and dismantled. It was subsequently restored by Henry IV. William Haliburton, of Fast Castle, took the fortress by surprise in 1419, but it was retaken the same year by the English, under Sir Robert Ogle, who made their way by a sewer from the Tweed to the kitchen. In both cases the garrison was put to the sword. In 1460 the Scots, provoked at the incursions of the garrison, crossed the Tweed and took the castle, leaving it in a ruinous condition. It was partially repaired by the English, but demolished again by the Scots before the battle of Flodden. It was afterwards repaired by the Earl of Surrey, and well fortified in anticipation of the approach of the Duke of Albany in 1523. The duke sent a force of Scots and French, to the number of 4000, and though they succeeded in carrying by storm the outer bailey, they were unable to gain the inner one, and retreated on the approach of the Earl of Surrey. George Buchanan the celebrated historian, carried arms in this expedition, and gives an interesting description of the castle as it then stood. The Earl of Sussex spent a night here in 1570, on his way to Teviotdale, where he destroyed more than fifty castles and peles, and about three hundred towns and villages. After the Union the much-battered stronghold was no longer needed, and gradually fell into ruins. It is remarked in "Denham's Tracts," concerning the old rhyme—

"Auld Wark upon the Tweed
Has been many a man's dead,"

that Wark's "prominent position as a Border fortress exposed it to repeated hostilities, and its history from the twelfth century down to, at least, the sixteenth century is perhaps without a parallel for *surprises, assaults, sieges, blockades, surrenders, evacuations, burning, restorations, slaughters.* These quickly-recurring events transformed the mount on which the castle stood into a Golgotha, and gave a too truthful origin to the couplet which still occurs on the borders of the once rival kingdoms."

The remains of the castle consist of the lower part of the tower, at the south-west corner, which formerly rose 120 feet above the Kaim, and the foundations of the north wall, a few feet in height, extending for about 100 yards in length. The east, west, and south walls also can be traced. During excavations made some years ago, a long flight of stone stairs was discovered, leading from the keep to the outer court, with a portcullis about half-way. A wide sewer to the north of the castle was also traced, up which the English found their way to the interior of the castle in 1419. On the margin of the river below the castle is a terrace, called "The Ladies' Walk." On the south side of the Kaim is a moss (the usual accompaniment of these ridges), which was crossed by a draw-bridge. It is now drained by a large cut at the east of the village, called "The Goat's Mouth," supposed to have been done by the enemy to reach the walls of the castle. A hill, about half-a-mile west of the village, is called "The Gallows Knowe," where the Scotch prisoners were formerly hanged. A quarter-of-a-mile to the north-east, close to the river, is the site of a great battle, which was fought in 1018 between Malcolm, King of Scotland, and Uchtred, Earl of Northumberland. The English earl had made a levy on the whole male population between the Tees and the Tweed, including the older men whose services on ordinary occasions would have been dispensed with, and his army was almost annihilated. So overwhelming was the calamity that the venerable Bishop Aldhune died of grief, and Uchtred seems to have had no alternative but to agree to any terms which were made to him. This battle of Carham, as it is called, is interesting from the fact that from this time the Tweed became the politically recognised limit between the eastern marches of England and Scotland. Half-a-mile west of Wark is a field called "Battle Place," the scene of a Border skirmish between Sir John Lilburne and Sir John Gordon, A.D. 1370. The Scots were driven from their ground five different times, but returned again to the charge, and finally obtained the victory, taking prisoner Sir John Lilburne and many of his followers.

Half-a-mile south of the village is Wark Station; half-a-mile east of which is Learmouth Bog, where several large staghorns and a curious oaken paddle have been found. This was a favourite hunting-ground of the botanist prior to recent draining operations, as it was the habitat of the marsh shield-fern (*Aspidium thelypteris*), prickly bog-rush (*Cladium mariscus*), lesser winter-green (*Pyrola rotundifolia*), lesser bladder-wort (*Utricularia minor*), slender-leaved carex (*Carex filiformis*), common mare's-tail (*Hippuris vulgaris*), great spear-wort (*Ranunculus lingua*), bog asphodel (*Narthecium ossifragum*), common drop-wort (*Spiræa filipendula*), etc.

A mile and three quarters from Wark, along the Kelso road, is the village of CARHAM, which also has its dark memories of Border warfare. "In the 33rd yere of Ecbright," (A.D. 833), says Leland, "the Danes arrived at Lindisfarne, and fought with the English at Carham, when eleven Bishops and two English Countes were slayne, and a greate numbre of people." A field to the south of the village marks the site of this battle. The adjoining field is known as *Wallace's Croft*, from the tradition that the Scottish hero encamped here in 1296, during one of his inroads into England. The *Church of St. Cuthbert* is a building of no architectural interest, built 1791. To the east of it are the remains of an Augustinian Monastery, founded at an early period by the Black Canons of Kirkham, in Yorkshire. It was destroyed by the Scots in 1297, and was probably never restored. *Carham Hall*, the residence of Mesdames Hodgson-Hinde and Hodgson-Huntley, is a handsome modern building, in the Elizabethan style, delightfully situated on the banks of the Tweed. At *Shidlaw*, half-a-mile south-east of Carham, the cattle which had been driven for safety within the walls of Wark Castle are said to have been "shed," or divided to the several owners. From the summit of the hill the eye may wander over a beautiful stretch of Border scenery. In a railway cutting, west of Carham, there is exposed a section of the Chert limestone—a rock which is only found in this district, and in small quantities near Dunse.

## HEIGHT OF PRINCIPAL HILLS.

| NAME. | FEET. | NAME. | FEET. | NAME. | FEET. |
|---|---|---|---|---|---|
| Cheviot | 2676 | Shielcleuch Edge | 1760 | Carter Fell | 1600 |
| Cairn Hill | 2545 | Standrop Rig | 1751 | Hindhope Law | 1504 |
| Hedgehope | 2348 | Shillmoor | 1734 | Blakeman's Law | 1501 |
| Comb Fell | 2132 | Preston Hill | 1724 | Wedder Hill | 1491 |
| Cushat Law | 2020 | Monkside | 1684 | Cold Law | 1484 |
| Bloody Bush Edge | 2001 | Hazelton Rig | 1655 | Woolbist Law | 1421 |
| Windy Gyle | 1963 | Shillhope Law | 1642 | Ewe Hill | 1327 |
| Dunmore | 1860 | Deels Hill | 1623 | Rooken | 1284 |
| Wether Cairn | 1834 | Wether Lair | 1622 | Weather Head | 1253 |
| Hogden Law | 1797 | Bell Hill | 1612 | Yeavering Bell | 1182 |

## CRAGS.

Callaley Crags
Cloudy Crags
Corbie Crags
Gunnerton Crags
Hebburn Crags
Kyloe Crags
Lorbottle Crags
Nine Nicks of Thirlwall
Ratcheugh Crags
Rothley Crags
Sewingshields Crags
Shafthoe Crags
Spindleston Crags
Thrunton Crags
Tiptoe Crags
Walltown Crags
Wanny Crags
Winshields Crags

## DENES.

Cawledge, near Alnwick
Denton, near Newcastle
Deepden, near Hexham
Denwick, near Alnwick
Hartburn, near Hartburn
Hartford, near Plessey
Holywell, near Hartley
Hareshaw, near Bellingham
Horncliffe, near Norham
Jesmond, near Newcastle
Roddam, near Wooler
Whittle, near Ovingham

## LOUGHS, LAKES, ETC.

Bavington Lake
Black Lough
Bolam Lake
Bromlee Lough
Capheaton Lake
Chartner's Lough
Crag Lough
Coldmartin Lough
Colt Crag Reservoir
Darden Lough
Doure Tarn
Fallowlees Lough
Gosforth Lake
Greenlee Lough
Hallington Water Ponds
Harbottle Lough
Harlow Hill Reservoirs
Holy Island Lough
Keemer Lough
Newham Lough
Pallinsburn Lake
Paston Lough
Sweethope Loughs

# PRE-REFORMATION CHURCHES.

## PERIODS OF ENGLISH ARCHITECTURE.

| | | | |
|---|---|---|---|
| Saxon | —— to 1066 | Geometrical Decorated | 1245 to 1315 |
| Norman | 1066 to 1145 | Curvilinear Decorated | 1315 to 1360 |
| Transitional | 1145 to 1190 | Perpendicular | 1360 to 1550 |
| Early English | 1190 to 1245 | | |

| Name of Place. | Dedication. | Benefice. | Period. |
|---|---|---|---|
| Alnham | St. Michael | V | Trans., E.E., & Perp. |
| Alnwick | St. Michael | V | Norm., Dec., Perp. |
| Alwinton | St. Michael | V | Norm., E.E., Dec. |
| Ancroft | —— | V | Norm., Dec. |
| Bamburgh | St. Aidan | V | E.E., Dec. |
| Bedlington | St. Cuthbert | V | Norm., E.E. |
| Belford | St. Mary | V | Norm. and Dec. |
| Bellingham | St. Cuthbert | R | Trans. and Perp. |
| Beltingham | St. Cuthbert | PC | Perp. |
| Bewick, Old | Holy Trinity | | Norm., Dec. |
| Birtley | St. Giles | V | Norm., E.E. |
| Blanchland | St. Mary | V | E.E. and Dec. |
| Bolam | St. Andrew | V | Sax., Norm., E.E., Dec. |
| Bothal | St. Andrew | R | Trans., E.E., Perp. |
| Bolton | —— | | Norman |
| Branxton | St. Paul | V | Trans. |
| Brinkburn | SS. Peter and Paul | V | Trans., E.E., & Perp. |
| Bywell | St. Andrew | V | Sax., E.E. |
| Do. | St. Peter | V | Norman, E.E., Dec. |
| Chillingham | St. Peter | V | Norm. |
| Chollerton | St. Giles | V | Norm., E.E. |
| Corbridge | St. Andrew | V | Sax., Nor., E.E., Dec. |
| Corsenside | St. Cuthbert | V | Norm. |
| Doddington | —— | V | E.E. |
| Edlingham | St. John the Baptist | V | Nor., Tr., Geom: Dec. |
| Eglingham | St. Maurice | V | Sax.? Trans., E.E. |
| Ellingham | St. Maurice | | E.E. |
| Elsdon | St. Cuthbert | R | E.E., Dec. |
| Embleton | Holy Trinity | V | E.E., Dec., Perp. |
| Falstone | —— | R | E.E., Perp. |
| Farne Island | St. Cuthbert | | Dec. |
| Felton | St. Michael | V | E.E., Dec. |
| Ford | St. Michael | R | E.E., Dec. |
| Halton | —— | | Norm. |

| Name of Place. | Dedication. | Benefice. | Period. |
|---|---|---|---|
| Haltwhistle . . . . | Holy Cross . . . . | V | E.E., Dec. |
| Hartburn . . . . | ——— | V | Norm., E.E., Perp. |
| Haydon . . . . . | St. Cuthbert . . . | | E. E., Curv: Dec. |
| Heddon-on-the-Wall | SS. Philip and John . | V | Sax., Norm., Trans., E. E. |
| Hexham . . . . . | St. Andrew . . . . | R | Sax., Tran., E. E., Dec., Per. |
| Holystone . . . . | St. Mary. . . . . | | E.E., Dec. |
| Holy Island . . . | St. Mary. . . . . | V | Trans., E.E., Dec. |
| Ilderton . . . . . | St. Michael. . . . | R | Trans., E.E. |
| Ingram . . . . . | St. Michael. . . . | R | Norman, E.E. |
| Kirkharle . . . . | St. Wilfrid . . . . | V | Dec. |
| Kirknewton. . . . | St. Gregory. . . . | V | Dec. |
| Kirkwhelpington . | St. Bartholemew . . | V | E. E. |
| Lesbury . . . . . | St. Mary. . . . . | V | E.E. |
| Longhoughton. . . | St. Peter. . . . . | V | Trans., E.E., Dec. |
| Long Framlington . | ——— | V | Trans., Dec. |
| Meldon . . . . . | St. John the Evangelist. | R | E.E. |
| Mitford . . . . . | St. Mary Magdalen . | V | Trans., E.E., Dec. |
| Morpeth . . . . . | St. Mary the Virgin . | R | Dec., Perp. |
| Newbiggin-by-the-Sea . | St. Bartholomew . . | V | E.E., Dec. |
| Newburn . . . . | St. Michael & All Angels | V | Norm., Trans., Dec. |
| Newcastle-on-Tyne . | St. Andrew . . . . | V | Trans., Dec., Perp. |
| " " . | St. John . . . . . | V | Norm., Dec., Perp. |
| " " . | St. Nicholas . . . | V | Nor., E.E., Dec., Perp. |
| Norham . . . . . | St. Cuthbert. . . . | V | Norm., E.E., Dec. |
| Ovingham . . . . | St. Mary the Virgin . | R | Sax., E.E., Perp. |
| Ponteland . . . . | St. Mary the Virgin . | V | Norm., E.E., Dec. |
| Rock . . . . . . | SS. Philip and James | V | Norm. |
| Rothbury . . . . | All Saints . . . . | R | E.E., Dec., Perp. |
| Ryal . . . . . . | All Saints . . . . | | Trans. |
| Seaton Delaval . . | St. Mary the Virgin . | | Norm. |
| Shilbotel. . . . . | St. James . . . . | V | Norm. |
| Simonburn . . . . | St. Mungo . . . . | R | E.E. |
| Stamfordham . . . | St. Mary the Virgin . | V | E.E. |
| Stannington . . . | St. Mary. . . . . | V | E.E. |
| Thockrington . . . | ——— | V | Norm. |
| Ulgham . . . . . | St. John . . . . . | V | Norm. |
| Warden . . . . . | St. Michael. . . . | V | Sax., E.E. |
| Warkworth . . . . | St. Lawrence . . . | V | Norm., Trans., Perp., Dec. |
| Whalton . . . . . | St. Mary. . . . . | R | Sax., Trans., E. E., Dec. |
| Whitley Chapel . . | St. Helen . . . . | PC | E.E. |
| Whittingham . . . | St. Bartholemew . . | V | Sax., E.E. |
| Widdrington . . . | Holy Trinity . . . | V | Dec. |
| Woodhorn . . . . | St. Mary. . . . . | V | Sax., Norm., Trans., E. E. |

## PRINCIPAL CAMPS OF THE ANCIENT BRITONS.

| CAMP. | NEAR | CAMP. | NEAR |
|---|---|---|---|
| Birtley Shields Dene | Birtley | Harelaw | Paston |
| Birtley West Farm | ,, | High Shields Green | Birtley |
| Brough Law | Ingram | Kettles | Wooler |
| Burgh Hill | Tosson | Lorden-shaw | Whitton |
| Callaley Hill | Callaley | Mill Knock | Birtley |
| Campville | Holystone | Monday Cleugh | Humbleton |
| Carry House | Birtley | Moneylaws | Barrasford |
| Castle Hill | Alnham | Old Bewick Hill | Old Bewick |
| Chatton Law | Chatton | Old Rothbury | Rothbury |
| Chesters | Ingram | Ringses | Beanley |
| Colwell Hill | Elsdon | ,, | Doddington |
| Countess Park | Birtley | Robert's Law | Trewhitt |
| Cup and Saucer | Wooler | Roseden Edge | Ilderton |
| Dod Law | Doddington | Rowting Linn | Ford |
| Fawdon Hill | Otterburn | Spindleston | Bamburgh |
| Greaves Ash | Linhope | Whitehall | Heathpool |
| Gunnar Heugh | Barrasford | Warden Law | Warden |
| Harehaugh | Hepple | Yeavering Bell | Yeavering |

## PRINCIPAL CASTLES AND PELE-TOWERS.

| | | | |
|---|---|---|---|
| Alnwick | Crawley | Hebburn | Rock |
| Aydon | Cresswell | Hexham | Shilbotel |
| Bamburgh | Dilston | Highfarlaw | Shittleheugh |
| Bellister | Doddington | Howtell | Shortflatt |
| Belsay | Dunstanburgh | Langley | Simonburn |
| Berwick | Edlingham | Lindisfarne | Staward-le-Peel |
| Bothal | Etal | Long Horsley | Thirlwall |
| Bywell | Elsdon | Mitford | Tosson |
| Cartington | Featherstone | Morpeth | Wark |
| Chillingham | Ford | Nafferton | Warkworth |
| Chipchase | Halton | Newcastle | Welton |
| Cockley Park | Harbottle | Norham | Whittingham |
| Cocklaw | Haughton | Ponteland | Whitton |
| Corbridge | Heathpool | Proctor Steads | Willimoteswick |
| Coupland | Hepple | Prudhoe | Woodhouses |

## ROMAN STATIONS AND CAMPS.

| NAME. | SITUATE. | NAME. | SITUATE. |
|---|---|---|---|
| Segedunum | Wallsend | Habitancum | Risingham |
| Pons Ælii | Newcastle | Bremenium | High Rochester |
| Condercum | Benwell | Corstopitum | Corbridge |
| Vindobala | Rutchester | Alione | Whitley Castle |
| Hunnum | Halton Chesters | Crawley Camp | |
| Cilurnum | Chollerford | Raylees Camp | |
| Procolitia | Carrawburgh | Chew Green Camps | |
| Borcovicus | Housesteads | Foulplayhead Camp | |
| Vindolana | Chesterholm | Outchester Camp | |
| Æsica | Great Chesters | Whitchester Camp | |
| Magna | Carvoran | | |

## RUINED CHURCHES AND CHAPELS.

| | |
|---|---|
| Alnmouth . | Church of St. Waleric |
| Bamburgh . | Chapel of St. Peter |
| Beadnel . | Chapel of St. Ebba |
| Belford . | Chapel of St. Mary |
| Bothal . | Chapel of St. Mary |
| Capheaton . | Chapel |
| Colwell . | Chapel |
| Etal . | Chapel of St. Mary |
| Gosforth, North | Chapel |
| Gunnerton . | Chapel of St. Margaret |
| Guyzance . | Church of St. Wilfrid of Gysnes |
| Hartington . | Chapel |
| Haughton . | Chapel |
| Heaton . | Chapel |
| Hexham . | Church of St. Mary |
| Inghoe . | Chapel |
| Jesmond . | Chapel of St. Mary |
| Lilburn . | Chapel |
| Lindisfarne . | St. Cuthbert's-in-the-Sea |
| Memmerkirk . | Chapel |
| Mindrum . | Chapel |
| Morpeth . | Chantry of All Saints |
| Newcastle . | Chapel of St. Lawrence |
| Prudhoe . | Chapel |
| Shaftoe, East . | Chapel |
| Tuggall . | Chapel |
| Wallsend . | Church of Holy Cross |
| Warkworth . | Church (Collegiate) |
| Wark . | Church of St. Giles |

## REMAINS OF MONASTIC HOUSES.

| | |
|---|---|
| Alnwick Abbey . | Premonstratensian |
| Alnwick—St. Leonard's Hospital. | do. |
| Amble Cell . | Benedictine |
| Bamburgh Friary . | Augustinian |
| Blanchland Abbey . | Premonstratensian |
| Brinkburn Priory . | Augustinian |
| Carham Cell . | Augustinian |
| Chibburn Preceptory . | Knights' Hospitaller |
| Coquet Island Cell . | Benedictine |
| Farne Island Cell . | Benedictine |
| Hexham Priory . | Augustinian |
| Hulne Abbey . | Carmelite |
| Holystone Nunnery | Benedictine |
| Lindisfarne Monastery . | Benedictine |
| Newcastle Black Friars Monastery . | Dominican |
| Newcastle Austin Friars . | Augustinian |
| Newminster Abbey. | Cistercian |
| Ovingham Cell . | Augustinian |
| Tynemouth Priory . | Benedictine |

## ERRATA.

Page 114.—The correct inscription on this bridge is as follows :—

GOD PRESARVE
WMFOIRA
ERENGTON
BELLDETE
THIS BREGE
OF LYME
AND STONE
1581

Page 142.—*Cymbularia* should be *Cymbalaria*

# PRINCIPAL HOTELS AND INNS IN THE COUNTY.

*Those Hotels marked by an asterisk are recommended as providing good entertainment and accommodation for the visitor.*

ACKLINGTON—Railway Hotel
ACOMB, W.—Queen's Arms ; Sun
AKELD—Black Bull, Bendor
ALLENDALE TOWN — Rose and Crown ; King's Head ;* Hare and Hounds
ALLENHEADS—Allenheads Inn
ALNMOUTH—Schooner;* Red Lion;* Hope and Anchor ; Sun
ALNWICK—White Swan and Northumberland Arms,* Bondgate Within ; Star Hotel,* Fenkle St. ; Nag's Head, Fenkle St.
ALWINTON—Rose and Thistle ;* Red Lion*
AMBLE–Dock Hot'l; Wellwood Arms
ANCROFT—Lamb
BACKWORTH—Backworth Hotel
BAMBURGH—Lord Crewe Arms ;* Victoria ;* Castle
BARDON MILL—Greyhound
BARRASFORD—The Board
BEADNELL—Craster Arms
BEAL—Plough
BEDLINGTON—King's Arms ; Turk's Head
BELFORD—Blue Bell ;* Black Swan
BELLINGHAM — Railway Hotel ;* Black Bull ; Fox and Hounds
BELSAY—Temperance Hotel ; The Highlander (two miles to the south)
BENTON, LONG—Sun ; Black Bull
BENWELL—Green Tree ; Fox and Hounds
BERWICK - UPON - TWEED — King's Arms Hotel,* Hide Hill ; Red Lion,* High St. ; Hen and Chickens,* Sandgate ; Royal Hotel, Castlegate ; Black Swan, Castlegate ; The Welcome Temperance Hotel, High St. ; Lorne Temperance Hotel, High Street
BIRTLEY (North Tyne)—Percy Arms
BLYTH—Station Hotel ; Waterloo Hotel
BLANCHLAND — Lord Crewe's Arms.*
BOULMER—Fishing Boat
CATTON—Unicorn ; Crown
CAUSEY PARK—Oak
CHATTON—Percy Arms*
CHARLTON, WEST—Tarsett Inn
CHESWICK—The Cat
CHIPCHASE—Chipchase Arms*
CHOLLERFORD—George*
CHOPPINGTON — Railway Hotel ; Travellers' Rest
CHRISTON BANK — Blinkbonny ; Sun
CLIFTON (near Morpeth)—Howard Arms
CORBRIDGE — Wheat Sheaf ; * Angel ;* Railway Hotel
CORNHILL—Collingwood Arms*
CRASTER—Jolly Fishermen's Inn
CROOKHAM—Blue Bell
CULLERCOATS—Huddlestone Arms Hotel
DIPTON (near Hexham) — Dipton Mill Inn
EACHWICK—Plough
EARSDON—Cannon ; Grey Horse
EGLINGHAM — Tankerville Arms ;* Ogle Arms
ELLINGHAM—Masons' Arms
ELSDON — Crown Temperance Hotel ;* Bird-in-Bush
ELTRINGHAM—Boat-House Inn
EMBLETON—Hare and Hounds * Grey's Inn
ETAL—Black Bull
FALSTONE—Black Cock *
FEATHERSTONE—Wallace Arms
FELTON — Northumberland Arms Hotel ;* Red Lion
FORD—Coffee Room

FOURSTONES—Railway Hotel
FRAMLINGTON—New Inn; Queen's Head
GLANTON—Queen's* Head Hotel; Red Lion Inn
GOSFORTH — Gosforth Hotel; County Hotel
GREENHEAD (near Blanchland)—Red Lion
GREENHEAD (near Gilsland) — Greenhead Hotel*
GREYSTEAD—Moor Cock*
HALTWHISTLE—Manor House
HARBOTTLE—Star; Forsters' Arms
HARTLEY—Delaval Arms
HARLOW HILL — Three Tuns Temperance Hotel
HAYDON BRIDGE—Anchor;* Black Bull; Scotch Arms
HEDLEY-ON-THE-HILL–Feathers Inn
HEDDON-ON-THE-WALL — Three Tuns; Royal French Arms
HENSHAW—Twice Brewed
HEUGH (Stamfordham)—Plough
HEXHAM—White Hart,* Fore St.; Royal,* Priestpopple; Grey Bull,* Priestpopple; North-Eastern,* Market Place; Temperance Hotel, Priestpopple
HOLY ISLAND — Northumberland Arms;* Iron Rails*
HOLYSTONE—Salmon
HORSLEY (Redewater)—Redesdale Arms*
HORSLEY (Near Wylam)—Crown and Anchor; Lion and Lamb
HORTON—Three Horse Shoes
HUMBLETON—Black Bull, Bendor
HUMSHAUGH—Crown.*
KENTON BAR—Kenton Bar Inn
KILLINGWORTH — Railway Hotel; Killingworth Arms
KIRKWHELPINGTON—The Board*
LEARCHILD—Ravensworth Arms
LESBURY—Blacksmith's Arms
LONG HORSLEY—Shoulder of Mutton; Rose and Thistle
LOWICK—White Swan; Commercial Inn; Golden Fleece
LUCKER—Apple
MATFEN, WEST—Black Bull; Temperance Hotel*
MELDON DYKE NEUK—Fox and Hounds
MELKRIDGE—Three Horse Shoes
MIDDLETON, NORTH—Ox Inn
MILFIELD—Red Lion
MITFORD—Plough Hotel*
MONKSEATON—Black Horse; Monkseaton Arms
MONKSHOUSE—St. Cuthbert's Inn*
MORPETH—Queen's Head,* Bridge Street; Grey Nag's Head,* Newgate Street; Newcastle Hotel,* Castle Square; Black Bull, Bridge Street; Turk's Head Hotel,* Bridge Street; Sun Inn, High Church
NETHERTON—Phœnix; Star
NETHERWITTON–Temperance Hot'l*
NEWBIGGIN-BY-THE-SEA—Old Ship Inn*; New Dolphin; Queen's Head
NEWBROUGH—Red Lion
NEWBURN—Northumberland Arms
NEWCASTLE—Alexandra,* 22 Clayton St. West; Central Exchange Hotel,* 95 Grey St.; County Hotel,* Neville St.; Crown Hotel, Clayton St. West; Douglas,* Grainger St. West; Norfolk Hotel,* 90 Grey St.; Royal Exchange Hotel,* 106 Grey St.; Station Hotel,* Neville St.; Turk's Head Hotel,* 73 Grey St.
*Temperance Hotels:*—Mrs. E. Avery, 118 Grey St. and 2 Higham Place; R. N. Ellis, Neville St.; R. Foster, 1 Charlotte Square; The Excelsior Temperance Hotel, 26 Clayton St. West
NEWTON-BY-THE-SEA—Ship
NEWTON-ON-THE-MOOR — Moor Cock and Barker Inn
NORHAM—Victoria;* White Swan; Masons' Arms; Salmon
NORTH SHIELDS — Ballarat, 42 Saville St. W.; Coburg, 1 Coburg St.; European and United States, 5 Railway Terrace

NORTH SUNDERLAND—White Swan
,, ,, (Sea Houses)—Bamburgh Castle
ORD, EAST—Salmon
OTTERBURN—Murray Arms*
OVINGHAM—New Inn
OVINGTON—Highlander; Ship
PALLINSBURN—Blue Bell
PONTELAND—Blackbird Hotel;* Seven Stars Hotel
POWBURN—Plough
PRESTON (North Shields)—Sportsman
PRUDHOE—Doctor Syntax; Fox and Hounds
RENNINGTON—Horse Shoes
RIDING—Wellington
RIDSDALE—Dun Cow
ROSEHILL (Gilsland)—Railway Hot'l
ROTHBURY-County Hotel;* Queen's Head*; Railway Hotel; Station Hotel; Turk's Head Inn
ST. MARY'S ISLAND—St. Mary's Island Inn
SEATON DELAVAL—Hastings Arms
SEATON SLUICE—Waterford Arms
SHILBOTTLE—Percy Arms
SLAGGYFORD-Malt Shovel; Railway
SLALEY—Travellers' Rest
SNITTER—Half-Moon Inn
SPITAL (Berwick)—Roxburgh Hotel; Blenheim Hotel; Spital Hotel
STAGSHAW BANK—Errington Arms
STAMFORDHAM—Swinburne Arms; Bay Horse; Masons' Arms
STANNERSBURN—Crown Inn
STANNINGTON—Howard Arms
STOCKSFIELD—Bywell Inn*
TONE PIT (Carrycoats)—Tone Pit Inn
THROPTON—Cross Keys; Three Wheat Heads
TWEEDMOUTH — Station Hotel;* Union Hotel
TYNEMOUTH—Bath Hotel,* Bath Terrace; Grand Hotel, Seabanks; Royal Hotel,* Oxford St.; Salutation Hotel, Front St.; Turk's Head Hotel, Front St.; Union Hotel, Percy St.; Kirby's Temperance Hotel
WALBOTTLE—Percy Arms
WALL—North Tyne Hotel; Smiths' Arms
WALLSEND—Station Hotel
WARDEN—Boat Inn
WARENFORD—White Swan
WARK—Black Bull; Grey Bull; Chipchase Arms*
WARKWORTH—Sun;* Hermitage;* Masons' Arms; Black Bull
WELDON BRIDGE—Anglers' Hotel*
WHALTON—Beresford Arms
WHITLEY-BY-THE-SEA—Victoria; Fat Ox
WHITLEY CHAPEL — Click 'em Inn
WHITFIELD—Temperance Hotel*
WHITTINGHAM—Castle; Bridge of Aln,* near Railway Station
WHITTINGTON, GREAT—Queen's Head
WHITTONSTALL—Anchor
WIDDRINGTON—Widdrington Htl.
WOODBURN, WEST—Bay Horse
,, EAST—Queen's Head
WOOLER—Tankerville Arms* (The Cottage); Black Bull; Red Lion
WYLAM—Fox and Hounds; Boat House

# INDEX.


## A.

Acklington Dam, Frank Buckland at, 371.
Acomb, West, 181.
Adderstone Hall, 442.
Æsica, Roman station of, 196.
Akeld, 504.
Allendale Town, 159.
Allenheads, 160.
Alnham, church, castle, and pele, 353.
Alnmouth: church, Saxon cross, camp at, 405; Synod, 406; naval engagements near, 406; Church Hill, 407.
Alnwick: history of, 372-373; Percy Tenantry Column, 373; Hotspur's Tower, 373; St. Paul's Church, 373; Market Place, 374; old houses, 374; Church of St. Michael, 374-376; chantry house, 376; castle, 376-383; history of the Percy family, 384-386; Alnwick Abbey, 386; Hulne Abbey, 388-390; Brislee Tower, 390; William the Lion's monument, 391; Lion Bridge, 392; St. Leonard's Hospital, 392; Malcolm's Cross, 392.
Alwinton, curious feature in church of, 349.
Amble, seaport of, cell at, 416.
Ancroft, 541.
Angerton Hall, 250.
Anick, 134.
Arthur's Chair, King, 191.
Ashington, 290.
Aydon Castle, description of, 141; Jack's Leap, 142.

## B.

Ballen Mill, prophecy fulfilled at, 225.
Bamburgh: village, 426; wreckers of, 427; sea-animal at, 427; duel at, 427; castle, its position, history, and charities, 427-431; description of, 431-434; Chapel of St. Peter, 434; parish church, 435, 436; Forsters of, 436, 437; Grace Darling's monument, 437; monastic remains at, 437.
Barcombe Hill, camp on, discovery of coins on, 166.
Bardon Mill, 165.
Barmoor Castle, 528.
Barrasford, British remains at, 211
Barrow Pele, 349.
Batinghope, 321.
Battle Bridge, 398.
Bavington Hall, 210.
Bavington, Little, 210.
Beacon Hill, near Holystone, 344.
Beadnell, pele, church, remains of chapel at and geology of, 449.
Beal, 447.
Beanley Moor, camps on, 400.
Beaufront, 134.
Bebside, 68.
Bedlington, 68, 69.
Belford, village, castle, plague at, church, 444; hall, crags, Chapel Hill, 445.
Belling Crags, 225.
Bellingham: church, 214; legend of, 215; Cuddy's Fair, 215; Hareshaw Linn, 216.
Bellister Castle, 170; legend of, 171.
Belsay: castle, 79; quarries, 79; crag, 80; Silky at, 80.
Beltingham Chapel, 163.
Bendor Stone, 503.
Benridge, West, 273.
Benwell, tower, 85; Roman station at, 86.
Berwick-upon-Tweed: description of, 530; history of, 531-534; remains of castle, 534, 535; water tower, 535; Lord Soulis's and Bell tower, 535; church, 535; town hall, 536; walls and gates, 537; bridges, 537.
Bewick: Old, Norman chapel of, 499; camp, incised rocks at, 500, 501.
Biddleston Hall, 352.
Bilton Junction, 405.
Bingfield, 209.
Birdhope Crag, Presbyterian meeting-house at, 323.
Birtley, church and castle of, 231.
Birtley Shields Dene Camp, 231.
Bishop's Linn, 178.
Bitchfield, West, pele at, 79.
Blackburn Linn, 223.
Black Callerton, George Stephenson at, 88.
Black Carts, 187.
Black Cock Hall, ruins of, 337.
Black Hedley, Lough born at, 133.
Black Heddon, Silky's pranks at, 84.
Black Lough, 396.
Black Middens, wrecks on, 52.
Blagdon Hall, 73; Kale Cross at, 74.
Blanchland: monastery, 116, 117; Edward III. at, 117; church, 117; Gibraltar Rock, 118.
Blaw Weary, 501.
Blenkinsopp: castle, 171; white lady of, 171, 172 hall, 172.
Blue Crag, camp on, 211.
Blyth, 67, 68; local Samson at, 68.
Bockenfield, 279.
Bogle Gap, 195.
Bolam: house, church, camp, 268; Dr. Angus born at, lake, 269.
Bolton, leper hospital, church, camp at, 399.

Bondicar Rocks, 417.
Bonnyrigg Hall, 194.
Borcovicus, Roman station of, 192-194.
Bothal, village, 286; castle, 287, 288; church, 289.
Boulmer, smuggling at, 419, 420.
Bower, The, the Charltons of, 220.
Bowmont Hill, coins found on, 510.
Bradford, 441.
Brainshaugh, 370.
Brandon, old chapel of, 364.
Branton, 363.
Brandy, Leish, grave of, 228.
Branxton, 518.
Bremenium, Roman station of, 322, 323.
Bridle Rock, 441.
Brierdene, 57.
Brinkburn, priory, 367-369; burial-place of fairies at, 369.
Brislee Tower, 390.
Bromlee Lough, legend of, 191.
Broomridge, 519.
Broom Park, 399.
Brough Law, antiquities of, 365.
Brown Dykes Camp, 188.
Brunton, remains of wall and turret at, 182.
Buckton Moor, camps on, 447.
Budle, bay, cockles, shales, hills of, 438.
Buller's Green, Dr. Morrison born at, 247.
Burgh Hill Camp, 338.
Burn Deviot, 195.
Burnstones, 179.
Burradon, 73.
Busy Gap, 191.
Buteland, camp at, 232.
Byrness, 324.
Bywell: castle, 144; Roger North at, 144, 145; St. Andrew's Church, 145; St. Peter's Church, 145, 146; hall, 146.

## C.

Caistron Camp, 341.
Callaley Castle, 356; legend of, 357; Castle Hill, 357; crags, 357, 358.
Caller Hues, 216.
Cambo, pele, incised grave-covers at, 259, 260.
Campville, camp at, 346.
Canny Bank, camp at, 346.
Capheaton: village, 238, hall, 239; Swinburnes of, 239; priests' holes at, 240; site of castle, 239; chapel, 241.
Carham, battles near, 556, 557; church and hall, 557.
Carraw, 188.
Carrawburgh, Roman station at, 187.
Carry House Camp, 230.
Carter Bar, affray with poachers at, 325.
Carter Fell, 326.
Cartington: castle, 355; nunnery, 355; cove, 330.
Carvoran, Roman station at, 197.
Castle Hill, Callaley, 353.
Castle Nick, 195.
Catcleugh, 324.
Cats' Stairs, 195.
Cateran Hole, 501.
Catton Beacon, 159.
Cawfields Mile-castle, 195.
Caw Gap, 198.
Cawledge Dene, 394.
Cawsey Park Tower, 278.
Chapel Hill, Mithraic temple at, 193.
Chapel House, Martin at, 88.
Charlton (No. Tyne), 222.
Chartner's Lough, rare waterlilies in, 336.
Chathill, fairy ring at, 443.
Chattlehope Spout, 324.
Chatton, 491.
Chatton Law, incised rocks on, 491.
Cheeseburn Grange, 81.
Cherryburn House, Bewick born at, 97.
Chesterholm, Roman station and milestone at, 167.
Chesterwood, peles at, 153.
Chesters, The, 185, 186.
Chesters, The (Breamish), 366.
Chesters, Great, Roman station of, 196.
Cheswick House, 541.
Cheviot: hills, 480; sheep, 480; ascent of, 480, 481; Defoe on, 481; Henhole, 481; Black Adam of, 482; hanging stone, 483; forest of, 483; routes to and from, 483.
Chew Green, Roman camps at, 350.
Chibburn, ancient preceptory at, 284.
Chillingham: church, 491, 492; castle, 492-494; toadstone, 493; gardens, 494; park, 495, 496; Ros Castle, 495; wild cattle, 495-498.
Chipchase Castle, 206-208; legend of, 208.
Chirdon Burn, waterfalls on, 220.
Chirton, 43, 44; Ralph Gardiner at, 43; Dobson born at, 44.
Chollerford, Jock o' the Side at, 183; Roman bridge at, 184, 185; Roman station at, 185, 186.
Chollerton, 209.
Chubden Hill, 363.
Cilurnum, Roman station of, 185, 186.
Cinder Kiln Hills, 230.
Cippus, Roman, 323.
Clavering's Cross, 274.
Clennel Hall, 346; pele, 351.
Clint Rocks, 230.
Cloudy Crags, 398.
Cloven Crag, 310.
Cocklaw Pele-tower, 209.
Cockley Park Tower, 278.
Colt Crag Reservoir, 211.
Colwell, 210.
Colwell Hill Camp, 311.
Comb Peles, 223.
Condercum, Roman station of, 86.
Coquet Island, cell on, capture by the Scots, wrecks on, 417.
Corbie Crags, 501.
Corbridge: Roman station at, 135; Roman stones at, 136, 137; Roman bridge at, 137; history of, 137, 138; church, 138-140; pele-towers at, 140; bridge, 140.
Cornhill, 544, 545.
Corsenside, 310.
Corstopitum, Roman station of, 135.
Countess Park Camp, 230.
Coupland Castle, 511.
Coventina's Well, 187.
Cowett Wells, 337.
Coxlodge, 72.
Crag Lough, 194.
Cragside, 331-333; hut-circles near, 333.
Craster, tower, 422.
Crawley Dene, camp, and tower, 363.
Cresswell, village and church, 293; family of, 294; old tower at, 294; white lady of, 294; house, 294.
Cresswell Bog, near Middleton, 478.
Crookham, 518.
Cuddy's Cave, 527.
Cuddy's Cove, 518.
Cullercoats, artists at, 55; Smugglers' Cave, 56; Sparrow Hall, 55.
Cullernose Point, 422.
Cummings Cross, 190.

Cunion Crags, 485.
Cupola Bank, 158.
Cup and Saucer Bank, 476.

D.

Dalley Bank, skirmish on, 211.
Dally Castle, 219.
Dalton, haunted house at, 81.
Dancing Hall, 356.
Darden Lough, 310.
Dead Water, 229.
Debdon, dancing green at, 355.
Deepden, 113.
Denton: narrow escape of John Wesley at, 86; dene, 87; hall, 87; Dr. Johnson at, 87.
Denwick, 394.
Derry Camp, 445.
Devil's Punch Bowl, 271.
Devil's Rock, 231.
Dewley Burn, 88.
Diamond Burn, 479.
Dilston: story of Earl of Derwentwater, 120-126; Earl's tree, 125; Countess of Derwentwater at, 126, 127; castle, 127, 128; chapel, 128; village of, 130; Mrs. Butler's description of, 130; old bridge at, 131.
Dissington Hall, 81.
Dissington, South, 81.
Doddington, pele-tower and church, 526.
Dod Law, camps, incised rocks on, 525.
Dolly Pit Colliery, 88.
Dotland Park, 113.
Doure Tarn, 324.
Downham, 510.
Drake Stone, 348.
Druridge Bay, 295.
Duddo, castle and stones, 542.
Dunstan Hall, Duns Scotus born at, 423.
Dunstanburgh Castle: history and description of, 452, 453; legend of, 454; crystals, 431-454

E.

Eachwick, 81.
Earle, 477.
Earsdon, 58, 59.
Easington, 455.
East Land Ends, Martin born at, 152.
Edlingham: church, 395; castle, witch of, 396.
Eglingham: church, 400; hall, Cromwell at, 401.
Elishaw, hospital, convivialities at, proverbs respecting, 322.
Ellingham: hall, 442; church, Haggerstones of, 443.
Ellington, 295.
Elsdon: ancient customs at, 302; mote-hills, 302; church, 303; castle, 305; rectors of, 305; humorous description of, 306-308.
Elyhaugh, 369.
Embleton: church, 450; tower of, 451; vicars of, 451; memorial of Andrew Barton near, 451.
Errington, 209.
Eshott, hall and castle, 279.
Eslington Hall, 362; Collingwoods of, 362.
Etal: village, church, castle, 523; remains of chantry near, 524.
Ewart Park, 511.

F

Falloden Hall, 443.
Fallowfield Fell, written rock on, 181.
Fallowlees' Lough, 336.
Fallowlees, Veitch at, 337.
Falstone, Saxon cross at, 224.
Farnham Low, Celtic antiquities at, 343.
Farne Islands, Fairway, House Island: hermits of, 466, 467; St. Cuthbert's Chapel, 468; Prior Castell's tower, 468; Wedums, 468; Crumstone, 469; Stapel Island, 469; Pinnacles, 469; sea-birds of, 469, 470; Brownsman, 470; Wawmes, cormorants of, 470; Harcars, 470; Longstone, 471; wreck of *Forfarshire*, 471, 472; Grace Darling, 472, 473; Goldstone wreck on, 473.
Fawdon Hill Camp, 311.
Fawdon Hill, fairies of, 363.
Featherstone Castle, 175.
Felton: village, 369; church, 370; park, 370.
Fenton, house, disused graveyard, 527.
Fenwick Tower, 84.
Fleehope, 508.
Fleetham, pele-tower, 450.
Flodden Hill, 512; battle of, 513-518.
Flotterton, 341.
Ford: castle, 519-521; village, 521; frescoes in school-room, 521, 522; church, 522.
Fourstones, 150.
Fowberry Tower, 490.
Framlington, Long, 354.
Frankham Fell, quarries on, 150.
Freemen's Well, 396, 397.
Frenchmen's Row, 89.

G.

Gallowhill, 268.
Gallowshill, 259.
Gallowshaw, 275.
Garleigh Hill, Celtic remains on, 335.
Gawen's Field, 369.
Gibb's Cross, 223.
Girsonfield, 311.
Glanton, 363.
Gled Law, incised rocks on, 526.
Glen Cune, 178.
Glen Dhu, 179.
Glenwhelt, 173.
Glororum, 442.
Gloster Hill, remains of manor-house, Roman antiquities at, 416.
Golden Pots, 351.
Gosforth, South, 70.
Gosforth, colliery, ball at, 71.
Gosforth Park, 72.
Greaves Ash Celtic Town, 365, 366,
Greenhead, 172.
Greenlee Lough, 194.
Greenrigg, Jacobite rendezvous at, 232.
Greensilhaugh, Sir A. Featherstonehaugh killed at, 175.
Gregory's Hill, camp on, 506.
Grindon Moor, skirmish on, 543.
Grizzy's Clump, 445, 446.
Grunstane Law, 148.
Gunnerton: the lady's well, 211; old chapel at, moneyhill of, 211; crags, camps, 212, 213.
Guyzance, ruined chapel of, 370.

H.

Habitancum, Roman station of, 234.
Haddrick's Mill, 71.
Hagg, monument near, 510.
Haggerstone Castle, 542.

Hallington, reservoir of, 210.
Halton Tower, 142, 143.
Halton Chesters, Roman station of, 143.
Haltwhistle: Castle Hill, 168; castle of, pele of, church, 168; fray of, 169.
Haly Chesters, 554.
Harbottle Castle, 346-348; birth of Margaret Douglas at, 347; Drake Stone, 348.
Harbottle Peels, 348.
Hardriding Hall, 167.
Harehaugh Hill, camp on, 344.
Harelaw, Earl of Northumberland in hiding at, 509.
Hareshaw Linn, 216.
Harkess Rocks, 438.
Harle Tower, Little, 237.
Harle Kirk, 237, 238.
Harlow Hill, 89.
Harnham Hall: ancient fortalice at, 269; Veitch at, Madam Babbington's grave, 270.
Hartburn: monuments in church of, 256; dene, "King and Queen" of, 257.
Hartburn Grange, 257.
Hartford Dene, 74.
Harthope Linn, 480.
Hartington, hall, remains of chapel at, 259.
Hartley, Old, 59.
Hartley Colliery accident, 65-67.
Hartleyburn, 178.
Hartside, 365.
Haughton Castle, 199, 200; Midhat Pacha at, 200; legend of, 200; paper mill near, 201; ferry at, 201.
Hauxley, 417.
Hawkhill, glacial action at, 394.
Hawkhope, 225.
Hawsden Burn, Celtic town near, 478.
Haw's Pele, murder at, 308, 309.
Haydon Church, curious epitaph at, 152; Cruel Syke, 152.
Haydon Bridge Church, 151; Martin at, 152; Ned Coulson, 152, 153.
Heathpool: castle, linn, Collingwood's oaks, 507; terrace cultivation at, 508.
Heaton Castle, old, 553, 554.
Heaton Hall, 36.
Heaton Main Colliery, 37.
Heavenfield, battle of, 182.
Hebburn, near Morpeth, 278.
Hebburn Tower and Crags, near Chillingham, 499.
Heddon-on-the-Wall, remains of wall, church, 89.
Hedgehope, 484.
Hedgeley Moor, battle of, 489.
Henshaw, 167.
Hepple, pele-tower, 341.
Hepple Woodhouses, pele at, 344.
Hermitage (Hexham), Latin inscription at, 181.
Hermitage (Warkworth), 412-415.
Hesleyside, 219.
Hetchester Camp, 343.
Hetha, Great and Little, camps on, 508.
Hexham: history of, 102-106; market-place, 106; abbey church, 106-110; remains of abbey buildings, 110; remains of St. Mary's Church, 111; Moot Hall, 111; Manor office, 111; old houses, 112; eminent natives of, 112.
Hexham, Levels, battle of, 114.
Highfarlaw Pele, 393.
High Street House, birthplace of George Stephenson, 94.
High Warden, camp at, 198.
Hirst, Low, pele at, 290.
Holburn, 527.
Holy Island: pilgrimage to, 456; history of, 456-459; priory church, 459, 460; priory buildings, 460; parish church, 462; petting-stone, 462; wreckers of, 462, 463; castle, 463; St. Cuthbert's Isle, 464; lough, 464.
Holystone, nunnery, church, and our lady's well at, 345.
Homer's Lane, 198: murder of Joe the Quilter, 199.
Holywell Dene, 59.
Homildon Hill, battle of, 503.
Horncliffe, Suspension Bridge, house, dene, 546.
Horsley (Wylam), nonconformists at, 91.
Horsley (Redewater), 322.
Horsley, Long, 277.
Horton, castle and church, 68.
Hot Bank Farm, 194.
Houghton, Long, 418, 419.
Housesteads, Roman station at, 192-194.
Howdon, John Martin at, 43.
Howick Hall, 420; Earl Grey of, 421; church, grounds, 421; pinetum, camp, submerged forest at, 422.
Huckhoe, camp at, 269.
Hulne Abbey, 388-390.
Humbleton, village, hill, camps, 582.
Humlie Dod, antiquities on, 272.
Hurl Stone, 499.

## I.

Ilderton, 487.
Ilderton Dod, 487.
Inghoe, 149.
Ingram Church, British antiquities near, 364.

## J.

Jesmond: dene, 35; Lady chapel, St. Mary's well, Stote's hall, 36.
Jolly's Close, 93.

## K.

Kenton, Thomas Atthey born at, 76.
Kettles Camp, 476.
Keyheugh, 310.
Kidland, 351.
Kielder Castle, 226; story of Cowt of, 226, 227; Cowt's grave, 227; camps near, 229.
Kilham, 511.
Killingworth, 72.
Kimmerston, 519.
King's Stone, 544.
Kirkharle: tower, 237; church, 237; village, 238.
Kirkhaugh Church, 180.
Kirkheaton, 149.
Kirk Hill, ancient chapel on, 342.
Kirkley Hall, 78.
Kirk Newton, 506.
Kirkwelpington, 236.
Knaresdale: hall, legend of, church, 179; curious epitaph at, 180.
Kyloe, hills church, pele, 447.

## L.

Lady Chapel of the Wansbeck, 285.

Lamberton Toll, 535.
Lambley Nunnery, 178.
Langlee, camp near, 478.
Langleeford, Sir W. Scott at, 479.
Langley Castle, 154, 155; mills, 155.
Langside Moor, 501.
Lantern, Jenny's, 399.
Lanton Hill, monument on, 511.
Leap Crag Pool, 231.
Learmouth Bog, 556.
Lee Hall, story of Long Pack at, 217.
Lee, St. John, 181.
Lemmington Hall, 398.
Lesbury, church, vicars of, 404.
Lewis Burn, 226.
Lilburn: tower, 486; remains of chapel, 487.
Limestone Bank, fosse of wall and vallum at, 187.
Linden House, 277.
Lindisfarne: dyke, 456; name, 456; bishops of, 456-458; priory of, 459, 460.
Linemouth, whale stranded at, 293.
Linhope Farne, 365.
Linhope Spout, 366.
Linnel's Bridge, hollin bush of, 114.
Linshiels, 349.
Lisle's Burn, 234.
Lipwood, 162.
Longframlington, 354.
Long Hirst Hall, 280.
Long Horsley, 277.
Long Houghton: church, market cross, 418; curious register at, 419.
Long Lonkin's Hole, 101.
Longridge Towers, 546.
Longwitton Hall, 275.
Lorbottle, 355; cubs of, 356.
Lorden-shaw Camp, 336.
Lowick, 529.
Lowlyn, 542.
Low Park End, 204.
Lucker, 442.
Lynnhead Waterfall, 234.

## M.

Macartney's Cave, 358.
Magna, Roman station of, 197.
Mare and Foal, 195.
Matfen, village, 147, 148; hall, 148.
Meldon: church, 245; water-mill, Cromwell at, 255; Hall, Meg of, 255.
Meldon Dyke Neuk, 254.
Melkridge, 167.
Memmerkirk, remains of chapel of, 351.
Middleton Hall, near Belford, 445.
Middleton Hall, near Wooler, 477.
Middleton Moss, British relics found in, 266.
Middleton, North, village community system at, 256.
Milbourne Hall, 78; grange, 78.
Milkhope Hill, entrenchments on, 351.
Millfield, ancient palace at, battle of, 512.
Mill Knock Camp, 231.
Mindrum, 510.
Minster Acres, 132.
Mitford: village, 251; church 251, 252; castle, 252, 253; manor-house, 253; hall, 253; Mitford family, 254.
Monday Cleugh, camp at, 502.
Monkridge Hall, 311.
Monkseaton, 58.
Monkshouse, 448.
Monk's Stone, legend of, 53.
Moot Law, camp on, 210.
Morpeth: history of, 242; castle, Ha' Hill, 243; parish church, 243, 244; prison, 244; Chapel of All Saints, 245; town hall, 245; clock tower, 245; Church of St. James, 245; old hostelries, 246; asylum, grammar school, Collingwood's house, 246; eminent natives of, 247; terrace, 247.
Morwick Hall and Mill, 415; incised rocks at, 416.
Moss Kennel Farm-house, 192.
Mote Hills, 302, 243, 346, 168.
Mount Huly, 508.
Mumps Ha', 174.

## N.

Nafferton Tower, Long Lonkin at, 100.
Netherton, 352.
Netherwitton: hall, 274, 275; Cromwell at, 275; "king and queen" oaks of, 275.
Newbiggen Dene, 552.
Newbiggin-by-the-Sea: port of, church, 292; fairy rocks, 293.
Newbrough: St. Mary's Well at, 150; town hall, 151.
Newburn: ancient ford at, 92; church, 92, 93; battle of, 93; George Stephenson at, 93; old hall, 94.
Newcastle: history of the town, 2-5; Norman Keep, 5-7; Black Gate, 8-9; South Postern, 9; St. Nicholas' Church, 10-15; All Saints' Church, 15, 16; St. Andrew's Church, 16, 17; St. John's Church, 17-19; town walls, 19, 20; Black Friar's Monastery, 20; Castle Garth, 20; Side, 20; Butcher Bank, 21; Guild Hall and Exchange, 21; Sandhill, 21; Close, 22; Quayside, 22, 23; Trinity House, 22, 23; Sandgate, 23, 24; Keelmen's Hospital, 24; Austin Friars, 24; Pilgrim Street, 24; Central Station, 25; Stephenson's monument, 25; Town Hall, 26; Grey Street, 26, 27; Blackett Street, Grainger Street, Clayton Street, 27; St. Mary's Cathedral, 28; Judges' lodgings, 28; Lord Armstrong's birthplace, 29; Lambert's Leap, 29; High Level Bridge, 29; Redheugh Bridge, 29; Swing Bridge, 30; Lit. and Phil., Public Library, 30, 31; museum, 32; Town Moor, Leazes Park, Elswick Park, 33; Heaton Park, King John's Palace, 34; Armstrong Park, Jesmond Dene, 35.
Newminster Abbey, 248-250.
Newton, hall, church, 147.
Newton-by-the-Sea, 450.
Newton-on-the-Moor, 403.
Newton, West, 508.
Ninebanks, 161.
Norham Castle: description of, 547, 548; history of, 548-550; Marmion at, 549; Monks' Well, 550; village and church, 550, 551.
North Shields, 44-47.
North Sunderland, 448.
North Sunderland Seahouses, piers at, 448.
Nunnykirk Hall, 276.
Nunriding Woods, 273.
Nunsbrough, Earl of Derwentwater at, 115.
Nunwick Hall, 203.

## O.

Ogle Castle, 78; family of, 78.

Old Bewick: village and chapel, 499; hill, camp on, incised rocks on, 500.
Old Slate Hill, 269.
Old Town, 158.
Ord, East, 546.
Otterburn: village, 311; tower, 312; Mad Jack Ha' of, 312; battle of, 313-318; Battle Stone, 318.
Outchester, Roman station at, 444.
Over Acres, 311.
Ovingham: church, 98; Bewick buried at, 98; cell of black canons at, 99
Oxhill, camp on, 211.

## P.

Pallinsburn House, lake, kaim, 544.
Parkhead Farm, Roman sculpture near, 235.
Paston Hall and Lake, 509.
Pauperhaugh, 367.
Peden's Pike, 322.
Peel Crag, 195.
Peel Fell, 229.
Percy's Cross (Hedgeley), 489.
Percy's Cross (Otterburn), 318.
Pigdon, 273.
Pigdon's Leap, 353.
Pinwell, 476.
Piperden, battle of, 510.
Plainfield Moor, 341.
Plane Trees Field, remains of wall at, 182.
Plashett's Colliery, 226.
Pleapiece, murder on, 487.
Plessey Mill, 74.
Poind and his man, 266, 272.
Ponteland Castle, church, pele at, 77.
Powburn, 363.
Presson, 510.
Preston Tower, 443.
Prestwick Car, 77.
Priest and clerk, 355.
Procolitia, Roman station of, 187.
Proctor Steads: pele at, Duns Scotus born at, 423.
Prudhoe Castle, 94-97; remains of chapel near, 97.
Pynkinscleugh, legends of, 177, 178.

## Q.

Queen's Cave, 112, 113.

## R.

Ramshope Crystals, 324.
Ratcheugh Crag, 394.
Raven's Crag, 162.
Raylees, Roman camp at, 310.
Redesdale, history and description of, 269-301.
Redesmouth, 230.
Redhouse Crags, camps on, 182.
Reed, Parcy ballad of, 320, 321; ghost of, 321.
Reidswire, raid of the, 325.
Reiver Crag, camp on, 211.
Reiver's Well, 331.
Rennington, 424.
Richardson's Stead, 540.
Riding Mill, 132.
Ridley Hall and Grounds, 162.
Ridsdale, 236.
Rimside Moor, legend of, 354.
Riplington, 268.
Risingham, Roman station at, 234.
Risingham, Rob of, 235.
Robert's Law, camp on, 352.
Rob Roy's Cave, 346.
Rochester, High, Roman station at, 322.
Rock: Norman church of, 424; hall, 425; Colonel John Salkeld and John Fenwick of, 425.
Roddam Hall, 487; dene, family of, 488.
Rory's Gair, 484.
Roseden Edge, camp on, 485.
Rosehill, Roman statue found at, 197.
Rose's Bower, 206.
Rothbury: name and history of, 327; ancient inn at, 328; church, 328; Saxon cross, 329; Bernard Gilpin at, 329; racecourse, 330; Cragside, 331-333; natives of, 334.
Rothbury, old camp of, 330.
Rothley: crags, castle, mill, 258; fairies at, 258, 259.
Rowting Linn, 527; camp, incised rocks near, 528.
Rutchester: Roman station at, tower, 89; giant's grave, 90.
Ryall, 148.
Ryehill, hospital at, 338.
Ryle, Little, old pele at, 353.
Ryle, Great, 362.

## S.

Saddle Rock, 451.
St. John Lee, church of, 481.
St. Lawrence, chapel of, 37.
St. Mary's Island, 58.
St. Ninian's Well, 361.
St. Oswald's Chapel, battle near, 182.
St. Oswald's Hill Head, centurial stone at, 181.
Sandhoe, 135.
Scots Gap, accident near, 256.
Scotch Coulthard, 195.
Scotswood, 92.
Scremerston, 540; immured frog at, 541.
Sea-houses, 448.
Seaton Sluice, 60.
Seaton Delaval: hall, 60-65; history of Delavals, 62, 63; statues at, 64; Lady chapel, 64; mausoleum, 65; obelisks, 65.
Selby's Cove, 336.
Seven Linns, the, 220.
Sewingshields, castle, 188; legend of, 189.
Shafthoe Crags, 270-272; Devil's Punch Bowl, 271; Shafthoe Hall, Tailor and his man, Piper's Chair, 271; Sawter's Nick, 272.
Shafthoe, East, remains of chapel at, 272.
Sharperton, 341.
Shawdon Hall, 399; hangman's oak near, 399.
Sheepwash, 290.
Shepherds' Law, 399.
Shidlaw, 557.
Shields, North, 44-47; site of St. Leonard's hospital at, master mariner's asylum, Dotwick Street murder, 46.
Shilbottle Church and Pele, 402.
Shillmoor, 350.
Shipley, 401.
Shitlington, 218.
Shittleheugh Pele, 321.
Shoreston Hall, 448.
Shortflatt Tower, 269.
Silver Lane, Roman vessels found in, 238.
Silvernut Well, 312.
Simonburn, church, Wallis curate at, 202; castle, Teckitt Linn, 203.
Simonside, 336.
Sinkside Hill, camp on, 502.
Skirlnaked, 478.
Slaggyford, 180.
Slaley, 115.

Smales' Leap, 221.
Snear Hill, 478.
Snitter, 352.
Snook Point, cave at, 449.
Soldier's Fauld, Celtic camp, 343.
Soneyrigg, Arthur's round table at, 226.
Southern Knowe, 508.
Spade Adam Waste, 174.
Spindleston Heughs, legend of, 438-441.
Spital, 540.
Spital Hill House, 250.
Stagshawbank Fair, 135.
Stamfordham, 81.
Standingstone Farm, 147.
Stannersburn, 221.
Stannington, 74.
Stanton Hall, Veitch at, 273.
Staward, Low, manor house at, 155.
Staward-le-Peel, 155, 156; Dicky of Kingswood at, 156, 157; Thief's Loup, Cyper's Linn, 157.
Steel Rig Gap, 195.
Stocksfield, 133.
Sunderland, North, 448.
Swansfield House, 395.
Swarland Hall, 370; monument of Nelson at, 370.
Sweethope Lough, 233.
Swinburn Castle, 210; standing stone at, 211.
Swinburn Tower, Little, 211.
Swine Hill, Roman camp, 232.
Swinhoe, 450.
Switcherdown, 478.
Sybil's Well, 512.

T.

Tallon's, grave, Tom, 506.
Tarset Castle, 222; story of, 222, 223.
Tecket Linn, 203.
Thirlwall Castle, 172; legend of, 173; nine nicks of, 196.
Thockrington, 211.
Thorneyburn, 223.
Thorngrafton, 166; Find, 166.
Three-mile Bridge, 72.
Three-stone Burn, Druidical circle at, 484
Throckley, gateway of mile-castle at, 89.
Thropton, 340.
Thrum, the, 331.
Thrunton Crags, 358, 361
Thruston Wells, 276.
Tillmouth, chapel at, 553.
Tindle House, 524.
Tiptoe Rocks, 524.
Titlington Hall, pike, 399.
Todlaw Mill, ghost of Parcy Reed at, 321.
Tone, 233.
Tosson: pele, hill, 338; fairies of, 339.
Tower Taye, 187.
Trewhitt House, 352.
Troughend Hall, dyke, 319.
Tuggall Church, 450.
Turvelaws, 525.
Tweedmouth Church, 538; Hang-a-Dyke-Neuk, 538, 539; Tweed House, 539.
Twizel: bridge, 514; castle, 552.
Twizell House, ornithological collection at, 442.
Tynemouth: castle, 47; priory, 48; oratory of St. Mary, 50; Jingling Geordie's Hole, 50; legend of Wizard's Cave, 51; Black Middens, 52; Harriet Martineau at, 52; aquarium, Monk's Stone, 53.

U.

Ulgham, 280; old oak near, 281.
Unthank, 543.
Unthank Hall, reputed birth-place of Bishop Ridley, 165.
Uswayford, 350.

V.

Vindolana, Roman station of, 167.

W.

Walker, 38, 39.
Walbottle, 88; Dene House, remains of mile-castle at, 88.
Wall, 209.
Wallington House, 260-267; pictures at, 262-265; remains of Border tower, 261; Fair Mabel of, 261; gardens, 266.
Wallsend: Roman station at, 39; Emperor Nicholas at, 40; ruined church, 40.
Walltown: King Arthur's well, 196; tower of, 196.
Walwick Grange, 199.
Wanehope Linn, 226.
Wanny Crags, 233.
Warden, 198.
Warden, High, camp at, 198.
Wardrew Spa, 174.
Warenford, 442,
Waren Mills, 438.
Wark: village, church, kaim, 554; castle, history of, 554-556; description of, 556.
Wark-on-Tyne, 204-205; mote hill at, 204.
Warksburn, petrified cascade on, 205.
Warkworth: history of, 407, 408; church, 408; castle, 409-412; hermitage, 412-415.
Warton, 341.
Waterfalls, Jacobite rendezvous at, 233.
Wedderburn's Cave, 361.
Wedder's Loup, 350.
Weetwood, camp, hall, bridge, 490.
Weldon Bridge, 369.
Welton Tower, story of old Will o', 90.
West Hills, Rothbury, camp at, 330.
West Moor, Geo. Stephenson's cottage, 72.
Whalton, pele, church, and camps, 267.
Whelpington, West, 237.
Whetting Stone, 476.
Whickhope Burn, 225.
Whitchester, 167.
Whitefield House, 310.
Whitehall, camps near, 508.
Whitelee, 324.
Whitfield, 158.
Whitley Castle, Roman station at, 180.
Whitley-by-the-Sea, 56-58; convalescent home, 57; singing sands, 58.
Whitsunbank, fair at, 490.
Whittingham, history of, 359; church, 360; pele, 361.
Whittington, Great, 149.
Whittle, Scots at, immured frog at, 403.
Whittle Dene, 99.
Whitton, tower and dene, 335.
Whittonstall, 133.
Widdrington Castle, 282; James I. at, 282; church 282; the Widdringtons of, 283, 284.
Willimoteswick Castle, 163; Ridleys of, 164; Lowes of, 165.
Willington Quay, 41; haunted house of, 41-43.
Windyhaugh, 350.
Wingates, 276.

Winshields Crag, 195.
Winter's Stob, 309.
Witton Shields, 275.
Witton, Long, 275.
Witton, Nether, 274.
Woodburn, East, terminal moraine near, 234.
Woodburn, West, 234.
Woodhall, old farm-house of, 346.
Woodhorn Church, 290, 291.
Woodhouses Pele, 344.
Wooler: Earl of Derwentwater at, 474; fairs, castle, bastle-house, church, Dalziel Bros. at, 475; Whetting Stone, Pin Well, King's Chair, Kettles Camp, Cup and Saucer Camp, 476.
Wooler Haugh Head, Surrey at, 486.
Woolsington, 76.
Wooperton, 489.
Wreighburn House, 340.
Wreighhill, 343.
Wydon Scar, 175.
Wylam, George Stephenson's birth-place, 94.

Y.

Yarrow, 221.
Yeavering: old palace at, 504; battle of, 504; white lady of, 504; Bell, antiquities on, 505.

THE WALTER SCOTT PUBLISHING CO., LTD., NEWCASTLE-ON-TYNE.
11-02